Does God believe in atheists?

This is Blanchard at his best: immensely thorough, crystal clear, devastating in his logic, compassionate at heart. No stone is left unturned: a brilliant defence of belief in God — and its implications!

The Rev. Andrew Anderson, B.Sc., B.D.,
International Baptist Church of Brussels

This book is a remarkable outcome of forty years or so experience of John Blanchard as an evangelist, Bible teacher and writer. His incisive style combined with his ability to draw upon a wide range of sources have resulted in a book in which the overall flow of thought provides an immensely readable and persuasive argument for the classical, biblical, Christian faith.

Professor J. M. V. Blanshard, M.A., FIFST,
St Albans, Herts, England

John Blanchard not only has the knack of answering a sceptic's questions with precision, clarity and subtle humour, he has the uncanny ability to answer questions before they arise in the sceptic's mind. This book is destined to be a classic on the subject.

The Rev. Wade Burleson, B.Sc.,
Southern Baptist Convention, USA

It is highly referenced with all the relevant literature, which is accurate and up to date. It is a book which any Christian would be glad to have on their shelves, not only from its useful reference point of view but because it presents the data in a readable and interesting way.

Professor Desmond Burrows, M.B., B.Ch., B.A.O., M.D., M.R.C.P., FRCP,
Belfast, N. Ireland

Anyone reading this volume will immediately see the level of study and research that has gone into its preparation. Its scope and subject matter are of the greatest importance today and it is to be hoped that it will have the impact upon people's thinking that it deserves.

The Rev. Dr A. T. B. McGowan, B.D., STM, Ph.D.,
Highland Theological College, Dingwall, Scotland

As a one-time atheist myself, I commend John Blanchard's keen and discerning intellectual and spiritual critique of atheism. No self-respecting atheist should be without it.

The Rev. Dr Nick Needham, B.D., Ph.D.,
Highland Theological College, Dingwall, Scotland

I read John Blanchard's chapters on scientific aspects of the subject with pleasure. They are lucidly written and thoroughly researched. He has amassed a great deal of information and presented it in a compelling way. I thoroughly recommend this work to the believer and the sceptic. The reader must react to it.

Dr J. H. John Peet, B.Sc., M.Sc., Ph.D., C.Chem., FRSC,
Guildford, Surrey, England

I have the highest regard for John Blanchard. His work is concise and biblically based. It is pertinent, applicable and relevant for Christians in the twenty-first century.

Dr Patrick Sookhdeo, Ph.D., D.D.,
Pewsey, Hants, England

The breadth and depth of John's reading is quite breathtaking and his grasp of modern scientific and philosophical trends stunning. This book is going to be a great help to any honest thinkers who are prepared to face the challenge which it presents. It is also an absolute gold-mine of 'quotable quotes'. Students will revel in it.

The Rev. Derek Swann, B.A., B.D.,
Cardiff, Wales

A veritable *tour de force*. Not only does the author fairly and squarely face the doubts and contradictions posed by unbelievers, but he also provides evidence that is both accessible and convincing.

The Rev. Daniel Webber,
European Missionary Fellowship, Welwyn, Herts, England

John Blanchard's arguments lead to the inevitable conclusion that atheism is both illogical and untenable. Anyone who remains an atheist after reading this volume does so in wilful contradiction of the overwhelming evidence for the existence of God.

Dr A. J. Monty White, B.Sc., Ph.D., C.Chem., MRSC,
Cardiff, Wales

Does God believe
in atheists?

John Blanchard

EVANGELICAL PRESS

EVANGELICAL PRESS
Faverdale North Industrial Estate, Darlington, DL3 0PH, England

Evangelical Press USA
P. O. Box 825, Webster, New York 14580, USA

e-mail: sales@evangelicalpress.org

web: www.evangelicalpress.org

First published March 2000
Second impression April 2000
Third impression June 2000
Fourth impression October 2000
Fifth impression September 2001
Sixth impression February 2003
Seventh impression August 2005

British Library Cataloguing in Publication Data available

ISBN 0 85234 460 0

Other titles by John Blanchard:
Evolution — Fact or Fiction?
Has Science got rid of God?
How to Enjoy your Bible
Is God Past his Sell-By Date?
Luke Comes Alive
Meet the Real Jesus
Read Mark Learn
Right with God
Truth for Life
Ultimate Questions
What in the World is a Christian?
Whatever Happened to Hell?
Where is God when Things Go Wrong?
Where was God on September 11?
Why Believe the Bible?

Printed and bound in Great Britain by Creative Print & Design Wales, Ebbw Vale

Contents

Dedicated to
MERVYN AND HELEN SNOW
with admiration, gratitude and affection

Foreword

by the Rev. Dr Sinclair B. Ferguson, M.A., B.D., Ph. D.

The book you are holding in your hands may well be unique and certainly is remarkable. It is very probable that you have never read anything quite like it before. *Does God Believe in Atheists?* belongs to no ordinary book category because it seems to belong to so many different categories. One does not need to be a prophet to predict that it will be frequently consulted and its material widely used.

John Blanchard is a widely respected author and communicator of the Christian faith. He is well known for his ability to talk about serious things without being lugubrious, and about deep and difficult things in a way that helps others to understand them. But even by his normal standards of excellence and clarity, this work is a *tour de force*.

Does God Believe in Atheists? is a one-volume encyclopaedia of information related to what the German philosopher Martin Heidegger said was the most basic question of all: why is there something and not nothing? In more commonplace terms, is there a God?

Over the thousands of years in which the library of human literature has been compiled, that question has been discussed, weighed and answered — often affirmatively, sometimes negatively and, in recent times, uncertainly. It is one of the extraordinary achievements of this volume that it provides an informed, coherent account of several millennia of these discussions and debates. In addition — and herein lies its genius — it does so in a manner that is both understandable and wonderfully readable.

Here is a college course on philosophy, anthropology, geology and the life sciences — yet packaged in such a way that a person of average intelligence will be able to follow, understand, enjoy and find it deeply relevant. If you are not a Christian, you will discover that these pages provide a fascinating account of the intellectual and ethical systems that, often un-known to you, have influenced the way you think as a twenty-first-century human being. If you are a Christian you will find this work to be an illuminating survey of what lies behind modern thought; and that survey will better equip you to explain the Christian faith to your own contemporaries. Whether Christian or not, you will quickly discover from John Blanchard's ability to clarify the big issues that being a Christian does not involve the sacrifice of the intellect, but rather leads to its truest and best use.

Here is a book on religion and theology. It is bulging with facts and fascinating information. The notes alone, which display John Blanchard's wide interests and reading, run into somewhere over 2,300. Yet nobody need be afraid of these pages for that reason. For John Blanchard takes great care not only to make everything clear, but also to make it enjoyable, by sharing with us all kinds of interesting information about the great thinkers and scholars in world history. Big ideas, complex thoughts, recondite philosophies and scientific theories are all explained in a way that even a modestly educated reader can understand. When all this comes packaged with a sense of humour and a love for golf (the latter without the former would surely be a grave philosophical aberration), you know that you have a book worth reading!

Most of all, however, this is a book that will challenge you to think and help you to do so.

Even in our post-modern (or has it become post-post-modern?) world, many young men and women enter college or university in the hope that there they may still discover learning that will provide a key to the meaning of life. Surely philosophy, whether moral or natural, can guide them? Surely the wisdom of the ages, recorded in history and literature, will direct them? But, alas, there seems to be an inbuilt frustration code in every branch of human wisdom and learning. The real meaning of existence still proves to be elusive. Indeed, if we are to listen to Richard Dawkins (who features frequently in these pages), the very idea that there is meaning of the kind we seek is a non-starter.

But the deep quest of the human mind and the thirst of the human spirit underline for us that Dawkins' answer will not do. It fails at stage one, simply because it does not take account of the way reality is, including — indeed perhaps especially — the reality of our own existence. The 'Why?'

question which scientists as scientists cannot answer will not allow itself to be satisfied by answers to the 'How?' question which they often can.

Enter John Blanchard. With his great apologist predecessor Saul of Tarsus, he is convinced that 'The world in its wisdom did not know God.' He recognizes that it takes a different kind of wisdom to find answers to ultimate questions. Paradoxically, the chief reason he excels as a guide to the history of human wisdom is just this: he has also been educated in another college, where divine wisdom is taught. He himself has been a diligent scholar in that school, and learned his lessons well. I think you will find him an outstanding and reliable professor in the classroom you are about to enter.

Sinclair B. Ferguson
St George's Tron
Glasgow

Preface

It has often been said that the most important questions anyone could ever ask are: 'Who am I?', 'Why am I here?' and 'Where am I going?' Dealing as they do with the issues of a person's identity, meaning and destiny, they are obviously of great significance, but even these are secondary when put alongside one which is both fundamental and inescapable: *'Does God exist?'*

This is *the* question, and every debate about human life and death, and about the universe in which humanity lives and dies, ultimately revolves around it. Several years ago, *Encyclopaedia Britannica* published a set of fifty-four volumes which marshalled the writings of many eminent thinkers in the Western world on the most important ideas that have been studied and investigated over the centuries. The subjects covered included law, science, philosophy, history and theology; the longest essay of all was on the subject of God. Addressing the question as to why this should be the case, co-editor Mortimer Adler wrote, 'More consequences for thought and action follow from the affirmation or denial of God than from answering any other question.'[1] The outstanding Latvian philosopher Isaiah Berlin, who died in 1997, elaborated the point in his book *Concepts and Categories*: 'The world of a man who believes that God created him for a specific purpose, that he has an immortal soul, that there is an afterlife in which his sins will be visited upon him, is radically different from the world of a man who believes in none of these things; and the reasons for action, the moral codes, the political beliefs, the tastes, the personal relationships of the former will deeply and systematically differ from those of the latter. Men's views of one another will differ profoundly as a very consequence of their general conception of the world: the notions of cause and purpose, good and evil, freedom and slavery, things and persons, rights, duties, laws, justice, truth, falsehood, to take some central ideas completely at random, depend entirely upon the general framework within which they form, as it were, nodal points.'[2]

If Adler and Berlin are right, looking into the subject addressed in this book is hardly a trivial pursuit. Those who disagree over the question of God's existence are not merely crossing paper swords over some interesting but ultimately irrelevant point of science, philosophy or theology. They are disagreeing over the greatest issue of all. The contemporary British philosopher C. Stephen Evans hits the nail on the head when he says that believing in God is not like believing in the Loch Ness Monster: 'The Loch Ness monster is merely "one more thing"... God, however, is not merely "one more thing". The person who believes in God and the person who does not believe in God do not merely disagree about God. *They disagree about the very character of the universe.*'[3]

As this also involves the fundamental basis of all human life and behaviour, it is hardly surprising that no issue provokes more controversy. The question of God's existence has raged for centuries — and 'raged' is the right word to use, with millions of people persecuted, punished, tortured, maimed or killed for their convictions on the matter. Theologians and philosophers, psychologists and psychiatrists, scientists and sociologists galore have fought tooth and nail over the issue, and the ongoing arguments would seem to indicate that nobody has succeeded in landing a decisive blow.

Yet this is an issue which not only profoundly affects all the other questions that humanity asks about its existence and environment; it is one in which both sides cannot be right. Either God exists, or he does not exist.[4] There is no point in looking for compromise, a kind of halfway house in which both sides can live in agreement. To say that God *is* and at the same time *is not* is a crass violation of the law of contradiction. The truth must lie on one side or the other — and to dismiss the question as irrelevant or unanswerable changes nothing.

This is the background against which this book is written — though it is not the one I had in mind. I originally set out to produce a brief, straightforward analysis of the historical, logical and existential problems facing those who believe that God does *not* exist, but I soon found myself drawn into taking a much broader approach. The further I went, the more I realized that atheists (and agnostics, for that matter) face a huge raft of questions to which, in nearly forty years of writing, broadcasting and public speaking all around the world, I had never heard convincing answers. Bringing these questions together, and asking them in their proper context, soon spilled over into something much larger than the book I first had in mind: what follows is the result.

Prefaces to quite slender volumes have been known to include thanks to all kinds of people, including numerous friends and family members, and have sometimes seemed to fall only just short of complimenting the family pet for remaining silent while the master of the house was at work. In this case, failing to thank those who have made significant contributions to the present book would be worse than churlish.

Firstly, I owe a huge debt to an unofficial team of men who have read through all or part of the manuscript, some of them meticulously, and have made numerous corrections and suggestions. It is humbling to realize how many flaws would have slipped through without their kind and careful work, and I am grateful to the following for the time and effort they have spent on my behalf: Rev. Andrew Anderson, Rev. Peter Anderson, Professor Edgar Andrews, Dr John Baigent, Professor John Blanshard, Ron Blows, Professor Desmond Burrows, Derek Cleave, Rev. Ian Densham, Rev. Noel Due, Professor Julian Evans, Dr. Niall Fraser, David Fryett, John Garvie, Rev. Graham Hind, Dr Andrew McGowan, Jonathan Morgan, Rev. George Murray, Rev. Philip Miller, Dr Nick Needham, Dr John Peet, Alan Radcliffe-Smith, Rev. Tony Seagar, Dr Patrick Sookhedo, Rev. Derek Swann, Michael Taylor, Rev. Daniel Webber, Dr Monty White and Rev. Alistair Wilson.

In addition to these, my special thanks are due to John Canales for his great help in the writing of chapter 13 and to Dr Andrew Blanchard for similar assistance in the writing of chapter 14. Without their expert input, I would have been sunk without trace.

It has been my privilege to serve Christian Ministries for the past twenty years, and I am indebted to my colleagues on the CM Board for generously allowing me to write this book in 'company time', and to CM's supporters, who have so faithfully sustained the work. I am especially thankful to some sixty men and women in Britain and elsewhere who have made this writing project a particular focus for their prayers. It would be impossible for me to overstate my gratitude to them. In the United States, Trey

Lee and David Henderson have 'hung in there' (as Americans would say) since the very beginning of the project, and their constant encouragement has meant a great deal to me.

For many years now, Evangelical Press has published almost all of my books. I am grateful to the entire EP team for their part in handling my work, not least to Executive Director David Clark and General Manager John Rubens, who have gently nudged me along throughout the long process of producing this particular volume. I would like to pay a special tribute to EP's indefatigable editor, Anne Williamson, who has once again brought her meticulous skills to bear on my manuscript. Her work is necessarily behind the scenes, but her significant contribution to the present book deserves to be expressed openly.

I have heard it said that a good book does not need a foreword and that a bad book does not deserve one. Be that as it may, Dr Sinclair Ferguson has honoured me by his generous commendation, which I greatly appreciate.

Finally, I must once again express my thanks to Joy Harling, who has been my secretary for the past twenty years. How she copes with my constant revisions (and dreadful scrawl) I will never know. This particular project has involved her in an immense amount of work, which she has undertaken cheerfully, swiftly and with great efficiency.

My sincere hope is that what follows will be of help to many who are genuinely seeking to find the truth, and a great encouragement to those who have already done so.

John Blanchard
Banstead
Surrey
March 2000

Introduction

As we begin to uncover the problems faced by atheists and agnostics, we need to bear in mind that theists can hardly be said to have everything their own way. Speaking at a conference of religious leaders in 1945, the universally respected scholar and author C. S. Lewis told his audience, 'It is very difficult to produce arguments at the popular level for the existence of God'[1] — and this in spite of the fact that he had by then been a totally convinced believer for almost fourteen years. The contemporary philosopher Os Guinness goes even further and says, 'God's existence not only *cannot* be proved, it *should* not be attempted.'[2]

In his recent book *Explaining Your Faith*, theologian Alister McGrath fine-tunes the point and writes, 'God's existence can neither be conclusively proved nor disproved.'[3] This seems fair comment, but it depends for its validity on the meaning he attaches to the word 'conclusively'. It is true only if he means that it is impossible to persuade everybody. Yet to say this is to say nothing; after all, the Flat Earth Society is still in business! George Mavrodes makes the point well: 'We are, of course, especially interested in whether there is any argument that will prove God's existence to everyone. Such an argument has apparently not yet been invented... The invention of such an argument would, of course, be a wonderful thing, just as would be the development of a drug that would cure all diseases. But there is not much reason to believe that either of these is possible.'[4]

Facing any issue in which diametrically opposed views seem to have both strengths and weaknesses, we need to examine the data with an open mind (or at least a readiness to listen to what both sides are saying) and then come to conclusions based either on what becomes satisfying evidence or, failing such evidence, reasonable probability. In other words,

when we can get no clear answer to the question, 'What does this *prove?*'
we should ask, 'Where does it *point?*'

God and Gallup

Proposition 1:   Only a minority of people are atheists.
Proposition 2:   Most people are atheists.
Proposition 3:   Nobody is an atheist.

This might seem a decidedly unpromising start, yet a case can be made in
favour of each one of these propositions. As we shall soon see, everything
hinges on the meanings given to the key words involved.

There may never have been a period in history when opinion polls
have been as widely used as at present. From politics to economics, morality to aesthetics, and sports to the arts, random sampling is assumed to
give a significant indication of what people as a whole are thinking. Not
surprisingly, religion has had a great deal of attention from the clipboard
crews and, as far as the existence or non-existence of God is concerned,
the results seem to point in the same general direction and to support
Proposition 1.

A worldwide poll taken in 1991 put the global figure for atheists at just
4.4%, and although a category labelled 'other non-religious' produced a
further 16.4%, this still left nearly 80% professing some kind of belief in
some kind of god.[5] These figures tie in fairly accurately with those quoted
in *Operation World,* which puts the 'non-religious/atheist' total at 970 million, some 20% of the world's population.[6]

In 1991, the prestigious Barna Report, an annual survey of values and
religious views in the United States, found that 74% of adults interviewed
agreed 'strongly' or 'somewhat' with a statement affirming the existence of
'only one true God'.[7] In 1986, average figures in a study of religious activity
and belief in ten countries in Western Europe suggested that 75% believed
in God, with only 11% believing in 'no god at all' and 16% registering as
'don't knows'.[8]

In a Marplan Survey taken in the United Kingdom in 1979, around
82% expressed a religious belief of some kind, while 73% specifically said
they believed in God.[9] A Gallup Poll undertaken in Great Britain in 1986
as part of a European Value Systems Study revealed that 76% of those

interviewed believed in God,[10] while *Britain Twenty Years On*, a survey taken a year later, gave the figure as 70%,[11] the same as that quoted in 1994 by the presenter of a radio programme in the *Believing in Britain* series.[12] In a 1989 review of social attitudes in Britain, 34% claimed to have 'no religion', a 3% increase on the 1983 figure.[13] At the end of 1999, a British survey conducted by Opinion Research Business suggested that 38% were 'not religious'.[14]

White lies...

Taken at their face value, these statistics seem to put atheists in a relatively insignificant minority, but the fact is that the numbers conceal at least as much as they reveal.

To make the most obvious point first, the surveys beg the all-important question as to what the pollsters had in mind when they used the word 'God'. Did they mean a personal being, or an impersonal life force; a conscious deity, or cosmic dust; a living entity totally 'outside' the universe, or some kind of universal energy woven into its fabric? The difference a clear definition would make to the statistics can easily be illustrated. In the Western European survey, 75% of those polled said they believed in God, but when just one qualification was added — as to whether they believed in 'a personal God' — the figure dropped dramatically to just 32%.[15] This simple example brings to mind the old saying that there are three kinds of lies — white lies, black lies and statistics. What is certain is that statistics cannot always be taken at face value; we shall need to dig deeper if we are to get beyond the figures to the facts.

It is already obvious that the place to begin digging is in the field of definitions. The eighteenth-century French philosopher François-Marie Arouet, who wrote under the pen-name of Voltaire, is quoted as saying, 'If any man will reason with me, let us first define our terms.' To talk about 'theism' and 'atheism' is to engage in a dialogue of the deaf until we determine what we mean when we use these words and, as the meaning of the second depends directly on that of the first, we must begin with 'theism'. This is not as simple as it seems. One dictionary defines theism as 'belief in existence of gods or a god',[16] but as the same dictionary's primary definition of 'god' is 'superhuman being worshipped as having power over nature and human fortunes'[17] it is immediately obvious that 'theism' is much too vague a term for us to use in this book. It allows too much scope for wriggling.

Nor is the problem solved by giving 'god' a capital 'G', because, as the British pop singer George Harrison put it in the 1960s, 'When you say the word "God" people are going to curl up and cringe — they all interpret it in a different way.'[18] The American scholar David Elton Trueblood took the same line: 'Nothing is easier than to use the word "God" and mean almost nothing by it. It is easy to be right if we are sufficiently vague ... in what we say.'[19] The influential British theologian John Robinson said much the same thing: 'The word "God" is so slippery and the reality so intangible that many today are questioning whether they have reference to anything that can usefully or meaningfully be talked about at all.'[20]

This is precisely the kind of problem we face, and vague answers will not help. When responding to particularly difficult questions on BBC Radio's *Brains Trust* some years ago, Professor C. E. M. Joad would often begin, 'It all depends what you mean by ...' We need to get that issue settled before we go any further.

Defining deity

Charles Dodgson, a professor of mathematics at Oxford University from 1855-1881, used his famous *nom de plume* Lewis Carroll in writing a number of children's stories that have charmed generations of readers ever since. In *Alice Through the Looking Glass* one of his best-known characters gets involved in verbal gymnastics:

> 'When *I* use a word,' Humpty Dumpty said in rather a scornful tone, 'it means just what I choose it to mean — neither more nor less.'
> 'The question is,' said Alice, 'whether you *can* make words mean so many different things.'
> 'The question is,' said Humpty Dumpty, 'which is to be the master — that's all.'[21]

That kind of delightful dottiness is fine for children's fiction, but it will hardly do when we are discussing the most important question human beings could ever ask. It may therefore be helpful if at this point I seek to establish a bench-mark by setting out what I mean when I use the word 'God' from here on. Put in a nutshell, I mean 'a unique, personal, plural, spiritual, eternally self-existent, transcendent, immanent, omniscient, immutable, holy, loving Being, the Creator and Ruler of the entire universe and the Judge of all mankind'. Let me elaborate a little.

- By *'unique'* I mean that there is only one God and that all other objects or ideas given that name are figments of misled imagination.
- By *'personal'* I mean that God is not a 'thing' or 'power', influence or energy, but that he lives, thinks, feels and acts.
- By *'plural'* I mean that there are distinguishable persons within a single Godhead.
- By *'spiritual'* I mean that God has no physical attributes or dimensions, that he does not have a body, or any characteristics that can be defined in terms of size or shape.
- By *'eternally self-existent'* I mean that he has always had the power of being within himself and has neither beginning nor end.
- By *'transcendent'* I mean that God is over and above all things, outside of time and space, completely distinct from the universe, and not to be confused with it in any way.
- By *'immanent'* I mean that, while remaining separate from it in being and essence, he permeates the entire universe.
- By *'omniscient'* I mean that he knows everything, including the past, the present and the future.
- By *'immutable'* I mean that he is unchangeable in every aspect of his being.
- By *'holy'* I mean that he is utterly without blemish or deficiency in his being, essence or actions.
- By *'loving'* I mean that he cares for all of creation and that in a very special way he demonstrates his love to humanity and communicates this to individuals.
- By *'Creator'* I mean that by his own choice and power he brought into being all reality other than himself.
- By *'Ruler'* I mean that he is in sole and sovereign control of everything that exists or happens, and that nothing can prevent him doing as he pleases.
- By *'Judge of all mankind'* I mean that he alone determines the eternal destiny of every member of the human race.

Four things need to be said about this conception of God.

Firstly, it is not a shot in the dark, or a random collection of ideas, but reflects what has been consistently accepted by millions of people over thousands of years and is now held by the largest religious grouping the world has ever known. This does not necessarily say anything in its favour, but does at least give it some kind of perspective.

Secondly, as we shall see much later in this book, it is no more than an outline, just sufficient to prevent the word 'God' from being so slippery that nobody can get hold of it.

Thirdly, although it gives a clear indication of what I will mean when I use the word 'God' in the course of this book, it is not necessarily what is always meant by the authors and speakers I will be quoting; this will be obvious in most cases.

Fourthly, as we shall see in later chapters, fine-tuning the definition of God in this way will obviously produce more atheists than would settling for deity as being no more than a vague, supernatural principle or power.

The other side

Accepting that theism is belief in the existence of God, what is atheism? Again, the answer is far from straightforward. A simple dictionary definition, based on the Greek words *a* (without) and *theos* (God) is 'disbelief in the existence of God or gods',[22] but the history and use of the word are much more complex.

In ancient Greece the word 'atheist' was used to describe three groups of people: those who were impious or godless; those who were without supernatural help; and those who did not accept the prevalent Greek idea of deity. The earliest Christians were often called atheists by their contemporaries because they refused to accept the existence of the popular pagan deities of their time, and one religious group has sometimes accused another of atheism even when both claimed to believe in a supernatural Being of whom at least part of our outline of who and what God is would be true.

Yet even these examples do not exhaust the uses of 'atheism'. Swami Vivekanada, an Indian who was instrumental in bringing Hinduism to the West, once said, 'Just as certain world religions say that people who do not believe in a personal God outside themselves are atheists, we say that a person who does not believe in himself is an atheist. Not believing in the splendour of one's own soul is what we call an atheist.'[23]

It would simplify things if we could settle for the general idea that atheism is the rejection of theism, but the difficulty of pinning down the meaning of theism makes the issue a lot more complicated than that. As long as our concept of God is sufficiently vague, our first proposition — that only a minority of people are atheists — is already proved. However, if we define God in the way I have suggested, our second proposition, which says that most people in the world are atheists, comes into play. It will take us twelve chapters to discover whether this is the case. We will then prepare the way for our third proposition, and follow it by examining some of its implications.

I should add one technical point. In recent years, authors have had to wrestle with the issue of inclusive language, and I have been caught up willy-nilly in the struggle. Rather than getting into the tortuous syntax which can sometimes be involved, I have often opted for the use of 'man', 'him', 'he', and 'his' when maleness is not necessarily implied, but in every case the meaning will be obvious. The same applies to 'mankind'.

1.

The Greeks had words for it

The theory has often been put forward that religion evolved slowly over many millennia, beginning with very primitive ideas and gradually developing into today's concepts. Wrapped up in this theory, and an important element in the thinking of many atheists, is the idea that monotheism (belief in one God) is a comparatively recent refinement. In the nineteenth century, two anthropologists, Sir Edward Tyler and Sir James Frazer, popularized the notion that the first stage in the evolution of religion was animism (which involved the worship of spirits believed to inhabit natural phenomena), followed later by pantheism (the idea that everything is divine), polytheism (belief in a multitude of distinct and separate deities) and eventually by monotheism.[1]

However, recent studies in anthropology have turned this scenario on its head and show, for example, that the hundreds of contemporary tribal religions (including many which are animistic) are not primitive in the sense of being original. Writing from long experience in India, and after extended studies of ancient religions, the modern scholar Robert Brow states, 'The tribes have a memory of a "High God", who is no longer worshipped because he is not feared. Instead of offering sacrifice to him, they concern themselves with the pressing problems of how to appease the vicious spirits of the jungle.'[2] Other research suggests that tribes 'are not animistic because they have continued unchanged since the dawn of history' and that 'The evidence indicates degeneration from a true knowledge of God.'[3] After working among primitive tribes for many years, one modern expert says, 'The animism of today gives us the impression of a religion that carries the marks of a *fall*,'[4] while another bluntly refers to 'the now discredited evolutionary school of religion' as being 'recognized as inadmissible'.[5]

The evidence of modern archaeology is that religion has not evolved 'upwards', but degenerated from monotheism to pantheism and polytheism, then from these to animism and atheism, a finding confirmed by the Scottish academic Andrew Lang in *The Making of Religion*: 'Of the existence of a belief in the Supreme Being among primitive tribes there is as good evidence as we possess for any fact in the ethnographic region.'[6] In *History of Sanskrit Literature*, the Oriental expert Max Muller, recognized as the founder of the science of the history of religions, came to the conclusion: 'There is a monotheism that precedes the polytheism of the Veda; and even in the invocations of the innumerable gods, the remembrance of a God, one and infinite, breaks through the mist of idolatrous phraseology like the blue sky that is hidden by passing clouds.'[7] In *The Religion of Ancient Egypt*, Sir Flinders Petrie, universally acknowledged as one of the world's leading Egyptologists, claimed, 'Wherever we can trace back polytheism to its earliest stages, we find that it results from combinations of monotheism.'[8] In *Semitic Mythology*, the Oxford intellectual Stephen Langdon, one of the greatest experts in his field, said, 'In my opinion the history of the oldest civilization of man is a rapid decline from monotheism to extreme polytheism and widespread belief in evil spirits. It is in a very true sense the history of the fall of man.'[9]

These statements make it clear that the scenario suggested by Tyler and Frazer will not fit the facts. There is no convincing evidence for any development in nature religions from animism through polytheism to monotheism. The idea that religion itself is something man invented has proved just as baseless. When the British naturalist Charles Darwin went to Tierra del Fuego in 1833, he believed that he had discovered aborigines with no religion at all. There are atheists today who still lean heavily on this, in spite of the fact that a scholar who went to the region after Darwin, and spent many years learning the language, history and customs of the Fuegians, reported that their idea of God was well developed and that he found *'no evidence that there was ever a time when he was not known to them'*.[10]

The same overall picture emerges in studies centred on the traditions of the oldest civilizations known to man: original belief in a 'High God', followed by degeneration into polytheism, animism and other corrupt religious notions.

To trace all the currents in the ebb and flow of man's religious thinking over the centuries is beyond anyone's ability, but it is possible to track down some of the people whose ideas not only made a marked contemporary impact but still affect the way many people think today on the issue of the existence of God. In this and the next eleven chapters we will make a high-speed pass over the last 2,500 years or so and identify some of the most influential characters and concepts. One point before we begin: animism, pantheism, polytheism (and some of the other '-isms' we shall touch on as we go along) are usually treated as facets of theism, but for the purpose of this book I want to draw the line elsewhere and to treat them as aspects of atheism, on the grounds that they fail to square with the definition of God proposed in the introduction.

Let me interrupt myself at this point. Readers with little or no exposure to philosophical thinking may find parts of the next few chapters a little difficult at first reading. However, it is important to realize that modern atheistic and agnostic theories are often a reworking of ideas put forward over previous centuries. In many cases, modern thinkers are standing on the shoulders of those who went before them, rather than producing totally new ideas. As recently as 1998, a survey carried out among students and academics found that the philosophers who have contributed most to the advancement of human understanding lived over 2,500 years ago, while the well-known contemporary French philosopher Jacques Derrida headed the list of thinkers 'whose contribution to the subject has been most overrated'.[11]

Getting even a general picture of how modern atheistic and agnostic ideas developed over the centuries will, I believe, prove a great help when reading the later parts of the book.

From myths to monism

Questions about the physical world in which we live and the nature of reality have fascinated men of all ages and cultures. The first written evidence we have of this is the Mesopotamian *Epic of Gilgamesh*, which dates from 2,000 B.C. and tells how the eponymous hero scoured the earth in his search for the meaning of the universe, life, death and immortality.

Other ancient writings record mythical accounts tying the origin and meaning of the cosmos to the forces of nature, with magic as the greatest force of all. In the eighth century B.C. the famous Greek poet Homer

wrote of gods and goddesses who were personifications of nature, presided over by Zeus, 'the Father of gods and men'. The distinction between these gods and human beings was one of power, not virtue. One
writer says, 'They connived, cheated and lied to help themselves and
their favoured patrons among men,'[12] while another adds, 'Among their
normal activities were perjury, war and adultery.'[13] Not surprisingly, in
Homer's scenario man was a meaningless and helpless nonentity, separated from the deities by an impassable gulf and doomed at the end
of his miserable life to complete annihilation. Anyone tempted to dismiss these polytheistic notions as ancient and irrelevant history, nothing
more than crude steps in man's early development, should think again.
As we shall see in chapter 11, some of today's largest world religions
are clearly polytheistic.

A sea change in men's thinking took place around the sixth century
B.C. and was centred at Miletus, a Greek colony on the coast of Asia
Minor. These so-called Milesian philosophers were headed by Thales (*fl. c.*
585 B.C.), usually thought of as the father of Greek philosophy, who rejected mythological explanations of the origin and nature of the universe
and substituted the basic ideas of natural science, believing that the physical world contained rational and intelligible evidence as to its origin and
meaning. Within this general framework, Thales embraced monism, the
theory that all reality consists of only one basic stuff or essence out of
which everything in the cosmos was made. He believed that this primal
substance was water, which was said to contain the cause of motion and
change, and therefore of life itself. In this sense it could be said to be
'divine'. This may be what lay behind his well-known saying, 'All things are
full of gods,' though scholars have disagreed as to precisely what he may
have meant by this. Similar uncertainty in being able to nail down the
precise meaning of their statements leads one modern philosopher to say
of the Milesian philosophers that 'Their place in the history of unbelief is ...
ambiguous.'[14]

Other philosophers of the same era focused their monism elsewhere.
Anaximenes (*fl. c.* 550 B.C.) taught that the primal substance was air;
Heraclitus (*fl. c.* 500 B.C.) saw fire as the first principle of reality, from
which everything flowed in a constant state of flux, guided by a kind of
universal reason; Parmenides (*fl. c.* 480 B.C.) believed that the only reality
was 'being', of which nothing can be said other than that it is. Empedocles
(*c.* 495 – *c.* 435 B.C.) taught that all matter was composed of four elements

— earth, water, air and fire — and that their interaction explained all motion and change.

Monism has taken various other forms over the centuries, some regarding the primal substance as material and others as spiritual, but it is in direct conflict with theism for several reasons. Firstly, the totality of things includes evil, whereas God is without evil of any kind. Secondly, the process, structure, substance and ground of monism are impersonal, whereas God is personal. Thirdly, monism implies that there is no essential difference between good and evil, because eventually everything flows into a single unity, an idea which runs counter to theism and has serious implications. Os Guinness says of monism, 'There are no moral absolutes; moral values are only relatively true or sociologically useful and the question of ethics is only the question of the optimal ground rules.'[15] But to say that right and wrong are ultimately the same is to destroy any basis for law, order and morality in society. We will look more closely at this in a later chapter.

There are modern echoes of monism's ancient ideas in the New Age Movement, which begins with the assumption that there is only one essential principle in the cosmos, into which all things, including humanity, are destined to merge. In the 1970s the hugely successful film *Star Wars* made use of the idea that good and evil were two facets of the same reality (the so-called 'Force') with the film's hero, Luke Skywalker, making use of its good side and its villain, Darth Vader (ultimately revealed to be Skywalker's father), tapping into the dark or evil side.

Socrates

The next landmarks were put in place by the three giants of ancient Greek philosophy. The first of these was Socrates (*c.* 470–399 B.C.) who rebelled against the natural approach adopted by his predecessors and changed the whole direction of philosophy. Although possessing 'one of the keenest minds of all time',[16] he left no written record of his ideas, but we know of these from his brilliant pupil Plato, who used Socrates as the main character in a series of *Dialogues*, or dramatized discussions on philosophy, and from the Greek historian Xenophon.

Socrates differed from the natural philosophers in that he was primarily concerned with ethical matters rather than the nature of the universe. In his own words, 'I have nothing to do with physical speculations.'[17] Socrates claimed to be driven by an inner voice to search within the human soul or psyche for a solid foundation for knowledge, though this 'inner voice' would have borne little or no resemblance to the God outlined in the introduction. Socrates was an optimistic rationalist, believing that reason was the only path to knowledge and that humanity could be perfected, not by the external influence of a divine Creator but by the acquisition of true knowledge. He also believed that evil would eventually disappear from an educated world: in the words of his famous dictum, 'He who knows what good is will do good.'

Socrates also held that the human soul was a prisoner of the body and that death released it to inhabit the eternal world of ideas. His views outraged many influential Athenians and at the age of seventy-one he was brought before a jury of 500 of his peers on a charge of disbelieving in the gods (in their view, atheism) and corrupting the youth of the city. By a narrow majority he was found guilty and sentenced to death by drinking hemlock within twenty-four hours, the form of capital punishment then prescribed by law. Gathering his friends around him, he continued to argue for the immortality of the soul until the poison took effect. Incidentally, Socrates provides us with an almost humorous example of the need to define our terms, because it could be said that an atheist was condemned by atheists for refusing to embrace atheism!

Plato

The second of the three Greek giants was Plato (428–347 B.C.), now acknowledged as one of the greatest thinkers of all time, who taught philosophy at his renowned Academy, the prototype of our modern university, which he established in Athens and which lasted for 1,000 years. His enduring influence is such that the twentieth-century British philosopher and mathematician A. N. Whitehead, one of the founders of mathematical logic, commented that all subsequent philosophy is merely 'footnotes to Plato'.

According to Plato's famous *Theory of Forms*, the world is divided between 'reality' and 'appearance', an idea that has percolated throughout the entire history of Western culture. He taught that whereas we can have nothing more than opinions about tangible things ('appearance', or the world of the senses) we can have true knowledge of things that can be understood by reason ('reality', or the world of ideas).

Within this world of ideas, he said that 'All mankind, Greeks and non-Greeks alike, believe in the existence of gods,'[18] though he qualified this by writing of 'the malady of atheism', an atheist being defined as 'a complete unbeliever in the being of gods'.[19] In his blueprint of the ideal state, Plato made 'impiety' a crime punishable by five years' imprisonment for the first offence and death on a second conviction.[20] Although he rejected relativism and believed in absolutes such as good and beauty, he did not believe in a transcendent Creator who brought the world into existence out of nothing, but in what he called a 'Demiurge', a divine architect who designed the world out of pre-existent materials.

With Socrates, he held that evil came about by ignorance rather than malice and that to know good was to become good. In this model, men and society were perfectible by the development of the moral values inherent in human nature, but every era of human history has shown this utopian idea to be a mirage.

Aristotle

Plato's most famous pupil, and the third of the Greek giants, was Aristotle (384–322 B.C.), a prolific philosopher who wrote extensively on most branches of learning, including ethics, politics, logic, rhetoric, psychology, botany, zoology, astronomy, history, mathematics and poetry. He founded a school in Athens, the remains of which were unearthed during excavations in 1997. Aristotle's Lyceum was an alternative to Plato's Academy and they became the Oxford and Cambridge of the ancient world. His direct influence, drawing the whole field of knowledge into a philosophical unity, extended well into the Middle Ages, and the discovery of the Lyceum's ruins in 1997 prompted the *Sunday Telegraph* to say that he has 'seldom been out of the news these last 2,000 years and more'.[21] One modern writer calls him 'not only the last of the great Greek philosophers', but 'Europe's first great biologist',[22] and many of his principles can be traced in the thinking of contemporary atheists.

Aristotle began by defending Plato's views, but he later became critical of them and eventually rejected all the essential features of his teacher's metaphysics. Although he covered a vast field of learning, his major contribution to our subject was his complete explanation of reality without any reference to a personal God. Aristotle rejected the idea of a transcendent world of changeless forms or principles and emphasized instead the existence of individual, material objects. Human beings, like all other objects, were a mixture of form and matter, though reason made them unique and able to attain union with the divine. God, on the other hand, was pure form, existing without matter and, as such, was separate from all material things and not subject to change. This 'Unmoved Mover', or 'First Cause', set the world in motion and would draw everything to its final end or purpose.

There are glimmers here of elements present in traditional theism (which certainly says that God is not *less* than the 'Unmoved Mover' or 'First Cause') but, as with Plato, Aristotle's notions of a Supreme Being were 'abstract, coldly intellectual, impersonal, detached, and unconcerned about the world'.[23] He once defined God as 'thought thinking itself'[24] — something far removed from a personal and transcendent Creator and Sustainer of the universe with whom people can have a living relationship.

The atomists

Other philosophers developed ideas which were variations on these themes. One was Democritus (*c.* 460–370 B.C.) who believed that reality consisted of empty space and an unlimited number of invisible, eternal and unchangeable building blocks which moved because of their own innate powers and for which he coined the word 'atoms' (the Greek *atomos*, from the negative *a* and the verb *temno*, 'to cut', means 'indivisible'). As to ideas of deity, he assumed the existence of extra-terrestrial beings which had more or less human forms but no interest or involvement in human activity.

Another atomist was Epicurus (341–270 B.C.) who, like Democritus, believed that even the human soul, thought and emotion could be explained by the movement and collision of atoms, while at death the soul's atoms disperse 'and when death is present we no longer exist'.[25] For these philosophers, man could be understood only as the sum of his physical parts. Epicurus believed in an infinite number of worlds, but no gods.

These atomists were among the Greek philosophers who laid the earliest foundations of the scientific approach to the cause, course and climax of human history that was to be so dominant many centuries later. Their philosophy was a basic form of naturalism, a view of the world that places it firmly in the atheistic camp because it totally excludes the supernatural or spiritual. Naturalism, which has been called 'the oldest philosophy in Western civilization',[26] says that our universe is a closed system in which everything has a 'natural' explanation. Not only does every event have its cause within the system, but no events within the system have any effect beyond it. Man's thoughts, ideals, attitudes and actions are all determined by biochemical laws, which in turn are governed by physical laws.

For the naturalist, the word 'nature' includes everything that exists, as philosopher William Halverson explains: 'If you cannot locate something in space and time, or you cannot understand it as a form or function of some entity or entities located in space and time, then you simply cannot say anything intelligible about it... *To be* is to be *some place, some time.*'[27] As the naturalist cannot allow the possibility of a theistic world, the existence of God is ruled out *a priori*, and any discussion about his being, nature or behaviour is futile; in other words, the naturalist pronounces the answer before he asks the question.

We will pursue this further in a later chapter, but we have already uncovered enough to know that the questions raised by the atomists and their ilk come not in a trickle but in a torrent. If man is part of nature, where, as human beings, can we find any personal significance for our existence? What is the meaning of 'purpose', or the purpose of 'meaning'? What basis is there for corporate or individual morality? What reference-point is there to distinguish good from evil? How can there be any rational sense of obligation to do or to be anything? If even our thoughts are pre-determined, what is the sense in speaking about choice, opinion, values, responsibility, self-awareness, convictions, or even aesthetic appreciation? If human beings are no more than sophisticated machines, what sense is there in trying to construct or defend a concept of personal freedom? C. S. Lewis hit the nail on the head: 'If naturalism were true then all thoughts whatever would be wholly the result of irrational causes. Therefore, all thoughts would be equally worthless. Therefore, naturalism is worthless. If it is true, then we can know no truths. It cuts its own throat.'[28] We are also entitled to ask how naturalists can possibly know that *their* beliefs are correct, when in order to be certain they would have to transcend this world.

American author George Roche dismisses naturalism like this: 'Contriving the theory required a great deal of thought and the finest scientific reasoning, only to conclude that thought and reasoning are meaningless. If the conclusion is correct, the theory is nonsense and no one need believe it. If the conclusion is false, it is just that, false; the theory is again nonsense. Naturalism, looked at philosophically rather than through the truncated thought of science, is an insult to the intelligence.'[29]

The sceptics

As we have seen, early Greek philosophy produced or promoted a bewildering array of religious and philosophical ideas, many of which flatly contradicted previous or contemporary theories. One Roman satirist suggested that it was easier in Athens to find a god than a man, while Xenophon called the city 'one great altar'. If it is true to say that this era was the first to aim at certain knowledge about reality, it is equally true to say that its legacy 'was one of uncertainty and confusion'.[30] It should therefore come as no surprise to discover that there were many thinkers who balked at the idea of religious and philosophical certainty and refused to commit themselves to any of the propositions on offer. One of the most important of these was Pyrrho (c. 360–270 B.C.), the prime mover in a school of thought whose adherents became known as the 'sceptics'. Pyrrho is hardly a household name today, but he is a highly significant figure in the history of scepticism. Until about 100 years ago Pyrrhonism was the name given to his particular position, which says that man is unable to know the real nature of the world or how it came into being.

According to the modern scholar James Thrower, Pyrrho's scepticism (the word is based on the Greek *skepsis*, meaning enquiry, hesitation, doubt) was motivated 'primarily by the search for tranquillity which he believed would follow from realizing perfect suspension of judgement'.[31] In other words, the violent clash of ideas gave Pyrrho a philosophical headache and he saw scepticism as the perfect pain-killer. Dogma was a disease, and the cure was to suspend judgement, not only on logical and metaphysical questions, but on those relating to moral values and conduct. One would then be able to live a peaceful life, following one's own instincts and inclinations and refusing to be threatened by other people's convictions.

That rings a very loud bell in our day, which has been called 'the age of scepticism'.[32] As the contemporary apologist Ravi Zacharias puts it, 'Never before has scepticism had such a brilliant halo around its head. There is a glory about "not knowing". A high premium is placed on the absence of conviction, and open-mindedness has become synonymous with intellectual sophistication.'[33] In the face of a barrage of religious and philosophical ideas offering a staggering variety of options in belief and behaviour, millions of people have reached for Pyrrho's pain-killer and decided that the best decision is indecision. In historian Paul Johnson's assessment, 'Scepticism towards or denial of the existence of God is the hallmark of modern *homo sapiens* — Thinking Man.'[34] Scepticism says that nothing can be known with complete certainty, and that the only sensible thing is neither to affirm nor deny anything. Even when faced with the massive implications of the issue, the sceptic adopts the popular political phrase and says, 'I am ruling nothing in and I am ruling nothing out.'

Scepticism obviously falls foul of both theism and atheism, each of which says we *do* have sufficient data to come to a judgement. The issues are so important and complex that scepticism sounds commendably humble and perfectly reasonable — but is it either? It can hardly claim to be humble. No reasonable theist, however zealous, would seriously suggest that anyone can know everything there is to know about God, and such a person will freely admit that there are grey areas within his overall belief system. Yet that is not the same as scepticism; there is a difference between a mystery and a mirage! The sceptic, on the other hand, makes the bold claim that he alone has a clear picture, in which the truth is that no truth is knowable. Yet this makes the sceptic every bit as dogmatic as the theist (or, for that matter, the atheist). He *is* a believer; he is convinced that we can know nothing about God. But surely nobody can ever *know* that he can know nothing about God? After all, the sceptic can hardly shelter behind the principle that the burden of proof lies with the theist, because the burden of proof is always on the one who believes *any* idea — and the sceptic is a believer. Far from being a modest position, full-blown scepticism is exactly the opposite.

More importantly, is it reasonable? The modern philosopher B. A. G. Fuller points out that 'The role of scepticism is to remind men that knowing with absolute certainty is impossible.'[35] But if this is the case, how can we know this statement with certainty? Scepticism claims that there is no objective truth, but in doing so it trips over its own feet. If the claim is true, then we *can* be sure about at least one thing, the claim itself, and if we can be sure about the claim, the claim itself must be false. Scepticism is self-contradictory, yet it seems happy to live with this, as it avoids the need to defend a dogma. It says that we must accept as certain truth that there is no such thing as certain truth and that we must cast doubt on everything except the statement that we must do so. Peter Kreeft and Ronald Tacelli, two professors of philosophy, pinpoint the clear contradictions in all forms of scepticism: 'They all amount to saying that it is true that there is no truth, or we can know that we cannot know, or we can be certain that we cannot be certain, or it is a universal truth that there are no universal truths, or you can be quite dogmatic about the fact that you can't be dogmatic, or it is an absolute that there are no absolutes, or it is an objective truth that there is no objective truth.' [36]

For all their superficial attraction, Pyrrho's ideas never became a settled part of the philosophical establishment and it was to be well over 1,000 years before scepticism resurfaced as a significant philosophical movement. We will pick up the threads of this in the next chapter.

The cosmic cop-out

The influence of the so-called 'Golden Age' of Greek philosophy was so powerful that in this high-speed survey we can jump 500 years to Plotinus (c. A.D. 205–270), who radically reshuffled the ideas of Plato and others, added a significant dose of mysticism and formulated the philosophical system which became known as neo-Platonism.

Plotinus' solution to the Greeks' age-old problem of trying to reconcile what they called 'the one and the many' was to say that ultimate reality is the one from which all existence flows and to which it strives to return. These 'flowings' are in the form of a kind of descending or widening stream — first ideas, then soul and finally matter, a system which was later to become known as 'the Great Chain of Being'. In this scheme of things, there is no essential distinction between a creator and his creation. Although the divine image becomes fainter as one moves 'downstream', everything that exists has divinity within it, or it could not exist at all. It also means, as Henry Morris notes, that 'There is no true beginning and no ending, neither of the cosmos nor of individuals.' [37]

What we have here is one of the earliest formal statements of pantheism, although the word, from the Greek pan (all) and theos (God), was not coined until 1705, when the Irish scholar John Toland used it of philosophical systems which identified God with the world. Fifteen years later he developed his idea into his famous statement: 'God is the mind or soul of the Universe.'[38] Stripped down to its bare essentials, pantheism is the idea that God is everything and everything is God. To put it even more concisely, all that there is is God. This makes it easy to see why pantheism can properly be called a form of atheism, because if God is everything in general, he is nothing in particular.

Although pantheism is one of the earliest philosophical theories known to man, it mixes well with modern, man-centred religious concepts, not least because it gets rid of a God to whom we are morally answerable. Yet that in itself proves nothing. After debunking the evolutionary religious model which sees pantheism as a development from more primitive ideas, C. S. Lewis warned, 'The fact that a shoe slips on easily does not prove that it is a new shoe — much less that it will keep your feet dry. Pantheism is congenial to our minds, not because it is the final stage in a slow process of enlightenment, but because it is almost as old as we are.'[39]

After speaking of 'the human impulse towards pantheism', Lewis added, 'It is nearly as strong today as it was in ancient India or in ancient Rome.'[40] It has certainly remained one of the world's most pervasive philosophies; as we shall see later, Buddhism, Hinduism, Theosophy and the New Age Movement are all basically pantheistic. So is the so-called Gaia hypothesis, first proposed by the British scientist James Lovelock and increasingly popular among environmentalists and others. This says that the earth is one single living organism, with the entire biosphere as a self-regulating system which controls and maintains the conditions for life.

Although Lovelock is 'regarded as something of a crank in the orthodox scientific community',[41] the Gaia hypothesis has attracted massive support. Pursuing its ideas has led many to personify 'Mother Nature' or 'Mother Earth' and others to speak of the earth as 'God's body'.[42] The Secretary-General of the United Nations told the 1992 Earth Summit in Rio de Janeiro, 'To the ancients, the Nile was a god to be venerated, as was the Rhine, an infinite source of European myths, or the Amazonian forest, the mother of forests. Throughout the world, nature was the abode of the divinities that gave the forest, the desert or the mountains a personality which commanded worship and respect. The Earth had a soul. To find that soul again, to give it new life, that is the essence of Rio.'[43] In her plenary address at a conference held under the title 'Re-imagining God, the Community and the Church', Chung Kyun Kyung summoned 'the spirit of Earth, Air and Water' and declared, 'For many Asians, we see god in the wind, in the fire, in the tree, in the ocean. We are living with god, it is just energy ... it is in the sun, in the ocean, it is from the ground and it is from the trees... If you feel very tired and you feel you don't have any energy to give, what you do is to go to a big tree and ask the tree, "Give me some of your life energy!" '[44] These are just two striking examples of a modern mixture of animism and pantheism which goes far beyond the respect we should properly have for the natural world and the corporate responsibility we have to care for it. Encouraging the sensible conservation and development of the earth's resources has a rationale that has become increasingly clear as the twentieth century has run its course; treating nature as a divine entity which calls for our worship has none. It is no coincidence that in Greek mythology Gaia was the name of the earth goddess.

In spite of its widespread appeal to concepts of unity and harmony, pantheism has seriously negative implications. Theologian Gene Edward Veith gives one example: 'If God, other people, pieces of quartz, individual dolphins, different planets and one's own soul are all the same, then loving God, loving other people and loving nature become just glorified ways of loving oneself. The whole universe becomes sucked into the black hole of introversion and egotism.' [45]

In that it posits God as immanent but not transcendent, pantheism is essentially one form of monism and faces the same kind of awkward questions. If there is no distinction between God and the world, between God and self and between self and the world, what is the basis for objective truth? If God and the universe are one, what is the source of human freedom? If we are nothing more than drops in a cosmic ocean, where do countless millions of people get their irresistible sense of individuality and personal identity? Where in nature can we discover a rationale for ethical principles? If we are part of nature, how can we have any moral dimension? How do we explain the existence of evil, alienation and ignorance? If these things are illusions, how can they at one and the same time be part of an indivisible whole? Kreeft and Tacelli add this clincher: 'If all is one, as pantheism claims, and if manyness is an illusion, where did the illusion come from? If all is a dream, who is the dreamer? Would a perfect God dream an imperfect dream? And if an imperfect, unenlightened human mind is the dreamer of this illusion of manyness, then these non-divine minds *do* exist, and *not* everything is God; thus pantheism is abandoned.'[46]

Plotinus did not invent pantheism, but he did give it an impetus which has lasted over 1,700 years and shows no signs of falling out of fashion.

There are millions of people today whose philosophy, religion and world-view are pinned to pantheism. Finding evidence for its popularity is child's play; finding evidence for its credibility is another matter altogether. Paul Johnson comes to the conclusion that pantheism 'is the negation of belief, an escape, a cop-out from all the difficulties of theology'. [47]

In passing, we should also include a note on panentheism, which is a kind of compromise between theism and pantheism. Panentheism denies on the one hand that God is eternal and transcendent, yet it does not identify him with the material universe. Instead, God and the universe are dependent on each other; God needs the world, because he exists only as its vital force, and the world needs God, because it cannot exist without his vitalizing power. In this scheme of things, God is no longer the Creator, but merely some kind of cosmic energy, and questions as to how the material world came into being and why it exists are ignored.

For all their prodigious output (Epicurus alone produced some 200 volumes) and the many valuable insights they brought to the world of their day, these ancient Greek philosophers left behind more questions than answers.

2.

Movers and shakers

Continuing our brief glance at some of the people who have significantly influenced atheistic or non-theistic thinking over the centuries, and at some of the ideas they proposed, we can virtually ignore the Middle Ages, often dated from about A.D. 500 to about A.D. 1500. In A.D. 529, the Roman Emperor Justinian I (483–565) closed down the ancient schools of philosophy in Athens, and it was to be at least 600 years before anything like their freethinking approach was to make any telling impact.

For the most part, theologians took over from philosophers as the movers and shakers in society. As the British theologian Colin Brown points out, 'By and large, the great minds of the Middle Ages were not interested in the physical universe for its own sake; they were interested in the reality which they believed lay behind it. They were not so much concerned with scientific questions about natural phenomena. What interested them was the relationship between the natural and the supernatural.'[1] These great minds were by now entrenched in ecclesiastical institutions, which monopolized education to such an extent that 'the medieval world was a church-state'.[2] Men's interests in science, art, music and economics were rooted in the (Roman Catholic) church and they gradually came to accept as certain only those things decreed by the church's authority. This was light years away from the freethinking approach of the ancient Greeks, and there was uproar when Aristotle's works were translated into Latin and scholars began to take his ideas on board. His classic works *On the Soul, Physics* and *Metaphysics,* in which he explained reality without any reference to a personal God, were banned as soon as they were published — a move which predictably guaranteed that they became best sellers!

The Italian connection

While some denounced the ancient Greeks as dangerous and heretical, others treated them very differently and tried to find a way of blending their basic ideas with what was then considered orthodox theism. By coincidence, two Italians were by far the most important of those who took this line.

Anselm (1033–1109), who served as Archbishop of Canterbury for the last sixteen years of his life, was the first great theologian of the Middle Ages. Using ideas from Plato, Aristotle and Plotinus, he gave philosophy a distinct role within theology. Leaning on Plato's idea that thought was more real than objects in the physical, external world, Anselm defined God as 'that than which no greater can be conceived' (by 'greater' Anselm meant 'more perfect') and aimed to show not only that faith was perfectly reasonable, but that God was infinitely greater than the conception his fellow monks had in mind. In Anselm's view, God is perfect in every way; existence is a perfection; therefore God exists. This so-called 'ontological argument' (from the Greek words *ontos* — the present participle of *einai,* 'to be' — and *logos,* 'word' or 'reason') has been playground and battlefield to theologians and philosophers ever since, and has been used to defend not only theism but several other metaphysical positions, including polytheism and pantheism. As theologian John Frame says, it is 'in some ways the most fascinating — and exasperating — of all the classical arguments ... to some it is a joke, to others the very foundation of reason and faith'.[3] Perhaps the simplest thing we can say about Anselm's argument here is that he used it to show that faith in God was reasonable, rather than to prove God's existence.

The second Italian scholastic giant in the Middle Ages was *Thomas Aquinas* (1224–1274), whose most important work was done at the University of Paris. Because of his size and ponderous movements he was nicknamed 'the dumb ox', but one of his professors saw beyond this crude assessment and forecast, 'The dumb ox will fill the world with his bellowing.' The professor got it exactly right; over 700 years later the British scholar Paul Helm can write, 'The influence of Thomas will always be felt where philosophical theology is pursued vigorously.'[4]

Aquinas' output was prodigious. Of his forty or so volumes, his most important work, *Summa Theologica* ('A Summary of Theology') ran to two million words and has been described as 'one of the most internally-consistent systems of thought ever devised'.[5] He rejected most of what Plato (and Anselm) had written, but reworked Aristotle's ideas of an 'Unmoved Mover', man as a rational animal and the priority of reason in the natural order so that they could be used to support orthodox theism rather than oppose it.

Although he taught that scientific knowledge and religious faith belonged to two different spheres, Aquinas believed that if a rational man would draw the right conclusions from the facts of nature he would have to accept the existence of God. He developed his natural theology at great length in *Summa Theologica*, laying down his now famous 'Five Ways' or proofs of God's existence (of which more later in this book). These came under heavy attack in the eighteenth century, and scientific knowledge and language have now moved even further, but it can still be claimed that Aquinas' influence is 'greater than ever'.[6] Nobody can seriously discuss God's existence without taking into account what Aquinas had to say on the subject.

By the fourteenth century, which historian Gordon Leff has called 'the sceptical century',[7] Aquinas' distinction between reason and faith had wrongly been taken to mean that each was self-contained and could contribute little or nothing to each other because they dealt with different worlds. In James Thrower's words, 'Theology and philosophy tended to fall apart.'[8] What is more, the focus of academic interest shifted increasingly from the metaphysical realm to the physical, and by the late Middle Ages there were the beginnings of a revival in culture and a mounting interest in classical art and literature. This undercurrent, in which intellectual interests gradually pushed aside men's preoccupation with religious issues, eventually forced its way to the surface: when it burst through, everything changed.

Renaissance

'Renaissance', the French word for rebirth, is the term rightly used to describe the revolution which took place over the next three hundred years and the effects of which remain as up to date as tomorrow's headlines. What was reborn was the classical culture which flourished during the 'Golden Age' of Greek philosophy but had been largely submerged during the Middle Ages. Architecture, literature, philosophy and music became all the rage. So did science, and especially the study of nature, which began to be seen as something worthy of man's closest attention in its own right and not necessarily within a religious context. Great emphasis was placed on the importance of empiricism, which says that all knowledge is based on experience or observation, using one or more of the five senses. Such was the emphasis on learning that Francis Bacon (1561–1626), who became Lord Chancellor under James I and has been called 'the prophet of modern science',[9] proudly declared, 'Knowledge is power.'[10]

One major feature of the Renaissance and the period which followed was the resurgence of confidence in humanity, what Os Guinness calls 'the eruption of the importance of the man'.[11] Epicurus and Aristotle had seen man as autonomous and self-sufficient; so had the Greek philosopher Protagoras (c. 490–421 B.C.), who coined the phrase 'Man, the measure'. This idea went into decline during the Middle Ages, but during the Renaissance man again moved centre stage and elbowed God into the wings. The idea of a supernatural Being was not always entirely rejected, but it was claimed that human reason alone was sufficient to enable man to understand the world in which he lived and to carve out a satisfactory way of living. One Renaissance thinker, Leon Battista Alberti, expressed the spirit of the age perfectly when he updated Protagoras and claimed, 'A man can do all things if he will.'[12]

It was during the Renaissance that the word 'humanism' came into existence. Initially, this meant nothing more than concern for man — his well-being, his pleasure and his freedom to understand, to explore and to develop his full potential within the natural world. One of the most significant outcomes of this was that huge advances were made in science and in the use of the scientific method, building on the work of Aristotle and other Greek philosophers whose conclusions were reached after they had carefully recorded, classified and explained their detailed observation of the world of nature.

This emphasis on humanity was not necessarily atheistic. In fact, among the first Renaissance thinkers given the name 'humanists' were those whose great concern was the rediscovery, not only of ancient secular learning, such as that represented by Socrates, Plato, Aristotle and others who flourished in the 'Golden Age' of Greek philosophy, but also of religious learning. A leader in this field was the Dutch scholar Desiderius Erasmus (c.1466–1536), whose motto was *Ad fontes!* ('To the sources!') and who sought to reform the church through the recovery of truth taught by the early Church Fathers and enshrined in its earliest manuscripts. Erasmus, one of the greatest Greek scholars of his age, has been called 'the first best-selling author in the history of printing',[13] one of his works running to 600 editions. What is certain is that his particular strand of humanism saw religion as an integral and important part of man's experience, growth and development. Such was the enduring importance of his work that he is seen by some as sowing the seeds of the great religious revival commonly known as the Reformation. Other Renaissance thinkers took a different line and were key players in the development of a modern philosophy which virtually deifies man and banishes God altogether. We will look at this in a later chapter.

The free-wheeling spirit of the Renaissance meant that naturalism, pantheism, scepticism and other ancient philosophies stifled during the Middle Ages resurfaced with a vengeance and were joined by a welter of other ideas which men now felt free to develop. In the ferment that followed there were many significant 'movers and shakers'; we can pinpoint just seven of them here.

The first was the English political philosopher Thomas Hobbes (1588–1679), who had a lot in common with Democritus and the ancient Greek atomists and taught that man was nothing more than a material entity moving through space. Although Hobbes believed in the existence of a transcendent Creator, his 'God' was merely 'the first of all causes' and had no ongoing relationship with nature or man. This model is known as 'deism'.

In its earliest form, deism was very similar to the natural theology of Thomas Aquinas and adopted what has been called 'the two-storey approach',[14] in which the ground floor is built by reason and the top floor by faith. Gradually, however, it came to teach that every aspect of faith must be shown to derive from reason; rationality reigned. Today, classical deism says that God is beyond the world and in no way identical to it or part of it. Although God brought natural order out of chaos, and set it in motion, he then left it to its own devices. God is therefore seen as an absentee landlord, or a cosmic clockmaker who wound the world up once and for all, and now lets it tick away on its own, without any attention or adjustment; the American philosopher Norman Geisler says, 'A deist believes that God made the world but does not "monkey" with it.'[15] Deism goes on to say that just as God has no interest in breaking into nature, so man has no ability to break out of it, and it is therefore impossible for man to have a direct, personal relationship with his Maker.

Deism quickly made massive strides, and leading figures in the early years of the United States, including the nation's third president, Thomas

Jefferson, were among those who considered themselves deists. In his record-breaking best seller *A Brief History of Time*, the remarkable contemporary scientist Stephen Hawking, Lucasian Professor of Mathematics at Cambridge University, seems to have the same picture of God in mind. Writing of the laws governing gravity he says, 'These laws may have originally been decreed by God but it appears that he has since left the universe to evolve according to them and does not now intervene in it.'[16] Later in the same book he suggests that with the success of scientific theories in describing events, 'Most people have come to believe that God allows the universe to evolve according to a set of laws and does not intervene in the universe to break these laws.'[17] Hawking says that his goal is 'nothing less than a complete description of the universe we live in',[18] but in the meantime he seems to give the impression that he has joined the deists in reducing God to a vague Supreme Being, a so-called 'god of the gaps' who fills in the bits that science cannot reach.

Deism's idea of God obviously falls a long way short of the one outlined in the introduction, and raises some tricky questions. What is the evidence that God has never taken any continuing interest in the world? Is it reasonable to think that a personal God would create the world and then deliberately disown it? If the world is uncontrolled, how can we trust natural law, or any individual's understanding of it? If there is no God actively present in the world, why does *anything* matter? Deism can be said to fit the presuppositions of modern science more comfortably than the model of an active, or 'interfering' God but, after examining its history and evaluating its tenets, Norman Geisler endorses the widely accepted conclusion that deism 'is defunct both historically and philosophically'.[19]

The doubter

One of the most interesting and influential characters during this period was the French mathematician René Descartes (1596–1650), who has been called 'the father of modern philosophy'. He lived at a time of great scepticism, when old belief-systems were being challenged by new scientific discoveries, and when many people were wondering whether anything at all could be believed with certainty. Because Descartes was anxious to hold religion and science together, he abandoned his idea of writing a book with the ambitious title *Project for Universal Science Designed to Elevate Human Nature to its Highest Perfection*. Instead, he tried to bring certainty into philosophy by discarding everything that could possibly be doubted in order to find something that was beyond *all* doubt. The great advances in science relied on the evidence of our senses — but how could we know that our senses were reliable? When we dream, we think that we are experiencing reality — but what if our feelings when we are awake are just as illusory? How can we know that we are not dreaming all the time? Descartes reached a point at which he wrote, 'I am constrained to admit that there is nothing in what I formerly believed to be true which I cannot somehow doubt.'[20]

In one sense, he had joined the sceptics, but he pressed on with his quest. On a cold day in the winter of 1619–1620 he entered a 'stove' (perhaps a small room heated by a stove) determined to doubt everything that could be doubted. After hours of mental contortions he came to the conclusion that, whatever doubts he might have, his own mind must exist in order to have them. Because he doubted, he must himself exist as a thinking, doubting being. Descartes had reached his goal: in his now famous words, *'Cogito ergo sum'* ('I think, therefore I am').

From what he took to be that unshakeably certain foundation, and using the levers of logic, Descartes went on to establish the existence of God and of the material world. Knowing that he was an incomplete and dependent being, the idea of a complete and independent Being presented itself to him so clearly (shades of Anselm!) that he wrote, 'I do not think that the human mind is capable of knowing anything with more evidence and certitude.'[21] This certainty was underlined by the related idea of God as a Perfect Being, who must therefore exist. Furthermore, as such a God would not deceive us as to the existence of our own bodies and the external world, these too must exist.

In building his philosophy, Descartes became one of the founding fathers of modern rationalism, which says that reason alone is the primary source of all human knowledge and is sufficient to solve all the problems relating to man's nature and destiny. At the same time (though he would not have intended this when he started on his quest) he prepared the way for those who would eventually embrace a rationalism which abandoned all belief in God, leaving nothing but nature and hard facts. According to Ravi Zacharias, Descartes 'put the knowledge of God on the road to scepticism'.[22] There are signs of this in his own words, in which he reduced traditional theistic teaching to 'the realm of religious sentiment and emotion, whereas my universal science is in the realm of reason and knowledge'.[23]

Yet for all his thoroughness, Descartes' thinking was defective. Having 'clear and distinct ideas' of things does not make them true, and defining something does not prove that it exists. We cannot jump from concepts to reality without the checks and balances of experience. What is more, logic only demonstrates possibility, not reality. As Norman Geisler rightly says, 'There are no rationally inescapable arguments for the existence of God because it is always logically possible that nothing ever existed including God.'[24]

At the end of the day, Descartes elevated reason to the place where it became the ultimate reference-point and reduced God to being nothing more than an innate philosophical idea. This explains why William Temple, who was Archbishop of Canterbury from 1942–1944, came to the conclusion that the day Descartes shut himself away in his stove alcove was the most disastrous moment in European history. That may be an overstatement; what is certain is that in one day the French philosopher made waves which are still rocking the boat nearly 400 years later.

An example of the survival of full-blooded rationalism is provided by the American novelist and philosopher Ayn Rand, who died in 1992: 'Reason is man's only source of knowledge and his basic tool of survival. Man is an end in himself — which means that each individual must live by his own mind and for his own sake.'[25] Building on this, Michael Berliner, executive director of the Ayn Rand Institute, told the *Washington Times*, 'There is no world beyond this one, no unknowable.'[26] Rand described herself as 'an intransigent but not militant atheist'.[27]

A 'hideous atheist'?

The Dutch thinker Benedictus (or Baruch) de Spinoza (1632–1677) has the rather odd distinction of having been described both as 'a hideous atheist' and as 'God-intoxicated'.[28] In fact, three other words give a much clearer picture: he was a rationalist, a monist and a pantheist.

Firstly, he was a *rationalist*. He began by setting down eight definitions, seven axioms and thirty-six propositions and then, like his contemporary rationalist Descartes, tried to build up a system of philosophy by geometrical reasoning.

Secondly, he was a *monist*. Like the Greek philosopher Thales a thousand years earlier (but unlike Descartes), he believed that 'There is only one Substance.'[29]

Thirdly, he was a *pantheist*, teaching that God existed within nature and not outside of it; in his own words, 'God is the indwelling and not the transcendent cause of all things.'[30]

In Spinoza's system, God is impersonal and as such has neither consciousness, intelligence, nor purpose. God's 'thoughts' are an amalgamation of all the thoughts of everyone in the world. Yet, as with all other forms of pantheism, Spinoza's idea self-destructs in that it requires the existence of a separate finite self to make the affirmation that all reality is one.

Even when they declined to accept all of Spinoza's ideas, European thinkers were fascinated by the general idea of seeing everything in terms of a single reality. Rationalism was to dominate continental philosophy for a very long time and Spinoza has been called 'the metaphysician of modern atheism'.

Lighten our darkness?

In summing up the position at the end of the seventeenth century, the French philosopher Pierre Bayle wrote, 'The champions of reason and the champions of religion were fighting desperately for the possession of men's souls, confronting each other in a contest at which the whole of thoughtful Europe was looking on.'[31] It was not long before rationalism was winning hands down: the Western world had already entered into what has since become known as the Enlightenment, or the Age of Reason, which was to dominate the eighteenth century.

No stone was left unturned in the dynamic drive to break out of the previously held belief-systems and to bring nature, law, society, morality — and religion — under the control of reason and of the scientific model. As nature was considered a closed system, everything that happens in nature must have a rational explanation in terms of something in nature. Since truth was considered as logical, orderly and systematic, everything in life should be seen in these terms.

Believing as they did in the inherent goodness of man, Enlightenment thinkers were also convinced that their all-embracing system would inevitably lead to human progress in every area of life. This utopian dream is brilliantly illustrated in the frontispiece to a book with the title *Reasonable Thoughts about God, the world, the human soul and just about everything else*, written by the rationalist philosopher Christian Wolff and published in

1720. The engraving shows a world shrouded in shadows and darkness, representing the old traditions and belief-systems. But on part of the scene, the sun has broken through, lighting up the hills and valleys and playing on the smiling faces of a group of peasants. It is impossible to miss the message: as 'reasonable thoughts' dispersed the gloom and darkness of traditional theism, humanity would come of age, striding confidently forwards in the radiant light of rationalism. Once the principles of enlightened reason had been recognized, man could then set about building a perfect society. Enlightenment thinking, with its two fundamental axioms, the autonomy of man and the primacy of reason, has left an indelible mark on history.

Seeing is believing?

While rationalism was taking continental Europe by the ears, a number of leading British scholars took a very different line, and John Locke (1632–1704) pioneered an empirical approach that was to become one of the most significant philosophical movements of the time. Empiricism, from the Greek *empeira* (experience), says that knowledge (other than pure logic) comes not from reason but from human sense perception. Unlike the rationalists, who said that the mind was pre-stamped with primary, self-evident notions, Locke said that the mind was a *tabula rasa* (blank slate) on which the five senses — sight, hearing, smell, taste and touch — trace whatever knowledge is to be found. In Locke's scheme of things, all ideas are acquired from experience. The senses convey data to the mind, and the mind reflects and interprets; for Locke, these two operations 'are the foundations of knowledge, from which all ideas we have, or can naturally have, do spring'.[32]

During the 'Golden Age' of Greek philosophy, Aristotle had rejected Plato's idea that men had a set of innate ideas by claiming, 'There is nothing in the mind but what was first in the senses.' Locke now used exactly the same phrase in rejecting the basic idea of Descartes, Spinoza and the other rationalists, though he agreed with Descartes that certain ethical principles applied to everyone and that man was inherently able to know that God exists.

It is not difficult to see that both rationalism and empiricism are ultimately self-centred. The individual is autonomous and is the final arbiter of truth and error, fact and fiction. Nor is it difficult to find a fatal flaw in Locke's line of thinking. James Mannoia puts his finger on it: 'If, as Locke held, all knowledge consists of ideas "drawn" in the mind by our sense experience of objects outside the mind, how can we know if the idea in the mind resembles the thing outside? How can we be sure that our senses do not introduce a "copy error" much as coloured glasses might distort our perception of a coloured object?'[33]

In spite of its weakness, the empiricist perspective became what Mannoia calls 'the spirit and hallmark of the new-born modern science',[34] and today it still underlies the thinking of those who say they will only believe something when they can see it. Although he realized that without God morals become a matter of taste, Locke had to admit that his empiricism did not establish the knowledge of God. What it did was to leave ajar the door to scepticism. It would soon be pushed wide open.

Pyrrho revisited

The man who did so was David Hume (1711–1776). Born in Scotland seven years after Locke's death, he was best known during his lifetime as a historian, but has subsequently been called the 'outstanding British philosophical mind of the age'.[35] Living in the Age of Reason, Hume bucked the trend and set out to show that reason was no more than custom and habit. He argued that perceptions of the mind were essentially impressions from sensations, emotions and ideas, and that it was impossible to prove whether these were true or false. All we could say about our experiences was that we were having experiences. Not only could we never really know what was going on outside of ourselves, we could not even prove empirically that the mind or the self existed. For Hume, any given substance was 'nothing but a collection of simple ideas'.[36] In effect, he whittled down Descartes' famous phrase, 'I think, therefore I am,' to 'I think, therefore thinking exists.' This is all very engaging, but it is easy to see how taking this approach reduces all knowledge to subjectivity — and why it has led to Hume being called 'the father of modern scepticism'.

Hume's thinking and writing covered vast areas of human knowledge. With regard to religion, he believed it had evolved from polytheism to monotheism, and he mounted a strong attack on traditional arguments for the existence of God. Like Locke, he was an empiricist, strongly opposing the idea that one could demonstrate the existence of God by human reason or sense experience. His rejection of the principle of causality (the law of cause and effect) led him to discard the whole idea of God as a First Cause, as well as the argument that the world's beauty, order and complexity proved the existence of a divine Designer. He did not deny that the universe had a cause; the issue for Hume was whether anything could be known about it

Paul Helm says of Hume, 'His work in religion can be regarded as one of the most fundamental attacks on natural theology in modern times,'[37] but he may now be best known for his classic assault on miracles. In his *Enquiry Concerning Human Understanding*, he said that a miracle was 'a violation of the laws of nature' and that miracles could be discounted by proof 'as entire as any argument from experience can possibly be imagined'.[38] He considered the possibility that a large number of witnesses testifying to an unusual event might be said to weaken or destroy his rational conclusions, but countered this in turn by saying that even the most unusual effect might still have a natural, that is to say non-miraculous, cause. It is worth noting here that in his long discussion Hume never examines a test case, but writes only in general, theoretical terms. According to Colin Brown, 'His technique is more a case of demolition by bluff and insinuation than of precise argument.'[39] Another serious flaw in his approach is that he builds up his proposition by using the kind of rational argument that he disowns elsewhere, a technique producing the wry comment that 'Hume was never one to be overburdened with anxiety for consistency.'[40]

Hume's ideas underlie many people's thinking today, but his strident scepticism runs into the same kind of problems we noted when we looked at the views put forward by Pyrrho some 1,400 years earlier. How can we deny the existence of self as an object without making use of self as a subject? One is reminded of the student at New York University who asked his professor, 'Sir, how do I know that I exist?' The professor paused for a moment, then peered over the rim of his spectacles and replied, 'And who shall I say is asking?' If what we call reason is based on nothing more than custom and habit, what foundation is there for universal and necessary scientific laws? How is it possible to rule out miracles without examining the testimony of those who say they have experienced them? How can we know we are telling the truth when we say there is no objective truth? How can we claim to be consistently sceptical unless we turn our backs on scepticism while making such a claim? The whole thing collapses in confusion.

Even Hume came to see that his ideas were leading him down a miser-able cul-de-sac, which is where huge areas of modern society are to be found. Using another picture, the British humanist Kathleen Nott says that among all the great philosophers, Hume 'hung his nose as far as any over the nihilistic abyss'.[41] At one point he wrote, 'I am affrighted and con-founded with that forlorn solitude in which I am placed by my philos-ophy.'[42] As Clark Pinnock points out, 'Scepticism in knowledge may be a nice game to play, but there is no way one can live on the basis of it.'[43] Nor is it any help when one comes to die. A woman who attended Hume on his deathbed is reported to have said that when his friends were with him he was cheerful, 'even to frivolity', but that whenever he was alone he was often overwhelmed with 'unutterable gloom' and had, in his hours of de-pression, declared that he had been in search of light all his life, but was now in greater darkness than ever.[44]

The Encyclopaedists

Enlightenment scepticism spread from England to France, where Denis Diderot (1713–1784) and Paul Henri d'Holbach (1723–1789) became two of its most influential exponents. Full-blown naturalists, they believed that man lived in a closed universe and that the massive advances in the natu-ral sciences had made God redundant, no longer needed as an expla-nation for existence and order in the universe. Diderot began as a deist but became an atheist, 'believing that all would be well with the world if only the idea of God could be obliterated.'[45] Baron d'Holbach was even more strident in his atheism and declared himself to be 'the personal enemy of God'.[46] When David Hume visited him at his home and said he had never met an atheist, he was told that he was in the company of seventeen of them![47]

Diderot and Baron d'Holbach belonged to a group of thinkers known as the French Encyclopaedists, a name taken from L'Encyclopédie, of which Diderot was one of the editors. Intended to be a complete review of the arts and sciences, thirty-five volumes were published between 1751 and 1780. It was said of the work, 'Everything is to be found here, from the way needles are made to the way cannons are founded,'[48] but this partly disguises the fact that it became a powerful voice for the freethinking en-emies of the French establishment's interpretation of traditional theism. Its stance can be seen from the way in which it was compiled. In previous encyclopaedias, information was classified under such headings as 'animal kingdom' and 'plant kingdom'. In Diderot's work the connecting link between previously related entries was broken and everything was arranged in alphabetical order. This arrangement does not normally imply anything, but in this case it carried a clear message: all entities exist independently of each other and the hierarchy of man and animals, things and ideas has disappeared. What is more, the supernatural element has been thrown out and all that is left is man and the nature that surrounds him. Scholar Ernst Cassirer says that French Encyclopaedism 'declares war openly on religion, on its claims to validity and truth',[49] and accuses religion of having been an eternal hindrance to intellectual progress and of having been incapable of founding a genuine morality and a just social and political order. This was certainly the case, though one should add the qualification that the Encyclopaedists were reacting against a Roman Catholic Church marked by widespread corruption.

Some 250 years later, many people take exactly the same line as the French Encyclopaedists, but one wonders whether they have thought through the implications. If all the elements in the universe, human and otherwise, are unconnected or unrelated, where can human life find meaning or purpose? Where is there any basis for law or morality? What does it mean to be human? What is the value of human life? The Encyclopaedists claimed to have liberated humanity; they did exactly the opposite.

No way over the wall?

The Enlightenment eventually peaked in Germany, where Immanuel Kant (1724–1804) became the dominant figure. A lifelong bachelor who had a quiet, religious upbringing, he spent virtually his entire life in the small town of Königsburg (now part of Russia and renamed Kaliningrad). Kant's self-discipline was such that neighbours could set their clocks by his habit of leaving home at precisely 4.30 every afternoon and walking up and down the street eight times.

A heavy lecturing schedule, eventually as Professor of Logic and Metaphysics at the local university, delayed the production of his first book until he was fifty-seven years of age, but his *Critique of Pure Reason* (1781), *Critique of Practical Reason* (1788) and *Critique of Judgment* (1790) were widely acclaimed and helped to establish his reputation as one of the greatest philosophers of all time. His relentless and meticulous approach prompted one of his students to write that 'Nothing worth knowing was indifferent to him.'[50]

As we have already seen, the Enlightenment glorified human autonomy, with rationalism (human reason) and empiricism (human sense experience) as the ultimate sources of knowledge. Some thinkers said that one or other of these rendered human beings capable of establishing the existence of God, while others used them to marginalize God or to abolish him altogether. Kant had been raised in a rationalist tradition, but said that David Hume's scepticism about human knowledge 'first interrupted my dogmatic slumber'.[51] He believed that humankind was coming of age and that the time had come to break out from the creeds and dogmas of previous generations. In a letter to a fellow professor he said that he wanted to reassess the whole field of pure philosophy, asking four questions: 'What can I know? What shall I do? What may I hope? What is man?' His approach was so radical that he called it a 'Copernican Revolution'[52] in philosophy. Just as the sixteenth-century Polish astronomer Nicolaus Copernicus had transformed the medieval world-view with his discovery that the earth was not at the centre of the universe, as had previously been believed, but that it moved around the sun, so Kant aimed to show that all valid knowledge was centred on man, not God.

Kant's writing was prodigious, but often ponderous. For our purposes, we will have to settle for a very brief outline of some of his conclusions. On the question of knowledge, Kant tried to marry empiricism and rationalism by saying that all knowledge comes from experiences that have been filtered through the mind, neither reason nor sense experience being able to provide knowledge by itself. He agreed with the empiricists that the *content* of all knowledge came by use of the senses, and with the rationalists that the *form* of all knowledge was 'pre-stamped' on the mind. In Kant's own words, he agreed that 'All our knowledge begins with experience,' but qualified this by saying that 'It does not follow that it all arises out of experience.'[53] Kant's failure to escape from scepticism has led to it being said that 'Hume gave Kant the problem of knowledge and Kant gave it back as if it were the solution.'[54]

When it came to knowledge about God, Kant went even further. His 'big idea' was to divide knowledge into two spheres. The first, which he called the *phenomenal*, is the world of space, time and appearances which can be explored by the senses, the world we can see, hear, smell, taste or touch. The second, which he called the *noumenal*, is the metaphysical world, which included both God and what Kant called philosophical 'essences', things about which we have no sense perception or empirical experience, and which cannot be scientifically demonstrated. He then erected a wall between these two worlds and said that man did not have the necessary apparatus to climb over it and move from the phenomenal to the noumenal. This meant that our normal, rational methods of knowing the physical world around us could not be used to discover anything about God. They were valuable for the study of the natural world, but not of the supernatural, useful for physics, but not for metaphysics. The American theologian R. C. Sproul calls this radical redefinition of knowledge 'a watershed moment in Western history' and explains his reason for doing so: 'Since then, multitudes of thinkers have succumbed to scepticism and have said that if we are to have any knowledge of God or any religious truth, that knowledge must be achieved not by reason or by scientific observations. We must conjure up a new way to get over that wall. This is done either through an existential experience or through mystical intuition. The result is that normal avenues of knowing are closed to the things of God.'[55]

In his *Critique of Pure Reason* Kant mounted a blistering attack on the traditional proofs for the existence of God, and dismissed the arguments from natural theology as 'null and void',[56] so that by the time he had bricked God away behind the wall dividing the noumenal and the phenomenal he seemed to many to have dispensed with him altogether. It is said that when he returned home one day and asked his servant why he was crying, the servant replied, 'You have taken away my God.'

Yet this was certainly not Kant's intention, and in his *Critique of Practical Reason* he argued that while pure reason was unable to establish God's existence, there was an area of human experience that demanded it. He said that everybody possessed a 'categorical imperative', a sense of duty or 'oughtness', and that this undeniable moral law presupposed three things — freedom, immortality and God. One of his most quoted statements, now carved on his gravestone, personalized this proposition: 'Two things fill my mind with ever new and increasing wonder and awe, the more often and more intensely the reflection dwells on them, the starry heavens above and the moral law within.'

It is interesting to notice how he established his idea of his 'categorical imperative'. Firstly, human experience tells us that the moral law is something we can obey or disobey — so freedom must be a reality even though it cannot be empirically demonstrated. Secondly, the moral law points to the soul's indefinite progress towards perfection — in Kant's famous dictum, 'ought implies can' — which in turn points to the immortality of the soul. Thirdly, we have a sense of justice, and make an instinctive connection between virtue and happiness, yet in the phenomenal world the connection is often missing; we see justice flouted, evil unpunished and virtue unrewarded. We must therefore presuppose that there is a world beyond the phenomenal where these wrongs will be righted — and this can only be brought about by a moral, omnipotent and omniscient Being who is perfectly just. Although we cannot prove anything about God on the basis of argument, we need the idea of God as the basis on which to build moral judgement. In other words, we must live as though there were a God.

Kant was perfectly right to point out that without God ethics and morality would be meaningless, virtue would be destroyed and society would disintegrate, but he smuggled God into his scheme of things only to provide support for his moral system. What is more, Kant's God was nothing more than an abstract logical principle created by human reason (in effect, the God of the deists) rather than one who personally intervenes in human history. As a result, man's spiritual progress and destiny lay entirely in his own hands: 'Man must make or have himself made into whatever, in a moral sense, whether good or evil, he is or is to become!'[57]

Although on his own terms he would have considered himself a theist, it has been rightly said that he 'laid the groundwork for future rejections of the idea of God',[58] and his teaching continues to have a massive impact today. For example, his fingerprints are all over the widely accepted notion that while science is a matter of fact, the supernatural is a matter of speculation at worst and faith at best. Ravi Zacharias goes so far as to say, 'In many ways, Kant is the single progenitor of modern man's confidence in the power of reason to grapple with material things and its incompetence to deal with anything beyond the material. All that is manifestly real is rationally justifiable, and all that is ultimate is rationally indefensible.'[59] The whole so-called conflict between science and religion (more of this in a later chapter) owes as much to Kant as to anyone in history. Kant's insistence that 'universal human reason' is 'the supremely commanding principle' lies beyond modern man's elevated belief in his own importance and his assertion that he is under no authority other than that of his own rationality. Yet, ironically, there is a sense in which Kant was trying to save religion from being judged or destroyed by philosophers and scientists on terms that were not its own; by placing it outside of rationality he was allowing it to survive. Kant also paved the way for relativism by claiming that religion and ethics must be removed from the realm of certain knowledge, and placed in the realm where they could only ever be matters of personal opinion.

Kant's pervasive influence over present-day thinking is partly because many people have fallen for what logicians call 'the argument from authority', in this case the idea that Kant's reputation is sufficient to guarantee the validity of his thesis. This is clearly not good enough, and in many areas his teaching has been shown to be fatally flawed. If everything our senses pick up is conditioned by our minds, how can we have clear and certain knowledge about anything? What evidence is there for his assertion that the human mind is the creator and sustainer of knowledge? How can we say that we are ignorant about ultimate reality unless we know something about it? How did Kant know that there was an invisible realm to which none of us has access? Ravi Zacharias makes an important point: 'To say, as Kant did, that one cannot cross the line of appearances is to cross the line in order to say it.'[60] Again, although Kant claimed to have torpedoed the traditional arguments for the existence of God, it has rightly been said that 'What he put in their place was scarcely more seaworthy.'[61]

Kant's model of philosophy was built around a number of stupendous assertions, but many of them were clearly mistaken, and his case is seriously weakened by the way he studiously ignored powerful evidence which contradicted it. As Colin Brown points out, 'His method was rather like writing a book about the Himalayas with the deliberate intention of ignoring Everest.'[62]

Kant's first name — Immanuel — means 'God with us'. It is ironic that, of all the 'movers and shakers' we have considered so far, none has been more influential in persuading man that this is not the case.

3.

Conflict and confusion

The Enlightenment, which ended almost exactly as the nineteenth century began, was dominated by three related ideas: the assertion that reason and logic were the only keys to unlock the truth about the universe and everything in it, a belief in human autonomy, and the conviction that individuals and society at large could be brought to perfection as a result. Voltaire, who was a typical Enlightenment thinker, spoke enthusiastically about 'the limitless perfectibility of the human species'.[1] As Enlightenment man paraded his optimistic views, the idea of a transcendent, personal, loving God who interacted with mankind was gradually sidelined, replaced at best by the Deists' impersonal clockmaker who had turned his back on the closed system he had brought into being. Yet towards the end of the eighteenth century, some of the most widely held beliefs began to run out of steam, and were eventually replaced by a variety of alternatives which, subtly or stridently, carried on the battle against traditional ideas of God. In this chapter we will link some of these to five major players. As it happens, all five were born in Germany.

From facts to feelings

The most dramatic change came during what historians now call the Romantic period, when people abandoned the ordered package proposed by rationalism and, in searching for the basis for truth, concentrated on their own emotions and experiences. Romanticism affected every part of European culture and was the driving force behind the music of composers such as Beethoven and Mendelssohn and the poetry of Wordsworth, Keats,

Shelley and others. As far as religion was concerned, the leading representative of Romanticism was the German liberal theologian Friedrich Schleiermacher (1768–1834) who has been called 'the first great theological thinker after Kant'[2] and 'the first great theologian of the modern world'.[3] One of the intellectual *avant-garde* of his day, Schleiermacher was an astounding member of a Berlin-based group of Romantic writers and poets who turned against the rationalism of the Enlightenment and concentrated on the importance of mystery, imagination and feeling.

Although he reacted against a firmly pietistic upbringing, Schleiermacher tried to unite romanticism and theism. In one of his earlier works, *On Religion: Speeches to its Cultured Despisers*, first published in 1799, he began with an indictment of unbelief that has a strikingly relevant ring to it 200 years later: 'The life of the cultivated person is removed from everything that would in the least way resemble religion ... in your tasteful dwellings there are no other household gods than the maxims of the sages and songs of the poets, and humanity and fatherland, art and science have taken possession of your minds so completely that no room is left over for the eternal and holy being that for you lies beyond the world.'[4]

Schleiermacher tried to show that, whatever man's apparent distaste for formal religion, he had an innate 'sense and taste for the Infinite'.[5] In a later work he developed his big idea, that of dependence. Just as man always finds himself relatively dependent on the world, so he has 'the consciousness of being absolutely dependent, or, which is the same thing, of being in relation with God'.[6] Those who look favourably on Schleiermacher's work argue that in making this statement he was 'unambiguously positing the existence of the objective God'[7] and 'pointing out that our experience fits with the reality that God is there'.[8] Be that as it may, a very different picture emerges when we read his view of the nature of God: 'All attributes which we ascribe to God are to be taken as denoting not something special in God, but only something in the manner in which the feeling of absolute dependence is to be related to him.'[9] This fits in perfectly with the Romantics' fundamental principle that placed man at the centre of all reality.

Following from this is the notion that all religions are 'good' and 'true' in an infinite variety of forms.[10] This at least sounds charitable and slots comfortably into today's multi-faith climate but, as we shall see in chapter 11, the theory leaks like a sieve. What is more, Schleiermacher's related idea that, as each individual human being is a compendium of humanity he can love himself as one in whom he has discovered the Infinite, seems only a whisker away from pantheism.[11]

Schleiermacher's teaching was to have loud repercussions in the twentieth century, especially through the work of the German theologians Albrecht Ritschl and Adolf von Harnack. The German theologian and philosopher Paul Tillich was another influential scholar in whose work one can see shades of Schleiermacher. Tillich saw God not as a person but as the 'infinite and inexhaustible depth and ground of all being'. Elsewhere he wrote, 'The God who is *a* being is transcended by the God who is Being itself, the ground and abyss of every being... God does not exist. He is being-itself beyond essence and existence. Therefore, to argue that God exists is to deny him.'[12] The Jesuit priest and palaeontologist Pierre Teilhard de Chardin fine-tuned this idea and maintained that the universe and mankind are in constant evolution towards a perfect state, describing his position as 'a superior form of pantheism'.

The twentieth-century German theologian Rudolph Otto said that Schleiermacher's intention was 'to lead an age weary with and alien to religion back to its very mainsprings',[13] but by relying so heavily on religious experience he was bound to fall short of this. Nor is it difficult to see that Schleiermacher's theory was thoroughly man-centred, with proof of God's existence totally dependent on human experience. As has often been pointed out, Schleiermacher turned theology (the study of God) into anthropology (the study of man) and an understanding of God was reduced to an understanding of human nature. Later in this chapter we will notice how one heavy-weight philosopher adopted this idea and used it to mount a withering attack on the whole idea of God's existence.

On to Utopia?

Our second key nineteenth-century thinker is Georg W. F. Hegel (1770–1831) whose career climaxed in his holding the chair of philosophy at the University of Berlin. Hegel is difficult to grasp and virtually impossible to summarize, largely because of the tortured way in which he tried to pull together a great raft of past ideas, particularly those formulated during the Romantic period. Years later, one of Britain's best-known thinkers was to say of him, 'Never has a philosopher written less clearly.'[14]

Hegel has been called 'one of the great philosophical system-builders'.[15] His particular system was built around the belief that, rather than being isolated from each other, successive philosophies over the centuries were part of an ongoing, dynamic process. This process is usually called a dialectic; when a thesis is found to be wanting it generates an antithesis; the interaction between the two produces a synthesis; and this in turn constitutes a new thesis. Hegel used the words 'Being', 'Not-Being' and 'Becoming' to describe what he called this 'basic triad' which he believed governed all existence. He taught that this constant flow (traces here of what Heraclitus said some 2,400 years earlier) was a development of the absolute, which he called 'spirit' or 'mind', leading to the ultimate existence of fully self-conscious thought.

While holding that the material was secondary to the spiritual and that 'Spirit alone is reality,'[16] he insisted that traditional theism had had its day and must give way to Absolute Idealism (the name usually given to Hegel's model). In this system, religion is nothing more than 'an imaginative, pictorial way of representing philosophical truth',[17] what he calls elsewhere 'the self-consciousness of God'.[18] Although it is extremely difficult to get a clear picture of who or what Hegel's 'God' might be, he taught that God was 'no longer a Being above and beyond this world', but that he had revealed himself as a 'world spirit', the inner being of nature and consciousness. This is clearly panentheism, which says that God is *in* the world, unlike pantheism, which says that God *is* the world (although in some sense pantheism's advocates still regard the universe as part of the reality of God). As far as religion was concerned, Hegel's idea was not entirely new. The ancient Greek philosopher Diogenes (412–322 B.C.) taught that God is in the world in the way the soul or mind is in the body, while both Plato's Demiurge and Aristotle's Unmoved Mover give the same kind of picture.

In developing his system, Hegel played down the importance of the individual and insisted on the supremacy of the state. In one of his most radical statements he claimed, 'The Universal [absolute] is to be found in the State ... the State is the Divine Idea as it exists on earth. We must therefore worship the State as the manifestation of the Divine on earth ... the State is the march of God through the world.'[19] It is not difficult to see how this became meat and drink to various dictators in later years, but one of Hegel's most acute critics came to a very different conclusion: 'Hegel makes men into heathens, into a race of animals gifted with reason. For in the animal world "the individual" is always less important than the race.'[20]

Hegel's central thesis gripped great swathes of Western intellectualism — Paul Johnson claims that 'Every rational thinker in the nineteenth century was a Hegelian of sorts'[21] — but he failed to establish the idea that human history is a steady progression from lower to higher forms and, as we shall see later, a worldwide system based on Hegel's idea brought untold misery to millions before its sensational collapse.

How can we say with Hegel that there is no 'eternal truth' and timeless reason without making an assumption that contradicts what we are saying? Peter Kreeft and Ronald Tacelli expose the problem: 'First, you have to assume the standpoint of timeless truth in order to say that truth is determined by time *at all times*, not just at this one time. Second, you have also to say that the old theory — that truth is timeless — is timelessly false, not that it was once true and then became false. For if it was *ever* true that truth is timeless, then truth could never become time-bound and changing, for the timeless is by definition unchangeable. But if you say that the old "timeless truth" theory was timelessly false, you are admitting a timeless falsity, and thus also a timeless truth.'[22]

In his day, Hegel was idolized, but many have long since concluded that he had feet of clay.

Wishful thinking?

While Ludwig Feuerbach (1804–1872) was a theological student at Germany's Heidelberg University, his two brothers led a revolt against the university's religious teachers. When they were severely punished for their actions, Feuerbach renounced his faith and decided to mount a sustained attack on theism. In 1824, he moved to the University of Berlin, where Hegel encouraged him to study philosophy, and he soon became one of his most outstanding students and eventually one of Europe's most influential thinkers.

Feuerbach embraced the now discredited notion that religion had evolved over the centuries, arising out of man's need to find an explanation for his own existence and for the events taking place in the material world around him. As we saw in chapter 1, many people have believed that from crude beginnings, then moving on through polytheism and other developments, man had gradually come up with the idea of the single, transcendent divine Being who had become the object of traditional theism. Feuerbach stopped short of buying the entire package by rejecting the whole idea of such a Being. In the preface to the first volume of his collected works, published in 1846, he wrote, 'The question as to existence or non-existence of God, the opposition between theism and atheism belongs to the six-teenth and seventeenth centuries, not to the nineteenth. I deny God.'

Yet he did not reject religion and agreed with Schleiermacher that at the heart of all religion was a sense of dependence, but he went further and said that 'That on which man depends and feels himself dependent is none other than nature.'[23] In doing so, he radically rewrote Hegel's script and said that nature, not 'mind' or 'absolute' spirit, was true reality. For Feuerbach, nature was totally and exclusively physical; the supernatural and spiritual did not exist. He was a full-blown materialist; in his own words, 'There is nothing beyond nature and man ... any solution that seeks to go beyond the boundaries of nature and man is worthless.'[24]

The oneness of man and nature was central to Feuerbach's thinking, leading him to make his famous statement: *'Der Mensch ist was er isst'* ('Man is what he eats'). In his view, human beings, like rivers, rocks, or trees, exist solely as the result of material processes, and in that sense are no different from any other object in the natural world. The whole of his philosophy was based on man. He would have enthusiastically endorsed Protagoras' famous maxim, 'Man, the measure'.

Then what did Feuerbach see as the nature and value of religion? Ac-cepting that, in contrast to animals, man is self-conscious, he claimed that religion was merely 'the dream of the human mind'. Drawing on his past experiences and future hopes, man builds up the picture of a deity who possesses to perfection all the virtues and powers which he himself lacks and which could comfort, protect and sustain him in an alien world. What man views as 'God' is nothing more than a projection of his own nature. To put it another way, religion is nothing more than man's consciousness of himself, to which he gives the name 'God'. This idea eventually led to Feuerbach's well-known statement: 'Theology is nothing else than anthro-pology — the knowledge of God nothing else than a knowledge of man!' In effect, God does not create man, but man creates God; in Feuerbach's own words, 'Man is the beginning, the centre and the end of religion.'[25]

At the height of his career, Feuerbach was one of the most celebrated philosophers in Europe, and 20,000 people attended his funeral. Since his death, millions have taken on board the ideas he put forward, yet although much of what he wrote showed unusual and helpful insight into the nature of religion, the basic structure he built wobbles when even the slightest pressure is applied. Firstly, it is logically invalid to say that an object of human wishes or desires has no real, objective existence beyond the mind of the person who wishes or desires it. We may at times long for things that do not exist, but to say that nothing we long for exists outside of our longing for it is absurd. As the nineteenth-century scholar Eduard von Hartmann pointed out, 'It is perfectly true that nothing exists merely because we wish it, but it is not true that something cannot exist if we wish it. Feuerbach's entire critique of religion and the proof of his atheism, however, rest upon this single argument — a logical fallacy.'[26]

Secondly, how can the argument that theists invent God's existence to support their wishes provide evidence that he does not exist? In fact (as we will discuss in a later chapter) how can anything *disprove* the existence of God?

Thirdly, the argument that the existence of God is nothing more than wish-fulfilment on the part of the theist can boomerang. Might it not be more to the point to suggest that the non-existence of God (certainly of a sovereign, holy God to whom mankind is answerable) could be wish-fulfilment on the part of the atheist? Surely there is more than a grain of truth in the saying that the atheist cannot find God for the same reason the thief cannot find a policeman?

Fourthly, it is important to remember that Feuerbach launched his attack on theism for personal reasons, not because he had any philosophical, theological or rational evidence that God did not exist.

Fifthly, by lumping all religions together Feuerbach overlooked the fact that there are some — Buddhism for example — which deny the existence of a personal God.

Sixthly, if man is wrapped into valueless nature, what is his basis for distinguishing between right and wrong? Feuerbach's reply was to say, 'Man is a god to man.' This may sound elevating and liberating, but at a personal level it amounts to nothing more than 'every man for himself' and is a recipe for social, moral and ethical chaos. Feuerbach reached for philosophical gold, but left us with a handful of dross.

Hammer and sickle

Hegel and Feuerbach had a powerful influence on many of their contemporary thinkers and on those who immediately followed them. One young German student who adopted their ideas might have seemed an unlikely candidate for inclusion with them in a survey of nineteenth-century atheistic Western philosophy, especially if it had been known that he would spend most of his life in poor health, psychological insecurity (he had a nervous breakdown while still a teenager) and financial difficulty. Yet he was to leave his mark on the lives of more millions of people than either of them, and his impact was such that we must give him additional space. His name was Karl Marx (1818–1883).

Marx came from a Jewish family and was born in the ancient Rhineland city of Trier. He was sent to a church school, but there was little or no pressure on him to commit himself to any religious cause, and eventually he declared himself an atheist. In his early twenties, he became the editor of a radical newspaper, a post which enabled him to spread his ideas widely until the paper was shut down by the authorities. In 1844, he met the political theorist and socialist revolutionary Friedrich Engels in Paris. Not only did they become lifelong friends, but Engels, a successful businessman, proved a vital source of funds for Marx, who was rarely in regular employment. Caught up in the revolutionary activity of the times, Marx was expelled from Paris and spent five years in Brussels. In 1848, he and Engels published *The Communist Manifesto*, a statement of principles urging workers to overthrow the ruling classes. One clause in the manifesto clearly reflected its authors' atheism: 'Communism abolishes all religion and all morality.' Although acquitted on a charge of sedition, Marx was expelled from Germany and in 1849, when thirty-one years of age, he moved to London, where he was to spend the rest of his life. For most of this time he lived in abject poverty. When one of their children died his wife had to beg money from a neighbour to buy a coffin, and in later years he was to write, 'I have sacrificed my whole fortune to the revolutionary struggle.'[27]

For many years, he spent up to nine hours a day studying and writing in the British Museum. In 1861 he began to concentrate on *Das Kapital*, which he considered his major work and which was published in 1867. Ironically, income from his writing eventually put him into the very economic bracket which *Das Kapital* condemned, but his final days were desperately unhappy, and he sank into deep depression before his death in 1883.

Marx was not a philosopher. He once said, 'Philosophers have always interpreted the world in various ways; the point, however, is to change it,'[28] yet he drew on many thinkers in the distant and immediate past in formulating his communistic system of society. His doctoral thesis examined the ideas of Democritus and Epicurus, two of the ancient Greek atomists we noted in chapter 1, and, like them, he believed our universe to be a closed system in which everything has a 'natural' explanation. From the generation immediately preceding his own he adopted Hegel's idea of history as a dialectical process, with thesis, antithesis and synthesis continuing to bring about higher stages of existence. However, Marx's basic world-view would not allow him to swallow Hegel whole, and in place of dialectical idealism he put dialectical materialism, in which he saw society's economic forces as the motor driving history on to the ideal. Marx reduced all of history to five stages: the primitive, communal stage, when people owned everything in common; the slave stage; the feudal society; the bourgeois or capitalist society (dominant in his day) and the socialist or communist stage, the goal for which he aimed. Within this framework, he saw the class struggle in which he immersed himself as a titanic effort to get from the fourth stage to the classless society of the fifth.

In its early development, Marxism owed a great deal to Feuerbach; at one point Engels said, 'We were all enchanted by him and for a time became Feuerbachians.'[29] Marx was particularly attracted to Feuerbach's emphasis on man, rather than on the supernatural and transcendent, and on the fact that he made 'the social relationship of "man to man" the basic principle of his theory'.[30] Yet he thought that Feuerbach was too abstract and that in wanting to get rid of theology but keep religion (even as nothing more than self-projection) he did not go far enough. Marx wanted to get rid of both, and made no bones about his position: 'Religion is the sigh of the oppressed creature, the sentiment of a heartless world, and the soul of soulless conditions. It is the opium of the people. The abolition of religion, as the illusory happiness of men, is a demand for their real happiness.'[31] Elsewhere he wrote, 'Religion is just the imaginary sun which seems to man to revolve around him, until he realizes that he himself is the centre of his own revolution.'[32]

As Marx saw it, religion caused people to think in terms of an afterlife in another world, when they should be working to change the one in which they now lived. They were driven to this, not by any inherent spiritual dimension, but by social injustice and the inhumane use of material power. What the masses failed to see was that the ruling classes were drip-feeding them with 'pie-in-the-sky' religion as some kind of consolation in their downtrodden condition. When social and economic oppression had been removed by communism, religion — which he once called 'flowers on the chains of our oppression' — would disappear and man would live contentedly in a classless society in which the supernatural would play no part in his thinking. Needless to say, Marx rejected all forms of theism out of hand. In the foreword to his doctoral thesis he openly declared, 'I harbour hate against all the gods.' What is more, he was sure that he was on the right track and would eventually lead humanity out of its religious ignorance and superstition: 'I will wander godlike and victorious through the ruins of the world. And giving my words an active force, I will feel equal to the creator.'[33]

In the early part of the twentieth century, massive strides were taken to put Marx's theories into practice. Leading this determined drive was the Russian leader Vladimir Ilyich Ulyanov (1870–1924), also known as Vladimir Ilyich, but best known as Lenin, a single-minded radical who became the century's most successful revolutionary. Hardened by working underground for over twenty years in Russia and elsewhere, Lenin and his Bolsheviks (roughly meaning 'those in the majority') seized control of the country soon after the Russian czar was deposed in 1917. In the seven years that remained before his death he ruthlessly set about applying Marx's theories.

Although he reshaped some aspects of Marxism to meet his goals, Lenin retained its essential principles, including its dogmatic atheism. On religion in general, he echoed Marx's own words: 'Religion is opium for the people. Religion is a kind of spiritual intoxicant in which the slaves of capitalism drown their humanity and blunt their desire for a decent human existence.'[34] In a letter to Maxim Gorky, sometimes known as the father of Soviet literature, he wrote, 'There can be nothing more abominable than religion.'[35] In Lenin's view, this dogma needed to be firmly applied at a personal level: 'Every religious idea, every idea of god, every flirtation with the idea of God is unutterable vileness... Any person who engages in building a god, or who even tolerates the idea of god-building, disparages himself in the worst possible fashion.'[36]

Early in the revolution, religion was seen as the major threat and steps were therefore taken to neutralize it. An avalanche of laws, increasingly oppressive, began to restrict religious activity. In 1918, priests and bishops were robbed of certain important rights, and were classed with idiots as being unproductive in the cause of Communism. The religious instruction of children and young people was slowly stifled and believers were forbidden to teach in schools and universities. Heavy financial burdens were imposed on churches, forcing thousands to close, and cathedrals in Kazan and Leningrad were turned into anti-religious museums. The Union of Militant Atheists, founded with the motto 'The fight against religion is the fight for socialism', produced a stream of films, plays, lectures and radio broadcasts. Many of those who refused to abandon their belief in God were sent to mental institutions, prisons, concentration camps or the grave.

After Lenin's death in 1924, his place was taken by Josef Stalin (1879– 1953). A one-time seminary student studying to be a minister of religion, Stalin turned his back on God, became one of the main architects of the Union of Soviet Socialist Republics (USSR), and remorselessly continued to impose his interpretation of Marxist-Leninist ideas on the vast numbers of people under his control. The Godless Union was founded, and by 1932 had seven million members organized into 80,000 cells. A League of Militant Godless encouraged young people to oppose religion of every kind, and in one year alone published some fourteen million pieces of atheistic literature.

On a wider front, upwards of twenty million people were herded into slave-labour battalions to help in developing a socialist state. Some fourteen million were imprisoned, often in vile conditions. Stalin was 'but old Lenin writ large'[37] and his contempt for God was especially demonstrated in his vicious persecution of believers, many of whom died for their faith in the course of a vicious purge which, in one authority's estimate, led to the systematic slaughter of some ten million people.[38]

Stalin was followed by a succession of leaders who presided over what was soon to become a spiralling decline in the great Marxist enterprise but, although they made token concessions under pressure from the international community, none of them renounced atheism. One year after his appointment as General Secretary of the USSR in 1985, Mikhail Gorbachev was calling for more aggressive atheistic education and describing the struggle with traditional religion as 'decisive and uncompromising', but other forces were at work and three years later the USSR collapsed.

In 1983, the dissident Soviet author Alexander Solzhenitsyn was presented with the prestigious Templeton Prize for progress in religion. In accepting the award, he gave this clear assessment of what lay behind the tragedy that had wrecked his country: 'I have spent well-nigh fifty years working on the history of our Revolution. In the process, I have read hundreds of books, collected hundreds of personal testimonies, and have already contributed eight volumes of my own towards the effort of clearing away the rubble left by that upheaval. But if I were asked today the main cause of the ruinous Revolution that has swallowed up some sixty million of our people, I could not put it more accurately than to repeat: "Men have forgotten God; that's why all this has happened."'

Although only eleven people attended Marx's graveside funeral in London's Highgate Cemetery in 1883, Engels said in his eulogy, 'His name will endure through the years, and so also will his work.' In one sense this has proved to be the case, because by 1980 some twenty-eight nations, representing 1.5 billion people (more than one-third of the world's population) were governed by Marxist regimes. More importantly from our present perspective, these regimes were all committed to an atheistic agenda and engaged to a greater or lesser extent in the repression and persecution of those who believed in God. Two countries in particular provide horrific evidence of what happened as a result.

In 1949 the Communist revolutionary Mao Tse-tung established the People's Republic of China and, in the course of imposing his regime, expelled all foreign missionaries, liquidated religious organizations and subjected believers to cruel and relentless persecution. Many thousands of them were put to death as Mao sought to accelerate the Marxist revolution in a gigantic piece of social engineering that was eventually to cost the lives of millions; at one stage, opponents of his plans were being executed at the rate of over 22,000 a month.[39] Towards the end of his life, as his diseased mind oscillated between religion and secular belief, Mao is reported to have said, 'My body is riddled with diseases. I have an appointment with God.'[40] Mao kept that appointment on 9 September 1976.

The Cambodian Marxist Pol Pot was another who tried to create instant atheistic Communism in his country. With his Khmer Rouge guerrillas as an instrument, Pol Pot set his sights on 'stripping away, through terror and other means, the traditional bases, structures and forces which have shaped and guided an individual's life' and then 'rebuilding him according to party doctrines by substituting a series of new values'.[41] The blood-letting in the 'killing fields' of Cambodia was terrible. Between April 1975 and January 1977, over 1,500,000 people, one-fifth of the country's population, were slaughtered.[42] As with his Marxist-Leninist heroes in the USSR, Pol Pot's atheism was one of the forces which drove his agenda. As part of his revenge on religion (he had been educated in a monastery)

Cambodia's religious leaders were prime targets in his programme of systematic slaughter and of the country's 60,000 monks only a few hundred survived. Ironically, Pol Pot died peacefully in his sleep in April 1998.

In giving these details I am not suggesting that atheism automatically leads to barbarity, nor am I claiming that all atheists would endorse this kind of cruelty. Nevertheless, atheists must face this question: in the absence of any moral law grounded in God, on what basis can we deny any the right to frame their own sets of values and seek to impose them on others? Pol Pot, for example, was not only a crude Marxist but a passionate nationalist. He believed that the way to Cambodian prosperity was to wipe out the urban élite — 'To spare you is no profit; to destroy you is no loss,' was one of his favourite slogans — and to give power to the peasantry. On what grounds can an atheist question what he did?

Marxism under the microscope

Mounting a critique of Marxist-Leninism is not difficult, though there are areas in which Marx pointed out features in society which needed to be addressed and corrected. He was undoubtedly right in much of what he said about economics, labour and the exploitation of the poor. Again, religion *has* sometimes been misused for social, economic and political oppression, though this is a long way from proving that every religion has done so. There *are* those who have used religion as a crutch, but this hardly warrants tarring everyone with the same brush, and Marx makes no contribution to the fundamental debate on the existence of God. In turning from this truly remarkable man, here are some of the key questions that need to be asked:

- If the state is self-sufficient, self-justifying and a law unto itself, where does this leave individual freedom of thought and direction?
- If there is no God, and no other absolute beyond the existence of matter, how can there be any ultimate source of truth as a reference-point by which an objective system of law and order can be assessed?
- If man has no soul, and all 'goodness' and 'truth' are relative to time and space, how can any abiding value be attributed to man as an individual?

As Charles MacKenzie asks, 'How can man experience, use and organize nature while being nothing more than a part of nature? Does not his capability to subdue and direct nature imply that man is above nature?'[43]

Marxism claims that human beings are completely material, biological entities, and are in that sense on the same level as animals, but what explanation does it offer for their spiritual self-awareness, or for their longing for the transcendent? If man is really nothing more than matter, where does he get his conscience, willpower, creative impulses, aspirations, creativity, hope and imagination, or concepts such as love and beauty?

A major plank in Marx's philosophy (lifted from Hegel) is the notion that mankind is inherently good and merely needs efficient leadership to bring it to perfection. Paul Johnson easily knocks this idea on the head: 'We can see ... that Hegel was wrong because we have had demonstrated, before our eyes, the catastrophic failure of the system based on the ideas of his most influential follower, Karl Marx. The collapse of the Communist empire, or realized Marxism, in total and unqualified ruin, has been a vivid and costly and utterly persuasive demonstration that Hegel's central proposition, translated by Marx into political and economic forms, is false. Humankind may improve and learn to behave better, at any rate up to a point, but it does not change in fundamentals, and "Utopian visions are dangerous fallacies".'[44] Nobody could show that Western capitalism has all the answers, but how does one square the socialist claim of leading the state's citizens to perfection with the pride, greed and ruthless cruelty of the leaders concerned? Why did a system based on reason and idealism spawn what Johnson calls 'every form of corruption known to man'?[45] Charles MacKenzie focuses on one specific failure: 'One hundred years after Marx's death no society has yet achieved pure Communism. Socialist countries have simply exchanged ownership of capitalists for that of party leaders who live as luxuriously and rule more absolutely than any capitalist ever did.'[46]

Where is the proof for Marx's fundamental assertion that religion is imaginary, nothing more than a projected longing, an idea which is absolutely basic to his communistic model?

If changing the system would cause the notion of religion to fade from people's minds as a matter of course, why did Communist dictators in the USSR and elsewhere find it necessary to close down countless thousands of churches and other places of worship, brutalize religious leaders, force atheism on to the educational curriculum and slaughter millions of believers?

What explanation can Marxism give for the fact that, in spite of massive and systematic attempts by one Communist government after another to eliminate religion, it has not only survived but emerged from persecution stronger than ever? Conceding (as some Marxists do) that religion will always have some kind of secondary role until a truly classless society is achieved is clearly special pleading.

The Marxist revolution and the subsequent government of China, Russia and Eastern Europe for most of the twentieth century has been called the greatest experiment in consistent atheism that the world has so far seen, yet it has proved a catastrophic failure. An East European once made the shrewd comment that the only difference between capitalism and Communism is that with capitalism man exploits man and with Communism the reverse is the case! It is said that an old woman once asked Mikhail Gorbachev whether Communism had been invented by a politician or a scientist. Gorbachev replied that he was not sure, but thought it was a politician. 'That explains it,' said the woman. 'If it had been a scientist he would have tried it on mice first.'[47]

There was a time when Marxism seemed to be establishing itself as a creditable alternative to theism, and many believed that it had God on the run. Now, at the beginning of the twenty-first century, it lies in a discredited and shameful heap on the graves of those massacred in pursuit of its godless ideas. *The Black Book of Communism*, written by a group of left-wing historians and published in 1997, puts the number of victims since the Russian Revolution eighty years earlier at between eighty-five million and 100 million.[48] Paul Johnson went even further and wrote that in the twentieth century alone the totalitarian state proved itself to be 'the greatest killer of all time' and that by the 1990s, 'State action had been responsible for the violent or unnatural deaths of some 125 million people during the century, more perhaps than it has succeeded in destroying during the whole of human history up to 1900.'[49] As Johnson notes elsewhere, Marxism, along with other modern totalitarian alternatives to God, has been 'demonstrated to be incorrigibly destructive and evil'.[50]

One might add that there is a tragic irony in Marxist governments spending vast fortunes trying to destroy religion which they claimed to have no foundation, and forbidding their people to worship a God they claim does not exist!

God's undertaker?

The fifth and last of the nineteenth-century's most influential atheists was the German philosopher and philologist Friedrich Nietzsche (1844–1900). The son of a minister of religion — and grandson of two others — Nietzsche is renowned for his often-quoted words, 'God is dead,' but, taken at its face value, this statement hides more than it reveals. Several other thinkers, including Hegel, had already spoken about God's death, but it was Nietzsche who gave the idea the dramatic impetus that led to his being described as 'the most imaginative and articulate modern spokesman for atheism'.[51]

Nietzsche's writing was intense, vivid, powerful and moving, as we can see from this defining passage in *The Joyful Wisdom*, published in 1882:

> Have you not heard of the madman who lit a lamp in broad daylight and ran up and down the marketplace shouting incessantly, 'I'm looking for God! I'm looking for God!'? But, because many of the people who were standing there did not believe in God, he aroused a good deal of mirth... But the madman thrust in between them and fixed them with his eyes. 'Where is God?' he shouted. 'I'll tell you! We have killed him — you and I! We are all his murderers! But how have we done it? How could we drink the sea dry? Who gave us the sponge to wipe away the horizon? What did we do when we uncoupled the earth from its sun? Where is the earth moving to now? Where are we moving to? Away from all suns? Are we not running incessantly? Backwards, sideways and forwards in all directions? Is there still an above and a below? Are we not wandering through an infinite nothing? Is not the void yawning ahead of us? Has it not become colder? Is it not more and more night? Do the lamps not have to be lit during the day? Do we hear nothing of the noise of the gravediggers who are burying God? Do we smell nothing of the decomposition of God? The gods are decomposing! God is dead! God is dead! And we have killed him!'[52]

For Nietzsche, the first response to God's passing was one of joyful relief. He wrote, 'We philosophers and "free spirits" feel ourselves irradiated as by a new dawn by the report that the "old God is dead"; our hearts overflow with gratitude, astonishment, presentiment and expectation. At last the horizon seems open once more ... perhaps never before did such an open sea exist.'[53] Nietzsche was a mythological atheist; he believed that the God-myth was once alive in the sense that man believed in it, but that the myth was dead and buried and was no longer workable. In other words, like Feuerbach, he dismissed God as mere wish-fulfilment. Man feels inadequate, longs for someone to meet his needs, so 'wishes' into existence a God who has no objective reality. In Nietzsche's view, God was created by man, and not man by God.

But he was not content to leave things there; he saw himself as a prophet for the liberation of the human race. He looked on the culture of the nineteenth century as 'decadent' and in the process of losing its authentic existence. The religious call to virtues such as meekness and humility produced what he called a 'herd morality'; men huddled together to find comfort and sympathy, instead of striking out to find their own personal values and significance. He despised weakness, meekness and subservience, which he saw as indications of a 'slave morality', an attitude accepted without question even though it was based on nothing more than the conventions of society. In this approach, he was taking naturalism to its logical conclusion. If mankind is locked into a closed system, with no transcendent God in control, things like truth, morals and ethics are up for grabs; they are no more than what we decide for ourselves.

What is more, Nietzsche taught that 'herd morality' impoverished man by depriving him of natural values and ethics. Looking to God for help and to heaven as a reward robbed man of his authentic existence and identity, and should be forcibly resisted: 'I entreat you my brothers, remain true to the earth, and do not believe those who speak to you of superterrestrial hopes! They are poisoners, whether they know it or not.'[54] Man's significance was to be found in biology, not theology. Kant had argued that moral activity implies a moral dimension; Nietzsche turned the coin over and saw that once God is abandoned, morality based on his existence must be thrown out.

In establishing something to take its place (he realized that values were imperative) Nietzsche called for 'biological heroism' in re-establishing authentic human existence. What was needed was a 'transvaluation of values' and a 'will to power' (one of Nietzsche's major phrases) which would impose these new values on others, whether they wanted them or not. Traditional values tended to preserve the weak and helpless, who could make little or no contribution to society. In the new order of things, only the strong would survive. For Nietzsche, there was no point in mankind aiming for the perfection (his word was 'supernature') alleged to have been his as God's creation. 'Supernature' was a future goal, and man should be looking for an *Übermensch* (usually translated 'Superman', but more accurately 'Overman') who would refuse to submit to political or religious authority or tradition, break out of the 'herd morality' and 'go beyond good and evil' in establishing his own value-system, triumphing over all weakness and despising it when he found it in others.

It is not difficult to see why the German dictator Adolf Hitler hijacked Nietzsche's writings as his philosophical blueprint when he set about building his infamous Third Reich. Fundamental atheism, which saw the world as a closed system, fitted perfectly into Hitler's scheme of things. So did the idea of the extermination of the weak, the mentally unstable and all who could not make a worthwhile contribution to the establishment of a superior race. Still preserved in the notorious Auschwitz concentration camp in southern Poland, where at one stage during the Second World War 12,000 people a day were gassed to death as part of Hitler's demented mass-murder of over six million Jews, his words reflect the outcome of taking Nietzsche's ideas to their logical conclusion: 'I freed Germany from the stupid and degrading fallacies of conscience and morality ... we will train young people before whom the world will tremble. I want young people capable of violence — imperious, relentless and cruel.'[55]

Nietzsche had forecast that, because God had died in the nineteenth century, the twentieth century would become the bloodiest century in history. His words proved tragically and sickeningly true. As Ravi Zacharias says, 'Hitler unintentionally exposed atheism and dragged it where it was reluctantly, but logically, forced to go. The denuding of people, in every sense of the word, that took place in concentration camps, brought about the logical outworking of the demise of God and the extermination of moral law... Disregard for the sanctity of life, and its resultant corollary of estimating the value of a life by its quality, provided some of the Third Reich's metaphysical moorings. The "inferior" were to be obliterated; the "superior" were to determine destiny, and the will and power of the superman would dominate.'[56]

Nietzsche disowned what Hegel, Feuerbach, Marx and others had said about the flow of history. Instead, he turned the clock back over 2,000 years and tried to revive the idea of history as an endless series of meaningless cycles. Tied in with this was his opposition to the then fashionable philosophy of optimistic humanism, including the idea that education would lead man to Utopia. Nietzsche was a tortured paradox. At times he wrote with life-affirming optimism, yet at other times seemed to reject every attempt to construct meaning and hope in human existence. In doing so he produced the seed-bed of nihilism (of which more in chapter 7), a philosophy which says that man began in nothingness, has no God-given values to stabilize him and ultimately ends in oblivion.

One of those who survived Auschwitz has no doubt that nihilism lay behind what took place there: 'If we present man with a concept of man which is not true, we may well corrupt him. When we present him as an automation of reflexes, as a mind machine, as a bundle of instincts, as a pawn of drives and reactions, as a mere product of heredity and environment, we feed that nihilism to which modern man is, in any case, prone. I became acquainted with the last stage of corruption in my second concentration camp, Auschwitz. The gas chambers of Auschwitz were the ultimate consequence of the theory that man is nothing but the product of heredity and environment — or, as the Nazis like to say, of "blood and soil". I am absolutely convinced that the gas chambers of Auschwitz, Treblinka, and Maidanek were ultimately prepared at the desks and in the lecture halls of nihilistic scientists and philosophers.'[57]

Nietzsche's tension in trying to marry this stifling pessimism to his passionate call for heroic living should not make it totally surprising to discover that this intense, tormented man 'flipped' in 1889 and spent the last years of his life in a state of madness, thought by many to have been accelerated by the venereal disease which he caught some time earlier. After a lifetime of exploring the anxiety, anger and pain of human existence, his quest for dignity ended in insanity. When he was confined to his house, his sister followed his principles and, instead of evoking pity and sympathy, exercised her 'will to power' by selling people tickets to come and see him in his tragic derangement.

It is doubtful whether anyone has written more incisively or vividly than Nietzsche about the consequences of atheism. As Ravi Zacharias puts it, 'He compelled the philosopher to pay the full fare of his ticket to atheism and to see where it was going to let him off. Nietzsche wanted to look life squarely in the eye, with no God to obstruct his vision, and the picture he saw was agonizing to the mind. He saw no vast mind behind the framing of the world, he heard no transcending voice giving counsel to this world, he saw no light at the end of the tunnel, and he felt the loneliness of existence in its most desolate form.'[58]

Colin Brown rates Nietzsche's influence upon European literature and philosophy as 'incalculable',[59] and we will look at one particular facet of this in chapter 6, yet for all his impassioned rhetoric he made no contribution to the question of the existence of God. Instead, all his brilliant and at times tortuous thinking was based on the unexamined assumption that God was non-existent. He lived just a few painful and deranged months into the twentieth century and, like the madman he created in the work from which we quoted earlier in this chapter, he ended his life 'wandering through an infinite nothing'. In one of his works he had written, 'Truths are illusions about which one has forgotten that this is what they are!' Cold comfort on one's dying day!

Some time ago a piece of graffiti scrawled on a wall in New York announced, '"God is Dead". Nietzsche.' Underneath, someone added, '"Nietzsche is dead". God.' Quite!

4.

Impossible things before breakfast

In his annual report for 1858, Thomas Bell, President of the Linnean Society of London (named after the eighteenth-century Swedish biologist Carolus Linnaeus) told its members, 'The year has not been marked by any of those striking discoveries which revolutionize the department of science on which they bear.'[1] This was to prove a stupendous gaffe, because it failed to recognize the potential impact of two papers that had been read to the society in July of that year. One was written by the naturalist Alfred Russel Wallace while recovering from illness on the small island of Ternate, between New Guinea and Borneo; the other was the work of a middle-aged naturalist whose ideas were about to take the world by storm. Those ideas penetrate so deeply into our subject that we will need to examine them at some length.

Origins

Charles Darwin was born in Shrewsbury in 1809. His father was a doctor but, after an abortive attempt to study medicine at Edinburgh University, Charles switched to Cambridge, where he read classics, mathematics and theology in preparation for what was hoped would be a career in the Church of England ministry. He did poorly in classics, and even worse in mathematics. His theology results helped him to leave Cambridge in 1831 with a BA degree, though he had already turned his back on the idea of entering the ministry. Instead, and in spite of having no training in the subject, he jumped at the offer of a place as a naturalist on HMS *Beagle*, which left that year for an extensive surveying expedition off the coast of South

America and elsewhere. The expedition was to last five years; its repercussions were to produce what has been called 'by far the most potent single factor to undermine popular belief in the existence of God in modern times'.[2]

This would not have been what Darwin intended when he set out, although pigeon-holing his religious beliefs is far from straightforward, and atheists, agnostics and theists have all tried to claim him as one of their own. We can assume that he was a traditional (if formal) believer when studying for the ministry, and there are indications of his being quite orthodox while on the *Beagle's* voyage, and of his being ridiculed for taking a traditionally theistic stance on a point of morality. It was after his return to England, when he increasingly realized the implications of his ideas on the evolution of species, that his beliefs began to erode; forty years later he was to write, 'Disbelief crept over me at a very slow rate, but was at last complete. The rate was so slow that I felt no distress.'[3] This seems to put him firmly in the atheists' camp yet, when Karl Marx's son-in-law Edward Aveling introduced himself as a fellow atheist, Darwin corrected him and referred to himself as an agnostic. This would tie in with his statement elsewhere that 'In my most extreme fluctuations I have never been an atheist in the sense of denying the existence of a God.'[4] A letter written two months before he died in 1882 took the same line: 'Whether the existence of a conscious God can be proven from the existence of the so-called laws of nature is a perplexing subject, on which I have often thought, but cannot see my way clear.'[5]

Theists can counter this (and his alleged atheism) with a quotation which gives a very different picture: 'I feel compelled to look to a First Cause having an intelligent mind in some degree analogous to that of a man; and I deserve to be called a theist.'[6] They can also point to his being so impressed with missionary work in Tierra del Fuego that he sent subscriptions to the South American Missionary Society, to his handing over the use of a rented schoolroom in his local village for religious services, and to his encouraging Lady Elizabeth Hope to hold similar meetings in his own summer-house.[7] Some of the evidence claimed to indicate Darwin's return to his early faith has been strongly contested, but even if it is valid it does nothing to lessen the impact of his teaching, which 'removed the ground from under the feet of traditional religion'.[8] It is not difficult to know why this should have happened. As Rousas John Rushdoony explains, 'Darwinism offered an account of origins which performed all the miracles of creation and yet was totally impersonal, materialistic, and held no man to account.'⁹ Needless to say, people jumped at the opportunity of abandoning a divine Creator to whom they would eventually be answerable and replacing him with what someone has called 'a god without thunder'. Yet there is a sense in which theists had the last word. Described during the BBC's 'Evolution Week' in 1998 as 'the man who killed God', Darwin was baptized into the Church of England as a nine-year-old, spent his most productive years living in an old parsonage in Kent — and is buried in Westminster Abbey.

Origin

Darwin had grown up with the more or less universally accepted belief that God had not only created the world but separately created different living species with characteristics suited to their environment. However, as the *Beagle's* expedition went on, he began to question this. A year after he returned home he wrote, 'I am almost convinced (quite contrary to the opinion I started with) that species are not (it is like confessing to a murder) immutable.'¹⁰ He was by no means the first person to come up with the theory of the evolution of species. Some of the earliest ideas can be traced back as far as the Greek philosopher Anaximander (*c.* 610 – *c.* 547 B.C.); there was considerable speculation on the subject in the seventeenth century; and in the eighteenth century three French scientists, Benoît de Maillet, Pierre de Maupertuis and the Comte de Buffon, produced material on most of the major themes that were later popularized by Darwin. Another Frenchman, naturalist Jean Baptiste de Lamarck, promoted a model of human evolution which greatly influenced Darwin, and a recent authority says that of the two 'Lamarck was the one possessing the most extensive and systematic knowledge of biological facts'.¹¹ Yet one of the biggest impacts on Darwin's thinking came from his own grandfather, Erasmus Darwin. A highly successful physician, who wrote many books of science and poetry, his biographer called him 'the greatest Englishman of the eighteenth century',¹² and in *Zoonomia*, published sixty-four years before Charles hit the headlines, 'He clearly anticipated practically all the basic arguments and mechanisms of evolution later made famous (possibly plagiarized) by his grandson.'¹³

For some twenty years, Darwin worked on the manuscript of an enormous volume on evolution, encouraged by Charles Lyell, a qualified lawyer who became the most influential (though amateur) geologist of his day. Meanwhile, in the course of his work in what was then Malaya, Alfred Wallace published a paper on species in 1855, and both Darwin and Lyell quickly realized that it came close to pre-empting the major work which they had in mind. In spite of increasing pressure from Lyell to get his book published, Darwin insisted on doing even more research, but in 1858 Wallace wrote to him setting out an evolutionary scheme, including the origin of species, which had suddenly come to him in the course of a tropical illness. Darwin was horrified, and wrote to Lyell, 'All my originality, whatever it may amount to, will be smashed... I never saw a more striking coincidence.'[14] The crisis, of which Wallace was blissfully unaware, was solved when Lyell and others arranged for Wallace's paper and one hurriedly compiled by Darwin to be read together at the Linnaean Society on 1 July 1858. To avoid an even greater crisis, Darwin reworked and condensed his massive manuscript and had it published the following year with the title *The Origin of Species by Means of Natural Selection or the Preservation of Favoured Races in the Struggle for Life*, now usually referred to as *The Origin of Species* or simply *Origin*.

Evolution rules — OK?

Writing about the part Wallace and Darwin played in popularizing the theory of evolution, Henry Morris comments, 'Herein was a marvellous thing! A theory that Darwin had been developing for twenty years, in the midst of a world centre of science and with the help and encouragement of many scientific friends, was suddenly revealed in full to a self-educated spiritist, halfway around the world, alone on a tropical island, and in the throes of a two-hour malarial fit. This is not the usual route to scientific discovery!'[15] Be that as it may, Wallace could have had no inkling that his ideas would cause such a stir, nor could Darwin have imagined that a century later *Origin* would be referred to as 'one of the most important books ever written'[16] and 'a book that shook the world'.[17]

A number of those involved were decidedly unsure about *Origin's* merits. The publisher, John Murray, had serious reservations about accepting it; as an amateur geologist, he considered Darwin's main theory 'as absurd as though one should contemplate a fruitful union between a poker and a rabbit'.[18] The editor of the prestigious *Quarterly Review* suggested that if Darwin wanted to become famous he should abandon *Origin* and write a book on pigeons! Darwin himself was very uncertain about both its contents and its likely reception. He reworked so much of the manuscript that he offered to pay the publisher for the cost involved, and in a letter to a friend wrote, 'You will be greatly disappointed ... it will be grievously too hypothetical.'[19] Later, he admitted to biologist Thomas Huxley, 'I had awful misgivings and I thought perhaps I had deluded myself,'[20] and asked Joseph Hooker, Director of London's Kew Gardens, 'not to say to anyone that I thought my book on Species would be fairly popular'.[21] Evolutionists sometimes claim that it was completely sold out on its first day of publication, but this is only technically correct. The first print run of 1,250 was taken up by dealers and book agents, but retail sales were only sufficient to earn it sixth place on the publisher's advertising list, and it was not reprinted until 1860.

The book got mixed reviews. Some were enthusiastic, but the *Daily News* thought it was merely repeating what had been said by Robert Chambers (who later gave his name to *Chambers' Encyclopaedia*) in his book *The Vestiges of the Natural History of Creation*, which was published in 1844 and went through eleven editions in the next fifteen years. The well-known geologist Adam Sedgwick wrote to Darwin, 'I have read your book with more pain than pleasure. Parts of it I admired greatly, parts I laughed at till my sides were almost sore; other parts I read with absolute sorrow because I think them utterly false and grievously mischievous.'[22] By 1872, when the last edition during Darwin's lifetime was published, he had become 'plagued with self-doubt and frustrated by the many objections which had been levelled at his theory'.[23] Forced to make numerous changes, he admitted, 'I cannot remember a single first-formed hypothesis which had not after a time to be given up or greatly modified.'[24] Nevertheless, the Australian molecular biologist and physician Michael Denton notes, 'Despite the weakness of the evidence, Darwin's theory was elevated from what was in reality a highly speculative hypothesis into an unchallenged dogma in a space of little more than twenty years after the publication of the *Origin*.'[25] Today, evolution dominates the entire philosophical, scientific and cultural landscape. No other theory about human and other life on this planet has done more to influence the way in which people view themselves and their relationship to the world in which they live. Almost all the books on biology issued by secular publishers in recent generations have been written from evolutionary presuppositions. No longer limited to biology, evolution has become a total philosophy which claims to explain the origin and development of everything within a closed universe, and thereby to rule out the existence of God. The evolutionary idea has become so pervasive that any student in a school, college or university who opposes it is likely to face open ridicule. This is hardly surprising when one reads of the sweeping confidence with which the theory has been endorsed and promoted. Here are some examples, listed without comment:

- The eminent American zoologist George Gaylord Simpson declared that 'Darwin ... finally and definitely established evolution as a fact.'[26]
- Astronomer Carl Sagan, whose *Cosmos* television series may have been seen by three per cent of the world's population, stated in the printed version of the series, 'Evolution is a *fact*, not a theory.'[27]
- In 1996 the celebrated geneticist H. J. Muller circulated a manifesto signed by 177 American biologists asserting that the organic evolution of all living things, man included, from primitive life-forms and even ultimately from non-living materials, is a fact of science as well established as the fact that the earth is round.[28]
- Theodosius Dobzhansky, another leading light in the world of modern genetics, underlined the contention that evolution is a complete worldview: 'Evolution compromises all the stages of the development of the universe: the cosmic, biological, and human or cultural developments.'[29]
- René Dubos, one of America's top ecologists, agreed: 'Most enlightened persons now accept as a fact that everything in the cosmos — from heavenly bodies to human beings — has developed and continues to develop through evolutionary processes.'[30]
- The prominent British biologist Sir Julian Huxley rammed the point home again and again. On one occasion he wrote, 'Evolution is the most powerful and the most comprehensive idea that has ever arisen on earth.'[31] Elsewhere he declared, 'The first point to make about Darwin's theory of evolution is that it is no longer a theory, but a fact. No serious scientist would deny the fact that evolution has occurred, just as he would not deny that the earth goes round the sun.'[32] Having served as the first Director of the United Nations Educational, Scientific and Cultural Organization (UNESCO) he argued, 'It is essential for evolution

to become the central core of any educational system, because it is evolution, in the broad sense, that links inorganic nature with life, and the stars with the earth, and matter with mind, and animals with man. Human history is a continuation of biological evolution in a different form.'[33]

- United Nations Assistant Secretary-General Robert Muller was just as emphatic: 'I believe the most fundamental thing we can do today is to believe in evolution.'[34]

- The Oxford zoologist Richard Dawkins, Simonyi Professor of Public Understanding of Science, who has virtually become the British media's 'atheist-in-waiting' and is never reluctant to let fly with both barrels whenever he has a creationist in his sights, does so with his customary panache: 'It is absolutely safe to say that, if you meet somebody who claims not to believe in evolution, that person is ignorant, stupid or insane (or wicked, but I'd rather not consider that.)'[35] One should add that Dawkins went on to say that what he particularly dislikes about creationists is that they are intolerant!

With that kind of artillery bearing down, what is the point of arguing? The evidence is apparently all around us: history proves the case; science confirms it; the experts have spoken. Evolution rules — OK? Not quite!

Windows on words

The overall subject of evolution is vast and complex. In Darwin's day a lawyer friend of his suggested that *Origin* was 'possibly beyond the comprehension of any scientific man living'[36] and nearly thirty years later Thomas Huxley complained, 'I have read the *Origin* for the sixth or seventh time, becoming confirmed in my opinion that it is one of the most difficult books to exhaust that ever was written.'[37] Now, at the beginning of the twenty-first century, many thousands of books and countless millions of words later, the subject bristles with even greater complexity, confusion and controversy, and it would be fatuous to attempt even a superficial overview of the subject in the course of a single chapter. Instead, we will pinpoint some of the 'atheist-friendly' claims evolutionists have made, and examine them through the eyes of experts in the field. Before doing so, we will need to nail down some definitions.

The word 'evolution' — which comes from the Latin *evolutio* ('unroll-ing') — and means an 'outfolding' or 'change'[38] — does not in fact appear in *Origin*, although 'evolved' is there from the sixth edition onwards. Put in its very simplest terms, evolution is the process by which nature is said to have constantly improved itself through gradual development. There was nothing new in the idea that life had evolved over millions of years, possibly from a single primitive organism. What Darwin did was to claim that an impressive mass of data supported the idea of natural selection as a mechanism for bringing this about. Yet 'evolution' is too broad a word, and in order to maintain our focus we need to distinguish between two different forms of evolution and two different concepts of it.

Micro-evolution is the theory that in organisms *of the same species* different characteristics emerge as the result of adaptation to differing natural environments. This began to dawn on Darwin after the *Beagle* had visited the Galapagos Islands, where he had made particular notes about differ-ent varieties of turtles and of a small group of land birds now known to the world as 'Darwin's Finches'. Seven chapters of *Origin* are taken up with micro-evolution, showing that great variations occurred within existing species by perfectly natural processes, and there was nothing remotely revolutionary about this. The respected biological evolutionist Ernst Mayr has pointed out, 'Darwin's choice of title for his great evolutionary classic, *On the Origin of Species*, was no accident. The origin of new "varieties" within species has been taken for granted since the time of the Greeks.'[39] Had Darwin kept to micro-evolution — his 'special theory' — he might now be little more than a footnote in history.

Macro-evolution — what we can call Darwin's 'general theory' — goes much further and claims that as a result of natural selection all life-forms have evolved from a common ancestor in a continuity of nature that goes back to a single primal origin. In *The Descent of Man*, published in 1871, Darwin made the massive leap which guaranteed both his fame and his infamy: 'The main conclusion arrived at, and now held by many natural-ists who are well competent to form a sound judgement, is that man is descended from some less highly organized form.'[40]

The first concept of our subject is *theistic evolution*, which attempts to harmonize both forms of evolution with belief in God. Theistic evolution basically says that while God remains the personal Creator of the uni-verse, he used (and still uses) the process of evolution to carry out his entire programme, including the development of the human race. In a different model, which he defined as a superior form of pantheism, Pierre Teilhard de Chardin taught that there is an ongoing evolution, not only of biology but of consciousness, mind and society, and that human history is evolving towards a climax of spirit — what he called 'the Omega point'[41] — which would be God himself. The major problem with theistic evolution is its acceptance of a theory which by definition is based on chance natural processes, and which is therefore difficult to reconcile with the purposeful actions of a supernatural God.

The second concept of our subject, and the one which directly concerns us, is *atheistic evolution*, which rules God completely out of the picture. As we have seen, not all evolutionists are atheists, yet the general theory of evolution, or something very much like it, is in one sense a necessity as soon as one rejects creation by God. If the earth was not created supernaturally, it came about naturally, as 'the result of natural laws operating upon primitive matter, producing complexity over time'.[42]

Darwin played a significant part in the development of this concept. Towards the end of *Origin* he made a few respectful allusions to God as Creator, but this may have been a tactical ploy to avoid criticism from certain quarters, including members of his own family, rather than something that fitted into the general thrust of his book. However, three years later, in *The Descent of Man*, he dropped any reference to God. In doing so, and at the same time relentlessly pressing home the alternative scenario, Darwin helped atheism to become respectable; he gave it a scientific gloss. In Richard Dawkins' judgement, 'Although atheism might have been logically tenable before Darwin, Darwin made it possible to be an intellectually fulfilled atheist.'[43] Today, 'evolution' usually means atheistic macroevolution, the vertical transformation of one kind of organism into another, from the most primitive submicroscopic form of life to man, all as the result of blind chance, and with no need or place for divine energy or interference. As the British writer and researcher Ian Taylor explains, 'The idea that life on earth originated from a single-celled organism and then progressed onwards and upwards in ever-increasing complexity to culminate in man himself is what the theory of evolution is all about.'[44] Macroevolutionists endorse this and Richard Dawkins provides a typical example of what they say: 'Charles Darwin showed how it is possible for blind physical forces to mimic the effects of conscious design, and, by operating as a cumulative filter of chance variations, to lead eventually to organized and adaptive complexity, to mosquitoes and mammoths, to humans and, therefore, indirectly, to books and computers.'[45] In fact, Darwin did no such thing, and neither, over a century later, has anyone else since, not even Dawkins. Michael Denton explains why: 'By its very nature, evolution cannot be substantiated in the way that is usual in science by experiment and direct observation. Neither Darwin nor any subsequent biologist has ever witnessed the evolution of one new species as it actually occurs.'[46] As we shall emphasize in the next chapter, macro-evolution is no more than a model, and one which can be accepted only by those whose faith can jump over a number of extremely high hurdles.

Mechanisms

Darwin proposed that evolution happens by a process which he called 'natural selection'. According to this idea, organisms prey on each other in order to survive and at the same time they develop new characteristics in order to cope with the environment in which they find themselves. Where these new characteristics become a permanent feature, a new species emerges in what Darwin called 'progress towards perfection', whereas those life-forms which adapt less well die out.

This amounts to 'the survival of the fittest', a phrase coined by the British philosopher Herbert Spencer in his *Principles of Biology*, published in 1865. Darwin originally thought that natural selection and the survival of the fittest were two different ideas, but he introduced Spencer's phrase in the sixth edition of *Origin* when he explained that it was a 'more accurate' explanation of what he had previously called 'natural selection'.

The idea of natural selection was thought to be Darwin's greatest contribution to science, but it has long since been pointed out that it leans heavily on circular reasoning: certain life-forms survive because they are the fittest, and they are the fittest because they survive. Ernst Mayr admitted that Spencer's idea simply meant that 'Those individuals that have the most offspring are by definition ... the fittest ones.'[47] Put even more concisely, those who survive, survive. Describing it as 'a vacuous statement', the well-known British evolutionist C. H. Waddington said, 'Natural selection is that some things leave more offspring than others; and you ask which leave more offspring than others; and it is those that leave more offspring; and there is nothing more to it than that. The whole real guts of evolution — which is, how do you come to have horses and tigers and things — is outside the mathematical theory.'[48] One might add a postscript here. If macro-evolution *is* taking place, why should we try to preserve creatures which are in danger of extinction? If they are inadequate to cope with their changing circumstances, surely we should let them die off to prevent them hindering evolution's progress?

Another major weakness in Darwin's presentation of the idea of natural selection is that although it provides a good working model of changes within species it provides no evidence of the creation of new ones. In *Evolution: A Theory in Crisis*, Michael Denton writes, 'It was not only his general theory that was almost entirely lacking in any direct empirical support, but his special theory was also largely dependent on circumstantial evidence. A striking witness to this is the fact that nowhere was Darwin able to point to one *bona fide* case of natural selection having actually generated evolutionary change in nature, let alone having been responsible for the creation of a new species. Even in the case of trivial adaptations Darwin was forced to use conditional language.'[49]

By the 1930s, classical Darwinism was being superseded by neo-Darwinism. This put forward the so-called 'synthetic theory', which said that, although organic evolution could not be brought about by natural selection alone, it could happen if mutations (inheritable genetic changes taking place over an immense period of time) were added to the process. Natural selection could merely eliminate unfit organisms and preserve the fit, whereas mutations could provide the variants in the life-form concerned, and from these nature could use those best suited for future development. Crudely put, mutations could give nature a bigger deck of cards from which to deal a winning hand. This is the 'hot number' in contemporary evolutionism, and Sylvia Baker, a well-known writer in the field, goes so far as to say that 'The modern theory of evolution ... stands or falls on this question of mutation.'[50] Yet for all the passion with which it is promoted, the theory runs into massive obstacles.

Firstly, natural mutations (as opposed to those induced in a laboratory) are extremely rare, one specialist suggesting that they occur once in approximately every ten million duplications of deoxyribonucleic (DNA) molecule. Pierre Grassé, one of the world's leading zoologists, who held the Chair of Evolution at the Sorbonne for over thirty years, made a particular study of mutations in generations of bacteria, which multiply 400,000 times faster than human generations. This means that in a short space of time scientists can trace mutational changes equivalent to millions of years of change within the human species. Yet Grassé found that these bacteria have not essentially changed during all these generations,[51] a discovery which led him to make the following comment: 'The opportune appearance of mutations permitting animals and plants to meet their need seems hard to believe. Yet the Darwinian theory is even more demanding. A single plant, a single animal, will require thousands and thousands of lucky, appropriate events. Thus miracles would become the rule: events with an infinitesimal probability could not fail to occur... There is no law against daydreaming, but science must not indulge in it.'[52]

The rarity factor is so important that it is worth including yet another endorsement of the heavy odds against mutations driving evolution, this time from as staunch an evolutionist as Julian Huxley: 'A proportion of favourable mutations of one in a thousand does not sound much, but is probably generous... And a total of a million mutational steps sounds a great deal but is probably an understatement... However, let us take these figures as being reasonable estimates. With this proportion, but without any selection, we should clearly have to breed a million strains (a thousand squared) to get one containing two favourable mutations; up to a thousand to the millionth power to get one containing a million. Of course this could not really happen, but it is a useful way of visualizing the fantastic odds against getting a number of favourable mutations in one strain through pure chance alone. A thousand to the millionth power, when written out, becomes a figure 1 with three million noughts after it; and that would take three large volumes of about 500 pages just to print! No one would bet on anything so improbable happening.'[53]

Secondly, far from contributing to the viability of the organisms in which they occur, mutations are almost universally harmful, if not lethal. Canadian medical professor Magnus Verbrugge has this comment on the rarity of mutations: 'This is fortunate, for in virtually all instances they are harmful. Recall that the DNA is a molecular message. A mutation is a random change in the message, akin to a typing error. Typing errors rarely improve the quality of a written message; if too many occur, they may even destroy the information contained in it. Likewise, mutations rarely improve the quality of the DNA message, and too many may even be lethal.'[54]

After something approaching a century of research, involving untold thousands of experiments, geneticists have still not been able to produce a single case of a mutation that was clearly and positively beneficial, other than at a very localized level. Verbrugge cites the results of experiments on fruit flies, chosen because of their very short life-span: 'Mutations do not create new structures. They merely alter existing ones. Mutations have produced, for example, crumpled, oversized, and undersized wings. They have produced double sets of wings. *But they have not created a new kind of wing. Nor have they transformed the fruit fly into a new kind of insect.* Experiments have simply produced variations within the fruit fly species'[55] (emphasis added).

Linking these two difficulties together, Sylvia Baker writes, 'Mutations are far from being able to produce new, vigorous genes which would enable a new species to evolve. They are extremely rare and detrimental events which do not alter the genetic structure of the race as a whole — except in some cases to weaken it. This even applies to the so-called favourable mutations such as the sickle-cell anaemia trait and the drug resistance of bacteria.'[56]

The third problem develops from the first. As all observed mutations are infinitesimally small, millions of such micro-mutations would be needed to change one kind of plant or animal into another. Verbrugge explains: 'How likely is it that random mutations will come together and co-ordinate to form just one new structure? Let's say the formation of an insect wing requires only five genes (a very low estimate). Most mutations are harmful, and scientists estimate that only one in 1,000 is not. The probability of two non-harmful mutations occurring is one in one thousand million million. *For all practical purposes, there is no chance that all five mutations will occur within the life cycle of a single organism*'[57] (emphasis added). Yet Verbrugge's 'no chance' verdict is against the possibility of one solitary structure, whereas an organism is made up of many structures *that must appear at the same time, working together as an integrated whole.* Little wonder that the French biologist Rémy Chauvin, Professor in the Laboratory of Animal Sociology at René Descartes University in Paris, comes to this conclusion on the overall theory of macro-evolution: 'I say, and I underline the fact, that if this mass of preconceived ideas did not exist, everyone would admit that since those forms of animal life which mutate very rapidly have remained the same during tens of millions of generations, *mutation could not be considered the motor of evolution.* This is a matter of good sense, but given the strength of prejudice within science as everywhere else, good sense loses its case in court'[58] (emphasis added).

The time needed to accommodate all the changes claimed by evolutionists to develop would require many times longer than the largest estimate for the age of the earth, yet even if we allowed this absurdity, other questions arise. How could evolving organs or structures interrelate effectively with other, unchanged organs or structures? What would be the survival value of a partially developed organ? How would beneficial mutations survive the loss over time by further (and more likely) disadvantageous mutations? How would mutations overcome the fact that the natural cell is conservative and tends to eliminate any change, good or bad?

The fourth difficulty faced by the mutation theory is that by their very nature mutations are completely random whereas, if evolution were to succeed, should we not expect it to follow an ordered design or plan? As we have seen, mutations are like typing errors. They result from mistakes in copying the genetic code and can therefore be thought of as accidental damage to the code. This leads Malcolm Bowden, a specialist in the subject, to suggest that 'The reliance of evolutionists upon damaging mutations as the means by which evolution progresses is rather like saying that using a hammer on a number of watches will eventually improve one of them! ... The mutation theory just does not work and is but one more inadequate attempt to provide a mechanism of how new species can arise.'[59] Ernest Chain, co-holder of a 1945 Nobel Prize for his work in the use of penicillin, is equally dismissive: 'To postulate that the development and survival of the fittest is entirely a consequence of chance mutations seems to me a hypothesis based on no evidence and irreconcilable with the facts. These classical evolutionary theories are a gross over-simplification of an immensely complex and intricate mass of fact, and it amazes me that they are swallowed so uncritically and readily, and for such a long time, by so many scientists, without a murmur of protest.'[60]

The whole neo-Darwinian package raises important questions.

- If it takes millions of years for evolution to occur, *how can we be sure that it is occurring?*
- Is humankind as we now experience it merely an intermediate stage leading to a more complex and intelligent life-form?

- If humans are the products of random mutations, sifted by the process of natural selection, how can we be sure that this statement is true?
- How can natural processes, operating by blind chance, generate complex, functioning mechanisms, let alone intelligent human beings, out of random particles?
- What objective value or dignity does humanity have if it owes its existence to nothing more than millions of accidents?

We will take a detailed look at these and related issues in chapters 15–17.

Fossils — facts and fantasies

When United States President Ronald Reagan said on national television in 1981 that the theory of evolution 'is not believed in the scientific community to be as infallible as it was once believed', a spokesman for the American Association for the Advancement of Science angrily responded that 100 million fossils, identified and dated, 'constitute 100 million facts that prove evolution beyond any doubt whatsoever'.[61] His outburst reflected modern evolutionary thinking: in the words of a leading modern zoologist, 'The most important evidence for the theory of evolution is that from the study of palaeontology. Though the study of other branches of zoology ... might lead one to suspect that animals are all inter-related, it was the discovery of various fossils and their correct placing in relative strata and age that provided *the main factual basis for the modern view of evolution*'[62] (emphasis added).

This was not the case in Darwin's day. Writing in *Origin* about the need for intermediate links between species, he said, 'Why then is not every geological formation and every stratum full of such intermediate links? Geology assuredly does not reveal any such finely graduated organic chain; and this, perhaps, is the most obvious and serious objection which can be urged against the theory. The explanation lies, as I believe, in the extreme imperfection of the geological record.'[63] Nobody is suggesting that we now have a perfect geological record, but we do have a vastly greater number of fossils to work on. What is the result? According to David Raup, Curator of Geology at Chicago's Field Museum of Natural History, 'The situation hasn't changed much. The record of evolution is still surprisingly jerky and, ironically, we now have *even fewer examples of evolutionary transition*

than we had in Darwin's time... Darwin's problem has not been allevi-
ated'[64] (emphasis added). This is hardly the message the man in the street
is hearing. Bombarded with trees, graphs, charts, columns and models
littered with polysyllabic names and claiming to prove wholesale evolution, he is inclined to assume that he can take the whole package for
granted as something scientists have long since settled as being beyond
dispute.

The particular importance of the fossil record is that, whereas all the
other evidence offered in favour of evolution is circumstantial, the evidence from palaeontology (the study of life-forms based on fossils found
in the earth) is the only one which claims to present proof of the history of
evolution, rather than its results and mechanisms. Evolutionists admit that
the functions of evolution may not always be clear, but the fact of evolution is usually said to be proved by the fossils. Yet even this claim is not
universally agreed. Writing in *Darwin Up To Date*, the leading evolutionist
Mark Ridley, of the Animal Behaviour Research Group, Oxford, has this to
say: 'The argument is about the actual historical pattern of evolution; but
outsiders, seeing a controversy ... unfolding, have imagined that it is about
the truth of evolution, whether evolution occurred at all. This is a terrible
mistake; it springs, I believe, from the false idea that the fossil record provides an important part of the evidence that evolution took place. In fact,
evolution is proven by a totally different set of arguments, and the present
debate within palaeontology does not impinge at all on the evidence that
supports evolution.'[65] If Ridley is right, the fossils contribute little or nothing
to the evolution debate but, because so many people set so much store by
them, we will take a closer look at this aspect of evolutionary claims.

The framework for palaeontology is provided by geology, the study of
the earth. Until the nineteenth century, most scientists believed that the
earth was no more than a few thousand years old. Everything changed
when Charles Lyell popularized the idea of uniformitarianism, which claims
that processes now operating to modify the earth's surface have always
done so in the same way and at the same rate over an immense period of
time. This means that the development of all things can be explained exclusively in terms of the laws and processes which are operating today, a
doctrine summed up by the eighteenth-century Scottish agriculturalist James
Hutton in his now famous phrase, 'The present is the key to the past.'
When Lyell's assumption was applied, it produced a geologic column in
which the units of rock were neatly stacked, with the oldest at the bottom

and the youngest at the top. However, it is important to note that these strata were arranged on the basis of another critical assumption, namely that organic evolution was an established fact, with complex chemicals leading to primitive living material, and in turn to simple and eventually increasingly complex creatures. Using these tools, geologists, biologists, palaeontologists and others, in the course of a century and a half, have commonly revised the age of the earth from a few thousand years to about 4,600 million years and suggested that virtually no living matter existed for the first 80% of that time.

The commonly accepted ages in the geologic column are the Pre-Cambrian or Pre-Phanerozoic Era, dated from 600–4,600 million years ago; the Palaeozoic ('ancient life') Era, dated from 225–600 million years ago and containing the simplest life-forms; the Mesozoic ('intermediate life') Era, dated from 65–225 million years ago and containing more advanced life-forms; and the Caenozoic ('recent life') Era, covering the last sixty-five million years and containing the most highly developed life-forms. In general terms, the Palaeozoic rocks are particularly characterized by relics of marine life and amphibians, the Mesozoic by those of reptiles (including dinosaurs and others popularized in recent years by the Hollywood film industry) and the Caenozoic by those of birds and mammals. When the entire package is presented it seems very impressive, but closer examination reveals serious flaws.

The first is fundamental, and was hinted at two paragraphs ago, namely that the geologic column was put together *on the assumption of evolutionary biology*. In fact, no complete geologic column actually exists (it would be well over 100 miles high if it did) except in the minds of evolutionary scientists. It is simply an idea, based on a presupposition and producing a clear case of circular reasoning, as Scott Huse explains: 'The only basis for placing rock formations in chronological order is their fossil content, especially index fossils. The only justification for assigning fossils to specific time periods in that chronology is the assumed evolutionary progress of life. In turn, the only basis for biological evolution is the fossil record so constructed. In other words, the assumption of evolution is used to arrange the sequence of fossils, then the resultant sequence is advanced as proof of evolution. Consequently, the primary evidence for evolution is the assumption of evolution!'[66] *Encyclopaedia Britannica* agrees: 'It cannot be denied that from a strictly philosophical standpoint geologists are here arguing in a circle. The succession of organisms has been determined by a study of their remains embedded in the rocks, and the relative ages of the rocks are determined by the remains of organisms that they contain.'[67] This fact alone means that the geologic column cannot properly be used as conclusive evidence of evolution, any more than it can be used to prove a vast age for the earth.

Ol' man river

A second weakness in uniformitarianism is its unquestioning faith in Hutton's dictum that 'The present is the key to the past', when the fact is that scientists are unable to subject to the rigorous examination and experimentation which true science demands events which happened millions of years ago. Instead, the evolutionist relies on extrapolation, which can be used to cover a multitude of omissions and produce some bizarre results. Writing under his famous pseudonym Mark Twain, the American novelist Samuel Langhorne Clemens provides a typically folksy comment on this: 'In the space of 176 years, the Lower Mississippi has shortened itself 242 miles. That is an average of a trifle over a mile and a third per year. Therefore any calm person who is not blind or idiotic can see that in the Old Oolithic Silurian Period, just a million years ago next November, the Lower Mississippi River was upward of 1,300,000 miles long and stuck out over the Gulf of Mexico like a fishing rod. And, by the same token, any person can see that 742 years from now the Lower Mississippi will be only a mile and three quarters long, and Cairo and New Orleans will have joined their streets together under a single mayor and a mutual board of aldermen. One gets such wholesale returns of conjecture out of such a trifling investment of fact.'[68] Twain's whimsy hardly qualifies as science, but it is a humorous way of suggesting a serious weakness in evolutionary claims based on Hutton's doctrine.

Unwelcome guests

The idea that the fossil record proves gradual development from simple to complex organisms is contradicted by evidence in strata said to be about 600 million years old. Nearly all the animal phyla suddenly 'appear' in the rocks of this period, with no evolutionary ancestors to back up the theory of gradual development. This so-called 'Cambrian explosion' of fossils represents nearly every major group of organisms alive today. To make matters worse, while the simplest life-forms are virtually absent, more complex creatures are found in their hundreds. As Richard Dawkins admits, 'It is as though they were just planted there, without any evolutionary history.' Not surprisingly, the Berkeley law professor Phillip Johnson describes the 'Cambrian explosion' as 'the single greatest problem which the fossil record poses for Darwinianism'.[69]

The missing missing links

A fourth and critical weakness in palaeontology's claim to prove evolution is the fact that, even when they are arranged in the most ingenious way, the fossils stubbornly fail to produce what evolutionists so desperately need, the smooth transition from one species to another, with a stream of intermediate organisms to 'cement' the index species together. Instead, as Henry Morris shows, 'All of the present orders, classes and phyla appear quite suddenly in the fossil record, without indications of the evolving lines from which they presumably developed.'[70] There are countless examples of deterioration and extinction — one modern ecologist has even suggested that the present rate could possibly be several thousand per year[71] — but if there is a complete absence of any fossils showing transitional structures leading to the evolution of more complex species the evolutionary model is seriously damaged. In his book *Macroevolution: Pattern and Process*, palaeontologist Steven Stanley is quite dogmatic about it: 'The known fossil record fails to document a single example of phyletic evolution accomplishing a major morphologic transition and hence offers no evidence that the gradualistic model can be valid.'[72] This is such a crucial statement — in layman's language, Stanley is saying that *there is no concrete evidence for one species evolving into another*— that we need to take a close look at the evidence. Ignoring at this point the stupendous rift between non-living matter and even the most primitive life-form (we will look at this in chapter 14) the other gaps are truly immense.

In the 100 million years of developmental time during which vertebrates (life-forms with a spinal cord and backbone) are said to have evolved from invertebrates, not one transitional form has been found. Questioned about this in 1979, David Raup tentatively offered one particular species of starfish as a candidate for the 'missing link', but then admitted, 'There is no direct documentation.'[73]

Evolutionists tell us that in the course of thirty million years fish evolved into amphibians — but nobody has been able to find a 'fishibian'. A group of fishes called the *Rhipidistia*, with certain skeletal features resembling those of early amphibians, including bones that looked as if they could have evolved into legs, was touted as evidence that an 'ancestral group' had been found, but further study has ruled it out. In her major work *Vertebrate History*, the scholar Barbara J. Stahl writes, 'Most of them lived after the first amphibians appeared, and those that came before show no evidence of developing the stout limbs that characterized the primitive tetrapods.'[74] For many years it was believed that the coelacanth, allegedly extinct for at least seventy million years, was closely related to the *Rhipidistia*, but its death notice had to be withdrawn when a living specimen was caught off the coast of East Africa in 1938, and the possibility that it would provide evidence of a link between fish and amphibians sank without trace when it showed no signs of having been pre-adapted for life on dry land. Some years later, it was accepted that some 500 coelacanth lived in the seas around the Comoros Islands, near Madagascar. In 1997, an American's scientist's wife spotted one in a fish market in Manado, Indonesia, leaving experts puzzled as to how the coelacanth had escaped the attention of biologists 'when local fishermen seemed to know it well'.[75] Another underwater example is the *Neopilina galatheae* mollusc, believed to have been extinct for some 350 million years until a living specimen was recently dredged up off the coast of Central America.

The next major gap to be bridged is that between amphibians and reptiles, but here again evolutionists draw a disconcerting blank in the fossil record. Although the amphibian *Seymouria* has some reptilian features, it can be ruled out because it appears too late in the fossil record — reptiles are found in the fossil record much older than the rock strata in which *Seymouria* is found. Another major problem with the supposed evolution of amphibians into reptiles concerns their eggs. Amphibians lay their eggs in water, whereas reptiles lay hard-shelled eggs, and no explanation has been found for the development of such a radically different method of reproduction.

Reptiles and mammals are commonly distinguished by the structure of their ear- and jaw-bones, and evolutionists claimed to have found a link between the two classes with the discovery of *Therapsida*, a species with a skull-bone structure intermediate between the two. However, the argument that skeletal similarities prove one species to be the direct descendant of another is punctured by the fact that there are similarities in many different species that are obviously outside of any possible line of descent. As Phillip Johnson notes, 'The case for therapsids as an ancestral chain linking reptiles to mammals would be a great deal more persuasive if the chain could be attached to something specific at either end.'[76] A contributor to *New Scientist* in 1982 highlighted the double-sided problem evolutionists have here: 'Each species of mammal-like reptile that has been found appears suddenly in the fossil record and is not preceded by the species that is directly ancestral to it. It disappears some time later, equally abruptly, without leaving a directly descended species.'[77]

The fifth major gap which needs to be filled before we can accept the smooth and seamless progress of macro-evolution is that between reptiles and birds, and in this case the evolutionists' prize exhibit has been *Archaeopteryx*, a small creature about the size of a crow said to have lived about 150 million years ago and of which there are two main specimens, one in the British Museum of Natural History and the other in the Berlin Museum. With teeth, a long tail and hooks on its wings, it certainly had reptilian features, while fully developed flight feathers would seem to have made it as capable of powered flight as any modern bird. Yet there are several question marks over its credentials as a 'missing link'.

Firstly, fossil birds younger than *Archaeopteryx* (and out of the supposed 'reptile-to-bird' evolution scenario) have been found, some with teeth and others with a similar hook on their wings. Perhaps the most striking is the modern hoatzin *(Opisthocomus hoatzin)*, officially placed in a family of its own but with some of the characteristics of *Archaeopteryx*. About two feet in length, and living along the river banks in northern South America, it was once thought to be a distant relative of the game birds, but is now considered to be related to the cuckoo. Secondly, no creature, fossilized or living, has scales that are halfway to developing into feathers, and there is not a shred of evidence that this has ever occurred in any creature. The only candidate which comes close is the *Longisquama*, a pseudosuchian reptile from the Triassic deposits in Kirghizia. This had a double row of elongated scale-like appendages on either side of its backbone which may have been used for flight — or at least for gliding purposes. Thirdly, an animal halfway between a reptile and a bird could not survive; Ernst Mayr states that it 'would not have the slightest chance of escaping elimination through selection'.[78] Fourthly, the fossilized remains of at least two undisputed birds have been found in rock strata said to be some seventy-five million years *earlier* than the dating evolutionists suggest for *Archaeopteryx*.[79] How could *Archaeopteryx* possibly be their ancestor?

If 'one swallow doesn't make a summer', two handfuls of *Archaeopteryx* hardly prove the case for macro-evolution. After a detailed study of the evidence, evolutionist Francis Hitching conceded, 'Every one of its supposed reptilian features can be found in various species of undoubted birds.'[80] The word *Archaeopteryx* comes from the Greek *archaios* (ancient) and *pterux* (wing); as evidence for macro-evolution this particular high-flier is turning out to be something of a *koutsi papia* (dead duck).

Monkey business

For obvious reasons, by far the most important and interesting gap in the macro-evolutionary model is the one between humans and their supposed ape-like ancestors. The widely believed theory is that between thirty and seventy million years ago apes and humans evolved from a common, unknown ancestor, a claim backed up by impressive-looking museum exhibits in major cities throughout the world, supported by text which strongly conveys the impression that this particular evolutionary transition can be taken for granted.

Darwin bit the bullet in *The Descent of Man* when writing of the way in which monkeys developed: 'Simiidae then branched off into two great stems, the New World (North and South America) and the Old World (Africa and India) Monkeys; from the latter, at a remote period, Man, the wonder and glory of the universe, proceeded.'[81] (We should add that nowadays, the *Simiidae* — or, more correctly, the *Pongidae* — are restricted to include only the anthropoid apes.) Darwin's declaration gave added impetus to the search for evidence in support of the idea, yet some 150 years later palaeontologist (and evolutionist) Niles Eldredge of the American Natural History Museum admits, 'The smooth transition from one form of life to another which is implied in the theory ... [of evolution] ... is not borne out by the facts. The search for "missing links" between various living creatures, like humans and apes, is probably fruitless, because they never existed as distinct transitional forms ... *no one has yet found any evidence of such transitional creatures*[82] (emphasis added). This damaging admission can best be illustrated by seven of the strongest claims to have hit the headlines since Darwin's time.

Neanderthal Man

In 1857, two years before the publication of *Origin*, quarrymen found a partial skeleton in a cave in the Neander Valley, near Düsseldorf in Germany. The bones appeared to be human, though unusual features included a grossly large eyebrow ridge and curvature of the thigh-bone. Over the next few decades, similar skeletons were found in Europe, Africa and Asia. Linked with the original find, they were given the common name Neanderthal, and eventually models were sculpted, drawn and painted showing semi-erect, barrel-chested creatures, with short legs, massive eyebrow ridges and strong lower jaws, said to have lived between 35,000 and 70,000 years ago. They certainly gave the impression of being ape-men but, as Ian Taylor says, 'It should be borne in mind that only bones had been found; all the rest of the reconstruction was speculation based on preconception.'[83]

Close examination of the original bones revealed strong evidence that the Neanderthals were not a cross between apes and humans. Rudolf Virchow, the eminent German scientist who laid the foundation for modern pathology, concluded that they were those of a middle-aged human, the unusual features in the skull and elsewhere resulting from 'pathological changes' caused by deforming diseases such as rickets and arthritis. Nearly a century later, after examining many of the Neanderthal specimens, a medical specialist reported that many of the remains found in Europe showed that the individuals concerned, including children, had suffered from Vitamin D deficiency, something known to cause osteomalacia and rickets, producing a subtle change in the shape of the face. Another medical specialist pointed to syphilis as a possible cause of some of the Neanderthal bone deformities.

There are many other major difficulties about promoting Neanderthals as a 'missing link', of which three will be sufficient to make the point here. Firstly, the cranial volume of Neanderthals is on average larger than that of modern humans, whereas evolutionary dogma teaches that the reverse should be the case. Secondly, Neanderthal people conducted religious rituals in burying their dead, something which clearly points to genuine humanity and not a sub-human species. Thirdly, the dating sequence required by the 'missing link' idea was destroyed when a typical Neanderthal skeleton, buried in a suit of armour, was found in a tomb in Poland in 1908.[84] This discovery delivers such a shattering blow to the current evolutionary ideas of Neanderthal Man that it is carefully left out of modern textbooks.

In his book *Bones of Contention*, the American scholar Marvin Lubenow writes, 'Simply put, evolutionists don't know where Neanderthal came from or where he went,' but he goes on to say that, after thirty-five years of researching the fossil issue, he had come to the conclusion that 'Neander-thal was a card-carrying member of the human family.'[85] In 1998, a report by American anthropologists added to the weight of evidence pointing in this direction by concluding that in Neanderthals the pencil-sized hypoglossal canal, which carries the motor nerve controlling the tongue, closely matched that of modern humans. This overturns the evolutionary model which relegates Neanderthal to the role of our crude and distant cousin. In a witty 1998 editorial, the *Daily Telegraph* commented, 'Now it has emerged that, far from being grunting oafs, the Neanderthals were accomplished conversationalists, with tongues quite as dextrous as our own. We have been wrong all along to use their name as a by-word for numbskulled immobilism. On the contrary, they were the chattering classes of Upper Pleistocene Europe... They were not watching in puzzlement while *Homo sapiens* invented new tool-making techniques. Instead, they were sitting in caves, discussing the fashionable causes of their day: how to preserve the woolly mammoth and other threatened species; what could be done to halt the proliferation of flint-axes; whether the fur trade could be stamped out... In an age when collective atonement is all the rage, perhaps it is time for our entire species to offer the Neanderthals an apology.'[86] Even allow-ing for journalistic licence, this seems much nearer the mark than the sug-gestion that Neanderthal was nothing more than a crude cousin connect-ing us to our ape-like ancestors.

Java Man

While excavating in Trinil, Java, in 1891–1892, the Dutch physician (and fervent evolutionist) Eugene Dubois found a skull fragment, a thigh-bone and three molar teeth. Although they were lying at least fifty feet from each other, and unearthed over a one-year span, Dubois announced that he had found *Anthropopithecus erectus* (upright, man-like ape). Later, he shifted it slightly up the evolutionary ladder and renamed it *Pithecanthropus erectus* (upright ape-man), but contemporary experts remained hopelessly divided about the validity of Dubois' conclusions, while Rudolf Virchow stated bluntly, 'There is no evidence at all that these bones were part of the same creature.'[87]

In 1920, by which time the focus of attention had switched to other candidates for the 'missing link' between apes and humans, Dubois admitted that he had also found genuinely human skulls in the same geological stratum. Hidden under the floorboards of his house for some thirty years, they provided clear evidence that Java Man (the popular name given to *Pithecanthropus erectus*) could not have been the transitional form Dubois longed to produce. Java Man is arguably the best-known human fossil, and for many years was paraded as our evolutionary ancestor, but the accumulation of evidence points with increasing clarity to the Trinil fragments as being truly human.

Piltdown Man

In 1912, lawyer Charles Dawson, an amateur fossil hunter, took a collection of bones, teeth and primitive implements to a friend at the British Museum for analysis, saying that he had found them in a gravel pit near Piltdown, Sussex. Experts said the remains were about 500,000 years old, and for the next forty years the so-called Piltdown Man — officially classified as *Eoanthropus dawsoni* (Dawson's Dawn man) — was hailed as 'the sensational missing link'.[88] Plaster casts were sent to museums around the world, over 500 doctoral dissertations were written on the discovery, and 'A whole generation grew up with Piltdown Man in their textbooks and home encyclopaedias.'[89]

Some ten years after Dawson's death in 1916, the three scientists responsible for establishing Piltdown Man's status in the monkey-to-man sequence had received knighthoods, but the story went downhill from then on and in 1953 the whole thing was exposed as a gigantic hoax. Piltdown Man was shown to be made up from a human skull and the jawbone of an orang-utan which had died about fifty years earlier and whose teeth had been filed to give them a more human look. Other fossil finds on the same site included fragments of rhinoceros, elephant, mastodon, beaver, red deer and a horse's tooth, all stained to conceal their age and origin. It was even shown that some of these had been found elsewhere and brought to the Piltdown site, presumably to make it more impressive.

As all the people associated with the Piltdown fraud are now dead, we shall never know for certain who perpetrated it. The finger of suspicion has been pointed at Pierre Teilhard de Chardin, local resident Arthur Conan Doyle (author of the famous Sherlock Holmes stories) and certain members of the British Museum staff. All we can say for certain is that Piltdown Man, once hailed as proof positive of man's evolutionary ancestry, can now be safely filed away under 'fiction'.

Nebraska Man

In 1922, the amateur geologist Harold Cook was looking for fossils in Nebraska when he found a single tooth in a Pliocene deposit, said to be between 1.7 and 5.5 million years old. Experts enthusiastically claimed it as belonging to an early type of Pithecanthropoid (ape-like man) and named it *Hesperopithecus haroldcooki* in honour of its founder. When the prestigious *Illustrated London News* published a double-page feature of the find on 24 June 1922, complete with an artist's impression of the 'ape-man' and his mate, Nebraska Man was trumpeted as a vital link in the history of humanity.

Six years later it was discovered that the tooth unearthed by Cook belonged to a type of peccary, a wild pig believed to have become extinct at the end of the Pleistocene era, about 10,000 years ago. *Hesperopithecus* was deftly dropped from reference books, and the next edition of *Encyclopaedia Britannica* coyly described it as 'a being of another order'![90]

Peking Man

In 1927, during excavations at Chou K'ou Tien, near Peking (or Beijing), China, the Canadian physician Davidson Black unearthed a single tooth which he believed had characteristics intermediate between ape and man. He named it *Sinanthropus pekinensis*, and the prestigious Rockefeller Foundation was so impressed with the potential of the discovery that it made a grant of $80,000 specifically for the study of human fossils. Two years later, with up to 100 labourers at a time having been employed at the site, Black discovered an almost complete brain case, which he was convinced came from *Sinanthropus pekinensis*. Black's reputation grew quickly. After his death in 1934, a skull was reconstructed around the original brain case, and plaster casts of this are what we now find in museums as part of a man-like ape renamed *Homo erectus pekinensis*, or Peking Man. The British Museum exhibit shows three naked specimens, but they are little more than an artist's impression of what they may have looked like if they had evolved from apes, that story-line being taken for granted.

However, later excavations at Chou K'ou Tien produced a number of clearly human skeletons, together with large quantities of bone and stone tools, and an ash heap twenty-three feet high, giving a strong impression of prolonged and organized human activity. The size of the original brain case, and of similar fragmented specimens found later on the same site, pointed to the distinct possibility that they belonged to large monkeys and were broken open by real men in order to extract the brains for food. When the famous French palaeontologist Marcellin Boule, Director of the Museum of Natural History in Paris, went to examine *Sinanthropus pekinensis* he was furious at having travelled halfway around the world to see what he determined to be nothing more than a battered monkey skull. Just as damaging to the reputation of Peking Man is the fact that although the excavations at Chou K'ou Tien covered a depth of 150 feet, there was no evidence in the fossils of any progression from ape to man. As Ian Taylor comments, 'One suspects that the only evolution that has occurred in the case of Peking Man has been in the imagination of those making the reconstruction.'[91]

Nutcracker Man

In 1959, the well-known palaeontologist Louis Leakey and his wife Mary uncovered a skull in the Olduvai Gorge, in East Africa. They called it *Zinjanthropus boisei* (honouring their American sponsor Charles Boise) but the news media picked up on the skull's huge jaw and named the find 'Nutcracker Man'.

On the basis of an ape-like skull and some crude stone tools found nearby, it was claimed that the creature concerned walked upright and was the world's earliest man, living some 600,000 years ago. Although the dating was guesswork, and not believed by many experts, *National Geographic* presented the find as new evidence of man's evolutionary descent from the ape, and when Charles Boise's funds ran out, the National Geographic Society began funding the Leakeys' work.

In 1961, tests at the University of California sensationally dated the skull at 1.75 million years, by far the oldest claim made for any hominoid fossil, but by 1968 further tests put fossil bones found *under* 'Nutcracker Man' at 10,100 years. As Ian Taylor notes, 'Had this been discovered a few years earlier, Leakey's claim to have found the most ancient ancestor of man would have been doubted even more strongly.'[92]

An earlier discovery was to do even more damage to 'Nutcracker Man'. In 1913, the German anthropologist Hans Reck had found a complete human skeleton immediately above the bed where *Zinjanthropus* was discovered. Leakey had examined this in 1928, but said nothing about it when presenting *Zinjanthropus* forty-six years later. The opening words of his *National Geographic* article claimed that the skull was 'quite obviously human'[93] but, as Ian Taylor says, he was 'allowing his preconceptions to get the better of good science'.[94] Later, Leakey withdrew his extravagant claims for *Zinjanthropus* and conceded that it was simply one of many *Australopithecines* found in various parts of Africa, and now believed by many to be extinct apes.[95]

Since Leakey's death in 1972, discoveries in the Olduvai Gorge have dealt additional blows to his scenario, especially evidence of a circular stone shelter, which conflicts with the idea that such shelters were not built until comparatively recently.[96]

'Lucy'

Our final example is a tiny skeleton, without hands or feet, found in 1974 by the American anthropologist Donald Johanson while working in the Afar region of the Great Rift Valley in southern Ethiopia, and said to be something over three million years old. Johanson announced his find to the world four years later at the Nobel Symposium on Early Man. Its official designation was *Australopithecus afarensis* (Southern Ape from Afar), but Johanson and his team nicknamed it 'Lucy', as the Beatles' hit song 'Lucy in the Sky with Diamonds' was being played on site during the evening when Johanson and his team were discussing their discovery; the name stuck.

In spite of Johanson's enthusiastic claim that he had unearthed the first ape to walk upright, and therefore the elusive link between primitive apes and humans, the experts have not been overly impressed with 'Lucy', not least because of evidence that genuine people walked upright long before her time. Johanson's case also suffered a severe blow when he admitted, in answer to a question following his lecture at the University of Missouri on 20 November 1996, that the knee joint cited as proof that 'Lucy' walked upright was found more than two miles away and 200 feet lower in the strata! When further asked how he could be sure that the bones belonged to 'Lucy', he weakly replied, 'Anatomical similarity'.[97]

'Lucy' is a good example of the way in which articulate evolutionists have used popular media presentation to perfect the art of passing off guesswork as fact. In February 1994 I watched a BBC2 television programme called *In Search of our Fathers*, in which Johanson told how 'Lucy' had been discovered and then drew a stream of fascinating conclusions about her lifestyle and the way in which she died. In his *Daily Telegraph* review the following day, television critic Max Davidson poked telling fun at Johanson's grandiose claims: 'Last night the reconstruction industry hit new lows with the death of "Lucy" three million years ago... She seems to have been a pert three-footer, with a 36D chest, a problem with body hair and a brain half way in size between Jeremy Beadle's and a pea...[98] She didn't have television and appears to have spent most of her day foraging for food. From an examination of male fossils of the period, it seems she may have had a partner who treated her as an equal because his teeth were the same size as hers; equally, because he was twice as tall, he may have beaten her and ducked out of the washing up. But it is Lucy's death which really concerns me. Instead of having the humility to recognize that, at this remove of time, any self-respecting coroner would have to return an open verdict, the programme staged a grisly reconstruction in which someone, presumably a child actor in a monkey suit, was seen wandering through the jungle, stumbling and drowning in six inches of water. There was no explicit reference to alcohol, but it was obvious that this could only have happened to someone in an advanced state of inebriation. I know Lucy's been dead a while but, if she's such an important figure in our history, surely she deserves better treatment than this?'[99]

These cases represent hundreds of others which have never hit the headlines, and they help to make the point that, in spite of the enthusiastic efforts of its supporters, the general theory of evolution, which says that all life on earth originated and evolved by a gradual process of chance mutations, remains what it has always been, a highly speculative idea without any clear and firm foundation. A stab in the dark has acquired the status of a dogma. In Phillip Johnson's words, 'Instead of a fact we have a speculative hypothesis that says that living species evolved from ancestors which cannot be identified, by some much-disputed mechanism which cannot be demonstrated, and in such a manner that few traces of the process were left in the record — even though that record has been interpreted by persons strongly committed to proving evolution.'[100] The last phrase is particularly important. Time and again we can see how the initial interpretation of new finds has confirmed the presuppositions of those who were looking for evidence to support their ideas. David Pilbeam, physical anthropologist at Yale University, openly admits this: 'I know that, at least in palaeoanthropology, data are still so sparse that theory heavily influences interpretations. Theories have, in the past, clearly reflected our current ideologies instead of the actual data.'[101] Yet in spite of this bias, usually concealed when the case is presented to the public, the fact remains that the microbe-to-man proposition is woefully weak. Little wonder that Darwin admitted in a letter to his friend Asa Gray that one's 'imagination must fill up the very wide blanks'.[102]

At the time this chapter was being written, my wife and I took a Christmas break in Cornwall, in the course of which we visited the National Seal Sanctuary in Gweek. One of the first display boards we read on entering announced that the seal had evolved fifteen million years ago and man ten million years later. This was the unblinking basis on which the seal's story was then presented. Later, as we toured the underground viewing area and had a close encounter with a particularly fine specimen on the other side of the plate glass, the message was being driven home through the sound system. I remained totally unconvinced — and there may even have been a shadow of scepticism on the face of the seal! All we can say with certainty about the 'missing links' is that they are still missing.

Alternatives

These yawning gaps in the fossil record, together with the abrupt appearance of various forms of life, are hugely embarrassing to dyed-in-the-wool evolutionists. One of their leading and most articulate spokesmen, Stephen

J. Gould, Professor of Geology and Palaeontology at Harvard University, and President of the American Association for the Advancement of Science, frankly confesses, 'All palaeontologists know that the fossil record contains precious little in the way of intermediate forms; transitions between major groups are characteristically abrupt.'[103] Elsewhere, he goes so far as to say that the extreme rarity of transitional forms in the fossil record 'persists as the trade secret of palaeontology';[104] in other words, generations of students and others have had the wool pulled firmly over their eyes! Niles Eldredge confirms the conspiracy: 'We palaeontologists have said that the history of life supports ... [the story of gradual adaptive change] ... *all the while knowing that it does not*'[105] (emphasis added). Evolutionist Jeremy Rifkin has been positively scathing about the attempt to make the fossils speak out in favour of Darwinism: 'What the "record" shows is nearly a century of fudging and finagling by scientists to conform with Darwin's notions, all to no avail. Today the millions of fossils stand as very visible, ever-present reminders of the paltriness of the arguments and the overall shabbiness of the theory that marches under the banner of evolution.'[106]

Ever since Darwin's time, scientists have wrestled with the problem of saltation (the apparent sudden jump to a new species or type) and come up with alternative theories to accommodate it. In 1940, the American geneticist Richard Goldschmidt proposed what has become known as his *'hopeful monster'* theory. Occasionally, Goldschmidt said, nature would throw up a genetic monstrosity such as a two-legged sheep or turtle, and if there were enough of these there might be one which would survive. In his view something like this had happened every time there was a gap in the fossil record. As part of his startling scenario, Goldschmidt even endorsed palaeontologist Otto Schindewolf's suggestion that the first bird was hatched from an egg laid by a reptile! Goldschmidt's ideas were met with derision, but have still not been totally discarded.

One of today's most widely accepted theories is that of punctuated equilibrium, an idea developed in the 1970s by Niles Eldredge and Stephen J. Gould.[107] In this model, many millions of years with little or no change (equilibrium) were followed by worldwide cataclysms (punctuations) causing wholesale extinctions and new life-forms. There then followed periods of stasis, or stagnation, which lasted for anything up to ten million generations, after which there would be another burst of life, in which new types and species suddenly appeared on the scene. The punctuational idea wriggles out of the problems caused to evolutionists by the stubborn gaps in the fossil record, but as yet it has offered no genetic or mechanical evidence in support of its own major premise. As Luther Sunderland notes, 'The theory of punctuated equilibria is causing much turmoil amongst evolutionists. They know that there is no actual mechanism that would explain large rapid jumps from one species to another, yet they also know the fossil record does not support gradualism. They are left on the horns of a dilemma.' Niles Eldredge admits that the idea is still very 'evolutionary'[108] and that arguments about mechanisms are still going on within the evolutionary camp.[109] Marvin Lubenow goes so far as to say that the punctuated equilibrium model of evolution was 'invented to explain why [transitional fossils] were not found', adding wryly, 'However, it is imperative to emphasize that the punctuated equilibria model does not *remove* the need for transitional fossils. It just explains why those transitions have not been found. Certainly, the punctuated equilibria theory is unique. It must be the only theory put forth in the history of science which claims to be scientific but then explains why evidence for it cannot be found.'[110]

Chance would be a fine thing

In *Mathematical Challenges to the Neo-Darwinian Interpretation of Evolution*, Marcel Schutzenberger of the University of Paris, working with other scientists, calculated the probability of evolution based on mutation and natural selection and came to this conclusion: 'There is *no chance* to see this mechanism appear spontaneously... We believe there is a considerable gap in the neo-Darwinian theory of evolution, and we believe this gap to be of such a nature that *it cannot be bridged with the current conception of biology*'[111] (emphasis added). Then why is atheistic macroevolutionism held on to with such tenacity? Writing in *Nature* as long ago as 1929, biologist D. M. S. Watson brazenly conceded, 'The theory of evolution itself [is] a theory universally accepted, *not because it can be proved by logically coherent evidence to be true*, but because the only alternative is special creation, which is clearly incredible'[112] (emphasis added). The palaeontologist L. T. More, of the University of Chicago, has said much the same thing: 'Our faith in the idea of evolution depends upon our reluctance to accept the antagonistic doctrine of special creation.'[113] So has the eminent British anthropologist Sir Arthur Keith: 'Evolution is *unproved and unprovable*. We believe it only because the alternative is special creation, which is unthinkable'[114] (emphasis added).

In his keynote address to the Darwinian Centennial Convention in 1959, Julian Huxley said, 'I am an atheist in the only correct sense that I don't believe in the existence of a supernatural being who influences natural events,'[115] and claimed that Darwin's real achievement was 'to remove the whole idea of God as the creator of organisms from the sphere of rational discussion'.[116] Simply put, the atheistic macro-evolutionist would have us believe that the cat and the cockroach, the wasp and the whale, the swan and the spider, the gerbil and the giraffe — and, for that matter, the hippopotamus and the human — are not essentially different, but are dramatic variations of unguided development from a single speck of inanimate matter. Weighing it all up, Professor Louis Bounoure, President of the Biological Society of Strasbourg and Director of the Strasbourg Zoological Museum before becoming Director of Research at the French National Centre of Scientific Research, came to this withering conclusion: 'Evolutionism is a fairy-tale for grown-ups. This theory has helped nothing in the progress of science. It is useless.'[117] One is reminded of an incident in *Alice Through the Looking Glass*. When Alice tells the White Queen, 'One can't believe in impossible things,' the queen replies, 'I daresay you haven't had much practice. Why, sometimes I've believed as many as six impossible things before breakfast.'[118]

5.
The legacy

At one point in *Origin*, Darwin wrote, 'I see no good reasons why the views given in this volume should shock the religious feelings of anyone,'[1] but one wonders whether his tongue was firmly in his cheek at the time. In the event, *Origin* sparked a furious row between those who supported his ideas of natural selection and traditional theists, who believed in purposeful creation by God. The most famous confrontation came at a meeting of the British Association for the Advancement of Science held in Oxford on 30 June 1880. Although we have no copies of the speeches, and there have been dozens of contradictory accounts of what happened, the meeting is still remembered because of a clash between Darwin's self-appointed 'bulldog' Thomas Huxley and the Oxford don Samuel Wilberforce, who was also a bishop in the Church of England and the son of William Wilberforce, who successfully campaigned for the abolition of slavery.

Wilberforce was an able naturalist and a brilliant debater, and is said to have made a reasonably good job of critiquing Darwin's theory, no doubt basing his remarks on a detailed review of *Origin* which he had just written, and which Darwin had acknowledged as being 'uncommonly clever'.[2] As a scientist, Huxley bitterly resented the clergy's superior status in society at that time, and saw the debate as an opportunity to ridicule the church for holding to what he considered outdated and prejudiced ideas. If the popular reports are correct, his opportunity came in an unexpected way. Towards the end of his speech, Wilberforce jokingly asked Huxley whether his descent from the apes was on his grandfather's or his grandmother's side. Dismissing Wilberforce's technical arguments as 'empty rhetoric', Huxley latched on to the question about his line of descent and replied, 'If ... the question is put to me, would I rather have a miserable ape for a grandfather or a man highly endowed by nature and possessed of great means and influence, and yet who employs that influence for the mere purpose of introducing ridicule into a grave scientific discussion, I unhesitatingly affirm my preference for the ape.'[3]

Little did he realize that this brilliant flash of cheap repartee was to give the debate an enduring place in history. Wilberforce apparently left the meeting quite happy that he had 'given Huxley a bloody nose',[4] while both Huxley and his fellow Darwinian Joseph Hooker were equally sure they had won the day. In fact, no vote was taken, and the audience seemed fairly evenly divided, but Huxley's unprecedented attack on a highly re- spected church leader guaranteed there would be repercussions. In spite of this, Huxley's reputation soared, and before long the Oxford debate had triggered off shock-waves which reverberated throughout scientific and religious society. Historian G. M. Trevelyan gives the following assessment: 'The whole idea of evolution and of "man descended from monkeys" was totally incompatible with existing religious ideas of creation and of man's place in the universe. Naturally the religious world took up arms to defend positions of dateless antiquity and prestige. Naturally the younger gener- ation of scientific men rushed to defend their revered chief, and to estab- lish their claim to come to any conclusion to which their researches led, regardless of the ... ancient traditions of the church. The strife raged through- out the sixties, seventies and eighties. It came to involve the whole belief in the miraculous... The "intellectuals" became more and more anti-clerical, anti-religious and materialistic under the stress of the conflict... The world of educated men and women was rent by a real controversy, which even the English love of compromise could not deny to exist.'[5] It is not difficult to understand why there was such an uproar. As Michael Denton explains, 'It was because Darwinian theory broke man's link with God and set him adrift in a cosmos without purpose or end that its impact was so funda- mental. No other intellectual revolution in modern times (with the possible exception of the Copernican) so profoundly affected the way men viewed themselves and their place in the universe.'[6]

Whether or not Darwin was really surprised at having caused such a commotion, the surprise now being expressed by many scholars concerns the question how the publication of this volume could have done so when it is now seen to be deficient in so many ways. After analysing the text of *Origin*, Henry Morris concludes, 'One can search the whole book in vain for any real scientific evidences for evolution — evidences that have been empirically verified and have stood the test of time... None of *Origin's* evidences or arguments have stood up under modern critical analysis, even by other evolutionists. One can only marvel that such a book could have had so profound an influence on the subsequent history of human life and thought.'[7] Michael Denton agrees: 'The influence of evolutionary theory on fields far removed from biology is one of the most spectacular examples in history of how a highly speculative idea for which there is really no hard scientific evidence can come to fashion the thinking of a whole society and dominate the outlook of any age. Considering its historic significance and the social and moral transformation it caused in Western thought, one might have hoped that Darwinian theory was capable of a complete, comprehensive and entirely plausible explanation for all the biological phenomena from the origin of life on through all its diverse manifestations up to, and including, the intellect of man. That it is neither fully plausible, nor comprehensive, is deeply troubling. One might have expected that a theory of such cardinal importance, a theory that literally changed the world, would have been something more than ... a myth.'[8] In this chapter we will note some other assessments of evolution and look at some dimensions of Darwin's legacy. PURPOSE

Science, philosophy, religion, life

The notion that 'Science proves evolution' is virtually taken for granted today. The *New Catholic Encyclopaedia* assures us that 'Evolution has been established as thoroughly as science can establish facts,'[9] and in the introduction to the 1996 edition of *The Blind Watchmaker*, Richard Dawkins calls evolution 'The Greatest Show on Earth, The Only Game in Town'[10] — but these claims are more than countered by other penetrating assessments. In *Teilhardism and the New Religion* the American mathematician and physicist Wolfgang Smith writes, 'We are told dogmatically that evolution is an established fact; but we are never told who established it, and by what means. We are told, often enough, that the doctrine is founded upon evidence ... but we are left entirely in the dark on the crucial question wherein, precisely, this evidence consists.'[11] Later he adds, 'If by evolution we mean macro-evolution ... it can be said with the utmost rigour that the doctrine is totally bereft of scientific sanction ... there exists today not a shred of *bona fide* scientific evidence in support of the thesis that macro-evolution transformations have *ever* occurred.'[12] In a monograph entitled *Evolution as Dogma: the Establishment of Naturalism*, Phillip Johnson brings his expertise in the evaluation of evidences to bear on the subject and comes to the conclusion: 'What the science educators propose to teach us as "evolution", and label as fact, is based not upon any incontrovertible empirical evidence, but upon a highly controversial philosophical proposition.'[13] Writing after years of hands-on experience, the British Museum of Natural History's senior palaeontologist Colin Patterson claimed, 'Nine-tenths of the talk of evolutionists is sheer nonsense, not founded on observation and wholly unsupported by facts. This museum is full of proofs of the utter falsity of their views. *In all this great museum there is not a particle of evidence of the transmutation of species*'[14] (emphasis added).

Yet the idea of evolution has become so ingrained into modern man's thinking that few people realize how difficult it is to pin down. As recently as 1986, Edgar Andrews, Emeritus Professor of Materials Science in the University of London, could write, 'A student cannot graduate in such a subject or even, generally, take a course of university lectures in the field.'[15] Instead, evolutionary concepts are scattered around a variety of scientific disciplines such as astronomy, botany, chemistry, geology, physics and zoology. Speaking on the BBC Radio 4 programme *On Giants' Shoulders* in December 1997, philosopher David Dennett called evolution 'the single best idea anyone ever had'. An idea is one thing; an established fact is something altogether different.

Evolution is usually referred to as a theory, but in strictly scientific terms this is also going too far, because, as Colin Patterson makes clear, it is not possible to prove or refute what it teaches: 'It is easy enough to make up stories of how one form gave rise to another, and to find reasons why the stages should be favoured by natural selection. But such stories are not part of science, for there is no way of putting them to the test.'[16]

In a keynote address at the American Museum of Natural History in 1981, Patterson illustrated the speculative nature of evolution's claims in an eye-opening way: 'Last year I had a sudden realization that for over 20 years I was working on evolution in some way. One morning I woke up and something had happened in the night, and it struck me I had been working on this stuff for 20 years and there was not one thing I knew about it. That's quite a shock to learn that one can be so misled so long. Either there was something wrong with me or there was something wrong with evolutionary theory. Naturally I know there is nothing wrong with me, so for the last few weeks I've been putting a simple question to various people and groups of people. Question is: Can you tell me anything you know about evolution, any one thing, any one thing that is true? I tried that question on the geology staff at the Field Museum of Natural History and the only answer I got was silence. I tried it on the members of the Evolutionary Morphology Seminar in the University of Chicago, a very prestigious body of evolutionists, and all I got there was silence for a long time and eventually one person said, "I do know one thing — it ought not to be taught in high school." ' [17]

This seems to mean that we would be nearer the mark if we called evolution a hypothesis or postulate, a supposition assumed without proof. Having drawn the distinction between a theory and a hypothesis, Edgar Andrews concludes that 'No matter how much one may sympathize with the difficulties of establishing a hypothesis, we must face the fact that the theory of evolution has not grown, and is never likely to grow, out of the infant hypothetical form.' [18] At one stage the renowned philosopher of science Sir Karl Popper was even more tentative and raised doubts as to whether it can even be called a hypothesis, as its claims are centred around unrepeatable events which cannot be adequately tested or falsified, though he later published a paper accepting that the study of origins is scientific. Professor Verna Wright, one of Britain's leading medical experts, strongly argued that we should use the word 'model' with regard to evolution and creation. He maintained that neither evolution nor creation could be considered a theory because the very definition of a theory meant that it could be tested. For example, the statement, 'Water boils at 100 degrees Celsius,' can be tested in the laboratory, but no one can test the 'theory' of evolution or the 'theory' of creation.

Yet, as Ernst Mayr shows, others see evolution in philosophical terms, as a system of principles governing people's view of the world in which we live. Mayr makes this clear when he writes, 'Man's view of the world today is dominated by the knowledge that the universe, the stars, the earth and all living things have evolved through a long history that was not foreordained or programmed.' [19] When this is the case, the principles framing evolutionary thinking will profoundly affect a person's attitude to the whole of life, because the cosmos of space, time and matter will be taken as the only ultimate reality.

It is only a short step from there to see why, consciously or unconsciously, evolution has for many people taken on a religious dimension.

The American history professor George Marsden writes, 'In modern culture "evolution" often involves more than biology. The basic ideologies of
the civilization, including its entire moral structure, are at issue. Evolution is
sometimes the key mythological element in a philosophy that functions as
a virtual religion.'[20] L. T. More is even clearer: 'The more one studies palaeontology, the more certain one becomes that evolution is based on faith
alone; exactly the same sort of faith which it is necessary to have when one
encounters the great mysteries of religion.'[21] This should hardly surprise us.
As we shall see in later chapters, no purely materialistic interpretation of
human existence can relate to our deepest instincts or meet our deepest
needs, and for many the place traditionally occupied by God is taken by a
new religion in which, as Edgar Andrews says, 'evolution becomes a mystical force and reason the new deity'.[22] In his introduction to the 1971
reprint of *Origin*, the British biologist Harrison Matthews writes that belief
in evolution is 'exactly parallel to belief in special creation' with evolution
simply 'a satisfactory faith on which to base our interpretation of nature'.[23]
George Roche is even more specific: 'Evolution is and always has been a
religious vision... Evolution must be taken on faith, and that is the whole of
its strength.'[24] Having shown that molecular biology has as yet been unable
to demonstrate the formation of a single species by mutations, Lynn
Margulis, Professor of Biology at the University of Massachusetts, comes
to the conclusion that neo-Darwinism is 'a minor twentieth-century religious sect within the sprawling religious persuasion of Anglo-Saxon
biology'.[25]

When evolutionary concepts and their corollaries are so firmly fixed in
people's minds they are bound to be reflected in their behaviour. In 1961
the British preacher Martyn Lloyd-Jones stated, 'The belief in evolution ...
has captured the public imagination for a hundred years and is perhaps the
greatest controlling influence on the thought of mankind in practically every
realm of life and living.'[26] To pick out one particular area not majored on
elsewhere in this book, Darwin's teaching has had a profound effect in the
world of psychology. In *Names in the History of Psychology*, Leonard Zuzne
writes, 'To psychology, his books *The Origin of Species* and *The Descent
of Man* are of particular importance. They spell out the basic assumption
underlying psychology, namely that man is on a continuum with the rest of
the animal world, and that, since animals can be studied by the scientific
method, so can man... The evolutionary viewpoint concerning the development of both structure and function, including the mental processes, is
now the accepted and pervasive point of view in psychology.'[27]

Questions of colour and class

In many instances, the influence of Darwin's teaching has been downright malign. *Racism* is an obvious example. The latter part of *Origin's* full title — *The Preservation of Favoured Species in the Struggle for Life* — pointed in this direction and in *The Descent of Man* Darwin argued that natural selection would eventually eliminate what he called 'the savage races' in favour of 'the civilized races of men'.[28] Herbert Spencer's phrase, 'the survival of the fittest', was an integral part of his Darwinian socialism, which said that 'superior races' would properly rule 'inferior' ones and that the strong were under no obligation to help the weak. Thomas Huxley, Darwin's most powerful advocate, stated, 'No rational man, cognisant of the facts, believes that the average negro is the equal, still less the superior, of the white man.'[29] Racism existed long before Darwin, but his evolutionary ideas appeared to give it scientific plausibility, leading Henry Morris to conclude, 'Darwin's notion that the various races were at different evolutionary distances from the apes, with Negroes at the bottom and Caucasians at the top ... was almost universal among the evolutionary atheists of the nineteenth century.'[30]

Racism led naturally to *imperialism*. As Gertrude Himmelfarb puts it, 'Social Darwinism has often been understood in this sense: as a philosophy, exalting competition, power and violence over convention, ethics and religion. Thus it has become a portmanteau of nationalism, imperialism, militarism and dictatorship, of the cults of the hero, the superman and the master race.'[31] It is not difficult to see the link here. If the evolutionary myth is taken on board, why should it be wrong for the more powerful or more intelligent among us to dominate or manipulate the less powerful or intelligent for whatever purposes they choose to call 'worthy' or 'good'?

The weakest to the wall

Eugenics (the production of superior offspring by the improvement of inherited qualities) and *euthanasia* (the killing of the incurable) are other offshoots of evolutionary thinking. The word 'eugenics' was coined by Francis Galton, Darwin's first cousin, whose stated aim was to upgrade the human race by giving 'the more suitable races or strains of blood a better chance of prevailing speedily over the less suitable'.[32] As Hitler was coming to power in Germany, Galton's ideas fitted in with the Führer's need to produce an Aryan super-race to spearhead the coming world conquest by the Third Reich. Human stud-farms were set up during the 1930s in an attempt to breed from a few thousand suitable specimens the nucleus of a master nation. Hand in glove with this, a policy of imposed sterilization was introduced which led to at least two million people being forcibly sterilized.[33]

Galton's ideas, driven by the doctrine of evolution, were carried on with devastating effect by the German biologist Ernst Haeckel, one of Darwin's most enthusiastic disciples, who faithfully reproduced his master's dogma: 'The history of selection teaches that in human life, as in animal and plant life everywhere, and at all times, only a small and chosen minority exist and flourish, while the enormous majority starve and perish miserably and more or less prematurely.'[34] Euthanasia was the chosen way to put the doctrine into practice and give nature a helping hand. As well as advocating 'the destruction of abnormal new-born children', arguing that this 'cannot be rationally classed as murder',[35] Haeckel went on to draw attention to the fact that 'Hundreds of thousands of incurables — lunatics, lepers, people with cancer, etc, are artificially kept alive ... without the slightest profit to themselves or the general body'[36] and to suggest that 'the redemption from this evil should be accomplished by a dose of some painless and rapid poison'.[37] As a result, prussic acid gas was used in the late 1930s to end the lives of thousands of innocent people deemed to belong to 'worthless race types'.

Holocaust

There is conclusive evidence that evolution was a major factor in the philosophy of those who steered *Nazism* to its destructive destiny. Arthur Keith had no doubts about this: 'To see evolutionary measures and tribal morality being applied rigorously to the affairs of a great modern nation, we must turn again to Germany of 1942. We see Hitler devoutly convinced that evolution produces the only real basis for a national policy.'[38] Later he added, 'The German Führer, as I have consistently maintained, is an evolutionist; he has consciously sought to make the practices of Germany conform to the theory of evolution.'[39] Hitler confirmed this: 'He who would live must fight, and he who does not wish to fight in this world where permanent struggle is the law of life has not the right to exist.'[40] All the Nazi leaders were committed evolutionists, with Heinrich Himmler, head of the secret police, the ruthless Gestapo, claiming that 'The law of nature must take its course in the survival of the fittest.'[41]

Darwin would have been horrified to see his ideas used as a justification for calculated brutality, but in Hitler's mind evolutionary thinking provided scientific justification for even the most appalling of his actions. As Purdue University biologist (and evolutionist) Edward Simon admits, 'I don't claim that Darwin and his theory of evolution brought on the holocaust, but I cannot deny that the theory of evolution, and the atheism it engendered, led to the moral climate that made a holocaust possible.'[42]

The red menace

As we saw in chapter 3, even Hitler's sickening record of suppression and slaughter was outdone by the savagery of those who assumed the leadership of *Marxism* — and these too were fuelled by evolutionary philosophy. Darwin's insistence that man is part of nature greatly influenced Marx in the development and application of his ideas. It explained away the need for a divine Creator, gave a scientific basis for his materialism and provided a parallel for his scenario of human development. At one stage Marx wrote, '*The Origin of Species* serves me well as a basis in natural science for the struggle in history,'[43] and after reading another of Darwin's works he told Engels, 'Although it is developed in a crude English way, this is the book that contains the natural history foundation for our viewpoint.'[44] Engels was equally enthusiastic, telling Marx, 'Darwin, whom I am reading, is splendid.'[45] In the course of his eulogy at Marx's funeral Engels declared, 'Just as Darwin discovered the law of evolution in organic nature, so Marx discovered the law of evolution in human history.'[46]

The affinity Marx felt between his own ideas and those of Darwin is reflected in his frequent attendance, during his residence in London, at Thomas Huxley's lectures on Darwinianism and in the fact that he sent Darwin a copy of *Das Kapital* soon after its publication. Six years later he wrote to Darwin asking if he might dedicate his next book to him but, presumably taken aback by Marx's direct denial of God, Darwin declined, explaining that it would pain certain members of his family if he were associated with such an atheistic presentation. The damage, however, had already been done.

Widening the lens

We have looked at some of the most baleful effects of atheistic evolution, but these represent only part of the total picture — and for obvious reasons. Darwin's materialism contradicted the widely held belief that human beings were created by an eternal and righteous God with a personal interest in their well-being and a benevolent plan and purpose for their lives. If Darwin was right, human beings were merely the result of a blind, random, selfish, natural process. Of course this takes the same line as undiluted atheism, and we will develop its relevance to human life and values more fully in chapters 15–17. In the meantime, we can note some of the more obvious repercussions of an evolutionary world-view.

In the first place, it robs life of all meaning and purpose beyond survival. Darwin himself made this clear in the closing words of *Origin*: 'Thus, from the war of nature, from famine and death, *the most exalted object which we are capable of conceiving*, namely, the production of higher animals directly follows'[47] (emphasis added). Utilizing the title of one of his best-known books, Richard Dawkins underlines the fact that this is built into the theory of evolution: 'Natural selection, the blind, unconscious, automatic process which Darwin discovered, and which we now know is the explanation for the existence and apparently purposeful form of life, has no purpose in mind. It has no mind and no mind's eye. It does not plan for the future. It has no vision, no foresight, no sight at all. If it can be said to play the role of watchmaker in nature, it is *the blind watchmaker*'[48] (emphasis added). William Provine, Professor of History and Biological Sciences at Cornell University, agrees: 'Modern evolutionary theory has shattered the hope that some kind of designing or purposive force guided human evolution and established the basis of moral rules. Instead, biology leads to a wholly mechanistic view of life... There are no gods and no designing forces.'[49] Evolution tells us that we are nothing more than pieces of flotsam thrown up on the beach of time, with no ultimate meaning, significance or destiny. This last point was endorsed by Provine on the BBC television programme *Science Friction* in 1996. Calling himself 'a total atheist', he said, 'We have always believed that as human beings we are so special that we can't even truly die, but somehow go over into another life. But evolution tells us that no one lives after he or she is dead. There is no life after death.'[50] C. S. Lewis often exposed the sterility of this line of thinking, and set his evaluation to verse in what he called an 'Evolutionary Hymn':

Lead us, Evolution, lead us
Up the future's endless stair:
Chop us, change us, prod us, weed us,
For stagnation is despair:
Groping, guessing, yet progressing
Lead us nobody knows where...

Ask not if it's god or devil,
Brethren, lest your words imply
Static norms of good and evil
(As in Plato) throned on high;
Such scholastic, inelastic,
Abstract yardsticks we deny.

Far too long have sages vainly
Glossed great Nature's simple text;
He who runs can read it plainly:
  'Goodness = what comes next.'
By evolving, Life is solving
All the questions we perplexed.

On then! Value means survival —
Value. If our progeny
Spreads and spawns and licks each rival
That will prove its deity.
(Far from pleasant, by our present
Standards, though it well may be).[51]

Paradoxically, an evolutionary world-view is also the platform on which
man stands to announce that he has taken over. Jeremy Rifkin makes no
bones about it: 'We no longer feel ourselves to be guests in someone else's
home and therefore feel obliged to make our behaviour conform with a
set of pre-existing cosmic rules. It is our creation now. We make the rules.
We establish the parameters of reality. We create the world and, because
we do, we no longer feel beholden to outside forces. We no longer have to
justify our behaviour, for we are now the architects of the universe. We are
responsible to nothing outside ourselves, for we are the kingdom, the power
and the glory for ever and ever.'[52] With a righteous God taken out of the
picture, people are free to fill the void in any way they choose — though

Rifkin concedes the dangers of this and says that the upshot of evolutionary pantheism will be the greatest calamity in history.[53]

Values

The third obvious corollary of evolution is that it denies the absolute significance of moral values. If man has been thrown together by chance, where does he find a framework for virtue, wisdom or truth? As humanist author S. S. Chawla wrote, 'Darwin's discovery of the principle of evolution sounded the death-knell of religious and moral values. It removed the ground from under the feet of traditional religion.'[54] William Provine endorses this and admits, 'No inherent moral or ethical laws exist, nor are there any absolute guiding principles for human society. The universe cares nothing for us and we have no ultimate meaning in life.'[55] Surely this must be the case? Once God is removed, there can be no absolute basis for moral standards, and the door to relativism is wide open. The only values that then exist are those we invent for ourselves, and the result is moral and social chaos. Arthur Keith makes clear that if we follow evolutionary ethics to its logical conclusion we must 'abandon the hope of ever attaining a universal system of ethics' because 'the ways of natural volition, both in the past and in the present, are cruel, brutal, ruthless and without mercy'.[56] What is more, as Edgar Andrews points out, embracing evolutionary ethics put us in an impossible moral dilemma: 'My definition of who is wise and what is good may differ from yours... The problem is: who is to decide? Who is to take control? Can any intellectual élite be trusted to remain incorrupt? And even if we did find someone whom everybody trusted, how capable is man of creating his own destiny, and then steering his ship safely home to it? We only have to look around the world today and down the recent history of man to find that, with all his education, knowledge, science, ability and powers, man inspires little confidence as the arbiter of his own destiny.'[57]

Hard-core evolutionists are reluctant to concede this point, and claim that evolution is capable of accounting for certain behavioural patterns. Richard Dawkins does precisely this in *The Selfish Gene*, where he argues that the evolutionary biological process is dominated by the need for survival. Many years earlier, Thomas Huxley had related this to human behaviour: 'It was cunning and ruthlessness that enabled man to evolve from the beasts... It is this law of the jungle that has to be the directive for all human progress.'[58] In this scenario, whatever will enable the individual to survive is good and right, both for the individual and for society at large; a contributor to a 1939 issue of *Science* wrote, 'Darwinianism consistently applied would measure goodness in terms of survival value.'[59]

Sociobiologist Edward Wilson and neo-Darwinian philosopher Michael Ruse take the point even further: 'In an important sense, ethics as we understand it is an illusion fobbed off on us by our genes to get us to co-operate... Ethical codes work because they drive us to go against our self-ish day to day impulses in favour of long-term group survival and har-mony... Furthermore, the way our biology forces our ends is by making us think that there is an objective, higher code to which we are all subject ... ethics is a shared illusion of the human race.'[60] In this extraordinary state-ment Wilson and Ruse are saying that a cruel, random, mechanical pro-cess tricks us into believing in a non-existent moral code because obedi-ence to it is the only means of our survival! This calls for stupendous faith — and flatly contradicts William Provine's comment on *Science Friction* that 'Evolution teaches us virtually nothing about morality... We humans are just on our own. We're put here by a process that doesn't care about us, and we have to figure out for ourselves how to behave with each other.'[61]

This leads to another question. What does the evolutionist offer as an incentive for seeking the well-being of his fellow humans? Julian Huxley replies that 'The development of man's potential realizable possibility pro-vides the prime motive for collective action,'[62] but it is not difficult to see that on the basis of Darwin's 'progress towards perfection' this is a totally inadequate basis. John Stott puts his finger on the flaw: 'If the unimpeded progress of evolution were our chief concern, why should we care for the senile, the imbecile, the hardened criminal, the psychopath, the chroni-cally sick, or the starving? Would it not be more prudent to put them to sleep like a well-loved dog, lest they hinder the evolutionary process?'[63]

Let me press a little harder here. If evolutionary dogma is taken to its logical conclusion, where is the rational basis for *any* sentimental feelings for the value of human life? If the survival of the fittest is one of the foun-dation stones in the evolutionary model, surely any concern to protect and save the defenceless, the weak and the sick must be deemed counter-productive? American author Dave Hunt is more specific: 'If evolution, not God, is responsible for our existence, then we should shut down all medical facilities and let the weak die naturally. Medically prolonging the lives of those with genetic disabilities or diseases allows such persons to pass on their defects to subsequent generations and thereby weaken the race and undermine the survival of the fittest... The sooner those with deficiencies die, the better for our species. That is the way evolution works!'[64] One thing is certain: the compassion, concern and care shown by human beings the world over for the weak, the sick and the underprivileged fits uneasily with an atheistic evolutionary framework. Millions have cause to be grateful that instinct triumphs over indoctrination.

Guilty or not guilty?

After reading *Origin*, geologist Adam Sedgwick wrote to Darwin pointing out the danger of breaking the link between man's understanding of the material world and human morality. He felt that Darwin had provided criminals with justification for their behaviour, and told him that if his teaching were to be accepted, humanity 'would suffer a damage that might brutalize it and sink the human race into a lower grade of degradation than any into which it has fallen since its written records tell of its history'.[65] Sedgwick's words have proved prophetic, and there is now clear evidence that evolutionary philosophy has had a profound effect on the approach which many in our modern judicial systems have taken towards wrongdoers. As Henry Morris notes, 'The modern opposition to capital punishment for murder and the general tendency towards leniency in punishment for other serious crimes are directly related to the strong evolutionary determinism that has characterized much of this century.'[66] The geneticist Theodosius Dobzhansky paints a fuller picture: 'Natural selection can favour egotism, hedonism, cowardice instead of bravery, cheating and exploitation... Evolution on the cosmic, biological and human levels are parts of one grand process of universal evolution.'[67] In 1981 the Chairman of Britain's Police Federation admitted, 'Long ago people in power stopped talking about the punishment of crime and began to talk about treatment, as if every thug was sick and in need of a prescription from the chemist.'[68] It would be 'over the top' to suggest that an increase in the crime rate is directly due to evolutionary teaching in our schools and elsewhere, but surely it is not difficult to see the connection between leniency in punishment and the idea that human beings are the product of a blind evolutionary process?

René Dubos certainly points in this direction: 'Many aspects of human behaviour which appear incomprehensible, or even irrational, become meaningful when interpreted as survivals of attributes which were useful when they first appeared during evolutionary development.'[69] If anti-social, or criminal, behaviour is genetically determined, how can those who exhibit these traits be held entirely responsible for their actions? Shoplifters, violent robbers, child abusers, rapists and even murderers are among those who have benefited from the efforts of lawyers and others leaning, even if unconsciously, on genetic determinism as an explanation of their behaviour.

Nobody would seriously suggest that macro-evolutionists are automatically driven to racism, fascism, imperialism or genocide, or to practise or support eugenics or euthanasia; nor would it make sense to say that evolutionary ideas inevitably lead to the other crimes I have just mentioned. The Oxford University professor Keith Ward makes the point well: 'Of course one cannot reject Darwinism just because it has unpleasant social consequences. But if one can see that it undermines some of the most important and strongly held human values, one will enquire very carefully into its credentials. Are we not more certain of some fundamental values, of the importance of morality, than we are of the metaphysically inflated world-view of social Darwinism?'[70] Yet there is no doubt that evolution has been used to explain certain anti-social behaviour and reduce or remove any element of guilt. One writer even makes the claim: 'Unbridled self-indulgence on the part of one generation without regard to future ones is the *modus operandi* of biological evolution and may be regarded as rational behaviour.'[71] What is certain is that while changes in Western value systems, as well as the judicial system, owe a great deal to other philosophical theories, the principles of evolution have often been used (and abused) in detrimental and, at times, destructive ways. As Richard Dawkins made clear in *New Humanist*, the deeper the commitment to evolution, the further God fades into the background: 'The more you understand the significance of evolution, the more you are pushed away from the agnostic position and towards atheism.'[72] Edgar Andrews makes the point precisely: 'The theory of evolution allows people to forget God.'[73]

Darwin died in 1882; his legacy is still very much alive.

6.

Every man for himself

After our excursion into the ramifications of Darwinism, we can now resume our briefer survey of other atheistic movements. As the twentieth century unfolded, the long war against God showed no signs of cooling. Philosophers, scientists, psychologists, sociologists — and theologians — pitched in and took it in turns to promote alternatives to traditional theism. As we shall see, these often borrowed heavily from ideas that had been put forward hundreds, or even thousands, of years earlier and dressed them up in words and concepts which fitted the contemporary culture. In the next two chapters we will look at several of these, and note some of their more obvious weaknesses.

Me, here, now

It has been said that the characteristic philosophy of the present time is existentialism, but defining it with precision is about as easy as nailing jelly to a wall because it is a position held by philosophers ranging from the strongly theistic to the stridently atheistic and there are profound differences between individual points of view.

The word is based on the German *existentialismus*, meaning 'to stand forth' or 'to stand out', and *The Chambers Dictionary* provides as good a one-sentence explanation as I have been able to find: 'A term covering a number of related philosophical doctrines denying objective universal values and holding that people, as moral free agents, must create values for themselves through actions and must accept the ultimate responsibility for those actions in the seemingly meaningless universe.'[1] Rather than dealing with the nature of the universe and objective philosophical problems, existentialism is concerned with an individual's attitude to life.

Some scholars trace the roots of existentialism as far back as the 'Golden Age' of Greek philosophy, but it will be sufficient for our purposes to pick them up in the nineteenth century. By far the best-known theistic existentialist during this period was the somewhat quirky Danish philosopher Søren Kierkegaard (1813–1855), who adopted a cynical approach, not only to Hegel's idealism, but to rationalism, romanticism and to organized religion and human behaviour in particular. As this note from his *Journal* makes clear, truth for Kierkegaard was not abstract and objective but something intensely personal: 'The thing is to understand myself, to see what God really wishes *me* to do; the thing is to find a truth which is true *for me*, to find *the idea for which I can live and die.*'[2] As he put it elsewhere, 'Truth is subjectivity.'[3]

Although he believed that God was the ultimate source of reality in the universe, Kierkegaard was so opposed to rationalism that he could write, 'God does not exist; he is eternal.'[4] This one statement shows that it is almost impossible to pin him down as to the nature of God. There are times when he appears fairly orthodox and others when 'his view of God seems to have a great deal in common with the Wizard of Oz'.[5] Kierkegaard sees men as thrashing about in a dangerous sea, finding meaning and security only when they take a risky and irrational 'leap of faith' across the chasm separating them from God.

Because he worked out his model (though he would have denied that it was anything so formal) within a theistic framework, we can leave Kierkegaard there, but his importance lies in the fact that current existentialist emphases on individual existence, subjectivity and inwardness, and commitment to existential involvement spring largely from this man, whose lugubrious approach to things has led to his becoming known as 'the melancholy Dane'.

Anxious and alone

The two key players in the history of modern atheistic existentialism were born within a few years of each other, one as the nineteenth century drew to a close and the other as the twentieth began. The first was the German philosopher Martin Heidegger (1889–1976) who once studied for the

Roman Catholic priesthood, but then turned to philosophy and was strongly influenced by the works of Plato, Kant and Nietzsche. For part of the 1930s he supported the National Socialists (Nazis), though he later turned his back on them.

His major work, *Being and Time*, was first published in 1927, and discussed the pressures and problems facing men living in a post-Enlightenment secular society, a world without God. Heidegger called this situation 'the dark night of the world', a world from which the light of God had been eclipsed and in which men were left to grope around as best they could, searching in the darkness for any scraps of meaning that might be found.

To emphasize man's dilemma and trauma, Heidegger invented the word *Geworfenheit*, which means 'having been thrown-ness'. It is a graphic description of the disorientation felt when finding oneself in bewildering circumstances. I vividly remember that a few years ago, on the first full day of a round-the-world speaking tour, I woke up with the feeling that I was completely out of touch with my surroundings. The whole atmosphere seemed strange to me. I felt as if I had been thrown into an unfamiliar setting with which I had no connecting link, but as my senses slipped into gear my bewilderment quickly dissolved. Bangkok, Thailand, was certainly a city I had never before visited, and the sights, sounds and smells were all new to me — but I no longer had any sense of *Geworfenheit*. I knew how I had got there, when I was due to leave and where I was going. What is more, I knew *why* I was there. My being there was something I had chosen, and the timing of my visit was something over which I had at least some measure of control.

In Heidegger's view of things, the sense of having been hurled into an alien, impersonal universe in which we can never feel at home produces *Angst*, a gnawing anxiety as to our existence and identity and a deep-rooted fear of meaninglessness in the face of what he called our 'propulsion towards death', the fact that in a few years at most death will reduce us to non-being. *Angst* is what grips the existentialist when he reflects on his belief that he came out of nothingness and is moving inexorably towards nothingness.

Existentialism rarely uses the word 'man' in its common, generic sense. Instead, we find expressions like 'thereness' (one of Heidegger's favourites), 'existence', 'ego', 'being there' and 'being for oneself'. For the existentialist, there is no such thing as collective man, only individual men and women. This intensely personal focus is in part a reaction against the dehumanizing factors in modern society — not only dictators who deny human rights and philosophical systems that reject individual freedom, but urbanization, industrialization, bureaucracy and technology, all of which tend to see people as anonymous units in the context of planning, consumption or production. Existentialism has been called '... basically a reaction against the extremes of scientific rationalism which, many feel, tend to dehumanize man to the level of a biochemical machine... The great emphasis on experience, irrationality and absurdity among *avant-garde* elements in the art world in the West is further evidence of this reaction against reason.'[6]

Existentialism's anxious self-concern is said to be what distinguishes men from the natural world and from brute animals, in that horses, trees, rocks and plants are not concerned with how they came into existence or how they arrived at where they are. For existentialists, this means that only human beings, aware of their existence, are said to exist (or, in one of their favourite phrases, to have 'authentic existence'). In Heidegger's own words, 'Rocks are, but they do not exist. Trees are, but they do not exist. Horses are, but they do not exist. God is, but he does not exist.'[7] As to what 'exist' means when used in this way, Heidegger says, 'The proposition "man exists" means: man is that being whose Being is distinguished by the open-standing standing — in the unconcealedness of Being, from Being, in Being.'[8] Clarity was not his strong point!

Heidegger is concerned that men should not settle down in 'inauthentic existence' as one of the crowd (what he calls 'irresoluteness'), seeing themselves as nothing more than skin-covered objects and treating death as something that happens to others. Instead, he calls on men to exercise their freedom (in modern jargon, to 'do their own thing') and bring their potential nature into being. There is therefore a sense in which, for the existentialist, selfhood is not something anyone has, but something which is being developed in the course of a person's life. As one writer puts it, 'Man is *possibility* because he stands before a *future*. He is always on his way and incomplete in his being; he has always to make himself and is not provided with a ready-made nature like a stone or an iceberg.'[9]

Along with 'Being' and *Angst*, another of Heidegger's major concerns is death, and it is important to see where this fits into the picture he creates. As there is no creator or judge, it is pointless for a person to think of any kind of reality before birth, or to be concerned about what might happen after death. B. A. G. Fuller explains how Heidegger relates this to the individual: 'Life is cast up between nothing and nothing. Death is its boundary and its supreme possibility. To freely accept death, to live in its presence, and to acknowledge that for it there is no substitute and into it one must go alone, is to escape from all illusions and to achieve genuine dignity and authentic existence.'[10]

Heidegger leaves us with the picture of a human being as someone who finds himself anxious and alone in an unfriendly world. To become 'authentic' he must create his own existence and essence and can do so freely and without any fear of future judgement. As Robert Brow explains, 'Existentialism ... denies that there is any ultimate purpose or end and ethics becomes an exhortation "to do something boldly anyway".'[11]

The media man

The second key player in the history of modern atheistic existentialism was Jean-Paul Sartre (1905–1980) the French philosopher, dramatist, essayist and novelist. The last three descriptions are particularly important, because Sartre's brilliant ability to use the popular media in getting his message across is one of the most significant reasons why huge swathes of human culture are drenched in existentialism today. Born in Paris, Sartre was the leading student in his philosophy year at the renowned Sorbonne. He worked for a time as a teacher but, after the Second World War, part of which he spent in a Nazi prison camp, he committed himself to writing and to supporting left-wing political causes. In looking for a way out of the upheaval caused by the war, he became increasingly involved with Marxism, and gradually established an international reputation as one of the most powerful and influential European thinkers and writers of modern times. He refused the 1964 Nobel prize for literature 'for personal reasons'. Here, we can touch on just three of the major issues with which he concerned himself — God, man and values.

As to *the existence of God*, Sartre called himself 'an atheistic existentialist', and said that the idea of God was 'contradictory'. He made the claim that his atheism was based in part on an experience he once had of sitting in a cafe and feeling that he was being stared at by another customer. Sartre felt that this dehumanized him by reducing him to an object and that, if God were omniscient, his all-seeing stare ('gaze' is Sartre's big word here) would do the same. This produced an intolerable conflict with Sartre's conviction that human beings were subjects, not objects; the only way to defuse the conflict was to deny the existence of God.

Along similar lines, the existence of God clashed with Sartre's fundamental assertion that human beings are totally free to define their own existence and essence by the way they choose to live. If God existed, men would not be free to choose their own values, ends, means and existence, because these would have been chosen by a transcendent Being who stood over them and, as Sartre saw it, reduced them to the level of objects. A God who laid down a moral code, and to whom men were answerable, would rob them of their moral autonomy, so God must go. Of course Sartre gives the game away here, and shows that his atheism is assumed, not proved.

On the question of *human identity*, Sartre's major idea was that existence precedes essence[12] and that it is pointless to think of 'human nature' because there is no God to conceive of such a thing. Put very simply, traditional theism taught that essence precedes existence and that God had humanness in mind before he created man (a modern analogy might be a car designer having the finished product in mind before the car is built), while in Sartre's existentialism a person begins with an awareness of his existence and then needs to determine his own personal identity or essence. Some of the most radical existentialists go even further and say that there is no such thing as essence and that only existence has reality. As Sartre saw it, human beings exist, not as part of an *a priori* essence of humanness, but as unique individuals who do not know what they are like or what meaning they have. Yet whereas everything else in the universe is a thing 'in itself', a fixed object, with no self-consciousness and no relationship to anything else, each individual person is a being 'for itself', a fluid entity with immense possibilities which can be developed by choice, commitment and action. People are free to become whatever they choose, and if they allow politics, society or religion to influence their values and choices they are acting in 'bad faith'.

It is not difficult to see the appeal of this kind of thinking, not least because it massages the ego and opens up endless possibilities for self-gratification — but Sartre was not finished. Some previous thinkers had argued that, although God could be ruled out of court, it was important to hold on to morality based on traditional theism. Quite rightly, Sartre would have none of this and taught that in rejecting God man had no option but to go it alone. In *Existentialism and Humanism* he wrote, 'And when we speak of "abandonment" — a favourite word of Heidegger — we only mean to say that God does not exist, and that it is necessary to draw the consequences of his absence right to the end.'[13] In the same work he underlined the point: 'Existentialism is nothing else but an attempt to draw the full conclusions from a consistently atheistic position.'[14] The Russian novelist Fyodor Dostoevsky, who died in 1881, had written, 'If God does not exist, everything would be permitted,' a statement which Sartre called 'the starting-point' of existentialism.[15] In his view, atheists who attempted to hold on to theistically based morality were trying to have their cake and eat it. He insisted that men who reject God must work out their own values, make their own choices, and live with the consequences. As Sartre saw it, men were not basically good or evil, because there were no values other than those they created for themselves.

However, far from opening the door to a blissful, unthreatened Utopia, Sartre saw that this line of approach resulted in human prospects becoming increasingly bleak. At one stage he wrote, 'If God does not exist ... man is in consequence forlorn, for he cannot find anything to depend upon, either within or outside himself.'[16] In other words, by ruling out God man finds himself without any other means of support. The story is told of an amateur mountain climber who fell off a steep precipice. Hurtling towards the ground hundreds of feet below, he managed to grab a solitary little bush growing on the side of the mountain, but the bush could not bear his weight and began to work loose from its roots. In utter terror, the climber looked to the sky and screamed, 'Is there anyone there who can help me?' To his amazement, a voice from the clouds said, 'Yes, I can help you, but you must trust me. Let go of the bush.' After a quick glance around him, the climber shouted, 'Is there anyone else up there who can help?' This was the kind of dilemma Sartre found he had created.

Even the freedom which he assigned to individual human beings proved to be a liability rather than an asset. In the first place it was limited by what Sartre called 'facticity', the body, ability and other factors which go to make up the current situation of the person concerned. Even more depressingly, without a Creator or any outside reference-point by which to assess meaning or values, man's freedom is a farce. Far from being liberated, Sartre said man is 'condemned to be free'.[17] As he explained, 'My freedom is the unique foundation of values. And since I am the being by virtue of whom values exist, nothing — absolutely nothing — can justify me in adopting this or that value or scale of values. As the unique basis of the existence of values, I am totally unjustifiable. And my freedom is in the anguish in finding that it is the baseless basis of values.'[18]

Bluntly put, Sartre had reached the point where values had no value. All the energy poured into the attempt to live an 'authentic' life was like water sprinkled on sand. 'Man,' he concluded, 'is a useless passion.'[19] It is only a short step from there to believing that the whole of life is irrational, meaningless and absurd — and Sartre took it. In his first and most famous novel *Nausea*, one of his characters, Roquentin, questions his right to exist at all and goes on, 'I existed like a stone, a plant, a microbe... I was just thinking ... that here we are, all of us, eating and drinking, to preserve our precious existence and there's nothing, nothing, absolutely no reason for existing.'[20] Sartre's bleak philosophy condemns everyone else to the same meaningless fate: 'Every existent is born without reason, prolongs itself out of weakness and dies by chance.'[21] In his best-known philosophical work, *Being And Nothingness*, Sartre explored the question, 'What is it like to be a human being?' and came to the conclusion that, as there was no explanation for the existence of anything, man must accept the fact that he has been dumped into a meaningless universe and is caught between 'the absurdity of life's origin and the fear of life's extinction'.[22] As R. C. Sproul comments, 'Sartre's grim conclusion is that all of our caring, our concerns, our deepest aspirations are empty of significance. Human life is meaningless. It is a cosmic joke and a cold, indifferent universe is the comedian.'[23]

Theory is one thing . . .

Not surprisingly, Sartre proved unable to apply his convictions with any consistency. As an entrenched existentialist, he claimed to be passionately committed to the idea of individual human autonomy, yet he strongly supported the Marxist cause, which in practice smothered the freedom of the individual in the interests of the state. All eight leaders of the *Angka Loeu* ('Higher Organization') who masterminded the horrendous blood-letting in Cambodia in 1975 had absorbed their ideas of 'necessary violence' while studying in France in the 1950s; in Paul Johnson's words, 'They were Sartre's children.'[24] Again, although he taught that ethics was an irrelevance, he became actively involved in the protest against the French occupation of Algeria, calling it an unjust and dirty war. He paid dearly for this U-turn; as soon as he signed the Algerian Manifesto he was regarded as an apostate, and lost his leadership of the *avant garde*. On a more intimate level, while claiming that his personal credo was 'Travel, polygamy, transparency', he had his publisher secretly prepare four copies of one of his books, each one bearing the name of one of his four current mistresses and indicating that she was the person to whom the book was dedicated.[25]

It is fascinating to place other glimpses of Sartre's own private experience alongside his public announcements. At one point, he wrote of how his religious upbringing had ironically contributed to his atheism. Everyone in and around his family believed in God 'for reasons of discretion', and 'An atheist was a fanatic whom you did not invite to dinner lest he "created a scandal".' Baptized and registered as a Roman Catholic, he confessed, 'Deep down it all bored me to death ... yet I believed: in my heart, kneeling on my bed, hands folded, I said my daily prayer but thought less and less about the good God... For several years longer I kept up public relations with the Almighty; in private, I stopped associating with him...'[26]

In the same autobiographical passage he wrote of an occasion when he was at home playing with matches and accidentally burned a mat in the bathroom. While trying to cover up the evidence he had an overwhelming sense that God was watching him: 'I felt his gaze upon my head and upon my hands.' He reacted angrily at feeling that he was 'a living target' and from then on his alienation from God accelerated. 'Unable to take root in my heart, he vegetated in me for a while and then died.'[27] Even more telling are his feelings about the incident many years later: 'Fifty years ago, without that misunderstanding, without that mistake, without the accident which separated us, there might have been something between us. Nothing happened between us... Atheism is a cruel, long-term business: I believe I have gone through it to the end.'[28]

The 'cruel, long-term business' was marked by what Paul Johnson calls 'extraordinary squalor, selfishness, confusion, cruelty and, not least, cowardice',[29] and his final years, sadly darkened by blindness, were 'squalid bordering on the horrific'.[30] Yet there was a final, surprising twist. For years, Sartre had unleashed a torrent of atheistic literature but, a few months before he died, he wrote in a left-wing journal, 'I do not feel that I am the product of chance, a speck of dust in the universe, but someone who was expected, prepared, prefigured. In short, a being whom only a Creator could put here: and this idea of a creating hand refers to God.'[31] That one brief statement turned Sartre's lifelong commitment to atheistic existentialism on its head. Simone de Beauvoir, his last mistress (and one of his earliest), was so shocked by this that, having given all the right signals at his funeral, she published *La céremonie des adieux*, in which she mounted a vicious attack on Sartre and described his statement as 'this senile act of a turncoat'.[32] Maybe — or did the blind old thinker finally see something he had missed in seventy-five years of searching?

Whether or not Sartre had an eleventh-hour conversion, he died as an icon of atheism and his funeral cortège was followed by thousands who had been influenced by his teaching. Today, millions of people (most of them without knowing it) are root-and-branch existentialists, in spite of the glaring weaknesses which questions like these expose:

- Although existentialism brilliantly reveals the human predicament, it provides no solutions. What can it offer the insecure, the lonely, the guilty and the fearful?
- How can existentialism sensibly distinguish between 'authentic' and 'inauthentic' experience? Colin Brown pinpoints the problem: 'If the world is irrational, and there are no objective values, how can playing bingo be described as less authentic than listening to Beethoven? To prefer one rather than the other is purely a matter of personal taste.'[33]
- In the absence of values and rationality in the world, how can we possibly 'authenticate' ourselves?
- If, as Kierkegaard put it, 'truth is subjectivity', how can we be sure we are getting the right message when it conflicts with other people's claims? Specifically, how can I contradict someone else's conviction that God exists?
- Sartre argues that man can be autonomous only if there is no God, but how can this be proved without first demonstrating that God does not exist?
- Sartre claims that getting rid of God makes genuine morality possible, but might it not be easier to show that Sartre's morality makes the non-existence of God *necessary*? In other words, does it not seem that Sartre's denial of God is wishful thinking?
- Sartre stands firmly against the existence of any objective values, but shoots himself in the foot by insisting that becoming 'authentic' (by

asserting one's own freedom and creating one's own meaning) is creditable. But how can we call anything creditable if there is no objective
standard by which to judge it?

- If pessimistic existentialism is right to say that everything is meaningless,
would this not include its claim that this is the case? If not, what else
might be excluded from the claim?

- If our actions have no ultimate meaning, why should giving to charity
be considered more worthy than robbing a bank? Morally speaking,
what do the words 'good', 'bad', 'better' and 'worse' mean?

- Because it is soaked in subjectivity, existentialism fails to give anything
like enough weight to reason, science and the objective world. Can we
honestly say that sensations, moods, emotions and personal opinions
are the *only* things which constitute reality?

- How is it possible for a self-authenticating person to live with other self-
authenticating people? What happens when my (self-authenticated) freedom conflicts with someone else's?

- If everyone practised atheistic existentialism and 'did his own thing',
surely the result would be total and universal anarchy? Does any existentialist seriously believe that he could live in such a world?

- One last question: is man's relentless search for freedom, meaning, dignity, significance and values not exactly what we would expect to find if
he had in fact been created by a God who is the ultimate reference-
point for all of these?

7.

Five steps to nowhere

In the last chapter we looked at one of the most pervasive notions being embraced today as an alternative to traditional theism. In this chapter we will pursue existentialism a little further and then take a much briefer look at four other alternatives to theism, each of which draws on ideas which have been circulating for centuries. As with the previous alternatives, we will also point out some of the inherent weaknesses in the ideas being put forward.

The existential explosion (EXISTENTIALISM)

The person most often associated with Jean-Paul Sartre in the development of twentieth-century atheistic existentialism is the French philosopher and novelist Albert Camus (1913–1960). Born in Algeria, Camus joined the Algerian Communist Party in his early twenties and later edited the French Resistance magazine *Combat* during the German occupation of France in the Second World War.

Camus was strongly influenced in his ideas by the work of the nineteenth-century French political theorist and economist Pierre Joseph Proudhon, who branded the God of traditional theism as 'evil' because he had deprived man of his creative powers. For Proudhon, this meant that 'The first duty of free and intelligent man is to chase the idea of God out of his conscience incessantly.'[1] This may have sounded courageous at the time, but towards the end of his life Proudhon was forced to accept that this kind of dogma had a serious downside: 'Today, civilization is indeed in a critical stage. All traditions are used up, all beliefs abolished... Everything contributes to sadden people of goodwill... We shall struggle in the night, and we must do our best to endure this life without too much sadness. Let us stand by each other, call out to each other in the dark.'[2] Camus was even more strongly influenced by the strident atheism of Friedrich Nietzsche, for whom the God of traditional theism was no longer a living reality.

Camus and Sartre came together in 1943 and, although they disagreed in their attitudes to war, they shared a large pool of existential ideas. Their emphasis on man's fundamental loneliness in a godless world, the tensions between self and society, and the issues of individual freedom and responsibility all caught people's imagination. In their novels and plays they spoke directly to the real, passionate issues of life and eventually attracted a cult following in France, especially among young people. Yet the real breakthrough for atheistic existentialism came when it crossed the Atlantic and took root in the United States, especially in the student community. This triggered an explosion of ideas in all the popular communication media — films, plays, novels, poetry and art — and the fallout is all around us. R. C. Sproul is not exaggerating when he says, 'The rapid spread and enormous impact of existential philosophy upon our culture has been uncanny... We encounter the influence of existentialism virtually every day of our lives and in virtually every sphere of our culture. Few people can define it or articulate its theory, but we are living under its influence every day.'[3]

As atheistic existentialism took hold in the world of the created arts, the themes of loneliness, emptiness, helplessness and pessimism began to dominate. Camus himself had popularized the idea of 'the Absurd', the word he gave to anything in human experience which is incompatible with man's desire for reason, justice, happiness and purpose. The 'Theatre of the Absurd', which had received rave reviews in France ten years earlier, crossed the Atlantic in the 1960s. It hit the headlines on Broadway with Samuel Beckett's play *Waiting for Godot*, in which two tramps, obviously representing the human race, do nothing but hang around waiting for Godot to turn up and give their lives some meaning and direction. Godot never appears, and the play ends with the two tramps rooted to the spot. The message is loud and clear: without God man is helpless and alone in a meaningless, silent world.

Eugène Ionesco, the Romanian-born French playwright who became the most widely performed dramatist writing in the French language, was another founder of 'the Theatre of the Absurd'. He defined humour as 'becoming aware of absurdity while continuing to live in absurdity'.[4] When he completed *Macbett*, a witty reworking of Shakespeare's tragedy, he commented, 'I have never written with such pleasure on such sinister themes... It was as though I was dancing on thousands of millions of corpses... I was happy in my unhappiness, happy in the unhappiness of others. And I do not have a bad conscience about it.'[5] Although as a young man he had toyed briefly with the idea of becoming a monk, his work became increasingly negative and concentrated on issues such as the loneliness of existence and the emptiness of language, and his later plays were full of angry pessimism. Six years before he died he told an interviewer, 'Life is a joke that God has played on man.'[6]

Camus was awarded the Nobel Prize for Literature in 1957, when he was cited as 'the one who illuminates the problems of the human conscience in our time'. What he failed to do was to provide any answers, admitting instead (and echoing Ionesco) that 'Life is a bad joke,' and saying that the only serious question left for philosophers to discuss was that of suicide. Elsewhere he wrote, 'Truth is a colossal bore,'[7] by which he meant that all attempts to invest the world in which we live with rational significance are a waste of time. A serial adulterer, whose continual philandering helped drive his mentally fragile wife Francine to clinical depression and an unsuccessful suicide attempt, Camus hardly set an attractive example of existentialism in practice in his own private life.

Camus was not alone in getting his existential message across at a popular level, and the same pessimistic world-view has been a recurring theme ever since. American playwright Tennessee Williams admitted, 'There is a horror in things, and our existence is meaningless.' The singer and songwriter Bob Dylan made a big hit with *Desolation Row*, which has been described as 'a catalogue of the absurdities of modern life'.[8] Many of the Beatles' songs were pure existentialism; to give just one example, their 'Nowhere Man' sits in his 'nowhere land, making all his nowhere plans for nobody'. In his massive 1980s' hit 'Born in the USA', American pop idol Bruce Springsteen could offer no improvement: 'I'm ten years burning down the road, Nowhere to run, ain't got nowhere to go.'[9] When the so-called 'Swinging Sixties' were at their peak, folk-singer Joan Baez (influenced, no doubt, by the threat of nuclear warfare) lamented, 'You are the orphans in an age of no tomorrow.' Best-selling author Arthur Koestler struck the same pessimistic note: 'Nature has let us down. God seems to have left the receiver off the hook, and time is running out.'[10] Glitter, glamour, colour, music and noise can do nothing to mask the pervasive emptiness of atheistic existentialism.

Not surprisingly, modern art has often reflected the alienation, chaos and absurdity of the age. There were signs of this in the early part of the twentieth century when, in a quest to discover what lay behind reality, the Spanish painter Pablo Picasso turned to cubism, a style which broke through the barriers of reality (faces with three eyes or three noses, for example) and pioneered a deliberate deformation of appearances. As Anthony O'Hear, Director of the Royal Institute of Philosophy, wrote in the *Daily Mail*, 'Things which artists in previous centuries had treated with reverence and dignity were disjointed and turned inside out... Art began to undermine confidence in human reason and morality.'[11] From 1913 onwards, French painter Marcel Duchamp (a notorious prankster, but taken very seriously by art critics and teachers) began to exhibit his 'ready-made' pieces, the most famous being a urinal entitled 'Fountain', which he said was a work of art because he, an artist, declared it to be so. Soon afterwards, the Russian artist Wassily Kandinsky produced the first completely 'abstract' painting, a style with no definable subject matter.

Today, almost anything goes, as just one exhibition is sufficient to illustrate. The prestigious Turner Prize for 1995 was won by the British artist Damien Hirst, who first came to fame when he exhibited a dead shark in a tank of formaldehyde and progressed from there to a pickled sheep in London and two rotting, copulating cattle in New York. His prize-winning presentation at another London exhibition was called 'Mother and Child, Divided' and consisted of a cow and calf, each dissected at the spine and placed in neighbouring tanks. Others short-listed for the 1995 Turner Prize included Mona Hatoun, who offered a video filmed by a camera crawling across her body and entering her various orifices. Her other entry was a 'sculpture' of wire cages with a bare light bulb moving up and down the middle. At the same exhibition, Mark Wallinger showed garish cut-outs of horses with their forequarters and hindquarters transposed. Another short-listed artist was Callum Innes, who covered a canvas with a single colour, then removed sections of pigment to reveal the canvas underneath, the finished effect being described by one art critic as resembling a badly stained wall.

We put existentialism in the witness box at the end of the last chapter. Here, it will be sufficient to add this comment by the British philosopher David Cook: 'The first and major problem with the existentialist is how to make sense of what he says. At its simplest, the existentialist message is that everything is meaningless. Immediately we must ask whether that message itself is meaningful or meaningless. This is not some verbal trick of twisting words to suit one's own purposes. Rather it is a realization that there are some things which cannot be said or thought. "Everything is meaningless" is such an unsayable... The existentialist message of absurdity is itself absurd for it is an attempt to say the unsayable, think the unthinkable, and to live the unliveable. It cannot be said, thought, believed as correct, or put into practice, it is self-contradictory. Thus it rules itself out as a serious view. From the very start, existentialism is a non-starter.'[12]

Long road to oblivion (NIHILISM)

A philosophy which runs parallel to atheistic existentialism goes under the name of 'nihilism'. The word 'nihilist' was coined by the nineteenth-century Russian writer Ivan Turgenev in his work *Fathers and Children*, when he used it to define a radical form of socialism. In the third quarter of the nineteenth century, nihilism became a key doctrine among the Russian intelligentsia, who advocated widespread terrorism and called for the rejection of all authority in favour of individual expression. The *Concise Oxford Dictionary* defines nihilism as 'negative doctrines, total rejection of current beliefs, in religion or morals', adding that in the field of philosophy nihilism is 'scepticism that denies all existence'.[13]

In its most popular form, nihilism says that there is no reason why the universe exists and no goal towards which it is moving; nothing is of real value; human existence is totally meaningless; human beings are biological accidents; there is no life after death and suicide could therefore be a more rational approach than the desire to go on living. As far as values, morals and ethics are concerned, nihilism makes no rules and draws no lines. The whole of life is an exercise in futility, and personal satisfaction at any given moment is sufficient justification for anything any individual chooses to do or not to do.

There is nothing new about nihilism. In one of his most famous phrases, William Shakespeare called life '... a tale, told by an idiot, full of sound and fury, signifying nothing'.[14] Friedrich Nietzsche, sometimes called the father of modern nihilism, came to the same depressing conclusion, his final verdict on human life being to call it *Das Nichtige* (the nothingness).

Nor is this bleak assessment something felt only by academics living in ivory towers. After decades spent in carefully probing the human mind-set, the distinguished Swiss psychiatrist Carl Gustav Jung said that in his considered opinion, 'The vast neurotic misery of the world could be termed a neurosis of emptiness,'[15] while Victor Frankl, his counterpart in the University of Vienna, speaks of an 'existential vacuum' in modern society, and has devised a 'logotherapy' to help patients break free from their inner emptiness.[16]

As is the case with existentialism in general, the performing arts have reflected nihilism in the most direct and challenging way. Samuel Beckett produced a play entitled 'Breath', which lasted just thirty seconds and had no actors or dialogue. The only props were miscellaneous pieces of rubbish scattered over the stage and the only 'script' was the sigh of human life, from a baby's cry to a dying man's last gasp. In 1952, the composer John Cage presented a piece of 'music' which he called 'Four Minutes Thirteen Seconds' and which consisted of total silence for that length of time, suggesting that the silence 'may then be filled by the sounds of the world itself'. Artist Yves Klein took exactly the same approach and produced paintings which were nothing but canvasses filled with unrelieved blue, leaving everyone who saw them free to give them their own meaning. Film-maker and pop artist Andy Warhol wrote, 'The world would be easier to live in if we were all machines. It's nothing in the end anyway. It doesn't matter what anything does.'[17] The American journalist and broadcaster Jon Casimir could offer nothing better: 'Here's what I think. There is no meaning of life. The whole thing is a gyp, a never-ending corridor to nowhere. What is passed off as an all-important search is basically just a bunch of philosophers scrabbling about on their knees, trying to find a lost sock in the cosmic laundromat.'[18] The renowned film director Robert Altman, interviewed for the *Observer* in 1995, looked back on a brilliant career and admitted, 'None of it — gambling, money, winning or losing — has any real value. It is simply a way of killing time, like crossword puzzles... I am sitting here today in this bleak atmosphere in the middle of winter, making this silly movie, and to me it is an adventure. I have no idea what it will be like. But even if it works, it will all be for nothing. If I had never lived, if the sperm that hit the egg had missed, it would have made no difference to anything.'[19]

Other artists have expressed the same philosophy, ignoring history, rejecting all convention and denying objective truth and moral absolutes. In the 1990s, London's Tate Gallery famously exhibited a huge oblong composed of ordinary building bricks, the presentation of which was acclaimed as a masterpiece comparable to Rome's Sistine Chapel. At the Saatchi Gallery's London show 'New American Artists', staged in 1996, one prominent exhibit was a video of a young man endlessly taking off and putting on his underpants. One woman's contribution was a 'sculpture' made from huge lumps of brown chocolate and white lard which she had chewed, licked and nibbled into its final form. Another artist, Jacqueline Humphries, offered an example of her speciality, which was nothing more than bright paint allowed to slither down over a static object — a 'skill' which led to her being known in the art world as 'Jack the Dripper'. Helen Chadwick, who died in 1996 at the age of forty-two, was described in her *Daily Telegraph* obituary as 'one of Britain's most innovative conceptual artists'. Ten years earlier she had hit the headlines with a sculpture entitled 'Carcass', a transparent pillar seven feet high and crammed with rotting vegetables. Another of her best-known creations was a collection of twelve white-enamelled bronzes cast from shapes made when she and her partner urinated into mounds of snow.

In 1997, writer-director David Cronenberg released his high-profile film *Crash*, which showed its central characters exploring car crashes as a way to achieve sexual ecstasy. The film attracted enormous attention and was hailed by some as a work of artistic genius and high moral tone, but a *Daily Mail* leader called it 'a disgusting and depraved film',[20] and the *Daily Telegraph's* reviewer referred to the film's 'pervasive nihilism'.[21]

Twenty years before these grotesque absurdities, the distinguished modern thinker Francis Schaeffer had seen which way the wind was blowing: 'What marks our own generation? It is the fact that modern man thinks that there is nobody home in the universe. *Nobody* to love man, nobody to comfort him, even while he seeks desperately to find comfort in the limited, finite, horizontal relationships of life. But it does not work — in his art, in his music, or anywhere else. In his literature, in his drama, it does not work. In the sexual act, in human relationships, he finds only the devastatingly sterile and the dreadfully ugly.'[22] In his unusual and challenging book, *A World Without Heroes*, George Roche says much the same thing: 'One looks in vain through this motley mayhem for any standard of manners or morals not violated or any commandment unbroken. What it conspicuously offers is an unrestrained quest for sensation, especially the physical. What it conspicuously lacks is a higher view of life, seeking beauty,

cultivation, character, knowledge and moral redemption.'[23] It is now virtually impossible to watch television, read a newspaper, or turn the pages of
a popular magazine without being exposed to a philosophy which says
that truth is irrelevant, absolutes are non-existent and subjective experience is everything. In the absence of any God-consciousness, man is adrift
and alienated from society and self. This is one of the clearest explanations
for the desperate attempts millions of young people and others are making
to escape from the screaming pain of the world they have made for themselves by means of drug abuse, Eastern mysticism, experimentation with
the occult and other means of disengaging themselves from reality. It is
also a major factor in the spiralling suicide rate in many of the world's most
developed countries; in the United States alone over 300,000 people a
year end their own lives and it has been estimated that more than five
million of that country's present population have tried to do so.

At least four things can be said in response to the nihilist. Firstly, nihilism
begins by assuming that God does not exist, or at least that the concept of
God is no longer respectable for modern thinkers. The major assumption,
that God does not exist, has the same effect on nihilism that it has on so
many of the other philosophies we have examined — it holes itself below
the water-line. To make such a controlling assumption without producing
any evidence cannot be taken seriously; it simply makes no sense. The
idea that the concept of God can no longer be believed by today's thinkers
is just as unreliable, because it flies in the face of the facts, as Paul Johnson
points out: 'The most extraordinary thing about the twentieth century was
the failure of God to die. The collapse of mass religious belief, especially
among the educated and prosperous, had been widely and confidently
predicted. It did not take place. Somehow, God survived, flourished even.
At the end of the twentieth century the idea of a personal, living God, is as
lively and real as ever, in the minds and hearts of countless millions of men
and women throughout our planet.'[24] In 1980, *Time* Magazine fine-tuned
the point: 'God? Wasn't he chased out of heaven by Marx, banished to the
unconscious by Freud and announced by Nietzsche to be deceased? Did
not Darwin drive him out of the empirical world? Well, not entirely. In a
quiet revolution in thought and arguments that hardly anyone could have
foreseen only two decades ago, God is making a comeback. Most intrigu-
ingly, this is happening not among theologians or ordinary believers ... but
in the crisp, intellectual circles of academic philosophers, where the consensus had long banished the Almighty from fruitful discourse.'[25]

Secondly, it is equally untrue that values do not exist. We will look at the question of values more closely in a later chapter, but the basic point can be made by using one chilling illustration. On 13 March 1996, Thomas Hamilton walked into Dunblane Primary School in Scotland, made his way to the gym, fired 105 bullets and killed sixteen children and their teacher. All but one of the children were five years old. Is there anyone — even the most entrenched nihilist — who would deny that what Hamilton did was wrong? And if the nihilist agrees that it was wrong, is he not ruling out the idea that there are *no* values? What is more, how can the nihilist say that truth does not exist when he claims that the statement he is making is true? Let me press the point. The nihilist says, 'There are no absolutes.' Is that statement absolute? If so, his premise is false. If not, his whole argument collapses. The nihilist is in a 'no-win' situation.

Thirdly, although some nihilists take a somewhat sceptical view of science, and see it as merely an alternative religion, nihilism usually assumes that science is at the cutting edge of human knowledge, that only what can be known and proved by science is rational, and that science has now proved that man is nothing more than a biochemical accident, living in a silent and uncaring universe. We shall look at the 'science versus faith' issue in chapter 19, but we can answer the point here by saying that this assumption shoots itself firmly in the foot, because it is not itself a scientific statement but a philosophical statement *about* science. As American author J. P. Moreland rightly says, 'One cannot turn to science to justify science any more than one can pull oneself up by his own boot straps.'[26]

Fourthly, no nihilist can consistently live as if there was no rational or moral order. A nihilist stepping out in front of moving traffic might not enjoy a long life during which to promote nihilism! Would a nihilist be happy to accept someone stealing his car, raping his wife, abducting his child or damaging his property on the basis that moral values were non-existent? Would it not be in the best interests of the nihilist if others rejected nihilism and treated him with the kind of respect that a moral law demands?

Nihilism is a philosophical, moral and practical dead-end. Far from showing that God does not exist, what it does (unintentionally of course) is to demonstrate the futility of finding any meaning in the universe as a whole, and in human life in particular, apart from the existence of God and the relationship which he bears to his creation. As John Frame concludes, 'The choice is between God and chaos, God and nothing, God and insanity.'[27]

Cosmic stand-off? (DUALISM)

A very different alternative to traditional theism is dualism, which comes in various forms. One says that the world exists, or can be explained, as two fundamental types of substance, such as mind and matter. In the seventeenth century, Descartes developed the idea of the human mind and body as two separate but interacting entities or 'substances' — now known as 'the theory of the ghost in the machine'. Later, Kant's ideas about noumenal and phenomenal reality constituted another radical form of dualism. Another form of dualism, very popular today, reflects the separation of religion and philosophy, the sacred and the secular, or faith and reason.

The dualism that concerns us here is painted on a wider canvas. From about the fourth century B.C., Chinese philosophy has taught that the cosmos is ruled by *yin* and *yang*. *Yin*, which is negative and passive, represents femininity, maternity, earth, cold, darkness, weakness and death, while *yang*, which is positive and active, represents masculinity, paternity, heaven, warmth, light, strength and life. Plato distinguished between two principles, his divine architect, or Demiurge, and the primary matter used in forming the world. In the third century, the Babylonian thinker Mani put forward a highly mythological collection of ideas built around the doctrine that two principles, Light and Dark, God and Matter, were eternal. Even the subsequently famous Augustine of Hippo (354–430) was attracted to Manichaeism for about ten years, and the Manichaean model had spread as far as China by the eighth century, after which it gradually went out of fashion.

The ultimate form of dualism, which says that the universe is governed not by one sovereign God but by two equal, uncreated, powerful forces, one good and one evil and both eternally opposed to each other, has had surges of popularity over the centuries, and we shall see examples of it in chapter 11 when we look at a number of contemporary major religions. This means that we need not stop to examine it more closely here, but merely note in passing that the concept has many serious built-in weaknesses, which emerge when we ask some fundamental questions. If there are two such forces, how can we explain the origin of evil on rational grounds? How can two such gods, or spirits, or powers each be independent and eternal? As C. S. Lewis pointed out, 'Neither of them chose this *tête-à-tête*. Each of them is therefore *conditioned* — finds himself willynilly in a situation, and either that situation itself, or some unknown force which produced that situation, is the real Ultimate.'[28] Is there some kind of unity behind these two competing forces? If so, does this not destroy their godlike status and reduce them to secondary players operating within a greater reality? By what objective principle can we say that one is good and the other evil? Would this not demand an ultimate ground of reality beyond them both, to which 'good' and 'evil' relate?

Finally, as R. C. Sproul shows, ultimate dualism leaves us with the problem of the irresistible force and the immovable object: 'If the immovable moves then it is not immovable. If it does not move, the irresistible force is resistible! It is rationally absurd to have two absolute, mutually exclusive entities. Even if it were hypothetically possible (which it is not) it could not account for real manifestations of good or evil. We would have a universe paralysed by ultimate moral inertia. Absolute evil would always be checked by absolute good. Absolute good would always be checked by absolute evil. In this scheme neither good nor evil would be possible.'[29] Dualism may seem an attractive alternative to theism, but it fails to deliver, and C. S. Lewis makes it clear that the only way to avoid monotheism and remain a dualist is 'by refusing to follow your thoughts home'.[30]

Cogs in a machine? (MATERIALISM)

A third alternative to theism is materialism. This had its earliest traceable roots among Greek philosophers such as Thales and Democritus (sometimes called 'the father of materialism') who tried to explain the universe and its working without any reference to the great gaggle of gods who were all the rage at the time. As we saw in chapter 1, Democritus taught that all reality consisted of nothing but a vast number of atoms whirling around in space and energized by their own innate powers. Over 2,000 years later, Feuerbach agreed: 'There is nothing beyond nature and man... Any solution that seeks to go beyond the boundaries of nature and man is worthless.'[31] Some 200 years after Feuerbach, the modern materialist takes the same line; all reality is either matter itself or is dependent on matter for its existence.

Put in a nutshell, the modern materialist says that the origin and nature of the universe, and the existence and characteristics of man, are all due to physical agencies, because nothing else exists. The universe began with a spontaneous gathering of atoms and will end with a stupendous scattering of atoms, neither event having any meaning or purpose. In this scenario, 'nature' is everything and there is therefore no point in debating the existence or relevance of non-material concepts such as God, the supernatural, the human soul, religion, morality, ethics, eternity or the afterlife; what we see is what we get.

Over the centuries, many thinkers have attempted to fine-tune this general idea and to apply it specifically to the form and functions of human beings. The nineteenth-century Irish physicist John Tyndall thought that all of life was 'once latent in a fiery cloud'.[32] The French historian and philosopher Hyppolite Taine stated, 'Man is a spiritual automaton... Vice and virtue are produced like sugar and vitriol,'[33] while his fellow-countryman Emile Littré defined the human soul as 'anatomically the sum of functions of the neck and the spinal column, physiologically the sum of functions of the power of perception in the brain'.[34] The nineteenth-century German biologist Ernst Haeckel took a somewhat different line and said, 'We now know that the soul [is] a sum of plasma-movements in the ganglion cells.'[35] On the other hand Feuerbach wrote, 'There is no thought without phosphorous and ... bluntly speaking, thoughts are in the same relationship to the brain as bile to the liver and urine to the kidneys.'[36] Before we are tempted to dismiss these as nothing more than crude conclusions reached long before the huge scientific advances made during the twentieth century, we need to read these words by the contemporary atheist Peter Atkins, a lecturer in physical chemistry at Oxford University: 'Free will is merely the ability to decide, and the ability to decide is nothing other than the organized interplay of shifts of atoms.'[37]

Atkins touches on an issue which is something of a materialist's mantra, and we shall come back to it in a moment, but before we do so we should spell out the bottom line of materialism's assessment of man, which sees him as nothing more than what 'nature' made him to be, a complex chemical machine. Man does not have a mind, self or soul which is different or distinct from his body. Essentially, he is on the same level as rocks and rats, a collection of atoms and sub-atomic particles which have accidentally come together and, as far as human beings are concerned, experience a variety of sensations and emotions when their physical ingredients are shuffled around. Materialism says that man's personality, hope, aspirations and ideals are merely biological functions and therefore have no meaning. All our human experiences such as knowing, imagining, feeling, tasting, loving and enjoying, are nothing more than chemical reactions, the meaningless by-products of random rustlings inside our craniums.

This cues us in to one major area in which materialism cuts across all human intuition and experience — the identifying of the mind with the brain. Even in the most extreme situations, human beings have an intrinsic awareness that they are more than the sum of all their physical parts, an awareness that ties in with the most recent evidence in the field of brain research. As physicist Michael Cosgrove writes in *The Essence of Man,* 'A simple materialistic explanation for all that man is and does will not fit with human experience or with what we know about the human brain.'[38]

Two other modern scholars have collected a mass of evidence to refute the materialists' identification of the mind with the brain, including the following example. While under a local anaesthetic, an epileptic's scalp was lifted away, and the cranium opened to allow the surgeon direct access to the brain tissue. Using an electrical probe, he touched that part of the brain which made the right hand move or twitch. As the hand moved, he said to the patient, 'You just moved your hand.' The patient replied, 'I didn't move it, you did.' Evidently the man's self-awareness was not directly related to his brain. The surgeon then directed the patient to will in his mind not to let his right hand move. The patient agreed to resist moving it in his mind and, as the hand began to twitch due to the application of the electric probe, the patient's left hand reached over and stopped the right hand from moving. The physician could control the brain and make it move the right hand, but the mind of the patient, which transcended the brain, moved the left hand to stop it. If the patient's mind and brain were identical, then the surgeon would have been able to control the patient's mind as well as his brain. In reality, the patient's mind was free from the physician's manipulation of the brain.[39]

The identification of the mind with the brain is a case in which materialism can be seen to be flawed when applied to one specific issue, but other major weaknesses show up when we take a broader view of what it claims. In *Blind Alley Beliefs*, David Cook exposes one of these by showing that even if one accepts that the notion may be theoretically true, there is no way in which it can be expressed as true, or believed in, without falling into a contradiction. To illustrate this, he pictures all the national newspapers coming out with the same front-page headline — 'Materialism is True' — and then running articles which show the theory to be totally proven. He then goes on, 'The ordinary man would ask, "What differences would that make at lunchtime or in the evening?" If it is correct that materialism is true, and that everything is simply matter, if there is no reality of the mental life, and if feelings are all simply reducible to pieces of matter, would we believe, think, feel or relate in any way differently at all? In other words, the ordinary man would deny that it would in fact make any difference. After the shock and novelty wore off, life would be the same. We would all continue to think, feel, say and believe that these things were real. We would continue to relate to each other on the basis of these, and to use normal societal structures even if materialism were true. The common-sense argument here suggests that there is something extremely odd about a view which is true and correct, but does not make any difference at all. What kind of view is it that is true, but does not in fact affect *anything* that we do? It seems a strangely remote kind of truth.'[40]

Yet this 'strangely remote kind of truth' is one of today's dominant philosophies, and one with which we are swamped from childhood onwards. As the British author John Benton comments, 'We are taught from an early age that the only things that matter, the only things which exist, are the things you can taste, touch, smell, hear and see. Death is the end, and therefore we must adopt the philosophy of "Eat, drink and be merry for tomorrow we die". So we are brainwashed into believing that success in life means business success, academic success, sporting success. The question as to whether a person is loving, patient, kind and loyal is viewed as largely irrelevant. "How much does he earn?" "What grades did he get?" These are the questions our society operates on, and that sort of attitude is producing a lonely and cut-throat world.'[41]

Materialism, which has rightly been called 'the natural accompaniment of atheism',[42] seeps into every part of modern society and has a massive influence on ethics, standards, lifestyle and relationships, yet as soon as we begin to examine what it says a whole raft of uncomfortable questions beg to be answered:

- If there is no absolute beyond the existence of matter, how can there be any source of eternal truth upon which an objective system of law and order can be based?
- If matter is everything and everything is matter, what do we say about theories, meanings, concepts, propositions, the laws of logic — and truth itself? Can we seriously deny that these things exist or say that they have no 'reality'?
- Again, what does the materialist do with universals (entities which can be in more than one place at the same time)? What about properties such as softness or blackness; or the relation of one object to another —

what we mean when we speak of something being larger than something else, or of objects being closer or further apart? Are these things not true because they are not comprised of matter?

- Materialism is obviously locked into empiricism, which says that all knowledge is limited to what can be tested with the senses; but how can that claim itself be valid when it cannot be subjected to empirical testing?

- If materialism is true, why is there no evidence that rocks feel, think or make decisions (as humans do) or that animals have moral emotions (as humans do)?

- If man is nothing more than one item in a universal mass of matter, how can any human being have individual value or personal worth?

- If matter is all there is, what possible meaning can we give to concepts such as good, evil, morality, reason, love, beauty, desire, intention or hope?

- How does the materialist explain creativity in the worlds of science, music, drama or art?

- How do things such as imagination, belief and memory fit into a materialistic concept of man?

- If man is just a mass of matter, how does he remember the past, evaluate the present and anticipate the future?

For all its dominance, materialism simply fails to deliver, as the modern American scholar Robert Morey explains: 'As a world view, materialism is neither philosophically nor logically valid because it carries within itself the seeds of its own destruction. It does not correspond to what the world is. It does not describe man as he is or does. It is unliveable on a personal level and unbearable on a political level. Materialism is thus a rotted pillar which cannot give any support to modern atheism. It has failed the tests of reason and experience.'[43]

Que sera sera? (DETERMINISM)

It is generally accepted that there is virtually a straight line from materialism to determinism. The *Concise Oxford Dictionary* defines determinism as 'doctrine that human action is not free but determined by motives regarded as external forces acting on the will'.[44] Put more simply, determinism says that everything we do can be totally accounted for by two determining factors, heredity and environment.

It is easy to see why materialism and determinism go together. If the universe came into being by a process of spontaneous generation, if there was, and is, no transcendent, independent, purposive power acting on it, what we have is a closed, mechanistic universe which is totally predictable. What is more, if we can get a scientific grasp of the make-up of its constituent parts, and work out their relationship to each other, we can describe how the universe will behave. This was one of the strands in Marx's thinking. As a dialectical materialist he rejected the traditional approach to the supernatural and believed that metaphysical ideas arose from the material world, depending on a certain interpretation of the material world for their existence. This was exactly the kind of lever he used in prising people away from their belief in God and forcing them into his programme of social engineering.

Feuerbach, who was a contemporary of Marx, showed his determinism when he made his famous statement, 'Man is what he eats,' but, as John Gerstner makes clear, the trouble with that statement is that the man who wrote it must be what he eats as well as the man who reads it. Gerstner's humorous dismantling of Feuerbach's formula is worth quoting: 'But if that is the case, then some of his ideas may have been the product of the spinach he had for supper, and things he wrote in chapter twelve may have been produced by pie *à la mode*. And the conclusion of all his volumes may have come right out of a can of beans... We should be wondering what the books would have been like if the author had eaten the spinach on Thursday instead of on Friday, and how different the conclusion might have been if it had followed a banana split rather than the beans. Moreover it is conceivable that if Feuerbach had had some smoked herring, he might have concluded that man is not what he eats. There is one thing we dare not do with such an author, and that is take him seriously. If man is what he eats, then he is not what he eats. If he is not what he eats, then there is some possibility that food, whatever influence it may have on him, does not altogether determine what he is.'[45]

Nobody seriously questions the fact that some chemical, psychological and sociological factors may affect a person's decisions and actions, but this falls a long way short of full-blown determinism, which says that all our decisions and actions are the inevitable result of determining factors over which we have no control. The recognition that certain factors affect behaviour leaves room for moral responsibility, whereas determinism obliterates it, a point not lost on legal, psychological and behavioural experts in arguing for the lenient treatment of criminals. When Richard Speck was found guilty a few years ago of killing eight nurses in Chicago, his psychologist wrote a book saying that Speck could no more keep from killing them than another man could keep from sneezing! Quite apart from the Pandora's box which this opens up when applied to every other illegal act, from unauthorized parking to embezzlement, this application of the doctrine of determinism raises three very serious questions, as Francis Schaeffer points out in *Death in the City*: 'First of all, what about the nurses who were killed, some of them in a very violent fashion? These must then be written off. With this kind of explanation they become zero. Second, what about society? Society and the problems of ordering it are also written off. In such a situation, order in society is merely like a big machine dealing on a machine level with little machines. Third, what about Speck himself? The psychologist's explanation does the most harm to him, for as a man he disappears. He simply becomes a flow of consciousness. He, too, becomes a zero.'[46]

Yet deep in the human heart there is a stubborn sense that man is more than a flow of consciousness. When the Czech novelist Franz Kafka claims, 'The conveyor belt of life carries you on, no one knows where. One is more of an object, a thing, than a living creature,' one's immediate instinct is to shout, 'Speak for yourself!' The fact that people ask such questions as 'Who am I?', 'Why am I here?' and 'Where am I going?' shows that determinism is unnatural, that it goes against the consistent grain of human experience. One has only to add the following questions to show why this is the case:

- How can there be any purpose in doing anything, and in life as a whole, if people are chemically determined, and how can they be held responsible for their actions if they are biologically or psychologically determined?
- Materialistic determinism treats the mind as being merely subjective, and the brain, with its atoms, molecules and electrons, as true reality but, as Carl Gustav Jung has pointed out, we can be more sure of the mind than of atoms, molecules and electrons: 'How on earth do people know that the only reality is the physical atom, when this cannot be proved to exist at all except by means of the psyche?'[47]

- If we are determined, how, for example, can the writer and reader of this book be responsible for their actions in writing and reading? Determinism would mean that I have no choice in writing whatever appears on these pages and that you have no choice but to read them; we are simply responding to the dance of the atoms. If I were to write that all materialists were ugly toads, the materialist would have to agree that nature itself forced me to say so, but would it mean anything?
- If we are determined, why should we trust our thought processes? What is more, why should a thoughtful assessment of a theory or a proposition be of any more value than a leaf falling from a tree?
- How is it possible to make the statement, 'Determinism is true,' without admitting that it cannot possibly correspond to objective reality by which I can judge it to be true or false?
- If our mental processes are totally determined, then surely they are totally determined to accept or reject determinism? If this is the case, how can we have any ground for holding that our judgement to accept or reject determinism is true or false? By its own definition, determinism is self-destructive, as David Cook shows: 'If determinism is true, it means that all my belief in determinism is determined. *All* beliefs are determined. Therefore, the materialist belief is in no way different from the belief in God, morality or in little green men at the bottom of the garden.'[48]
- Specifically, how can a determinist deny the existence of God without admitting that such a denial is not based on evidence of any kind?

Does anyone really live on the basis that determinism is true? Do we seriously treat inanimate objects on the same basis as we treat our fellow humans, or hold them in any way responsible for what they do? Much as it would inflate my ego, I know there is no point in blaming my word-processor for its annoying tendency to misspell certain words, any more than it makes sense to hold my golf ball responsible when it plunges into deep rough instead of soaring down the fairway.

In one form or another, determinism colours the thinking of a vast number of people, with demoralizing and dehumanizing consequences. What it conspicuously fails to do is to suggest any reason why anyone should adopt it as a personal world-view; nor does it provide any reason for questioning the existence of God.

8.

Protagoras rides again

The focus in our present chapter will be secular humanism, which Os Guinness calls 'the daily climate of our time'.[1] As it is unquestionably one of the most prevalent expressions of contemporary atheism, we need to be particularly clear as to what the term 'humanism' means.

Roots

Humanism is usually traced back to the 'Golden Age' of Greek philosophy, and especially to Protagoras, Epicurus and Aristotle, whose literally down-to-earth ideas contrasted with Plato's belief that values such as beauty, truth and goodness have their source in a higher world. Protagoras is hardly a name you will hear bandied about at school or university, let alone in the supermarket or the office, but he is virtually the patron saint of humanism and his slogan, *Homo mensura* ('Man, the measure'), is the humanists' basic creed. For Protagoras, and others like him, man became the focal point around which everything centred, and by the time the 'Golden Age' came to an end this idea had led to massive strides being taken in the fields of politics, mathematics, literature, art and drama. On the other hand, issues that went beyond the immediate and the physical were pushed into the background and treated as irrelevant. It was also the era during which Socrates and others pioneered what has become known as the critical method of thinking, an approach in which man is free to question and explore anything he chooses, brushing aside any limitations or rules which religion, society or anything else might seek to impose upon him.

As we saw in chapter 2, the freethinking spirit of the 'Golden Age' was eventually swept away and during the Middle Ages man's thinking about the physical universe, and his own place in it, was more or less limited by what was allowed by the (Roman Catholic) church, which claimed to have cornered the market not only on theology but on every other area of learning, while concentrating heavily on the importance of man's welfare after death. Through a closely controlled web of monasteries and other institutions, the church exercised its self-assumed monopoly, a policy which inevitably led to widespread ignorance and superstition.

Instead of being preoccupied with personal immortality, scholars began to concentrate people's thinking on the need to achieve the best life possible in the present world, something which they said could be attained through one's own efforts. As they pushed this agenda, the movers and shakers of the age gradually dislodged the authority of the church and relied more and more on reason. At the same time, there was a rediscovery of the values of classical Greek and Roman civilization in politics, the arts and elsewhere, and those at the cutting edge of this movement came to be known as 'humanists'. Technically, a humanist was someone who taught Latin grammar, but the word later came to mean someone who read the classics and sought to mould his life on what he read. Eventually, 'humanism' was the word used to reflect the whole idea of man's freedom to explore every part of the natural world and to cultivate and control it for his own well-being and happiness. According to Os Guinness, 'The Renaissance was an intoxicating phase of humanism, an explosive confidence of the human mind, the celebration of art, morals, thought and life on an eminently human scale.'[2] As the new movement rapidly gathered pace, it led to far-reaching developments in science and in the use of the scientific method, and there were inevitable clashes with the traditional teaching of the church. One classic example is worth quoting.

In the Middle Ages, the standard textbooks on astronomy were still the ancient work of the second-century Egyptian astronomer and geographer Claudius Ptolemy, whose major thesis was that all the heavenly bodies in the universe revolved around the earth. This view was not seriously challenged until the sixteenth century, when the Polish astronomer Nicolaus Copernicus, unable to square his own discoveries about the movement of the planets with Ptolemy's system, rejected it outright and said that the sun, not the earth, was at the centre of our planetary system. As the result of his revolutionary use of the telescope, Galileo Galilei (1564–1642), a high-profile Italian astronomer and physicist, came to the conclusion that Copernicus was right, and in his *Dialogue of the Two Great Systems of the Universe*, published in 1616, confirmed that the earth rotates on its own axis and revolves around the sun. He was immediately in serious trouble with the ecclesiastical authorities and warned against promoting his unorthodox views. When Galileo (as he has come to be called) refused to comply, he was hauled before the notorious Inquisition, forced to recant and eventually placed under house arrest for the remainder of his life.

The story is worth telling because it is sometimes used by humanists to argue that science gets rid of God, but that argument can easily be demolished. In the first place, Galileo's disagreement was not merely with the church but with orthodox seventeenth-century science as a whole. As R. C. Sproul points out, 'It wasn't merely the bishops who refused to look through his telescope. His fellow scientists were equally reluctant to take a peek.'[3] In other words, the debate was not between God and Galileo, but between astronomers who supported Ptolemy and those who supported Copernicus. Secondly, to say that certain seventeenth-century theologians giving their blessing to a faulty scientific model from ancient Egypt destroys the whole idea of a God who transcends humanity is illogical nonsense. We can add a modern footnote to this medieval fracas. In his 1998 encyclical *Fides et Ratio* (Faith and Reason), Pope John Paul II used Galileo's writings in support of his own pronouncements and underlined the fact that 'The two truths of faith and science can never contradict each other.'

The third major historical contribution to modern humanism came during the eighteenth-century Enlightenment, which was characterized by <u>five major developments.</u> The first was *rationalism*, which said that the unaided power of human reason could produce clear and certain knowledge about reality. The second was *empiricism*, which said that knowledge is drawn not from reason but from sense perception. The third was another surge in *science*, which was increasingly claiming to provide an explanation of the origin and development of the universe without any need for a divine Creator and Sustainer. The fourth was *romanticism*, which emphasized man's creative ability to produce beauty in art and life. The fifth was *utilitarianism*, which said that the greatest happiness of the greatest number should be the guiding principle of human conduct.

It is impossible to miss the point that these five Enlightenment characteristics were all determinedly man-centred. Knowledge was to be found in man's reason or sense perception; man was able to unpack the universal 'machine' and discover what made it tick; man was capable of creating a society of beauty and progress; and man could engineer his own happiness. When this package was fully developed there was little or no room for God, so that for men like David Hume religion was 'no more than a dim, meaningless and unwelcome shadow on the face of reason'.[4]

Humanist Orgs.   Nothing in the nineteenth century stemmed the flow, and in 1896 the Ethical Union was established to draw together the large number of secular humanist societies which existed at that time. Three years later the Rationalist Press was founded, and in 1963 the two groups united to form the British Humanist Association. Across the Atlantic, the American Humanist Association, founded in 1941, gradually gathered momentum. In 1952, the International Humanist and Ethical Union was formed 'to meet the moral needs of the post-war period'. Today, it claims to have nearly 100 member organizations from over thirty countries, representing nearly five million members. The organizations include specialist bodies such as publishers, universities and development agencies. This particular expression of humanism is well organized, articulate and influential, draws support from an impressive pool of scientists, philosophers, politicians and other leaders in society and has a clear and dogmatic agenda. IHEU has representative status at the United Nations, the United Nations Educational, Scientific and Cultural Organization (UNESCO), the United Nations International Children's Emergency Fund (UNICEF), the Council of Europe and the European Union and Parliament. Yet even these formal arrangements are just the tip of the iceberg, and there are many millions of people outside of IHEU's membership whose world-view is basically humanistic.

Branches

Having traced some of the roots of modern humanism, it is equally important to identify some of its branches, not least because, left on its own, the word 'humanism' goes beyond the particular focus of this chapter. We caught more than a hint of this by noting that when the word was coined during the Renaissance it originally referred to those who taught Latin grammar, then to those who read the classics and sought to use them as a basis for their lives, and eventually to those who joined in the celebration of man's new-found freedom. It was as humanism developed that it produced the deists' distant and unconcerned deity — and then, for many, banished God altogether.

In trying to get a picture of modern humanism, we must begin by making sure that we do not confuse it with humanitarianism, which concerns itself with the well-being of the human race, especially those who are in particular physical, material or mental need. Some of the most fervent humanitarians in history have also been the most determined opponents of any kind of secular humanism. Humanitarians may be fervent theists, militant atheists or anything in between.

Somewhat in the same area is what we might call *uncommitted humanism*. The uncommitted humanist is not primarily concerned about God's existence or non-existence; he can take it or leave it. If someone else's belief in God helps such a person to set commendable standards for his or her own life and to be concerned about integrity, freedom, justice and the needs of others, well and good; the all-important issues are those relating to man's individual and corporate well-being.

Religious humanism is another kettle of fish altogether, best illustrated by a few recent examples. In 1963 the liberal theologian John Robinson, then Bishop of Woolwich, wrote a runaway best seller (reprinted seven times in the first four months) entitled *Honest to God*, in which he bluntly argued that we should give up thinking of God as a transcendent Being who enters into a personal relationship with us, and use the word 'God' to denote 'the ultimate depth of all our being, the creative ground and meaning of all our existence'.[5] He went on: 'To say that "God is personal" is merely to say that "reality at its very deepest level is personal", that personality is of *ultimate* significance in the constitution of the universe, that in personal relationships we touch the final meaning of existence as nowhere else.'[6] Robinson's ideas attracted massive media attention, but they were far from original and one critic called the book 'just a plateful of mashed-up Tillich'.[7] Robinson also pulled together concepts proposed by two other German theologians, Rudolf Bultmann and Dietrich Bonhoeffer, but one finishes reading *Honest to God* realizing that large chunks of it could have been written by a naturalist, a pantheist or a straightforward atheist.

In the 1980s the writings of Don Cupitt, a Church of England minister and Fellow of Emmanuel College, Cambridge, triggered the founding of Sea of Faith, an organization which flatly rejects traditional beliefs about God. With an estimated membership of 800, and now drawing support from a wide spectrum of Roman Catholic and Protestant churches, Sea of Faith sees God as a human creation, what Cupitt calls 'a symbol of man's highest ideals'.[8] In the run-up to Christmas 1997, one of its members, asked by the *Sunday Times* how in conscience he could prepare his people to celebrate events he denied had ever happened, replied, 'I wouldn't tell them that Father Christmas didn't exist — it's the same as that.'[9] Supporters of Sea of Faith reject the charge that they are atheists on the grounds that they believe in the human invention of a deity, yet this takes us all the way back to our introduction. Is any individual or group of individuals entitled to invent its own deity? Would such a deity have any credibility? Could he (or she, or it) be revamped to fit any developing culture — or discarded when considered obsolete? Sea of Faith turns out to be faith at sea.

In 1993 <u>Anthony Freeman</u>, a Church of England clergyman, attracted a great deal of attention in the British media with the publication of a small paperback entitled *God In Us*. In the book, he strongly endorsed Sea of Faith and dismantled the traditional picture of an eternal and sovereign God, stating that 'We no longer live in a world where such an idea has any place.'[10] Religion, he claimed, was 'a purely human creation' with 'no place in our understanding of the real world', in which 'we do not need to bring in the supernatural at all'.[11] There was no mistaking the book's humanistic emphasis: 'All aspects of our life — physical, mental, aesthetic, moral, spiritual — all are human in origin and content. To involve the supernatural is unnecessary, because we can explain all aspects of life without it.'[12]

Freeman went on to make it clear that, in his view, God was on a par with the ancient gods of the Greeks and Romans and had 'no independent existence'. The 'absolute existing-out-there God has gone... There *is* nothing "out there" — or if there is, we can have no knowledge of it.'[13] A new definition was needed: 'Now I have decided to change my use of the term "God". Instead of referring it to a supernatural being, I shall apply it to the sum of all my values and ideals in life.'[14] Although sixty-five clergymen wrote to the left-wing *Independent* newspaper in his support, the ecclesiastical authorities gave him twelve months to retract his views and, when he failed to do so, he was sacked, giving the media a second bite at what they saw as a very juicy cherry. In a *Daily Telegraph* article, written to coincide with his unfrocking, Freeman underlined his central belief: 'I think of myself not so much as an atheist but as a Christian humanist. God is not a person, not a being at all, but the sum of our values and of our spiritual experience: the ideal,'[15] while in *The Times* he defined God as 'no more than the potential for good within the human spirit'.[16]

This obviously represents one form of humanism, but it remains a bizarre brand, as two simple questions will make clear. Firstly, how can anyone who says that God is 'not a being at all' square this with the opening words of the Apostles' Creed, 'I believe in God the Father Almighty, maker of heaven and earth,' which Freeman solemnly repeated as he conducted his farewell service? Secondly, how is it possible to come up with any explanation of how we can worship or pray to 'the sum of our ideals'? When broadcaster Joan Bakewell was asked whether she believed in God she replied, 'People have suggested that God is an internal view of the ideal — well, I can go along with that.'[17] One wonders how such a fluent speaker can be such a fuzzy thinker.

[margin note: B's objections to Religious Humanism]

In 1994 John Shelby Spong, the notoriously unorthodox Bishop of Newark, New Jersey, aired his religious humanism when in the course of an interview he said, 'An intervening, personalistic deity who affects the life of this world by an intervention of any sort is a concept I find difficult to understand.'[18] Yet this statement raises issues which are even more difficult to understand. If God is not personal, how can the controversial cleric approach him (or her, or it) in prayer? Even if one did, what would be the point of praying if God does not intervene in the affairs of the world in any way?

The world-view under discussion in this chapter is *secular humanism*, and it is the adjective 'secular' which brings it sharply into focus. The word comes from the Latin *saeculum*, meaning a generation or age. In the Middle Ages the word 'secular' meant 'belonging to the world or the present age', as distinct from the church, so that a secular priest was one who served out in the parishes rather than exclusively in a monastery. Today 'secular' refers to thinking which says that this present time and place are all there is and that reality has no supernatural content and no eternal dimension. The word 'secularism' was invented by the eighteenth-century rationalist George Holyoake, who campaigned for the regulation and improvement of human life without any reference to religion or theology. This takes 'secular' one step further. It is the deliberate policy of excluding God and interpreting life solely in terms of time and space. In John Gerstner's words, 'Secularism in simpler language is merely worldliness; or "this-worldliness" in contrast to "other-worldliness". This one-world-at-a-time philosophy sees the future as an irrelevance, if not an impertinence. It supposes that one world in the hand is worth two in the bush.'[19] Theologian Dan Beeby puts it more bluntly: 'Secularism is when the creature declares the Creator redundant.'[20]

The manifestos

In 1933, a group of secular and religious humanists joined forces in drafting *A Humanist Manifesto*, which became the accepted creed for secular humanism. The manifesto reflected the general optimism of the time and the widespread belief that, with the horrors of the First World War receding into the distance, mankind could look forward to a triumphant future. It listed fifteen major tenets of humanism, and included statements asserting that the universe is self-existing and not created, that man is the product of an ongoing natural process, that there is no supernatural and that man's goal is the development of his own personality, which ceases to exist at death. Paul Kurtz, one of those involved, summed up the aims of those who drafted the document: 'Though we consider the religious forms and ideas of our fathers no longer adequate, the quest for the good life is still the central task for mankind. Man is at last becoming aware that he alone is responsible for the realization of the world of his dreams, that he has within himself the power for its achievement. He must set intelligence and will to the task.'[21]

So much for the rhetoric. In reality, man's dreams turned into yet another nightmare with the outbreak of the Second World War, followed by the lingering menace of the Cold War, which was to hang over Europe for forty years. Humanist leaders began to see that their confidence in human goodness and perfectibility was overblown and they eventually admitted that the 1933 manifesto had been 'far too optimistic'. As a result, *Humanist Manifesto II* was published in 1973. Yet for all its authors' confession that too much had been taken for granted in 1933, the new document reflected an even harder atheistic line and strongly asserted that humanism alone 'can provide the purpose and inspiration that so many seek' and 'give personal meaning and inspiration to human life'.[22] The seventeen statements of *Humanist Manifesto II* cover such overall subjects as religion, philosophy, mankind, society, one-world government and science. Within the framework of our present study, excerpts from four of these propositions are particularly worth examining. We will take them out of order but be careful not to use them out of context.

Presumption or proof?

The first article in the manifesto includes the words:

①
> *Rejection of Supernatural*
> We find insufficient evidence for the existence of a supernatural;
> it is either meaningless or irrelevant to the question of the survival
> and fulfilment of the human race.

This blunt dismissal of deity is underlined by the manifesto's co-authors: 'As in 1933, humanists still believe that traditional theism, especially faith in the prayer-hearing God, assumed to love and care for persons, to hear and understand their prayers, and to be able to do something about them, is an unproved and outmoded faith.'[23] A promotional leaflet issued by the International Humanist and Ethical Union makes it clear that the movement 'presents the case for understanding the world without reference to a god'. In 1997, the well-known British humanist Sir Ludovic Kennedy told readers of the *Daily Telegraph* that he had nearly finished writing a book in which he sought 'definitively to disprove the existence of God'. In announcing this demolition job, Kennedy assured us that '[God] exists only in the mind and is otherwise completely redundant.'[24]

The point being made is certainly clear, but is it cogent or coherent? The non-existence of God is not being floated as a possibility, or as a theory which is open to discussion or examination; it is being asserted as an article of faith. Yet nowhere in humanistic literature have I been able to discover even a remotely credible basis for such a belief. Instead, humanism falls back on old arguments from anthropology, sociology and psychology to explain the universal phenomenon of religion. In particular, it leans heavily on the general idea that man invented religion to counter his overwhelming sense of inadequacy as he faced up to pressures in this life and concerns about a possible life to come; in Julian Huxley's words, 'Man invented the gods to protect himself from loneliness, uncertainty and fear.'[25] Feuerbach's notion of self-projection, in which 'Theology is nothing less than anthropology,' is also recycled, with the Irish writer George Bernard

Shaw claiming that 'Man has created God in his own image, rather than the reverse.'[26] These jaded theories are of passing interest, but surely they fall a long way short of evidence that God is non-existent? It is one thing to claim that wishing for something to exist is not evidence that such a thing exists, but it is quite another thing to suggest that longing for something to exist is evidence for its non-existence, especially when that longing has been the experience of vast numbers of people over thousands of years.

This points to another weakness in humanism's case for the dismissal of deity. The manifesto's statement that humanists find 'insufficient evidence' for the existence of God is based on its insistence that any account of nature 'should pass the tests of scientific evidence'. The flaw here is that humanists begin by assuming that the scientific method is the only way of discovering certain truth about anything, an assumption that is not only decidedly unscientific but seriously outdated. As has rightly been said, 'What counts today as the scientific method doesn't even claim to deliver what we mean by certain knowledge.'[27]

Writing in the *Daily Telegraph* in 1993, Richard Dawkins blithely brushed this obvious fact aside and announced, 'Faith is a cop-out, an excuse to evade the need to think and evaluate evidence.'[28] Dawkins is a compelling communicator and as entertaining a writer as I have ever come across, but as a contribution to our subject his claim is as crass as the one broadcast by Moscow Radio on Christmas Day 1960: 'Our rocket has bypassed the moon and is nearing the sun, and we have not discovered God. We have turned out lights in heaven that no man will be able to turn on again.' To demolish the idea of God with such sweeping statements is ignorance masquerading as intelligence. Molecular biologist Andrew Miller is on much safer ground: 'To suggest that recent advances in our understanding of life rule out belief in God is only valid against a very simplistic, though once popular concept of a "God of the gaps"... *It is certainly not a scientific matter to decide whether or not there is a God'* [29] (emphasis added).

An important question needs to be asked here: are humanists and others approaching the issue with their minds already made up? The seventeenth-century French mathematician, philosopher and scientist Blaise Pascal claimed, 'The evidence of God's existence and his gift is more than compelling, but those who insist that they have no need of him, or it, will always find ways to discount the offer.'[30] One suspects that many humanists are doing exactly that.

'Nothing-buttery'?

The second article in the manifesto includes the statement:

Reductionism

② As far as we know, the total personality is a function of the biological organism transacting in a social and cultural context.

The philosophy behind this statement is technically known as 'reductionism', which begins by saying that, in examining any phenomenon, the scientific explanation is the only valid one available to us. Reductionism then goes on to say that various key sciences explain each other: psychology can be explained in terms of biology, biology in terms of chemistry and chemistry in terms of physics. Applying this to the manifesto article we are now considering, reductionism implies that human beings are nothing more than accumulations of matter and can therefore be explained in terms of atoms and molecules.

Reductionism has many high-profile supporters. Francis Crick, the Brit- *R's supporters* ish biophysicist who, in partnership with James Watson, discovered the double helix structure of deoxyribonucleic acid (DNA), has put forward what he called an 'astonishing hypothesis': ' "You", your joys and sorrows, your memories and ambitions, your sense of personal identity and free will, are in fact no more than the behaviour of a vast assembly of nerve cells and their associated molecules.'[31] Peter Atkins, quoted along similar lines in our previous chapter, says of decision-making, 'At the deepest level, decisions are adjustments of the dispositions of atoms in the molecules inside large numbers of cells in the brain.'[32] In his book *The Selfish Gene*, Richard Dawkins claims that we are 'survival machines — robot vehicles blindly programmed to preserve the selfish molecules known as genes'.[33] In *The Blind Watchmaker* he adds, 'The body is a complex thing with many constituent parts, and to understand its behaviour you must apply the laws of physics to its parts, not to the whole. The behaviour of the whole will then emerge as a consequence of interactions of the parts.'[34] British astronomer Sir Fred Hoyle writes that living creatures, humans included, are 'no more than ingenious machines that have evolved as strange by-products in an odd corner of the universe',[35] while the American psychologist B. F. Skinner claims that 'Man is a machine in the sense that he is a complex system behaving in lawful ways.'[36]

R's objectors

In the 1950s the distinguished British scientist <u>Donald MacKay</u> called reductionism 'nothing-buttery' and mounted a withering and effective attack on the theory that human beings could be reduced to nothing but atoms and molecules. Since then, an impressive array of scientists at least as eminent as the reductionists just quoted have agreed with MacKay and opposed the idea that men are just machines. <u>Steve Jones</u>, Professor of Genetics at University College, London, provides a good example of this very different approach: 'It is the essence of all scientific theories that they cannot resolve everything. Science cannot answer the questions that philosophers — or children — ask: why are we here, what is the point of being alive, how ought we to behave? Genetics has almost nothing to say about what makes us more than just machines driven by biology, about what makes us human. These questions may be interesting, but scientists are no more qualified to comment on them than is anyone else.'[37]

The essential difference between humanity and machinery can be illustrated by asking questions about the most advanced technology known to man. I can remember being told years ago that <u>a machine capable of performing the functions of the human brain would need a structure the size of the Empire State Building to house it and all the water pouring over Niagara Falls to cool the engine.</u> Technology has long since made that illustration sound prehistoric — but has it made any difference to the point being made? Modern computers can store almost unbelievable amounts of information, crunch numbers at mind-boggling speed, produce complex graphics in seconds — and occasionally beat world chess champions at their own game. As I write these words, computers in Pasadena, California, are steering a tiny buggy across the surface of Mars, over 200 million miles away. Yet computers can do such things only because they have been built and programmed by human beings with vastly superior qualities, and with attributes infinitely beyond even the most complex machines.

Emotions Can a computer express love, hatred, pride, prejudice, sympathy, jealousy, fear or joy? Can any machine known to man lose its temper, change its mind, express its independent approval or exercise self-control? Is there any machine that can set out to make an impression, influence people's thinking or make moral judgements? Can any machine enjoy good music or a beautiful sunset? Does any machine ask questions about its origin, character or destiny? Does a computer know it is a computer? The American philosopher <u>Paul Ziff</u> punctured the idea that man is just a machine by pointing out these distinctions between them: 'A machine uses power, but a man has lunch. A machine can take, but a man can borrow. A machine can kill, but a man can murder. A machine can calculate, but a man can be calculating. A machine can break down, but a man can have a break-down.'[38] To say that human beings are just machines contradicts every-thing we know about both. A totally new dimension would need to be added to machinery before it would even approximate to humanity, and a vital dimension would need to be removed from humanity before it could ever be reduced to machinery. As Robert Morey says, 'The fact that man remembers the past, perceives the present and anticipates the future re-veals that he is a transcendent self as well as a body.'[39]

Someone who read this chapter in draft form wrote to tell me that the previous paragraph was 'an argument from credulity' and went on to say, 'The fact that computers can't do something in no way means that they won't be able to do it in future. Artificial intelligence is a rapidly growing field of research and it is quite possible, though by no means certain, that a truly cognitive machine could be made.'

This might seem to torpedo much of what I have said in this section, *Rebuttal* especially as my expertise in computer technology is roughly on a par with that of a retarded gorilla in the field of astrophysics, but my response is to ask even more questions. Could a 'cognitive machine' be designed by a non-cognitive machine? Could any item of inanimate hardware have a sudden flash of inspiration that would lead to its creating something vastly more sophisticated than itself? Could it ever have a motive, purpose, goal or objective in producing such a thing? Or is it a simple fact that something capable of 'artificial intelligence' could be envisaged, designed and pro-duced only by a human being exercising the real thing?

In 1998, IBM unveiled a new supercomputer called Pacific Blue. Some 15,000 times faster than the average PC, and with 80,000 times more memory, it can carry out 3.9 trillion operations per second. Staggering as this may be — the *Daily Mail's* Science Correspondent David Derbyshire said that Pacific Blue made the average personal computer 'seem like an abacus'[40] — it is significant to note that Pacific Blue was not designed by a computer, but by human intelligence, and was powerless to operate on its own. Even a supercomputer is only as good as the data fed into it.

Reductionism raises many more problems than it claims to solve. It cannot explain why a whole person *seems* to be infinitely more than the sum of his physical parts. It provides no basis for conscience, imagination, intention, desire for freedom and the power of reflective choice. It fails to satisfy the demands of reason and human experience. Above all, it has one fatal defect, pointed out by the British biologist (and atheist) J. B. S. Haldane fifty years before Richard Dawkins began assuring us that we were nothing more than human hardware: 'If my mental processes are

Main Objection to R

determined wholly by the motions in my brain, I have no reason to suppose that my beliefs are true ... and hence I have no reason for supposing my brain to be composed of atoms.'[41] *No humanist has yet been able to produce a credible response to that.* To reduce the human personality to 'a function of the biological organism' is to step outside of reality. It is also to destroy any credible sense of purpose or hope. H. R. Blackman, one-time Director of the British Humanist Association, admitted that the greatest problem humanism faced was 'the pointlessness of it all' and asked how it was possible to escape the nihilism of Friedrich Nietzsche and the absurdity of Jean-Paul Sartre if at the foundation of our existence there is nothing but blind chance.[42]

Ethics à la carte?

The third article in the manifesto begins:

Relative Morals (Relativism)

> We affirm that moral values derive their source from human experience. Ethics is autonomous and situational, needing no theological or ideological sanction. Ethics stems from human need and interest.

For the secular humanist, man himself is the only standard by which his own behaviour is to be assessed. Man is to be the sole arbiter in all matters of justice and law, right and wrong. In the words of the *Encyclopaedia Americana*, 'Since there is no God, man is the creator of his own values.'[43] The British author John Hick bluntly asserts, 'There is no God; therefore no absolute values and no absolute laws.'[44] Another writer elaborates: 'There is in reality no absolute standard by which we judge... In the final analysis our guide in moral affairs should be that which gives to the individual the greatest possible happiness.'[45] Even writing as what I have called a religious humanist, Anthony Freeman comes to the same conclusion: 'Not only the absolute existing-out-there God has gone. So have the absolute existing-out-there values such as peace, joy, goodness, beauty, love, etc...

The only difference from the old idea that they were created by God is that we now acknowledge them to be ours: we made them and therefore we must look after them, cherish them and commit ourselves to them, because no one else is going to.'[46]

These quotations underline the manifesto's assertion that moral values are rooted in human experience, human interest and human need. There is no place here for any objective standard. *Homo mensura!* Protagoras would sign up in a heartbeat. The British author D. H. Lawrence, who hit the headlines with his controversial novel *Lady Chatterley's Lover,* first published in Britain in 1961, even went so far as to say, 'Morality which is based on ideas, or on an ideal, is an unmitigated evil.'[47] Lawrence has been called 'one of the great architects of the twentieth-century mind-set',[48] but the flaws in his thinking are glaringly obvious. The greatest and the most obvious is that in the absence of transcendent absolutes there is no basis on which anyone can say that anything is true or false, right or wrong, good or bad.

C. S. Lewis made this point when writing about the time when he was an atheist: 'My argument against God was that the universe seemed so cruel and unjust. But how had I got this idea of *just* and *unjust?* A man does not call a line crooked unless he has some idea of a straight line. What was I comparing this universe with when I called it unjust? If the whole show was bad and senseless from A to Z, so to speak, why did I, who was supposed to be part of the show, find myself in such violent reaction against it? ... Thus in the very act of trying to prove that God did not exist — in other words, that the whole of reality was senseless — I was forced to assume that one part of reality — namely my idea of justice — was full of sense. Consequently atheism turns out to be too simple. If the whole universe has no meaning, we should never have found out that it has no meaning.'[49] Lewis hit the nail on the head. In the absence of transcendent values, we are left floundering about as best we can. As Ravi Zacharias rightly says, 'Thinking atoms discussing morality is absurd.'[50]

One of the manifesto's alternatives to God-given values is to say that 'Ethics is autonomous and situational.' What this means is that people must be given freedom to choose their own 'truth', make their own rules for living, set their own moral standards. This may seem liberating and enriching, but as we noted in chapter 6, this leads to what Jean-Paul Sartre called a 'baseless base of values'.[51] The person who takes this route finds himself in a world with particulars but no universals, relatives but no absolutes, valuations but no values. Francis Schaeffer tells of speaking at a student leaders' conference in Washington with John Gardner, head of the Urban Coalition. Gardner spoke on restoring values in our contemporary culture, and when he was finished there were a few moments of complete silence. Then someone from Harvard stood up and asked, 'Sir, upon what base do you build your values?' Gardner thought for a moment, looked down and said, 'I do not know.' In relating the incident, Schaeffer adds, 'I have never felt more sorry for anybody in my life... Here was a man crying to the young people for a return to values, but he offered nothing to build on.'[52]

What we have here is relativism, which begins by saying that knowledge is relative, not absolute, and ends by saying the same thing about morals and ethics. Far from being a fringe factor, relativism has become what Paul Johnson calls 'one of the principal formative influences on the course of twentieth-century history'.[53] In *The Closing of the American Mind*, Allan Bloom claims, 'There is one thing a professor can be certain of. Almost every student entering the university believes, or says he believes, that truth is relative.'[54]

Two of the roots of modern relativism can be found in eighteenth-century philosophy and twentieth-century science. Immanuel Kant was not a relativist — he said that reason could establish what he called the 'categorical imperative' of universal moral principles — but he opened the door to relativism by placing religion and ethics (for our present purposes, God and morals) on the other side of his famous 'wall', where their truth could not be rationally verified. One hardly has to be a genius to see how easy it became for others to develop this idea and to decide that this left people free to come to their own moral judgements.

In the twentieth century, the unlikely (and innocent) culprit was the German-born American physicist Albert Einstein, whose theory of relativity ushered in the atomic age and changed the world for ever. Einstein's work showed (among other things) that the world is finite, parallel lines eventually bend, time slows down in certain circumstances and all motions are relative to particular points of reference. As his own religious ideas incorporated firm commitment to absolute standards of right and wrong, Einstein was horrified when philosophers hijacked his theory, made the massive leap from relativity to relativism, and in effect reduced his conclusions to seven words: 'Everything is relative; there are no absolutes.'

As we saw in an earlier chapter, Fyodor Dostoevsky showed that without God 'everything is permitted'.[55] Friedrich Nietzsche agreed: '... the

(margin handwritten note: 2 roots of Rela.)

advantage of our times, nothing is true, everything is permitted.'[56] Yet whatever possibilities it might seem to offer, open-door morality, with values reduced to nothing more than items laid out on a behavioural buffet from which we can pick and choose as we like, is a concept that grates against our deepest instincts. In June 1997 *The Times* carried the obituary of a man who had worked in turn as secretary to Britain's Joint Intelligence Committee in World War II, a priest and an 'unshockable and permissive' sex therapist. The obituary reported him as saying that 'A perversion is only what someone perceives to be a perversion.'[57] Can we live with that? It is one thing to be told that truth is a matter of personal opinion and morality a matter of preference, but surely those who make these claims react very differently when they read of things like genocide or child abuse?

Moral relativism has other serious defects, one of which is the obvious fact that it is impossible to live it out consistently. What may sound attractive as a proposition proves absurd in practice. Does anyone really believe that other people's views on abortion, euthanasia, homosexuality, psychedelic drugs, racism or divorce are just as valid as his own? *Humanist Manifesto II* says that ethics and values are based on 'human experience ... need and interest', but is it seriously suggested that a stable society or personal happiness (a major goal of humanism) is possible if the foundations for ethics, morality and behaviour are constantly shifting? If each one of us is operating from a personal set of values, what gives any of us the right to say that others are wrong? Is the car thief happy to have his own car stolen, or the rapist to have his own daughter violated? It is one thing to mouth pious platitudes about respecting the views of others, but do we honestly believe that those with whom we profoundly disagree on important moral issues are every bit as right as we are?

Relativism produces chaos, not cohesion, as Josh McDowell and Don Stewart show when commenting on a later clause in *Humanist Manifesto II*. The manifesto comes out strongly against intolerant attitudes which 'unduly suppress sexual conduct' and those who 'wish to prohibit, by law or social sanction, sexual behaviour between consenting adults', but it also makes clear moral assertions about 'mindless permissiveness' and 'unbridled promiscuity'. Yet what right do humanists have to say they do not approve of certain sexual activity? As McDowell and Stewart say, 'What if an individual *likes* such sexual activity? If the humanists were to reply that such activity denies the rights of other parties, we must ask, what right have the humanists to say that those others' rights should come before the particular individual's rights? In short, without an absolute standard of

ethics by which his sexual attitudes are determined, one cannot successfully argue for the universal adoption of his own subjective ethics. The
secular humanists may have decided among themselves that certain forms
of sexual behaviour are "wrong", but they have no right to enforce their
ideas on anyone who disagrees.'[58]

If one person decides that his values are correct and another comes to
a different conclusion, who is to arbitrate? In the absence of transcendent
law, moral imperatives are based on nothing more than subjective personal preferences; football or tennis, spaghetti or steak? The only absolute
is the absence of absolutes. Reviewing the cult American television show
Melrose Place in June 1997, the *Daily Telegraph's* Cristina Odone quoted
one of the actors as saying, 'What's right is what you feel.'[59] This is an
empty echo of Ernest Hemingway's creed: 'What is moral is what you feel
good after, and what is immoral is what you feel bad after.'[60] Would that
make sense to both parties after a violent rape? The American author Neale
Donald Walsch, who at one stage in 1997 had two volumes of his *Conver-
sations With God* (claiming to be precisely that) in the top ten hardbacks
on the *New York Times* best-seller lists, says much the same thing: 'Feelings are your truth... Feeling good is the soul's way of saying, "This is who
I am".'[61] Very exciting — but what if others feel differently?

Finally, relativism collides with logic. It has no possibility of being true
because it eliminates the very possibility of truth by robbing it of any rational
meaning. The confident chorus, 'Everything is relative,' is nonsensical,
because the statement itself claims to be an absolute and therefore *not*
relative. Philosopher Roger Scruton drives the point home: 'A writer who
says that there are no truths, or that all truth is "merely negative", is asking
you not to believe him. So don't.'[62] How can the humanist be absolutely
sure that everything is relative? Relative truth is of no more value or substance than relative error, and relativists' attempts to wriggle out of the
jaws of logic can only produce dishonest contortions. In *Lucifer's Handbook*, secular activist Lee Carter advises atheists to counter a theist's logical argument by saying, 'Actually, logic is whatever people find to be convincing,'[63] and then goes on to claim that logic is a matter of personal
preference — yet later in the same book he establishes another point by
treating Aristotle's logic as absolute truth!

Relativism also ruins the humanist's insistence that morality is about
trying to produce the greatest good for the greatest number of people. Not
only does this fail to produce any basis for right and wrong, but the idea

can be manipulated by rulers, politicians, scientists and others to justify anything they choose. Even Hitler's policy of eliminating millions of Jews, gypsies, blacks and other 'inferiors' whom he considered to be a drain on society was motivated by his determination to develop a superior race, where the greatest good of the greatest number would be guaranteed. If humanism is right, how can it categorically insist that Hitler was wrong? Whatever merits the idea may seem to have, promoting the survival of the human race as the ultimate value is derailed by history.

Everyone should welcome humanists' emphasis on justice, freedom, the 'preciousness and dignity of the individual' and their concern for peace and harmony throughout the world. The problem is to find how they can have a rational and consistent motive for it; as one writer has pointed out, 'If man is only part of nature and nature is indifferent to the human venture, why should man have any special concern or compassion toward fellow human beings?'[64] By ruling God out, humanism presents a picture in which the universe serves no purpose, humanity has no lasting meaning, ethics has no transcendent basis and morality has no fixed reference-point, and in which acts and events have only the significance we choose to give them. As Francis Schaeffer wryly says, 'The humanist has both feet firmly planted in mid-air.'[65]

All dressed up . . .?

The second article in the manifesto begins with the words:

No Afterlife

Promises of immortal salvation or fear of eternal damnation are both illusory and harmful. They distract humans from present concerns, from self-actualization, and from rectifying social injustices.

Later it adds:

There is no credible evidence that life survives the death of the body. We continue to exist in our progeny and in the way that our lives have influenced others in our culture.

The idea that death marks the end of conscious human experience has always been the humanists' party line. Confirming that on humanist assumptions 'Life leads to nothing', a one-time director of the British Humanist Association gave this graphic illustration of what this means: 'If there is a bridge over a gorge which spans only half the distance and ends in mid-air, and if the bridge is crowded with human beings pressing on, one after another they fall into the abyss. The bridge leads nowhere, and those who are pressing forward to cross it are going nowhere... It does not matter where they think they are going, what preparations they have made, how much they may be enjoying it all.'[66] In the light of the previous four extracts from *Humanist Manifesto II*, he could hardly say otherwise. If man has no Creator, if he is nothing more than an accidental collection of animate atoms, if he has not been given any distinctive dignity and is free to write his own moral agenda, then his annihilation at death is inevitable. Not that this is a new idea: well over 2,000 years ago the Greek philosopher Epicurus wrote, 'Death, the most dreaded of evils, is ... of no concern to us; for while we exist death is not present, and when death is present we no longer exist.' In 1938, the British philosopher Bertrand Russell took the same line: 'No fire, no heroism, no intensity of thought and feeling can preserve an individual life beyond the grave ... all the labour of the ages, all the devotion, all the inspiration, all the noonday brightness of human genius are destined to extinction.'[67] Less elegantly, he made it crystal clear what he meant: 'When I die I shall rot.'[68] Corliss Lamont, a contemporary spokesman for humanism, cheerfully chimes in with, 'While we're here, let's live in clover; for when we're dead we're dead all over.'[69]

Several things need to be said in response to what *Humanist Manifesto II* says.

In the first place, the claim that promises of an afterlife of salvation or damnation are 'harmful' because 'they distract from present concerns, from self-actualization, and from social injustices' could hardly be more at odds with *the evidence of history*. Over the centuries, no identifiable group of human beings has had a more positive impact on this world than that comprised of those with a firm belief in the world to come and in the very promises dismissed by humanists as 'illusory and harmful'. Writing of the 'humanizing influence' of the object of their faith, John Stott traces the way in which they founded schools, hospitals and refuges for the outcast. He then goes on: 'Later still they abolished the slave trade and freed the slaves, and they improved the conditions of workers in mills and mines and of prisoners in gaols. They protected children from commercial exploitation in the factories of the West and from ritual prostitution in the temples of the East. Today they bring leprosy sufferers ... modern methods of reconstructive surgery and rehabilitation. They care for the blind and the deaf, the orphaned and the widowed, the sick and the dying. They get alongside junkies and stay alongside them during the traumatic period of withdrawal. They set themselves against racism and political oppression. They get involved in the urban scene, the inner cities, the slums and the ghettos, and raise their protest against inhuman conditions in which so many are doomed to live. They seek in whatever way they can to express their solidarity with the poor and hungry, the deprived and the disadvantaged. I am not claiming that all ... at all times have given their lives in such service. But a sufficiently large number have done so to make their record noteworthy.'[70] For *Humanist Manifesto II* to say that all of this stems from promises that are 'illusory and harmful' and that those who believe in such promises are distracted from helping the needy and seeking to rectify social injustices is to allow prejudice to stand truth on its head. What is more, it invites the question whether humanism can produce anything to match what these 'distracted' believers have done. Is there a long-standing and consistent record of self-effacing and sacrificial service covering such a wide field and involving millions of humanists *driven by their denial of God's existence* and motivated by their conviction that 'When we're dead we're dead all over'?

The second thing to be said is that the humanistic theory seems at odds with *reality*. If we assume for the sake of argument that there *is* a God who created man, gave him a unique dignity, instilled in him a sense of human solidarity, commanded him to behave in a responsible, generous and compassionate way towards others and told him of an afterlife which relates in some way to life lived here on earth, would we not expect those who believe these things to respond in ways which would contribute to the welfare of others? On the other hand, where is the motivation for blobs of animate matter on the way to extinction to be concerned for the temporary well-being of similarly doomed blobs?

Something also needs to be said about Corliss Lamont's phrase, 'While we're here, let's live in clover.' Is he not unknowingly letting the cat out of the bag? With no hope of salvation and no fear of damnation, surely man's first instinct is his *own* well-being, not the well-being of others? Countless millions of people today take the line, 'Eat, drink and be merry, for tomorrow we die,' a phrase coined by the followers of Epicurus (though he himself, while teaching that man was free to follow the self-centred pleasure principle, also realized that excess would be self-defeating). Yet when earthly positions, possessions, achievements and pleasures form his entire agenda, man still finds himself frustratingly unfulfilled. There is something in man which can never be satisfied, by even the finest things the material world has to offer; even Sartre admitted, 'There comes a time when we ask, even of Shakespeare, even of Beethoven, "Is that all there is?"' [71]

John Gerstner rightly says that the world itself proves to be 'a mere shadow', and he goes on to identify the trouble with being preoccupied with the present world and rejecting the idea of a future one: 'Those who are most successful in acquiring it suffer the greatest disillusionment... They are always piling up but never possessing anything... Animals can eat, drink and be contented, but man cannot. He cannot be content without these physical gratifications because he has his animal appetites, but being more than an animal he cannot be content with only them. He cannot live without bread, but neither can he live by bread alone.' [72]

What of the manifesto's statement, 'There is no credible evidence that life survives the death of the body'? On the humanist's own terms, one wonders what kind of evidence could ever be accepted as being credible; on the other hand there are powerful signs that the manifesto's statement is puerile.

In the first place, *history* is against it, in that in every culture known to man there is evidence of a common belief in the afterlife, what the British author G. K. Chesterton called 'the democracy of the dead'. [73] Life beyond the grave is a major theme in the ancient Egyptian *Book of the Dead*, one of the oldest pieces of literature in the world. The coffins of those buried in the great pyramids were called 'chests of the dead' and contained directions for the journeyings of the deceased. Many other cultures showed their belief in an afterlife by burying certain items with their corpses; Indians included arrowheads, Norsemen a horse and armour, Greenlanders a dog to act as a guide. These may seem primitive or even faintly ridiculous, but candles placed at the heads of coffins today have been called 'the modern representatives of the primitive man's fire which was to light the way of the soul on its dark journey'. [74]

These customs do not of themselves prove anything, but Canadian scientist Arthur Custance is justified in saying that 'In every culture, and apparently throughout history, it has been normal for man to assume that he has some continuance beyond the grave.' [75] As far as we can tell, this belief has been embedded in man's history from the very beginning and has never been absent. As Dave Hunt puts it, 'At the same time that death is acknowledged to be inescapable, there is an equally universal and overpowering conviction that death does not end human existence. That man is a spiritual being, who survives the death of his physical body, is a basic human instinct which is denied only with the greatest effort.'[76] Humanism certainly makes the effort, and many in today's younger generation cheerfully claim to reject the whole idea of the afterlife, but the instinct of immortality proves impossible to eliminate.

Secondly, *morality* is against the idea that death is the end. As we shall examine more closely in a later chapter, man has a conscience, a moral sense of right and wrong. The human conscience is not in itself a law, but a faculty by which our intellect and emotions respond to a perceived law. Our intellect assesses the issues in relation to that law (in terms of whether things are right or wrong) and our emotions tell us what we ought or ought not to do in response. Man also has an inbuilt sense of rightness, fairness and justice, which cannot be adequately explained in terms of disguised self-interest, social conditioning or cultural programming. Even if he shows a remarkable ability to bend the rules when it suits him to do so, man generally wants justice to be 'done, and seen to be done'. Yet far too often in life, that does not happen. People get away with murder (literally and metaphorically), the good die young, the innocent suffer, cheats prosper, crime pays — not always, of course, but often enough to stand our cosy clichés on their heads. If humanism is right in telling us that there is no life after death, we are left to grit our teeth and accept that 'the ultimate triumph of good over evil' is yet another piece of romantic nonsense; there will be no post-mortem justice, no ultimate righting of wrongs; good will remain unrewarded and evil unpunished. When the time comes for them to die, the serial killer and the tiny baby, the child molester and the gracious old lady, the ruthless dictator and the gentle nurse, together with all they have been and done, will be wiped out of existence. To accept that scenario requires a determined and unnatural effort that goes against most people's instinctive grain.

Thirdly, *humanity* itself is against it. We will examine the issue of human dignity in a later chapter, but at this point it will be sufficient to ask what anybody's dignity amounts to if it disappears at death. What is the point of high-flown phrases at a funeral if at that point the deceased has no more value than a few kilograms of potassium or peat? There is not much dignity in fertilizer! As Francis Schaeffer insists, 'There is a direct link between one's convictions about human dignity and the afterlife: all men ... have a deep longing for significance, a longing for meaning... It is quite clear: no man — no matter what his philosophy is, no matter what his era or his age — is able to escape the longing to be more than merely a stream of consciousness or a chance configuration of atoms now observing itself by chance. In an extreme form the longing for significance expresses itself most clearly in *the fear of non-being*. It has been obvious for centuries that men fear death, but depth psychologists tell us that such a fear, while not found in animals, is for man a basic psychosis: no man, regardless of his theoretical system, is content to look at himself as a finally meaningless machine which can and will be discarded totally and for ever.'[77] Does the humanist who believes that 'When we're dead we're dead all over,' have an answer to this? Does he draw any inspiration from realizing that he is ultimately nothing more than manure in the making?

Fourthly, our reaction to *time* is against it. In his moving book *A Severe Mercy*, Sheldon Vanauken writes of the fact that human beings consider time precious, yet never wholly satisfying, whereas animals seem unaware of it, untroubled by it, and act as if time was their natural environment. He goes on: 'Not only are we harried by time, we seem unable, despite a thousand generations, ever to get used to it. We are always amazed at it — how fast it goes, how slowly it goes. Where, we cry, has time gone? We aren't adapted to it, not at home in it. If that is so, *it may appear as proof, or at least a powerful suggestion, that eternity exists and is our home*'[78] (emphasis added).

The idea that we merely 'continue to exist in our progeny and in the way that our lives have influenced others in our culture' is totally at odds with this. When someone asked the American film producer Woody Allen if he was not greatly encouraged by the thought that after his death he would live on in the hearts of his countrymen through his work, he replied, 'I'm not interested in living on in the hearts of my countrymen; I'd rather live on in my apartment.'[79]

The secular humanist has not only to demolish all these arguments, he has also to assume the burden of proof in relation to his own position. It is one thing to say that 'There is no credible evidence that life survives the death of the body,' but where could we possibly find the 'credible evidence' that it does not?

From nothing to nowhere

Secular humanism is a distinct and dogmatic world-view. In 1961, the United States Supreme Court defined it as a religion, endorsing the fact that, although it denies the existence of God, it is a carefully structured belief system. The core of that system is the bizarre conviction that man exists by accident and will end in annihilation, but that in the brief blip separating the two he is of immense value and dignity and bears important rational and ethical responsibility. The humanist believes that he comes from nothing and is going nowhere, yet insists that the journey itself is of monumental significance. Small wonder that R. C. Sproul calls modern secular humanism 'one of the stupidest beliefs ever concocted'![80]

9.
The dogmatists

Thus far we have been making a somewhat oblique approach to our subject by looking at some of the major philosophical systems that are atheistically inclined, or which eventually lead to a denial of God's existence. In this chapter we will make a more direct approach, beginning with two dogmatic atheists who had a profound effect on the thinking of millions of people during the major part of the twentieth century.

All in the mind?

The first was the Austrian psychiatrist Sigmund Freud (1856–1939). After years of working with hysterical and neurotically disturbed patients, he developed a particular approach to the study of human personality, one which involved the vigorous probing of an individual's personal problems, motives, goals and attitudes to life in general. Freud coined the word 'psychoanalysis' to describe his method of treatment, which aimed at helping patients to identify repressed and unconscious traumas and bring them out into the open where they could be given attention. He even went so far as to say that 'The unconscious is *the* major motivating force behind all human behaviour.'[1] Another major feature of his work was based on his claim that the interpretation of dreams was 'the royal road to a knowledge of the unconscious activities of the mind'.[2]

Freud's initial ideas were treated with considerable scepticism by others working in the same field, but he was a dominating personality and refused to compromise. When people disagreed with him he would brush them aside, sometimes suggesting that they themselves were suitable cases for psychiatric treatment! Freud's most notable clash was with his brilliant colleague, Carl Gustav Jung, who eventually parted company with him in 1913.

Psychoanalysis began as a primary form of therapy, aimed at liberating patients from their repressed traumas, but it has been said that 'By the time Freud had finished ... it had virtually become a global hypothesis, capable of explaining just about anything.'[3] His concept of the unconscious has been described as 'probably the most revolutionary change in thought which this century has produced',[4] while one scholar says that Freudian concepts 'have completely revised the way we look at human nature',[5] and that 'It is probably accurate to say that no single individual has so revolutionized the way we view ourselves as Freud did.'[6] Of more direct interest to us is the fact that he was a convinced atheist; one writer notes that he grew up 'devoid of any belief in God or immortality and does not appear to have felt the need of it'.[7] His atheism becomes particularly significant when we realize that his dynamic communication skills made him 'one of the most influential figures of the twentieth century'.[8]

Leaning heavily on the notion that all knowledge comes through the sciences, Freud described religion as 'the universal obsessional neurosis of humanity'. This blanket rejection of religion was based on his theory that even the most advanced civilizations had been unable to protect man against the brutal forces of nature, leaving him feeling terrified and helpless. In his own words, 'There are the elements which seem to mock at all human control: the earth, which quakes and is torn apart and buries all human life and its works; water, which deluges and drowns everything in a turmoil; storms, which blow everything before them; there are diseases, which we have only recently recognized as attacks by other organisms; and finally there is the painful riddle of death, against which no medicine has been found, nor probably will be. With these forces nature rises up against us, majestic, cruel and inexorable; she brings to our mind once more our weakness and helplessness, which we thought to escape through the work of civilization.'[9] With this as a starting-point, Freud went on to say that, in order to deal with this dramatic situation, man projected personality into the elements of nature, enabling him to react to them on a personal level. In his view, this explained the appearance of animism (the worship of inanimate objects said to be inhabited by spirits) and its development into polytheism and eventually monotheism, whose single, all-powerful God provided a benevolent father-figure as the sole object of worship.

Tied in with this were Freud's highly speculative ideas on the origin — what he called the 'psychogenesis' — of personal religion. He pictured an ancient tribe over which the father had complete authority, including sexual rights over all the females. The young men rebelled against this dictatorship and killed the father, but were then racked with guilt and anxious about the loss of the leadership, security and comfort which he had provided. In an attempt to remove their guilt and reduce the spreading tension in the tribe, a series of rituals was devised. Freud saw this as a plausible explanation for the origin of monotheistic religion, in which men invented a variety of ways by which they hoped to appease the wrath of a God who had the power and ability to bring good or ill into their lives and who controlled their destiny. In other words, he saw the need for a single, all-powerful God in terms of the human psyche's need for a father. As a human father gives life and protection, and lays down rules for the well-being of his family, so God becomes the Creator and Sustainer who gives commands for the well-being of the human race; as Freud put it, 'The face which smiled at us in the cradle, now magnified to infinity, smiles down upon us from heaven.'[10] Freud saw this as man making himself believe what he wanted to believe, instead of realizing that science had revealed the natural laws which explained everything and made God redundant. As far as Freud was concerned, belief in God was an infantile delusion, and religious observance a public version of a private obsession, with no more rational basis than some people's insistence on walking on one particular side of the road. As Ravi Zacharias shows, 'Freud desacrilized ethics, beliefs and practices, and grabbed the church by the seat of the pants to throw it over the wall of civilization.'[11]

A third element in Freud's thinking was his insistence (based on his tribal model) that sex lay at the root of almost all forms of human behaviour. In particular, he saw a close connection between sex and religion, seeing the latter as a universal form of neurosis associated with sexual repression and marked by psychotic hallucinations.

Sigmund fraud?

As Freud has been described as one whose influence in popular ideas about religion 'can hardly be exaggerated',[12] it is important to put him under the microscope. When we do, the picture that emerges is very different from the one he presented at the time. The following questions and comments reveal some of the more obvious Freudian flaws.

Firstly, Freud's reputation in his own field has taken a fearful battering in recent years. Writing in *Modern Times*, Paul Johnson says, 'We now know that many of the central ideas of psychoanalysis have no basis in biology. They were, indeed, formulated by Freud before the discovery of Mendel's laws, the chromosomal theory of inheritance, the recognition of inborn metabolic errors, the existence of hormones and the mechanism of the nervous impulse, which collectively invalidate them.'[13] In 1955, *Newsweek* magazine spoke of many of Freud's tenets as having become obsolete, and reported science historian Frank Sulloway's conclusion: 'His model of the mind and notion of dreaming are in total conflict with modern science. His major edifice is built on quicksand.'[14] This is borne out by many of today's psychiatrists, who suggest that there is little if any solid experimental data to prove that psychoanalysis is effective in treating or curing mental illness. Peter Moore picks out Freud's constant emphasis on sex: 'Freud may have been right that young men subconsciously want to kill their fathers and marry their mothers. But most post-Freudians think his need to explain everything (art, religion, ethics, society) by sex tells us more about his obsessional neuroses than ours.'[15] Carl Gustav Jung brought this particular issue into balance when he wrote, 'Common sense will always return to the fact that sexuality is only one of the life-instincts — only one of the physiological functions.'[16]

Secondly, and especially in his approach to religion, he committed what is known as the 'genetic fallacy' of deciding the truth or falsehood of a view on the basis of its origins. For example, the fact that many people believe in God in order to seek solutions to their psychological needs does not mean that God does not exist. As Peter Moore explains, 'Even if it could be shown quite conclusively why a person does or does not hold a particular conviction, nothing has been said about its truth or falsehood.'[17] What is more, the psychological motive cuts both ways. It is one thing to say that men can invent a benevolent, comforting God to meet their needs, but would those burdened with guilt seek to invent a *holy* God to whom they are accountable and by whom they would expect to be punished for their wrong-doing? Man is certainly able to create a tailor-made 'God' to meet his own psychological need or desire, and many do so, but this provides no evidence that the true God does not exist. Man has proved prolific at conjuring up religious ideas, as we shall see in chapters 11 and 12, but even this prodigious output proves nothing about the existence or non-existence of God; nor does Freud's explanation of religions and religious experience.

Thirdly, Freud assembled his religious data in a very selective way. To bolster his case, he caricatured all the major religions and singled out the worst individual examples of neurotic religious experience and behaviour. As Clark Pinnock points out, 'Many of the things he said about neurotic religion of course were true and perceptive, but nowhere in his writings is there the slightest indication that he recognized religion at its best and what it can mean to honest people every bit as intelligent as himself.'[18] Freud simply refused to face up to the basic possibility that a universal sense of need for God might exist because man could never find fulfilment outside of the relationship with God for which he was created.

Fourthly, there is overwhelming evidence against Freud's claim that religion is a universal neurosis geared to repressed sexuality and producing psychotic hallucinations. Carl Gustav Jung came to exactly the opposite conclusion, and found that the vast majority of those who came to him for psychological treatment (and all who did so in middle age) lacked a religious dimension to their lives. Jung believed that everyone had an innate need for God and a capacity for having that need met. The prestigious Alister Hardy Research Centre at Manchester College, Oxford, has gathered a massive amount of data on religious experience, showing that those with a religious dimension to their lives are generally better balanced and behave more ethically. Even more impressively, Freud's conclusions are contradicted by millions of people who would claim that their faith in God has had a morally transforming effect on their lives and has given them a stability and balance that were previously missing.

Fifthly, Freud's idea of God as a self-projected father-figure proves to be a double-edged sword. Countless people with very negative, even traumatic, memories of their human father have become strong believers, claiming that they are committed to worshipping, loving and serving God. They may of course have invented the idea of a romanticized father-figure but, on Freud's theory, surely they would have become atheists, or at least God-haters?

Sixthly, Freud did not get into the detailed study of religion until *after* he had decided what its origins were. He had already accepted Ludwig Feuerbach's theory that religion was no more than a psychological projection, and in a letter to a friend he grumbled about having to study the subject at all: 'I am reading books without being really interested in them, since *I know the results*; my instinct tells me that.'[19] It has been said that Freud's pet hates were religion and America; as far as religion was concerned, Freud determined to find nothing in its favour. As he made his wife move out of their bedroom so that he could sleep with his own sister, he would hardly have wished to discover a holy God to whom he was morally accountable.

All of this means that Freud was not addressing the question, 'Does God exist?'; he had decided the answer to that question before examining it. Instead, he was addressing the question, 'Since God does not exist, why is there such a thing as religion?' This was the starting-point for the prejudiced speculation which he then attempted to present as truth. The fact that he convinced so many adds nothing to the value of his ideas, and it is difficult to disagree with Alister McGrath's bleak verdict: 'On the relatively few points at which Freud's hypothesis is capable of being tested experimentally, it is generally accepted that it is wrong... Freud's psychoanalytical atheism must now be regarded as a hypothesis that has not been, and indeed cannot be, proved.'

Making the best of a bad job?

Another dogmatic twentieth-century atheist was the British philosopher, mathematician and essayist Bertrand Russell (1872–1970), who did important work in the fields of mathematics and logic, but was also involved in education, liberal politics and international affairs. He was a pacifist in both World Wars, and served as President of the Campaign for Nuclear Disarmament. Awarded the Nobel Prize for Literature in 1950, he wrote some sixty books over 'one of the widest selection of topics ever covered by a single writer'.[20] Colin Brown calls him 'not only one of the most prolific but perhaps the most lucid and witty philosophical writer of modern times', adding that his *History of Western Philosophy* 'is perhaps the only treatment of the subject that can be read in bed'.[21]

Russell's atheism was partly founded on theories put forward by the French philosopher Auguste Comte (1798–1857), who profoundly shocked his religious parents by declaring himself an atheist while in his mid-teens and later went on to develop a system of belief which came to be known as 'positivism'. Comte taught that the human history of ideas went through three stages: the theological, when the focus was on the supernatural; the metaphysical, when philosophy was at the centre of man's thinking; and the scientific, when man broke free from his early superstitions and speculations and came to discover 'positive truth' by experiment and observation.

During most of his career, Russell enthusiastically endorsed and developed an approach very similar to this. At one point he wrote, 'Whatever knowledge is attainable must be attained by scientific means; and what science cannot discover, man cannot know,'[22] a statement which neatly disposes of God, who is by definition intangible and cannot be verified by scientific investigation. Russell also took up a position very similar to one form of the general theory known as 'logical positivism', which said that only statements which can be verified by the senses have any meaning. The point here is not whether a thing is true or false, but whether it is meaningful or meaningless. Following this principle, the statement 'God exists' can be thrown out as it can never be tested by empirical observation; for the logical positivist, it simply has no meaning.

Russell's whole life could be characterized by the word 'contradiction'. He supported peace movements, yet showed great personal hatred towards people he disliked; he argued for pacifism, yet wanted the United States to take pre-emptive military action against the Soviet Union; he wrote passionately against both Communism *and* capitalism; he supported women's rights, yet belittled their intellectual capacities; he hated being deceived, but was often trapped in his own deceit.[23] Russell's work can sometimes be very confusing, as he often changed his views; a Cambridge professor has said that he 'produced a brand new philosophy every few years'.[24] Yet perhaps the overall sense one gets when reading Russell on religion is that while his output was massive, the outcome of what he says was minute. He said so much, but offered so little, as the following examples show.

Firstly, he offered *no basis for reality*. Logical positivism says that what cannot be proved scientifically — by what it calls the 'verification principle' — is nothing more than subjective experience and cannot therefore be treated as reality or knowledge. Yet this idea is suicidal, because the verification principle is itself incapable of verification. To put it very simply, if the only meaningful statements are those which are analytical or which can be verified empirically, what happens to the law of verification? Some thirty years ago, the headmaster of a school in Cornwall challenged something I said to the students because, as he put it, 'You cannot say that in these days of logical positivism.' He obviously felt that he was in tune with the times, and that I was wallowing ignorantly in his wake, but logical positivism's days were already numbered. Even A. J. Ayer, whose book *Language, Truth and Logic* gave logical positivism an enormous boost, was later to admit that the positivist approach was a blind alley and, in an interview with *The Listener* in 1978, said that 'Nearly all of it was false.'[25] Professor of Philosophy Ronald Nash nails the coffin down: 'Today, it is quite difficult to find any philosopher who is willing to claim publicly the label of logical positivism. The movement is dead and quite properly so.'[26]

Secondly, Russell offered *no rationale for the existence or structure of the world*. As far as he was concerned, the entire cosmos is a brute fact which we have to accept without looking for any reason or purpose which may lie behind it; in his own words, 'The world is simply there and is inexplicable.'[27] Elsewhere he wrote, 'Academic philosophers, ever since the time of Parmenides, have believed that the world is a unity... The most fundamental of my beliefs is that this is rubbish... I think the universe is all spots and jumps, without unity, without continuity, without coherence or orderliness.'[28] As we shall see in a later chapter, this could hardly be further from the facts.

Thirdly, he offered *no meaning or purpose for human existence*. In the course of one of his best-known attacks on religion he wrote, 'That man is the product of causes which had no prevision of the end they were achieving; that his origin, his growth, his hopes and fears, his loves and his beliefs, are but the outcome of accidental collocations of atoms ... all these things, if not quite beyond dispute, are yet so nearly certain that no philosophy which rejects them can hope to stand.'[29] His final phrase is not only a gross exaggeration, it fails to suggest any reason as to why it should be believed.

Fourthly, he offered *no sound basis for a moral philosophy*. In a famous debate with the philosopher Frederick Copleston he was asked how he differentiated between right and wrong. He answered that he did so on the same basis that he differentiated between yellow and blue. When Copleston challenged the analogy because colours were distinguished by sight, and again asked how one separated right from wrong, Russell lamely replied that he did so on the basis of his feelings! On another occasion he said, 'It is for us to determine the good life, not for Nature — not even for Nature personified as God.'[30] It is not difficult to see that this approach leads directly to relativism and to personal and social chaos. It also helps to explain his reputation as a notorious womanizer; in a BBC2 television documentary screened in 1997, a family member told of his having an affair with his own daughter-in-law when he was seventy-nine and she was fifty-three years younger.

Fifthly, he offered *no reasonable explanation for religion*: 'Religion is based, I think, mainly on fear. It is partly the terror of the unknown and partly, as I have said, the wish to feel that you have a kind of elder brother who will stand by you in all your trouble and disputes.'[31] This is a rather tame reworking of ideas we have already examined and seen to contain more flaws than facts. One glaring weakness in Russell's argument here is that the God posited in this book is far from the sort of being people would want to project. A celestial sugar-daddy or comforter is one thing, but a holy God who knows me through and through, requires me to respond to him by living a life of holiness and makes it clear that there is to be a day of eternal judgement has decidedly limited appeal! As J. P. Moreland explains, 'If one were going to project a god to meet one's needs, a being much tamer, much more human, much more manageable would be a better candidate.'[32] Russell badly missed the mark here.

Sixthly, he offered no hope beyond death, as this statement shows: 'Brief and powerless is man's life; on him and on all his race the slow, sure doom falls pitiless and dark. Blind to good and evil, reckless of destruction, omnipotent matter rolls on its relentless way; for man, condemned today to lose his dearest, tomorrow himself to pass through the gate of darkness, it remains only to cherish, ere yet the blow fall, the lofty thoughts that ennoble his little day.'[33] This is all that the materialist, humanist or straight-forward atheist has to offer. Man has put in an accidental appearance on a meaningless planet, has no transcendent values by which to find direction or purpose and, within a very short time, death will wipe him out. In the meantime, he might as well make the best of a bad job, doing whatever he can to 'ennoble his little day'. This approach usually adds the rider that there is nothing to fear about death, because nothing lies beyond, but the truth is that when fear moves out, despair has a tendency to move in, and at one point Russell gave an example of this. He said that as 'the whole temple of man's achievement must inevitably be buried beneath the debris of a universe in ruins ... only on the firm foundation of unyielding despair can the soul's habitation henceforth be safely built'.[34] What on earth does this mean? How can 'unyielding despair' be a 'firm foundation' for any-thing? As has been pointed out, the whole idea is 'psychologically imposs-ible and logically contradictory'.[35] Far from being a foundation for anything, despair is exactly the opposite. Logical inconsistency is a sure sign of error and this is a good example. Bertrand Russell's aversion to religion was formidable; his case against God was feeble.

The real thing

As we saw in previous chapters, atheists come wrapped in a variety of ideas such as rationalism, empiricism, materialism, existentialism and humanism. Others, sometimes less sophisticated, are either muted, moderate or militant in their atheism. Muted atheists may be the brand A. J. Ayer had in mind in *Language, Truth and Logic*, when he wrote, 'It is characteristic of an atheist to hold that it is at least probable that no god exists.'[36] William and Mabel Sahakian paint the same kind of picture in *Ideas of the Great Philosophers* when they write of certain atheists who argue that, while absolute proof of the existence or non-existence of God is not available, 'The evidence favours the assumption of non-existence.'[37] The muted atheist is one for whom the evidence for God's existence has never seemed convincing, nor perhaps important. He would not be capable of defending his position with any great vigour, nor would be interested in attacking theism. He is simply happy to 'go with the flow', assume that God does not exist, and get on with the much more interesting business of living.

The moderate atheist is much firmer in his beliefs, and more dismissive of those who disagree. Isaac Asimov, one of the world's most prolific authors in the scientific field, with some 300 books to his credit, is a good example: 'I am an atheist, out and out. I've been an atheist for years and years, but somehow I felt it was intellectually unrespectable to say one was an atheist, because it assumed knowledge that one didn't have. Somehow it was better to say one was a humanist or an agnostic. I finally decided that I'm a creature of emotion as well as of reason. Emotionally, I'm an atheist. I don't have the evidence to prove that God doesn't exist, but I so strongly suspect that he doesn't that I don't want to waste my time.'[38] Two things are worth noting here. The first is that Asimov goes no further than to suspect that God does not exist. The second is the significant admission that, for all his achievements and reputation, he confesses to having no evidence to support his atheism.

The militant atheist goes much further and asserts, 'Atheism is the deliberate, definite, dogmatic denial of the existence of God... It is not satisfied with approximate or relative truth, but claims to see the ins and outs of the game quite clearly — being the absolute denial of the Absolute.'[39] The *Encyclopaedia of Philosophy* is emphatic in defining an atheist as 'a person who maintains that there is no God; that is, that the sentence "God exists" expresses a false proposition'.[40] It has been said that 'There are few zealots for the cause of atheism,'[41] but, as in almost every other field, those who are the most passionate about their positions are those who get the most attention and whose views most often percolate through the media into society at large. Madalyn Murray O'Hair, the founder of American Atheists Inc., who became known as 'the most hated woman in America' and who mysteriously disappeared without trace on 28 September 1995, had eight years earlier succeeded almost single-handedly in persuading the United States Supreme Court to ban prayer in the nation's state schools. In her book *What on Earth is an Atheist?* she stated, 'I am an atheist and this means at least: I do not believe there is a god, or any gods, personal or in nature, or manifesting himself, herself, or itself in any way.'[42] A few pages later she added, 'There are no supernatural forces, no supernatural entities such as gods, or heavens, or hells, or life after death. There are no supernatural forces, nor can there be.'[43] In the *Encyclopaedia of Unbelief*, editor Paul Edwards turns the heat up and, after describing religious principles as 'sick dreams', asserts, 'The sooner these sick dreams are eliminated from the human scene the better.'[44]

When we get into that league we would be better to use the word 'antitheism', which is certainly the position Richard Dawkins takes. In a 1989 issue of the *Daily Telegraph Science Extra* he declared, 'Religion is no longer a serious candidate in the field of explanation. It is completely superseded by science.'[45] In his 1992 Voltaire Lecture, delivered to the British Humanist Association, he called religious belief 'a virus of the mind', something which spreads like a computer virus. This is a modern reworking of Freud's idea that belief in God is like a mental illness causing deep psychological problems, but surely it leaves open the possibility that Dawkins' own atheistic beliefs are themselves a viral infection? When the *Independent* carried a leader supporting author Susan Howatch's endowment of a Cambridge University lectureship in science and theology, Dawkins vented his spleen in a letter to the editor: 'What has theology ever said that is of the smallest use to anybody? ... The achievements of theologians don't do anything, don't affect anything, don't achieve anything, don't even mean anything. What makes you think that theology is a subject at all?'[46] In 1994, he backed this up by saying that he wanted to see all academic chairs of theology removed from British universities.[47] This outburst generated more heat than light, but it gives us a clear picture of what full-blown atheism, or antitheism, is saying.

A world of believers

The second major point to establish about atheism is that it is a belief system. Some of the most militant atheists have tried to deny this, but in order to do so they have had to come up with a skewed definition of atheism, one which says it is not so much belief in the non-existence of God as the absence of belief in his existence. Gordon Stein, editor of *An Anthology of Atheism and Rationalism*, provides a good example: 'An atheist is a person *without* a belief in God... Atheism is not a belief as such. It is a lack of belief.'[48] Another leading atheist backs him up: 'Atheism, therefore, is the absence of theistic belief ... in its main form, it is not a belief; it is the absence of belief.'[49] By defining atheism in this way, these writers wriggle out of any responsibility to explain or prove anything about their case. By saying that atheism makes no assertions or claims, they evade the kind of rigorous investigation which can be made into any system of belief which makes both. Yet, as Robert Morey shows, they end up scoring a spectacular own goal: 'Atheists attempt this definition for only one reason; to allow themselves to bring in any ideas they wish without having to prove anything. But, in so doing, they have rendered atheism incapable of falsification or verification. And, if it is true (as they claim when attacking theism) that a word or an idea is nonsense if it is not capable of falsification or verification, then atheism is nonsense and should be dismissed as meaningless.'[50] Only by radically changing the rules can atheists get away with this dishonest manoeuvre.

The reason why atheism can never escape the responsibilities of a belief system is that there are no such people as unbelievers or, more strictly, non-believers. (This is not the same as the third of the propositions we considered in our introduction and which suggested that nobody is an atheist: we will come to that in a later chapter.) The question here is not *whether* we believe, but *what* we believe and *why* we do so. As someone rightly pointed out, 'We can choose what to believe, but not whether to believe.'[51] What is more, our beliefs have practical implications; they radically affect the way we live. This is obviously true at the most basic levels.

We believe that our water supply has not been contaminated, that objects will fall if we let them drop, that stairs will take our weight, that it will get dark at night. The same principle applies at the metaphysical level. As Martin Robinson says, 'Those who characterize themselves as "unbelievers" do not believe in nothing. On the contrary, they often have a very definite set of beliefs, which may be held just as passionately as so-called "believers" hold to the tenets of their faith.'[52]

This is as true of atheists as it is of any others. The president of American Atheists Inc. once declared, 'This world would be the best of all possible worlds if "faith" was eradicated from the face of the earth,'[53] but this misses the whole point that all honest atheists themselves exercise great faith — and claim they have a sound basis for believing as they do. The adjective used here of atheists is not accidental; the only *honest* reason anyone can have for believing anything is that he or she thinks it is true. For anyone to say that he believes in something because he thinks it is false is a contradiction in terms. By definition, faith means giving assent to something about which the person concerned is satisfied that he has sufficient evidence to justify his belief. In those terms, an atheist can be said to have much greater faith than a theist. Francis Collins, Director of the Human Genome Project, 'arguably the most important biological project of the twentieth century',[54] was a vigorous atheist up until the age of twenty-seven. Now, as a convinced theist, he writes, 'Of all choices, *atheism requires the greatest faith*, as it demands that one's limited store of human knowledge is sufficient to exclude the possibility of God'[55] (emphasis added).

Burden of proof

This leads to the next point, which is that atheists have a responsibility to prove their case. Atheists are reluctant to admit this, and again try to escape under the cover of redefining atheism to mean the absence of belief rather than the presence of unbelief, but we have already seen that this will not work. Nevertheless, atheists insist that the burden of proof falls exclusively on the theist. The atheologian Antony Flew claims, 'The debate about the existence of God should properly begin from the presumption of atheism, that the onus of proof must lie upon the theist.'[56] The Australian philosopher Michael Scriven agrees: 'We need not have a proof that God does not exist in order to justify atheism.'[57] *Why not?* In effect, what Flew and Scriven are saying is that theism is to be taken as being wrong unless or until it can be proved to be right, but that atheism is to be taken as right unless or until it can be proved to be wrong. Flew calls this 'the presumption of atheism' (using 'presumption' to mean something that may reasonably be taken for granted) but would it not be nearer the mark to call it presumptuousness? How can it be reasonable to assume that one belief-system is true and its opposite false, unless both are subjected to the same criteria? Scriven goes on to say that the proper attitude to 'the absence of any evidence for God's existence ... is not merely suspension of belief ... it is disbelief'.[58] Yet surely this is a blatant case of moving the goalposts to suit one's own side? If the theist is required to defend his belief in the existence of God, surely the atheist has a similar responsibility to defend his belief in God's non-existence? Ronald Nash is right to insist: 'The sensible person will reject the claim that theism should be presumed guilty until proven innocent.'[59]

What is more, for the person who signs up to 'the absolute denial of the Absolute' the burden of proof is even greater. Although philosophy tells us that it is impossible to come to certainty about things by pure deduction, the militant atheist claims that he has done so. As we shall see in a later chapter, the theist has another avenue of proof which is denied to the atheist by his own convictions, but the atheist says that he has come to a definite conclusion on the issue by using his powers of reason. That being so, one is surely entitled to ask some questions: 'What is the evidence that reason offers so as to produce the conclusion that God does not exist? Is there scientific evidence? Is there evidence from experience? Is there evidence of *any* kind?'

At this point, the atheist runs into even greater difficulty, brought about by his belief that the material world is all there is, and that human beings are merely complex organizations of atoms and molecules. Nobody has exposed this particular difficulty more clearly than C. S. Lewis. This was his reply to a question put to him in a 'One Man Brains Trust' held in 1944: 'If the solar system was brought about by an accidental collision, then the appearance of organic life on this planet was also an accident, and the whole evolution of man was an accident too. If so, then all our present thoughts are mere accidents — the accidental by-product of the movement of atoms... Why should we believe them to be true? I see no reason for believing that one accident should be able to give me a correct account of all the other accidents. It's like expecting that the accidental shape taken by the splash when you upset a milk jug should give you a correct account of how the jug was made and why it was upset.'[60] Does the atheist have an answer to this?

In the introduction to this book we saw that the right approach to the subject of the existence of God is to assemble and assess all the data we can and then come to a conclusion based on what we consider satisfying evidence or reasonable probabilities. However, the card-carrying atheist goes beyond this and says (or at the very least gives the impression) that he has reached the point where he has bedrock proof on which to base his convictions. In *The Atheist Debater's Handbook* we are told, 'Atheism ... is an intellectually respectable viewpoint ... the atheist may *know* that God does not exist.'[61] Is this really 'intellectually respectable'? Is it even reasonable? Can anyone be absolutely sure of his grounds for making what we saw earlier described as a 'deliberate, definite, dogmatic denial of the existence of God'?

For all the advances made in science, philosophy and elsewhere, absolute certainty has proved tantalizingly elusive. Do we know with *absolute* certainty that Alexander the Great was born in 356 B.C., or do we merely believe this to be true on the basis of what we consider to be sound evidence? Can we be certain about scientific theories and discoveries in the sense that we can prove them to be *absolutely* true or false? Those who argue that science has disproved the existence of God sometimes give this impression, but this is not how science works. Instead, scientists make the best judgements they can on the evidence available, but keep an open mind as to whether these may have to be changed or abandoned in the light of new discoveries, as Karl Popper makes clear: 'The old scientific idea of *episteme* — of absolutely demonstrable knowledge — has proved to be an idol. The demand for scientific objectivity makes it inevitable that *every scientific statement must remain tentative for ever*'[62] (emphasis added).

The attempt to establish primary truths on which we can build absolute knowledge has proved to be futile. As Alister McGrath points out, 'The dream of finding self-evident truths, known with total certainty, and upon which an entire system of beliefs could be erected, is now seen as a delusion... All our knowledge about anything that really matters is a matter of probability.'[63] Yet the hard-core atheist sweeps this aside and maintains that he has all the evidence he needs to make a 'deliberate, definite, dogmatic denial of the existence of God'. When Richard Dawkins says that faith in God means 'blind trust, in the absence of evidence, even in the teeth of evidence',[64] the clear inference is that there is conclusive evidence in favour of atheism. The militant atheist is prepared to go beyond lower standards of proof such as those required in civil cases, which call for 'the balance of probabilities', and in criminal cases, which call for evidence 'beyond reasonable doubt'. Instead, he claims that his case can be proved *beyond all possible doubt.* Even when it is reduced to the four words, 'There is no God,' the atheist's creed is a statement of the absolute.

There are two obvious reasons why this is 'over the top'. In the first place, philosophical proof is incapable of reaching that far. As one modern thinker concedes, 'We know that there are *no* philosophical beliefs anywhere that are supported by conclusive evidence.'[65] In the second place, this 'in-your-face' approach collides headlong with the simple fact that it is impossible to prove a universal negative. For someone to know with absolute certainty that God does not exist would mean that person being in possession of every single fact contained in reality. *If even one fact was unknown, God's existence could not honestly or rationally be ruled out, as it might be the fact in question.* God is a possible fact, and anyone claiming to rule him out of existence is claiming to have infinite knowledge that there is no being in existence with infinite knowledge — in other words, to possess nothing short of the omniscience which theism says belongs to God alone.

Some years ago, a friend of mine was involved in an incident in which this kind of thinking came into play. He got into conversation with a strapping young freethinker who was soon pouring out his views on philosophy, life and religion nineteen to the dozen and with an air of great assurance. As my friend was elderly, very quietly spoken and barely came up to the young man's shoulder it must have seemed like a decidedly uneven contest. Eventually, the young man came to his triumphant summary and declared, 'I am an atheist.' 'Are you sure of that?' my friend asked. 'Absolutely', the young man replied, 'I have thought it through, studied the issue from every angle, and am quite certain that I can say, "There is no God".' He was probably trying to stir my friend up by announcing his faith with such a flourish, and must have been very surprised at his response. The conversation went something like this:

'Then would you please give me the great privilege of shaking your hand?'

'You can certainly shake my hand, but I don't see why you should think that's a privilege.'

'But it is. You have no idea how excited I am. If you would allow me to shake your hand I would remember this day for the rest of my life.'

'Why on earth do you say that?'

'Because you are by far the most remarkable and outstanding person I have ever met.'

'This is becoming ridiculous. There is nothing unusual about me. I am just an ordinary person, convinced that God does not exist. Why are you making such a song and dance about that?'

'Because I have never met anyone who has been alive throughout all time, visited every spot in the universe and knows every single thing that it is possible for a human being to know.'

'Well, you still haven't.'

'Then let me ask you some questions. If you have not been alive throughout all time, won't you accept that it is possible that God does exist, but that he revealed himself to humanity at some point before you were born? If you have not been everywhere in the universe, won't you accept that it is possible that God does exist, but that he is somewhere in the universe that you have never visited? And as you admit that you don't know everything it is possible to know, won't you admit that there may be evidence of God's existence within that body of knowledge you don't possess?'

My friend's arguments were far from original, but in this particular case they had an amazing and immediate effect, because the young man suddenly said, 'I see what you mean, and you are right. It is *impossible* for me to be an atheist. I have just become an agnostic'! It was a spectacular and embarrassing climb-down, but it did at least have the virtue of being honest. The question we now need to ask is whether his new position was any more tenable than the previous one.

10.
The impossible option

Giving the eleventh Eric Symes Abbott Memorial Lecture at Westminster Abbey in 1996, the playwright David Hare made the following statement: 'Although you might feel the question of God's nature and existence *ought* to be obsessively important to each and every one of us, the simple fact of the modern world is that it is not felt to be. Most of us have little idea of what we believe, and are also extremely confused on the subject of whether we would be willing to die for it. At least until the approach of death, the majority of Westerners are willing to tick the box in which they profess that they have some generalized religious belief but they are jiggered if they can actually say what it is.'[1]

As I read the edited version of David Hare's lecture in the *Daily Telegraph*, I felt pretty sure that he was including himself among those who were uncertain about their religious belief. In surveys of the kind we looked at in the introduction, he and the people he had in mind would almost certainly tick the box marked 'Don't know'. For just over 100 years, another word has been available to those in a similar position. It was provided by Darwin's 'bulldog', Thomas Huxley.

The fox's tail

Huxley records that when he had reached 'intellectual maturity' he began to ask himself whether he was 'an atheist, a theist, or a pantheist, a naturalist or an idealist', and confessed, 'The more I learned and reflected, the less ready was the answer.' He noted that those who held to these and other positions seemed sure they had solved the problem of existence, 'while I was quite sure I had not, and had a pretty strong conviction that the problem was insoluble'. He was certain he had never left 'the straight road' mapped out by Hume and Kant, but was becoming dismayed that this road led into the depths of 'a wild and tangled forest'. Nevertheless, he decided to go straight on 'until I either come out on the other side of the wood, or find there is no other side to it, at least, none attainable by me'.[2]

At this stage, he joined the Metaphysical Society, which met to discuss all kinds of philosophical and religious issues, but he was uneasy at being the only member without clear convictions, especially on the greatest question of all, the existence of God. He felt like the proverbial fox which escaped from a trap but left its tail behind, and then felt out of place when rejoining what he delightfully called its 'normally elongated companions'. Looking for a word to describe his own position, Huxley dug back 2,000 years into church history and latched on to the word 'gnostic', which translates the Greek *gnosis* (knowledge). The Gnostics, who belonged to a variety of religious movements, claimed to have attained personal salvation through a special, secret and exclusive knowledge. This was exactly the kind of assurance Huxley lacked, but it provided him with the basis of the word he needed: he simply added the prefix 'a' (without) and described himself as an 'agnostic'. He goes on to tell how 'I took the earliest opportunity of parading it at our Society, to show that I, too, had a tail, like other foxes.'[3] That particular meeting was held in 1869. Since then, the same fox's tail has been used by countless millions of people.

Huxley may have given us a word, but his position was hardly original. In Plato's *Republic*, Socrates was praised for being aware, not only of what he knew, but of what he did not know. Although we have previously labelled Protagoras a humanist, there was a time during which he provided a model for agnostics: 'With regard to the gods I cannot feel sure either that they are, or that they are not, nor what they are like in figure, for there are many things that hinder sure knowledge: the obscurity of the subject and the shortness of human life.'[4] One scholar has called Protagoras' view 'a humanistic agnosticism'.[5] As we saw in chapter 1, Pyrrho jibbed at the strident dogmatism of his day and tried to find a position where he could follow his own instincts and inclinations without feeling threatened by the convictions of others. In the eighteenth century, David Hume took a stronger line and rejected any attempt to prove the existence of God or the immortality of the soul. For Hume, the existence of God was a matter of imagination rather than knowledge; any book on divinity or metaphysics could safely be burned, 'for it can contain nothing but sophistry and illusion'.[6] Immanuel Kant was another major player in the development of agnosticism, bricking up God behind the wall which he said separated the noumenal world from the phenomenal.

The output and influence of these men and others meant that by the time Thomas Huxley appeared on the scene agnosticism provoked little intellectual opposition. For most, natural theology had failed, knowledge was said to be limited to human experience, religious beliefs seemed to be buckling under the onslaught of science, and the divine government of the world was being seriously questioned. Huxley recorded his great satisfaction that in no time at all 'the term [agnosticism] took', the influential magazine *The Spectator* 'stood godfather to it', and any suspicion in the minds of respectable people as to where the word came from 'was completely lulled'.[7]

A term for our times

If the word 'agnosticism' slipped quietly into our language in 1869, it is easy to see why it fits the contemporary scene like a glove. The term most often used to identify today's culture is 'post-modernism'. It is virtually impossible to give a satisfactory definition of it, partly because scholars are unable to agree on the 'modernism' it is said to supersede. For our present purposes we shall have to settle for a few comments on each.

'Modernism' is the name given to the world-view established by the Renaissance and the Enlightenment. In this system, reason is the key to finding the rules and criteria for discovering absolute truth and for understanding the world. Great faith is placed in education in general, and science in particular, to produce a world of health, wealth, equality, freedom and happiness for all who tap in to their endless resources. By his own unaided efforts, man is capable of defining morality and thus improving the well-being of the human race. What is more, modernism endorses the Enlightenment conviction that reason alone is the source of anything we might know about God. This idea became so entrenched that in his contribution to *The Myth of God Incarnate*, published in 1977, one liberal theologian wrote, 'We must accept our lot, bequeathed to us by the Enlightenment, and make the most of it.'[8] Yet by then serious cracks had already begun to appear in Enlightenment-based modernism. In 1979 the French author Jean-François Lyotard identified some of these in his book *La condition postmoderne*, and by the time this was published in English five years later a new, post-modern mood was gathering pace.

Unlike Enlightenment-based modernism, which sees history as rooted in meaning, post-modernism rejects both. For post-modern man, 'There is no past and no future, there is only a perpetual and dominant present.'[9] Neither are there any foundations, fixed certainties or absolutes. Post-modernism utterly rejects the whole idea of a rational, cohesive package and brings into play at least three words which relate directly to agnosticism.

The first is *'deconstruction'*, which says that in any written work the text will have meanings which the author did not intend and could not have intended, and that in any case the author could never have adequately expressed what he or she meant. One hardly has to be a genius to see where this leads: words are nothing more than words, and we can invest them with whatever meaning (or lack of meaning) we choose. In his fine book *The Gagging of God*, Don Carson elaborates: 'Because meaning finally resides in the interpreter, there are as many meanings as there are interpreters, even if interpreters are multiplied indefinitely. That means no one meaning can ever be thought to be superior to any other meaning; there is no objective basis on which to evaluate them.'[10]

The widespread phenomenon of 'spin-doctoring' is a classic example of deconstruction at work. In the world of politics, ministerial aides are constantly used in imparting to their masters' statements whatever 'spin' is most likely to make them more beneficial to their party or more acceptable to the public. When United States President Bill Clinton was embroiled in allegations of sexual and other offences dating back many years, and which in 1999 led to his becoming only the second president in his country's history to be impeached, he and his public relations staff showed a remarkable ability to turn the tables on his accusers (and to keep the majority of Americans on his side) by their dextrous manipulation of the meanings of words. Was telling someone to be evasive the same as telling him or her to twist the truth? Would 'misled' sound better than 'lied'? Did deviant sex count as adultery? Could he admit to 'sexual contact' but not 'sexual relations'? Even more bizarrely, could it be argued that while a woman had sexual relations with Clinton, he did not have sexual relations with her? This is classic post-modernism at work. If truth is not absolute, it can constantly be revised without any concern about contradiction. If there is no such thing as truth, how can anything be a lie? Interpretation, or 'spin', is everything.

In this particular area, post-modernism has further implications. As Gene Edward Veith explains, 'Values such as consistency, unity and personal integrity are "fundamentalist" and thus wrong. Instead of having a single core identity, human beings are free to have many identities, compartmentalizing them so they do not impinge on each other. Religion, sexual desires, job demands, family role and political beliefs are all part of one's make-up, but none of these compartments need have any bearing on any of the others.'[11] This is exactly the line taken by President Clinton, enabling him to give dazzling public performances while wrestling with disastrous private problems. Intending it as a compliment, the post-modernist psychologist Robert Jay Lifton described him as 'the nation's first post-modern president' and added, 'Not bound by objective standards of truth, Mr Clinton is able to continually reinvent himself, flexibly adapting his ideology, his behaviour and his very personality to the needs of the moment.'[12]

The second word brought into play by post-modernism is 'pluralism', another product of the so-called 'philosophy of doubt' which is so pervasive in contemporary thinking. Pluralism says that truth cannot be known and that doubting is the mature approach to life. As far as our specific subject is concerned, pluralism claims that religious orthodoxy is a matter of preference and that the only heresy is to call anything heresy. No religious philosophy is entitled to pronounce itself right or true and others false or untrue. The Observer's Martin Wroe noted, 'The consumer is champion and personal choice is everything... This is the era of do-it-yourself faith, of making your own god.'[13]

Nor does the post-modernist feel forced to choose any of the pre-packaged systems. Sociologist Tony Walter says, 'A new stage has been reached; people do not choose between different religions, they choose their own religion from the elements they like in all the others... Orthodox, institutionalized religion is out, but home-made, make-it-up-as-you-go-along spirituality is in.'[14] The Daily Telegraph's Clifford Longley puts his finger on the spot: 'Post-modernism has no soul of its own, but borrows selectively from past or distant cultures which do. It is essentially a culture in search of an experience, not in search of truth (in which it does not believe)... In religion, long-standing differences over belief are boiled down, in this post-modern perspective, to mere cultural styles, all of them deemed equally "valid". The one measurement that matters is the spiritual high they give, as if worship was something you snorted through your nose.'[15] In a post-modern climate, any individual is entitled to declare that his 'pick'n'mix' world-view is right and true for him. This sounds wonderfully liberating but, as we shall see in the next chapter, the differences between religions are so fundamental and so enormous that trying to reduce all religions to their lowest common denominator is both illogical and unworkable.

The third word is *'relativism'*, which says that all moral principles are matters of the individual's own choice. There are no objective moral standards; only the person concerned, reacting to a particular situation, can decide what is right and what is wrong. As Don Carson says, 'There is very little consensus left in Western countries over the proper basis of moral behaviour.'[16] He goes on to speak of the influence of the popular media and to suggest that for millions of people the talk show is the only forum in which moral questions are discussed. The outcome is totally predictable. Carson tells of a talk show on the subject of pornography, during which one guest enthused, 'The great thing about our society is that you can have your opinion and I can have mine.'[17] In a post-modern setting, self is the epicentre of ethics; morality is privatized. Richard Rorty, one of America's most articulate post-modernists, bluntly claims, 'There is nothing deep down inside us except what we have put there ourselves, no criterion that we have not created.'[18] At this point we can see that, for all their superficial differences, modernism and post-modernism both flow from the idea that human beings derive their knowledge from themselves. Yet as Ranald Macaulay indicates, they also share the same problem: 'If human knowledge really does have no higher reference point than "man", then no one can say for sure what life is about.'[19] In this environment, where religion has no transcendental nature and moral values are matters of personal preference, agnosticism feels right at home. Don Carson goes even further and declares, 'Post-modernism ruthlessly applied ... deifies agnosticism.'[20]

Although post-modernism says there are no moral absolutes, the real world keeps showing the opposite. Writing in *The Times* in 1996, James Jones, then Bishop of Hull, cited political events in South Africa from 1960–1990 to frame a clear example of this: 'We are told that in this relativistic climate it is no longer possible to speak of moral certainties. Yet in this decade the so-called post-modern world has behaved with surprising moral certainty. It has revealed a captivity to absolute truth. When condemning, for example, the barbarities of apartheid, the post-modernists did not say they were relatively wrong. They did not concede that moral issues of justice depended on how you were brought up. The oppression of one race by another was not, and is not, relatively wrong, but absolutely wrong. Such was the worldwide recognition of these universal and absolute truths that a sovereign nation was forced to change.'[21]

Deciding to be undecided

Agnosticism is obviously related to scepticism, which we examined in a previous chapter, but for our present purposes we will focus on its relevance to the issue of the existence of God. There are two distinct kinds of agnostic, which we can define as soft-core and hard-core, but their differences are so marked that we shall need to look at them separately.

The soft-core agnostic is simply not sure whether God exists. He accepts that there may or may not be sufficient data to show that he does, but he has not yet come to any conclusion on the matter and, at least for the time being, he would prefer to suspend judgement. This seems to be the kind of agnosticism A. J. Ayer had in mind when he wrote, 'It is a characteristic of an agnostic to hold that the existence of a god is a possibility in which there is no good reason either to believe or disbelieve.'[22] The British industrialist Cecil Rhodes, best known for his tremendous influence in the development of South Africa and Rhodesia, once said, 'I've considered the existence of God and decided there's a 50-50 chance that God exists, and therefore I propose to give him the benefit of the doubt.'[23] Even if he were to feel that the odds were about the same, the soft-core agnostic would give the benefit of the doubt to his doubts. He is open to believing that God exists and he does not rule out the possibility that somewhere down the road he might come to the conclusion that he does. In the meantime, he would typically not choose to defend his case with any great enthusiasm, nor would he want to attack those who take a different position. The British consultant surgeon Bernard Palmer calls this 'unconscious atheism' and writes of those who have not deliberately renounced belief in God but who behave as if God is nothing more than 'an optional extra for those who have a need!'[24]

For obvious reasons, soft-core agnosticism almost always extends to questions of death and the afterlife. The sixteenth-century French philosopher François Rabelais said, 'I am going to the great Perhaps.' In the seventeenth century the political philosopher Thomas Hobbes spoke of taking 'my last voyage, a great leap in the dark'.[25] His contemporary John Dryden, the first Poet Laureate, wrote, 'Death in itself is nothing; but we fear to be we know not what, we know not where.'[26] For the soft-core agnostic, both God's existence and his own final destiny are matters on which he remains uncommitted.

Soft-core agnosticism is obviously not a direct threat to theism — in countless cases it has been the prelude to it — but it does face one obvious challenge. In his powerful defence of theism, the renowned American psychologist and philosopher William James discussed the question of options, the decision between two hypotheses, which he said might be living or dead, forced or avoidable, momentous or trivial. A dead option does not relate in any way to the person to whom it is being proposed; a trivial option is one in which there is no kind of compulsion. As James clearly pointed out, the question of the existence or non-existence of God is 'living, forced and momentous'.[27] The soft-core agnostic's response is to duck. The point to discuss here is not whether such a response (or non-response) is possible, but whether it is sensible. Is it rational to settle for agnosticism in the light of the issues involved, and especially when the agnostic confesses to be ignorant of the facts? This is how James makes the point:

> When I look at the religious question as it really puts itself to concrete men, and when I think of all the possibilities which both practically and theoretically it involves, then this command that we shall put a stopper on our heart, instincts, and courage and *wait* — acting of course meanwhile more or less as if religion were *not* true — till doomsday, or till such time as our intellect and senses working together may have raked in evidence enough — this command, I say, seems to me the queerest idol ever manufactured in the philosophical cave.[28]

Soft-core agnosticism is not the avoidance of option; it *is* an option. Not making a decision *is* a decision, an act of faith, a commitment to being uncommitted. What James is saying is that the issues involved demand more. Let me illustrate. For as many years as I can remember, people have argued over whether a yeti, or 'abominable snowman', roams the high Himalayas. The reasoning for and against has been fascinating and I imagine people will still be arguing the pros and cons long after I am dead and buried. Yet on this particular issue, I am happy to remain a soft-core agnostic, knowing that, whatever they might be, the true facts cannot have any effect on my life, and firmly believing that they will not affect me in any way after death; but surely the issue of the existence or non-existence of God is in another league? I can duck the question of the abominable snowman without giving it a second thought. Even if the yeti is alive and well and living in Nepal I can see no way in which it could possibly have any relevance to my present life or lifestyle or to what may happen to me after I die. The same cannot possibly be said about the existence of God; in Stephen Evans' words, 'The question of God cannot finally be avoided because it is a question about what kind of universe we live in. This is a real question and it must have a real answer. We need to know the truth about God if we are to live our lives rightly.'[29]

Agnostics sometimes point to the fact that, just as open-mindedness is the proper approach to science, the same approach is valid in religion, but this ignores the fact that, for the honest scientist, open-mindedness is a live base from which he presses relentlessly on in the search for evidence in which to ground his developing beliefs. Serious attention should surely be given to what claims to be the most serious question anyone could ever face, and which has apparently attracted mankind's attention for as far back as we have been able to trace. An agnostic who is actively trying to come to a settled conclusion either for or against the existence of God must surely have realized this! The apathetic soft-core agnostic is not thinking straight.

These are some of the questions one would like to ask the soft-core agnostic:

- Are you seriously interested in discovering the truth, or are you merely playing mind games? Have you honestly examined the claims of theism?
- Can you think of any question which, to quote William James, is more 'living, forced and momentous' than the existence of God? How can you settle for uncertainty over an issue which claims to affect you for ever?
- Do you think it wise (or possible) to wait until all your questions are answered before getting to grips with ultimate issues?
- Have you given any thought as to the kind of evidence which would convince you that God exists? What kind of evidence would convince you that he does *not* exist?
- Are you using agnosticism as an excuse not to examine the arguments?

- Are you asking questions because you want to believe or because you want to disbelieve?
- Are you sure you are not trying to avoid getting to grips with the reality of a God who is said to have the prior claim on your life and lifestyle?
- Is John Gerstner not right when he states, 'The merest possibility of the eternal world completely outweighs the utmost certainty of this one'?[30]
- If giving an account of yourself to a holy and righteous God who will decide your eternal destiny is a possibility, would it not make sense to do everything you can to discover whether this idea is fact or fiction — and to do so urgently? Would you honestly be happy to die in the dark and risk the worst?

Retreat from reality

The hard-core agnostic is in an altogether different league. Not only does he say that he has insufficient data to know whether God exists, he claims that everybody shares his ignorance. Simply put, he says it is impossible to know whether God exists. Even the most dogmatic and well-informed the- ist will admit to a measure of agnosticism and confess he does not know everything about God. Norman Geisler is not exaggerating when he says, 'One would have to be God in order to know God exhaustively. Finite man can have only a finite knowledge of the Infinite.'[31] Yet the hard-core agnostic asserts that nothing outside of the natural world can be known or proved and that, as the God of traditional theism is by definition outside of the natural world, he is out of reach as far as human knowledge is con- cerned. What can be said in response?

In the first place, the hard-core agnostic helps to confirm that, although it is rarely done, we are technically correct in classifying agnosticism as a form of atheism. As theism is belief in God (or, in a broader use of the word, belief in one or more gods) atheism means everything outside of theism and this, by definition, includes agnosticism, which neither asserts nor denies God's existence.

Secondly, even the hard-core agnostic is a believer. In 'You've Gotta Serve Somebody', Bob Dylan sings, 'You've either got faith or you've got unbelief, there ain't no neutral ground.' The title of the song points to the fact that there can be no neutrality on the issue of God's existence, but the lyric misses an important point we have made elsewhere, namely that even unbelievers have faith. They believe they are right in saying that theists have got it wrong. The hard-core agnostic is an obvious case in point. He may not belong to a church, engage in worship, or realistically be able to pray to any supernatural being, but he does have a creed: it reads, 'I believe it is impossible for finite human beings to know whether God exists.' This is not being offered as a tentative proposition, but is being put forward as a solid, clear statement of fact. The hard-core agnostic has set up camp on the phenomenal side of Immanuel Kant's wall and come to the conclusion that there is no way to get over it and reach the noumenal world in which God may or may not exist. In fact, he out-Kant's Kant and declares that not only are the normal avenues of knowing closed to the things of God, but there is no existential experience or mystical intuition which can establish God's existence.

However modest this may sound, it is exactly the opposite, because agnosticism literally means 'not-knowingness' and the hard-core agnostic's claim is tantamount to saying, 'My ignorance equals factual impossibility.' In this sense, he almost renders the word 'agnostic' misleading, because there seems very little difference between his position and that of the atheist. This is what led Karl Marx's co-worker Friedrich Engels to call the agnostics of his day 'shame-faced atheists',[32] people who wanted a more comfortable and socially acceptable label for their unbelief. The British novelist Somerset Maugham conceded that this was the case: 'In religion above all things the only thing of use is an objective truth. The only God that is of use is a being who is personal, supreme and good, and whose existence is as certain as that two and two makes four. I cannot penetrate the mystery. I remain an agnostic, and *the practical outcome of agnosticism is that you act as though God did not exist*[33] (emphasis added).

This is an interesting admission, and for the hard-core agnostic it sometimes proves a damaging one. Whereas Immanuel Kant asserted, 'We must live as though there were a God,' the hard-core agnostic rarely takes this line. He usually approaches life on the assumption that God does not exist, rather than on the assumption that he may. I have never met a hard-core agnostic who is trying to build the moral fabric of his life on the basis that he *may* be answerable to a God of infinite holiness who has invested human life with eternal significance. Instead, the hard-core agnostic typically lives as if God's existence could be ruled out. At this point, very little separates his approach to life from that of the out-and-out atheist who rejects the ideas of God and meaning and says he is free to live as he chooses. The British novelist Aldous Huxley (grandson of Thomas) was perfectly frank about what this meant for him: 'I had motives for not wanting the world to have a meaning; consequently I assumed that it had none, and was able without any difficulty to find satisfying reasons for this assumption. The philosopher who finds no meaning in the world is not concerned exclusively with a problem in pure metaphysics, he is also concerned to prove that there is no valid reason why he personally should not do as he wants to do... Most ignorance is vincible ignorance. *We don't know because we don't want to know.* It is our will that decides how and upon what subject we shall use our intelligence. Those who detect no meaning in the world generally do so because, for one reason or another, it suits their books that the world should be meaningless'[34] (emphasis added)

Sitting in a coffee bar in North Devon some years ago, I got into a very heated discussion with two young men who produced an avalanche of atheistic and agnostic arguments. When the rocks stopped flying, I asked them a very simple question: 'If I could prove to you that God did exist, would you commit yourselves to him if it meant changing your lifestyles in order to meet his demands?' When they immediately chorused, 'No!' I replied, 'Then your problem about the existence of God has nothing to do with science or philosophy; it has to do with the way you want to run your lives.' They both agreed, and many hard-core agnostics refuse to budge because they have a vested interest in ignoring the possibility of God's existence.

Thirdly, the hard-core agnostic can properly be asked to produce the evidence on which, as a believer, he bases his faith. As we saw in chapter 9, when addressing the subject of atheism, nobody can seriously hold to a position which he or she judges to be false. Then what evidence does the hard-core agnostic have for saying that man is inevitably ignorant of God's existence? How can he know that it is impossible to know and be certain that we must for ever remain uncertain? What are the sources of information that enable him to say that reality is unknowable? Can he really say that ultimate reality is unknowable unless he knows enough about ultimate reality to know that this is the case?

Fourthly, is the hard-core agnostic right to rule out any possibility that he might be wrong? Has he seriously, fairly and carefully examined what theism proposes? If he has, is he sure he can dismiss it all? Does he see nothing in the natural world to suggest that he might want to rethink his position? Even an entrenched sceptic like David Hume, who relentlessly criticized all the traditional proofs for the existence of God, admitted that 'A purpose, an intention, or design strikes everywhere the most careless, the most stupid thinker; and no man can be so hardened in absurd systems as at all times to reject it.'[35] G. K. Chesterton said there was 'a choking cataract of human testimony in favour of the supernatural'.[36] Does the hard-core agnostic not see anything in the experience of others which gives even the slightest hint that he may be on the wrong track? Millions of people, over thousands of years, have claimed that their lives have been transformed for the better because of a living relationship with God. Is there a credible reason for rejecting all of this, or is there something else which prevents the hard-core agnostic accepting any evidence which might contradict his creed?

The story is told of a man who thought he was dead and was persuaded by a friend to visit a psychiatrist. After listening to the patient's unusual problem, the psychiatrist made a determined effort to convince him of one fact that would prove him wrong — that dead men do not bleed. After several weeks, the patient was convinced, but when the psychiatrist then punctured his arm with a needle and blood seeped out, the man was shocked and cried, 'I knew I was right! Dead men do bleed after all!' Is the hard-core agnostic being any wiser when he refuses to consider any of the evidence for the existence of God offered by the natural world or the torrent of human testimony?

Fifthly, as the hard-core agnostic is a religious sceptic, he runs up against most of the fatal flaws we saw to be associated with scepticism. How can he be consistently agnostic? How is it possible to rule out all knowledge of supernatural reality without knowing anything of what such reality might mean? As Norman Geisler shows, 'It will not suffice to say that his knowledge about reality is purely and completely negative, that is, a knowledge of what reality is not. For every negative presupposes a positive; one cannot meaningfully affirm that something is *not*-that if he is totally devoid of a knowledge of the "that". It follows that total agnosticism is self-defeating because it assumes some knowledge of reality in order to deny any knowledge of reality.'[37]

We might add that agnosticism is a dismal pall-bearer. Robert Green Ingersoll was one of America's most eloquent agnostics, but in the course of his brother's funeral oration this was the best he could offer: 'Whether in mid-sea or amongst the breakers of the further shore, a wreck must mark at last the end of each and all. And every life, no matter if its every hour is rich with love and every moment jewelled with joy will, at its close, become a tragedy, as deep and as dark as can be woven out of the warp and woof of mystery and death... Life is a narrow vale between the cold and barren peaks of two eternities. We strive in vain to look beyond the heights. We cry aloud, and the only answer is the echo of our wailing cry.'[38]

Answering hard-core agnostics is a never-ending business, because as soon as one argument is answered or compromised another is produced. I have long since discovered that while some people ask questions because they want to believe, others ask questions because they want to disbelieve. Hard-core agnostics are usually found in the second category, seemingly unaware that their position is untenable because the non-existence of God can never be demonstrated. Surely openness to the alternative is wiser? After listening to an address given by a friend of mine, Sir Hector Hetherington, then Principal of Glasgow University, made the following significant comment: 'There are issues on which it is impossible to be neutral. These issues strike right down to the roots of man's existence. And while it is right that we should examine the evidence, and make sure that we have all the evidence, it is equally right that we ourselves should be accessible to the evidence.'[39]

Most people seeking to make themselves accessible turn to one of the multitude of religious groupings on offer but, as we are about to see, many who do so end up by embracing some form of atheism rather than avoiding it.

11.
Masks

Watching television at home in Guernsey in the early 1960s, I heard the well-known Jewish philosopher Martin Buber make a statement which has remained embedded in my mind ever since: 'Nothing so tends to mask the face of God as religion. It can be a substitute for God himself.' I have long since forgotten the context in which Buber was speaking, but his statement warns us that following some form of religion cannot automatically be equated with finding God.

To include religious movements in an overall summary of atheism may seem either reckless or ridiculous, but I am doing so in the context of the concept of 'God' outlined in the introduction. With this in mind, it can be shown that many of the world's religious movements have concepts of God which are in one way or another at variance with this, while others have those which bear little or no resemblance to it. This will become clear as we take an overview of these in the next two chapters, though we should begin by entering one caveat. Because the treatment of these movements is necessarily brief, there is always the possibility of straying into generalization, but I have tried to avoid this and at the same time to base these summaries as fairly as possible on the statements of the movements concerned or on the comments of reliable authorities. I have listed the movements in alphabetical order rather than by age or size.

In the beginning, Bab?

The origins of Baha'ism lie in Shi'ite Islam. Its tortuous early history centres around Sayyid Ali Muhammad of Shiraz, the self-styled 'Bab' (meaning 'Gateway') who became the leader of a Shi'ite sect from 1844 until he was executed in 1850. One of his successors, Baha, born in Persia in 1817, took upon himself the title of 'Baha'u'llah' ('the glory of God'). When he moved into the Bahji Palace in Akka, Turkey, countless Baha'is made pilgrimage there to gaze for a few seconds upon the one they called the 'Blessed Perfection'.

Baha was a prolific author and wrote over 100 books. Baha'is regard all his writings as the word of God and he himself pointed to one of his titles, *Al-Kitab Al-Aqdas*, written in Arabic in 1872, as 'the most holy book'.[1] With Baha's writings as its sacred scriptures, Baha'ism is now governed by the Universal House of Justice in Haifa, Israel, and according to one reference work lays claim to be the fastest growing religious movement in the world.[2]

Baha'ism emphasizes the value of service to others and its concern for universal peace and love. 'Bab' and 'Baha'u'llah' are thought to be manifestations of God, transcending anything known in any other religion, but Baha'ism's notion of God is so vague as to place him beyond human knowledge in this world.

One principle; no personality

Siddhartha Gautama, the founder of <u>Buddhism,</u> was born about 563 B.C. into an aristocratic family living in north-eastern India. His arrival there at that time is said to have been the last of at least 550 reincarnations during which he moved gradually closer to the enlightenment he sought. He left his privileged surroundings when he was twenty-nine years of age and some years later, after a week of meditation sitting under a fig tree (later renamed the *bodhi* or bo tree, 'the tree of wisdom') he claimed to have reached 'nirvana', the highest spiritual plane possible for any human being.

From then on he became known as Buddha ('the enlightened one'). By the time he died some fifty years later, his complex teaching had taken hold on many of his fellow countrymen who had become disillusioned with Hinduism. Now one of the largest religious groupings in the contemporary world, Buddhism has a strict moral code that outlaws, among other things, all killing (even the killing of insects), stealing, adultery and lying. Yet on wider issues it is depressingly bleak: the human soul does not exist, personality is an illusion and, because his existence is temporary, man is essentially worthless. In the words of one of Buddhism's own authorities,

'The man who perceives his true self grasps the fourfold emptiness disclosed in the words, "I am nowhere a somewhatness for anyone".[3]

Buddhism has so many different sects that it has been described as 'a family of religions rather than a single religion'.[4] The most widely known in the West is Zen Buddhism, which has been called 'a world of bewildering dialogues, obscure conundrums, stunning paradoxes, flagrant contradictions and abrupt *non sequiturs*, all carried off in the most urbane, cheerful and innocent style'.[5]

Buddha avoided all claims to divinity and refused to speculate upon the existence of deities, with the result that in many Buddhist countries today no word exists for a supreme divine Being. Gautama himself is considered by many Buddhist and non-Buddhist scholars to have been an atheist. Although there are Mahayana Buddhists who now worship Gautama, along with many other gods borrowed from older Hindu ideas, the Buddhist world-view is basically monistic (teaching that only one ultimate principle or being exists), a philosophy in which a universal, personal and transcendent God plays no part.

The emperor's ethics

Confucianism has had 'a monumental impact upon the life, social structure and political philosophy of China'.[6] About 530 B.C. a divorced tax collector by the name of Kung Fu-tzu (Confucius in Latin) left his government post to become a teacher, convinced that he could be instrumental in changing society. He lived during the horrific period of 'the Warring States', which saw hundreds of thousands of people slaughtered *en masse*, and his greatest longing was to restore communal harmony. In one expert's assessment, 'His philosophy was very simple: namely, virtue is the foundation of happiness.'[7]

As his moral views took hold on others, his stock rose and he was appointed minister of justice in 500 B.C., later resigning after a dispute with his superiors. He spent the next ten years wandering from state to state in an unsuccessful attempt to elicit a response to his moral challenge, before devoting the last five years of his life to compiling what have become known as his 'Five Classics', though these were largely an anthology of other men's work. By the time he died in 479 B.C., Confucius had established himself as the most important teacher in Chinese culture. Within sixty years of his death he was given the title 'Duke Ni, All-complete and Illustrious', and successive promotions led in the eleventh century to his elevation to the full rank of emperor. In 1906 an imperial prescript raised him to the status of 'Co-assessor with the deities Heaven and Earth', but there is no evidence that Confucius himself would have laid claim to this inflated accolade.

Confucianism is an ethical system rather than a religion (Confucius had only a shadowy concept of impersonal deities) and is wholly concerned with man's present well-being within earthly society. It sees stability rooted in custom and tradition, an acceptance of one's 'place' in life, and leaves no room or need for God. After twenty-three years spent working in China, British missionary Leslie Lyall concluded, 'Had Confucius lived in the twentieth century, he would surely have been the patron saint of the humanists.'[8]

Of gods and cows

Hinduism is not so much a religion as 'a family of religions ... fluid and changing'.[9] Unlike closed systems of beliefs and practices, it cannot be traced to a single founder and is virtually impossible to define. Its roots go back at least as far as 3,000 B.C., when Dravidians invaded India and established themselves in the Indus River valley, from which the word 'Hindu' is derived. Their civilization was overcome about 1,500 B.C. by other invaders from Asia Minor and Iran, who added their religious ideas to the polytheism and naturism they found being practised. The invaders' language was Veda, but this eventually gave way to Sanskrit, which became the sacred language in which their religious literature came to be written after many centuries of oral tradition.

The Hindu scriptures developed over hundreds of years into a massive collection of philosophical and religious material. In broad terms they are divided into the *sruti* ('what is heard'), said to be eternal truths conveyed to ancient seers, and the *smriti* ('what is remembered'), a secondary authority based on the *sruti*. The earliest Hindu scriptures are known as the *Vedas*, a collection of mantras, prayers, rituals and magical formulae and incantations. Other treatises, epics, myths and poems were committed to writing over the centuries, each one adding further ingredients to the stew. The best-known of these is the *Bhagavad-Gita*, written in the first century A.D. and now considered Hinduism's most sacred book.

Core doctrines that have persisted in most sects of Hinduism include 'karma', the culminating value of one's actions in determining human or other form in future incarnations; 'nirvana', the final emancipation from the chain of rebirths; the caste system, dividing Hindu society into four main closed social groups based on heredity; and the sacredness of the cow as a revered symbol of the earth's bounty.

Yet Hinduism goes far beyond these, and over the centuries has assimilated a bewildering assortment of philosophical and religious ideas, said to accommodate no fewer than thirty-three million gods.[10] Os Guinness notes, 'There is a great range in Hindu theology. Seen one way, there are as many gods as there are Indians.'[11] This has resulted in Hindus showing great tolerance of other religions, in the belief that they are all reflections of one universal truth, but it has also robbed Hinduism of any coherent theology of its own. One authority goes so far as to say, 'Hindus have an extraordinarily wide selection of beliefs and practices to choose from: they can (to use Western terms) be pantheists, polytheists, monotheists, agnostics, or even atheists.'[12]

There are over 600 million Hindus in the world, including more than 80% of the population of India. A *Sunday Telegraph* report in 1998 said that 'Visiting temples to make offerings to gods remains the nation's favourite pastime,' and that a recent poll had shown that 'Most Indians under 30 were highly religious, regularly observing India's many religious festivals, praying daily and visiting temples.' It also told of religious temples and organizations setting up websites on the Internet, enabling worshippers to 'receive the *darshan* or audience of their favourite god, goddess or guru at the click of a mouse'.[13]

Submit!

The second youngest (and second largest) of the world's great religions is Islam — the word is the infinitive of an Arabic verb and means 'to submit' — which has been called 'one of the outstanding phenomena of history'.[14] As it is now the majority religion in about forty countries, claims some 900 million adherents (about one sixth of the world's population) and is growing at such an impressive rate, it warrants much more attention than others.

Between A.D. 570–580, a posthumous son of an unknown father was born in the Arabian city of Mecca. His mother named him Muhammad

('Praised') and, after her death six years later, he was brought up by various
members of the family. When he was twenty-five, he married a wealthy
widow who bore him three sons and four daughters. By this time,
Muhammad had already become intensely religious. Mecca's idolatrous
polytheism centred around the Ka'aba, a cube-shaped building known as
'house of Allah' but filled with sacred stones and images of 360 male and
female deities, and Muhammad became increasingly incensed by the situation. Almost certainly influenced by the teaching of Jews, Christians and
Hanifs, a group of monotheistic Arabs, he became firmly convinced that
there was only one true God.

   When he was about forty years of age, he claimed to have received the
first of many visions that came to him in the course of mystical and sometimes ecstatic experiences. He thought that he might have been possessed
by *jinn*, spirits said to inspire Arab poets and soothsayers, but his wife
persuaded him to believe that these revelations, which were to continue
intermittently for over twenty years until his death in A.D. 632, came from
Allah. These revelations, and statements based on his teaching, were later
incorporated by his disciples into the *Qur'an* (Arabic for 'recitation'), every
word of which orthodox adherents to Islam now believe to be divinely
inspired.

   Muhammad never claimed divinity, and according to orthodox Islam
he was only a human being chosen by God to live an exemplary life and to
introduce to the world the purest and most perfect religion of Islam: 'Every
previous prophet of God was sent to a particular people, but Muhammad
was sent to all human beings of the world until Doomsday.'[15] This position
of exclusive eminence is enshrined in Islam's basic confession, the *shahada*:
'There is no God but Allah, and Muhammad is the messenger of Allah,'
and the Muslim scholar Wilfred Cantwell Smith underlines the remarkable
veneration of Muhammad by noting, 'Muslims will allow attacks on Allah
... but to disparage Muhammad will provoke from even the most "liberal"
sections of the community a fanaticism of blazing vengeance.'[16]

   This is in tune with a variety of Islamic sources. The *Ahādith*, a collection of sacred Islamic traditions, depicts Muhammad as pre-existent and
the purpose of all creation. *Qawwalis*, a popular cultural presentation, is
equally fulsome and says, 'If Muhammad had not been, God himself would
not have existed.'[17] The popular doctrine of *Nur-i-Muhammadi*, or 'light of
Muhammad', is reflected in many traditional Islamic books which teach
that God first created the light of Muhammad and from that light proceeded

to make the rest of creation.[18] The Islamic scholar Michael Nazir-Ali writes of the prophet being venerated to an astonishing degree in modern Pakistan through the mass media, school books and cultural presentations, including one particular poem which reads, 'Though my link with the Divinity of God be severed, may my hand never let go of the hem of the Chosen One [i.e. Muhammad].'[19]

His character seems to have been a curious mixture, and the *Qur'an* expressly alludes to his mortality[20] and imperfection.[21] The British scholar Sir Norman Anderson, an acknowledged expert in Islamic history, literature and law, notes that while Muhammad was 'generous, resolute, genial and astute', he 'could be cruel and vindictive; he could stoop to assassination, and he seems to have had a sensual streak'.[22] This last comment seems to be borne out by the fact that after the death of his first wife Muhammad married someone new every year for the next fourteen years (including the divorced wife of his adopted son), claiming that revelations from Allah gave him exclusive authority to exceed the quota of four wives permitted to other men. The reference to assassination is based on evidence that he ordered people to be put to death for composing poems that mocked him. These flaws in his character would certainly appear to be at odds with a Muslim classic by Kamal ud Din ad Damiri, in which the prophet is described as 'the most perfect of mankind in every variety of perfection'.[23]

After Muhammad's death there was a bitter power struggle for the leadership of the religion he had founded. Muhammad is said to have predicted that his followers would become divided into seventy-three sects, all but one of which would go to hell,[24] but protracted fragmentation has resulted in about 150 different sects of Islam at the present time, of which the best-known are the Sunnis and the Shi'ites.

By far the most important issue for us to consider here is whether Islam's 'Allah' is identical with the God defined in our introduction. Although the exact etymology of 'Allah' is virtually impossible to define with certainty, some critics are adamant that Allah is not simply the Arabic word for God. For example, Dave Hunt writes, 'Allah is a contraction of *al-Ilah*, the personal name of the moon god, chief of the gods in the ancient Ka'aba. The fact is still reflected in the crescent moon on the minarets and shrines and mosques and national flags of Islamic countries. If Allah were merely the Arabic word for God, then the Muslims would not hesitate to use the word for God in other languages. But in each language it is insisted that the name of Allah be used; it would be blasphemy to call the Muslims' god anything but Allah.'[25]

Others take a different view and say that although the Ka'aba was filled with gods, the existence of Allah as the supreme God was acknowledged long before the foundation of Islam, and that this can be seen by the negative form of the Muslim creed: 'There is no god except Allah.' In *The Call of the Minaret*, Kenneth Cragg, a highly respected scholar of Islam, maintains that 'The Prophet's mission was not to proclaim God's existence but to deny the existence of all lesser deities.'[26] He goes on to say, 'There can be no doubt that the Prophet's contemporaries knew of a Supreme Being, but he did not dominate their minds. Rather they thought more directly and frequently of the lesser gods, the daughters, perhaps even the sons, of Allah, who were far more intimately related to their daily lives, their wars, their harvests, and their fertility.'[27]

It may be safest to go along with the well-known Muslim author Maurice Bucaille: 'Al'Lah means "the Divinity" in Arabic; it is a single God, implying that a correct transcription can only render the exact meaning of the word with the help of the expression "God"',[28] although we also need to bear in mind that there are subtle, yet far-reaching, differences between the Muslim understanding of the supreme Being and that of the non-Muslim theist. The nature and qualities of Allah are reflected in ninety-nine 'most beautiful names' (a popular devotional book gives Muhammad 201)[29] which are frequently repeated by devout Muslims as they finger their rosaries. Some of these names seem to tie in very well with our working definition of God — the *Qur'an* certainly teaches that Allah is eternal, independent and omniscient, and the Creator and Sustainer of the universe — but closer examination reveals a subtly different picture.

For example, the fundamental concept of Allah is his unity, but in the doctrine of *mukhalafa* this has been pressed to the point where, according to Norman Anderson, 'God is declared to be so different from his creatures that it becomes virtually impossible to postulate anything of him.'[30] One of the 'most beautiful names' is *Al-Quddus* (the Holy), but the phrase occurs only twice in the *Qur'an* and does not refer to moral purity or perfection. Instead, according to the respected Islamic commentator Beidhawi, it means nothing more than 'the complete absence of anything that would make him less than he is'.[31] One student of the subject has said, 'It is a hopeless case to look for the doctrine of the holiness of God ... in the *Qur'an*.'[32] Again, although Allah is said to be *Ar-Rahman* (the Merciful) and *Ar-Rahim* (the Compassionate), his love is hardly ever mentioned in the *Qur'an*, and even then means nothing more than his actions in giving men laws and warnings. After many years of study and observation, one expert came to the conclusion that 'The chief lack in the Islamic doctrine of God is the lack of love,' and added that 'No orthodox Muslim could say, "God is love." '[33]

By the same token, the very word 'Muslim' (one who submits) indicates that man's required response to Allah is not devotion but rigid obedience. In his classical study of Islam, Johannes Hauri goes so far as to say, 'Muhammad's idea of God is out and out deistic. God and the world are in exclusive, eternal opposition. Of an entrance of God into the world or any sort of human fellowship with God he knows nothing.'[34]

Although the *Qur'an* teaches that God is nearer to man than a man's jugular vein, it does not develop the theme of an intimate relationship between God and the believer, something which leads a leading Muslim author to state, 'Beyond their speculations concerning God, the necessity of his existence, and his properties, Muslim theologians apparently felt no need to question the possibility and reality of a human experience of God.'[35] In orthodox Islam, Allah is so remote from his creation that he is unaffected by people's actions or attitudes, and does not intervene personally in their lives. Nor does he have an ongoing relationship with them; Allah is not a personal God, for he is 'so far above every man in every way that he is not personally knowable'.[36] Allah's 'names' are drawn from what it is claimed he does, rather than from what he reveals himself to be. In other words, Islam says nothing about his essence, a fact which leads one authority to say of its followers, 'If they think at all deeply, they find themselves absolutely unable to know God... Islam leads to agnosticism.'[37]

In Islam, Allah is seen as the source of both good and evil — his 'most beautiful names' include *Al-Hadi* (the One who Guides) and *Al-Muthill* (the One who Leads Astray), and his power and judgement are dominant factors in the working out of his inflexible decrees, leading to a strong element of fatalism in Islamic belief. Not surprisingly, the *Qur'an* has no word for 'conscience'. In carrying out his decrees, God is said to employ various means. For example, every human being has two angels; one on his right records his good deeds and one on his left his sins. Immediately after a person's death and burial, two other angels, Munkar and Nakir, make the corpse sit up while they examine the deceased's spiritual orthodoxy. For those who pass the test, the *Qur'an* promises an eternity of luxury and pleasure: 'Allah will deliver them from the evil of that day and make their countenance shine with joy. He will reward them for their stead-fastness with robes of silk and the delights of Paradise... Reclining there upon soft couches ... they shall ... be arrayed in garments of fine green silk and rich brocade, and adorned with bracelets of silver. The Lord will give them a pure beverage to drink.'[38] Colin Chapman comments, 'Many Muslims would not interpret passages such as these in a literal way. But when every allowance has been made for metaphor and symbol, the Muslim cannot hold out any hope of enjoying a personal relationship with God. So that although he can speak of man's goal as being to "glorify God", he cannot consistently add ... "and to enjoy him for ever".'[39]

For unbelievers, the prospects are bleak. The *Qur'an* teaches that for them, 'We have prepared fetters and chains, and a blazing fire.'[40] In the words of one well-informed interpreter, they will 'suffer and swelter in the hot blasts, foul smoke and molten metal of hell'.[41] Nor can anyone be certain of escaping this disaster: for all its dogmatism on so many issues, there is no assurance of salvation in Islam. One authority says that 'Great as it may be in the eyes of Islam for any person to make the decision to enter the faith, the entry constitutes no guarantee of personal justification in God's eyes.'[42]

One very important aspect of Muslim law is 'jihad', interpreted either as righteous war or as spiritual striving. The first interpretation looks for its basis to instruction in the *Qur'an* to 'fight and slay the Pagans wherever ye find them',[43] and there have been numerous attempts to obey this to the letter. In March 1944 the Grand Mufti of Jerusalem, broadcasting on Radio Berlin, urged all Arabs to 'Kill the Jews wherever you find them! This pleases God and religion and saves your honour. God is with you!'[44]

One recent high-profile example of militancy at an individual level came in 1989 when Ayatollah Khomeini, then Iran's undisputed spiritual and political leader, issued a 'fatwa' (a verdict, or legal opinion, given by a mufti, an expert in Islamic law) against the author Salman Rushdie, decreeing that he should be executed for 'blasphemy' in his book *The Satanic Verses* and urging 'brave' Muslims to 'quickly kill' him. In 1996, Kalim Siddiqui, the leader of Britain's self-styled Muslim parliament at that time, said that the fatwa 'was and remains an order that must be carried out as and when it becomes possible to do so', and went on, 'Any weakness on this position will undermine our moral standing and long-term prospects. By standing firm on our commitments we shall build our place in society.'[45] In 1997 Ayatollah Sheikh Hassam Sanei, head of the Iranian religious foundation Khordad-15, raised the bounty on Rushdie's head from $500,000 to $2.5 million and declared, 'Imam Khomeini's fatwa is a divine decree and all Muslims are duty-bound to execute it. This is not exclusive to a certain person. It concerns all Muslims.'[46]

These cases hardly reflect a reasoned application of orthodox Islamic doctrine, and the widespread bloodshed resulting from fundamentalist activities in the Middle East and elsewhere led journalist Bernard Levin to ask in *The Times*, 'Why has one of the world's most beautiful and profound religions ... been turned into a monstrous charnel house of fanatacism?'[47] One clue to the answer came in a letter to the *Daily Telegraph* in 1996: 'By its very nature [Islam] cannot live and let live; rather, the ultimate aim is to dominate, "to change the existing society and to make Islam supreme" — a plain statement from the Islamic Foundation in Leicester.'[48]

The size, influence and dynamic growth of modern Islam have warranted the extra attention we have given it. Norman Anderson provides a helpful summary of the major point that concerns us here: 'The Muslim God can best be understood in the desert. Its vastness, majesty, ruthlessness and mystery — and the resultant sense of the utter insignificance of man — call forth man's worship and submission, but scarcely prompt his love or suggest God's.'[49]

Higher spirits

The origins of Shinto, the national religion of Japan, and one of the oldest in the world, are virtually impossible to trace with certainty. Clark B. Offner, author of *Modern Japanese Religions*, says that they are 'lost in the hazy mists enshrouding the ancient period of Japanese history'.[50] According to a modern Shinto scholar, it denotes 'the traditional religious practices which originated in Japan and developed mainly among the Japanese people along with the underlying life attitudes and ideology which support such practices'.[51] The word 'Shinto' derives from the Chinese *Shen-tao*, meaning 'way of the higher spirits'. One of its central ideas is that of *kami* (literally, 'superior beings') which implies the concept of sacred power in both animate and inanimate objects, the sun goddess Amaterasu being the most important. In Shinto mythology, the islands of Japan (and eventually the rest of the world) were formed by drops which fell from the spear of Izanagi and Izanami, second-generation male and female *kami*, when they withdrew it after stirring up the primordial brine which lay beneath their celestial dwelling-place.

The Japanese are said to be directly descended from the celestial *kami*, and their emperors from Amaterasu. Shrine worship is central to Shinto practice, with elaborate rituals conducted both in private homes and at communal sites. The nation's imperial shrine, the most sacred spot in all Japan, is located at Ise, 200 miles south-west of Tokyo.

Shinto has no founder, no written canon, no systematic body of doctrine and no unified code of behaviour. Not surprisingly, it has acquired a vast amount of cultural, and at times superstitious, baggage in the course of its long history, making it virtually impossible to define. In Shinto, vagueness is the vogue; it is 'an amalgam of attitudes, ideas and ways of doing things that through two millenniums and more have become an integral part of the *way* of the Japanese people'.[52]

Shinto is primarily concerned with man's personal and communal well-being and pays little attention to the concept of an afterlife. It is essentially polytheistic.

Merging with the abstract

A comparatively recent religion, Sikhism, is based on the teaching of an Indian mystic by the name of Nanak, who was born to working-class Hindu parents near Lahore around 1469. He claimed to have received divine illumination in his early thirties and, by the time he died nearly forty years later, he had pulled together selected strands of Hindu and Islamic teaching to form a body of doctrine later formalized by some of his followers (*'sikh'* is Hindi for 'disciple') into the *Granth Sahib* — 'the Lord's book' — which forms the sacred scriptures of Sikhism.

Sikhism rejects Hinduism's polytheism, ritualism and asceticism, but accepts the ideas of karma and reincarnation. It rejects the ruthless and violent elements in its deity, but accepts Islam's concept of a supreme and absolute ruler. However, Sikhism's God is remote and impersonal and is equated with 'the abstract principle of truth or reality',[53] while its system of salvation, as in certain strands of Hinduism, involves 'a pantheistic merging of the individual self with the mystical world soul'.[54] Speaking in 1999 at the 300th anniversary of the founding of the Sikh brotherhood Khalsa,

Prince Charles commended Nanak's teaching that 'God's light pervades every creature and every creature is contained in this light.'[55] There may be as many as twenty million Sikhs in the world.

Tune in, drop out

The ancient Eastern religion of Taoism is clearly atheistic. Its founder is said to have been a Chinese philosopher by the name of Lao-tze, otherwise known as Lao-zi or Lao-tsu. He was reputedly born between 604 and 570 B.C., but as his names mean no more than 'old teacher', he may be a purely legendary figure.

Based on poems entitled *Tao-te-eching* ('The Way of Life') said to have been written by Lao-tze, Taoism is a mystical concoction of political, philosophical and religious ideas, but with no positive agenda, though teaching that *Tao* ('the Way') can be attained by virtues such as compassion and humility. One summary of its teaching sees it as 'recommending doing nothing and resisting nothing',[56] a philosophy somewhat similar to the 'tune-in, drop-out' mentality of the hippie generation which flourished in the United States and elsewhere in the 1960s.

At one point in Taoism's development, Lao-tze became a divinity. Eventually, the forces of nature, including the sun, moon, stars and tides, were among hundreds of elements that were deified and worshipped. As one experienced observer puts it, 'Taoism quickly degenerated into what it is today — a polytheistic system of spiritualism, demonism and superstition.'[57] Today Taoism as an entity is virtually non-existent, though one authority says that in modern China 'many still cling to it as magic'.[58]

The divine duo

Sometimes known as Zarathustrianism or Mazdaism, Zoroastrianism was founded by the Persian priest Zoroaster, or Zarathustra (*c.* 628 – *c.*551 B.C.). Zoroaster formulated the idea of a cosmic battle between two co-equal powers, Ahura-Mazda (later called Ormazd), the spirit of light and goodness, and Angra Mainyu (later called Ahriman), the spirit of evil and darkness. Although it has had considerable influence (it was the dominant religion of Persia for over a thousand years and spawned several other religions), Zoroastrianism is now reduced to about 100,000 Parsis living in India and Pakistan and a few thousand followers in other countries.

Stressing the eternal conflict between good and evil, Zoroastrianism is basically dualistic, though in practice it has sometimes broadened into polytheism with Zoroaster himself being deified by many. Its practices involve occultism, and the drinking of the hallucinogenic *haoma* (*soma* in India) is a central rite in Zoroastrian worship.

Many paths to the summit?

It has wittily been said that all the study of comparative religion does is to make people comparatively religious. Whatever we make of that, our glance at the core beliefs of nine major world religions ought to disabuse us of the nonsensical notion that all religions are basically saying the same thing.

In the nineteenth century, scholars made a determined effort to discover a common essence in all religions. This led to the now well-known metaphor which sees them as so many different paths traversing a mountain in a variety of ways but all eventually reaching the summit of God's presence. In recent years, this enticing idea has resulted in a vast number of enthusiastic attempts to promote active expressions of unity by means of ecumenical movements and inter-faith events.

One notable example was a Day of Prayer for World Peace held at Assisi, Italy on 20 October 1986. Organized by Pope John Paul II, it drew together 130 religious leaders, including the Archbishop of Canterbury (representing the worldwide Anglican Communion), leading representatives of Buddhism, Islam, Shinto, Sikhism and Zoroastrianism, the Dalai Lama (the spiritual ruler of Tibet, whose national religion, Lamism, is a mixture of Buddhism and animism), as well as snake worshippers, fire worshippers, spiritists, animists and a gentleman rejoicing in the name of John Pretty-on-Top, chief medicine man of the Crow Indians of Montana. Even if we assume that everyone attending the event was genuinely concerned for world peace, it is difficult to see how they could unite in praying about it. To whom were they praying? To the supreme, sovereign, yet loving God of the Roman Catholics and Anglicans? To some or all of Hinduism's millions of deities? To Islam's austere Allah? To the spirits of inanimate objects revered in Tibetan animism? To fire or snakes? To whatever object of worship commends itself to the Crow Indians? And how does one pray to Buddhism's ultimate principle or Zoroastrianism's spirit of light and goodness?

Nor is the problem solved by airy assertions about 'the universal fatherhood of God and the universal brotherhood of man', or by suggesting that each person could contribute meaningfully to the event by addressing the deity or deities of his or her choice, because the point of conflict that divides these religions from virtually all the others is not peripheral but central. Can God exist and not exist? Can there be a personal God who is not personal? Can it be true at one and the same time that there are millions of deities but only one? However well-meaning, Assisi was an exercise in absurdity.

The same kind of woolly thinking lay behind the 1996 decision to extend the interdenominational chapel at London's Heathrow Airport by including a non-denominational prayer room in which, as one of the resident chaplains put it, 'All faiths will feel at home.' This sounds suitably charitable, but the *Daily Telegraph*'s Patrick Sawer (perhaps unintentionally) unravels the whole thing: 'Airline passengers of all faiths will soon be able to settle their pre-flight nerves with a quiet word with *their own particular Almighty*'[59] (emphasis added). The problem sticks out like a sore thumb. Whether one 'Almighty' exists can be sensibly debated, but there cannot possibly be more than one, and perhaps the most appropriate thing to say about the idea that air travellers can invent one tailor-made to deal with their fear of flying is that it never gets off the ground!

Prince Charles seems to have missed this point when announcing in 1996 that in the event of his accession to the British throne he would envisage himself as 'defender of faith' rather than 'defender of *the* faith'. As journalist Janet Daley pointed out in the *Daily Telegraph*, 'You cannot defend all faiths — at least not at the same time — because each has beliefs that render those of the others false.'[60]

Even among those who might seem to share common ground, vagueness can render this unity virtually useless. One is reminded of the wry comment of the British writer Malcolm Muggeridge after attending the Fourth Assembly of the World Council of Churches in Uppsala, Sweden in 1968: 'At Uppsala, as one clearly saw, they were able to agree about almost anything because they believed almost nothing. They reminded me of a pub turn-out in my youth, with ten or a dozen drunks holding on to one another, swaying to and fro, but managing to remain upright. Alone, they would infallibly have fallen into the gutter... If ever in human history there was a non-event, this was it.'[61]

There are obviously social and moral issues on which the followers of many religions can usefully unite, but this can hardly validate their religion, because these are issues on which the same stance could be taken by many atheists. To illustrate this very simply, and at a personal level, an act of kindness by an atheist is just as valuable to the beneficiary as one performed by a theist, but this is a long way from saying that all religions are essentially the same. The simple fact is that all religions *cannot* be the same. To be so, they would need to be united on the very issue where they are most widely divided: the existence and nature of God.

There is no 'lowest common denominator' which allows all conceptions of deity to be both inclusive *and valid*. As R. C. Sproul rightly says, 'There are only two possible ways to maintain the equal validity of all religions. One is by ignoring the clear contradictions between them by a flight into irrationality; the other is by assigning these contradictions to the level of insignificant non-essentials.'[62] It is one thing to defend the right of everyone to freedom of worship; it is quite another thing to say that everyone's choice is right. Toleration is not the same as validation. Theoretically, all religions may be wrong; logically, they cannot all be right. The idea that all religions are the same is clearly ridiculous, but it is no more sensible to say that they point in the same direction or lead to the same destination.

12.

Deviations

In the last chapter we took an overview of some of the world's major religions in order to pinpoint their conceptions of deity and to show how these were at odds with the model on which this book is based. Yet this by no means gives us the whole picture. In the last 150 years or so, hundreds of religious cults have sprung up, attracting millions of followers. One authority suggests that their membership is nearly 100 million, over two per cent of the world's population,[1] but even this is likely to be a conservative estimate.

Many of these groupings are too small to be included here, but it will be helpful to examine the basic doctrines of some of the best-known. As with the overview of religions, these are listed in alphabetical order rather than by age or size.

Mind over matter

'The Church of Christ, Scientist' is a diverting label for a cult that is neither Christian nor scientific. It was founded in the United States in 1879 by the intensely religious but psychologically unstable Mary Anne Morse Baker Glover Patterson Eddy (more simply known as Mary Baker Eddy) who had been greatly influenced by Phineas Quimby, a hypnotist and self-styled healer who called his principles 'Christian Science'.

In 1875, Eddy published a book called *Science and Health*, followed eight years later by *Key to the Scriptures*. Her claim that they came to her by divine revelation and that she was 'only a scribe echoing the harmonies of heaven in divine metaphysics'[2] is tarnished by evidence that the material needed to be corrected by a hired clergyman.

Christian Science teaches that there is no reality except mind or spirit, and insists that sin, disease and death are mere illusions, a concept that sits strangely with the fact that Mary Baker Eddy wore dentures and spectacles and frequently had morphine injections.

Christian Science's theology is plainly pantheistic. Mary Baker Eddy defined God as 'a divine whole, an all-pervading intelligence and love, a divine, infinite principle'[3] and asserted that 'God is identical with nature.'[4]

Light from the East?

The Divine Light Mission was founded in 1960 by the Indian guru Shri Hans Ji Mahoraj. Its present leader is Guru Mahoraj Ji, who in 1966, at eight years of age, announced himself as 'the Perfect Master' and encouraged people to recognize, obey and adore him. There was an immediate and widespread response to his claims and by 1970 he was addressing a crowd of almost two million in Delhi and declaring, 'I will establish peace in this world.'[5]

After he had moved his home to the United States and begun to indulge in a luxurious and extravagant lifestyle, funded by his disciples and numerous business enterprises, his mother disowned him and declared his older brother, Bal Bhagwan Ji, to be the legitimate 'Perfect Master'. This produced a breakaway movement, but the Divine Light Mission regrouped and expanded and now claims to have upwards of five million followers worldwide. Mahoraj Ji claims to be the exclusive channel of spiritual truth to mankind and 'the treasure house of unlimited happiness and peace'.[6] His doctrine of deity is a form of pantheism in which he sees God as nothing more than cosmic energy.

Pot-pourri

EST (Erhard Seminars Training) was established in 1971 by Werner Erhard — he changed his name from John Paul Rosenberg — a one-time encyclopaedia and used-car salesman whose 'enlightenment' came while driving along a Californian highway. Erhard had previously experimented with Scientology, Zen Buddhism, hypnosis, yoga and at least five other disciplines for transforming human life, and elements of many of these are woven into his system.

EST has been called 'one of the most popular and influential self-improvement groups flourishing in the vacuum of Western society'.[7] It consists of sixty hours of intensive training which promise 'a transformation — an essential shift in the context in which the facts, circumstances and positions of one's life are held'.[8]

In EST there are no absolutes and no system of truth: 'Wrong is actually a version of right. If you are always wrong you are right.'[9] One writer underlines the philosophy behind this absurdity by saying, 'In EST, you are God.'[10] Erhard's pantheistic and humanistic principles are clear: 'I would prefer someone who is ignorant to someone who believes in God... To pay attention to personality is to pay attention to illusion or effects. That's all there is, there isn't anything but spirituality, which is just another word for God, because *God is everything*.'[11]

The saffron robes

The International Society for Krishna Consciousness, commonly known as Hare Krishna, was founded in the 1950s by Abhay Charan De Bhaktivedanta Swami Prabhupade, who abandoned his wife and five children to devote himself to the worship of the Hindu god Krishna.

Krishnaism has a long and tortuous history. The Hindu sect of Vishnuism taught that Vishnu, the supreme God, manifested himself to mankind as Krishna but, in the fifteenth century, Chaitanya Mahaprabhu turned this doctrine on its head and taught that Krishna was the supreme God who had revealed himself in the form of Vishnu. The essential difference between pure Hinduism and both sects is that Hindu's god is impersonal and unknowable, whereas Vishnuism and Krishnaism both encouraged interaction with personalized aspects of deity.

In 1965, at seventy years of age, Prabhupade left India for the United States and within a few weeks the International Society for Krishna Consciousness (ISKCON) was founded in New York. It has grown rapidly ever since and its devotees, easily recognizable in their saffron robes, spend hours every day in chanting, worship and the study of the Hindu scriptures, *Bhagavad-Gita*, and in soliciting donations from the public to fund their movement.

Doctrinally, Hare Krishna is a mishmash of ideas. It embraces Hindu traditions of both monism and pantheism, and has elements of both polytheism and monotheism. Its followers live in buildings housing numerous Hindu gods (which must be washed every day in a mixture of cows' urine, milk and rose-water) yet they acknowledge Krishna as the supreme deity, living on a heavenly planet, though they believe him to be unable to understand man and devoid of feelings towards humanity.

Unreliable Witnesses

The Jehovah's Witnesses form one of today's most active cults. Originally called 'Russellites' after their founder Charles Taze Russell (1852–1916), a Pittsburgh haberdasher, they were briefly known as Millennial Dawn, then the International Bible Students' Union, then the Watchtower Bible and Tract Society, which is currently the cult's official name.

Russell had an orthodox theistic upbringing, but while still a teenager became fascinated by ideas relating to the precise date of the end of the world and by pyramidology. He also became convinced by an atheist that man had no soul and therefore faced no judgement after death. Russell poured himself into the propagation of his developing ideas, and the movement grew very rapidly, mainly through a series of books and a weekly sermon which was syndicated in some 2,000 newspapers in North America and Europe.

However, Russell's fame was marred by several court cases which exposed his blatant dishonesty, and in 1913 his wife obtained a divorce, the court finding his conduct towards her 'so insulting and domineering' as to 'make her condition intolerable'.[12] After his death, Russell's place was taken by Joseph Franklin Rutherford, whose output included twenty major books and who claimed divine revelation for the name 'Jehovah's Witnesses' ('Jehovah' is the anglicized version of an ancient Hebrew name of God). Russell had taught that the world would come to an end in 1874 (later revised to 1914), but Rutherford found ways of blurring the issue and subsequent teaching has produced a whole string of failed prophecies. Russell's idea that out of the whole of humanity only an élite group of 144,000 (he and his followers) would receive eternal life also had to be revised when the cult's membership went over that number.

It has been said that the cult is 'probably the most authority-ridden religious body in the world',[13] with not the slightest deviation allowed from its rigid teaching. This claims to be 'God's sole collective channel for the flow of biblical truth to men on earth',[14] denies both plurality within the

Godhead and the immortality of the human soul, and refuses to allow cult members to receive blood transfusions. Outwardly, the movement gives the appearance of being fairly orthodox, but its theology unravels when one begins to get into the detail, and perhaps as many as three million people are pinned to what one of Russell's contemporaries described as 'the destructive doctrines of one man, who is neither a scholar nor a theologian'.[15]

Salt Lake and gold plates

With a worldwide membership in excess of six million, the Church of Jesus Christ of Latter-Day Saints, better known as <u>Mormonism,</u> is the most pervasive cult in the Western world.

In 1820, an American teenager named Joseph Smith claimed to have had a vision in which God forbade him to join any of the established Christian churches. In another vision three years later, an angel called Moroni is said to have told him that God's true message for humanity was written in Egyptian hieroglyphics on gold plates buried at Palmyra, New York. Four years later he was given permission to unearth the plates, and claimed that when he did so he was able to translate the writing. Eventually entitled *The Book of Mormon*, his work was published in 1830 and in the same year Smith and five friends founded 'The Church of Christ', later to be given its present, longer title.

Its membership grew rapidly, but opposition forced the group to move to Illinois, where Smith was shot dead in 1844 while being held in police custody on a number of serious charges. His place was taken by Brigham Young, who convinced most of the Mormons that he was their rightful leader and eventually led them on a trek of over 1,000 miles to Salt Lake, arriving in the summer of 1847. Young was an organizational genius, and supervised the emergence of Salt Lake City, which became part of Utah when it was incorporated into the United States in 1896.

Mormonism is popularly associated with polygamy (Joseph Smith had seventeen wives and Brigham Young twenty-five). The official church renounced the practice in 1890, but a significant breakaway group still holds to it. Although Mormonism claims to be God's only true church, Joseph Smith's pretensions have long since been shown to be fraudulent and the *Book of Mormon*, the integrity of which was said to have been guaranteed by fifteen angelic visits during its translation and printing, and which was described by Joseph Smith as 'the most correct of any book on earth',[16] has been altered about 3,000 times since its first edition.

Mormons believe in many gods and teach that Mormon males have the potential of attaining eternal divinity. Joseph Smith stated that God 'has a body of flesh and bones as tangible as man's',[17] and lived on earth as a human being before progressing to his present state. The finitude of Mormonism's God is underlined by another of Smith's statements: 'I am going to tell you how God came to be God. We have imagined and supposed that God was God from all eternity. I will refute that idea and take away the veil so that you may see.'[18]

The spiritual supermarket

With millions of followers, the New Age Movement is one of the fastest-growing social phenomena in the world today, though its title hides the fact that its principles go back for centuries and can be found in many ancient occult traditions and mystical religions.

The present movement exploded on to the scene during the 1960s, when many people, spiritually restless and disillusioned by traditional assumptions about life, the nature of reality and the future of the planet, became attracted to the vision of a new age in which cultural, religious and political differences would give way to universal unity and love. Borrowing terms from astrology, New Age looks beyond the futility and failure of the present so-called 'Age of Pisces' to the 'Age of Aquarius', beginning around the year 2000, when humanity will eventually achieve 'holistic health'. New Age proclaims itself as 'a bridge to the future and the hope of humanity',[19] and looks to the total restructuring of civilization into a One-World Federation in which geographical, ethnic and cultural boundaries are obliterated and humanity realizes its own divinity.

Marilyn Ferguson, author of the New Age manifesto *The Aquarian Conspiracy: Personal and Social Transformation in the 1980s*, makes it clear that the New Age Movement sees itself as much more than just another cult: 'Broader than reform, deeper than revolution, this benign conspiracy for a new human agenda has triggered the most rapid cultural realignment in history. This great, shuddering, irrevocable shift overtaking us is not a new political, religious, philosophical system. It is a new mind — the ascendance of a startling world-view.'[20] New Age teaches that in order to bring this about there needs to be a 'Consciousness Renaissance' in which man achieves higher states of 'god-consciousness' until he sees that 'Heaven is here on earth every day.'[21]

This idea is reinforced by another overlapping branch of New Age, a 'Quantum Leap of Consciousness', the gist of which can be gathered by this quotation from promotional material: 'We are on the brink of a new age, a whole new world. In the twinkling of an eye, mankind's awareness, our collective consciousness, is going to make an instant quantum leap into heaven. Everything will change in a flash of Divine light. Get ready. Your heavenly heritage awaits. Come on in; the water's fine... He who chooses life is found.'[22]

With no central organization controlling agenda, activities or doctrine, New Age has become a confusing cocktail of philosophies and phenomena including paganism, monism, pantheism, theosophy, reincarnation, mythology, astrology, spiritism, witchcraft, occultism and yoga. Once a high-profile New Age spokesman, Randall Baer underlines the pantheistic element: 'In a neo-paganistic revival, New Agers bow to the god they think is contained in every aspect of creation. Stars are god, trees are god, planet Earth is god, dolphins are god, everything is god.'[23] New Age author Benjamin Creme confirms this: 'In a sense there is no such thing as God. And in another sense there is nothing else but God — only God exists... All is God. And because all is God there is no God.'[24] Among tools and methods used for inducing altered states of consciousness in order to contact and interact with higher forces and energies Baer lists New Age music, self-hypnosis, chanting, New Age deep relaxation exercises, psychedelic drugs, subliminal tapes, guided creative visualization and crystal power techniques.[25] Eileen Campbell, Editorial Director of the New Age publisher Aquarian Press, opens up an even larger can of worms: 'As an umbrella term, New Age encompasses aromatherapy, astrology, Bach Flower remedies, biofeedback, channelling, crystals, colour healing, dowsing, earth mysteries, EST, firewalking, geomancy, guided imagery, herbal medicine, hypnosis, I Ching, iridology, isolation tanks, Jungian psychology, ley lines, meditation, magic, mysticism, massage, numerology, palmistry, psychic phenomena, past life therapy, radionics, rebirthing, reflexology, runes, Shaminism, shiatsu, tarot, tai chi, UFOs, Wicca, yoga and Zen.'[26]

Put very simply, New Age invites people to embark on the ultimate 'power trip' and to make up their own menu for life, choosing their own truth, their own values, their own reality. Baer calls it 'spiritual humanism' and says, 'The cornerstone of this humanism is the belief that man is divine in nature, and is therefore essentially "God" or an enlightened "God-man".'[27] When actress Shirley MacLaine embraced the New Age idea, ABC Television created a five-hour, two-part mini-series, allowing her to share her exotic notions with millions. She could not be more specific about New Age's humanism: 'Each soul is its own God. You must never worship anyone or anything other than self, for you are God. To love self is to love God.'[28] Standing on the Pacific shoreline, she affirmed her personal creed with her well-publicized chant: 'I am God! I am God! I am God!' If the exuberant lady is to be believed, her present exalted status is the climax of several previous visits to our planet, as she claims to have committed suicide on the legendary island of Atlantis, served as a handmaid to Nefertiti, Queen of Egypt (c. 1372 – 1350 B.C.), posed as a model for the nineteenth-century French artist Henri Toulouse-Lautrec and been raised by elephants after her parents died.

In chapter 5, we quoted Jeremy Rifkin in the context of evolution's claims to provide a platform for human progress. As Rifkin is a well-known New Age spokesman, it is worth reminding ourselves of what he says: 'We no longer feel ourselves to be guests in someone else's home and therefore obliged to make our behaviour conform with a set of pre-existing cosmic rules. It is our creation now. We make the rules. We establish the parameters of reality. We create the world, and because we do, we no longer feel beholden to outside forces. We no longer have to justify our behaviour, for we are now the architects of the universe. We are responsible to nothing outside ourselves, for we are the kingdom, the power and the glory for ever and ever.'[29]

This all sounds very exhilarating, but as John Benton points out, it begs some fundamental and inescapable questions: 'How can this possibly work out in real life? For example, how can two people who both believe that they are God possibly live together? When there is an argument, as real life dictates there will be, who backs down? Which one can possibly admit to being wrong if they are both supposed to be inherently good? Because a person believes that he or she is God, does that mean that this person believes that he or she must dominate in all relationships with other people, or indeed ignore the laws of a country and its judiciary? And how does this "God" account for things like a headache or, worse still, cope with cancer? Can "God" do nothing about death?'[30] As soon as one begins to apply its philosophy to the real world, the New Age Movement is shown to be nothing more than a massive metaphysical fraud, whose God is nothing more than the product of hyperactive imagination.

Mission improbable

Shree Rajneesh is another Indian guru who left his normal life behind to seek spiritual enlightenment and share it with the world. Having assumed the name 'Bhagwan' ('God'), he moved to the United States in 1981 and established the Rajneesh Foundation, paying six million dollars for a site in Oregon which he developed as 'a world centre of enlightenment'.

One writer has described his teaching as 'a mixture of Eastern mysticism, American if-it-feels-good-do-it philosophy and holistic medicine',[31] yet, with millions of followers, he is one of the most influential players on today's religious scene. His techniques include meditation, Sufi dancing, rebirthing, hypnosis and psycho-drama.

For Rajneesh, 'God', 'Void', 'Silence', 'Brahman' and 'Beingness' are used synonymously to describe the whole of reality. His theology is essentially pantheistic, Rajneesh himself stating, 'The very world, the very being is God.'[32]

Little gods

There is no official doctrine of God in the Church of Scientology, a quasi-philosophical cult founded in 1949 by the American science-fiction writer L. Ron Hubbard and recognized in the United States as a religion for tax purposes in 1993. Hubbard's own writing on dianetics, his self-made system of therapy aimed at clearing the mind, assumes some kind of impersonal deity, but Scientology's members are free to believe what they choose about whatever divine being may exist.

Among Scientology's exotic doctrines is one which says that human beings, animated by immortal spirits called Thetans, willed themselves into existence trillions of years ago and later brought the material world into existence. Now trapped in their physical bodies, people need to be released to resume their original god-like status. For fees which sometimes run to £200 per hour, the cult's ministers are available to help in this exciting enterprise. A year-long 'special briefing course' is also on offer for upwards of £15,000.

Hubbard died in 1986. His obituary in *The Times* called him 'a highly influential figure among the myriad inventors of magical and religious systems who have appeared in modern times',[33] and his bizarre beliefs are embraced by perhaps as many as twenty million people worldwide, in spite of the fact that, in pursuing the church's aggressive recruitment programme, members have been involved in a long list of criminal offences.

God in the ashtray

The Theosophical Society was founded in New York in 1875 by a Russian spiritist medium, Madame Helena P. Blavatsky, who claimed to be the first person to receive messages from 'adepts', said to be 'beings perfected spiritually, intellectually and physically, the flower of human and all evolution'.[34] Theosophy, which literally means 'wisdom of God', was later popularized by Mrs Annie Besant. The daughter of an English clergyman, she had also been involved in spiritism and had a conviction for publishing immoral literature.

Both leaders were impressed by aspects of Buddhist and Hindu teaching and took on board certain elements of Eastern mysticism, including the concepts of reincarnation, karma and nirvana. Theosophy's doctrine of man says that he has three souls, Buddahi, Manas and Kamamepha, while its doctrine of God is a mixture of monism and pantheism: 'We believe in a universal divine principle, the root of all, from which all proceeds, and within which all shall be absorbed at the end of the great cycle of being.'[35] The abstract nature of Theosophy's deity was established by its founder: 'We reject the idea of a personal ... God.'[36] When someone suggested that if her pantheistic ideas were true, God would be in the ash of a cigar just as he is in the soul of men, she replied, 'To be sure, God is in the ash just as in my soul.'[37]

Reluctant religion

The International Meditation Society, better known as Transcendental Meditation, or TM, is yet another cult to come out of an Indian background.

After several failures, Mahesh Prasad Warma, later known as Maharishi Mahesh Yogi, found widespread recognition for his meditation techniques in the 1960s, when he enlisted a number of famous devotees, including the British pop music group, the Beatles. The Maharishi, as he is commonly called, had moved to the United States in 1959, when the process began of setting up a world plan of 350 teaching centres of the Science of Creative Intelligence to be established in major cities around the world.

Although professing to be non-religious, TM is a thoroughly Hindu meditation technique, using secret Sanskrit words as mantras to connect with the spirit world. In 1977, a New Jersey Federal Court, having considered over 1,500 pages submitted by the movement, barred the teaching of TM in state schools and ruled that it had 'failed to raise the slightest doubt as to the facts or as to the religious nature of the teaching'.[38]

Although its founder claims that TM is the only way to salvation and success in life, its claims have proved vacuous, and they ignore the dangers inherent in cultivating altered states of consciousness. TM's theology is thoroughly pantheistic: 'Everything in creation is the manifestation of the unmanifested absolute impersonal being.'[39] It also promotes the confusing idea that 'Each individual is, in his true nature, the impersonal God.'[40]

Moonshine?

One of today's best-known cults is the Unification Church. Founded in Korea in 1954 by Sun Myung Moon and popularly known as 'the Moonies', the church claims over three million members in over 120 countries, though these figures have been disputed by objective observers.

Moon claims that in 1945 he had a titanic struggle with the forces of evil, from which he emerged as 'the absolute victor of heaven and earth ... and the Lord of creation'.[41] From then on, his pronouncements were to be given precedence over all other religious teaching. The church's ultimate authority is *Divine Principle*, in which Moon wrote 'hidden truths presented to you as a new revelation'.[42] Said to be worshipped by his followers as endorsement of his own claim to be the Messiah, Moon told *TIME* magazine, 'God is now ... establishing a new religion, and this religion is the Unification Church.'[43] Elsewhere, he went further and said, 'God is living in me and I am the incarnation of himself. The whole world is in my hand and I will conquer and subjugate the world,'[44] claims which fit somewhat uneasily with a prison record tied to bigamy, adultery, social disorder and tax evasion.

Dualism (with each part of existence having a dual aspect), reincarnation and universalism all have a part in the creed of the Unification Church. The God posited in this book does not.

Fillimores and followers

'Unity' is at least the fifth title given to a cult founded in the United States in 1889 by Charles and Myrtle Fillimore, who added a number of Eastern concepts, such as reincarnation, to ideas adopted from Phineas Quimby and Christian Science.

Myrtle Fillimore died in 1931 and her husband in 1948. The leadership of Unity then passed to their two sons and the movement now has a world-wide membership of about two million.

Unity's emphasis is on the importance of material and earthly happiness and it teaches that 'No one need be poor.'[45] Its world-view is basically Gnostic (believing that what is spiritual is good and what is material is evil) and pantheistic, asserting that 'God is all and all is God.'[46] Unity rules out any idea of a personal relationship with God; in Charles Fillimore's words, 'God is not loving. God does not love anybody or anything.'[47]

Body and soul

Although yoga is most popularly thought of in the Western world as being no more than a series of therapeutic physical exercises, it is very much more for millions of devotees in the East and elsewhere. The word 'yoga' stems from the Hindi verb *yuj*, which has the basic meaning 'to bind together', and the philosophy has the general idea of union with the absolute. Its roots lie deep in ancient Indian philosophies and religions and it maintains many of their ideas, including that of reincarnation.

For many, yoga is a complete way of life, with very strict physical, mental and moral regimens. In the Western world it has gained acceptance in medical, psychological, educational and religious circles through disciplines such as 'centring', relaxation therapy, self-hypnosis and creative visualization. These are designed to lead to 'the realization of one's true "godhood" through an inward meditative journey that finally locates the ultimate source of everything within the human psyche'.[48] As to its theology, yoga is wholeheartedly pantheistic, seeing God as being 'the ultimate substratum of all there is'. [49]

To recap . . .

For the last twelve chapters we have been seeking to establish the second proposition put forward in our introduction, namely that most people are atheists. Has the case been made out?

We began with a brief reference to animism (the worship of spirits said to inhabit natural phenomena) and polytheism (belief in a multitude of distinct and separate deities), two philosophies which are widely held today.

We then glanced at the 'Golden Age' of Greek philosophy and at early expressions of monism, naturalism, scepticism and pantheism, all of which still attract millions of people nearly 3,000 years later.

As we skipped to the sixteenth and seventeenth centuries we came across further philosophies current in today's world: deism, which reduces God to the status of a cosmic clockmaker; rationalism, which sees God as nothing more than an innate philosophical idea; empiricism, which leaves the whole idea of God up for grabs; and a further development of scepticism, which rules out everything supernatural.

A century later came Kant, who shut God away behind his famous 'wall', rendered him unknowable, and paved the way for countless numbers of people in every generation since to disown him altogether.

Moving on to the nineteenth century, we heard Schleiermacher providing a model for those who speak of God not as a living person but as 'the ground of all being'; we listened to Hegel promoting panentheism, in which God is 'no longer a Being above and beyond this world'; we saw how the development of Darwin's ideas on evolution gradually rubbed God out of the picture; we heard Feuerbach speaking of God as being nothing more than wish-fulfilment and listened to Nietzsche shouting, 'God is dead'.

Turning to the twentieth century, we observed how previously held ideas developed not only into atheistic existentialism but also into the barrenness of nihilism, both of which begin by denying God's existence. We saw how many today embrace materialism and deny any other absolute beyond physical matter. We noticed the claims of dualism, which suggests not one deity but two, neither possessing supreme power. We caught the drift of secularism, which says that this time and world are all there is. We looked at the hopeless void of determinism, in which both God and man become zeros. We recognized the tremendous grip of secular humanism, which puts man firmly in God's place. We took a specific look at classical, philosophical atheism, the complete and consistent denial of God; and on the other hand, we noticed the appeal of agnosticism, which deceives count-less millions of people into believing that they are sitting on the fence.

This led us to a brief overview of nine major world religions, none of them subscribing to our working definition of God and together claiming vast numbers of followers. Finally, in this chapter, we have looked at four-teen religious cults, all with eccentric definitions of deity and together rep-resenting another 100 million people.

Our working definition of God says that he is a unique, personal, plural, self-existent, eternal, independent, transcendent, immanent, perfect, holy, loving, spiritual Being, the Creator, Sustainer and Ruler of the entire uni-verse and the righteous Judge of all mankind.

Using that definition, the proposition that most people are atheists is surely difficult to deny? Most of the remainder of this book will be taken up with examining some of the specific problems they face.

13.

Matter matters

Late in the evening of 23 March 1997, I stood in the Suffolk garden of my friends Philip and Dorothy Miller. The night was crystal clear and, as we were out in the country, there was none of the diffusion one gets from city lights. Thousands of stars put on a glittering display above our heads, but our eyes were focused on just one thing — the Hale-Bopp comet. Some twenty-five miles across (about the same as Greater London), it was a riveting sight as it hurtled towards the sun at 100,000 miles an hour, trailing its bluish tails of dust and plasma. Two thoughts made the experience awe-inspiring. The first was that the last terrestrial sighting of Hale-Bopp had been some 4,000 years ago, in 2214 B.C. The second was that, although it was brilliantly clear to the naked eye and seemed tantalizingly close, the comet was some 122 million miles away.

No place like home

The British philosopher George Moore once said that the first and primary aim of philosophy was to give 'a general description of the *whole* of this universe'.[1] One has only to grasp something of the sheer immensity of the physical cosmos as we know it to realize that this is a pretty big preliminary step!

At this point in our study, we turn to look at some of the problems faced by atheists, of which none is more fundamental than the very existence of all known matter. For obvious reasons, we begin with the earth on which we live. For all our familiarity with it, its form, dimensions and characteristics continue to fascinate. It is common knowledge that the earth has a diameter of about 8,000 miles (more accurately, 7,926.5 miles at the equator and 7,900 miles through the north and south poles) and a circumference of nearly 25,000 miles. Its total surface area is about 197 million square miles, of which about two-thirds is water. Once every twenty-four hours it spins on its north-south axis, which is tilted at an angle of 23.45 and once every year, travelling at about 66,500 miles an hour, it orbits the sun, 93 million miles away.

Bewilderingly rich as it is in natural resources, which enable it to sustain thousands of varieties of vegetable and animal life, there is, as far as we know, no place remotely like it in the entire universe. Yet for all its size, complexity, richness and energy, our earthly home is hardly more than an inconspicuous dot on the cosmic map. In his record-breaking best seller *A Brief History of Time*, the British physicist Stephen Hawking, Lucasian Professor of Mathematics at Cambridge University (a post once held by Sir Isaac Newton), and arguably the best-known contemporary scientist in the world, calls it 'a medium-sized planet orbiting around an average star in the outer suburbs of an ordinary spiral galaxy, which is itself only one of about a million million galaxies in the observable universe'.[2] This statement obviously raises a fascinating question: what else is out there?

Neighbours

The story is told of a lecturer who had just finished addressing an audience on astronomy. At the end of the lecture a little old lady stood up and said, 'What you have told us is rubbish. The world is really a flat plate supported on the back of a giant turtle.' The scientist smiled condescendingly and asked, 'What is the turtle standing on?', to which he got the reply: 'On the back of a larger turtle.' 'But what holds up the larger turtle?' the lecturer asked. Not at all disconcerted, the lady retorted, 'That's easy. It's turtles all the way down'! We may be a very long way from being able to see the complete picture, but we can certainly do better than that!

Earth is the fifth largest of nine planets revolving around the sun in elliptical orbits. The word 'planet' translates the Greek *planetes* (wanderer), the description the ancient Greeks gave to any celestial body which did not remain in a fixed position. In order of their mean distance from the sun, the eight other planets are as follows:

- *Mercury,* some 35.9 million miles away, is closest to the sun. It is also one of the smallest, with an equatorial diameter of 3,024 miles, and the fastest-moving, spinning on its axis three times during every eighty-eight-day orbit.
- *Venus,* which is just over sixty-seven million miles from the sun, has a diameter of 7,520 miles. Mercury and Venus are known as the 'inferior' planets because they are closer to the sun than the earth, and orbit the sun more rapidly.
- *Mars,* the first of the 'superior' planets, is slightly over 141 million miles from the sun and has a diameter of 4,213 miles. Space probes to Mars have confirmed an extinct volcano three times as high as Mount Everest, as well as a number of massive canyons, one of which is four times the size of the Grand Canyon.
- *Jupiter,* by far the largest of the planets, has a diameter of 88,700 miles. Weighing nearly 318 times as much as the earth, Jupiter is at a mean orbital distance of 483 million miles from the sun.
- *Saturn,* nearly 885 million miles from the sun, has a diameter of 74,980 miles. It would be the clear winner in a planetary 'beauty contest' because of its intriguing halo of hundreds of rings, some of them 160,000 miles wide.
- *Uranus,* nearly 1,780 million miles from the sun, has a diameter of 31,750 miles. A unique feature of this planet is that its rotational axis is tilted at an incredible 98°, with the axis of its magnetic field inclined at 60° to its rotational axis. These factors cause Uranus to spin or rotate clockwise, whereas all other planets rotate anticlockwise. These phenomena led one wag to suggest it must have been designed by a committee!
- *Neptune,* 2,788 million miles from the sun and 30,950 miles in diameter, comes next.
- *Pluto* is the furthest planet from the sun, at a mean orbital distance of 3,658 million miles, though the eccentricity of its orbit, which at three miles per second takes 248 years to complete, has sometimes brought it several million miles 'inside' that of Neptune. Pluto is by far the smallest of the planets, with an estimated diameter of just 1,416 miles, and its inclined orbit and nearby moon give it the appearance of a double planet.

All the planets except Mercury and Venus have other bodies, generally known as moons, which orbit around them. Mars has two, Jupiter sixteen, Saturn at least twenty-three, Uranus eighteen, Neptune eight and Pluto just one. Of course the earth also has one — the moon — which in space terms is virtually on our doorstep. On 24 November 1997, an international team of scientists beamed laser light to the moon from telescopes in Texas, Hawaii, France, Germany and Australia, bounced it off mirrors placed on the moon by Apollo astronauts, and measured the distance by marking the time the laser pulses took to make the round trip. The precise time taken was 2.6525830468690 seconds, enabling the scientists to announce that at 16.425145 seconds past 3.42 p.m. on that day the distance from Earth to the moon was 15,654,023,458 inches. This will be sufficiently accurate for our purposes!

With a diameter of 2,155 miles, the moon is much larger in relation to Earth than any of the other planets' satellites are to them (with the exception of Pluto) and many astronomers think of it as Earth's companion planet. The moon takes 27.3 days to complete one revolution of its orbit, and exactly the same time to spin once on its axis, a phenomenon known as captured or synchronous rotation.

Further afield

Other natural objects swirling around within the planetary system include untold numbers of asteroids (small planets revolving around the sun, mainly between the orbits of Mars and Jupiter), thousands of comets (relatively insubstantial concoctions sometimes described as 'dirty snowballs'), and countless millions of loose pieces of matter, sometimes no larger than a grain of sand, which burst into flame when they enter the earth's atmosphere. These are known as meteors or shooting stars, and those which manage to reach the ground are called meteorites.

Yet all the bodies we have noted so far are dominated by the sun, which gives the solar system its name. With a diameter of 864,400 miles and a volume over one million times that of Earth, the sun is truly massive compared to our home planet. The visible surface of the sun has a temperature of 6,000 degrees Celsius, rising to at least fourteen million degrees Celsius at the core. As its hydrogen is converted into helium, the energy released keeps the sun 'shining', with about one billionth of this energy reaching

Earth. The sun loses four million tons of its mass every second, yet such is its stupendous size that it still has sufficient fuel to last another 5,000 million years. These statistics are already mind-boggling, yet it is no more than an average-sized star in the 'suburbs' of the Milky Way, a gigantic disc-shaped galaxy which stretches some 621,000 million million miles across. This single galaxy contains about 100,000 million stars, the nearest of which is about twenty-three million million miles away.

Elsewhere...

That takes care of our galaxy — but there are others. The nearest of these are the twin accumulations of stars known as the Magellanic Clouds, yet even these are so far away that we need to make their distance a little more manageable by switching from miles to light years. Light travels at just over 186,282 miles per second, or about 5,878,000 million miles per year. At this speed we would reach the sun in just eight minutes, but to reach the Magellanic Clouds, the nearest star clusters associated with our own galaxy, would take 170,000 years, and they are therefore said to be 170,000 light years away.

Another thirty galaxies complete what astronomers often refer to as the 'Local Group', even though one of them, the Andromeda Spiral, is some 2.2 million light years away from us.

Beyond the Local Group, the measurements of distances become more difficult, and the values less accurate, but astronomers already know of galaxies more than 13,000 million light years away. As a point of comparison with these staggering statistics, Sirius, which appears to be the most brilliant evening star, is just 8.8 light years away, the familiar Polaris, or North Star, is 350 light years away, and one of the spiral galaxies in the Ursa Major (Great Bear) constellation is seven million light years away. Yet even these figures give only a one-dimensional picture, as they tell us nothing about the number of galaxies (estimates range from 100,000 million upwards), nor about the size of their stars. The largest stars are the red giants such as Beteleguese in the Orion constellation. It is over 200 million miles in diameter, while the largest known object in the universe has been labelled DA240 and is six million light years in extent. Nor do they tell us anything about the number of stars in each galaxy. Only about 6,000 stars are visible from Earth with the naked eye, but one writer has suggested that if the known stars were to be divided up among the world's present population, each person would receive two trillion of them.[3] Another has said that if each star were represented as a pea, and the peas were then spread over the whole of Great Britain, they would make a pile a quarter of a mile high.[4] In less graphic terms, the total number of stars is currently put at 10,000 million million million.

In 1996, I came across a newspaper advertisement which offered readers an opportunity to name a star, in the constellation of their choice, to celebrate an event such as a birthday or a wedding, or for any other reason.[5] Those taking up the offer would be sent a computer chart showing the star's location, a certificate of registration and copyright, and several other goodies, all for £39.95 (including packing and postage). There seems little danger of Universal Star Listing running out of stock!

This is all breathtaking enough to the layman, but even the experts are still being surprised and excited by the new discoveries they are making. Until very recently it was thought that the furthest objects in space were quasars, mysterious sources of light upwards of ten billion light years away and variously said to be exotic stars, exploding galaxies or collisions between black holes (star remnants with such massive density and gravitational pull that not even light can escape from their surfaces); but in 1996 the Hubble Space Telescope found six massive objects that appear to be fourteen billion light years away.[6]

Even one year can make a huge difference to our understanding of the universe. At the beginning of 1997 the *Daily Telegraph's* science correspondent reported that at a meeting of the Royal Astronomical Society in London new data had been released showing that the universe is ten per cent larger than we thought.[7] Later that year, astronomers found what might be the brightest star in the Milky Way. The Pistol Star (so named because of the shape of its surrounding dust cloud) is about 25,000 light years away, measures between 180-250 million miles in diameter, and glows with the intensity of ten million suns.[8] Towards the end of the same year, Hubble showed that a small patch of sky which appeared pitch black when viewed through other telescopes was packed full of the most distant galaxies ever discovered. The *Sunday Times* reported that 'Several hundred galaxies in this deepest view of the universe have since been identified in a piece of night sky no bigger than the thumbnail of an outstretched arm.'[9] Finally, and still in 1997, it was announced that the Next Generation Space telescope was due to be launched in 2005, with the ability to see objects 400 times fainter than those currently being picked up by Hubble.[10] Sadly for the little old lady featured near the beginning of this chapter, no turtles have yet been sighted.

The big questions

'Space is big. Really big. You just won't believe how vastly mind-bogglingly big it is. I mean you may think it is a long way down the road to the chemist, but that's just peanuts to space.'[11] The author of the best-selling *Hitchhiker's Guide to the Galaxy* is right and, as we have already seen, the magnificent immensity of the natural world is truly amazing. Interviewed for the *Observer* in 1995, Richard Dawkins told Andrew Billen that he experienced 'a colossal sense of awe and wonder at the universe',[12] and it is difficult to imagine how anyone can avoid being affected to some degree by what we see. It is just as difficult to avoid some fundamental questions clamouring to be answered as we contemplate the world around us. What exactly is it that we are seeing? How does it work? Has it always existed? If not, when and how did it come into being? Will it go on for ever? If not, when and how will it come to an end? Why is it there at all? Does it have any meaning or purpose? Even touching briefly on these will take a long chapter and involve a certain amount of technical discussion, but I have kept things as clear and straightforward as possible. Ducking the issues altogether was not a sensible alternative.

Questions as to what we are seeing and how it all works might appear to have been answered by now. We have the technology to access information billions of light years into space. We can discuss the contents of black holes and the constituent elements of the stars. We have identified particles and antiparticles, molecules, atoms, protons, neutrons, quarks, electrons, positrons, photons, mesons and neutrinos. Our understanding of the laws of nature is vastly greater than it was even one generation ago, and physicists are enthusiastically pursuing the idea of a 'Theory of Everything'. Peter Atkins even goes so far as to say that 'There is nothing that cannot be understood.'[13] However, his fellow Oxford academic Keith Ward exposes this as enthusiastic blarney: 'This is a remarkably bold statement of faith. It goes well beyond all available evidence, since at present *there are millions of things we do not understand*, including the fundamentals of quantum physics'[14] (emphasis added). Having shown that there is absolutely no way in which, as humans, we could ever have an understanding of, for example, other universes that might exist, Ward adds this teasing comment: 'So it seems, after all, that if everything can be understood, only a God could understand it, so Atkins is committed to theism. In fact, I am rather puzzled by the fact that he does not seem to realize it.'[15]

Nobody has made a greater contribution to the twentieth century's understanding of the universe than Albert Einstein. Until his paper *On the Electrodynamics of Moving Bodies* was published in 1905, people believed in a stable, infinite, eternal universe in which heavenly bodies moved in completely predictable patterns, straight parallel lines would never meet and time was absolute. Einstein turned all these ideas upside down and, by the time he had added his general theory of relativity in 1915, he had shown that the universe was finite, not infinite, that straight parallel lines may eventually bend because of the curvature of space and that, in certain circumstances, time slows down. Yet, for all his greatness, Einstein recognized that he was an intellectual pygmy when faced with cosmic issues. Again and again he acknowledged a wisdom beyond any to which humanity could aspire. On one occasion he wrote, 'My religion consists of a humble admiration of the illimitable superior Spirit who reveals himself in the slight details we are able to perceive with our frail and feeble minds. That deeply emotional conviction of a superior reasoning power, which is revealed in the incomprehensible universe, forms my idea of God.'[16] Elsewhere he said, 'Everyone who is seriously interested in the pursuit of science becomes convinced that a spirit is manifest in the laws of the universe — a spirit vastly superior to man, and one in the face of which our modest powers must feel humble.'[17] Atheists attempting to understand the universe (or even, like Peter Atkins, claiming it is possible to do so) show an absence of the humility that properly characterizes true science.

Einstein was on much safer ground, and this is now being recognized. Noting that in contrast to the 'jaunty confidence' of nineteenth-century scientists, the present mood is 'chastened', the British physicist Donald MacKay wrote, 'Particularly in the physical sciences, cocksure dogmatism has given place to a much more cautious and tentative way of presenting conclusions. Arrogant postures may occasionally be struck by a few exponents of the newer sciences, such as molecular biology and anthropology; but these attitudes are widely deplored by fellow scientists as atypical.'[18]

Strictly speaking, even the first question posed in this section remains unanswered: what exactly is it that we are seeing? In the 1930s the Swiss-

American astronomer Fritz Zwicky noted that a mysterious, invisible force seemed to be preventing some galaxies from taking part in the expansion of the universe. He eventually decided that this force was the gravity of unseen 'dark matter' to be found in and around galaxies, and more sophisticated research has since confirmed the existence of this 'dark matter' on a massive scale. Theories of the origin, size and eventual end of our universe depend extensively on this 'dark matter', yet what it is, and how much of it exists, is still unknown. This is just one of the factors which, in spite of the vast accumulation of data now at our disposal, makes the composition of the universe what *Sunday Telegraph* Science Correspondent Robert Matthews calls 'a vast cosmic conundrum'.[19] Towards the end of his book *Exploring The Galaxies*, Cambridge astronomer Simon Mitton confirms that so much remains unanswered: 'How can we arrive at a picture of the total contents of the universe if we do not even know what fraction of the whole each of the observable forms occupies? ... Can we be sure that the great clusters of galaxies are the most important components of the universe? *We are even today not at the end of accumulating an elementary picture of the true contents of the universe,* although we can paint parts of the picture in exquisite detail'[20] (emphasis added).

World without end?

The ancient Greeks believed that the world sat fixed in the centre of the entire universe, with the sun, moon, planets and stars orbiting around it in concentric spheres, and this static arrangement, which had neither beginning nor end, was reflected in other cultures. The Hungarian philosopher of science Stanley Jaki notes that Hindu belief, Mayan culture and Chinese philosophy, along with almost every other form of pre-scientific thought, had 'a deep-seated aversion to time and history'.[21] Even when Galileo took his historic look at the planets through his telescope in 1609, confirming Copernicus' theory that the earth and other planets revolve around the sun, there was still no scientific evidence that the universe was anything other than unchanging. The stars were still believed to be other suns like our own, spread evenly throughout an infinite universe.

Nor did this particular picture change radically when the eminent British scientist Sir Isaac Newton published his theory of gravity in 1687. Newton realized that if stars gravitationally attract one another, they would also eventually collapse together unless the universe was infinitely large, with an infinite number of stars, so that the gravitational attraction of each star would be balanced out by the gravitational force of every other star. Yet even with this new view of things, there was still no proof that the universe was not static. Before the twentieth century, as Stephen Hawking reminds us, 'It was generally accepted that either the universe had existed for ever in an unchanging state or it had been created at a finite time in the past more or less as we observe it today.'[22]

Einstein and the cosmic balloon

The picture changed dramatically in 1915, when Einstein published his general theory of relativity, which unexpectedly predicted that cosmic space expands. The idea that the universe was not static or eternal was initially so distasteful to Einstein that two years later he added a 'cosmological constant' to his equations, a hypothetical force which compensated for the cosmic expansion and made the universe static once more. It was left to two other men, the Russian physicist Alexander Friedmann and the Belgian cosmologist Georges Lemaître, to develop the original thrust of Einstein's general theory of relativity and propose in the 1920s that the universe *was* expanding. Their next step was to have far-reaching consequences. They reasoned that if the universe is expanding over time, as Einstein's original equations indicated, then at some point in the past all the matter in the universe must have been packed closely together into an infinitesimally small and infinitely dense point. This dramatic conclusion produced the first version of what is now universally known as the 'Big Bang theory' and proposed that, contrary to the static model of the universe which had prevailed for centuries, the universe had a definite starting-point in time and that it has been changing ever since.

The next breakthrough was in 1929. Working at the Mount Wilson Observatory in California, the celebrated American astronomer Edwin Hubble came to the conclusion that, no matter where you look in the sky, all other galaxies are moving rapidly away from us. The significance of this can be appreciated by picturing the universe as an inflating balloon. If we mark a spot anywhere on the balloon to represent our galaxy, and any number of other spots to represent other galaxies, and then inflate the balloon, all the other spots will move away from the first spot. Although Hubble was unfamiliar with the Big Bang model, his observations have confirmed experimentally that we live, not in a static universe, but in one which is expanding. Where did this leave Einstein? After meeting Hubble and Lemaître at the Mount Wilson Observatory and examining the new evidence, he confessed that adding the 'cosmological constant' to his general theory of relativity was 'the biggest blunder' of his life.

The discovery that the universe is expanding threw up a whole new raft of questions for astronomers, two of which were fundamental: How fast is the universe expanding? Is the rate of expansion slowing down or speeding up? Even a layman can see that the answers to these two questions would seem to determine the ultimate end of the universe as we know it. If the cosmic expansion is rapidly slowing down due to the gravitational attraction between the galaxies, the universe will eventually stop expanding, then collapse once again into the tightly packed point from which it emerged. On the other hand, if the expansion is vigorous enough to overcome the deceleration caused by gravity, then the universe will simply go on expanding for ever. There is a third option: if the expansion of the universe is perfectly balanced by the deceleration caused by gravity, the universe will expand for ever, but with the rate of expansion gradually slowing down and never quite coming to an end.

Although scientists do not yet know with certainty which of these three possibilities best describes the likely fate of our universe, both astronomical observations and mathematical models such as the one proposed in 1998 by Stephen Hawking and his fellow Cambridge physicist Neil Turok point to the third one, which indicates that our universe is at what scientists call 'critical density'.[23]

World without end — or beginning?

Not everyone welcomed the Big Bang concept, some disliking the idea that the universe had a beginning because it strongly implied a supernatural creation. In 1948 Sir Fred Hoyle helped to formulate the 'steady-state' theory. This maintained that the universe was infinite and eternal and that the entire cosmic process was kept in balance as matter simply sprang into existence out of nothing at a regular rate to replace the matter which had 'died' through expansion. The biggest problem with this view is that it violates the First Law of Thermodynamics, sometimes known as the law of conservation of mass and energy. This fundamental law, which Isaac Asimov called 'the most powerful and most fundamental generalization about the universe that scientists have ever been able to make',[24] states that matter and energy can neither be self-created nor destroyed. Matter can be converted into energy and energy into matter, but their sum total must remain the same, as expressed in the well-known dictum *Ex nihilo, nihil fit* ('Out of nothing, nothing comes'). Hoyle's 'steady-state' theory, proposing that matter was continually created out of nothing and without any cause, clearly violated this law. There has never been any real evidence to support it, and the philosopher William Lane Craig says that 'The steady state model has been abandoned by virtually everyone.'[25] The First Law of Thermodynamics clearly supports the idea that an expanding universe must have had a beginning but could not have created itself.

The Second Law of Thermodynamics, which states that any physical system becomes less ordered and more random over time, provides another piece for the cosmic jigsaw. Applied very simply and generally, it means that our entire universe is running down. As the rotation of the planets and their moons slows down, and as stars (and whole galaxies) burn themselves out, the matter in our universe is becoming more and more disorganized as its energy is dissipated. The logical consequence of this is that the universe cannot be eternal. If it were, the stars would have ceased to shine long ago and all the energy in our universe would have long since been evenly spread throughout space. At the same time, this suggests that if the universe is becoming less ordered, it must have been more ordered in the past, and have had a highly ordered beginning.

In the same year that Hoyle advanced his 'steady-state' theory, the Russian cosmologist George Gamow took things one step further. He published a paper explaining that, as matter becomes hotter whenever it is compressed to a greater density, the early universe must have been extremely hot, and must have been unimaginably so when the entire universe was packed closely together into an infinitesimally small and infinitely dense point. Gamow then went on to say that, although the universe would have cooled as it expanded, the incredible heat released by the Big Bang would have left an afterglow of cosmic background radiation as a 'thermal signature'. In 1965, the American physicists Arno Penzias and Robert Wilson first detected this cosmic background radiation, a landmark finding repeatedly confirmed by other scientists. The American scientist Michael Behe says that this discovery finally put the 'steady-state' theory 'out of its misery' and is taken by many to be 'the crowning glory of the Big Bang theory'.[26]

Another alternative on offer is the oscillating model, in which the universe 'expands, collapses back again, and repeats the cycle indefinitely'.[27] Crudely put, this model sees these events following each other in an endless sequence — Big Bang, Big Crunch, Big Bounce. This idea obviously holds great appeal for the atheist, as it avoids the need for the universe to have an absolute beginning, but it runs headlong into the fact that it contradicts the known laws of physics. Professor Beatrice Tinsley, of Yale University, explains that in an oscillating model, 'Even though the mathematics *says* that the universe oscillates, there is no known physics to reverse the collapse and bounce back to a new expansion.'[28] Even scientists supporting the oscillating model have admitted, 'There is no understanding of how a bounce can take place... We have nothing to contribute to the question of whether and/or how the universe bounces.'[29]

Despite the evidence to the contrary, others beside Hoyle have continued to resist the idea that the universe is not eternal and have produced a range of theoretical alternatives. One suggests that the portion of the universe which we observe is simply a bubble in an infinite universe. Another says that our universe is one of an infinite number of universes. In 1982, Stephen Hawking and the University of California cosmologist James Hartle employed what they called 'imaginary time' to support yet another theory although, as Hawking explains in *A Brief History of Time*, this 'imaginary time' is simply a mathematical device which he and Hartle used to construct a model of the universe.[30] As they see it, the universe exists in both imaginary time and in the real time in which we live and in which the Big Bang marked its beginning. In imaginary time, which is the underlying reality behind our universe's existence in real time, 'the universe would be completely self-contained and not affected by anything outside itself. It would neither be created nor destroyed. It would just *be*.'[31] According to this model, there was no precise moment at which the universe began, as time was transformed into a kind of space. This is a mind-stretching concept but, as Robert Matthews reminds us, the problem with Hawking's proposal of an infinite universe is that *'There is not a scrap of evidence that this idea is right.'*[32]

The same can be said of other alternatives to the concept of a non-eternal universe. No observational evidence has been found to support any of them, and none of them can even be experimentally verified. As the American biochemist Michael Behe points out, 'They do science no good. Their only use is as an escape hatch from the supernatural.'[33] It seems quite clear that Einstein's general theory of relativity, the laws of thermodynamics and numerous astronomical observations (such as those made by Hubble and Penzias and Wilson) all point to a universe which is not eternal and static, but to one which had a definite beginning and is changing over time.

BANG — and here we are!

Most of today's scientists subscribe to one form or another of the Big Bang model. The one most widely held currently is known as the inflationary version, which says that the early universe underwent a period of very rapid expansion, inflating at an increasing rate rather than at the decreasing rate we observe today. This is important because it would explain how the force of gravity was able to form galaxies, stars and planets. It is also important to note that the universe did not expand into *existing* space after the Big Bang, but rather it was space itself which expanded outwards, the cosmic expansion *creating* space as it went along. A broad summary of what is said to have happened runs like this:

1. Between ten and twenty billion years ago (fifteen billion is the current favourite) all the matter of the universe was concentrated in a speck of matter smaller than a pinhead, and commonly defined as a 'singularity'. The temperature was so hot that no atoms or even subatomic particles could exist in it, and the matter was so dense that the laws of physics would not have applied. It is therefore commonly accepted that any description of the universe can go back only until a point one ten-millionth of a trillionth of a trillionth of a trillionth of a second (10^{-43}) after the Big Bang — that is 0.0000000000000000000000000000000000000000001 of a second!

At this point, the universe underwent a period of cosmic inflation, and this rapid, accelerating expansion created ripples (the so-called 'quantum fluctuations') in the fabric of space. This ensured that matter was not evenly distributed in the newly expanding universe, preparing the way for the later formation of galaxies, stars and planets.

This cosmic inflation also ensured that the resulting universe would be at critical density, so that it would keep expanding for ever, though the rate of expansion would slow down endlessly.

2. After one ten-billionth of a trillionth of a trillionth (10^{-34}) of a second, the temperature had dropped below 1,000 trillion trillion(10^{27}) degrees, enabling quarks (the components of protons and neutrons) and electrons to form. By this time, the cosmic inflation had already ended, having expanded the universe a million trillion trillion (10^{30}) times, and from this point on the expansion was gradually slowed down by the pull of gravity.

3. At about one-ten-thousandth of a second into the life of the universe, the temperature had cooled to 10^{15} degrees, enabling quarks to bind together to form protons and neutrons, which (along with electrons) are the building blocks of the atom.

4. After some three minutes, the temperature had dropped to about a billion degrees, enabling protons and neutrons to bind together and form the nuclei of hydrogen and helium, the component elements of stars. At this stage, the universe was about the density of water, and would continue to expand and cool in this state for about 300,000 years.

5. After 300,000 years, the temperature fell to 3,000 degrees, allowing electrons to bind together with the hydrogen and helium nuclei to form hydrogen and helium atoms.

6. Over the course of the next billion years, gravity began to pull clusters of hydrogen and helium atoms together to form the first quasars and stars, leading eventually to the formation of the Milky Way and other galaxies.

7. Another five billion years on (about five billion years ago), the burning of hydrogen and helium in the interior of stars produced heavier elements such as carbon, nitrogen, oxygen and iron, which were dispersed by stellar winds and supernova explosions. Some of these elements produced new stars, while others condensed around stars to create planets. In this way, the system of planets orbiting our sun was formed, planet Earth becoming one of these.

8. Two billion years later (about three billion years ago) our planet had produced a suitable atmosphere and sufficient water to sustain life.

Even this brief overview shows the essential part which gravity would have played in the formation of the universe as it exists today. In *Wrinkles in Time*, American astrophysicist George Smoot points out, 'The evolution of the universe is effectively the change in distribution of matter through time — moving from virtual homogeneity in the early universe to a very lumpy universe today, with matter condensed as galaxies, clusters, superclusters, and even larger structures.'[34] This was possible only because of the brief period of cosmic inflation in the life of the early universe, which created ripples in the fabric of space, ensuring that matter was not evenly distributed.

Had the universe remained perfectly homogeneous, no galaxies, stars or planets would have formed. However, the early rapid acceleration caused some areas to be denser than others and over time these denser areas, with their somewhat stronger gravitational fields, attracted surrounding matter to form stars and galaxies, while the less dense areas became voids of space. When the first atoms were formed, a burst of radiation, released in all directions, created a 'snapshot' of how matter was distributed in the early universe. Using the Cosmic Background Explorer (COBE) satellite, George Smoot and a team of scientists from Berkeley University, California, discovered this radiation, which slotted perfectly into current Big Bang ideas. Although some of their conclusions have occasionally been disputed, Michael Turner, of the University of Chicago, declared that they had found 'the Holy Grail of cosmology',[35] while Stephen Hawking called it 'the most important discovery of the century, if not all time'.[36]

Loose ends

Despite all the apparent confirmations of the current Big Bang model, many significant questions remain. Some of them are fundamental: Where did the original material come from? What do we mean by 'original'? What was the source of such energy? When did time begin? What came before 'time zero'? Although the theory has held up remarkably well, new information in the future could force even its strongest supporters to rethink their view of how the universe was formed. After all, until Galileo peered through his telescope in 1609, man's observation of the heavens fitted the centuries-old view that the earth was the centre of the universe. Until Hubble discovered the expansion of the universe in 1929, the long-standing idea that the universe was static seemed to have been confirmed by scientific observation. As Stephen Hawking points out, 'No matter how many times the results of experiments agree with some theory, you can never be sure that the next time the result will not contradict the theory. On the other hand, you can disprove a theory by finding even a single observation that disagrees with the predictions of the theory.'[37]

The fact is that many aspects of the Big Bang model, still only a few decades old, need further examination. For example, astronomers estimate that as much as 90% of the universe could be made up of invisible 'dark matter', whose make-up is unknown, leading the British astrophysicist David Wilkinson to comment, 'It is somewhat humbling to realize that for all our discoveries we still do not know what 90% of the universe is made of!'[38] Many calculations about the Big Bang rely on estimates about the amount and content of this 'dark matter', and if present estimates changed by even 10%, Big Bang equations would produce a universe vastly different from the one in which we now live. Stephen Hawking goes so far as to say that it would disprove the idea altogether.

Other key components quoted in the Big Bang model are also no more than estimations. To understand the size of the universe, astronomers have to know the distance to the furthest known galaxies. The best they can do is to measure the distance to nearby bright stars in our own galaxy and then 'leapfrog' from similar stars to nearby galaxies, and from there to more distant galaxies, a procedure plagued by the fact that galaxies are thought to evolve at different rates. George Smoot calls the estimation of galaxies' distances based on their brightness 'a risky manoeuvre, based on the unproven assumption that all galaxies of the same type have similar absolute brightness'.[39]

Another crucial element of the Big Bang model which relies heavily on estimation is the rate of the universe's expansion, which is based on how fast other galaxies are moving away from ours. We know that stars are grouped together to form galaxies, and that galaxies group together to form clusters of galaxies, which in turn are grouped into superclusters, but we have no clear understanding of the way in which the expansion velocity of the galaxies is retarded by their gravitational fields. As Berkeley professor and popular science writer Timothy Ferris notes in *The Whole Shebang*, 'Until astronomers understand these effects, there will continue to be troubling uncertainties in basing estimates of the cosmic expansion rate on the velocities of nearby galaxies.'[40] To put this another way, the rate of expansion depends on the value of what has become known as the Hubble Constant. However, this 'Constant' has been given a wide variety of values over the last sixty years. The problem is therefore that the value of the constant is constantly changing!

Stephen Hawking provides other reasons for caution. In *A Brief History of Time* he writes, 'Today scientists describe the universe in terms of two basic partial theories — the general theory of relativity and quantum mechanics. They are the great intellectual achievements of this century. The general theory of relativity describes the force of gravity and the large-scale structure of the universe, that is the structure on scales from only a few miles to as large as a million million million million (1 with twenty-four zeros after it) miles, the size of the observable universe. Quantum mechanics, on the other hand, deals with phenomena on extremely small scales, such as a millionth of a millionth of an inch. *Unfortunately, however, these two theories are known to be inconsistent with each other — they cannot both be correct*'[41] (emphasis added). This certainly underlines the limitations of the generally accepted Big Bang model.

In 1997, BBC Television ran a six-part series entitled *Stephen Hawking's Universe*, in which the physicist developed his belief that we are on the verge of discovering 'the Theory of Everything', a total explanation of the universe that could be expressed in a single line of mathematics. The programmes pointed to the launch of the satellite Planck Explorer early in the twenty-first century as being a vital tool in achieving this goal, but one did not have to listen too carefully to the voice-overs to hear the bets being hedged: 'The *hope* is that soon we *may* be able to see the heat of the early universe in enough detail to answer our questions about how it was formed. *If* the data is detailed enough, it *could* offer observational evidence that *may* clarify how everything began.'[42] Commenting in the *Sunday Telegraph* on the attempt of the series to have us believe that we are on the brink of knowing the origin and nature of the universe, Robert Matthews wrote, 'It is a trick that the series attempts with the skill of an estate agent [selling] a house with dodgy foundations. It directs our attention towards the well-appointed theories and the spacious extent of current cosmological knowledge, while keeping quiet about the nasty cracks in the scientific cellar and the intellectual doors that won't shut properly.'[43]

These reservations alone (and there are many others) are sufficient to remind us that, for all their popularity in certain circles, Big Bang ideas constitute a model, not a verifiable theory. The earliest moment of the universe's formation of which others claim to have experimental verification is some three hundred thousand years *after* the Big Bang, when the radiation released by the formation of the first atoms was detected by the COBE satellite in 1992. Yet even COBE's findings are fudged, and everything thought to have happened before that time, especially in the initial moments of the Big Bang, is *pure speculation and mathematical conjecture.*

Simply put, it is a matter of guesswork, and that being the case we would be wise to listen to Plato's advice to Socrates: 'As being is to becoming, so is truth to belief. If then, Socrates, amid the many opinions about the gods and the generation of the universe, we are not able to give notions which are altogether and in every respect exact and consistent with one another, do not be surprised. Enough if we adduce probabilities as likely as any others; for we must remember that I who am the speaker and you who are the judges are only mortal men.'[44]

Natural causes?

In 1999, the BBC ran an eight-part television series under the title *Planets*, exploring many facets of their composition and behaviour. Reviewing the first programme in the series, the *Daily Mail's* Shaun Usher wrote, 'The real forehead-wrinkler for agnostics or atheists was how, from microscopic material one modern scientist compared with cigarette smoke, the planets came about.'[45] A good question — but there is an infinitely greater 'forehead-wrinkler': where did the 'cigarette smoke' come from in the first place? Even if we were to accept that the universe as we now know it evolved in some incomprehensible way, we would not have begun to address the question of how the necessary 'ingredients' came to exist.

As we have already seen, the First and Second Laws of Thermodynamics prove as certainly as science can prove anything that the universe could not have begun itself but that it did have a beginning. As we go backward in time, we reach the point where energy and matter (to say nothing of time and space) must have come into existence. If an eternal, infinite, transcendent and omnipotent God is ruled out, where can science turn to explain their origin? Science is by definition the study of what *is*, but it cannot go any further back than the moment at which the laws on which it leans began to operate. Edgar Andrews puts it simply and well: 'No matter how close to the instant of origin one may be able to press the scientific model of the cosmos, it remains impossible for such an explanation to be applied at or before the zero time point. Thus it follows that *science, even at its most speculative, must stop short of offering any explanation or even description of the actual event of origin*[46] (emphasis added).

This seems pretty obvious, but it does not prevent hard-core atheists from suggesting a number of ingenious alternatives to God. Although *Ex nihilo, nihil fit* is a fundamental axiom of natural law, Peter Atkins blithely kicks it into touch and assures us that, for all its immensity and brilliant diversity, the entire universe is 'an elaborate and engaging rearrangement of nothing'.[47] He does this by endorsing what has become known as the quantum fluctuation hypothesis, in which, to quote Atkins in *Creation Revisited*, 'space-time generates its own dust in the process of its own self-assembly'.[48]

It has been suggested, with some justification, that 'Nobody understands quantum mechanics,'[49] and in a recent issue of *New Scientist*, David Darling takes an earthy swipe at what Atkins and others are suggesting: 'What is a big deal — the biggest of them all — is how you get something from nothing. Don't let the cosmologists try to kid you on this one... "In the beginning," they will say, "there was nothing — no time, space, matter or energy. Then there was a quantum fluctuation from which ..." Whoa! Stop right there. You see what I mean? First there was nothing, then there is something. And the cosmologists try to bridge the two with a quantum flutter, a tremor of uncertainty that sparks it all off. Then they are away, and before you know it they have pulled a hundred billion galaxies out of their quantum hats.'[50] This points out the basic self-contradiction in the quantum fluctuation hypothesis. It talks about beginning with 'nothing' but then, as Keith Ward points out, demands 'an exactly balanced array of fundamental forces, an exactly specified probability of particular fluctuations occurring in this array, and an existent space-time in which fluctuations can occur'. As Ward wryly adds, 'This is a very complex and fine-tuned nothing'![51]

Atkins describes the idea that 'time brought the points (non-spatio-temporal entities) into being, and the points brought time into being' as 'the cosmic bootstrap',[52] but how can a cause bring about an effect without already being in existence? Keith Ward easily exposes the fallacy here: 'If time brought points into being, time must already have existed before the points. And if the points brought time into being, they must have existed before time. But to say that two things have each existed before the other is a simple contradiction. Since contradictions convey absolutely no information, the cosmic bootstrap turns out to be vacuous. *Far from being an ultimate explanation, it says nothing at all*'[53] (emphasis added).

C. S. Lewis tells of hearing about a woman who considered that in 1944 her son narrowly escaped death at the Battle of Arnhem because the bullet which just missed him was following the laws of nature. When Lewis began to permutate all the factors involved, including the person who fired the bullet, the atmospheric conditions and the earth's gravitation, he came to see that none of these factors were laws; they were facts or events. Commenting on this, Lewis wrote, 'The dazzlingly obvious conclusion now arose in my mind: *in the whole history of the universe the laws of nature have never produced a single event* They are the pattern to which every event must conform, provided only that it can be induced to happen. But how do you get it to do that? How do you get a move on? The laws of nature can give you no help there... The laws are the pattern to which events conform: the *source* of events must be sought elsewhere.'[54]

Chance? Necessity?

In the absence of theories which can be tested, some people have suggested that the universe exists by chance, for no reason at all. In the eighteenth century, the arch-sceptic David Hume taught that some things were just brute facts and had to be accepted without any further explanation. There are those who apply this approach to the Big Bang model, but most scientists reject this view, mainly because its simple name conceals a very complex series of events, every one of which demands some kind of explanation. Keith Ward reminds us, 'The whole of science proceeds on the assumption that a reason can be found for why things are as they are,'[55] and adds, 'It seems odd to think that there is a reason for everything except for that most important of them all — that is, the existence of *everything*, the universe itself.'[56] Nothing daunted, Peter Atkins goes so far as to say, 'We can even begin to discern how the universe could come from absolute nothing as time induced (by chance) its own existence,'[57] but this is less than helpful. Chance is not an explanation so much as an abandonment of explanation.

Others suggest that, as the laws of physics are as they are, they developed out of sheer necessity. For example, Stephen Hawking says that if his proposal of a self-contained universe is correct, then God (assuming he exists) would have had no choice in how to construct that universe;[58] he would have been constrained by the necessary operation of the laws governing the universe. Whatever its attractions for some, this idea runs into serious problems. One is the question of infinite regression. How far back can we go in searching for ultimate reality? In 1983 the Russian physicist Andrei Linde proposed that our universe expanded in the Big Bang as a bubble arising out of the space-time of a pre-existing universe due to a particular configuration of scalar energy fields.[59] A fascinating idea — but where did the scalar fields or the pre-existing universe come from? Stephen Hawking's idea of a self-contained universe also seems to play down the need for any divine involvement: 'So long as the universe had a beginning, we could suppose it had a creator. But if the universe is really completely self-contained, having no boundary or edge, it would have neither beginning nor end: it would simply be. What place, then, for a creator?'[60] Yet this still fails to avoid the problem of infinite regression, as it depends on the presumption of a previous system.

Another fundamental problem is that of the limitations of knowledge. As Keith Ward asks, 'To say that the existence of the universe is necessary is to say that no other universe could possibly exist. But how could one know that without knowing absolutely everything? Even the most confident cosmologists might suspect that there is something they do not know. So it does not look as though the necessity of this universe can be established.'[61] To make the point as simply as possible, the idea that the universe came to exist by necessity can be proved only if we know everything there is to know. In the absence of omniscience, the 'necessity' model must remain just that — a model.

Referring to the story about the little old lady's view that the universe is a flat plate resting on an infinite number of turtles, the English theoretical physicist Paul Davies, currently Professor of Natural Philosophy at the University of Adelaide, came to this conclusion: 'The search for a closed logical scheme that provides a complete and self-consistent explanation for everything is doomed to failure... We will inevitably end up with turtle trouble: either an infinite regress, or a mysterious self-explaining turtle, or an unexplained ring of turtles. There will always be mystery at the end of the universe.'[62] No sensible theist will deny the element of mystery here, but is it less scientific (or sensible) to believe that the universe came into being by design than to believe that it just happened?

God's fingerprints?

One of the oldest and most enduring cases for the creation of the universe by God is the teleological argument (from the Greek *telos*, the end or goal), popularly known as the argument from design. Just as a product points to a producer (the cosmological argument) so, it is argued, design points to a designer.

As long ago as 390 B.C., the Greek historian Xenophon quoted Socrates as saying, 'With such signs of forethought in the design of living creatures, can you doubt that they are the work of choice or design?'[63] Plato argued that the two things that 'lead men to believe in the gods' were the argument from the soul and the argument 'from the order of the motion of the stars, and of all things under the dominion of the mind which ordered the universe'.[64] Aristotle said that a race of men who had always lived underground and who saw the wonders of the night sky for the first time 'would have judged ... that all these marvellous works are the handiwork of the gods'.[65] The Roman orator and statesman Cicero (106–43 B.C.) asked, 'When we see a mechanism such as a planetary model or a clock, do we doubt that it is the creation of the conscious intelligence? So how can we doubt that the world is the work of divine intelligence?'[66] When Greek Epicureans claimed that the universe was nothing more than a chance accumulation of atoms, the third-century scholar Minucius Felix gave them very short shrift: 'I feel the more convinced that people that hold this universe of consummate artistic beauty to be not the work of divine planning, but a conglomeration of some kind of fragments clinging together by chance, are themselves devoid of reason and perception.'[67]

The argument from design was the last of the famous 'Five Ways', which Thomas Aquinas put forward in the thirteenth century, not to prove God's existence, but to demonstrate that reason was capable of pointing in God's direction. Noting order and goals in nature, he wrote, 'Their behaviour hardly ever varies, and will practically always turn out well; which shows that they truly tend to a goal, and do not merely hit it by accident. Nothing that lacks awareness tends to a goal, except under the direction of someone with awareness and understanding; the arrow, for example, requires an archer. Everything in nature, therefore, is directed to its goal by someone with understanding, and this we call "God".'[68]

Some of the greatest scientists in history have seen the universe as God's handiwork. Nicolaus Copernicus (1473–1543), whose writings on astronomy set down some of the most significant discoveries in history, described what he saw as 'this divine work of the great and noble Creator'.[69] The German astronomer Johannes Kepler (1571–1630), the father of modern physical astronomy, spoke of being 'carried away by unutterable rapture'[70] at the ordered intricacy of the universe. Robert Boyle (1627–1691), the father of modern chemistry, saw the factors governing his particular discipline as 'the phenomena which [God] intended should appear in the universe'.[71] The universally acclaimed scientist Sir Isaac Newton (1642–1727) declared, 'This most beautiful system of the sun, planets and comets could only proceed from the counsel and dominion of an intelligent and powerful Being.'[72]

Paley's watch

The most famous and popular argument from design was put forward by the Anglican scholar William Paley (1763–1805), whose writings had long-lasting influence, especially as university textbooks. In his *Natural Theology*, published three years before his death, Paley presented a massive accumulation of evidence for design in nature to back up his famous 'watchmaker argument', the key part of which reads as follows:

In crossing a heath, suppose I pitched my foot against a stone, and were asked how the stone came to be there. I might possibly answer that, for anything I knew to the contrary, it had lain there for ever; nor would it, perhaps, be very easy to show the absurdity of this answer. But suppose I found a watch upon the ground, and it should be enquired how the watch happened to be in that place, I should hardly think of the answer which I had before given — that, for anything I knew, the watch might always have been there. Yet why should not this answer serve for the watch as well as for the stone? Why is it not as admissible in the second case as in the first? For this reason, and for no other, viz., that, when we come to inspect the watch, we perceive (what we could not discover in the stone) that its several parts are framed and put together for a purpose, e.g. that they are so formed and adjusted as to produce motion so regulated as to point out the hour of the day; that, if the different parts had been differently shaped from what they are, if a different size from what they are, or placed after any other manner, or in any other order than that in which they are placed, either no motion at all would have been carried on in the machine, or none which would have answered to the use that is now served by it...[73]

Later, he made the point of the analogy that, just as we infer a watchmaker from the design of the watch, so we should infer an intelligent designer of the universe: 'For every indication of contrivance, every manifestation of design, which existed in the watch, exists in the works of nature, of being greater and more, and that in a degree which exceeds all computation. I mean, that the contrivances of nature surpass the contrivances of art, in the complexity, subtlety and curiosity of the mechanism; and still more, if possible, do they go beyond them in number and variety: yet, in a multitude of cases, are not less evidently contrivances, not less evidently accommodated to their end, or suited to their office, than are the most perfect products of human ingenuity.'[74]

Endorsement of this idea has come from many unexpected sources. Voltaire, who was always bitterly opposed to the (Roman Catholic) church, nevertheless held strongly to its natural theology and wrote, 'I shall always be convinced that a watch proves a watchmaker, and that a universe proves a God.'[75] As we saw in chapter 2, Immanuel Kant mounted a merciless attack on the traditional proofs for God. Yet even though he dismissed the overall efforts of natural theology as 'null and void',[76] and flatly denied the possibility of arguing from nature to God, he confessed in his *Critique of Pure Reason* that 'by one glance at the wonders of nature and the majesty of the universe', man's reason is 'at once aroused from indecision of all melancholy reflection, as from a dream'.[77] In the same section he said of the argument from design, 'This proof always deserves to be mentioned with respect. It is the oldest, the clearest, and the most accordant with the common reason of mankind.'[78]

David Hume, who waded into the argument from design with even greater thoroughness and passion than Kant, never questioned that the natural world was an amazing and awe-inspiring phenomenon. In *Dialogues Concerning Natural Religion* he wrote, 'Look around the world: Contemplate the whole and every part of it: You will find it to be nothing but one great machine, divided into an infinite number of lesser machines, which again admit of subdivisions to a degree beyond what human sense and faculties can trace and explain. All these various machines, even their most minute parts, are adjusted to each other with an accuracy which ravishes into admiration all men who have ever contemplated them. The curious adapting of means to ends, throughout all nature, resembles exactly, though it much exceeds, the productions of human contrivance — of human design, thought, wisdom and intelligence.'[79] Elsewhere in the same book he wrote that 'A purpose, an intention, or design strikes everywhere the most careless, the most stupid thinker; and no man can be so hardened in absurd systems, as at all times to reject it.'[80]

Coincidental cosmos?

One of the words we use when referring to the universe, or the totality of the natural world, provides another pointer. Our English word 'cosmos' is the direct equivalent of the Greek *kosmos*, which is always connected with the idea of order. Its earliest use conveys the thought that there is an order of things in the natural world which corresponds to the order of human law. Later it came to mean the totality constituted by this order, giving us a picture of something 'well assembled or constructed from its individual parts'.[81]

Along the same lines, our English word 'cosmetic' is related to the Greek verb *kosmeo*, which includes meanings such as 'to order', 'to regulate' and 'to adorn'. This means that to refer to a chaotic, disordered cosmos is, strictly speaking, a contradiction in terms, at least when speaking of its original state. To speak of the cosmos is to imply that it came into being as a planned, arranged, integrated and harmonious whole, and science provides us with powerful pointers in this direction. (I might add that visitors to our home sometimes refer to my study as 'organized chaos', but this is because they fail to understand what I am doing!)

Nowhere is the ordered integration and unity of the cosmos more clearly demonstrated than in the fact that, in so far as we have been able to test them, the laws of science are consistent throughout all of time and space. Oxford scholar Richard Swinburne notes, 'There is ... this vast coincidence in the behavioural properties of objects at all times and in all places ... such as the fact that all electrons are produced, attract and repel other particles, and combine with them in exactly the same way at each point of endless time and space.'[82] Stephen Hawking confirms that 'The whole history of science has been the gradual realization that events do not happen in an arbitrary manner, but that they reflect a certain underlying order.'[83]

Is this remarkable harmony accidental or designed? Speaking during the interval in a BBC broadcast of Haydn's *Creation* from the Royal Albert Hall in London, Richard Dawkins said, 'The world looks as though it had been designed by a master craftsman — but it hasn't.' His basic thesis in *The Blind Watchmaker* is, 'We don't need to postulate a designer in order to understand life or anything else in the universe.'[84] There is nothing original in atheists asserting that the incredibly adaptive harmony we see all around us is a gigantic fluke, but this hardly qualifies as an explanation, let alone a scientific one. The Irish-born author Jonathan Swift (1667–1745), best known for his *Gulliver's Travels*, a satirical attack on the politics, philosophy and science of his time, coined an illustration which has often been quoted and adapted: 'That the universe was formed by a fortuitous concourse of atoms, I will no more believe than that the accidental jumbling of the alphabet would fall into a most ingenious treatise of philosophy.'[85] In a modern reworking of the same idea, the British author Rod Garner writes, 'We could suppose that the plays of Shakespeare came into being as a result of random typing by monkeys. But it is not a proposition that any reflective person would rush to defend. A more cogent explanation — and one we should note that is deeply embedded in human consciousness — is that the existence of a complex yet structured world leads us to the notion of a supreme cause or being. Creation supposes a creator.'[86]

Even scientists vehemently opposed to such an idea are forced to exercise their disciplines on the basis of faith in the existence of dependable order throughout the universe. When the American astronaut Neil Armstrong took his 'giant leap for mankind' on 20 July 1969 by becoming the first human being to set foot on the moon, he was able to do so only because every scientist and technician involved in the project — theist, agnostic and atheist alike — believed without question not only that the cosmos was governed by laws which could be trusted implicitly, but that their own judgement bore a true relationship to the orderliness of those laws.

Albert Einstein went so far as to say that true science demanded another dimension: 'To the sphere of religion belongs the faith that the regulations valid for the world of existence are rational, that it is comprehensible to reason.'[87] The British scientist Sir John Houghton is even more specific:

'The size, the complexity, the beauty and the order we find in the universe are expressions of the greatness, the beauty and the orderliness of the Creator. How does all this tie up with the scientific description of the world and the laws which we deduce from that description? The conflict which is often thought to be present between the scientific description and the description of God as Creator arises, I believe, from a misunderstanding of what both descriptions are about. Rather than a conflict there is a close connection; the order and consistency we find in our science can be seen as reflecting orderliness and consistency in the character of God himself.'[88]

As we implied earlier in this chapter, the Second Law of Thermodynamics demonstrates that the universe began in a highly ordered, energy-packed state, but that over time it has become increasingly disordered as its energy has dissipated. This clearly presents a problem to those relying on a 'natural' Big Bang origin, since random, purposeless events produce highly disorganized states of matter. If a drinking glass falls off a table and shatters on the floor, we can assume that the shards will never reorganize themselves into another highly organized system, such as a glass ornament, but will remain a disorganized mess. If the Big Bang was a random, chance event, the resulting universe would have started out at a high level of *disorder*, with little energy available to organize matter into the ordered structures we see all around us today. The British mathematician and physicist Roger Penrose, who worked with Stephen Hawking to develop our current understanding of black holes, computed the odds of the Big Bang producing by accident our ordered universe as opposed to a chaotic disorderly one, and estimated them as 'one in $10^{10^{123}}$'.[89] This number is so absurdly large that it is said to have more zeros than the total number of particles in the entire universe!

While atheistic thinking wrestles with the problem of overcoming these odds and finding a credible naturalistic explanation for this phenomenon, the concept of a tailor-made cosmos is steadily gaining ground in scientific circles. George Smoot quotes Princeton physicist Freeman Dyson as saying, 'The more I examine the universe and the details of its architecture, the more evidence I find that the universe in some sense must have known we were coming.'[90] Smoot himself adds, 'Nature is as it is not because it is the chance consequence of a random series of meaningless events; quite the opposite. More and more, the universe appears to be as it is because it *must* be that way; its evolution was written in its beginnings — in its cosmic

DNA, if you will.'[91] Paul Davies agrees: 'Through my scientific work I have come to believe more and more strongly that the physical universe is put together with an ingenuity so astonishing that I cannot accept it merely as brute fact... We human beings are built into the scheme of things in a very basic way.'[92] After developing this theme, Davies concludes, 'Far from exposing human beings as incidental products of blind physical forces, science suggests that the existence of conscious organisms is a *fundamental* feature of the universe. We have been written into the laws of nature in a deep and, I believe, meaningful way... I cannot believe that our existence in this universe is a mere quirk of fate, an accident of history, an incidental blip in the great cosmic drama. Our involvement is too intimate... *We are truly meant to be here*'[93] (emphasis added).

Fine-tuned facts

In recent decades, science has uncovered a growing mass of evidence in many areas to suggest that the universe has in some way been fine-tuned to sustain intelligent life on our planet, and in this section we will pull some of these together, beginning with the relationship between the relative strengths of the four fundamental forces of nature — gravity, electromagnetism, the strong nuclear force and the weak nuclear force.

The relationship between the relative strengths of the gravitational and electromagnetic forces is remarkable. In *God and New Physics*, Paul Davies states, 'Both forces play an essential role in shaping the structure of the stars. Stars are held together by gravity, and the strength of the gravitational force helps determine such things as the pressure inside the star. On the other hand, energy flows out of the star by electromagnetic radiation.'[94] For these two forces to balance out in such a way as to produce stars like our sun, the range of the relative strengths of these two forces must be very narrow. Physicist Brandon Carter points out that if gravity were altered by 'a mere one part of 10^{40}' (1 followed by forty zeros) 'stars like the sun would not exist, *nor, one might argue, would any form of life that depends on solar-type stars for its sustenance*'[95] (emphasis added). If gravity were even slightly stronger or weaker, planets could simply not form, but the forces of gravity and electromagnetism are perfectly balanced to sustain life in our universe. Interviewed in *Newsweek* magazine in 1994, physicist Edward Kolb of the Fermi National Accelerator Laboratory said, 'It turns out that "constants of nature", such as the strength of gravity, have exactly the values that allow stars and planets to form... The universe, it seems, is fine-tuned to let life and consciousness flower.'[96]

The strong and weak nuclear forces together determine how protons, neutrons and electrons interact in order to form atoms, the fundamental building blocks of matter, and again, their precise relationship is truly remarkable. Physicists have shown that if the strong nuclear force were even slightly weaker, atoms which require more than one proton in their nucleus would never have been formed. If this had been the case, the whole universe would have consisted of hydrogen, which has only one proton in its nucleus, and we would have none of the richness and diversity which surround us. On the other hand, if the strong nuclear force had been slightly stronger, all the hydrogen in the early universe would have converted to helium, and without the presence of hydrogen at a later stage stars could not have formed.

Minute variations in the weak nuclear force would have devastating effects on life, but it is at just the right level to allow hydrogen to burn at a slow and steady rate in the fiery interior of the stars. If this were not the case, the rate at which stars burn hydrogen would not be conducive to life, which depends on their energy. Stephen Hawking underlines the general issue of the precise balance of fundamental forces, and concludes, 'It seems clear that *there are relatively few ranges of values for the numbers that would allow the development of any form of intelligent life*[97] (emphasis added).

A second pointer towards fine-tuning is that the ratio of the proton and the electron, two of the three subatomic particles which form the atom, is also precisely that which enables life to subsist. Though physicists have no idea why the proton is 1,836 times more massive than the electron, science writer Fred Hereen points out that if the ratio of proton to electron mass were much different, 'the required molecules would not form, and there would be no chemistry, no life, and no physicists to wonder about it'.[98] If the difference in mass between a proton and the neutron (the third subatomic particle) were not twice the mass of an electron, the various atomic nuclei necessary to produce the elements of the universe could not have formed, a fact which leads Stephen Hawking to say, 'The remarkable fact is that the values of these numbers seem to have been very finely adjusted to make possible the development of life.'[99]

A third area indicating a cosmos tailor-made for life is the slight excess of matter over antimatter. Mirroring ordinary particles of matter, antipart-icles have the same characteristics as their counterparts, except that their electrical charges are opposite. While antimatter has been created in the laboratory, none has been found naturally, because whenever matter en-counters antimatter they annihilate each other. As George Smoot says, this means that had the universe come into being with equal amounts of matter and antimatter, 'a vast annihilation event would have occurred, leaving only very few particles of matter and antimatter in scattered, iso-lated remnants'.[100] Simply put, the universe as we know it would not exist.

Cosmologists who subscribe to the Big Bang idea believe that, immedi-ately after the event, particles of matter outnumbered those of antimatter to the extent that, when the process of mutual annihilation had taken place, exactly sufficient matter was left behind to form the universe we observe today. If too little matter had remained, there would not have been enough to form the universe; if too much had remained, the universe would have collapsed too quickly after the Big Bang to allow the formation of galaxies, stars and planets. As a variation as slight as about one particle per ten billion would have been enough to prevent our life-sustaining universe from coming into being,[101] we can certainly speak of fine-tuning!

A fourth pointer is found in the critical density of the universe. As we saw earlier, the gravitational attraction between the cosmic structures of the universe affects the rate of the universe's expansion, yet this expansion is balanced by the deceleration caused by gravity. If the density (the amount of matter) in the universe were greater, the gravitational attraction be-tween galaxies would cause the rate of expansion to slow down to such an extent that the universe would eventually stop expanding and collapse back in on itself. Nor, as Stephen Hawking tells us, would the density need to be much greater: 'If the rate of expansion one second after the Big Bang had been smaller by even *one part in a hundred thousand million million*, the universe would have recollapsed before it ever reached its present size'[102] (emphasis added). The balance between the effects of expansion and contraction is so precise that Paul Davies likens it to aiming at a target an inch wide on the other side of the observable universe and hitting the mark.[103]

On the other hand, if the universe had less matter (and therefore a lower density) its expansion would overcome the influence of gravity and the universe would expand for ever. However, as astronomers John Barrow and Joseph Silk point out, a universe expanding much faster than the critical rate 'would almost certainly be devoid of stars and galaxies and hence the building blocks of which living beings are made'.[104]

Yet current cosmology tells us that the universe is at critical density, containing precisely the right amount of matter to ensure that it will keep expanding for ever, even though gravitational deceleration will cause the rate of expansion to slow down endlessly without ever quite ceasing. Timothy Ferris says that we have no more reason to expect this critical density to have arisen by chance 'than to expect a pole vaulter's pole to remain standing, poised on its tip, for centuries following his vault'.[105]

Fred Hoyle is the unlikely guide to yet more evidence for fine-tuning. In the 1950s he discovered how carbon and oxygen, the two elements essential for life, were created through the burning of hydrogen and helium in the fiery interior of stars. As Timothy Ferris explains, the whole process hinges on the formation of the carbon atom: 'To make one takes three helium nuclei. The trick is to get two helium nuclei to stick together until they are struck by a third. It turns out that this feat depends critically on the internal resonance of carbon and oxygen nuclei. Were the carbon resonance only four per cent lower, carbon atoms wouldn't form in the first place. Were the oxygen resonance level only half a per cent higher, virtually all the carbon would be "scoured out", meaning that it would not have combined with helium to form oxygen. *No carbon, no us, so our existence depends in some sense on the fine-tuning of these two nuclear resonances*[106] (emphasis added). The precise quantities of these energy levels led Astronomer Royal Sir Martin Rees and science writer John Gribbin to state, 'This combination of coincidences, just right for resonance in carbon-12, just wrong in oxygen-16, is indeed remarkable. *There is no better evidence to support the argument that the universe has been designed for our benefit* — tailor-made for man'[107] (emphasis added). Rees and Gribbin reject the idea of a personal Creator, but when Fred Hoyle grasped the implications of what he had found he confessed, 'Nothing has shaken my atheism as much as this discovery.'[108]

A fifth sign of fine-tuning is more generally known, and was referred to in the early part of this chapter. Compared with those of all the other planets of the solar system (except Pluto) our moon is so abnormally big that astronomers refer to the earth-moon system as a 'double planet'. In addition, because the earth's axis is tilted at 23.45 degrees relative to the plane of its orbit, our moon orbits the earth along its orbital plane, while every other moon in the solar system orbits its planet around the equator. Although this phenomenon remains a mystery to astronomers, we do know that only this configuration allows oceanic tides to exist on Earth, and that without them life could not exist.[109]

These are only some of the indications that life on Earth is a cosmic function, something which needs an extremely complex and precise arrangement of terrestrial and extra-terrestrial elements before it can subsist. There are many others. Earth's size, rotational speed, distance from the sun and land-water ratio must be just right. We need light, but not too much ultraviolet; heat, but not too much infra-red. The atmosphere above our heads shields us from meteorites and from many harmful cosmic rays, while a screen of rock under our feet prevents us from being incinerated. Oxford scholar J. L. Mackie, one of the most influential atheists of our time, admits in his book *The Miracle of Theism,* 'It is ... surprising that the elements of this unique set-up are just right for life when they might easily have been wrong.'[110]

Back to square one

The extent of fine-tuning in the universe is a truly remarkable phenomenon, and one which demands our concentrated attention, yet to begin there is to put the cart before the horse, as there is an even more fundamental issue. The eighteenth-century German mathematician and philosopher Gottfried Leibniz put his finger on it: 'The first question which should rightly be asked will be, *Why is there something rather than nothing?*That is, why does anything at all exist?' There must be an answer to this question because, as Leibniz went on, 'Nothing happens without sufficient reason'[111] — but where do we look for it? It is obviously no good expecting to find it within the universe itself, which is a vast accumulation of things, every one of which needs an explanation for its own existence.

None of the Big Bang models provides an answer, not even one which suggests taking matter back to infinity, as this merely begs the questions as to what we mean by 'infinity' and why it was necessary for matter (let alone energy, time and space) to come into existence at all. Richard Swinburne elaborates: 'The existence of the universe is something evidently inexplicable by science... A scientific explanation as such explains the occurrence of one state of affairs in terms of a previous state of affairs and some law of nature that makes states like the former bring about states like the latter... It may explain the existence of the universe this year in terms of the existence of the universe last year and the laws of cosmology. But either there was a first state of the universe or there has always been a universe. In the former case, science cannot explain why there was the first state; and in the latter case it still cannot explain why any matter exists (or, more correctly, matter-energy) for the laws of nature to get a grip on, as it were. By its very nature science cannot explain *why* there are any states of affairs at all.'[112]

In the second, revised edition of a *A Brief History of Time*, Stephen Hawking is perfectly frank about this: 'Even if there is only one possible unified theory, it is just a set of rules and equations. What is it that breathes fire into the equations and makes a universe for them to describe? The usual approach of science of constructing a mathematical model cannot answer the questions of why there should be a universe for the model to describe. Why does the universe go to all the bother of existing? Is the unified theory so compelling that it brings about its own existence? Or does it need a creator and, if so, does he have any other effect on the universe? And who created him?'[113]

Most scientists honestly recognize the limitations of what science can explain in this area. Danish physicist Niels Bohr (1885–1962), who pioneered quantum mechanics, wrote, 'It is wrong to think that the task of physics is to find out how nature *is*. Physics concerns what we can *say* about nature... Our task is not to penetrate into the essence of things, the meaning of which we don't know anyway, but rather to develop concepts which allow us to talk in a productive way about phenomena in nature.'[114] Like Hawking, Bohr understood that a scientist's task is to describe the universe around us, using mathematical laws of physics. However, by its very nature, science cannot explain *why* the universe exists, or *why* these laws exist, or *why* the universe follows these particular laws. In his book *The Mind of God*, Paul Davies makes the point in this way: 'However successful our scientific explanations may be, they always have certain starting assumptions built in. For example, an explanation of some phenomenon in terms of physics presupposes the validity of the laws of physics... *But one can ask where these laws came from in the first place. One could even question the origin of logic upon which all scientific reasoning is founded.* Sooner or later we all have to accept something as given, whether it is God, or logic, or a set of laws, or some other foundation for existence.

Thus "ultimate" questions will always lie beyond the scope of empirical science as it is usually defined' [115] (emphasis added).

Theories which propose an infinite number of universes, or completely self-contained universes with no beginning, also come up empty on the issue of existence. 'Strictly speaking,' says Keith Ward, 'the question of whether the time of this universe had a beginning is not relevant to the question of whether the whole universe is created, or whether it exists without a creator. The question is the same whether time began or has always existed. *The question is, what explains the existence of space and time, or is there no explanation?'* [116] (emphasis added).

This whole issue points up a fundamental difference between theism and atheism, and has inescapable implications as far as human existence is concerned. If the universe in which we live is a meaningless mass of matter and anti-matter controlled by mindless forces, it is difficult to see how life can have any significance or purpose. Stephen Weinberg asserts, 'The more the universe becomes comprehensible, the more it becomes pointless,' and concedes that human life is 'a more-or-less farcical out-come of a chain of accidents'. [117] But if this is the case, why should these farcical biological blobs worry their (accidental) minds over questions of meaning, purpose, dignity or morality? Yet they never stop doing so, and many with no religious agenda are convinced that to dismiss the issue of the universe's existence by saying with Bertrand Russell, 'It's just there,' solves nothing. As Roger Penrose said in a televised debate, 'Some people take the view that the universe is simply there and it runs along — it's a bit as though it just sort of computes, and we happen by accident to find ourselves in this thing. I don't think that's a very fruitful or helpful way of looking at the universe.' [118] The day after receiving the prestigious Templeton Award in 1995, Paul Davies wrote much the same thing in the *Guardian*: 'I am ... impressed by the extraordinary ingenuity, felicity and harmony of the laws of physics. It is hard to accept that something so elegantly clever exists without a deeper reason or purpose... I have no idea what the uni-verse is about, but that it is about something I have no doubt.' [119]

Welcome to Wales

In 1963 the American philosopher Richard Taylor gave a new twist to the argument from design. He imagined a passenger looking out of a train window and seeing on a hillside a series of white stones spelling out, 'The British Railways welcomes you to Wales.'[120] Reflecting on this, the passenger might think that the stones fell into that arrangement accidentally (something entirely possible). On the other hand, she might conclude that they had been intelligently placed there for a purpose.

If the passenger were to decide, solely on the evidence of the stones, that she *was* entering Wales, it would be inconsistent for her also to assume that the stones were there by accident. By presupposing that the stones were saying something significant, she would also be presupposing that they had been arranged by an intelligent being, or beings, for the purpose of conveying a message that has nothing to do with the stones themselves. It would be bizarre of her to think that the stones got there by chance and at the same time to believe, solely on the evidence they provided, that she was indeed entering Wales.

The application is obvious. Just as the interesting arrangement of the stones might be accidental, so might our human sense organs. Atheistic biologists and others argue that this is the case, but even those individuals who view their sense organs as the product of chance accept as true the information they deliver about the world. As Taylor put it, 'We suppose, without even thinking about it, that [our sense organs] reveal to us things that have nothing to do with themselves, their structures or their origins.'[121]

Surely there is something fundamentally irrational in a person claiming that sense organs with a natural, non-purposeful origin reveal truth about something other than themselves and which is not merely inferred from them? As Taylor goes on to say, 'If, on the other hand, we do assume that they are guides to some truths having nothing to do with themselves, then it is difficult to see how we can, consistently with that supposition, believe them to have arisen by accident, or by the ordinary workings of purposeless forces, even over ages of time.'[122]

Taylor is not saying that theists have a cast-iron case, but he adds another telling dimension to the argument from design. In his book *Faith And Reason*, Ronald Nash drives the point home: 'Everything we find in nature that points to harmony, design, purpose and intelligence is consistent with the ... presupposition that God exists and provides supporting evidence for it. If I believe in ... God ... I should expect to find that the world is lawlike and exhibits signs of purpose and design; I should expect to discover that my sensory organs give me reliable information about the world; I should expect to find that my rational faculties enable me to draw sound inferences and discover truth.'[123] Atheists make the same claims, yet they reject the only presupposition which gives them rational credence.

No silver bullet

A large part of this chapter has been taken up with the argument from design, but even the most fervent theist needs to recognize that for all its attraction it is far from being knock-down proof of God's existence. Not even the combined forces of science and philosophy can produce this, and there is no point in making the attempt.

That being said, the theist can certainly claim that the order, beauty, precision and elegance we see in the world are consistent with the idea of God. The contemporary British author and one-time atheist Robert Frost summarizes the alternative: 'If the scientist prefers to suggest that there is no "God", no "Creator", and no "first cause", what does atheism offer him intellectually? The atheist must, of necessity, believe that matter without mind created reason and logic. Matter without intelligence created understanding and comprehension. Matter without morals created complex ethical codes and legal systems. Matter without conscience created a sense of right and wrong. Matter without emotion created skills and art, music, drama, architecture, comedy, literature and dance. Matter without design created in humankind an insatiable hunger for meaning and purpose.'[124]

We can take this one step further. As human beings, we depend on elements in the universe for our existence, yet what it takes for the universe to exist cannot be identical with the universe itself or with any part of it. Surely this pushes us towards the idea of an infinite, transcendent and creative source? After a long career in research and the political aspects of science, John Wright says, 'The very nature of the universe which modern science reveals encourages a belief in God. It does not prove God exists in any strict, logical sense. But the balance certainly tilts in favour of a reasoned faith.'[125]

Critics of the argument from design say that it is not rational to argue from our known world to one which is unknown. *Why not?* If there is no natural explanation for the origin and form of the universe as we know it, why is it irrational or illogical to presume that the explanation is supernatural? Without a finite cause of the effects we see all around, why not suppose that there must be an infinite one?

Nevertheless, the argument from design does not give theists a 'silver bullet' and the question to ask when reviewing it is not, 'What does it prove?' but, 'Where does it point?' Do the order, harmony and beauty all around us suggest that what we are seeing is a purposeless, irrelevant and senseless mess, or do they point towards transcendent and creative intelligence? When Richard Dawkins claims, 'We animals are the most complicated and perfectly designed pieces of machinery in the known universe,'[126] do most people instinctively sense that this is an illusion, or that they have been created with genuine purpose and value which go beyond the reproduction of the next generation of purposeless and valueless successors?

When the theist points to God as the only credible source of natural reality, the atheist produces a whole range of arguments against the idea. By far the most powerful is the fact that as well as order, harmony and beauty, the world also exhibits disorder, disharmony and ugliness. When we take account of these, surely talk of a perfect, omnipotent and benevolent Creator falls apart? This is a crucially important and complex issue, and one which theists need to face. We will tackle it head-on in a later chapter.

Why not God?

For centuries, we have been learning through science about the nature of our universe, and our growing scientific knowledge is steadily whittling away the possibility that the universe came into being by chance, or that it must necessarily exist as it does. In pulling the main strands of this chapter together, we can settle for the fact that if something exists now, one of three things must be true of it: it is either eternal, created by something that is eternal, or self-created. The first option clashes with the Second Law of Thermodynamics, since an eternal universe would have dissipated all its energy long ago. The third clashes not only with the First Law of Thermodynamics, but also with the law of contradiction, because in order to create itself it would have to exist before it existed, to be and not to be at the same time, a proposition which is scientifically and philosophically ridiculous.

This leaves the second option, and the God posited in the introduction to this book satisfies all the necessary criteria.

This is not a battered theist's desperate ploy to invent a 'God of the gaps', something to plug the holes science is unable to fill. Instead, it identifies a Being whose existence explains why science can explain anything — and why it cannot explain everything. As Keith Ward puts it, 'To grasp the idea of God is to grasp an idea of the only reality that could form a completely adequate explanation of the existence of the universe, for God is the only reality which, in being supremely intelligible or comprehensible to itself, explains itself.'[127]

A growing number of scientists in many disciplines are turning in this direction and being drawn to the conclusion that divine intelligence preceded and planned the natural universe and the laws by which it is governed. Although not attached to any religious tradition, Paul Davies writes, 'The delicate fine-tuning in the values of the constants, necessary so that the various different branches of physics can dovetail so felicitously, might be attributed to God. It is hard to resist the impression that the present structure of the universe, apparently so sensitive to minor alterations in the numbers, has been rather carefully thought out.'[128] Stephen Hawking goes even further: 'It would be very difficult to explain why the universe should have begun in just this way, *except as the act of a God who intended to create beings like us*'[129] (emphasis added).

In response to atheistic attempts to find some other kind of explanation, theism points to a simple, transcendent, eternal, self-sufficient, omnipotent Being with freedom to bring about anything he wishes (including matter, time and space), who chose to do so for his own purposes, and who sustains the whole of his creation by laws of nature which he ordained and whose limits he determined. The hard-core atheist may dismiss all of this as wishful thinking, but surely the issue deserves closer attention than that? Without such a God, the most basic questions of all can scarcely be considered, let alone answered. Why should a universe exist at all? Why should it be as complex and orderly as it is? If it was not the result of a natural process governed by natural law, must it not be the result of something supernatural? Is the fact that in human beings matter has become personal and self-conscious not a clue that the universe has a transcendent and personal origin and meaning? How else can we explain the emergence of personality? Why should the rationality we claim for ourselves harmonize with the rationality we find in the rest of the universe? How can we make rational sense of the cosmos unless the cosmos *does* make sense and we *do* have the power of reasoning? And how can either of these things be true if the whole shooting match is a gigantic, senseless fluke? Is atheistic prejudice a good enough basis for refusing to consider that there might be a theistic answer to all of these questions?

The subject matter of this chapter has demanded that I rely to a great extent on the views and conclusions of experts in the fields of astronomy, physics, the philosophy of science and other related disciplines. I make no apology for doing this, nor for closing with two further quotations, one from a theist and the other from an agnostic. The first, from William Lane Craig, gets right to the heart of the one fact I have been trying to establish, namely that the existence of the entire matter-energy-space-time package raises a massive problem for the atheist:

> Since everything that began to exist has a cause of its existence, and since the universe began to exist, we conclude, therefore, that the universe has a cause of existence. We ought to ponder long and hard over this truly remarkable conclusion, for it means that transcending the entire universe there exists a cause which brought the universe into being *ex nihilo*... This conclusion ought to stagger us, ought to fill us with a sense of awe and wonder at the knowledge that *our whole universe was caused to exist by something beyond it and greater than it*[130] (emphasis added).

The second statement is from a high-profile astronomer with no religious axe to grind. Writing in the *New York Times* in 1978, Robert Jastrow, Director of NASA'S Goddard Institute for Space Studies, asked the question, 'Have Astronomers Found God?', and came to the conclusion that they had, or had at least come close to doing so. After determining that the universe had a beginning in time, and accepting that its creation by an act of God was a reasonable possibility, he then went on to say that the astronomical evidence points to a theistic view of the origin of the world: 'The details differ, but the essential elements ... are the same; the chain of events leading to man commenced suddenly and sharply at a definite moment in time, in a flash of light and energy.'[131] The closing words in Jastrow's article are particularly telling, not least because they are written by an agnostic:

This is an exceedingly strange development, unexpected by all but the theologians... We scientists did not expect to find evidence for an abrupt beginning because we have had until recently such extraordinary success in tracing the chain of cause and effect backward in time... At this moment it seems as though science will never be able to raise the curtain on the mystery of creation. For the scientist who has lived by his faith in the power of reason, the story ends like a bad dream. He has scaled the mountains of ignorance; he is about to conquer the highest peak; as he pulls himself over the final rock, he is greeted by a band of theologians who have been sitting there for centuries. [132]

14.

Such is life

Atheists satisfied that they have arrived at an explanation for the existence of matter, time and space without needing to bring God into the picture are immediately faced with an even greater conundrum — the existence of life. Strange as it may seem, life is easier to discern than to define. We all recognize the difference between life and non-life; life is something we find in barley but not in battleships, in cockatoos but not in computers, in people but not in platinum. Yet what do we mean by 'life'? Not even the world's leading scientists can agree on the answer to this fundamental question.

Biologists, who are among those closest to the subject, can do no better than supply a list of features possessed by living things, including the ability to reproduce, the existence of genetic information, complexity and organization. Standard lexicons tend to go round in circles over the issue. In defining 'life', The *Concise Oxford Dictionary* includes the phrase 'animate existence',[1] yet it defines 'animate' as 'living';[2] not much help there! Even *Encyclopaedia Britannica* surrenders:

> A great deal is known about life. Anatomists and taxonomists have studied the forms and relations of more than a million separate species of plants and animals. Physiologists have investigated the gross functioning of organisms. Biochemists have probed the biological interactions of the organic molecules that make up life on our planet. Molecular biologists have uncovered the very molecules responsible for reproduction and for passing hereditary information from generation to generation, a subject that geneticists had previously studied without going to the molecular level. Ecologists have enquired into the relations between organisms and their environments, ethologists the behaviour of animals and plants, embryologists

the development of complex organisms from a single cell, evolutionary biologists the emergence of organisms from pre-existing forms
over geological time. Yet despite the enormous fund of information
that each of these biological specialities has provided, it is a remarkable fact that *no general agreement exists on what it is that is being
studied. There is no generally accepted definition of life*[3] (emphasis
added).

Yet, even without general agreement as to precisely what constitutes
'life', we all recognize that our planet is teeming with it in millions of different species and forms, from the tiniest organisms (the prokaryotes, which
include all bacteria) to the largest living thing on earth, the General Sherman
tree, a 272-foot high wellingtonia in Sequoia National Park, California.
The qualities, properties and implications of what we call 'life' are such
that nobody can think seriously about it without asking some very important questions. Nor is it difficult to think of the first one: how did it all
begin?

Space invaders?

One response to the riddle of life on earth is to say that it did not begin
here in the first place. This raises the fascinating question of whether there
is such a thing as extraterrestrial life. In the hugely-popular television series
The X Files, agent Mulder is convinced that 'The truth is out there', while
Carl Sagan goes as far as to say, 'The search for life elsewhere is something which runs so deep in human curiosity that there's not a human
being anywhere in the world who isn't interested in that question.'[4] Sagan
is over the top here, but there are many people who look beyond our own
planet, not merely for the existence of life, but for its source. This approach
takes in panspermia, the theory that germs of life are to be found all over
the universe. The word 'panspermia' — from the Greek *pan* (every) and
sperma (seed) — was coined by the Swedish physical chemist Svante
Arrhenius, though the development of the idea is largely based on work
by the nineteenth-century German chemist Justus von Liebig.
     There are two main groups of ideas as to how life reached our planet
from outer space. The first is *accidental panspermia*, which includes a
number of fascinating suggestions. These go back at least as far as the
early eighteenth century, when the British astronomer William Herschel

made the tongue-in-cheek suggestion that life first came to earth by means of falling meteorites. Somewhat to his surprise, the idea caught on for a while, but interest in the subject was to blow hot and cold over the next 200 years. Among those who advocated the idea were Arrhenius himself, whose *World in the Making* suggested that spores of living matter could be propelled by light rays from one celestial body to another, and the German biologist H. E. Richter, who taught that the bodies' own rapid motion caused spores to be detached and flung out into space. In 1932, the American scientist C. B. Lipman claimed to have isolated viable bacteria in nine separate meteorites, leading him to conclude, 'Stony meteorites bring down with them from somewhere in space a few surviving bacteria, probably in spore form.'[5] Lipman's claims were hotly contested, and most scientists who ran the relevant tests decided that the material he used had been contaminated, one researcher concluding that the 'supposition of the presence of living bacteria in meteorites is nonsense'.[6]

More detailed research has been equally dismissive of life on earth resulting from accidental panspermia. In *Life Sciences and Space Research* the Russian scientist A. A. Imshenetsky concluded that all previous reports of bacteria in meteorites were due to terrestrial contamination, and a 1972 report published by the New York Academy of Sciences, and based on the study of 432 meteorite samples, revealed no sign of any micro-organisms.

This would seem to go a long way towards putting the lid on accidental panspermia, but the idea has persisted and in 1981 it was taken up by the British astronomer Fred Hoyle and his colleague Chandra Wickramasinghe, Professor of Mathematics at Cardiff University, in their book *Evolution From Space*. In an earlier work, Hoyle had already derided the idea that life on earth had arisen spontaneously from some kind of primeval 'soup': 'It is remarkable that over the past half-century the scientific world has, almost without exception, believed a theory for which there is not a single supporting fact.'[7] It was this which drove him to seek a solution in panspermia and at one point he wrote that unless panspermia were true, 'life has little meaning, but must be judged a mere cosmic fluke'.[8] In *Evolution From Space* he and Wickramasinghe argued that life could not possibly have originated on earth, but they left their options open as to how our planet came to be seeded from space. It may be worth adding that in *Diseases From Space*, published two years later, Hoyle floated the idea that AIDS, Legionnaire's Disease, influenza and other diseases are all due to an endless aerial bombardment of viruses and other micro-organisms.

The rise and fall of ALH 84001

In 1996, those attracted to the idea of accidental panspermia seemed to receive a boost when NASA, the American space agency, released the results of a study which raised the possibility of early life on the planet Mars. NASA's administrator Daniel Goldin spoke of 'unbelievable excitement'[9] among the world's space scientists, and the *Sunday Times* splashed the headline 'Earth Welcomes Martian Invasion' across two pages.[10] The story began in 1984, when American scientists working in Antarctica found a piece of heavy grey stone about the size of a small potato. The rock was bagged and tagged (it became ALH 84001) and then ignored for nearly twelve years, when NASA revealed details of what it called 'a fascinating detective story'. In a nutshell, NASA theorized that ALH 84001, thought to be about 4.6 billion years old, was gouged out of the surface of Mars when the planet collided with a comet or meteorite about sixteen million years ago. After wandering around the solar system under the influence of its own velocity and then different gravitational pulls until about 13,000 years ago, it was finally snared by the earth's gravity and landed as a fireball in Antarctica. Examined under massive magnification, the rock revealed a few 'strange substances' about 100 times smaller than the tiniest terrestrial microfossils and a pattern of organic molecules which could possibly point to evidence of past life on its parent planet.

The story generated huge media coverage, but from day one many scientists unconnected with NASA were by no means convinced. Monica Grady, curator of meteorites at London's Natural History Museum, and whose photographs of carbonates in ALH 84001 were chosen by NASA as a key exhibit, said, 'I think it's a very valuable piece of work. I just don't believe the final interpretation. They admit themselves that there are inorganic explanations for everything they have found.'[11] Sir Martin Rees was equally cautious: 'It is still early days and we should await further details before we start analysing the implications of this discovery. All we know at the moment is that a series of complicated molecules has been found. We should be careful not to jump the gun.'[12]

NASA scientists' own summary of their findings went no further than to speak of '*possible* relict biogenic activity in Martian meteorite ALH 84001', and to say that the features found in the rock '*could* thus be fossil remains of a past Martian biota'[13] (emphasis added). This falls a long way short of proof that our planet was seeded from outer space, and the anti-climactic sequel to the story came less than two years after the original NASA report. In the *Daily Telegraph* the story was relegated to an inside page under the deflating headline 'Life on Mars? No, it came from earth after all.'[14] The story reported the finding of scientists at the prestigious Scripps Institute of Oceanography in California and the University of Arizona, both teams having come to the conclusion that ALH 84001 had been seriously contaminated by its surroundings in Antarctica. The California team analysed amino-acids in a sample of the meteorite and decided that they were 'clearly terrestrial', while the Arizona team examined the carbon isotopes and concluded, 'It looks like regular terrestrial organic material.'[15]

ALH 84001 may have taken over sixteen million years to fall from Mars to earth, but it took just seventeen months to fall off the front pages of the national press, leaving little or nothing to justify the earlier excited claims that had been made. By July 1998, the American scientist John Bradley could tell the news media, 'I think the 1996 claims of evidence of life in the ALH 84001 meteorite have now been disproven because all of their lines of scientific evidence have been shown to be either wrong or have significant weaknesses. Even their logic — i.e. several "possiblys" add up to a "probably" — is fundamentally flawed. This is now the consensus view of meteoriticists and planetary scientists (with the exception of the folk who made the 1996 announcement).'[16]

All aboard?

The second group of ideas comes under the heading of *directed panspermia*, which says that life from outer space reached earth not by accident but by design. In 1954, J. B. S. Haldane, who is said to have loved 'taking a swipe at God',[17] suggested that intelligent space beings had seeded earth with what he called 'astroplankton'. The Soviet biochemist (and, like Haldane, committed Marxist) A. I. Oparin said that in the distant past astronauts from elsewhere in space made an exploratory landing on earth, and that life on our planet developed from debris they left behind. On the other hand, the Japanese biochemist Tairo Oshima believed that the most basic elements of life were somehow placed on earth as a cosmic message from a superior civilization from outer space.

Today's most articulate 'directed panspermians' are the celebrated theoretical biologist Francis Crick and his colleague Leslie Orgel. Like Hoyle,

Crick has long since abandoned the idea of life originating on earth in some kind of primeval 'soup'. He has also rejected the idea that any form of life carried by meteorite could have survived radiation damage on its way here, and has turned to directed panspermia as what he considers to be the only alternative. In *Life Itself: Its Origin and Nature*, Crick paints a picture in which 'micro-organisms travel in the head of an unmanned space-ship sent to earth by a higher civilization which developed elsewhere some billions of years ago'.[18] Once here on earth, these primitive deposits became the basis for the cellular life-forms which led to the processes of competing and reproduction, and eventually to natural selection and the whole Darwinian package.

Crick is no less fascinating than Hoyle, but equally bereft of solid evidence for his particular brand of panspermia; even a sliver of substance from a spacecraft would be helpful! There are several major problems with directed panspermia, one of which can be summarized as follows: Assuming (as an atheist like Crick does) that macro-evolution is an established fact and that complex, intelligent life on earth arose by chance, why would a super-intelligent civilization have taken the process right back to square one by dumping nothing more than spores on our planet? If their aim was to colonize the earth, we might have expected those master-minding the operation to send a more advanced product, one much more likely to survive.

Be that as it may, all the present theories of panspermia crash into a wall of silence, as there is not the slightest solid evidence of life as we know it existing anywhere else in the universe. On the other hand, space programmes have yielded massive amounts of data suggesting that extra-terrestrial conditions are so brutally hostile to life that none would be possible. Henry Morris calls panspermia 'the refuge of desperation'[19] and in Michael Denton's view, 'Nothing illustrates more clearly how intractable a problem the origin of life has become than the fact that world authorities can seriously toy with the idea of panspermia.'[20]

One other thing: even if (and it is a monumental 'if') some form of panspermia were to be proved, it would only sweep the basic problem of life's origin under some other corner of the cosmic carpet. As Manfred Eigen explains, 'Attempts at explanation by shifting the location of the origin of life from earth to outer space do not offer an acceptable solution to the dilemma.'[21] This is a rather elegant way of saying that panspermia tells us absolutely nothing about how life began, a point driven home by

V. A. Firsoff in his book *Life Beyond the Earth*: 'The greatest weakness of any explanation by implantation from without is that it does not really solve the problem of the origin of life; it merely "passes the buck", for life would still have arisen elsewhere at some time and this would have to be explained.'[22] The idea of invaders from outer space has been the stuff of science fiction for years; there seems no serious reason to consider reclassifying it.

From nothing to nature?

At this point we need to consider the idea that life could arise anywhere from inert or inanimate matter, the so-called 'spontaneous generation' theory, otherwise known as *abiogenesis*, built up from the Greek words *a* (without), *bios* (life) and *ginomai* (to form). This notion has been around for a long time. The Greek philosopher Anaximander believed that living organisms developed from mud exposed to the sun, and when Aristotle endorsed this idea (he taught that insects and worms were born of dew-drops and slime, that mice were generated by dank soil and that eels and fish sprang forth from sand or mud and putrefying algae)[23] it gained considerable credibility, and was to be widely held for some 2,000 years. The Roman poet Lucretius (99–55 B.C.) wrote that the earth was called 'mother' because 'all things are produced out of the earth', and even as late as the seventeenth century we find one of William Shakespeare's characters in *Antony and Cleopatra* saying, 'Your serpent of Egypt is now bred out of your mud by the operation of your sun.'[24] Today, the same idea is held among the Hakka Chinese.

The spontaneous generation idea took quite a battering during the seventeenth and eighteenth centuries, when a number of scientists conducted experiments which showed it to be seriously flawed, but early in the nineteenth century Erasmus Darwin took a leading part in a movement promoting the idea that only the simplest forms of life came into being spontaneously, and that these slowly evolved into more complex varieties. These lines from his poem 'The Temple of Nature', hugely popular when it was first published in 1803, give us the general drift of what he taught:

Organic Life beneath the shoreless waves
Was born, and nurs'd in Ocean's pearly caves;
First forms minute, unseen by spheric glass,

Move on the mud, or pierce the watery mass;
These, as successive generations bloom,
New powers acquire, and larger limbs assume.

This all sounds delightfully romantic, but where in the writings of Erasmus Darwin, or of his more famous grandson Charles, do we find any clear data to take it beyond this?

The emperor's wine

About sixty years after Darwin's charming composition, the abiogenesis idea was dealt a massive blow by the French chemist Louis Pasteur, the founder of modern microbiology, who later gave his name to the process we now know as pasteurization. At one point in the 1860s, Emperor Louis Napoleon III asked Pasteur to discover what was causing a mysterious disease which had been plaguing the prestigious (and profitable) French wine industry. Until that time, it had generally been thought that microbes appearing in fermentation vessels were caused by reactions in alcohol and carbonic acid gas, a theory which apparently pointed to abiogenesis. After some two years of work, Pasteur not only proved that this was not the case (the microbes were introduced to the process by yeast, itself a microbe) but that contamination had been caused by bacteria already existing in unfiltered air.

Pasteur, a devout theist, had no doubts as to what abiogenesis would mean. In 1864 he wrote, 'To bring about spontaneous generation would be to create a germ. It would be creating life; it would be to solve the problem of its origin. It would mean to go from matter to life through conditions of environment and of matter (non-life). God as author of life would then no longer be needed. Matter would replace him.'[25] Macro-evolution is crucially dependent on the spontaneous generation of life from non-life; published just five years after Darwin's *Origin*, Pasteur's work showed how flimsy a foundation this is.

Back to earth

Before examining in detail the question of how life began here on earth, we ought to bear in mind the so-called 'anthropic principle', which is that the universe is specifically designed to sustain human life (see pp. 269-81), and realize that life of any kind anywhere in the universe is in itself astonishing. Physicist Paul Davies has estimated that for every time a Big Bang produced a universe which could sustain life, there would be others where life would be impossible. How many? In Davies' estimate, 1,000 billion billion billion. In other words, the odds against life appearing anywhere as an accidental consequence of natural forces are somewhat remote! What is more, those who argue that, however astronomical the odds, this is what happened, have not a shred of proof that there is even one other universe than ours, let alone the 1,000 billion billion billion that might be required.

Even if we narrow the issue down to the universe as we know it, we are faced with a mass of amazingly 'coincidental' factors which had to be just right before life could be viable anywhere in the universe. J. P. Moreland gives some examples:

> Had the ratio of carbon to oxygen been slightly different, no life could have formed. If the mass of a proton were increased by 0.2 per cent, hydrogen would be unstable and life would not have formed. For life to form, the temperature range is only 1-2 per cent of the total temperature range, and earth obtains this range by being the correct distance from the sun, just the right size, with the right rotational speed, with a special atmosphere which protects earth and evens out temperature extremes. In addition, the planet which had these factors just happened to contain the proper amount of metals (especially iron), radioactive elements to provide the right heat source, and water-forming compounds. Perhaps the temperature range could have been obtained in another way. But earth shows how delicate and multifaceted are the independent factors involved in maintaining the correct temperature for life.[26]

Progress?

In a letter written in 1871, Charles Darwin offered an attractive speculation: 'It is often said that all the conditions for the first production of a living organism are now present which could have ever been present. But if [and oh, what a big "if"!] we could conceive in some warm little pond, with all sorts of ammonia and phosphoric salts, lights, heat, electricity, etc. present, that a protein compound was chemically formed ready to undergo still more complex changes, at the present day such matter would be instantly devoured or absorbed, which would not have been the case before living creatures were formed.'[27] About fifty years later, scientists began to look more closely at this kind of model and to suggest that progress had been made in the search for life's origins.

In 1924 A. I. Oparin published a booklet entitled *The Origins of Life*, outlining experiments in which he claimed to have produced results analogous to the division of living cells. Oparin quickly became a star in the scientific firmament and was highly honoured in his own country. Later, he suggested that organic molecules could have formed by chance in the lifeless seas of the early earth (a global version of Darwin's 'warm little pond') and that, given enough time, chance would bring some of them together to form amino-acids, one of the building-blocks of life. More time and chance could then have led to the first protein molecules which, given yet more time and chance, could have combined to form the first primal organism.

Oparin's work attracted the interest of J. B. S. Haldane, who in 1929 published an article in *Rationalist Annual* suggesting that life on earth had its origin in a 'hot dilute soup' composed of an accidental accumulation of organic compounds. Today, the Oparin-Haldane theory that life originated spontaneously in the distant past and developed in some kind of primeval 'soup' is taken for granted in virtually all textbooks on biology.

By far the most famous follow-up to the Oparin-Haldane primeval 'soup' idea was the work carried out in 1953 by Stanley Miller, a graduate biochemistry student at the University of Chicago, in association with the Nobel Prize-winning chemist Harold Urey. Using a surprisingly simple piece of apparatus, Miller circulated a boiled mixture of water, methane, hydrogen and ammonia for about a week, at the same time passing it through an electrical discharge of about 60,000 volts, a set-up meant to simulate lightning flashing over the early earth's atmosphere. A receptacle at the bottom of the apparatus caught the lighter products and after a week it was found to have trapped small amounts of three amino-acids. This caused great excitement in scientific circles, and biologist L. R. Croft says that it was not long before 'a small cottage industry of primeval-soup workers was busily creating new concoctions'.[28] These produced a variety of amino-acids and other substances related to the genetic process, with the result that 'The more optimistic researchers concluded that the chemicals needed to construct life could have been present in sufficient abundance on the early earth.'[29]

For all their popularity, Miller's conclusions have not ended scientific studies on the subject, and the drive to find an alternative to the divine creation of life *ex nihilo* goes on. In 1995, a team led by Shinichi Shirono, of the Department of Earth and Planetary Sciences at Hokkaido University in Sapporo, Japan, published a fascinating report which turned a great deal of previous thinking on its head. It had always been believed that comets and meteorites smashing into an early earth would have inhibited the creation and progress of life, but Shirono and his colleagues suggested that these massive impacts may instead have been a critical factor in getting it started. They mixed together chemicals thought likely to exist in the primordial ocean — water, ammonia and formaldehyde — and then, to simulate the violent impact of extraterrestrial objects striking the earth, fired projectiles into their 'soup' at speeds of over 5,000 miles per hour. The high temperatures and pressures triggered certain chemical reactions and, as with Miller's experiment, produced small amounts of amino-acids. Writing in the academic journal *Icarus*, the Japanese team concluded, 'Oceanic impact could be an effective energy source for synthesizing amino-acids,'[30] adding that this could have been boosted by chemicals carried aboard the comets and meteorites themselves.

Problems

Oparin, Haldane, Miller, Shirono and others have provided a fascinating collection of ideas as to how the spontaneous generation of life's building-blocks might have occurred but, far from supplying a satisfying model, their work has left us with a bewildering tangle of loose ends.

In the first place, there are obvious physical problems. Miller's optimism has now all but evaporated, as experiments based on his model have failed to produce a number of components essential to life. A few basic amino-acids are almost infinitely less complex than the simplest protein molecules, leaving Miller's results far short of those needed to suggest abiogenesis. His experiment was conducted in a 'reducing' atmosphere, one containing no oxygen, yet there is no evidence that this was the case on the early earth. Amino-acids occur in two fundamentally different forms (popularly known in the trade as 'right-handed' and 'left-handed'), and all known life-forms use only the 'left-handed' kind. The addition of a single 'right-handed' one could destroy an entire amino-acid chain; Miller's experiment produced a lethal mixture of both. Chemists have shown that chemical reaction would have rendered primeval organic compounds unsuitable for constructing life, as the sun's ultraviolet light would have destroyed the methane and ammonia. When these are replaced by the more likely broth of carbon monoxide, carbon dioxide and nitrogen, Miller's experiment fizzles out; simply put, his soup had the wrong ingredients.

In the second place, there are conceptual problems, not the least of which being that there is no reason to believe that it is possible for amino-acids to combine randomly to form anything useful. As Phillip Johnson explains, 'Let us grant that, one way or another, all the required chemical components were present on the early earth. This still leaves us at a dead end, because there is no reason to believe that life has a tendency to emerge when the right chemicals are sloshing about in a soup. Although some components of living systems can be duplicated with very advanced technology, scientists employing the full power of their intelligence cannot manufacture living organisms from amino-acids, sugars and the like. *How then was the trick done before scientific intelligence was in existence?*[31] (emphasis added). Edgar Andrews agrees: 'The spontaneous synthesis of even the simplest protein or nucleic acid would represent a vast extrapolation of anything yet demonstrated in the laboratory or theoretically envisaged. Even if it were eventually shown that such molecules could be made from the kind of chemicals which *may* have existed in a primitive earth atmosphere, it would only emphasize the absolute necessity of the intelligent control of the synthesis by the chemist himself. The most that can be said is that certain *small* steps in such a process might plausibly be explained by known chemical reactions. The rest is pure speculation.'[32]

Amazing acids

In the third place, none of the theories or experiments can bridge the massive gap between the contrived production of tiny amounts of amino-acids and the initial generation of life. Amino-acids have to be held together in a specific way to make proteins, long chain-like molecules which form an essential part of all living organisms. But proteins are unstable and degrade and need to be replaced, a very complex process involving two substances which have achieved high-profile status in the last fifty years — DNA (deoxyribonucleic acid) and RNA (ribonucleic acid). The properties and powers of DNA are such that when in 1953 Francis Crick and James Watson discovered its now famous double helix structure (produced by two sugar-phosphate backbones twisting about on the outside), Crick walked into their local pub in Cambridge and airily announced to everybody within earshot that they had found 'the secret of life'. We can begin to understand what he meant when we realize that DNA governs all biological reproduction and the transmission of all inherited characteristics, but how does the process work?

DNA is a chemical made up of four components, adenine, guanine, cytosine and thymine (usually referred to as A, G, C and T). These link together side by side in large numbers to form huge strings, or chromosomes, comprising apparently random combinations of each of the four components. Watson and Crick's big breakthrough was the discovery that DNA is double-stranded, with the two strands held together by exclusive interactions between the A and T components and the G and C components on opposite strands. This means that a strand which contains the linear sequence AGGGTTC could be matched only with, or paired to, a strand containing the sequence TCCCAAG. This suggested that as cells divide and an organism grows, DNA could provide the means of passing on information from one cell to another. If the two strands were to unzip and each act as a template for the synthesis of a new strand, the result would be a perfect duplication of the original DNA molecule.

So much for passing on genetic information, but how does DNA direct and orchestrate the synthesis of the specific set of proteins that will enable a particular cell to carry out its normal function when DNA is a quite simple molecule consisting of just four basic elements? It does so by copying a relatively short stretch (a gene) of just one of the strands of a chromosome. This newly copied strand incorporates A, C and G together with another base, uracil (U). The new strand then separates from the template to form ribonucleic acid (RNA). Acting as a 'messenger', the RNA moves out of the nucleus and becomes attached to a ribosome, a complex structure which 'reads' the particular sequences of A, C, G and U in groups of three and starts making protein by using the RNA as a template and adding the appropriate amino-acid. For example, if the ribosome sees the sequence triplet CGU it adds the amino-acid arginine; if it sees AAG it adds lysine. The newly formed proteins, regulated by the copying process, then control the growth and activity of the cell, which in turn controls the growth and activity of the whole organism.

Even this greatly simplified outline explains why Crick spoke of having found 'the secret of life'. DNA forms the blueprint for the production of all the proteins that an organism needs to grow and survive, and is constructed in such a way that it is simply passed on to progeny cells so accurately that continuity of structure and function is preserved both within the organism and through reproductive cells to subsequent offspring.

Surely this all presents an obvious — and enormous — problem for the atheist? Reporting Shirono's findings in the *Sunday Telegraph*, Robert Matthews asked, 'Where on earth — or beyond it — did self-replicating molecules like DNA come from? Without their instructions, amino-acids are merely like so many Lego bricks lying forlornly in a box.'[33] As DNA forms the blueprint for the synthesis of all functional proteins, how could amino-acids and possibly proteins have arisen spontaneously *as a first step in evolution?* The bottom line here is that *you cannot invent DNA from proteins.*

The atheist's problem is hardly reduced when we realize that DNA is a marvel of miniaturization far beyond anything achieved by the most advanced technology. When the *Viking* space probe landed on Mars it carried a biology unit measuring just one cubic foot in volume yet containing some 40,000 functional components and capable of carrying out as many chemical operations as a university laboratory back on earth. Very impressive — but when put alongside DNA's credentials the *Viking* module looks as crude as the first bicycle! In DNA, the information needed to specify the design of a human being, including physical characteristics such as hair, skin, eyes and height, and determining the arrangement of components including over 200 bones, 600 muscles, 10,000 auditory nerve fibres, two million optic nerve fibres, 100 billion nerve cells and 400 billion feet of blood vessels and capillaries is packed into a unit several thousand million million times smaller than the smallest piece of functional machinery ever used by man, and weighing less than a few thousand-millionths of a gram. On the same scale, all the information needed to specify the design of all the species of organisms which have ever existed on our planet, a number put by George Gaylord Simpson at approximately 1,000 million, could be held in a teaspoon, and there would still be room left over for all the information contained in every book ever written.[34]

Fine-tuning the problem only compounds it. To give just one example, the chemical instructions for the construction of a complete human being exist in every fertilized human egg, and it has been shown that one chromosome may contain the information equivalent to 500 million words.[35] At 400 words to a page, it would take 5,435 books, each 230 pages long, to record the information contained in a single chromosome, and a library of 250,000 such books to store all the information secreted in the forty-six chromosomes in a single human egg. In a 1993 BBC television programme *Cracking the Code* presenter David Suzuki told viewers, 'If we could unravel the DNA in a human body it would reach to the sun and back more than 100 times.'[36] As if this were not amazing enough, all this information is encoded in a 'language' that has only four 'letters' and whose dictionary contains only sixty-four three-letter words.

A further complication for the atheist lies in the fact that DNA can be replicated only with the help of specific enzymes which, in turn, can be produced only by the controlling DNA molecule. In other words, each is absolutely necessary for the other, and both must be present before replication can occur. As they are completely interdependent, what is the explanation of the original synthesis? Carl Haskins, President of the Carnegie Institute of Washington, asks, 'Did the code and the means of translating it appear simultaneously in evolution? It seems almost incredible that any such coincidence could have occurred, given the extraordinary complexities of both sides and the requirement that they be co-ordinated for survival.'[37] We will return to the problem of the origin of inter-related proteins later in this chapter, but computer scientists agree that information does not, and cannot, arise spontaneously.[38] *As DNA is essentially information, how can the atheist deny that it was formed by intelligence?* The simple fact is that an atheistic (that is, evolutionary) explanation for the origin of DNA and its genetic code remains obstinately out of reach. As Leslie Orgel puts it, 'We must ... explain how a pre-biotic soup of organic molecules, including amino-acids and the organic constituents of nucleotides evolved into a self-replicating organism. While some suggestive evidence has been obtained, I must admit that attempts to reconstruct this evolutionary process are extremely tentative.'[39] In the September 1978 edition of *Scientific American*, devoted entirely to the subject of evolution, Richard Dickerson, Professor of Physical Chemistry at the California Institute of Technology, underlined the problem: 'The evolution of the genetic machinery is the step for which there are no laboratory models; hence *one can speculate endlessly, unfettered by inconvenient facts*'[40] (emphasis added).

One particular line of speculation followed work done in the 1980s by a scientist named Thomas Cech, who showed that some RNA had modest catalytic abilities. This led other scientists to propose the so-called 'RNA world' in which RNA — not protein — started earth on the road to life. However, Gerald Joyce and Leslie Orgel, acknowledged experts in the field, have called the notion 'unrealistic in the light of our current understanding of prebiotic chemistry', and one that 'should strain the credulity of even an optimist's view of RNA's catalytic potential'.[41] The idea of an RNA world became quite trendy during the 1990s, but a highly qualified biochemist claims that it 'ignores known chemistry' and likens it to the Stanley Miller phenomenon, which he calls 'hope struggling valiantly against experimental data'.[42]

Odds against

Useful proteins come from amino-acids, but it has been impossible to demonstrate either the spontaneous generation or the evolution of this genetic machinery. Where does the atheist turn for help? In *Implications of Evolution*, G. A. Kerkut, of the Department of Physiology and Biochemistry at the University of Southampton, wrote, 'It is ... a matter of faith on the part of the biologist that biogenesis did occur and he can choose whatever method of biogenesis happens to suit him personally; the evidence for what did happen is not available.'[43] Many hard-core evolutionists latch on to luck as the only avenue of escape from their dilemma, but many experts with no theistic flag to fly admit that the odds against are stupefying.

It has been said that Francis Crick 'understands the nature of living substances as well as any man living',[44] yet when he calculated the probability of the spontaneous origin of even a simple protein sequence of just 200 amino-acids (far simpler than a single DNA molecule), he arrived at a figure of one out of approximately 10^{260}. As we saw in chapter 4 that one chance in 10^{15} is considered to be 'a virtual impossibility', it is hardly surprising that Crick came to this conclusion: 'An honest man, armed with all the knowledge available to us now, could only state that in some sense the origin of life appears at the moment to be almost a miracle, so many are the conditions which would have to be satisfied to get it going.'[45] As a committed atheist, 'almost a miracle' was as close as he could get to acknowledging the possibility of divine creation, but it was his conviction that it was impossible for life to arise spontaneously here on earth that made him turn to the exotic notion of panspermia as an alternative explanation.

Fred Hoyle, who could hardly be labelled a creationist, dismissed spontaneous generation in typically down-to-earth terms: 'Anyone with even a nodding acquaintance with the Rubik cube will concede the near impossibility of a solution being obtained by a blind person moving the cube faces at random. Now imagine 10^{50} blind persons (standing shoulder to shoulder, these would more than fill our entire planetary system) each with a scrambled Rubik cube and try to conceive of the chance of them all simultaneously arriving at the solved form. You then have the chance of arriving by random shuffling (random variation) of just one of the many biopolymers on which life depends. *The notion that not only the biopolymers but the operating programme of a living cell could be arrived at by chance in a primordial soup here on earth is evidently nonsense of a high order*'[46] (emphasis added).

In *Evolution from Space*, Hoyle and Wickramasinghe wrote that the odds against the spark of life igniting accidentally were one in $10^{40,000}$, and then explained how those who rely on abiogenesis to kick-start their evolutionary model try to get around it: 'The tactic is to argue that although the chance of arriving at the biochemical system of life as we know it is admitted to be utterly minuscule, there is in nature such an enormous number of other chemical systems which could also support life that any old planet like the Earth would inevitably arrive sooner or later at one or another of them. This argument is the veriest nonsense, and if it is to be imbibed at all it must be swallowed with a jorum of strong ale.'[47]

Interviewed for the *Daily Express*, Wickramasinghe said that one chance in $10^{40,000}$ 'is such an imponderable that I am 100 per cent certain that life could not have started spontaneously on earth'.[48] He went on to illustrate the odds involved: 'For life to have been a chemical accident on earth is like looking for a particular grain of sand on all the beaches in all the planets of the universe — and finding it.'[49] Significantly, he told the newspaper that the conclusion to which his mathematical calculations had driven him came as 'quite a shock', as from his earliest training as a scientist he was 'strongly brainwashed to believe that science cannot be consistent with any kind of deliberate creation'. Now he had come to realize that 'The probability of life originating at random is so utterly minuscule as to make it absurd,' and that 'The only logical answer to life is creation — and not accidental random shuffling.'[50] Elsewhere Wickramasinghe was equally emphatic: 'Living systems could not have been generated by random processes, within a finite time-scale, in a finite universe.'[51]

Speaking on the BBC Radio programme *Science Today* later that year, Hoyle gave his often-quoted illustration of the same point: 'There is no way in which starting from a system without information, in a chaotic condition, one is going to produce that enormous degree of organization. If you imagine a whirlwind sweeping through a junkyard, what is the chance that all the pieces of metal that it stirs up will smash themselves together and produce a brand new Boeing 747? That is the kind of situation that is supposed for the origin of life on earth, and I think that the two cases are just as absurd.'[52] Hoyle's critics would argue that a whirlwind might indeed result in the joining together of two pieces of material, and that over an immense period of time a vast number of whirlwinds might result in a fully equipped aircraft. However, this misses the point that what is required to bring even a simple organic molecule into being is equivalent to a single whirlwind producing the complete aircraft *in one fell swoop*.

Vying with Hoyle's comment as the most-quoted statement on the subject is something written by the Princeton professor Edward Conklin. In a contribution to the January 1963 edition of *Reader's Digest* he stated, 'The probability of life originating by accident is comparable to the probability of the unabridged dictionary resulting from an explosion in a printing shop.'[53] The fact of the matter is that nobody has calculated the probability of a random search finding, in even the largest estimate of the finite time available, the sorts of complex systems that we find throughout nature. As Michael Denton says, 'It is surely a little premature to claim that random processes could have assembled mosquitoes and elephants when we still have to determine the actual probability of the discovery by chance of one single functional protein molecule!'[54]

So much for Tyche

As many atheists lean heavily on it as an explanation of how the universe in general, and life in particular, came into existence, we should add a postscript on the whole question of chance. The *Concise Oxford Dictionary* gives a selection of definitions of the word 'chance', including 'possibility' and 'undesigned occurrence'.[55] These uses of the word 'chance' are quite different from the statisticians' use of the word 'probability', and we must not confuse the two. For example, experts could use statistical data to calculate the probable number of marriages which will take place in Wales next year, but we could hardly call any of these events an 'undesigned occurrence'!

The laws of scientific probability are an important factor in many fields such as physics, biology and genetics, and they have many industrial applications, but they are very different from the popular view of chance as an undesigned occurrence. In ancient Greek mythology, Tyche was the goddess of chance or fortune, and people today still speak of 'Lady Luck' in a somewhat similar way, as if chance were a living, intelligent entity, able to think, determine and design. They may only be using a figure of speech, yet to suggest that chance causes anything to happen is to talk nonsense, because chance is merely a concept, unable to conceive, create or do anything.

As far back as the seventeenth century, John Locke wrote, 'Man knows by an intuitive certainty that bare nothing can no more produce any real being than it can be equal to two right angles.'[56] Applying this to the overall question of the existence of the universe, R. C. Sproul claims, 'To say that the world was created by chance is to say that it was created by nothing and was "self-created". Call it spontaneous generation or call it chance, but a rose by any other name... What are the chances that the universe was created by the power of chance? Not a chance.'[57]

Several other points can be made here. Firstly, how can we say with certainty that the universe (or life) arose by chance unless our knowledge is absolute? As science lecturer Michael Poole points out in *A Guide to Science and Belief*, 'The difficulty about not being "in the know" surrounds all our judgements of randomness. We may deny the appearance of a plan in chance processes or random events. But we are not in a position to deny the existence of a plan unless we have all the facts.'[58]

Secondly, as we saw in the last chapter, it can hardly be claimed that chance is the simplest or the most obvious explanation of the universe, or of life on our particular planet. For the universe to exist, there has to be a precise balance of gravity, electromagnetism and nuclear forces. For life to exist here, Earth has to be exactly the right size, to consist of certain elements, to be at a precise distance from the sun, to be tilted at a particular angle, to rotate at the right speed, and to meet a mass of other criteria with amazing precision. *Why should this rule out intelligent design?*

Thirdly, if the universe came into existence by pure chance, and is developing in a random, chaotic way, why should we assume (as we do) that human experience mirrors the reality of the world around us? If we have emerged by chance in the course of an ongoing, accidental process, what guarantee do we have that any of our perceptions can be relied on? The eighteenth-century French philosopher Baron de Montesquieu put his finger firmly on the spot: 'Those who have said that blind fatality has produced all the effects that we see in the world have uttered a great absurdity;

for what greater absurdity than a blind fatality which has produced intelligent beings?'[59] John Frame fine-tunes the question: 'Why should we assume that chance has equipped me with eyes and a brain so that when I think I'm a seminary professor typing at my desk in California, I am really a cockroach running around the New York subway?'[60]

Fourthly, many things which may appear to have happened by chance can equally well be explained by intelligent design. If we toss a coin, the odds against its coming down 'heads' or 'tails' are identical, one in two. Yet if we come across a coin lying somewhere, it would be wrong to assume that it must be 'heads' or 'tails' by chance. If a new golfing partner of mine were to notice that every time he saw an American twenty-five cent piece marking the position of my ball on the green it was lying 'heads', he might assume that this was a remarkable fluke, but he would be wrong; I deliberately choose to have George Washington looking at me just before I putt!

When the sceptic says that the universe and all life within it came about by chance, and that this rules out intelligent design, he is going too far. In John Benton's words, 'The account of chance is overdrawn at the bank of credibility.'[61]

The factory

The mind-boggling odds against life originating and developing by chance have been lengthened even further by recent advances in our understanding of the structure and function of individual cells. From Darwin's day until quite recently, a few more cells here and there may have seemed like a small change, and to have provided little in the way of conceptual difficulties in imagining alterations in their appearance and function, but given what we now know about the extraordinary complexity of a living cell and the processes going on within it, our understanding of what is involved in a 'small change' must be radically revised. The brilliant French molecular biologist (and atheist) Jacques Monod explains: 'The simplest living system known to us, the bacterial cell ... in ... its overall chemical plan is the same as that of all other living beings. It employs the same genetic code and the same mechanism of translation as do, for example, human cells. Thus the simplest cells available to us for study have nothing "primitive" about them ... no vestiges of truly primitive structures are discernible.'[62] In

Evolution: A Theory in Crisis, Michael Denton elaborates, 'Although the tiniest bacterial cells are incredibly small, weighing less than 10^{-10} gms, each is in effect a veritable micro-miniaturized factory containing thousands of exquisitely designed pieces of intricate molecular machinery, made up altogether of one hundred thousand million atoms, far more complicated than any machine built by man and absolutely without parallel in the non-living world.'[63] Later in the book, he gives an amazing illustration of what this means:

> Perhaps in no other area of modern biology is the challenge posed by the extreme complexity and ingenuity of biological adaptations more apparent than in the fascinating new molecular world of the cell. Viewed down a light microscope at a magnification of some several hundred times, such as would have been possible in Darwin's time, a living cell is a relatively disappointing spectacle appearing only as an ever-changing and apparently disordered pattern of blobs and particles which, under the influence of unseen turbulent forces, are continually tossed haphazardly in all directions. To grasp the reality of life as it has been revealed by molecular biology, we must magnify a cell a thousand million times until it is twenty kilometres in diameter and resembles a giant airship large enough to cover a great city like London or New York. What we would then see would be an object of unparalleled complexity and adaptive design. On the surface of the cell we would see millions of openings, like the portholes of a vast space ship, opening and closing to allow a continual stream of materials to flow in and out. If we were to enter one of these openings we would find ourselves in a world of supreme technology and bewildering complexity. We would see endless highly organized corridors and conduits branching in every direction away from the perimeter of the cell, some leading to the central memory bank in the nucleus and others to assembly plants and processing units. The nucleus itself would be a vast spherical chamber more than a kilometre in diameter, resembling a geodesic dome inside of which we would see, all neatly stacked together in ordered arrays, the miles of coiled chains of the DNA molecules. A huge range of products and raw materials would shuffle along all the manifold conduits in a highly ordered fashion to and from all the various assembly plants in the outer regions of the cell.

We would wonder at the level of control implicit in the movement of so many objects down so many seemingly endless conduits, all in perfect unison. We would see all around us, in every direction we looked, all sorts of robot-like machines. We would notice that the simplest of the functional components of the cell, the protein molecules, were astonishingly complex pieces of molecular machinery, each one consisting of about 3,000 atoms arranged in highly organized 3-D spatial conformation. We would wonder even more as we watched the strangely purposeful activities of these weird molecular machines, particularly when we realized that, despite all our accumulated knowledge of physics and chemistry, the task of designing one such molecular machine — that is one functional protein molecule — would be completely beyond our capacity at present and will probably not be achieved until at least the beginning of the next century. Yet the life of the cell depends on the integrated activities of thousands, certainly tens, and probably hundreds of thousands of different protein molecules.

We would see that nearly every feature of our own advanced machines had its analogue in the cell: artificial languages and their decoding systems, memory banks for information storage and retrieval, elegant control systems regulating the automated assembly of parts and components, error fail-safe and proof-reading devices utilized for quality control, assembly processes involving the principle of prefabrication and modular construction. In fact so deep would be the feeling of *déjà-vu*, so persuasive the analogy, that much of the terminology we would use to describe this fascinating molecular reality would be borrowed from the world of late twentieth-century technology.

What we would be witnessing would be an object resembling an immense automated factory, a factory larger than a city and carrying out almost as many unique functions as all the manufacturing activities of man on earth. However, it would be a factory which would have one capacity not equalled in any of our own most advanced machines, for it would be capable of replicating its entire structure within a matter of a few hours. To witness such an act at a magnification of one thousand million times would be an awe-inspiring spectacle. [64]

Behe's bombshell

Denton is right! The complexity, order, elegance and sheer efficiency of a
single living cell are truly amazing, and anyone who fails to be astonished
by all of this is simply not thinking straight. The theist's explanation for it is
that it was created by a God of supreme power, inconceivable imagination
and brilliant originality. The atheist may be equally awestruck by what he
sees. Richard Dawkins writes about this with great feeling and obvious
integrity, and rightly marvels that every cell contains in its nucleus 'a digit-
ally coded database larger ... than all 30 volumes of the *Encyclopaedia
Britannica* put together'.[65] Yet with no God available to create this amazing
phenomenon, some other explanation is needed. Finding one is proving
increasingly difficult, and the task is not being made any easier by the
emergence of a growing number of scientists who have come to the conclusion that molecular systems could not possibly have come into being by
a gradual step-by-step evolution but point unmistakably to intelligent design.

The biggest headlines in this impressive attack on Darwin's ideas are
currently being made by the American scientist Michael Behe, Associate
Professor of Biochemistry at Lehigh University. Behe is not a card-carrying
creationist and disclaims any religious agenda, but in his runaway best
seller *Darwin's Black Box*, first published in 1996 and subtitled 'The Biochemical Challenge to Evolution', he deals a devastating blow to the nineteenth-century notion that life arose spontaneously from non-living matter
and then developed by natural means. His central case is based on the
concept of irreducible complexity, which he explains as follows: 'By *irreducibly complex* I mean a single system composed of several well-matched,
interacting parts that contribute to the basic function, wherein the removal
of any one of the parts causes the system to effectively cease functioning.
An irreducibly complex system cannot be produced directly (that is, by
continuously improving the initial function, which continues to work by the
same mechanism) by slight, successive modifications of a precursor system, because any precursor to an irreducibly complex system that is missing a part is by definition non-functional.'[66]

As an ultra-simple mechanical example of such a system he cites a
mousetrap, consisting of a flat wooden platform, a metal hammer, a spring,
a sensitive catch and a metal bar to hold the hammer back when the trap
is set. He then asks, 'Which part could be missing and still allow you to
catch the mouse? If the wooden base were gone, there would be no platform

for attaching the other components. If the hammer were gone, the mouse could dance all night on the platform without becoming pinned to the wooden base. If there were no spring, the hammer and platform would jangle loosely, and again the rodent would be unimpeded. If there were no catch or metal holding bar, then the spring would snap the hammer shut as soon as you let go of it; in order to use a trap like that you would have to chase the mouse around while holding the trap open.'[67]

Behe's illustration brings his main thesis into focus. None of the mouse-trap's individual parts has any trapping ability, yet each is essential for the trap to work. In the same way, many molecular systems could never have evolved by randomly accumulating separate pieces, because there would be no function to select until all the pieces were properly organized to work together. Darwin himself admitted this: 'If it could be demonstrated that any complex organ existed which could not possibly have been formed by numerous, successive, slight modifications, *my theory would absolutely break down*'[68] (emphasis added). Behe tackles Darwin's dilemma head-on and shows quite clearly that irreducibly complex systems *do* exist.

Stopping the bleeding

Of the examples he gives, none is more fascinating than one to which most people pay very little attention – blood-clotting. When any other container of liquid springs a leak, the fluid drains out without resistance, yet when the human body's pressurized fluid system is punctured it nor-mally bleeds for only a short time before a clot stops the flow. Yet what we take for granted is a very complex, intricately woven system consisting of a score of independent protein parts. If any of these is missing, or there are significant defects in the system, the puncture could prove fatal. What is more, if the sealing mechanism kicks in by mistake somewhere in the sys-tem, it can result in a circulation blockage, a stroke or a heart attack.

Behe goes into great detail about how the clotting mechanism works; here, we will settle for a layman's sketch, specifically avoiding the technical terminology. The protein that physically enables a clot to form does so by forming a sticky fibrous mesh which traps escaping blood cells. The organ-ism's problem is how to prevent this happening all the time. It solves this by storing the protein in a form which only becomes sticky when it is needed. This conversion is carried out by another protein which is also stored in an inactive form and itself needs to be converted to the active form that allows it to convert the final protein to its sticky form! This process of sequential alteration and acquisition of function by proteins is known as a 'cascade', since an initial signal is cascaded down to the final point of need by an ordered sequence of events and involving twenty-eight separate proteins and enzymes, at least six times more complex than the summary I have given. In the case of an invasive event (a cut), a protein which is found only on the outside of cells not in contact with the blood is brought into the bloodstream locally and triggers off the cascade which results in localized clotting and the sealing of the wound. The all-important point about this whole process is that the cascade is formed in a specific way with a defined number of known interacting molecules; in other words, it is an irreducibly complex system, *precisely the kind of thing Darwin admitted would scupper his whole scheme.*

Needless to say, attempts have been made to show how the blood-clotting system could have evolved, the leading spokesman in the field being Russell Doolittle, a biochemist at the University of California, who has devoted forty years to the problem, but nobody has been able to get beyond speculation about gene mutations and the random duplication and shuffling of existing genes. Yet Behe insists that the odds against the inactive precursor protein and its activator getting together 'would not be expected to happen even if the universe's ten-billion year life were compressed into a single second and relived every second for ten billion years'.[69]

No evolutionist has been able to explain how the blood-clotting process was set up, nor how all the clusters of proteins involved come to be inserted all at once (as they must be) into the cascade. In Behe's bottom line, 'The fact is, *no one on earth has the vaguest idea how the coagulation cascade came to be...* Blood coagulation is a paradigm of the staggering complexity that underlies even apparently simple bodily processes. Faced with such complexity beneath even simple phenomena, Darwinian theory falls silent.'[70]

This is such a powerful argument that it deserves to be restated. While the 'sticky' protein (fibrin) is potentially very useful (it prevents the excessive loss of blood and the entry of germs), it is as deadly as the most powerful toxin when unregulated; fibrin floating around in the body would soon lead to death. On the other hand, the 'non-sticky' precursor (fibrinogen) is useless. If we put these two facts together, it is easy to see the problem they present to the evolutionist. Unregulated fibrin is lethal, and as fibrinogen is useless it would not have been retained in the course of evolution's upward march. Nor would there have been any evolutionary pressure for the formation and retention of the regulatory cascade enzymes.

In science, a theory is the best explanation of the known facts. If a set of observations cannot be explained by the accepted theory, the theory must be modified or scrapped. As no modification of evolutionary theory can account for the blood-clotting cascade, it is right to look for an alternative explanation. *Why should divine creation be ruled out?*

Back to the beginning

In the evolutionary model of life, nothing is more difficult to explain than the formation of self-replicating molecules from complex combinations of chemical elements. Natural selection could not have taken place until there had been reproduction, and science has never found a way of showing how a reproducing cell might have formed spontaneously without first having the products of living organisms. The best that Dawkins can offer (in *The Selfish Gene*) is the idea that a remarkable molecule which he dubs the 'Replicator', and which has the astonishing property of being able to create copies of itself, came into being by accident at some point in the earth's prehistory. He accepts that the emergence of self-replicating life-forms is 'exceedingly improbable',[71] yet in *The Blind Watchmaker* brushes the difficulty aside by suggesting that 'Given enough time, any-thing is possible.'[72] This is a popular ploy among those determined to avoid bringing God into the frame, but in his excellent book *God, Chance and Necessity*, the Oxford scholar Keith Ward knocks it neatly on the head: 'There is no reason why even one state should ever come into existence. There is no reason why, if there are *n* possible states, they should all come into existence one after another, or at some time... If, as seems likely, there is an infinite number of possible states, they cannot all come into exist-ence, since however many of them have existed, there will still remain an infinite number that have not existed. Moreover ... some possible states (like the state with a creator God in it) exclude many other possible states (like the state with no creator in it). So it is logically impossible for all possible states to exist. That is why Dawkins' statement embodies a fallacy.'[73]

An even more fundamental missing piece is an explanation for the exist-ence of the basic laws of physics which enable atoms to club together into molecules which eventually lead to organic life-forms. Where did they come from? Why do they operate so efficiently? Unless there is a satisfying explanation for the very existence of these laws, no scientific study can be undertaken with any degree of confidence. Keith Ward makes the point well: 'Suppose the basic laws of physics popped into existence for no reason at all. One day, they did not exist. The next day, there they were, governing the behaviour of electrons and atoms. Now if anything at all might pop into existence for no reason, there is actually no way of assessing the probability of laws of physics doing so. One day, there might be nothing. The next day, there might be a very large carrot. Nothing else in existence whatsoever, but there, all alone and larger than life, a huge carrot. If anything is possible, that certainly is. The day after that, the carrot might disappear and be replaced by a purple spotted gorilla. Why not? We are in a universe, or a non-universe, where anything or nothing might happen, for no reason. Why does this thought seem odd, or even ridiculous, whereas the thought that some law of physics might just pop into existence does not? Logically, they are exactly on a par.'[74]

For the theist, orderly, efficient and trustworthy laws of physics fit perfectly with the concept of God as the source and root of all existence. The atheist has to look elsewhere for an explanation, and the only one available to him is that of self-existent and self-organizing matter, operating by random natural processes over whatever amount of time it takes to produce the results we see. In *The Chemistry of Life*, Harvard scientist George Wald, winner of the 1967 Nobel Prize for physiology, put forward the idea that the sheer elapse of time would solve the evolutionists' problems about the origin and development of life: 'Time is the hero of the plot. Given enough time, anything can happen — the impossible becomes probable, the improbable becomes certain.'[75] But is this really the case? Writing in *Nature* magazine, Utah State University scholar Frank Salisbury discussed the staggering odds against the spontaneous production of a single gene. He asked his readers to imagine 10^{20} (one hundred million trillion) planets, each with an ocean two kilometres deep and fairly rich in gene-sized DNA fragments, which reproduce one million times per second, with a mutation occurring at each reproduction. Under such favourable conditions, Salisbury calculated that it would take trillions of universes to have much chance of producing a single gene in four billion years — even if 10^{100} different DNA molecules could serve the same gene function![76] In his entertainingly readable book *Climbing Mount Improbable*, Richard Dawkins puts the odds in an equally staggering form. Pointing out that there are a fixed number of twenty amino-acids, he shows that the probability that any particular sequence of, say, 100, amino-acids will form spontaneously is one in 20 x 20 x 20 ... 100 times, or one in 20^{100} and accepts that this 'is an inconceivably large number, far greater than the number of fundamental particles in the entire universe'.[77]

Figures like these simply defy imagination, and George Wald provides a good example of how the committed atheist is forced to respond: 'When it comes to the origin of life on this earth, there are only two possibilities: creation or spontaneous generation. There is no third way. Spontaneous generation was disproved 100 years ago, but that leads us only to one other conclusion: that of supernatural creation. We cannot accept that on philosophical grounds; therefore *we choose to believe the impossible*: that life arose spontaneously by chance'[78] (emphasis added). Elsewhere, Wald conceded that 'The spontaneous generation of a living organism is impossible,' then added, 'yet here we are — as a result, I believe, of spontaneous generation.'[79] This is hardly the kind of thinking we should expect from a distinguished scientist!

Richard Dawkins is equally firm in refusing to give God house-room. In a *New Scientist* article he wrote, 'The more statistically improbable a thing is, the less can we believe that it just happened by blind chance. Superficially the obvious alternative to chance is an intelligent Designer... I am afraid I shall give God very short shrift ... as an explanation of organized complexity he simply will not do. It is organized complexity we are trying to explain, so it is foolish to invoke as an explanation a being sufficiently organized and complex to explain it.'[80] This not only makes the mistake of imagining that the theists' God is complex in a way similar to the human mind — a fusion of thoughts, plans, desires and feelings — rather than what Keith Ward calls 'the one self-explanatory and supremely integrating reality';[81] it also suggests that it makes more sense to explain effects by causes that are not adequate to produce them than to concede the possibility that there should be a supreme cause more than adequate to do so. One should never underestimate the power of prejudice!

The chicken or the egg?

It should be clear by now that, far from being an established fact, abiogenesis is an article of faith, yet one with no supporting proof. In an article written for *Journal of Theoretical Biology* in 1997, molecular biologist

Hubert Yockey, a convinced evolutionist, openly confessed that there is no evidence whatever for the spontaneous evolution of even the simplest life-forms: 'One must conclude that, contrary to the established and current wisdom, a scenario describing the genesis of life on earth by chance and natural causes which can be accepted on the basis of fact and not faith has not yet been written.'[82] If we are still not able to determine the actual probability of the discovery by chance of one single functional protein molecule, how can we dogmatically claim that every one of earth's life-forms came into being in this way?

C. S. Lewis takes up the point with his usual clarity: 'If there ever was a life which sprang of its own accord out of purely inorganic universe, or a civilization which raised itself by its own shoulder-straps out of pure savagery, then this event was totally unlike the beginnings of every subsequent civilization... On any view, the first beginning must have been outside the ordinary processes of nature. An egg which came from no bird is no more "natural" than a bird which had existed from all eternity. And since the egg-bird-egg sequence leads us to no plausible beginning, is it not reasonable to look for the real origin somewhere outside sequence altogether? You have to go outside the sequence of engines, into the world of men, to find the real originator of the Rocket.[83] Is it not equally reasonable to look outside nature for the real Originator of the natural order?'[84]

It is, but the entrenched atheist dare not look too closely for fear of what he might find. Towards the end of his monumental *Tractatus*, Ludwig Wittgenstein, the leading analytical philosopher of the twentieth century, conceded, 'The solution of the riddle of life in space and time lies outside space and time.'[85] Looking at the issue from a scientific angle, Michael Behe goes a significant step further: 'As we reach the end of this book, we are left with no substantive defence against what feels to be a strange conclusion: that life was designed by an intelligent agent.'[86]

15.
Glory and rubbish?

Bertrand Russell is reported to have said that if (to his great surprise) he found himself confronted with God immediately after death, and God asked why he had not believed in him, he would look him straight in the eye and reply, 'Not enough evidence.' Yet whenever in the latter stages of his life Russell looked in a mirror, what he saw represented a massive accumulation of data which contradicted his passionate atheism.

The mirror would have reflected a peer of the realm (he was the third Earl Russell), a world-famous philosopher, mathematician and essayist, an articulate champion of liberal ideas, a powerful civil rights activist, a Nobel Prize winner, the author of some sixty books and a distinguished intellectual whose teaching had radically affected the thinking of millions of his contemporaries for the best part of a century. However, the case against atheism was presented by neither his record nor his reputation, but by something to which he contributed nothing — the fact that *he was a human being*.

But what is a human being, and why should humanness point away from atheism towards theism? Noteworthy definitions of humankind are scattered over centuries of literature, with Blaise Pascal providing one of the most memorable: 'What a freak, what a monster, what a chaos, what a subject of contradiction, what a marvel! Judge of all things and imbecile earthworm; possessor of the truth and sink of uncertainty and error; glory and rubbish of the universe.'[1] Pascal's purple prose is hardly a clinical definition, but it does suggest that human beings are remarkable creatures.

Body language

Then what did 'Bertie' Russell see when he looked in the mirror? C. E. M. Joad once famously said that an average human body consists of enough fat for seven bars of soap, enough iron to make one medium-sized nail, enough sugar to sweeten seven cups of tea, enough lime to whitewash one chicken coop, enough phosphorous to tip 2,200 matches, enough magnesium to provide one dose of salts, enough potash to explode one toy cannon and enough sulphur to rid one dog of fleas.[2] All of that sounds very clever, but it is not quite the full story! There are some twenty to thirty commonplace elements present in the earth's dry dust and found in scores of ordinary objects, but in the human body they exist in thousands of complex chemical compounds, many of which do not exist in the non-living world. What is more, they are arranged in such a staggering variety of ways, and function in such impressive harmony, that someone's description of a human being as 'an ingenious assembly of portable plumbing'[3] joins Joad's amusing assessment in falling some way short of being an adequate description.

Although human beings are arguably the most complex organisms on this planet, over ninety per cent of the human body consists of water and proteins. The rest is made up of inorganic salts, lipids (mainly fats), carbohydrates (sugar) and the two nucleic acids DNA and RNA. The smallest living units in the human body are some 10,000 billion cells, of more than a hundred different types, each one answering to Michael Denton's illustrated description from which we quoted in the previous chapter, and leading the Nobel Prize winner Linus Pauling to say that just one living cell in the human body is 'more complex than New York City'.[4]

The human *frame* is an engineering marvel. A baby is born with 305 bones, but some of these fuse together as the child grows, leaving just over 200, operated by about 600 muscles and 100 joints, each one formed in such a way as to function in perfect harmony with all the others. The framework is also remarkably strong; the tendons which anchor the muscles to the bones could stand a stress of eight tons per square inch.

The human *hand* has been called 'one of the finest, most delicate yet strong, and most minutely adjusted tools ever conceived ... the most perfect and precise instrument in a world bristling with the mechanical wonders of the atomic age'.[5] In his widely acclaimed book *The Human Body*, first published in 1998, the British author Anthony Smith writes, 'Next to its brain, the hand is probably *Homo sapiens'* greatest asset. Other species

may run faster or have keener senses, but none comes even close to match-
ing our manual skills.'[6] Referring to the forms of manual grip which 'out-
class the capabilities of any other creature', he says that the strength and
delicacy involved have 'permitted the human hand to be more gifted,
more capable and more manipulative than any limb ever seen'.[7] Powerful
enough to wield a pickaxe, yet precise enough to conduct microsurgery,
the human hand is uniquely designed to perform thousands of different
functions, a fact sometimes cleverly exploited by those promoting their
products: for example, one advertisement for a particular brand of golf
clubs asked, 'Ever wondered why you were born with 652,497 nerve endings in your hands?'

Each human _ear_ has a set of the smallest bones we possess — the
malleus, the incus and the stapes. The malleus picks up sound vibrations
from the eardrum, and by the time they have travelled to the incus and
then the stapes they have increased twenty-fold. Whereas a grand piano
has 240 strings and eighty-eight keys by which a gifted musician can produce beautiful sounds, the inner ear has 24,000 'strings' and 20,000 'keys',
enabling us to hear an amazing variety and range of sounds. Even an
airwave movement across the eardrum lasting one millionth of a second is
immediately translated into intelligible sound by processes involving 30,000
nerve centres contained in an area a fraction of an inch long. The ear
canal has some 4,000 wax-producing glands to prevent insects, dust and
other foreign bodies from reaching the delicate hearing mechanism, and
also serves as an effective air-conditioning system, while the inner ear,
deep within the skull, where it is one of the best-protected parts of the
human body, contains the structures essential for maintaining balance.
Small wonder that the complex construction of the ear has been said to
make a computer look as crude as a concrete-mixer!

The human _eye_ is a truly amazing phenomenon. Although accounting
for just one four-thousandth of an adult's weight, it is the medium which
processes some 80% of the information received by its owner from the
outside world. The tiny retina contains about 130 million rod-shaped cells,
which detect light intensity and transmit impulses to the visual cortex of
the brain by means of some one million nerve fibres, while nearly six
million cone-shaped cells do the same job, but respond specifically to colour variation. The eyes can handle 500,000 messages simultaneously, and
are kept clear by ducts producing just the right amount of fluid with which
the lids clean both eyes simultaneously in one five-hundredth of a second.

The inside story

If the outer organs of the human body are amazing, the internal ones are equally so. Not much bigger than a clenched fist, and weighing just 10-11 ounces, the *heart* automatically beats some 100,000 times a day, over 2,500 million times in an average life-span. It pumps blood through the body's 80,000 miles of blood vessels at a rate which means that every day the blood cells travel an accumulated distance of 168 million miles, equivalent to 6,720 times the world's circumference.

The average person has a supply of 6 - 8.5 pints of *blood,* totalling roughly 7% of body weight. A single drop of blood contains more than 250 million separate blood cells, floating in a straw-coloured plasma composed of thousands of different substances, including proteins, glucose, salts, vitamins, hormones and antibodies. There are three distinct types of blood cell. Some 250,000 million red cells carry oxygen from the lungs and drive it around the body, while 2,500 million so-called white cells (they are actually colourless) form a crucial part of the body's defence system, destroying dead and virally-infected cells, producing antibodies, detoxifying foreign substances and eating up bacteria. The smallest particles in the blood cells are the platelets. Whenever they are exposed to air, or any other foreign substance, they disintegrate, releasing an enzyme which causes the blood to clot, preventing the person concerned from bleeding to death. In the previous chapter we saw something of the amazing way in which this clotting process works.

Each red blood cell passes through the body's massive mileage of arteries, veins and capillaries some 300,000 times during its life-span of 120 days. The capillaries, tiny blood vessels which alone have a total area larger than a football field, are just five one-thousandths of a millimetre wide, so narrow that the red cells can only pass through in single file. After this amazing itinerary, the red cells are replaced in the bone marrow at the rate of three million per second. White cells have a much shorter life, and are replaced every twelve hours. Haemoglobin, which consists of four polypeptide chains of atoms linked in a unique and precise way, picks up oxygen atoms at the lungs, where oxygen concentration is high, and drops them off in the tissues, where it is low.

The human *brain*, shaped somewhat like an oversized walnut, and with the consistency of a mushroom, has been described by Isaac Asimov as 'the most complex and orderly aggregation of matter in the universe',[8] although it weighs just three pounds, and accounts for only about 2% of a person's body weight. Of the major organs, only the heart, kidneys, spleen, pancreas and lungs weigh less.

In an article based on her 1994 Royal Institution Christmas Lectures, Oxford University neurochemist Susan Greenfield wrote, 'If you were to prise the brain apart and strip it down to its most basic components, you would end up with about a hundred billion neurones, roughly as many trees as there are in the 2.7 million square miles of Amazonian rain forest. Even more astronomical are the connections that are formed between these cells: somewhere between 10,000 and 100,000 inputs from other neurones will converge on to each individual brain cell. Each particular neurone will in turn become one of tens of thousands of inputs stretching out to target neurones within a dense network.'[9]

According to experts in the field, a human brain processes ten tera-bytes of data over an eighty-year lifetime, the equivalent capacity of 7,142,857,142,860,000 floppy discs. How impressive is this? British Telecom's official futurologist projects, 'If current trends in the miniaturiz-ation of computer memory continues at the rate of the past twenty years, a factor of 100 every decade, today's eight megabyte memory chips will be able to store ten terabytes in thirty years' time.'[10]

Then are we to think of the human brain as being some kind of compu-ter, mysteriously and massively ahead of its time? Although there are cer-tain similarities (both are equipped with electrically powered mechanisms for storing, retrieving and processing information) there are some very basic differences, as Susan Greenfield explains: 'First and most obviously, the brain is fundamentally a chemical system... A wealth of chemical reac-tions is occurring incessantly in a bustling but closed world inside the cell... These events do not have a direct electrical counterpart or any easy anal-ogy with a computer. Second ... there is no separate and unchanging hard-ware distinguishable from some kind of neurological software... [Third] of course computers can "learn", but few are changing all the time to give novel responses to the same commands... True, advanced devices can seemingly organize and reorganize their own circuits to adapt to certain inputs; but they are still following a set of rules, algorithms that have been programmed in. The brain does not operate necessarily according to algo-rithms: what would be the rule for common sense, for example?'[11] She then went on to underline this crucial difference: 'In fact, no one pro-grammes the brain at all: it is a proactive organ, operating spontaneously.

Of course computers are able to do some of the things that brains can do, but that does not prove that the two entities work in a similar way or serve a similar purpose. A computer that does nothing defies its prime function: a person doing nothing is nevertheless having some kind of experience.'[12]

No computer can decide to reprogramme itself, be instinctively creative or perceive meaning. No computer knows it is a computer. No computer can relax, daydream, be amused or frustrated, become bored or fall in love. No computer can contemplate the reason for its existence and, in doing so, recognize the possibility of the existence of God.

The largest internal organ is the wedge-shaped _liver,_ which weighs between three and four pounds and serves as the body's chemical processing factory. It has over 500 essential functions, including the production of bile, the storage of sugars, vitamins and minerals, the maintenance of hormone balance and the manufacture of over 1,000 different enzymes. The liver processes ten million degenerating red blood cells every second.

The _kidneys_ are not much bigger than a standard bar of soap, and weigh just four ounces, yet they have over a million nephrons, filtering units which would stretch for over fifty miles if they were uncoiled and laid end to end. The nephrons process about forty gallons of fluid every day, filtering poisons and other impurities from the blood, regulating its volume and adjusting its chemical composition, and recycling water, minerals and nutrients. The kidneys have the remarkable ability to extract only toxic material and surplus water, leaving the bloodstream's valuable constituents untouched.

The _lungs_ are literally vital to a person's survival, as they take in oxygen and exhale carbon dioxide, the body's main waste product. This 'laundering' is carried out by some 300,000 million capillaries, which run in the walls of the alveoli, balloon-like structures found at the very end of the bronchial 'tree'. If these alveoli were spread out, they would cover an area the size of a tennis court. Filled and emptied like bellows by the action of a complex system of respiratory muscles, the lungs operate at a pace which means that the average person breathes just under twenty times every minute, something over 700 million times during his or her lifetime.

The human body comes encased in three integrated layers of flexible waterproofing, the _skin,_ the outer layer of which is unobtrusively and automatically replaced every few weeks. The body's first line of defence against harmful invaders such as microbes, the skin contains millions of nerve endings (up to 1,300 per square inch in sensitive areas such as the fingertips and lips) to detect pain, heat, cold, pressure and contact. Its waterproofing is provided by the *stratum corneum*, the topmost, 'dead' layer of skin, while a dark pigment called melanin protects the owner from the sun's potentially dangerous ultraviolet rays as well as determining the colour of skin and hair. The skin also houses a complex air-conditioning system comprising six miles of ducts one-fifth of an inch long. This system's membranes allow water to escape from the body in the form of sweat in order to prevent overheating, yet never allow water to enter the body. It has been calculated that the number of living organisms on the skin of one human being is roughly equivalent to the number of people currently living on our planet.

Accident or design?

We have only sketched in an outline of some of the components of the human body, but it is impossible to escape the question: 'How did the whole package come about?' It is interesting to read how Darwin wrestled with the issue: 'I cannot anyhow be contented to view this wonderful universe, *and especially the nature of man,* and to conclude that everything is the result of brute force. I am inclined to look at everything as resulting from designed laws, with the details, whether good or bad, left to the working out of what we may call chance. Not that this notion at all satisfies me. I feel most deeply that the whole subject is too profound for the human intellect... Let each man hope and believe what he can'[13] (emphasis added). This certainly covers all the options — he includes phrases that would satisfy the theist, the atheist and the agnostic! Others are less equivocal, and have no hesitation in stating that for all his staggering complexity and ability, *Homo sapiens* is a freak of nature. As we noted in an earlier chapter, Bertrand Russell wrote man off as 'the result of accidental collocations of atoms'.[14] In a 1997 *Daily Telegraph* feature in which he rightly debunked astrology, Martin Rees nevertheless claimed, 'The atoms in our bodies were once inside a star. We are literally stardust — or (in less romantic language) the nuclear waste from long-dead stars.'[15] Speaking in 1984 on the American television programme *60 Minutes,* Stephen Jay Gould said, 'If the history of life teaches us any lesson, it is that human beings arose as ... a kind of glorious cosmic accident resulting from the catenation [linking] of thousands of improbable events.'[16]

This has become a familiar tune — but by no means everybody has joined the choir. Isaac Newton has been reported as saying, 'In the absence of any other proof, the thumb alone would convince me of God's existence.' Elsewhere he asked, 'Was the eye contrived without skill in optics, and the ear without knowledge of sounds?'[17] James Le Fanu, a general practitioner who regularly contributes to the *Sunday Telegraph* and the *Daily Telegraph*, concluded a 1997 article entitled 'Why God is in everyone's blood', by stating, 'Just as [the seventeenth-century physician and anatomist William] Harvey could be certain that, as it was impossible for the body to create three times its own weight in blood every hour, the blood must circulate, we can now be certain that the blood-clotting system *(and, indeed, any physiological system one cares to examine)* could not have arisen by chance alone — it must have been designed [or created]. Hence, *there must be a designer*'[18] (emphasis added).

C. Everett Koop, one-time Surgeon General of the United States, is in no doubt as to what his medical research and practice reveal: 'If I didn't believe that I had a God who was solid and dependable, a God who makes no mistakes, I couldn't continue what I'm doing. I never operate without having a sub-conscious feeling that there's no way this extraordinarily complicated mechanism known as the human body just happened to come up from slime and ooze... When I make an incision with my scalpel, I see organs of such intricacy that there simply hasn't been enough time for natural evolutionary processes to have developed them.'[19]

Looking at the whole package, the renowned statistician George Gallup is quite emphatic: 'I could prove God statistically. Take the human body alone; the chance that all the functions of the individual would just happen is a statistical monstrosity.'[20] Philosophers may want to quibble over Gallup's use of the word 'prove', but is there credible evidence to show how the astonishing complexity and harmony of the human body could have arisen from a speck of inanimate matter, and reached its present level of sophistication by a process which began with the senseless stirring of primordial sludge?

Risen apes?

Determined atheists swat all this aside and look elsewhere for answers. As we saw in an earlier chapter, pantheism teaches that there is no difference between mankind and the rest of the universe, and that ultimately a human being is at one with all the rest of material reality, a cosmic coincidence essentially the same as any other object or being. The British zoo and club owner John Aspinall has no hesitation in lumping humans and nature together: 'I have an oak tree that is 500 years old. Its existence is more important than any human life because it supports 70 different species.'[21] Whatever mysterious attraction this idea may have to some, most people agree with David Cook: 'It seems obvious to most that there is a difference between grass thinking that man is grass, and man thinking that man is grass. In other words, there is a fundamental distinction between human-ity over and against natural phenomena. None of us is very sure what the thought-life of grass is like, but we are very sure about the thought-life of man. We think and we know it.'[22]

Many atheists take a somewhat 'softer' line than pantheism and say that, for all his sophisticated construction, man is merely the highest form of animal, the latest arrival on the evolutionary scene. This idea has been popularized by the British zoologist Desmond Morris in best-selling books such as *The Naked Ape*. Morris's message is simple: 'Human beings are animals. They are sometimes monsters, sometimes magnificent, but always animals. They may prefer to think of themselves as fallen angels, but in reality they are risen apes.'[23] Nobody seriously questions the fact that in general terms human beings do have many things in common with certain other life-forms — hardly surprising when we realize that they share the same genetic code — but this falls a long way short of establishing an evolutionary relationship.

There are over five million known species of living organisms in the natural world, of which over 90% are animals,[24] and the atheistic evol-utionist who sees man as evolution's finest achievement has to face the awkward fact that many creatures he would place a long way down the evolutionary 'tree' have characteristics not found in human beings. Fish can live permanently under water and birds can fly without mechanical help. Human beings are midgets compared to the 100-ton blue whale, or the largest land mammal, the African elephant, which weighs in at up to eight tons. They are dwarfed by the giraffe, which sometimes reaches a height of eighteen feet, left standing by the cheetah, which can sprint to forty-five miles per hour in two seconds from a standing start, and easily outlived by the aldabra giant tortoise.

Certain faculties are much more highly developed in other creatures than in humans. The buzzard has eyesight eight times as keen, enabling it to pick out from a great height an object as small as a beetle on the ground.

A 1998 study at the University of California concluded that the common housefly has 'the fastest visual system on the planet',[25] with eyes that can move ten times faster than a human's, while it can react to danger in under three-hundredths of a second, enabling it to change course five times faster than an Olympic sprinter can leave the starting-blocks. A dolphin's hearing is so acute that it can pick up underwater sounds at a distance of fifteen miles. It has been said that a dog's sense of smell is to a man's what a symphony orchestra is to a penny whistle. Whereas a human being has some five million olfactory cells, an Alsatian (or German shepherd-dog) has no fewer than 220 million. Experiments have suggested that these make it a million times better than a human at detecting odours — an obvious reason for using Alsatians in drug detection and other police work.

Nor do humans win any prizes for their breeding capacity. As I write, the British press is reporting that termites *(reticulitermes)* have established a colony in Britain for the first time. The insects have wrecked a £200,000 house in North Devon, and experts fear they could rapidly spread throughout the country, not least because queen termites, which often live for fifty years, can lay their first batch within hours of mating and can produce up to 36,000 eggs per day.

Many creatures have sophisticated systems not possessed by humans. Bats have what amounts to built-in radar, an ultrasound system enabling them to fly safely in the dark and to swarm in their thousands without colliding. Bees are sensitive to ultraviolet light, enabling them to locate the exact position of the sun even when it is completely obscured by clouds. The greatest distinction between humans and other living organisms usually cited is that of brain size, but even that factor has to be qualified. To give just two examples, some monkeys have a brain weighing nearly 5% of body weight, while in 1996 a *New Scientist* report revealed that the African Elephant Nose Fish *(Gnathonemus peterii)* has a brain which weighs 3.1% of its body weight, again a larger proportion than in humans, where it ranges from 2% to 2.5%.[26]

Nor can humans claim to be the only useful living organisms on our planet. As the common earthworm burrows, it passes soil, leaves and manure through its body, enriching the land with minerals and improving crop yields, while its network of tunnels drains and ventilates the earth. A well-known eighteenth-century English naturalist wrote, 'The earth without worms would become cold, void of fermentation and sterile,' while in Charles Darwin's opinion, 'It may be doubted whether there are any other animals which have played such an important part in the history of the world.'[27]

In 1994, the British media reported that in the space of a few months over ten people had died of necrotizing fasciitis, a flesh-eating disease caused by a common bacterium, some dying within hours of contracting a sore throat. Commenting that 'No bacteria in history has had such generous press coverage,' James Le Fanu went on to show the positive role bacteria played, and claimed that 'Quite simply, life on this planet would be impossible without them.'[28] Explaining the part they played in plant growth, animal welfare and human digestion, he also quoted from *Power Unseen: How Microbes Rule the World*, in which the British science writer Bernard Dixon tells us that bacteria 'make a massive contribution to global cleansing, attacking the waste that arrives in an unceasing stream at sewage disposal plants, rendering it safe and innocuous', and that 'Microbes accept this cocktail of filth and turn it into water sufficiently pure to be discharged into the cleanest of rivers.'[29] Le Fanu concluded that 'Man, in all his glory, is utterly dependent on these, the most primitive single-cell organisms on the face of the earth. The elegance of it all is awe-inspiring.'[30]

Bacteria also easily beat humans at the numbers game. In July 1998, geneticist Steve Jones reported the outcome of a global census of the world's bacteria, based on samples in the oceans, in the soil and elsewhere: 'The numbers are impressive; the world has 10 with 30 zeros after it of these single-celled creatures. Within them are most of the globe's living reserves of nitrogen and phosphorus — both essential to keep the energies of ... other animals in balance.' As an indication of what these vast numbers meant, Jones added, 'I have in my own guts ten times as many bacterial cells as I have cells of my own; some 10,000 times as many as there are people in the world.'[31]

· A dog's life?

The amazing features and abilities of some creatures have led to various human responses. In March 1998, Britain's National Lottery Charity Board gave £220,000 to a farm supplying pigs with underfloor heating, snout-operated showers and snacks in the shape of toys to prevent them from being bored.[32] At The Total Dog, Inc., in Los Angeles, pets are offered physical therapy, swimming, homeopathy, electro-acupuncture and Chinese herbs, while at the nearby Beverly Hills Animal Clinic, those deemed to need it are given the controversial antidepressant Prozac.[33] Meanwhile, at the Dog House in rural Wales, pets are 'pampered to the hilt with everything they want', including heated kennels, champagne and caviar, outings to the beach and 'plenty of television by a roaring log fire'.[34]

Much more significant than these and similar exotica is what we can loosely call the animal rights movement, many of whose supporters take the line that animals have the same rights as humans and should be treated accordingly. We dare not get sidetracked into animal rights issues here, but it is not difficult to see how a philosophy of radical equality breaks down. Linda McCartney, the (now deceased) wife of the well-known British musician Paul McCartney, chose to be a vegetarian, yet used medicine which had been tested on animals. Is there not a contradiction here? Can an atheist be consistent on this issue unless he or she is just as happy for animals to eat humans as for humans to eat animals? Why are we all in favour of people killing microbes, but all against microbes killing people?

The Australian bioethicist Peter Singer is one of today's most passionate animal rights campaigners. He strongly promotes the principle that, where their interests are similar, animals deserve the same consideration as human beings, and insists that what he calls 'speciesism' is just as wrong as racism or sexism. Interviewed by the *Daily Telegraph's* Boris Johnson in 1998, he was asked what he would do if he could save either a child or the last Bengal tiger. He immediately replied, 'I'd save the child.' But suppose the child was a disabled orphan, the tiger was starving and about to die along with the species, and could not catch the child without assistance? Presented with such a scenario Singer concluded: 'Assuming there were [no other ways of feeding the tiger] I guess ... I'd shoot the orphan.'[35] Most people might be horrified at that, but can the consistent atheist, who believes that both tigers and humans came about by different shakes of the evolutionary dice, find a reason to disagree with Singer's choice?

Are animals really on a par with humans? Do all living creatures have intrinsic moral values? Do they have codes of moral conduct? Can animals have similar rights to humans if those rights are not balanced by responsibilities? Are animals answerable for their actions? Are foxes 'guilty' if they bite the heads off chickens, or (and I write with some feeling here!) if they steal golf balls? Should cats who play with wounded mice be brought to account? Do ants, sheep and kangaroos wrestle with moral issues? If we should give 'rights' to whales, dolphins and gorillas, why not to hyenas, jellyfish and dung-beetles? The logic seems unanswerable. The plain fact is that there is a massive chasm separating humankind from everything else we see or know. Those who argue that as apes are almost genetically identical to humans they should be accorded the equivalent of human rights are missing a crucial point made by *New Scientist*: 'Genomes are not recipes. A creature that shares 98.4% of DNA with humans is not 98.4% human any more than a fish that shares, say, 40% is 40% human.'[36]

The hunter?

In a 1994 BBC television series broadcast under the general title *The Human Animal*, Desmond Morris presented a programme called *The Hunting Ape*, in which he claimed that hunting is what lifts humans above all other animals. In the light of what we see all around us, this seems to be a remarkable claim, even by Morris's adventurous standards. He tried to make his point by insisting that everything humans do is a form of hunting; in particular he cited buying food in a supermarket, spotting trains, playing football and waging war. Even traffic wardens were brought in as grist to the mill, stalking their prey before moving in for the kill. Morris presented this idea with his usual enthusiasm, but his theory lost its usefulness by going grossly over the top. There are scores of human activities that could clearly not be included, and *The Times* television critic was on target when he described *The Human Animal* as 'an entertaining series which would be more credible if it did not lay claim to scientific truth'.[37]

The fact is that human beings are separated from the rest of the animal world, not by a slight shading in a handful of features, but by a whole raft of fundamental distinctions. In his unusual book *Black Mischief: the Mechanics of Modern Science*, the philosopher and mathematician David Berlinski gives a sample of these, using what evolutionists usually call man's nearest relative as a reference-point: 'Chimpanzees do not talk, and apparently have nothing to say; they cannot read; they do not write; they do not paint, or compose music, or fashion sculpture; nor do mathematics, or metaphysics; they form no real communities, only loose-knit wandering tribes; they do not dine and cannot cook; there is no record of their achievement — not surprising of course; beyond the superficial, they show little curiosity; they are born, they live, they suffer, they die... One may insist, of course, that all this represents only a difference of degree. One can also say that only a difference of degree distinguishes man from the Canadian goose.'[38] Ongoing experiments seem to suggest that Berlinski's claim may eventually need some fine-tuning, but this in no way invalidates the general point he is making.

This already takes us far beyond Morris' simplistic analysis — and we can go much further. Most people do not question that human beings are animals. What needs explaining is why we are the only animals that *know* we are animals. Other species show no awareness of this. As George Roche comments, 'They all give every appearance of accepting what they are without question; certainly none publishes treatises or holds seminars on its animal status.'[39] Animals may have a degree of consciousness but, as Karl Popper points out, 'Only man can make an effort to become a better man; to master his fears, his laziness, his selfishness; to get over his lack of self-control.'[40] Do we have any evidence of animals having moral regrets about their actions or trying to discipline their emotional responses? Do animals set goals, cherish ambitions, assess their performance or adjust their lifestyle for other than instinctive reasons? The historian and philosopher Herbert Schlossberg provides the answer: 'Animals do not act morally or immorally; they only act naturally. A system of ethics that says human beings ought to base their behaviour on nature therefore justifies any behaviour, because nature knows no ethic.'[41] Sketching in the other side of the same coin, the nineteenth-century British essayist and critic William Hazlitt wrote, 'Man is the only animal that laughs and weeps, for he is the only animal that knows the difference between what things are and what they ought to be.'[42]

Distinctives

Schlossberg and Hazlitt touch on a major factor in distinguishing humans from the rest of the animal kingdom, but there are at least thirteen major areas in which fundamental differences can be clearly identified.

1. Man *intrinsically walks upright*. This is an obvious visible difference between humans and other creatures, and is much more significant than might at first appear. Man is not merely an erect ape (the relative size of his upper and lower limbs is the exact opposite of what is found in apes) and the curved shape of the human spine gives unique advantages for seeing,

face-to-face body language, and speaking without any change of head position. (The hoary chestnut about human back problems dating back to the time when hominids first stood upright is long past its sell-by date, as it is now well established that there are animals with even greater back problems.) The other major physical distinction is that humans have two hands and two feet.

2. Man has *vastly superior intelligence.* He can accumulate, remember and evaluate masses of information on an immense variety of subjects, and then act rationally as a result. Man's superior intelligence is illustrated or proved in many ways, and the remaining distinctives listed below help to make the point.

3. Man is *a historical and political being,* one who is aware of his past, has developed a cultural tradition and makes laws and rules of behaviour to govern his social life.

4. Man possesses qualities not only of consciousness, but of *self-awareness,* which lead him to reflect on his identity and relevance. He instinctively senses that he is neither an atomic accident nor an educated ape. All other living creatures are conscious; man alone is self-conscious. If a kangaroo could say, 'I am a kangaroo,' it would cease to be a kangaroo. Unlike anything else we know of in the universe, man asks 'Why?' as well as 'What?' He thinks about meaning and purpose. He longs for significance. He conceives goals and aspirations. He has an inbuilt sense of dignity, which leads him to be concerned about such things as human values and rights. He is able to look beyond his own immediate and direct experiences, and wonder about his origin and destiny. He thinks (more often than he cares to admit) about death and what may lie beyond.

5. Man has the unique ability to use *propositional language,* employing sophisticated syntax. This phenomenon leads Arthur Koestler to claim, 'The emergence of symbolic language, first spoken and then written, represents the sharpest break between animals and man,'[43] while Ludwig Wittgenstein points to language as being essentially social and of prime importance in conferring selfhood on humans.

Man can write prose and poetry, translate languages, and express the whole gamut of human emotions in spoken and written words. Experts in the field have concluded that 'Apparently human beings, and only humans, are specifically designed to acquire just the range of language systems that we see manifested in the world's five thousand-plus languages.'[44] The eminent Jewish linguist Noam Chomsky explains that the ability to learn language is a unique feature of what it means to be human: 'The rate of vocabulary acquisition is so high at certain stages of life, and the precision and delicacy of the concepts required so remarkable, that it seems necessary to conclude that in some manner the conceptual system with which lexical items are connected is already substantially in place.'[45] Chomsky also shows that even the higher apes are incapable of dealing with the number system or with abstract properties of space, or in general with an abstract system of expressions.[46]

The Gorilla Foundation tutored a lowland gorilla named Koko in sign language for twenty-five years at its California facility before being able to claim that she understood 2,000 words of spoken English and had a working vocabulary of 500 signs. In 1998, the foundation arranged for Koko to respond to questions during a forty-five minute 'chat' on the Internet — but she ignored most of the questions. At one point, she apparently asked for 'food and smokes' for her birthday, though her tutor, Francine Kennedy, said she was a non-smoker. Even the redoubtable Koko seems to confirm the assertion of linguistic experts: 'If all the aeons of the space-time world could be multiplied clear to infinity, the material world would still fail to account for the abstract conceptions that any human can easily conceive of through the gift of language.'[47] More recent tests have suggested that monkeys can count, and in 1999 researchers at Georgia State University, Atlanta, presented a pygmy chimpanzee and an orang-utan which could 'speak' by pressing buttons on an electric keyboard linked to a voice synthesizer, but nobody claims that they can acquire or develop any of these skills unless trained by a superior species.

6. Man is capable of *complex reasoning,* lateral thinking and the development of theories and insights. This is related to the fact that human brain size alone is not a reliable guide to intelligence; it is the *type* of brain. Not only is the human cortex far bigger than that of any animal, it has a much larger uncommitted area, which is free for the higher mental processes.

7. Man has *mathematical skills.* He has the ability to count to immense numbers, construct algebraic equations, apply the rules of reason to sets of axioms, and use mathematical language to discuss issues in mathematics,

statistics and science generally, including the nature of the universe and the laws of planetary motion.

8. Man's *cultural and scientific achievements* are on a vastly different scale from anything accomplished by any other creatures. Nowhere is this clearer than in the construction of sophisticated tools in order to make use of natural resources for his benefit or enjoyment. As John Benton points out, 'Beavers may build dams, but men develop quantum mechanics, paint the Mona Lisa and fly to the moon! To say that animals and man are the same is like saying that coal and diamonds are the same. They are, yet they aren't, are they? There is something essentially different.'[48] The British author John Peet makes the same point: 'Human beings are the only creatures that have developed a technology that can change their way of life.'[49]

9. Man has *an aesthetic dimension*, an innate sense of beauty which, like goodness and truth, eludes scientific analysis. He is able to assess the relative qualities of form, texture, colour, order and design. He is endlessly creative in composing music and making pictures and other objects, not merely for practical purposes, but for his personal enjoyment or to express meaning. There is a world of difference between animal instinct and apparent ingenuity and the prolific imagination of human beings. In his book *Darwinism Defended*, evolutionist Michael Ruse is forced to admit that 'Nothing even yet scratches at an explanation of how a transformed ape could produce the magnificence of Beethoven's Choral Symphony.'[50] Nor is there an atheistic explanation as to why we can detect and interpret elements of creative designs in the work of an artist, composer or craftsman.

At a practical level, man's aesthetic tastes often generate very strong feelings. In 1984 Prince Charles caused a furore in British architectural circles by describing a proposed ultra-modern extension to the National Gallery in Trafalgar Square, London as a 'monstrous carbuncle'. Ten years later, author Christopher Booker commended the Prince for his role in leading the revolt against 'the megalomaniac excesses of the modern architects' and giving public voice to 'widespread feelings of popular revulsion against the dehumanized, soulless, moonscape architecture produced by the modern movement, and which in the sixties inflicted on our cities the greatest social disaster to hit this country since the war'.[51] The note struck in these stirring words was echoed in an article in the first issue of *Perspective*, sponsored by Prince Charles' Institute of Architecture, which spoke of the need for 'that critical spiritual dimension'. Is this kind of thing a factor in the non-human world? Is beauty for beauty's sake an issue anywhere else in creation other than among human beings?

Coming at this from another angle, is there no objective reality which gives content to the word 'beauty'? If not, is there any reason for thinking that a Mozart concerto is more beautiful than the sound of a pneumatic drill, that a Constable masterpiece is an improvement on an oil slick, or that the Taj Mahal has more to commend it than a garden shed? Even when we have made allowances for subjectivity related to such factors as age and localized culture, the concept of beauty is universally recognized.

At the non-practical level, the British physician John Rendle-Short makes another telling point about aesthetics: 'Compare the most beautiful of bird songs with a Beethoven symphony, or the elegant but repetitive mating dance of the bird of paradise with a human ballet production ... the bird's efforts are always the same. You can recognize the kookaburra by his in-imitable laugh even when he is a quarter of a mile away. Certain birds make certain sounds; spiders build a unique but constant web; animals have stereotyped habits — they seldom vary. But man has original ideas, he can create new things, and does so constantly.' Rendle-Short has no doubt as to why this is so: 'In his own small way he mimics God the Cre-ator.'[52] It is reported that when Albert Einstein first heard Yehudi Menuhin playing the violin as a child prodigy he said, 'Now I know there is a God in heaven.'

Predictably, Richard Dawkins takes the well-worn atheistic line in treat-ing values as nothing more than subjective reactions, matters of personal taste which vary from person to person, yet how can he possibly know this without being able to transcend the point he is making? In *River Out of Eden*, he kicks the whole 'beauty' issue into touch and comes to the astonishing conclusion that 'Beauty is not an absolute virtue in itself,'[53] a verdict which leads Keith Ward to retort that as the appreciation of, and the happiness that comes from, contemplating something of beauty is 'an intrinsic value if anything is', Dawkins' dismissal leaves him 'speechless'.[54] Dawkins is certainly at odds with H. R. Rookmaaker, one-time Professor of the History of Art at the Free University, Amsterdam, who sees true beauty as a reflection of the character of God, and goes on to say, 'Our being cannot be satisfied unless the thirst for beauty is quenched.'[55]

10. Man is *not governed by instinct*. When Irish Republican terrorists detonated a car bomb in Omagh on 15 August 1998, killing twenty-nine

men, women and children and injuring hundreds more, Mo Mowlam, who
was Northern Ireland Secretary at the time, told reporters, 'The people
who did this are not human, they are animals,'[56] but this scathing condemnation does an injustice to the animals, whose behaviour is governed by
instinct alone, whereas human beings can knowingly and deliberately act
in callous, perverted or destructive ways. In *The Brothers Karamazov*,
Fyodor Dostoevsky showed the basic fallacy of equating animal and human behaviour in this way: 'People talk sometimes of bestial cruelty, but
that's a great injustice and insult to the beasts; a beast can never be so
cruel as a man, so artistically cruel. The tiger only tears and gnaws, that's
all he can do. He would never think of nailing people by the ears, even if
he were able to do it.'[57] John Benton gives a simple illustration of how this
principle works out: 'At the less serious level of the more common misde-
meanours, people take a delight in actually *knowing* that what is being
done is "naughty" or "wrong". "Go on, enjoy yourself", people say. That
is something that would never occur to an animal.'[58] The difference between what governs animal and human behaviour in this area — the reason why, as Mark Twain noted, 'Man is the only animal that blushes or
needs to'[59] — is radical and defining, and it defies evolutionary diagnosis.

11. Man is *unique in his relationships with the opposite sex*. Man is free
to love one person before another, and is free to choose the level of his
affection. As John Peet says, 'Mankind has freedom from the rigorous
chemical control of the reproductive functions, whereas animals are constrained by these periodic functions. Human beings, on the other hand,
are essentially free to mate at any time of the year, responding to love
rather than simple chemical or environmental factors.'[60] In developing this
point, Peet adds another distinguishing mark: 'The role of people in the
care of offspring is unique in creation. The family unit in animals is relatively superficial; in humans it is for a lifetime and over great distances.'[61]

12. Man has *a moral dimension*, a stubborn perception that there is a
difference between right and wrong. He can use and understand words
like 'temptation', 'offence', 'wickedness', 'crime', 'sin', 'fault', 'blame' —
and 'forgiveness'. Tied in to this is a sense of ethical responsibility. In C. S.
Lewis' simple phrase, 'Human beings, all over the earth, have this curious
idea that they ought to behave in a certain way, and cannot get rid of it.'[62]
Even more simply put, man has a conscience. Time and again he responds
to this, not only by restraining certain instincts, but by exercising and

promoting kindness towards people completely outside his acquaintance and from whom he can expect no benefit in return. Do we see this anywhere else in nature? As one modern writer puts it, 'Rats, after all, as far as we know, show no particular enthusiasm for moral issues and questions of meaning; and chimpanzees, delightful though they are, are not normally to be seen on our streets collecting money for impoverished chimpanzees they will never meet.'[63]

13. Most significantly in the context of our present study, man has *a spiritual dimension*. He has what theologians call *sensus divinitatis*, a sense of deity. It has sometimes been said that man is incurably religious but, as the scholar R. B. Kuiper comments, 'Religion not being a disease, it is much better to say that man is *constitutionally* religious.'[64] Any fair reading of history, ancient and modern, would seem to justify this verdict of the British scientist Sir John Houghton: 'There is general evidence that most human beings, from whatever part of the world and from the earliest times, have exhibited a fundamental belief in a divine being or beings, and in some sort of spiritual world.'[65]

Why do only humans have this sense of spirituality? As George Roche rightly points out, 'Nature is amoral. There is not a hint of the other-worldly in the workings of nature or the behaviour of beasts. There is nothing around us from which to conceive a spiritual basis for life. *We literally could not imagine such a thing, for even imagination must have something, some hint, to start with. A world with only beasts can have no gods*'[66] (emphasis added). There is not a shred of evidence for spirituality anywhere else in the world. Religion is not an issue among reindeer; not even a praying mantis prays!

These are by no means the only characteristics which set humanity apart from anything else of which we have any knowledge, but they are sufficient to make the point. In a broader context, they also present massive problems for the macro-evolutionist. In the words of Ronald Nash, 'Even if, for the sake of argument, we assume the truth of a universal evolutionary hypothesis, the fact that this process produced creatures with intelligence, creativity, moral awareness, self-consciousness and God-consciousness demands an explanation that Naturalism seems powerless to provide.'[67]

In the course of his 1967 Reith Lectures, the humanist scholar Edmund Leach claimed, 'There is no sharp break between what is human and what is mechanical.' In the light of the evidence we have sketched out, can we not dismiss that statement as poppycock? The more we examine the evidence, the clearer the 'sharp break' becomes. In the next two chapters we will take a closer look at some of the distinctives we have just listed.

16.

Pointers

One of the clearest divisions in the living world is that while animals have an impressive set of instincts to guide their behaviour they appear to have no concept of meaning, whereas human beings have an insatiable curiosity about the significance of the world and of their place in it. Writing in *The Times*, Bernard Levin suggested, 'There are probably more people today seeking some larger meaning or purpose in their lives and in life in general than there have been, certainly in the West, since the day of unquestioned faith.'[1]

A 'passing show'?

As far back as historical records go, there are traces of this relentless refusal to accept that we are nothing more than biological blips surrounded by cosmic chaos. The British writer Andrew Knowles makes the point well: 'Am I really a random coincidence, adrift in a cosmic accident, meaning nothing, going nowhere? Surely I have a dimension that animals and vegetables lack? After all, a carrot is oblivious of the size of Jupiter. A cow cares nothing for the speed of light. But I am in a different class. I observe and appreciate. I create and choose. I criticize. Sometimes I even criticize myself.'[2]

As soon as we abandon the idea that the world is significant and that human life has meaning, we end up in philosophical confusion and moral chaos. In one of his Pantyfedwen Trust Lectures, the Welsh scholar Rheinallt Nantlais Williams claimed, 'There is nothing which arises more spontaneously from man's nature than the question about life's meaning...

Human nature, like material nature, abhors a vacuum ... for if to be shovelled underground, or scattered on its surface, is the end of the journey, then life in the last analysis is a mere passing show without meaning, which no amount of dedication or sacrifice can redeem.'[3] Yet a 'passing show' is all that atheists have to offer, as we can see from the following examples of their miserable mantra.

The Russian novelist Leo Tolstoy looked back to a time when he asked, 'What is life for? To die? To kill myself at once? No, I am afraid. To wait for death till it comes? I fear that even more. Then I must live. But what for? And I could not escape from that circle.'[4]

Bertrand Russell poured scorn on the possibility that human life had any meaning or purpose by dismissing man as 'a curious accident in a backwater'.[5]

The novelist Rebecca West confessed, 'I do not believe that any facts exist, or, rather, are accessible to me, which give any assurance that my life has served an eternal purpose.'[6]

Stephen Jay Gould, approaching the question as a palaeontologist, came to the same conclusion: 'We are here because one odd group of fishes had a peculiar fin anatomy that could transform into legs for terrestrial creatures; because comets struck the earth and wiped out dinosaurs, thereby giving mammals a chance not otherwise available (so thank your lucky stars in a literal sense); because the earth never froze entirely during an ice age; because a small and tenuous species, arising in Africa a quarter of a million years ago, has managed, so far, to survive by hook and by crook. We may yearn for a "higher" answer — but none exists.'[7] (Wisely, he does not try to tell us how he knows this!)

In George Gaylord Simpson's opinion, 'Man is the result of a purposeless and natural process that did not have him in mind.'[8]

According to William Provine, 'No moral or ethical laws exist, nor are there absolute guiding principles for human society. The universe cares nothing for us and we have no ultimate meaning in life.'[9]

Driving to the south coast to speak at a convention in July 1993, I was able to catch an edition of BBC Radio 4's *In the Psychiatrist's Chair*. Dr Anthony Clare's 'victim' that day was Professor Colin Blakemore, one of Britain's most prominent research scientists and a Fellow of the Royal Society, which awarded him the Michael Faraday Award for services to the cause of science. The whole of the interview was fascinating, not least because Blakemore denies any religious faith, but what interested me most was his answer to what was intended to be Clare's final question: 'So if I were to ask you ... what do you feel is the purpose of your life, the point of your life, what would you say?' Even with his remarkable record of academic and practical achievement, Blakemore replied, 'I don't feel that life has a purpose in the sense that you could ask a question, "Why are we here?" It doesn't have a purpose in the sense that there are goals to be achieved... When it has ended, as far as I'm concerned, there is nothing left.'[10]

Richard Dawkins takes a slightly different tack. Asked in a 1995 issue of the *Observer* (in which he was introduced as 'increasingly our most militant atheist') about the purpose of life, he replied, 'Well, there is no purpose, and to ask what it is is a silly question. It has the same status as "What is the colour of jealousy?"'[11]

However, coming at things from another angle, he does offer one limited purpose, though not one with any moral, philosophical or religious content, by promoting the idea that, although 'we animals are the most complicated and perfectly designed pieces of machinery in the known universe',[12] we are nothing more than 'survival machines — robot vehicles blindly programmed to preserve the selfish molecules known as genes',[13] with the preservation of our genes (bits of DNA) as 'the supreme rationale for our existence'.[14] The *Sunday Telegraph's* science correspondent Robert Matthews summarizes the position of those who take this line: 'Their claim is that all the diversity of life is the product of selfish genes fighting to be passed on to the next generation. Every living thing, from the lowest bacterium to Richard Dawkins himself, is supposedly designed to act in ways that boost the chances of their genes being passed on. The genes do not have scruples, either. If it is a choice between the survival of the genes or the death of the organism they inhabit — tough. The selfish genes come first, and everything else a poor second.'[15]

Dawkins' passionate promotion of this scenario (which was primarily the invention of the American biologist George Williams and Dawkins' Oxford colleague William Hamilton ten years earlier) has succeeded in convincing millions of people that its bleak, uncompromising lesson is beyond question, but Robert Matthews says that many experts in the field have written it off as 'clapped-out and wrong'.[16] One of the most distinguished dissenters is Stephen Jay Gould, who passionately argues that the idea of evolution being the result of a war between selfish genes is hopelessly simplistic: '[Dawkins'] argument is wrong. It is not just a question of being inadequate. It's wrong.'[17] Niles Eldredge agrees, based on the fact that the vast majority of organisms indulge in sex: 'If the name of the game is to leave as many copies of your genes behind as possible, it is pure folly to mix them with someone else's on a 50-50 basis.'[18] This is a compelling argument, and I have yet to come across anything to refute it. Keith Ward dismisses the whole 'selfish gene' idea out of hand: 'As a matter of fact, nothing more pointless, no less convincing rationale, could be imagined for the existence of bodies than this. Who could give a fig for the survival of bits of DNA?'[19] The idea that human beings are little more than what someone called 'computers made of meat', and that their only purpose is to pass on their genes to the next generation, grates against the over-whelming consensus of human instinct and experience. Richard Dawkins complains, 'We humans have purpose on the brain,' and calls it 'a nearly universal delusion',[20] yet purpose must be grounded in consciousness and, as Keith Ward comments, 'It is absurd to think that it can be found in small unconscious bits of DNA, pursuing their "selfish" goals.'[21]

Meaning, motive and morals

The meaning, or meaninglessness, of life is closely tied in with the ques-tion of the existence or non-existence of God. Ludwig Wittgenstein de-clared, 'To believe in God means to see that life has a meaning,'[22] while atheism and meaninglessness are a perfect fit. This explains why there are many for whom denying that life has any ultimate meaning or purpose is not an intellectual conviction based on credible evidence, but a conven-ient way of dispensing with a God whose demands clash with their chosen lifestyle. Nobody has made a clearer admission of this than Aldous Huxley. Looking back on his early days, he wrote, 'I had motives for not wanting the world to have a meaning; consequently I assumed that it had none, and was able without any difficulty to find satisfying reasons for this as-sumption. Most ignorance is vincible ignorance. We don't know because we don't want to know... Those who detect no meaning in the world gen-erally do so because, for one reason or another, it suits their books that the world should be meaningless... For myself, as no doubt for most of my contemporaries, the philosophy of meaninglessness was essentially an in-strument of liberation, sexual and political.'[23] His honest confession of in-tellectual dishonesty is very significant. It shows that in order to embrace the idea of meaninglessness he had to stifle his natural intuition; he realized that meaning implied morality and that as he preferred immorality, meaning must go.

This points us to the fact that the question of the meaning or meaninglessness of life is not a philosophical toy; it has serious <u>practical implications</u>. If people believe that human life has no ultimate meaning or purpose, but is simply an extension of a struggle for existence and the survival of the fittest, they will tend to behave accordingly, with disastrous results. As Eugène Ionesco conceded, 'Cut off from his religious, metaphysical and transcendental roots, man is lost; all his actions become senseless, absurd, useless.'[24] Have those who claim that life is meaningless thought through the moral and personal implications? Addressing the general subject of reality at a religious leaders' conference in 1994, the distinguished theologian Lesslie Newbigin pointed out, 'If you exclude purpose from your categories of explanation then you have no way of knowing that it is good or bad. If there is no public doctrine about what the purpose of a human being is, then there is no way of saying that any kind of behaviour is good or bad... Talk about values is bleating nonsense.'[25]

Newbigin pressed all the right buttons. In the absence of meaning, where is the basis for morality or responsible behaviour? Why should anyone seek to exercise responsibility for his own life, or for the lives of others? If the whole of existence is materialistic and therefore purposeless, to whom is one responsible? What is the point of speaking about responsibility for others when one's own opinion is the only standard? The British politician Lord Eccles once said that such a person 'is hard put to it to say why his life is more significant than that of a turnip'.[26] Describing a nursing home for the elderly, he went on, 'Contemplate the colourless, senile, dribbling bodies and ask yourself what can be the meaning of an individual life if there is no kind of time but nature's cycle. What is there to stop you treating these old people, male and female husks, as if they were as disposable as a screw of paper, a beer can or a cellophane bag?'[27] Does the atheist have an answer to that? Would he or she cheerfully settle for being treated in that way?

Animals may be satisfied to have their lives driven by brute instinct unfolding automatically and moment by moment, but human beings are in a totally different class. They have memory and ambition, and can act intentionally to affect their future. Above all, they sense that they are part of a greater whole, and they want to know where they fit into the bigger picture. Is it possible to live otherwise within the limits of reason and common sense? If human beings are nothing more than biological accidents, cobbled together from bits of their ancestors, why should anyone seek to preserve or improve life? What is the sense in talking about 'quality of life' or 'values'? Why be concerned about love, care, honour, prudence or honesty? Why trouble ourselves with aims and aspirations? It has been said, 'If God is lacking, nothing a man does is of any more consequence than the acts of a mouse.'[28] This is a massive problem for the atheist, who knows in his heart that he cannot be reduced to that level, dares not concede that God alone gives life its ultimate reference-point, yet can find no other way out of the dilemma. Small wonder that Albert Einstein once wrote, 'The man who regards his own life and that of his fellow creatures as meaningless is not merely unfortunate but almost disqualified for life.'[29]

The faith factor

Of all the factors separating humankind from all other animal species, none is more striking than its religious dimension, something that seems to have been present throughout human history. It is sometimes claimed that prehistoric man lived in ignorance and fear and that the earliest religions, spawned in this climate, give a false picture of life. Atheists and agnostics lean heavily on this, but where is the evidence to back it up? As our prehistoric ancestors kept no records, how do we know they lived in ignorance and fear? George Roche says of this claim, 'It seems singularly difficult to compress much more ignorance and prejudice into a proposition than this one.'[30] After extensive research, Joseph Gaer came to this conclusion: 'As far as we can determine, religion has existed in every society, from the most primitive to the most culturally advanced. The more keys modern science finds with which to open the locked doors of the past, the more we learn about the early days of man on earth, the more evidence there is that all the societies in the past had one thing in common — some form of religion.'[31] Richard Cavendish agrees: 'Religion is one of the things which distinguishes man from the other animals. Apes and dolphins, as far as we know, have no religions, but no group of human beings has ever been discovered which did not have religious beliefs.'[32]

What does the atheist say to this? If humans have evolved from 'lower' animals, we should expect to find some primitive tribes — past or present

— with no religion at all, but this is not the case. As the Princeton scholar Samuel Zwemer discovered, 'Religion is as old as the oldest record and is universal among the most primitive tribes today.'[33] What is the atheist's explanation for this historical and universal phenomenon? As we saw in earlier chapters, it will need to be something more convincing than the ideas floated by Feuerbach, Nietzsche and others who wrote off religion as something man conjured up at some point in his history.

Even when no one Supreme Being is in mind, the faith factor, however vague or unfocused, is still there. Humans seem to have a stubborn sense that there are unseen powers that can influence their lives. It is said that after attending a literary luncheon at which all the agnostics confessed to carrying around such things as rabbits' paws and lucky shamrocks, G. K. Chesterton commented, 'When people stop believing in God, they don't believe in nothing, they believe in anything.'[34] There is ample evidence to back up his claim. In Great Britain alone, millions of people regularly read their horoscopes, which appear in hundreds of newspapers and magazines. It is said that some 250,000 people attend services in 500 official spiritualist churches and that there are at least 1,000 recognized mediums practising clairvoyance and so-called spirit healing.[35] After careful research, my colleague Peter Anderson estimated that in some areas of our country up to 80% of teenagers at school had tried to reach into the spirit world by using a Ouija-board.[36]

In his book *In Harm's Way*, a fascinating account of his experience as a war correspondent, the British journalist Martin Bell writes, 'I came to put much faith in certain routines and rituals which may be considered superstitions, but which none the less worked for me.'[37] Among these he included the wearing of his famous white suit and (slightly less famous) green socks, and carrying items which were 'matters of life and death' because they had to do with the tokens of good fortune. These included 'a silver threepenny bit, a four-leafed, and even a five-leafed clover, a fragment of water-snake skin in an envelope, a brass pixie, countless silver crosses and Saint Christophers, and tapes of [the singer] Willie Nelson'. Commenting on this collection of talismans, Bell says, 'I carry them all ... and who can tell which will work and which will not? Better to be safe by accumulation than sorry by preferring one to another.'[38]

An even greater problem for the atheist is to explain why, for all the diversity of religious ideas, from the crudest forms of animism to the buffet-bar menu offered by the New Age movement, belief in the existence of one supreme deity has remained so dominant in the majority of religions. In his masterly study *Origin of the Idea of God*, the German scholar Pere Wilhelm Schmidt, said to be 'by any realistic measure the greatest modern authority on the origin of religions',[39] gives this summary: 'A belief in a Supreme Being is to be found among *all* the people of the primitive culture, not indeed everywhere in the same form or the same vigour, but still everywhere prominent enough to make his dominant position indubitable.'[40] Why should this be the case if religion is the product of man's unfettered imagination?

Just as impressive as the antiquity of human belief in God is its obstinacy. In one century after another, ruthless efforts have been made to remove religion from man's agenda, but every attempt at replacing it with atheism has failed; belief in God has stubbornly outlived all those claiming to be its undertakers. Recent examples of this are among the most striking. Surveying the latter part of the twentieth century, Paul Johnson notes, 'What is important in history is not only the events that occur but events that obstinately do not occur. The outstanding event of modern times was the failure of religious belief to disappear. For many millions, especially in the advanced nations, religion ceased to play much or any part in their lives, and the ways in which the vacuum thus lost was filled, by Fascism, Nazism and Communism, by attempts at humanist utopianism, by eugenics or health politics, by the ideologies of sexual liberation, race politics and environmental politics, form much of the substance of the history of our century. But for many more millions — for the overwhelming majority of the human race, in fact — religion continued to be a huge dimension in their lives.'[41]

Even with all the tools of totalitarianism at its disposal, militant atheism has failed to dislodge the roots of religion among the millions it has persecuted. Nowhere is this more clearly seen than in the case of Marxism, as the Jewish author Don Feder confirms: 'Communism's inability to eradicate man's spiritual instinct must rank among the great failures of history. During the nineteenth century, high noon of rationalism, the demise of religion was considered inevitable. As enlightenment spread and reactionary, church-dominated governments fell, mankind would shrug off this ancient superstition, it was confidently predicted. But even with atheism enshrined as the official policy of a state that exerted pervasive influence over the lives of its subjects, faith survived. Consider the forces mobilized in this total warfare: mass propaganda, educational brainwashing, punishment for believers ranging from loss of employment to gulags. Yet with all of the weapons, atheism was routed.'[42] Feder could have added that the revival of religion in countries where it was brutalized but never destroyed has been nothing short of amazing, especially in Eastern Europe. Atheistic states may have driven institutional religion underground, but they have never succeeded in destroying faith in God.

Ebb and flow

In 1867, the British author Matthew Arnold wrote the haunting poem 'Dover Beach', in which he expressed his sadness at the decline of faith in God:

> The Sea of Faith
> Was once too, at the full, and round earth's shore
> Lay like the folds of a bright girdle furl'd.
> But now I only hear
> Its melancholy, long, withdrawing roar,
> Retreating, to the breath
> Of the night-wind, down the vast edges drear
> And naked shingles of the world.

Arnold's metaphor is striking, and the poem reflects what many people were thinking at the time, but it misses the point that tides not only withdraw and retreat, they also return and advance. There have undoubtedly been times when the outward expression of religion in general, and monotheism in particular, has been less than vigorous, but that is very different from claiming that either religion or monotheism has been obliterated. In 1995, the *Observer's* Melanie Phillips insisted, 'The secular society is a modern myth. This authorized version holds that religion is doomed by the spread of modernity. We are all now enlightened, rational beings who have no truck with the supernatural. In fact, the evidence is to the contrary... The retreating tide is washing away not spirituality but organized religion. There's a difference.'[43] A year later, while admitting her own atheism, the *Sunday Telegraph* columnist Minette Marrin agreed: 'It always surprises me how much there is about. I have not dipped even a toe in the Sea of Faith, but Matthew Arnold was surely being short-sighted when he wrote that it was receding with a "melancholy, long, withdrawing roar". On the contrary, we have seen a rise of religiosity. Scientific materialism has done little to stem it, and in my experience people who truly believe that there is no ultimate meaning in anything and that there is no survival of the individual after death are very rare.'[44] As to the current situation, Paul Johnson claims, 'The withdrawal has halted. There may be no more positive atheists than in Arnold's time. There are without doubt many more agnostics. But equally there are many more believers ... clearly, the event which Arnold thought would in time be completed, and which he tried to depict metaphorically, has not occurred.'[45]

Evidence for the persistence of man's religious instinct is everywhere. *The Encyclopaedia of Religion and Ethics* runs to thirteen large volumes. In the four-year period from 1992 to 1996, the number of religious books published in the United Kingdom rose by 84%, one researcher claiming, 'This rate of increase is unmatched by any other publishing category. One book in 25 now published is a religious book.'[46] A survey conducted on behalf of the *Economist* showed that no fewer than 4,452 new religious books were published in the United Kingdom in 1995 alone, more than those on history, economics, medicine and computers, and twice as many as those relating to social welfare, political science, art, education, travel and law put together.[47] In 1997, the Internet search engine Alta Vista listed 410,000 pages referring to God and identified 20,000 religious discussion groups now available on the World Wide Web.[48] Some references to God may be in an atheistic or agnostic context, but even they help to make the point that the idea of God is pervasive.

Any resurgence of faith comes as something of a shock in an age when people are so often conditioned by the media to believe that it is irrational or irrelevant. *Science Friction — Creation*, a 1996 programme in BBC Television's *Everyman* series, which comes under the umbrella of its religious output, led the *Daily Telegraph's* Cristina Odone to write, 'The only divinity these programme-makers believe in is Darwin 'n' Dawkins, and the only credo they subscribe to is that faith is fiction.' She went on to point out to her readers that 'Plenty of scientists believe in God, and plenty of "God-botherers" believe in science. Just not on *Everyman*.'[49] As the Jewish scholar Jonathan Sacks says in his book *The Persistence of Faith*, 'For some reason, religious conviction in the modern world produces in us a mixture of surprise, fascination and fright, as if a dinosaur had lumbered into life and stumbled uninvited into a cocktail party.'[50] Yet the party *has* been interrupted. In many parts of the world there seems to have been a revolt against the idea that literally everything (humankind included) is explained in terms of atoms and molecules and the laws governing them. It is no longer taken for granted that science offers a complete and satisfying explanation of what we are and how we got here. This revolt has led to such a rising tide of religion that whereas in 1966 *TIME* magazine announced God's demise, the front cover of a 1969 issue asked the question: 'Is God coming back to life?'[51] By 1980, the same magazine was telling its readers, 'In a quiet revolution that no one could have foreseen only two decades ago, God is making a comeback. Now it is more respectable among philosophers than it has been for a generation to talk about the possibility of God's existence.'[52]

In Asia, Africa, South America and elsewhere there are signs that belief in God is increasing, not declining. Writing in *USA Today* in 1996, George Gallup noted, 'What happened in this country is a slow but unmistakable shift from materialism to spirituality as Americans have come to the end of their emotional resources.'[53] Another observer of the current scene goes so far as to say, 'How will our time be viewed by history? I believe these days will be remembered as a time of remarkable spiritual awakening. The greatest revival of religion in modern times is breaking out across the globe.'[54]

Needless to say, none of this impresses the hard-core atheist whose mind is firmly made up. In a debate at Oxford in 1996 Peter Atkins protested, 'It is deplorable that in modern-day Oxford the study of theology is taken so seriously that there is a professorship. It is a chair in the study of fantasy.' Never one to be outdone when theism is under fire, Richard Dawkins dismissed Paul Johnson's theistic system of beliefs as 'ignominious, contemptible and retarded',[55] but surely one is entitled to ask on what authority he can say this? Elsewhere, he described faith as 'a cop-out, an excuse to evade the need to think and to evaluate the evidence',[56] but has he made a careful and unprejudiced study of theology? Does he understand what theism is saying, or is he using invective to cover up his ignorance? Is it sensible to dismiss the worldwide phenomenon of religious experience and expression out of hand as some kind of neurosis, illusion, wish-fulfilment or defence mechanism, rather than to accept that there may be an objective reality behind it? Dawkins reportedly once told a friend, 'I am not arrogant. I merely get impatient with people who don't have the same humility in front of the facts,'[57] but can he be so confidently (not to say crudely) dismissive of a torrent of testimony involving millions of people over thousands of years?

Specifically, how does he respond to the fact that countless believers in God have been martyred for their faith (more in the twentieth century than in any of the previous nineteen)? History teems with the stories of men and women of outstanding moral fibre who have allowed themselves to be put to death, often in the most barbaric fashion, rather than deny their conviction that God had transformed their lives. Some of the most famous of these were burned at the stake within a few minutes' walk of where Richard Dawkins now works, sealing their testimonies with words of quite brilliant courage and assurance. Is he qualified to brush their beliefs aside as 'ignominious, contemptible and retarded'? Has he missed the point that *if just one theist in history was right, the case for the existence of God would be established?* Can he be certain that every one of theism's multiplied millions have been deceived while he has remained unscathed? Could anything these millions of believers have said or done persuade him otherwise? His only recourse has been to invent what he calls a 'meme', a unit of cultural inheritance transmitted like genes to explain religious attachment. Yet, as Melanie Phillips pointed out in the *Observer*, 'The evidence for the existence of this meme doesn't exist.'[58] In spite of what Dawkins says about having humility in front of the facts, his dogmatic attitude is a contradiction of this. One is reminded of the car bumper sticker being displayed during a General Election campaign: 'My mind is made up, please don't confuse me with facts.' The evidence of religious experience is universal and impressive, and Clark Pinnock is on safer ground than any sceptic when he writes, 'The claim to be in touch with divine reality is so stupendous in itself and has been so regularly made that it cannot possibly be swept aside, but must enter into any reasonable account of the nature of reality.'[59]

Devout sceptics

Just as telling as the statistics previously quoted are the comments of many people they would not usually include. In 1993, the British chess player Nigel Short played an elimination match in Spain against Jan Timman for the right to meet the world champion Garry Kasparov. At noon, precisely three hours before the start of each day's game, Short went to a local church and prayed for victory. When a reporter asked why he did this, since he had thought him to be an atheist, Short replied, 'So I am, but I am also an opportunist.'[60] When the presenter of a 1997 BBC radio programme in the series *Devout Sceptics* said that his guest, journalist John Humphrys, 'showed no sign of religion whatsoever', Humphrys immediately countered, 'I didn't say that I do not believe in God.'[61] Writing in the *Sunday Telegraph* feature 'Me and my God', broadcaster Jonathan Dimbleby used the title of the *Devout Sceptics* series to explain his own position: 'I come across too many people who are too serious, too intelligent, and who have faith, simply to be able to say that it is some aberration, some psychological malfunction on their part... There's something out there. I don't have an image of a personal God. I just have a strong sense that we cannot explain ourselves to ourselves in merely material terms. And because I can't, there has to be something beyond me.'[62] The British actress Kate Winslett, who starred in the hugely successful films *Sense and Sensibility* and *Titanic*, told the *Sunday Times* magazine in 1998, 'I'm not an early to bed person, though I'm full of good intentions. It's usually around a quarter to one. I light a candle and have a bit of a chat with a god or something, though I'm not a religious person.'[63]

The eighteenth-century English playwright Edward Young once claimed, 'By night an atheist half believes in God,'[64] while it has been famously said that there are no atheists in foxholes or rubber rafts. What is certainly true is that life-threatening situations often unearth hidden religious instincts. Interviewed for the 'Me and my God' series in 1997, art critic Brian Sewell insisted at one point that his faith was 'permanently gone', but admitted that when he was in hospital for a heart-bypass operation a year earlier and the ward sister recorded him as an atheist, he told her, 'Oh no, I'm an agnostic — but if anything goes wrong, get me a Roman Catholic priest.'[65] When the overloaded car ferry *Gurita* sank in shark-infested waters off the coast of Indonesia in January 1996, almost 200 passengers were drowned, but Steve Nicholson and his friend Caroline Harrison escaped after spending eighteen hours in raging seas. Speaking to reporters after their rescue Nicholson said, 'We thought it would be foolish not to have a natter [talk] with God. We're not really religious, but when you see people dying out there, you realize it makes sense to talk to him.'[66] Recalling in *The Impossible Voyage* his experiences while making the fastest single-handed sailing journey around the world, the British yachtsman Chay Blyth wrote, 'Ten months of solitude in some of the loneliest seas of the world strengthened every part of me, deepened every perception and gave me a new awareness of that power outside of man which we call God. I am quite certain that without God's help many and many a time I could not have survived to complete my circumnavigation.'[67] Later in the same book he added, 'No one will ever say to me that there is no God without my remembering all these situations. To atheists I say, go sailing single-handed for a few weeks.'[68]

We can even find pointers towards God in statements made by atheists. Jean-Paul Sartre wrote, 'God is silent and that I cannot possibly deny — everything in me calls for God and that I cannot forget.'[69] Bertrand Russell admitted, 'The centre of me is always and eternally a terrible pain — a curious wild pain — a searching for something beyond what the world contains, something transfigured and infinite — the beatific vision — God — I do not find it, I do not think it is to be found — but the love of it is my love — it's like passionate love for a ghost.'[70] Sigmund Freud promoted the idea that religion was only the illusion of a father-figure, invented to shelter mankind from inner and outer forces it could neither understand nor control, but even he was forced to admit that religion is 'perhaps the most important item in the psychical inventory of a civilization'.[71] This ties in with a remarkable statement by Carl Gustav Jung: 'Among all my patients in the second half of life — that is to say, over thirty-five — there has not been one whose problem in the last resort was not that of finding a religious outlook on life. It is safe to say that every one of them fell ill because he had lost that which the living religions of every age have given to their followers, and none of them has been really healed who did not regain his religious outlook.'[72]

The God-shaped blank

In the course of his Eric Symes Abbott Memorial Lecture, David Hare said he was persuaded that 'However incoherent our religious beliefs and practices, we are still aware of the spiritual side of our nature.'[73] Coming from an atheist, this is a telling admission, because it points to the fact that as human beings we have a deep-seated need to transcend ourselves. As Fyodor Dostoevsky put it, 'The one essential condition of human existence is that man should always be able to bow down before something infinitely great. The Infinite and the Eternal are as essential for man as the little planet on which he dwells.'[74] In none of the investigations into the history of animals has any trace been found of their seeking to relate to a higher spiritual power, whereas signs of people's compulsive instinct to worship can be traced wherever they have been. Other animals seem satisfied when their basic physical and material needs are met, but this is not the case with mankind. The human spirit can never be satisfied with creature comforts and material possessions, and there is widespread evidence that some of the world's wealthiest people in history have been among the most miserable and unfulfilled.

This 'God-shaped blank' in human hearts is a historical and universal phenomenon, setting humanity apart from every other species. Man is irresistibly religious, regardless of whether this is what he wishes, and the desire to reach out beyond himself to a superior spiritual power deeply affects the whole of life. It has even been said that 'Every effort to prove there is no God is in itself an effort to reach for God,'[75] while G. K. Chesterton dared to claim that even a man who knocks on a brothel door is looking for God. In his *Reflections on the Revolution in France*, the eighteenth-century British politician Edmund Burke wrote, 'We know, and it is our pride to know, that man is by his constitution a religious animal; that atheism is against not only our reason but our instincts.'[76]

What is the explanation for this universal spiritual phenomenon? Is it seriously suggested that if molecules of muck are left lying around for long enough they will develop ideas about God? C. S. Lewis supplied a more rational answer: 'Creatures are not born with desires unless satisfaction for these desires exists. A baby feels hunger; well, there is such a thing as food. A duckling wants to swim; well, there is such a thing as water. Men feel sexual desire; well, there is such a thing as sex. If I find in myself a desire which no experience in the world can satisfy, the most probable explanation is that I was made for another world.'[77] Malcolm Muggeridge said much the same thing: 'If I could point to one single basic feeling out of which the structure of my mind and thought and belief grew, it would be this — that I do not belong here.'[78]

Sixteen centuries ago, an African theologian whose writings have massively influenced Western thought ever since, fine-tuned his view by addressing God with the words, 'You have made us for yourself, and our hearts are restless until they rest in you.'[79] No atheist has yet been able to produce an effective counter to Augustine's conviction.

The last dance

At 6.21 a.m. on 21 April 1992, Robert Alton Harris became the first man in a quarter of a century to be executed in a Californian gas-chamber. He had been sentenced to death almost fourteen years earlier but, by the expert use of every legal process open to them, his lawyers had succeeded in obtaining four stays of execution, the last one at four o'clock that morning, when he was already strapped into the death chair. When the final appeal failed, Harris asked prison officials to make a note of his last words and to release them after his death: 'You can be a king or a street-sweeper, but everybody dances with the Grim Reaper.'[80]

It was an interesting final flourish, but it hardly broke new ground; death, after all, is the ultimate fact of life. Fred Carl Kuehner calls it 'the most democratic institution on earth' and adds, 'It allows no discrimination, tolerates no exceptions. The mortality rate of mankind is the same the world over: one death per person.'[81] Death comes to young and old, good and bad, rich and poor, educated and ignorant, king and commoner. It has no age exemption, no colour bar, no sex discrimination and no preference for time or place. About 100 human lives came to an end in the time it took me to write that sentence.

It is said that the fourth-century B.C. Greek ruler Philip of Macedon had a servant with a standing order to present himself at the door of his master's tent every morning and announce, 'Philip, remember you must die.' The king clearly had his reasons for this unusual command, but most people try to avoid the subject if at all possible. King Louis XV of France is alleged to have forbidden his servants to mention the word 'death' in his presence. Elizabeth Kuebler-Ross, who has majored for many years on the subject of death and dying, recalls that when she asked the staff of a 600-bed hospital to identify which of their patients were at a terminal stage of life, so that her students could do some research with them, nobody would admit that there was even one. There is a powerful denial dynamic at work here. Sigmund Freud noted, 'No one really believes in his own death,'[82] and Alex MacDonald writes, 'If the nineteenth century tried to conceal the facts of life, the twentieth has tried to conceal the facts of death.'[83]

Death is the last taboo. We are stubbornly reluctant to face up to our own mortality, and have invented a truckload of terms to avoid the dreaded 'D… word'. We say that someone has 'passed away', 'passed on', or is 'no longer with us'. More crudely (and to avoid being serious) people speak of those who have 'kicked the bucket', 'snuffed it', 'cashed in their chips' or 'popped their clogs', and are now 'six feet under' or 'pushing up the daisies'. There is a growth industry in euphemisms employed to sanitize the subject. Some hospitals in the United States refer to a death as 'negative patient care outcome', undertakers are 'grief therapists', the funeral home has become the 'slumber room', the cemetery is the 'memorial park' and the gravestone a 'horizontal marker'.

It is hardly surprising to find an almost universal reluctance to get to serious, personal grips with the subject of death, not least because it points so powerfully to human mortality, to what Alister McGrath calls 'the trauma of transience'.[84] Nor is this unsettling sensation limited to the weak, the sick or the elderly, as McGrath shows in this moving personal testimony: 'When I was about twelve or thirteen, I used to lie in my bed on winter evenings, gazing out through the bedroom window at the night sky. I had become interested in astronomy and knew the names of most of the major constellations, as well as some facts about some of their stars. Although I was always impressed by the beauty of the night sky, I nevertheless found it made me feel rather melancholy. Why should something so beautiful make me feel so sad? Because I knew that the light from some of those stars had taken thousands of years to reach the earth. And I knew that I would be dead and gone long before the light now leaving those stars would ever reach earth. The night sky seemed to me to be a powerful symbol of my own insignificance and mortality. I found it unbearable.'[85]

As time trickles on, the pressure mounts. Writing in the *Daily Telegraph* in 1994, Mary Kenny put her own feelings into print: 'Once you hit 50, death hovers ever nearer as friends, family and contemporaries are picked off one by one by the grim reaper. The thought is detestable, and always has been. Yet curiosity about how we die *and what happens afterwards* remains central to our concerns.'[86] Malcolm Muggeridge wrapped his concerns in a maritime metaphor: 'Now the prospect of death overshadows all others. I am like a man on a sea voyage nearing his destination. When I embarked I worried about having a cabin with a porthole, whether I should be asked to sit at the captain's table, who were the more attractive and important passengers. All such considerations become pointless when I shall so soon be disembarking.'[87]

Some try to disguise their concerns (and protect their image?) by lacing them with humour. In a 1996 article in the *Daily Express*, jazz musician and entertainer George Melly wrote, 'Turning 70, that is to say passing through the creaking turnstile of old age, has aroused in me an increasing obsession with time. I am acutely aware of the old gentleman with the beard and the fast-emptying hourglass talking shop with his seriously undernourished colleague with the scythe. And they are not very far away either. The body, like an old car, spends more and more time in the garage. Something, though not necessarily serious, is always going wrong. Soon it won't be worth paying for the repairs.'[88] Later in the article he wrote of gathering 'in the elegant abattoir of a church or the battery system of a crematorium' to take leave of friends, and referred to people 'terrified of the void'. He then signed off with a hollow flourish of which Nietzsche might have been proud: 'I have always found atheism a great comfort. Been there! Done that! All over!'[89]

Others see no value in evasion, and say quite openly that the prospect of life being swallowed up in death produces a relentless trauma. In a diary entry dated 22 August 1963, when he was at the peak of his career, the popular British actor and comedian Kenneth Williams agonized: 'The madness screaming up inside me. So many awful thoughts — this terrible sense of doom hanging over me. I wonder if anyone will ever know about the emptiness of my life. I wonder if anyone will ever stand in a room that I have lived in and touch the things that were once a part of my life and wonder about me? How could they ever be told? How to explain that I only experienced vicariously, never first hand, that the sharing of a life is what makes a life... Now I am thinking all the while of death in some shape or another. Every day is something to be got through. All the recipes of the past are no longer valid. I've spent all my life in the mind. I have entered into nothing.'[90]

The valley of the shadow

To some degree, the fear of death is virtually universal, however much whistling in the dark goes on, and even those with long-standing faith in God are not always exempt from it. In his classic work *Pilgrim's Progress*, John Bunyan expressed this perfectly at the point where his hero comes to the river separating this world from the next: 'Here he in a great measure lost his senses, so that he could neither remember nor orderly talk of any of those sweet refreshments that he had met in the way of his pilgrimage. But all the words he spoke still tended to discover that he had horror of mind, and heart-fears that he should die in that river...'[91]

The fear of death has many different strands to it. In a sense, some kind of stress is natural because death is unnatural, an unwelcome intrusion into the settled order of things. This partly explains why man goes to such lengths to postpone it. The so-called science of cryonics even claims to be able to go one better and provide the ultimate safety net. Immediately after death, blood is drained from the corpse, which is then filled with freezer fluid, encased in aluminium and suspended in a bath of liquid nitrogen. When a cure has been found for the disease from which the person concerned died, the body can then be thawed out and treated, so that normal life can be resumed. At the time of writing, cryonics has yet to register its first success.

Tied into the sense of death being unnatural is the obvious factor that it brings with it the fear of the unknown. Human beings are creatures of habit and comfort. We always feel more secure in familiar surroundings, but by its very nature death does not fit into this category. Even if we have been intimately involved in someone else's death, we have not actually shared in it. At the moment of death, a person enters unknown territory, and no experience, wealth, expertise or knowledge provides sufficient landmarks or signposts. The whole thing is dark, mysterious and frightening.

The wrenching apart of secure and rewarding family relationships can be an obvious source of distress. A husband may sense the grief his wife will suffer and be concerned at the extra responsibilities she will have to bear. A wife may grieve for children soon to be left motherless. More crudely, but no less really, some approach death in distress at having to leave behind the trappings of material success which one writer has described as being 'like grappling-irons in the soul, holding their affection to what they can touch'.[92] Others may agonize as they see their dreams of future success or prosperity being snatched from their grasp. For such people, McGrath's 'trauma of transience' is linked to the devastating disappointment of life coming to an untimely end just when the future seemed so bright, the possibilities so great. In a cemetery in Reading there is a tombstone in the form of a granite pillar which looks for all the world as if it has been broken off by vandals. Yet, like many similar tombstones in Europe, it was deliberately built like that, as the wording at the bottom explains: 'His life was broken off, unfinished.'

For many, the fear of death is firmly rooted in the process of dying, as Mary Kenny explained: 'Most of us will not experience a final exit of peace, serenity and graceful farewells as our grandchildren gather devotedly around the deathbed: most of us will move towards death painfully, dishonestly (denying to ourselves what is happening) and will be lucky to yield up the ghost in a haze of narcotics which may dull consciousness but not entirely eliminate distress.'[93] This is the aspect of fear that triggered Woody Allen's quirky comment, 'It's not that I am afraid of dying. I just don't want to be there when it happens.'[94]

And then?

The onset of death obviously brings into focus the question of what, if anything, lies beyond it, and I have examined this in detail elsewhere.[95] Here, it will be sufficient to agree with Mary Kenny that faith in an afterlife has been a universal concept: 'In all cultures and at all times, human beings have conceived of a spiritual life beyond the body.'[96] An atheistic model can obviously give no explanation for this phenomenon, and the idea that the experiences of this life meet all the latent needs and aspirations of a human being is not only miserable but downright morbid. Malcolm Muggeridge asserted, 'I wonder whether, in the history of all the civilizations that have ever been ... there was ever a more abysmally pessimistic [notion] than that we, who reach out with our minds and aspirations to the stars and beyond, should be able so to arrange our lives, so to eat and drink and fornicate and learn and frolic, that our brief span in this world fulfils all our hopes and desires.'[97]

The absence of an afterlife deals a devastating blow to the human ego. As Ernest Becker states in his book *The Denial of Death*, 'Man is literally split in two. He has the awareness of his own splendid uniqueness in that he sticks out of nature with a towering majesty, and yet he goes back into the ground a few feet in order blindly and dumbly to rot and disappear for ever.'[98] On the other hand, the possibility of existence beyond the grave brings with it another raft of concerns by raising issues of judgement, reward and punishment. Bunyan's hero was 'much in the troublesome thoughts of the sins he had committed, both since and before he began to be a pilgrim'.[99] Surely nobody can think seriously about any possibility of future punishment for his sins without a measure of fear? Is anyone so transparently faultless that he or she can cheerfully settle for an eternal destiny relative to his earthly life?

As far as our present subject is concerned, three things can be said. In the first place, human preoccupation with death clearly separates human beings from all other creatures. Eric Kast notes that no animal experiences 'the disease of conceptualizing death'.[100] As far as we know, animals live entirely for the present, driven by instinct, ungoverned by moral issues and totally unconcerned about the certain approach of death. Lizards never fret about the future; polar bears have no 'trauma of transience'; apes never muse on the afterlife.

Secondly, why is there such a radical distinction? If lizards, polar bears, apes, humans and the millions of other living species on our planet are all part of the so-called 'Great Chain of Being', separated by nothing more than the fluky fluctuation of atoms over millions of years, why should death be an irresistible issue for just one species and of no concern whatever to all the others? If humans are nothing but grown-up germs, at what point in the growing-up process did death begin to be a factor? Why should it have done so?

Thirdly, death is a subject on which the atheist can make no positive or sustainable contribution. Writing about his pre-theistic days, Malcolm Muggeridge tells of going to Lourdes, where a woman asked him to visit her sister, who was seriously ill: 'So of course I went along. The sister was obviously at the point of death and, like any other glib child of twentieth-century enlightenment, *I had nothing to say*'[101] (emphasis added). Ravi Zacharias points out, 'Here, atheism meets its nemesis. Any system that does not know the origin of man and cannot give his reasons for being, certainly must remain silent on his destiny or, at best, argue for nothing-ness.'[102] Later, he adds, 'The questions about death demand answers, but atheism has none because there is no heaven to be gained and no hell to be shunned. Life finishes with the last heartbeat: all relationships are sev-ered, all endeavours are ended, the arm of justice is cut short, eternity in the heart has been swallowed by the finality of experience. There is nothing to fear or to hope for, no God to meet, and no hope to anticipate — all is truly and ultimately ended.'[103]

For the atheist, death is not only a great leveller, it clinically exposes the futility of pursuing a godless, self-centred life. As British author Stephen Travis asks, 'Whoever heard of a Marxist on his deathbed asking for *Das*

Kapital to be read to him, or a let-us-eat-drink-and-be-merry man asking for a reading from *Playboy*?'[104] With all of life's interests, passions, possessions and pursuits disappearing, and convinced that there is nothing to follow, to what can the atheist aspire? Ravi Zacharias is right to say, 'In the end, the atheistic view reduces the botanist from studying daffodils to fertilizing them, the scientist from measuring the "Big Bang" to becoming a small fizzle, and the geologist from investigating the geological column to becoming embedded in one of its layers.'[105] Of course, none of this proves that the atheist's beliefs are invalid, and many show great courage in accepting the logical and inevitable outcome of their beliefs. Nevertheless, most serious-minded people struggle with the idea that their ultimate future is to become fertilizer. This may give the phrase 'pushing up the daisies' an added dimension, but it hardly matches most people's deepest instinct.

The thinker

The three human distinctives we have considered so far — a sense of meaning, religious awareness and concern about death — can be discussed only when we recognize a fourth, namely that human beings are self-conscious and rational personalities with an insatiable need to know and to understand. Although a scaled-down version of much of what we said in chapter 15 about the human brain could be said about that of other animals, this is not the case when we go beyond the physical 'hardware' to the processes in which the brain is involved. We cannot reason with rats or debate with dogs. The seventeenth-century English poet John Donne once noted, 'The difference between the reason of man and the instinct of the beast is this, that the beast does not know, but the man knows that he knows.'[106] C. S. Lewis fine-tuned the fact: 'One of the things that distinguishes man from the other animals is that he wants to know things, wants to find out what reality is like, simply for the sake of knowing. When that desire is completely quenched in anyone, I think he has become something less than human.'[107] As human beings, we are not only aware of sensations, we reflect on them, we engage in complex reasoning and lateral thinking, we evaluate data, develop ideas, exercise imagination and make decisions; in other words, *we think*. What is more, as Anthony O'Hear points out, 'In our knowledge-seeking we ... seek something more than beliefs conducive to survival and reproduction. We seek truth for its own sake.'[108]

Atheists paint a very different picture. Richard Dawkins contends, 'We are jumped-up apes and our brains were only designed to understand the mundane details of how to survive in the Stone Age African savannah.'[109] Another approach is to see the brain and its activities, together with everything else that goes to make up a human being, as the random products of natural selection, with the mind as a kind of biological computer. Richard Dawkins often uses the language of computer technology to describe the human brain. He speaks of the brain's evolution as an 'electronic arms race',[110] and describes the optic nerve as 'wires leading from a bank of three million photocells to the computer that is to process the information in the brain'.[111] Francis Crick takes the same line and claims, 'Our minds can be explained by the interaction of nerve cells and molecules.'[112] Peter Atkins says, 'At the deepest level, decisions are adjustments of the dispositions in the molecules inside large numbers of cells in the brain.'[113] According to Don Cupitt, 'Consciousness is just electronic waves of excitation. What we are used to calling the mind or the soul is entirely on the surface of our heads and bodies — understanding finds its origins in the motor nerves that give rise to language and speech and a sort of fluttering that occurs in the soft palate and ends up in the ear.'[114] These are some examples of what Donald MacKay called 'nothing-buttery', which says that if there is an explanation for any phenomenon in scientific terms, then that is the only valid explanation. We touched on the basic weaknesses of 'nothing-buttery' in an earlier chapter; here, we will ask whether it is possible to live with its implications.

In the first place, if human reasoning is just an electro-chemical operation taking place in the brain, how can we ever say that a thought is rational, or that a premise, theory or conclusion is 'true'? After all, this cannot be said about other physical functions. During a recent medical examination, my blood pressure and temperature were taken, but these could not be said to be 'true'. In and of themselves, they were merely phenomena waiting for intelligent clinical interpretation.

Secondly, intelligent reasoning does not fit into full-blown naturalism. In a paper originally read at the Oxford Socratic Club in 1946, C. S. Lewis spoke of the way in which naturalism claimed to be the explanation, firstly of inorganic matter, then of life, then human life, including man's emotions.

He then went on, 'But when it takes the final step and we attempt a naturalistic explanation of thought itself, suddenly the whole thing unravels. The last fatal step has invalidated all the preceding ones: for they were all reasonings and reason itself has been discredited. We must, therefore, either give up thinking altogether or else begin over again from the ground floor... There is simply no sense in beginning with a view of the universe and trying to fit the claims of thought in at a later stage. By thinking at all we have claimed that our thoughts are more than mere natural events.'[115] Does the atheist have an answer to this? If rational thinking is nothing more than a natural process, why should it be trusted? It is surely stretching things too far to believe that intelligent reasoning came into being as the result of the accidental amalgamation of particles of mindless matter.

Thirdly, huge swathes of atheistic argument lean heavily on laws of logic which are held to be absolute, universal and invariable. Yet in a materialistic universe these (immaterial) laws can only be matters of convention or consensus, subject to the kind of change that might, at least theoretically, lead to something accepted as logical becoming illogical. Can atheists seriously live with that? Can it really be said that logic is cultural, and therefore flexible? If not, how can atheists account for the laws of logic without a transcendent lawgiver? Is there any atheistic explanation as to why such laws exist, or why they can be trusted as being reliable? Without transcendent intelligence putting the laws of logic and reason into place, how can we explain the mind's capacity to move logically from premises to conclusions? How can we trust this thinking process? Theists claim that the laws of logic reflect the way God thinks and the way he wants us to think, and that if God did not exist we could not logically prove anything. Can atheism find a basis on which to counter this claim?

Fourthly, if the mind is the product of evolution, how can we be sure that at this point in time it is anywhere near ultimate truth or reality? What if it is in the early stages of an ongoing process that will one day lead us to see that today's most dogmatic principles are a long way wide of the mark? As atheists generally accept that their logic is culturally specific, and is in an ongoing process of evolution, would a hefty dose of humility not be in order? How can logic be reliable if it is a matter of personal opinion or contemporary consensus which, like the price of certain advertised goods and services, is 'subject to change without notice'? Even Darwin entertained doubts about this: 'With me the horrid doubt always arises whether the convictions of man's mind, which has been developed from the mind of the lower animals, are of any value or at all trustworthy. Would anyone trust in the convictions of a monkey's mind, if there are convictions in such a mind?'[116]

Fifthly, how does an evolutionary model account for human personality? Richard Dawkins has described life as 'just bytes and bytes of digital information' but, as Francis Schaeffer argues, 'No one has presented an idea, let alone demonstrated it to be feasible, to explain how the impersonal beginning, plus time, plus chance, can give personality. We are distracted by a flourish of endless words, and lo, personality has appeared out of the hat!'[117]

Sixthly, all attempts to treat thought as a natural event involve the fallacy of excluding the thought of the person making the attempt. How can rational thoughts arise in a non-rational world? Would we trust a computer print-out if we knew it had been programmed by random forces or non-rational laws? Darwinians are well and truly hoist by their own petard at this point, as one of their number admits: 'Darwin's "horrid doubt" as to whether the convictions of man's evolved mind could be trusted applies as much to abstract truth as to ethics... The armies of science are in danger of destroying their own base. For the scientist must be able to trust the conclusions of his own reasoning. Hence he cannot accept the theory that man's mind was evolved wholly by natural selection, if this means, as it would appear to do, that the conclusions of the mind depend ultimately on their survival value and not on their truth, thus making all scientific theories, including that of natural selection, untrustworthy.'[118]

Finally, the atheist can deny the existence of God only by destroying the basis on which such a denial is made. In one of his famous *Broadcast Talks*, C. S. Lewis pointed out that if there was no creative intelligence behind the universe, the human brain was never created for the purpose of coming to any rational conclusions. 'It is merely,' he said, 'that when the atoms inside of my skull happen for physical or chemical reasons to arrange themselves in a certain way this gives me, as a by-product, the sensation I call thought. But if so, how can I trust my own thinking to be true? And if I can't trust my own thinking, I can't trust the argument leading to atheism, and therefore I have no reason to be an atheist. Unless I believe in God, I can't believe in thought, so I can never use thought to disbelieve in God.'[119] Elsewhere, he wrote, 'If minds are wholly dependent on brains, and brains on biochemistry, and biochemistry (in the long run) on the meaningless flux of the atoms, I cannot understand how the thought of those minds would have any more significance than the sound of the wind in the trees.'[120] Does the atheist have an answer to this? How can he make an intelligent assertion that God does not exist, and at the same time admit that his thoughts are determined by chemical reactions and not by rational analysis? It may have been this kind of dilemma which led Voltaire to write, 'What is the verdict of the vastest mind? Silence! The book of fate is closed to us. Man is a stranger to his own research. He knows not whence he comes or whither he goes. Tormented atoms in a bed of mud, devoured by death, a mockery of fate.'[121]

In his work *Basic Questions in Theology*, Wolfhart Pannenberg says, 'In one sense, man does not ask the question about God, man's very existence raises the question of God.'[122] In this chapter we have seen that, in contrast to the members of all other living species, human beings are concerned about meaning, have spiritual awareness, think about their mortality and engage in rational thinking. Nobody could claim that even these unique distinctions *prove* the existence of God, but it can surely be argued that they point to some kind of transcendent reality beyond humanity?

17.

Status and standards

In the previous chapter, we looked at four unique features which separate humankind from all other species and can be said to point to a transcendent Creator. Before we can leave this general subject we must examine several other aspects of human life which do the same thing.

A different league

Although they come at it from very different angles, theists, atheists and agnostics generally agree that human beings are creatures of great dignity. Even *Humanist Manifesto II*, while saying there is 'no divine purpose or providence for the human species', begins its fifth article by stating, 'The preciousness and dignity of the individual person is a central humanist value.' There are some interesting words here. The root of 'preciousness' is the Latin *pretium*, meaning 'price', and it is commonly used of something highly cherished, valued or esteemed. The root of 'dignity' is the Latin *dignus*, meaning 'worthy', but there is also a link with *gloria*, the usual translation of an older Hebrew word carrying with it a sense of 'weightiness' and used to describe something significant. By employing both words, the manifesto is saying that individual human beings are important in their own right, with weighty, personal significance.

This conviction is deeply embedded in the human psyche. As R. C. Sproul says, 'We want our lives to count. We yearn to believe that in some way we are important. This inner drive is as intense as our need for water and oxygen. We argue about religion and politics, abortion, homosexuality, nuclear weapons and welfare programmes. We bicker about a host of things, but at one point we are all in harmony: *every person among us wants to be treated with dignity and worth*[1] (emphasis added). Even as we go about the ordinary business of daily living, we are convinced that we are in a different league from every other living thing we see around us, that we have a dimension denied to plants and animals, and that we are more than random collections of bits and pieces. Andrew Knowles puts it well: 'I am a mystery. I wake up in the morning. I find myself the sole occupant of a complex, sensitive and extremely useful body. I am also the proud owner of an intricate, imaginative and highly resourceful brain. Everything about me is unique: my face, my fingerprints, my "self". I am alive. I develop. I grow. So does a vegetable. But I am more than a vegetable. Vegetables don't fall in love, or read the paper, or go on holiday... I am a body with a brain; an animal. But — I am more than an animal. Animals don't peer through telescopes, or send birthday cards, or play chess, or cook...'[2]

Indications of this universal sense of being unique can be seen and heard everywhere, and 'dignity' is often the word used to pinpoint it. In 1996 the policy of having female prisoners in labour wards handcuffed to prison staff was attacked by the Royal College of Midwives as 'violation of a woman's dignity'.[3] In the same year, Funeral Plans Ltd, Britain's largest funeral planning group, launched a package offering burials 'tailor-made to your personal wishes', in which clients could choose funeral arrangements which reflected their chosen lifestyle: the new scheme was called 'The Dignity Plan'.[4] In 1997, after winning a legal battle allowing her doctor to administer drugs that would relieve the terrible pain of motor-neurone disease but also hasten her death, Annie Lindsell told the press, 'I've had a wonderful life over which I've had control. Now I want a dignified death over which I have control.'[5] The fundamental contention of the London-based organization EXIT is that individuals have the right 'to die with dignity'. Speaking against a background of unrest and bloodshed, the pope ended a visit to Nigeria in 1998 by telling leaders, 'Respect for every human person, for his dignity and rights, must ever be the inspiration and guiding principle behind your efforts to increase democracy and strengthen the social fabric of your country.'[6]

Dignity and brutality

The issue of human dignity is obviously wrapped up in questions about man's origin and destiny, to which the atheist gives a desolating reply. One philosopher concludes, 'Man is a grown-up germ, sitting on one cog of one wheel of a vast cosmic machine that is slowly but inexorably running down to nothingness'[7] — but does that harmonize with the instinctive and virtually universal reaction to what the Scottish poet Robert Burns called 'man's inhumanity to man'?[8] Four incidents, from comparatively recent history, one involving millions, another hundreds and the others just two individuals, will help to bring the question into focus.

In 1994, the world's media swarmed to Rwanda to cover the brutal civil war between the Hutu and Tutsi tribes, which was tearing the country apart. The sheer scale of the bloodshed was horrifying. At one stage it was reported that 500,000 people — one in every fifteen Rwandans — were slaughtered in the course of a few weeks. In the worst single incident, perhaps as many as 20,000 were butchered at the Nyarubuye parish convent in one day. An official in neighbouring Uganda said that between 25 April and 11 May over 26,000 bodies from Rwanda had floated down the Kagera River into Lake Victoria. Fishermen in Kasensero, a village near where the river runs into the lake, claimed that 50,000 bodies had done so in six weeks.[9]

Nearly two million Rwandans fled to other countries, but makeshift refugee camps were unable to cope with the numbers. With no food or sanitation, and polluted water supplies, up to 3,000 a day died of cholera in camps around Goma, in Zaïre. There was no time or space to bury the dead; bodies were collected by the lorry load, thrown into huge pits and incinerated *en masse*. A logistics co-ordinator with Care International told the media, 'We've got three categories of refugee here; the living dead, the dying dead and the dead dead.'[10] One reporter called the power struggle 'a calamity without precedent in modern times',[11] and there was worldwide response to appeals for help. Yet if human beings are nothing more than 'grown-up germs', why should anyone find what happened in Rwanda not only a moral obscenity but an offence against human dignity? Are Rwandans any better or more important than baboons or bacteria? Why should we care if one colony of germs decides to eliminate another? If human life comes about by an accidental accumulation of atoms, why should we be concerned to preserve it, or be remotely interested in how or when it comes to an end?

The second incident took place in Bosnia Herzegovina, when a Serbian firing squad worked all day, on or about 16 July 1995, to kill 1,000 Muslim prisoners, systematically and in cold blood, at Benjevo Farm, north of

Zvornik. Martin Bell reported, 'Many who did not die immediately pleaded with their executioners for the mercy of being put out of their pain. One soldier alone finished off 700 of the victims with a handgun shot to the head.'[12] One would hope that every decent human being would find such appalling savagery utterly repulsive, but if Peter Atkins is right in saying that mankind is 'just a bit of slime on a planet',[13] why should the massacre at Benjevo Farm be any more reprehensible than stamping on a swarm of ants?

The third incident was in Sierra Leone, on Africa's west coast, where civil war was raging during the time of the Rwanda conflict. In January 1996 the BBC's George Alagiah reported on the atrocities and spoke of one case in which soldiers who had come across a pregnant woman made bets with each other as to whether the unborn child was male or female, then murdered her and slit her open to see who had won the bet.[14] Merely hearing his report was almost literally sickening — but why? If humanity is nothing more than a coincidental link in the so-called 'Great Chain of Being' which joins all living matter together, why should we think that what those soldiers did was any worse than betting on how many pips an orange contains, then slitting it open to find out who won the wager? Surely the basic answer is our instinctive conviction that a human being has more intrinsic value than an orange?

There are few areas in which human dignity is more clearly at stake than in that of race relations. In 1998 forty-nine-year-old James Byrd, a partially disabled black man, was walking down a road in Jasper, Texas, late at night when he was picked up by three young white men driving a truck. All reportedly linked to white supremacist groups, they took Byrd to a deserted spot, beat him senseless, chained him to the back of the truck, then dragged him along the road until he was dead. Police investigators later found seventy-eight pieces of his disintegrated body scattered along a two-mile stretch of road. As the media reflected the outrage felt around the world, one of the recurring themes was that the murder had not merely been an attack on one human being but an offence against the dignity of humanity. Black leader Al Sharpton told reporters, 'As brother Byrd's body was torn, so America's spirit was torn... This crime was not against a person, it was against a people.'[15]

Millions of atheists in America and elsewhere would presumably agree, but what is the atheistic rationale for doing so? Debating civil rights with an atheist, Robert Morey asked him, 'Where do you get the idea that human beings have dignity? You fight for the blacks to get the dignity they de-serve. But what if no one deserves any dignity? If the blacks are just one species of primates which spun out of a different origin than the white race, and the blacks as well as the whites are only animals, why shouldn't they treat each other as animals? What's wrong with southern whites using cattle prods on black animals if that is all they really are? Since you assume evolution to be true, doesn't your civil rights work stand in the way of the survival of the fittest? If the whites are stronger, shouldn't they make the blacks slaves?' The atheist replied, 'I really don't care what you say. I don't believe in God, but I do believe in civil rights. And nothing you will ever say can change that.'[16] Does that really answer the question? With God out of the picture, why bother with civil rights? Why should anyone give two hoots about whether black blobs of humanity have the same rights as white blobs? According to the atheist, the whole of mankind is a doomed race in a dying universe, and it makes no difference whether it ever existed. William Lane Craig shows what this means: 'Mankind is thus no more significant than a swarm of mosquitoes or a barnyard of pigs, for their end is all the same. The same blind cosmic process that coughed them up in the first place will swallow them all again.'[17]

What are we worth?

Our self-conscious conviction about the special value and worth of human beings radically affects the way we treat each other and, in particular, our instinct to care for those in need. In the words of a contemporary author, 'A society's maturity and humanity will be measured by the degree of dignity it affords to the disaffected and the powerless.'[18] Some years ago, I spoke at a school for seriously disabled children, some of them so badly de-formed that they were strapped to mechanized chairs on which they trundled around. Specially adapted vans ferried them between home and school, where carefully trained teachers tended to their needs with immense devo-tion and patience. If anyone had dared to question such an expenditure of money, energy and manpower on children who were unlikely to make any significant contribution to society, they would have been told that every human being in the world, however sick, deformed or incapable, has dig-nity and worth which goes far beyond his or her physical or mental con-dition. The French biologist Jean Rostan has expressed it perfectly: 'For my part I believe that there is no life so degraded, debased, deteriorated or impoverished that it does not deserve respect and is not worth defending with zeal and conviction... I have the weakness to believe that it is an honour for our society to desire the expensive luxury of sustaining life for its useless, incompetent and incurably ill members. I would almost measure society's degree of civilization by the amount of effort and vigilance it imposes on itself out of pure respect for life.'[19] The outworking of this conviction often comes sharply into focus when it is concentrated on one individual. For example, in a highly-publicized case in 1993, a tiny child in the United States — identified only as Baby K — was born with a terrible brain disease which meant that it could never experience any physical sensation, yet $510,000 was spent in a vain attempt to save its life.

This kind of commitment, rooted in an entrenched sense of human dignity, fits perfectly into traditional theism. If a human being is the pinnacle of God's creation, invested with unique significance, given reason, awareness and a sense of morality which we can see nowhere else in the universe, and charged with bringing honour to God by the moral and spiritual quality of his life, he should be treated in a way that reflects his true worth, whatever his physical or mental condition and regardless of his ability or talents. This lies behind C. S. Lewis' statement: 'There are no ordinary people. You have never talked to a mere mortal.'[20] By contrast, it is difficult to see how people's ingrained sense of dignity fits into an atheistic, evolutionary framework. Unless human worth is grounded in something or someone outside of ourselves, any value we have is self-generated and limited to the brief moment of time we spend on this earth. Where is the 'preciousness' or dignity in being an accident of nature, a biological freak? The best that humanism can offer is to say that man has special value because (at least for the time being) he is the latest product of the evolutionary process; in the words of one humanist, 'What distinguishes man from animals is that he evolved by a mechanism that belongs to him alone, and which he alone can modify and improve.'[21]

This grandiose claim fails to mention that man is said to have achieved his exalted status purely as a matter of chance. If Jacques Monod is right in saying that we are what we are because 'our number came up in a Monte Carlo game',[22] how can we claim to have any dignity or significance? Are these things dependent on a person's wealth, ability or influence, or his likely contribution to society? The American news network CNN reported that as part of Rio de Janeiro's clean-up operation in advance of the Earth

Summit in 1992, destitute children were shot and disposed of.[23] On the other hand, the media reported in 1998 that the computer tycoon Bill Gates had became the world's wealthiest man, with an annual income of over nine billion pounds and total wealth of £31.6 billion, equivalent to £5.44 for every man, woman and child on earth.[24] Does this give him more dignity than a child treated as part of Rio's rubbish? If human life is an atomic accident, it might be thought logical to value an individual by his or her contribution to what philosophers call 'the common good', but does this assessment sit easily with what we instinctively feel about ourselves? Why do we immediately resent it if others treat us as if we were dumb animals? Yet why should we be treated otherwise if humankind is just another link in the 'Great Chain of Being'? Humanists buy eagerly into the evolutionary hypothesis, which involves a mechanism devoid of any purpose or intention, but where, in the absence of these, can they find any basis for saying that a human being has greater value, dignity or sanctity than an alligator, a cockatoo or a duck-billed platypus?

By the same token, what rationale does the atheistic humanist give for serving others, especially those in serious need? Julian Huxley tries to find one in what he calls 'the development of man's vast potential of realizable possibility'[25] (in other words, the securing of man's place in future stages of evolutionary progress) but, as John Stott points out, this is a hopelessly inadequate basis: 'If the unimpeded progress of evolution were our chief concern, why should we care for the senile, the imbecile, the hardened criminal, the psychopath, the chronically sick, or the starving? Would it not be more prudent to put them to sleep like a well-loved dog, lest they hinder the evolutionary process?'[26]

Far from seeing this as creating a dilemma for them, radical humanists agree. At the 1988 San Francisco Conference of the World Federation of Right-to-Die Societies, the humanist Joseph Fletcher declared, 'Humans without some minimum of intelligence or mental capacity are not persons, no matter how many of their organs are active, no matter how spontaneous their living processes are... [Idiots] are not, never were, and never will be in any degree responsible. Idiots, that is to say, are not human.'[27] Peter Singer goes even further: 'Mental defectives do not have a right to life, and therefore might be killed for food — if we should develop a taste for human flesh — or for the purpose of scientific experimentation.'[28] Nor is he alone in this gruesome suggestion. Writing in a 1983 edition of the *Edmonton Journal*, the Columbia University anthropologist Paul Tidsall maintained,

'Surely there can be no special pride in the practice of letting millions of soldiers rot on the battlefield because of a taboo against cannibalism? One can even argue that, nutritionally, the best source of protein for human beings is human flesh, because the balance of amino-acids is precisely that which the body requires for its own proper functioning.'[29] Revolting as these views must seem to the majority of people — including, to be fair, most humanists — it can hardly be denied that they fit in logically with the atheist's conviction that man's origin lies in sludge and his destiny in the dust. To make high-faluting claims about human dignity within that framework is a blatant case of having one's cake and eating it.

Facing facts

In recent years, some evolutionists have begun to get to grips with the implications of their theory as it relates to the value of human life. In his book *Created From Animals*, philosopher James Rachels bites the bullet. After accepting that theists can claim a special place for human beings in God's plan, giving them a nature radically different from that of animals, he admits, 'Darwinism must make do with skimpier materials.'[30] He then tries building a case for the value of human life using only these 'skimpier materials', but is eventually forced to admit, 'We have found no reason to support a policy of distinguishing, in principle, between the kind of consideration that should be accorded to humans and that which should be accorded to other animals.'[31] Bluntly put, he is saying that in terms of intrinsic value a man is worth no more than a mouse, a woman no more than a wombat, a child no more than a chaffinch. Yet he is at least being honest, keeping to the ingredients available to him. In reviewing Rachels' work, Marvin Lubenow comments, 'To value individual life in an evolutionary scenario is a contradiction in concepts. In evolution, the individual has no value. It is the population gene pool alone that has value, because it is out of that gene pool that the alleged new species will develop as evolution proceeds over time. Since there are over five billion individuals making up the human gene pool today, it does not take a rocket scientist to figure out how much value one individual has. For all practical purposes, the value of the individual in an evolutionary scenario is zero.'[32]

Far from dignifying man, atheism degrades him. The atheist begins by saying there was no dignity in man's origin, which came about as a result of the accidental stirring of primeval sludge. He then sees no dignity in human life itself. In a 1998 debate beamed live to forty-four universities across North America, and carried on the World Wide Web, Peter Atkins asserted, 'The reasons for believing in God are vacuous,' and went on: 'It is time to respect the nobility of the human spirit... It is time to stand four-square in front of this glorious world and accept we are alone.'[33] This was hardly an original idea, though it would have been one had Atkins explained how cosmic solitude produces nobility. If we are truly alone, we might as well echo Shakespeare's statement that 'Life ... is a tale, told by an idiot, signifying nothing.'[34] Nor does the atheist hold out any hope of dignity after death. In the *Sunday Telegraph's* 'Me and my God' series, the novelist and restaurant critic Jonathan Meades described himself as a 'more or less militant atheist' and said that in his opinion God was 'a hugely successful fiction ... no different from fairies at the bottom of the garden'.[35] Asked by John Morrish what he anticipated happening to him after death, he replied, 'I don't expect anything to happen to me except that I become humus — I don't mean as in taramasalata, I mean as in leaf mould.'[36] Very witty; perfectly honest; totally tragic. Atheism says that man began as a fluke, lives out a farce and will end as fertilizer. Where does dignity find a place in that scenario?

For Socrates and most of the Greek fathers of philosophy, the chief dignity of man lay in his exercise of reason in search of truth, but this hardly provides a sufficient basis for the weighty claims man makes for himself, nor does an honest assessment of his moral record over the centuries. Theism, on the other hand, does: it says that without God, man would have no reference-point by which to define himself, but that man has immense dignity, directly derived from his status as the crown of God's creation, honoured with the capacity to enter into a living and eternal relationship with him.

Rights

The issue of human dignity is closely tied in with that of human rights. This concept goes back at least as far as Plato and Aristotle, and Thomas Aquinas reworked Greek thought to promote the idea of 'natural rights'. The famous Magna Carta, which King John was forced to sign in 1215, and the Bill of Rights passed towards the end of the seventeenth century were milestones in British history. The American Declaration of Independence in 1776 affirmed as 'self-evident' that all men had 'certain inalienable rights', while a few years later France's Declaration of the Rights of Men and of Citizens spoke of 'the natural, inalienable and sacred rights of man'.

Other countries have made declarations along somewhat similar lines, but the atrocities of the Second World War brought the issue to the top of the world's agenda. The preamble to the charter of the United Nations Organization, which was established in 1945, affirmed 'fundamental human rights' and 'the equal rights of men and women and of nations large and small', while Article 55 of its charter said that the organization would promote 'universal respect for, and observance of, human rights and fundamental freedoms for all, without distinction as to race, sex, language or religion'. In 1948, the United Nations General Assembly adopted a 'Universal Declaration of Human Rights' which affirmed that 'All human beings are born free and equal in dignity and rights.' This declaration was followed by the establishment of the European Convention for the Protection of Human Rights in 1950, the European Commission on Human Rights in 1953 and the European Court of Human Rights in 1958. Ten years later, 1968 was declared to be the International Year for Human Rights and in 1976 the International Bill of Human Rights came into being.

Issues about the rights claimed by one group or another are constantly in the media and often hit the headlines. To name just a few, we hear of children's rights, students' rights, women's rights, so-called 'gay rights' for homosexuals and lesbians, workers' rights, senior citizens' rights, civil rights, coloured people's rights, prisoners' rights, patients' rights, rights for the disabled, the poor, the unemployed, the homeless and the refugee. The rights of those as yet unborn are a major issue in contemporary medical ethics, campaigns for the right to live are matched in passion by those advocating the right to die, and specific rights are claimed on behalf of those who are dead and buried.

Rights are claimed or touted by all kinds of people, sometimes in the most unlikely contexts. In 1998 London hosted a conference promoting tall people's rights. In the same year, the winner of the Eurovision Song Contest, Dana International, who underwent a sex change operation four years earlier, called her (or his) victory 'a blow for human rights'.[37] Speaking a month later against the genetic modification of food crops, Prince Charles was hardly exaggerating when he said, 'We live in an age of rights.'[38] In his 'Sacred and Profane' column in the *Daily Telegraph*, Clifford Longley agreed: 'The most significant moral transition of the past 50 years, which shows no sign of slowing down, is the change from the idea of sin to the idea of rights... Time and again, when philosophers, lawyers, politicians and teachers turn their attention to what might be the bedrock of modern morality, they select "human rights" as the best option.'[39]

In the context of our overall study, there are at least four categories of question raised by the contemporary preoccupation with 'rights'.

The first is to ask whether the atheist has an explanation as to why rights granted to humans should not be extended to all other animals. We touched briefly on animal rights in chapter 15, and need not get deeply into the subject here. It will be sufficient to point out the confusion caused by the evolutionary notion that there is no clear distinction between humans and other animals. To give just one example of this confusion, there is mounting pressure in these days to avoid testing drugs and cosmetics on animals, yet in 1992 the *Sunday Times* reported that vast numbers of abortions in Russia were fuelling the French cosmetics industry with tons of human placentas to produce face creams which give the skin a 'softer, smoother look' and, according to one producer, enable the user to age 'serenely and in total beauty'.[40]

Peter Singer adds to the confusion with his idea of 'speciesism', which leads him to state, 'We can no longer base our ethics on the idea that human beings are a special form of creation, singled out from all other animals... Once the religious mumbo-jumbo has been stripped away, we may continue to see normal members of our species as possessing greater capacities ... than members of any other species; but we will not regard as sacrosanct the life of each and every member of our species... Species membership alone ... is not morally relevant.'[41] He claims that some animals (whales, dolphins and apes, and possibly monkeys, dogs, cats, pigs, seals and bears) are 'non-human persons' and that it is just as wrong to hurt or kill them as it is to hurt or kill a human being. Yet he then gets into a tangle by removing the automatic rights of protection from unborn babies and those up to one month old: 'Killing a defective infant is not morally equivalent to killing a person. Very often it is not wrong at all.'[42]

The second batch of questions follows naturally from the first. Who is capable of making an unquestionable judgement as to which organisms are capable of experiencing happiness or misery and should therefore be accorded 'rights'? Can such a critical decision be left in the hands of a small minority of people with a highly controversial agenda? Can rights be graded to correspond to the levels of the various organisms' sensory perception? If so, who is qualified to make the decisions involved?

Searching for sources

In the third place, on what atheistic basis do human beings have *any* rights? Where in his creed does the atheist discover rights to such things as justice, freedom, possessions, health, happiness, security, or even to life itself? If human beings are nothing more than complex biological machines which came into existence by accident, why should they have any more rights than any other objects in the universe? At what point in the 'Great Chain of Being' did rights of any kind come into the picture? Did primeval 'soup', or amino-acids or eukaryotic cells or enzymes have rights? Did the first fish, amphibians, reptiles, birds or hominids have rights? If not, why not? If they did, when and why did some or all of them lose some or all of those rights?

As far as human rights are concerned, it must be obvious that if rights were self-determined, society would collapse in a chaotic heap, but arguments about a social contract and the common good are also very rickety platforms. If human rights are merely benefits granted by international organizations, national governments or other ruling bodies, or loosely agreed at some social level or other, how can we object when (as is often the case) they are later denied as emphatically as they were granted?

Fourthly, if there is no transcendent basis for human rights, why should anyone be concerned about the needs of other people? According to Keith Ward, 'When we speak about "human rights", we are not speaking about some purely personal preferences which vary from one country to another. We are speaking about giving everyone access to some share in the intrinsic values that make humans worthwhile.'[43] Ward is right, but what do 'intrinsic values' mean if, to quote Richard Dawkins, our existence and survival are only 'means to an end', the end concerned being 'reproduction'?[44] If this is the case, why should disablement, mental derangement, unemployment, hunger, poverty or drug dependency be causes for concern?

What does the materialist have to say to this? If Jacob Bronowski is right to state that 'Man is not different in kind from other forms of life ... living matter is not different in kind from dead matter,' that 'Man is an assembly of atoms that obeys natural laws of the same kind that a star does,' and that 'It seems self-evident to say that man is a part of nature, in the same sense that a stone is, or a cactus, or a camel,'[45] how can we claim that a human being has any unique value, or is entitled to any specific rights? If people are merely a different (and accidental) arrangement of molecules, any talk about their rights is gobbledegook. R. C. Sproul underlines the point: 'Why should we care at all about the plight of insignificant grown-up germs? What difference does it make if the white germs subjugate the black germs and make them sit at the back of the bus? Who cares if meaningless blobs of protoplasm are exploited in a steel mill or robbed in the halls of justice? Oh, you say, the black germs care and the little blobs of protoplasm cry out. Again I say, "So what?" A creature with no ultimate value, one who is ultimately insignificant, is not worth any sacrifice. Tell it to the idiot, as he alone can live with empty sound and fury. If man is valueless then we can sleep in tomorrow morning.'[46]

The concept of human rights is virtually impossible to square with an atheistic world-view, but it fits perfectly into a creationist world-view. The radical British author Thomas Paine (1737–1809) was the most famous deist of his day, believing in an unknown (and probably impersonal) deity rather than the God posited in this book, yet in his famous book *The Rights of Man,* first published in 1791 in support of the French Revolution, he pinpointed a crucial factor: 'The error of those who reason by precedents drawn from antiquity, respecting the rights of man, is that they do not go far enough into antiquity. They do not go the whole way. They stop in some of the intermediate stages of an hundred or a thousand years... But if we proceed on, we shall at last come out right; we shall come to the time when man came from the hand of his Maker. What was he then? Man. Man was his high and only title, and a higher cannot be given him.'[47]

Fifteen years earlier, the American Declaration of Independence, drafted by another deist, Thomas Jefferson, claimed that the 'inalienable rights' of human beings, including those to 'life, liberty and the pursuit of happiness', were not acquired or invented at some point in human history but were 'endowed by their Creator'. The American and French Revolutions were pivotal in raising the profile of human rights, and it is striking that the deistic leaders of both took a Supreme Being as their starting-point and insisted that man's rights are inherent in his creation.

On this issue at least, theists confirm what these deists claimed. Human rights can properly be discussed only when we have established what it means to be human. When his Cape coast home was ransacked in 1998 for the second time in a year, and members of his neighbour's family were brutally murdered by an intruder, the South African golfer Ernie Els made an impassioned plea to the government to curb 'the sickening wave of crime which is engulfing and destroying our country'. Speaking to Johannesburg's *Sunday Times*, he protested, 'Our rights as human beings are being taken away from us.'[48] Els was not making a religious statement, but in speaking about 'our rights as human beings' he was unconsciously putting his finger on the neglected truth that it is as human beings created by God that we have whatever 'rights' we can properly claim. John Stott puts the theistic position like this: 'The origin of human rights is creation. Man has never "acquired" them. Nor has any government or other authority conferred them. Man has had them from the beginning. He received them with his life from the hand of his Maker. They are inherent in his creation. They have been bestowed on him by his Creator.'[49]

This is not to say that animals have no rights, for they too are part of God's creation, but these fall short of those granted to beings who, as we shall see in a later chapter, stand in a unique relationship to God. Theism sees 'human rights', not as personal preferences which we can demand to be met, but as privileges granted by God and which he requires us to respect in others. This theistic picture provides the perfect framework for *equal* rights, as it says that man's highest worth (and therefore his most valid claim to 'rights' of any kind) lies in a creative act which bestows equal status on all human beings without any discrimination of any kind. It also points powerfully towards our responsibility to secure and defend other people's rights, even if we have to forgo our own in order to do so.

The moral maze

One of the greatest problems humanity presents to atheism concerns ethics and morality. The moral argument is an important part of natural theology, and formed the fourth of Thomas Aquinas' famous 'Five Ways'. Aquinas drew attention to the gradation of moral values in the world, with some things being said to be better or nobler than others. He then argued that just as 'good' and 'better' point to the 'best', so this gradation pointed to the necessary existence of a Supreme Being possessing a perfection of all moral values: 'There is therefore something which causes in all other things their being, their goodness and whatever other perfection they have.

And this we call "God".'[50] Aquinas' arguments have come under fierce attack, especially from the eighteenth century onwards but, as we shall see, they contain elements which it has proved impossible to dislodge. We touched briefly on ethics and morality in chapter 8, when assessing some of the statements in *Humanist Manifesto II*, but we need to pursue them here. Although people often use the words 'ethics' and 'morals' interchangeably, as if they meant the same thing, this is not the case. The word 'ethics' comes from the Greek *ethos* meaning 'foundation' or 'character', whereas 'morals' comes from the Latin *mores*, meaning 'customs' or 'manners'. Ethics sets a standard and establishes why one kind of behaviour is better than another, while morals describe people's behavioural patterns. In other words, ethics is concerned with what ought to be done, while morals are concerned with what is being done.

With these definitions in mind, we can begin by saying that everybody operates within some kind of ethical framework. Some people may be sceptical about morality in general, but they rapidly change their tune if they feel they have been wronged in some way. Although morality differs from person to person, and from one society to another, the existence of some kind of moral law seems fundamental and pervasive. As Stephen Evans points out, 'It is right to be kind, generous, honest, courageous and just. It is wrong to be selfish, cruel, deceptive and cowardly. It is wrong to be abusive, unfriendly and ungrateful. These are truths which human beings discover. We do not invent them; in their own way they are as objective as the laws of science or mathematics.'[51]

Surely it is difficult to disagree? Every rational person has some sense of right and wrong. There is no more reason to deny the objective existence of moral values than to deny the objective reality of the physical world. If we are unable to make clear, moral distinctions, we become incapable of making any judgements at all. When a lawyer tries to persuade a judge that a guilty client does not know the difference between right and wrong, he pleads that he is rationally defective, or in some other way incapable of acting as a normal human being. This gives us a clue that moral law seems programmed into our psychological 'software'. Over 2,000 years ago Cicero wrote, 'Only a madman could maintain that the distinction between the honourable and the dishonourable, between virtue and vice, is a matter of opinion, not of nature.'[52] As we noted in chapter 2, the 'moral law within' was one of the things which filled Immanuel Kant with 'ever new and increasing wonder and awe',[53] and led him to argue that, although we cannot know anything for certain about God, we must live as if he exists or society would collapse into moral chaos. In writing about his scepticism 'generally slipping away', Jonathan Dimbleby said that humankind's obvious instinct for good and evil was a major factor: 'We know intuitively that something is good or not good. We have a sense of what perfectibility is. We all therefore know when we are falling short. I can't explain that in mere neurological or chemical or societal terms. Therefore I am tempted by that clarity of faith which I see in some of my friends.'[54] But what is the source of this sense of morality which, whether we like it or not, none of us can completely escape and which glues us all together as a species? Where can morality find a secure point of reference? There is no shortage of answers on offer.

The Sinatra syndrome?

Running in parallel to a universal sense of morality is the widespread belief that there are no moral absolutes, a conviction that has been called 'one of the axioms of our contemporary Western culture'.[55] The American scholar David Wells goes so far as to say of his own country and other parts of the West, 'This is the first time that a civilization has existed that, to a significant extent, does not believe in objective right and wrong. We are travelling blind, stripped of our own moral compass.'[56] When the American singer Frank Sinatra died in 1998, all his obituaries reminded us that his most famous song was 'My Way', but few, if any, pointed out that it was an anthem for our times.

For millions of people, morality has become a matter of preference rather than principle. A Bradford University professor told the *Independent*, 'Anyone who teaches undergraduates today will tell you that the most prevalent reactions they have to most social and moral issues is a jejune selectivism: "It's all a matter of opinion, isn't it?"'[57] Writing in 1998, the *Sunday Times* journalist Bryan Appleyard agreed: 'Nowadays we don't have universal rules. Every situation in which people find themselves is different and every moral choice they make is surrounded by a complex, compromising halo of cause and effect... Modern morals, if any, tend to be entirely subjective.'[58] However 'adult' and liberating this may sound to some, a few illustrations of how it works out in practice will soon expose weaknesses in the 'Sinatra syndrome'.

During Northern Ireland's 'troubles' a few years ago, the Republican terrorist Dominic 'Mad Dog' McGlinchey boasted of murdering at least thirty people in his struggle for Irish independence. A *Times* columnist said McGlinchey had been 'consumed by blood-lust virtually from the cradle' and that 'The only progress he could see ... was via slaughter and the piled-up bones of those who opposed him.'[59] Yet at McGlinchey's funeral (he was shot dead in 1994 by three gunmen believed to be settling a ten-year feud) the political activist Bernadette McAliskey described him as 'incorruptible' and called him 'the finest republican, who never did an inglorious deed'.[60] In the absence of absolutes, how can we dismantle her eulogy of a serial killer who was doing what he believed to be right?

The day after his seventieth birthday in 1996, Hugh Heffner, the so-called 'Peter Pan' of soft porn, and founder of the Playboy empire, who brags of having slept with over 1,000 women, told the *Daily Telegraph's* William Cash, 'I'm a very ethical guy. I've managed to live on the edge, but I've done it with a lot of class.'[61] When Heffner was asked what important lessons he had learned in seventy years, Cash reported that 'without a glimmer of irony' he replied, 'Moderation is the key.'[62] The mind boggles, and to say that Heffner has the morals of an alley cat may be slandering alley cats, but if all morality is a matter of personal preference, who are we to argue with his definition of moderation?

In 1994, Bryce Taylor surreptitiously took photographs of Diana, Princess of Wales, while she was exercising in her London gym, then sold them to the tabloid press. When challenged about the morality of this, he said it was an opportunity for him and his family to make some money, and that 'It was within the bounds of my ethical and moral parameters at the time because of my circumstances.'[63] As the *Daily Telegraph's* Henry Porter commented when reporting the story, 'The logic is so bizarre that one almost giggles,'[64] yet Taylor's words deserve framing as a perfect illustration of what I have called the 'Sinatra syndrome'. The circumstances set the scene and, from all the ethical options available, he chose the one which produced the biggest personal pay-out. If ethics can be pulled around to fit our personal needs at any given moment, who can blame him?

When Woody Allen was challenged about having an affair with the adopted teenage daughter of his live-in partner Mia Farrow, he defiantly replied, 'The heart wants what the heart wants'; in other words, 'I will decide what is good or bad, right or wrong, and my decision is none of your business.' If the 'Sinatra syndrome' holds good, who can disagree? If arch-humanist Paul Kurtz is right in claiming, 'The moral principles that govern our behaviour are rooted in habit and custom, feeling and fashion,'[65] how can *anything* be commended as being right, or condemned as being wrong ?

Not surprisingly, the 'Sinatra syndrome' is hugely popular, yet even the most dogmatic unbelievers admit that privatized morality is hopelessly inconsistent. An entrenched atheist like Bertrand Russell vehemently opposed war, yet denounced restrictions on sexual freedom. In a letter to the *Observer* in 1957, he admitted that he could not live as though ethical values were a matter of personal taste, that he therefore found his own views 'incredible' and that 'I do not know the solution.'[66] In the absence of objective moral truth, this is hardly surprising. As John Benton also points out, 'If morality is just a matter of personal opinion, then we have no basis for a legal system. You can't send people to prison over differences in personal opinion.'[67]

Privatized morality has many other weaknesses, two of which C. S. Lewis identified with his usual clarity: In the first place, how do ethical standards come into being? In Lewis's words, 'The human mind has no more power of inventing a new value than of planting a new sun in the sky or a new colour in the spectrum.'[68] Secondly, in the absence of absolutes, how can we talk of moral progress? As Lewis put it, 'If things can improve, this means that there must be some absolute standard of good above and outside the cosmic process towards which that process can approximate. There is no sense in talking of "becoming better" if better means simply "what we are becoming" — it is like congratulating yourself on reaching your destination and defining destination as "the place you have reached".'[69]

Something new?

In the 1960s, John Robinson, then Bishop of Woolwich, used his book *Honest to God* to promote what he called the 'New Morality'. This says that there is no coherent system which lays down consistently valid rules for conduct, that the right course of action should be determined by the situation itself and that within any situation the only absolute should be love. Making the point positively and negatively, Robinson maintained that 'There is nothing prescribed — except love,'[70] and that 'The only intrinsic evil is lack of love.'[71] The idea got widespread publicity, and fitted in perfectly with the mood of the so-called 'Swinging Sixties', but it begs the question as to why we should call even love an obligation. As Colin Brown makes clear, 'The mere fact that other people are there does not mean that we should love them, unless there is some authority over and above us which tells us what we should do. In practice, people recognize such an authority when they say that stealing, adultery and murder are wrong and caring for others is right. But this in turn raises the whole question of the nature and *otherness* of this authority.'[72]

The 'New Morality' also ignores the fact that as human beings we are incapable of knowing the full nature of our actions, or all their consequences. As the American theologian James Montgomery Boice writes, 'There is too much guilt, too many entrenched patterns of unfaithfulness, and even too many unforeseen and unwanted children to make the new morality a valid or satisfying option.'[73]

Follow the crowd?

A third response to the question of the origin and basis of morality is to say that it should be determined by the prevailing culture, with written and unwritten law providing a collective social conscience which reflects public opinion. In this model, ethical principles are seen as a particular culture's way of organizing social relations, without any higher reference-point applicable to all cultures. The nineteenth-century American scholar Oliver Wendell Holmes, who eventually became a Chief Justice of the Supreme Court, promoted this idea with great effect during his term of office. He had come to the conclusion that, as it is impossible for human beings ever to know any supreme, absolute objective law, all laws must simply be a reflection of whatever the majority, or the strongest group, in a given society wants. Gertrude Himmelfarb, whose principal field of study has been Victorian England, shows that during the past century virtues have become 'values' and that they may now mean nothing more than a preference, belief, feeling, habit or convention — 'whatever any individual, group or society happens to value, at any time, for any reason'.[74]

In a debate held a few years ago at the University of California at Irvine, Gordon Stein, vice-president of Atheists United, and introduced as 'one of America's foremost scholars of atheism', indicated exactly what cultural morality is saying: 'People's moral values are an accommodation they have made with their particular environment and have taught their children. It is a survival mechanism.' Addressing the subject of evil, he went on, 'Evil is by definition in an atheist's universe that which decreases the happiness of people. That thing is evil which causes more people to be unhappy. How do we know this? Well, we don't know it. It's a consensus, just like morality in general is a consensus.'

This overall concept now has massive support, but it runs into serious difficulties. In the first place, how can we be sure that public opinion is any more reliable than personal opinion? Is there any guarantee in numbers? What kind of majority would define 'right' and 'wrong'? Would a million wrongs make a right? As Peter Kreeft and Ronald Tacelli put it, '"Society" only means more individuals. What right do they have to legislate morality to me? Quantity cannot yield quality.'[75] The notion that society produces morality is also torpedoed by the fact that some of the most honoured people in history are those who recognized the moral *failings* of their society and fought against them until radical changes were made.

Secondly, if morality is a mere product of culture, how can we compare cultures and claim that some cultural practices are morally superior? David Broughton Knox illustrates this well: 'It is a great mistake to think that the law should simply enshrine public opinion. For if a law is simply relative to culture then, of course, it is impossible for one culture to judge another; each has its own law and each law is justified by the public opinion of its own people. But when the crunch comes we know that this view of law is wrong. At the Nuremberg trials the Nazis charged with war crimes said that they had simply been carrying out the orders and laws of the government of Germany. But this rationale was seen to be false. The Nuremberg trials were based on the concept that there is a higher law by which the laws of Nazi Germany could be tested.'[76]

One has only to scan the newspapers to see that, in the detailed legislation of morality, culture points to confusion, not consistency. In 1994 Peter Hillmore wrote a piece for the *Observer* in which he pointed out that in Sweden criminal responsibility starts at fifteen, but in Ireland it starts at seven, and that in Spain the age of consent is twelve, while in Turkey it is eighteen. As a further illustration of his contention that legislation is 'a chaotic mixture of local prejudices and customs', he reported that in some Canadian provinces the minimum age for unaccompanied drinking is nineteen, while a girl can marry at twelve.[77]

Other differences are even more striking. In 1995 the *Daily Telegraph* carried this news item: 'Minibuses in Teheran are to be segregated to stop male and female passengers from brushing against each other, which is a sin in Islam. A transport official said that with 370,000 women passengers a day being brushed ten times each, 3.7 million sins were being committed.'[78] A few months later, the *Observer* reported a husband's brutal murder of his wife in Pakistan according to a tribal tradition called *karo kari*, under which any man who sees a female relative with a man to whom she is not married is *obligated* to kill both individuals to preserve his family's honour. A human rights lawyer explained that under the Pakistani Penal Code a *karo kari* murder was a justifiable offence which the court would consider 'an honour killing'.[79]

To many millions of people, the first of these illustrations will seem ludicrous and the second horrific, but on what basis can the cultures they represent be criticized? Writing as 'an agnostic Jew with no religious axe to grind', the *Daily Telegraph's* Janet Daley made an important point: 'It is a fundamental logical error to think that you can choose between cultures when a given culture, with its explicit moral programme, is the only equipment we have for making social choices. Carried to its logical conclusion, cultural relativism produces not tolerance, but nihilism. *If everyone is right, then no one is*'[80] (emphasis added).

The greatest good?

Cultural morality is often tied in with the concept of doing that which promotes 'the greatest good of the greatest number'. In a debate held in 1998, Peter Atkins claimed that moral values were simply a social contract produced by intellect and evolution to protect communities but, as John Benton shows, 'The idea of the greatest good for the greatest number can be manipulated to justify almost anything, including the greatest evils.'[81] For example, Hitler would have had no problem in signing up to the 'greatest good of the greatest number' idea; Nazi culture acted in line with an ethic which said that the extermination of Jews, gypsies and others was morally justified in the long-term interests of a superior race. If we say that culture can define ethics, how, in the absence of ethical absolutes, can we pass judgement on any culture that does not agree with ours? The Holocaust can be condemned only from an ethical vantage-point that transcends culture and gives an ultimate standard of right and wrong.

This raises another radical problem. At a seminar on the ethical dilemmas arising from medical advances, one contributor made this telling comment: 'When you talk about the greatest good of the greatest number you are still left with the question, "In the name of what is this called good for anyone?" *You are driven back to some interpretation of what it means to be a human being*'[82] (emphasis added). Peter Atkins ignores this when assuring us in *Creation Revisited* that 'Everything is driven by motiveless, purposeless decay.'[83] So does Richard Dawkins when insisting that human beings are nothing more than robots for passing on bits of DNA to the next generation. The best the evolutionist can do is to join Darwin in reducing morals to an extension of animal instincts, but this falls a long way short of showing that culture is a reliable basis for morality. Dawkins himself admits that if one wants to build a society in which people co-operate generously and unselfishly towards a common good 'you can expect little help from biological nature'.[84] He ends *The Selfish Gene* by conceding that 'pure disinterested altruism' never existed before human beings appeared on the earth,[85] a statement which, as Anthony O'Hear says, 'simply emphasizes the *irrelevance* of Darwinism'.[86]

The idea that morality is a matter of self-preservation is frankly absurd, as we often exercise moral judgements on issues that have no direct bearing on our personal well-being, let alone our preservation. To suggest that morality can be explained by natural selection, and that our sense of obligation can be reduced to instinct, simply fails to square with our moral experience. As Peter Kreeft and Ronald Tacelli indicate, 'We do not experience morality as an instinct, but as a law which tells us which instinct to follow in which situations. No instinct is itself always right, but morality is always right, therefore morality is not just an instinct. Rather, morality transcends instinct, as sheet music transcends the notes on a piano. Instincts are notes; the moral law tells us how and when to play these notes.'[87]

One other point: how can any culture be an absolute guide for morality if those who drive it have no transcendent reference-point? The story is told of a man who stopped outside a clockmaker's shop every morning on his way to work and synchronized his watch with a large clock standing in the shop window. One day, the owner of the shop got talking to him and asked him what kind of work he did. Rather sheepishly, the man told him he was the timekeeper at a nearby factory, and that one of his responsibilities was to ring the closing bell at five o'clock every evening. As his watch kept very poor time, he synchronized it every morning with the clock in the shop window. The shop-owner, even more embarrassed, replied, 'I hate to tell you this, but the clock doesn't work very well either, and I adjust it every time I hear the factory's closing bell!' When the movers and shakers in any given society have no moral absolutes to guide them, how can their culture claim to have any ethical integrity? Human beings in a given society might agree, for selfish mutual benefit, not to harm each other, but how does this social contract give any meaning to words such as 'rights', 'justice', 'fairness', 'right' and 'wrong'? As Os Guinness says, 'With the death of absolutes the prospects are grim for any lover of justice, freedom and order.'[88] Even Voltaire had an inkling that social morality needed some objective basis, and may not have been entirely cynical when he said, 'I want my lawyer, tailor, valets, even my wife to believe in God. I think that if they do, I shall be robbed less and cheated less.'[89]

Natural causes?

Another response to the problem of morals and ethics is that of the materialist, who says with Michael Ruse and Edward Wilson that they are the by-products of blind evolution: 'Morality or, more strictly, our belief in morality, is merely an adaptation put in place to further our reproductive ends... Ethics is seen to have a solid foundation, not in divine guidance, but in the shared qualities of human nature.'[90] Elsewhere, they wrote, 'No abstract moral principles exist outside the particular nature of individual species.'[91] According to the materialist, the idea that there is a divine source of ethical absolutes and guiding principles for human society can be dismissed as a religious illusion; blind, godless evolution explains everything. This ties in with what Francis Crick called his 'Astonishing Hypothesis: '"You", your joys and your sorrows, your memories and ambitions, your sense of personal identity and free will, are in fact no more than the behaviour of a vast assembly of nerve cells and their associated molecules.'[92]

This is the standard line now taken by atheistic biologists, yet even they are forced to admit its weaknesses and limitations. On BBC television's 1998 programme *The Darwin Debate*, the chairman, Melvyn Bragg, asked the Cornell University anthropologist Meredith Small, 'Does the evolution theory have anything to say about altruism, tenderness or morality?' She replied, 'Sure, but at a ground level, a population level, not at any individual level.' When Bragg asked, 'And do you think there's any evolutionary answer to that?', Small replied, 'No, not really.'[93] Interviewed by the

Daily Telegraph's Mick Brown, Richard Dawkins conceded that, as nature was 'red in tooth and claw', Darwinianism could offer no model for goodness. He himself claimed to have 'an ordinary citizen's view of goodness', paying his taxes and feeling compassion for the disadvantaged and unfortunate. He then went on, 'I have all the right emotions against injustice. I do have a strongly developed sense of good. But as a biologist I haven't a very well worked-out story where that comes from... I would sweep *good* into the same receptacle as music and philosophy and say that it is just something that has emerged.'[94] Later in the interview he said that love was 'a product of highly complicated equipment of some sort, nervous equipment or computing equipment of some sort' — but is this an adequate explanation of the profound and life-changing experiences we associate with the word? Is this his assessment of relationships within any of his own marriages? The notion that morality is merely 'something that has emerged' and can be put down to what I have called 'natural causes' may satisfy some, but it runs headlong into a flurry of questions.

Opening the debate on *God — For or Against?* televised from Oxford University in 1998, Peter Atkins stated, 'We must find the origin of the way we behave and therefore our judgement about what is good and what is wrong in the fact that we have found a way of surviving,'[95] but where is the connection between survival and morality? If human beings come from nothing and are going nowhere, what is the value of survival, let alone of having ethical standards in the process?

If the universe is no more than matter, energy, time and chance, how can 'right' and 'wrong' have any meaning? How can we derive personal morality from a fundamentally impersonal universe? What do we do with the law of causality, which says that you cannot get more out of less? How can we jump from molecules to morality? How can we explain concepts of good and evil in mechanistic terms? In an atheistic universe with no moral obligations, and in which human beings are merely shrink-wrapped bags of biological elements governed by the laws of physics, where can we find any basis for exercising moral judgement about anything? How could an impersonal reality make me feel any moral obligation to be honest, kind or truthful? Ravi Zacharias puts his finger on the spot when he says, 'Thinking atoms discussing morality is absurd.'[96]

If love can be written off as the product of some kind of physico-chemical equipment, can we not say the same of hatred? Why should one be considered better or worse than the other? Thomas Huxley conceded the point without blinking: 'The thief and the murderer follow nature just as much as the philanthropist. Cosmic evolution may teach us how the good and evil tendencies may have come about; but, in itself, it is incompetent to furnish any better reason why what we call good is preferable to what we call evil than what we had before.'[97]

If people are simply genetically programmed machines, determined biologically or in some other way, why should we be concerned over issues of justice or fairness, or feel any obligation to treat other human beings with respect? Scientist Rodney Holder elaborates: 'If we are nothing but atoms and molecules organized in a particular way through the chance processes of evolution, then love, beauty, good and evil, free will, reason itself — indeed all that makes us human and raises us above the rest of the created order — lose their objectivity. Why should I love my neighbour, or go out of my way to help him? Rather, why should I not get everything I can for myself, trampling on whoever gets in my way? After all, I am nothing but a "gene survival machine", and my sole purpose is to propagate my own genes. The best we can do can be to come to some kind of agreement in our mutual interest along utilitarian lines to live in peace, but if it suits us we shall be free to break any such agreement. Our behaviour could degenerate to that which we see in the animal world — after all, we are just animals anyway.'[98]

Holder might even be painting too bright a picture. One of today's liveliest 'nothing-buttery' scholars is Steven Pinker, a professor of philosophy at the Massachusetts Institute of Technology. In a 1997 issue of the *Sunday Telegraph* he claimed, 'Nothing in the mind exists except as neural activity.'[99] In a *New York Times* article, he backed this up by suggesting that women who murder their new-born babies may not be mad or evil, but unconsciously obeying primeval instincts to sacrifice their children for the good of the tribe.[100] This is the logical outworking of materialism, *but if reducing the brain's activity to electrical impulses can sanction murder, what can it condemn?*

It is one thing for Michael Ruse to say, 'Morality is no more ... than an adaptation, and as such has the same status as such things as teeth and eyes and noses,'[101] but what happens when we are faced with moral choices? If, as Ruse goes on to say, 'morality is a creation of the genes',[102] what is the criterion for making moral decisions? Have we no option but to do whatever our genes have programmed us to do? In other words, how can the materialist escape from the stranglehold of determinism? In *Objective Knowledge: An Evolutionary Approach*, Karl Popper makes the point that if determinism were true it could not be argued, since any argument is presumably itself determined by purely physical conditions, as are any opposing arguments.[103] We can illustrate this from the life and teaching of the French novelist commonly known as the Marquis de Sade (1740–1814), who gave his name to sadism, in which a person derives sexual satisfaction from inflicting pain and humiliation on others. De Sade argued that as everything is chemically determined, whatever is, is right. Is there any way in which an atheist can avoid that conclusion? If we are genetically programmed machines, how can we be right in saying that de Sade was wrong?

It is easy to see that determinism has serious social implications. In 1996, Steve Jones suggested in his book *In The Blood* that criminal behaviour was largely determined by genetic make-up. In discussing the book, Janet Daley insisted that if genetics is responsible for 'bad' traits it must also account for many good ones, adding that 'If we can never be truly guilty, then we can never be truly virtuous either.'[104] Showing that the debate was 'less about how we should treat criminals than about whether we can talk about morality at all', she pointed out the implications of determinism: 'Human beings are only capable of being moral insofar as they are free to choose how they behave. If they have no power to make real choices — if their freedom to decide how to act is severely limited by forces outside their control — then it is nonsense to make any ethical judgements about them. It would be wrong, as well, to base a judicial system on the assumption that people are free to choose how they will act. The idea of putting anyone on trial for anything at all becomes absurd.'[105]

If Darwinian evolution is true, and people are as much a part of nature as other creatures, how can any complaint be made against anything they do, any more than against any other part of nature? Why should we criticize vandals, but not vultures? The problem is not that atheists necessarily have wrong values, but that they have no objective foundation for their morality. To be morally minded, evolutionists have to rise above their fundamental beliefs, as Richard Dawkins, Desmond Morris, Peter Singer and four others did in 1997 when they wrote to a national newspaper protesting that it was 'morally repugnant' for the Department of Health to propose conducting certain experiments on apes.[106] Their genuine concern hardly tied in with their materialistic convictions; it was much more in line with Anthony O'Hear's contention that as human beings 'we are not the unwitting victims of purely natural or historical processes'.[107]

We might add here that some people have tried to use determinism as a defence for their actions by bringing God into the picture. In his autobiography, first published in 1998, the well-known football pundit Jimmy Hill wrote about his womanizing exploits and confessed, 'I am not proud of my record with women. I have always had an appetite to explore the delights of love and lust and, I am afraid, one partner was never going to be enough for me. It was simply the way God made me.'[108] It would be difficult to concoct a more confused assessment; the 'God' Hill has in mind is clearly not the one being put forward in this book.

Trying to locate a basis for morality in the blind outworkings of nature is futile. In Dave Hunt's words, 'There are no morals in nature. Try to find a compassionate crow or an honest eagle — or a sympathetic hurricane.'[109]

Anything goes?

Another response is that of the nihilist, who says with Friedrich Nietzsche and Albert Camus that, as human beings are biological accidents, with no meaningful origin or destiny, there is no rational justification for adopting an ethical stance about anything. Jean-Paul Sartre once stated, 'Nowhere is it written that Good exists, that we must be honest, that we must not lie: because the fact is that we are on a plane where there are only men.'[110] Elsewhere, he wrote, 'The existentialist finds it extremely embarrassing that God does not exist — for there disappears with him all possibility of finding moral values in an intelligible universe.'[111] More recently, Michael Ruse agreed and claimed, 'There is no justification for morality in the ultimate sense.'[112]

For the nihilist, life is absurd and there are no absolutes (except, presumably, the absolute that there are absolutely no absolutes!), and the only motivation for any kind of morality is the self-interest of the moment. J. P. Moreland summarizes how a nihilist would put this: 'If I find a moral life satisfying, or if doing what society says is moral will help me enjoy the moment, then I will be motivated to be moral on that occasion. But if the demands of morality go against my own personal interests, then morality has no rationally justifiable demands on me.'[113] This may sound liberating and fulfilling, but, as we saw in chapter 7, nihilism self-destructs. All the evidence is against the idea that there are no absolute values and the notion that we can never know with certainty whether particular actions are right or wrong. Is rape ever right? Is child molestation ever commendable? In the words of Peter Moore, 'Every time we make a moral judgement on someone else ... we are assuming a moral order to the universe under which both we and they must stand.'[114]

Fyodor Dostoevsky reminded us that 'Without God, everything is permitted.' If we deny objective ethics we are left in a moral jungle. In Francis Schaeffer's words, 'Without absolutes, man's endeavours degenerate into absurdity.'[115] In a godless universe, what one animal does to another is ethically irrelevant, whether the animals concerned are male or female, have two legs or more, or none. Can the nihilist honestly live with this? How could a nihilist base his behaviour on self-interest if every other person in the world did the same thing? The nihilist may want to argue for his philosophy, but could he recommend it to anyone else?

The calling card

It is impossible to discuss morality without reference to the conscience, which plays a powerful role in all human behaviour. In the first century B.C., the Roman author Publilius Syrus wrote, 'Even when there is no law, there is conscience,'[116] while in his famous 'To be or not to be' speech, Shakespeare's Hamlet admits, 'Conscience does make cowards of us all.'[117]

Nobody can seriously deny the place people give to the conscience, or the power it exercises. We feel its presence as really as our eyes see objects in the material world. In his hilarious autobiography *Dear Me*, the multi-talented actor Peter Ustinov admits, 'There has never been an anthem which sets my feet tapping, never an occasion which brings a lump to my throat. I can take no allegiance to a flag if I don't know who's holding it. *My only allegiance is to my own conscience*, and who is to tell that it is not higher than any flag, or any mediocre tune written by a third-rate bandmaster to the words of a fourth-rate poet, to which men rise as a mass with a look of inane pity on their faces?'[118] (emphasis added).

Ustinov's 'oath of allegiance' is a remarkable endorsement of the fact that we can no more evade our conscience than we can escape from our shadow. Whatever we may call it, we all recognize an insistent inner voice telling us to do certain things and not to do others. It may be neglected, smothered or suppressed at times but, as Paul Johnson reminds us, 'It is made of psychic indiarubber and springs back, however unwanted or unheeded, to wag a finger at us.'[119]

No part of life escapes the conscience's influence. It insists on having its say in politics, business, family life, sexual relationships, the use of time and money, social behaviour, our attitudes to other people — and religion — and will not even leave us alone at the table or on the sports field! It sits in moral judgement over everything we think, say and do — and its presence is one of the hallmarks of humanity. G. K. Chesterton once said, 'When a crocodile devours its tenth explorer you do not say to him, "Come, now, be a crocodile!" But when a human being breaks the moral law, the conscience says, "Be a man!"'[120] To disown the claims of conscience is to reduce oneself to the level of a beast, which has no ability to distinguish between 'ought' and 'ought not'. Rodney Holder elaborates: 'Man is the only animal endowed with a self-conscious mind enabling him to choose freely whether to follow the selfish path or a nobler, altruistic way... The other animals behave purely instinctively, as programmed by their genes, whether in preying on other species, or defending their own territory, or competing aggressively against rivals of their own species for space, food or mating partners. Their behaviour can hardly be described as having any moral dimension at all. In contrast man, while possessing such drives and instincts, does not have to obey them. He has a moral sense, a conscience, and is able to distinguish between right and wrong.'[121]

Put very simply, we have within us a sense of 'ought', a mysterious moral monitor which distinguishes between right and wrong, good and bad, and tells us where our responsibility lies. Where does this come from? What ethical guidelines are there in random collisions of subatomic particles? Do we owe any allegiance to accidents? If not, why should we feel under any obligation to do what conscience says? After all, we are past masters at the art of turning a deaf ear to it, or rationalizing our response to what it says; why not go the whole hog and snuff it out altogether? Why is it there in the first place? Where does it find an absolute moral basis on which to operate? As C. S. Lewis makes clear, it is no good looking for it in nature, as nature has no morals: 'If we are to continue to make moral judgements (and whatever we say we shall in fact continue to do so) then we must believe that the conscience is not a product of Nature. It can be valid only if it is an offshoot of some absolute moral wisdom, a moral wisdom which exists absolutely "on its own" and is not a product of non-moral, non-rational Nature.'[122] It might be argued that evolution could provide an explanation for certain instincts, but it cannot possibly explain consistent moral order. It is one thing to say that human beings are grown-up germs, but is it seriously suggested that in the process of growing up they deliberately installed a moral monitor to regulate their behaviour? Did people suddenly say, 'We ought to have an "ought"?' Why should they even think of doing such a thing?

The clearest clue as to the significance of the conscience comes from the fact that the word 'ought' is based on the Old English verb *agan*, meaning 'to owe'.[123] To say that we 'ought' to do something is to say that we 'owe it'. Nor is this merely a social impulse or a matter of emotion. People who have deliberately dulled their consciences are often obligated to do certain things, yet have no feelings of obligation. On the other hand, people with unusually sensitive consciences often feel obligated to do things which no reasonable person would claim they really ought to do. Feelings and obligation are obviously not the same. An indebtedness is involved, and as a debt can be owed only to a person, the universal conscience points to an absolute personality. In John Frame's words, 'If obligations arise from personal relationships, then absolute obligations must arise from our relationship with an absolute person.'[124] C. Stephen Evans calls the conscience 'God's calling card',[125] a reminder of the moral order which points us to a transcendent lawgiver to whom we are all responsible. Søren Kierkegaard made the point well: 'A man could have nothing upon his conscience if God did not exist, for the relationship between the individual and God, the God-relationship, is the conscience.'[126] Without God, moral order would make no sense; as geneticist Francis Collins writes, 'This moral law, which defies scientific explanation, is exactly what one might expect to find if one were searching for the existence of a personal God who sought relationship with humankind.'[127]

Even the most hardened atheist, who claims that there are no transcendent moral principles, has a sense of unease when disobeying his own private conscience. Why should this be the case? Why does even the atheist submit (at least theoretically) to this one universal moral authority and feel uncomfortable when ignoring the voice of conscience? Where did conscience get such amazing power? Peter Kreeft and Ronald Tacelli claim that there are only four possibilities: from nature, from the individual concerned, from society or from God. It is unreasonable to be obligated by nature, such as animal instinct, or the need for survival. It is difficult to see how an individual can be self-obligated, as such an obligation can be cancelled as clearly as it can be imposed. Society (even on a global scale) has no inbuilt right to impose any moral obligations on one individual. As Kreeft and Tacelli show, this leaves only one alternative: 'The only source of absolute moral obligation left is something superior to me... Thus God, or something like God, is the only adequate source and ground for the absolute moral obligation we all feel to obey our conscience.'[128]

We can give the last word on morality to the scholar Richard Taylor. In *Ethics, Faith and Reason* he writes, 'The concept of moral obligation [is] unintelligible apart from the idea of God. The words remain but their meaning is gone.'[129] No theist could have said it better. Richard Taylor is a committed atheist.

18.

The book that speaks for itself

Among the ancient artefacts carefully preserved in Magdalen College, Oxford, are three tiny papyrus fragments, the largest of which is no bigger than a postage stamp. Papyrus was once a cheap form of writing material made from the inner bark of a plant which grew along the banks of the Nile. Bequeathed to the college in 1901, these particular fragments were believed to date from the second century, but in 1994 the German papyrologist Carsten Thiede, one of the world's leading experts in his field, redated them to the third quarter of the first century. All very fascinating — but why should this be of the slightest interest to the atheist or agnostic or, for that matter, to the theist? The reason is that the writing on those tiny scraps of parchment is from the Bible.

For many people today, the idea that the Bible has any bearing on our subject, let alone that it constitutes a problem for the atheist or agnostic, seems ludicrous. After all, the Bible is a higgledy-piggledy assortment of fantasy and folklore, long ago discredited by science, virtually irrelevant in today's educated, sophisticated, post-modern world, and hardly worth the papyrus on which it was written — or is it?

In his *Introduction to Research in English Literary History*, military historian C. Sanders lays down three tests for assessing the reliability of ancient documents.[1] The first is the *bibliographical test*, which asks such questions as these: How many manuscripts (handwritten copies) do we have? How good are they? How close are they to the original? The second is the *external evidence test*, which asks whether there is other contemporary evidence to confirm the statements of the document in question. The third is the *internal evidence test*, which asks whether the author concerned was writing truth or error, fact or fiction. How does the Bible measure up when subjected to these tests?

The message of the manuscripts

To begin with the first question in the bibliographical test, how many copies of biblical material do we have?

Since the discovery of the Dead Sea Scrolls in 1947 (more about this later), we have had well over 100 scrolls of Old Testament material to add to nearly 25,000 copies of all or part of the New Testament. The significance of these figures can be seen when we contrast them with some examples of those relating to other ancient documents. We have no more than ten copies of Caesar's *Gallic War* (58–50 B.C.) and just twenty copies of Livy's *Roman History* (59 B.C. – A.D. 17). For our knowledge of the Roman emperors from Augustus to Nero we have to lean heavily on ten copies of works by the Roman historian Cornelius Tacitus (born *c.* A.D. 52). We have only seven copies of the letters of the Roman author Pliny the Younger (*c.* A.D. 61–113), eight copies of the works of the Roman historian Suetonius (*c.* A.D.69–140) and nothing we can completely trust about the King of Macedonia, Alexander the Great (356–323 B.C.), even though many later books have been written about him. The closest any ancient document can get to the Bible in terms of the handwritten copies now available to us is Homer's famous *Iliad*, with just 643.

The Bible obviously wins the numbers game hands down, but the sceptic will quickly — and rightly — point out that quantity does not imply quality, and that there would be no virtue in having thousands of pieces of inferior material. This brings us to the second question in the bibliographical test: *how good are the copies?*

At first glance, the Bible seems to be in serious trouble, because in the material we now possess there are about 200,000 differences (technically known as 'variants'). At first sight this may seem to make it virtually impossible to get anywhere near the original text, but that is not the case. For example, if the same misspelling appears in 3,000 manuscripts it is counted as 3,000 variants, whereas in fact it is only one variant copied 3,000 times, and two modern experts in the field, Norman Geisler and William Nix, have pointed out that the 200,000 variants are confined to 10,000 places in the text.[2]

This is still a huge number, but also a very misleading one. The great Cambridge scholar F. J. A. Hort, who spent a lifetime in critical study of the material concerned, came to this conclusion: 'The proportion of words virtually accepted on all hands as raised above doubt is very great, not less, on a rough computation, than seven-eighths of the whole. The remaining eighth, therefore, formed in great part by changes of order and other comparative trivialities, constitutes the whole area of criticism.'[3] When Geisler and Nix had excluded 'mechanical matters such as spelling or style' they stated that 'Only about one-sixtieth rise above "trivialities", or can in any sense be called "substantial variations",' leaving us with a text that in their view is '98.33 per cent pure'.[4]

Hort's Cambridge colleague Brooke Westcott researched every known text available and decided that the amount of the New Testament where there is any significant variation in the various sources 'can hardly form more than a thousandth part of the entire text'.[5] In view of the issue at stake, not even this tiny discrepancy can be ignored, but we need to do another piece of fine-tuning. Historian Philip Schaff has shown that only 400 variants could have any possible effect on the meaning of the passage concerned and that only fifty of these are of any importance.[6] Even more significantly, Schaff says that not a single one of these variants altered 'an article of faith or a precept of duty which is not abundantly sustained by other and undoubted passages, or by the whole tenor of Scripture's teaching'.[7] This gives a very different picture from the sweeping statement that manuscripts contain 200,000 differences!

How do other ancient documents compare? Very badly. Geisler and Nix have pointed out that in the *Mahabharata*, the national epic of India, some 10% of the lines are textual corruptions,[8] while Homer's *Iliad* (the runner-up in the manuscript count) has twenty times more instances than the Bible where the original words are in doubt. Sir Frederic Kenyon, one-time director and principal librarian of the British Museum, summed up as follows: 'It cannot be too strongly asserted that in substance *the text of the Bible is certain: especially is this the case with the New Testament.* The number of manuscripts of the New Testament, of early translations from it, and of quotations from it of the oldest writers in the church, is so large that it is practically certain that the true reading of every doubtful passage is preserved in some one or other of these ancient manuscripts. This *can be said of no other ancient book in the world'*[9] (emphasis added). F. F. Bruce, another acknowledged leader in the field, endorsed this in very similar language: 'There is no body of ancient literature in the world which enjoys such a wealth of good textual attestation as the New Testament.'[10]

However impressive this may seem, the sceptic will want to apply the third part of the bibliographical test: how close in time are the earliest manuscripts to the original documents? As far as the New Testament is concerned, the Bible once again seems to get off to a bad start. Even if Carsten Thiede is right in his dating of the Magdalen College fragments, the best we can manage are a few scraps of the New Testament which go back to within about fifty years of the events they record. After these comes the *John Rylands Fragment*, a piece of papyrus measuring two and a half inches by three and presently housed in the John Rylands Library, Manchester; it contains five verses from the New Testament and is thought to date from A.D. 117–138. Next we have the *Bodmer Papyri* and the *Chester Beatty Papyri*, both dating from around A.D.200.

Then come the oldest major manuscripts. The first of these is the *Codex Vaticanus*, stored in the Vatican Library for over 500 years and containing seventy-six papyri manuscripts containing fourth-century copies of almost the entire Bible. The second is the *Codex Sinaiticus*, which was found at Mount Sinai in 1859. It contains over 50% of the New Testament and, like the *Codex Vaticanus*, is dated around A.D. 350.[11]

A gap of 300 years between the earliest major manuscripts of the New Testament and the events they claim to record may seem fatally large, yet it compares very favourably with the time-lag involved in the cases of other documents. For only one fragment of Livy's *Roman History* is the gap less than 400 years; for the letters of Pliny the Younger it is 750 years and for those of Suetonius 800 years. As far as the works of Tacitus are concerned, we have to bridge a gap of 900 years, and in Caesar's case one of over 1,000 years. It is crystal clear that on this issue no other known piece of ancient literature, religious or secular, has anything remotely approaching the Bible's credentials. As far as the New Testament is concerned, Frederic Kenyon came to this conclusion: 'In no other case is the interval of time between the composition of the book and the date of the earliest extant manuscripts so short as that of the New Testament ... and the last foundation for any doubt that the Scriptures have come down to us as they were written has now been removed. *Both the authenticity and the general integrity of the New Testament may be regarded as finally established*'[12] (emphasis added). Small wonder that Isaac Newton wrote, 'There are more sure marks of authenticity in the Bible than in any profane history.'[13]

The scrolls and the scribes

Until 1947, the earliest text of the Old Testament was dated around A.D. 900, some 1,300 years after the events of the Old Testament era. This compared badly with the gaps we noted concerning the works of Pliny the Younger, Suetonius, Tacitus and Caesar, but the picture was transformed with the accidental discovery, in a series of caves in and around Wadi Qumran, north-west of the Dead Sea, of a mass of material including 100 scrolls representing thirty-eight of the Old Testament's thirty-nine books. The experts are agreed that these scrolls date from as far back as 200 B.C., which means that by this one discovery the time-span between the original documents and extant manuscripts was narrowed by 1,000 years. It also means that the Old Testament manuscripts have now 'overtaken' most of the secular sources we mentioned earlier.

This should certainly arrest our attention, yet it immediately leads on to another question, which also relates to the second part of the bibliographical test: how closely do these Dead Sea Scrolls correspond to the earliest Old Testament material we possessed prior to their discovery in 1947? The answer is that they are astonishingly similar. Geisler and Nix give a typical example, based on one particularly important chapter: 'Of the 166 words in Isaiah 53, there are only seventeen letters in question. Ten of these letters are simply a matter of spelling, which does not affect the sense. Four more letters are minor stylistic changes, such as conjunctions. The remaining three letters comprise the word "light", which is added in verse 11, and does not affect the meaning greatly... Thus, in one chapter of 166 words, there is only one word (three letters) in question *after a thousand years of transmission* — and this word does not significantly alter the meaning of the passage'[14] (emphasis added). Anyone remotely familiar with the way in which mistakes can occur even when using today's sophisticated printing technology will have all the more reason to be impressed that handwritten documents, copied time and again for 1,000 years, should remain virtually identical.

However, sceptics reluctant to be convinced by this are entitled to ask yet another vital question: how do we know that the earliest copies we had prior to the Dead Sea Scrolls were accurate copies of the centuries of manuscripts that had gone before? The answer to that question is truly remarkable. There is no evidence of any dispute over the Old Testament contents during the period of time it covers, and a Jewish council held at Jamnia, near the modern city of Tel-Aviv, between A.D.90–100, officially recognized the text that had already been accepted for some 500 years. This should hardly surprise us when we read of the Alexandrian philosopher Judaeus Philo saying, 'The Jews would die 10,000 times rather than permit one single word to be altered of their Scriptures.'[15]

From A.D. 100–500, the task of transcribing the text fell to the Talmudists, whose work was strictly governed by a set of minutely detailed regulations. Even a summary of the rules laid down for copying words regarded as sacred will give an idea of the care that was taken. The text had to be copied on to the skins of ceremonially clean animals, and the skins had to be prepared and fastened together in a particular way. All the skins, throughout the whole text, had to contain a prescribed and equal number of columns. Each column had to be between forty-eight and sixty lines in length, and each line had to consist of exactly thirty letters. Only black ink, prepared to a definite recipe, could be used. No word or letter, not even a *yod* (the tenth and smallest letter of the Hebrew alphabet) could be written from memory and without reference to the document from which the scribe was copying. There had to be the breadth of a hair or thread between consonants, the breadth of nine consonants between sections, and three lines between books. The fifth book of Moses had to terminate exactly with a line. In addition, the copyist had to sit in full Jewish dress, having washed his whole body before beginning his work. He was forbidden to write the name of God except with a pen newly dipped in ink, and should anyone, even a king, talk to him while writing that name, he was not permitted to take any notice.

This impressive attention to detail was buttressed in two ways. Any scrolls written without the strict observance of these rules were buried in the ground, burned or 'banished to the schools, to be used as reading-books'. Secondly, as soon as a completed manuscript became defaced or damaged in the passage of time, it was immediately condemned as being unfit for use. This is a vitally important point as it goes a long way towards explaining why we do not have much older manuscripts. The Talmudists were convinced that when they had finished transcribing a manuscript they had an exact duplicate of the one from which it had been copied. As a result, the new transcript was given exactly the same authority.[16] As Frederic Kenyon explains, 'The same extreme care which was devoted to the transcription of manuscripts is also at the bottom of the disappearance of the earlier copies. When a manuscript had been copied with the exactitude prescribed by the Talmud, and had been duly verified, it was accepted as authentic and regarded as being of equal value with any other copy. If all were equally correct, *age gave no advantage to a manuscript.*[17] Again, because this meticulous care was unique to the Bible, this can be said of no other ancient piece of literature.

Between A.D. 500–900, the work of preserving and standardizing the Old Testament text passed to a group of Jewish teachers and scholars known as the Masoretes. In addition to straightforward copying, the Masoretes gradually introduced vowel 'points' (to aid pronunciation) and punctuation. Like the Talmudists before them, the Masoretes submitted to a meticulous set of rules in order to ensure the accuracy of their work. They counted the number of words and letters in each book, noted the middle letter of each line, and the middle letter and word of each book, of the Pentateuch (the first five books) and of the whole of the Old Testament. They even counted the number of verses which contained all the letters of the alphabet, or a certain number of them; as one scholar comments, 'Everything countable seems to be counted'![18] As if this were not enough, they even made up mnemonics by which the various totals might be more easily remembered. This may seem to have been overdoing things but, as Frederic Kenyon points out, it 'had ... the effect of securing minute attention to the precise transmission of the text ... the Masoretes were indeed anxious that not one jot or tittle, not one smallest letter, nor one tiny part of a letter, of the law should pass or be lost'.[19]

This meticulous attention to detail over centuries of time gives an added dimension to the Bible's credibility, and is a serious obstacle to those who airily dismiss it as a dubious collection of inconsistent literary relics. In his excellent book *Nothing But the Truth*, Brian Edwards rightly makes the point that this kind of argument is rarely used about other writings from the ancient world. Quoting the example of Plato, who died in 347 B.C., he said that few suggest that the words of his *Republic* may not be his words after all: 'As a matter of fact I was not even told that for his work I was relying upon manuscripts copied thirteen hundred years after his death.'[20] The contrast with biblical material could hardly be greater, and we are certainly safe in saying that no other ancient literature has been transmitted with such accuracy as the collection of documents we call the Bible. Not only does it pass the bibliographical test, it does so with unique distinction.

The man from Princeton

This brings us to the external evidence test, which forms the second part of the examination for assessing the reliability of ancient documents: is there any contemporary evidence to confirm the statements made in the literature concerned?

In the early part of the nineteenth century, scholars in England and Germany led a popular school of thought which denied the accuracy of the Bible and spawned generations of amateur critics who came to believe that, whatever its religious message, the Bible could not be trusted in matters of historical fact. This idea has become so pervasive that it is common to hear people who have never even read the Bible confidently saying that it is full of mistakes and contradictions. If this is the case, we need not treat the Bible with any more respect than a daily newspaper or the works of Shakespeare — but is it?

Of all the witnesses we could call to challenge the liberal scholars who questioned the factual integrity of the Bible, none was more outstanding than Robert Dick Wilson, one-time Professor of Semitic Philology (the language and literature of the Middle East) at Princeton Theological Seminary in the United States. In his student days, he set himself an astonishing forty-five year schedule: fifteen years of language study, fifteen years studying the text of the Old Testament and fifteen years in publishing his findings. In the course of the first fifteen years, studying under some of the leading professors of his day, he became familiar with twenty-six languages and dialects, including the three biblical languages, Hebrew, Greek and Aramaic. In the second slot of fifteen years, he collected over 100,000 quotations from these languages and compared them with related statements in the Old Testament. As the result of this massive piece of research Wilson declared, 'I have come to the conclusion that no man knows enough to assail the truthfulness of the Old Testament.'[21] Wilson's work was so outstanding — Brian Edwards says, 'His brilliance was unequalled and we are fully justified in accepting his conclusions'[22] — that it is worth noting a number of his findings.

In *A Scientific Investigation of the Old Testament*, first published in 1926, he wrote, 'In 144 cases of transliteration from Egyptian, Assyrian, Babylonian and Moabite into Hebrew and in 40 cases of the opposite, or 184 in all, the evidence shows that for 2,300–3,900 years the text of the proper names in the Hebrew Bible has been transmitted with the most minute accuracy.' In particular, he focused on the Bible's record of kings who lived during a period of about 1,600 years and concluded, 'There are about forty of these kings living from 2,000 B.C. to 400 B.C. Each appears in chronological order ... with reference to the kings of the same country and with respect to the kings of other countries ... *no stronger evidence for the substantial accuracy of the Old Testament record could possibly be imagined* than this collection of kings. Mathematically, it is one chance in 750,000,000,000,000,000,000,000,000 that this accuracy is mere circumstance.'[23] Strictly speaking, this would not rule out what we might call 'accuracy by accident', but it clearly merits serious consideration by any honest sceptic!

Another example of the way in which Wilson routed the Bible's critics relates to the dates of four Old Testament books — Ezra, Nehemiah and 1 and 2 Chronicles. Critics claimed that these books must have been written as late as 300 B.C. because they used the title 'King of Persia' which was 'contrary to all contemporary usage'. From a mass of accumulated evidence, Wilson showed not only that such a title was commonly employed at least 100 years earlier, but that it was specifically used by Nabuniad of Babylon in referring to Cyrus in 546 B.C., seven years before its first appearance in the Bible. He also demonstrated that the same title, said by the critics to be 'contrary to all contemporary usage', was employed thirty-eight times, by eighteen authors, in six different languages, between 546 and 365 B.C.! In dismissing their puerile efforts to discredit the Bible, Wilson concluded, 'Having read carefully and repeatedly what these critics have to say on this title, I have failed to find any hint indicating that they have ever appealed for their information to any original sources outside of Greek, Hebrew and Aramaic.'[24]

A final illustration of the way in which Wilson demolished the arguments of those who sought to undermine the Bible's integrity relates to its account of the raid of Chedorlaomar, a King of Elam, against the Kings of Sodom and Gomorrah, and his subsequent defeat by Abraham, the founding father of the Jewish nation.[25] The German scholar Julius Wellhausen (1844–1918) stated that the biblical accounts were 'simply impossible', and other liberals claimed that between 900 and 300 B.C. an unknown Jewish archaeologist must have invented the story in Abraham's honour, using names he had discovered. With the vast resources of his research at his disposal, Wilson showed that such raids were quite common at the time, that the Bible's names for the kings concerned are also found in contemporary literature from the surrounding nations, and that Abraham is mentioned in this literature as early as 1950 B.C. In a devastating response to the critics, he wrote, 'Against the historical character of this narrative we have the assertion of Wellhausen and other critics of our times (only about 4,000 years after the supposed expedition!) that the expedition was "simply impossible", and that it is probable that the account may have been fabricated by some person unknown, at some time unknown, for reasons unknown. Not one item of evidence in the way of time, place, logic, psychology, language, customs, has been produced against the trustworthiness of the document... But a German professor says it is "simply impossible", English followers echo "simply impossible" and the Americans echo again "simply impossible". And this assertion of "simply impossible" is called an "assured result of scientific criticism"!'[26]

The evidence grows

In his book *Is Higher Criticism Scholarly?*, first published in 1922, Wilson wrote, 'I try to give my students such an intelligent faith in the Old Testament Scriptures that they will never doubt them as long as they live.'[27] He was able to do so from a position of far greater strength than that occupied by the liberal critics, and experts in archaeology, philology, religion and geography are constantly adding to the mass of evidence confounding the critics and supporting the Old Testament's accuracy.

Abraham was one of the sceptics' prime targets in the early nineteenth century. The Bible tells of him spending his early years in the Chaldean city of Ur, and records that he also lived at various times in the cities of Haran, Sodom and Gomorrah. Critics said that as there were no signs of ancient civilization in these areas, Abraham must have been a primitive nomadic tribesman, and stories about him must have been invented at a much later stage. Archaeology has since delivered a very different verdict. The ruined city of Ur (now 120 miles north of Basra, Iraq) was discovered in 1854 and extensive excavations carried out by Leonard Woolley from 1922–1934 produced clear evidence of an advanced state of civilization centuries before Abraham's time. Built around a seventy-foot high artificial hill made of solid brick, and surrounded by ornate staircase systems, the city of Ur boasted a massive temple, shops, law courts, a school, offices and a great number of houses, many with colour-washed plaster ceilings. Brian Edwards notes that thousands of official records reveal 'a bustling city of merchants and businessmen trading across into Syria and down to the Persian Gulf', and that they record 'purchases, marriages, and all the events of a busy city'. He goes on to say, 'Cities of the same date, excavated in the same region, reveal that these people had a correct understanding of mathematics and geometry, including the theory of Pythagoras, nearly fifteen hundred years before the Greek philosopher wrote it down!'[28] So much for the sceptics' claim that the whole region consisted of uninhabitable desert.

The Bible indicates that its first five books were written by Moses, the great Jewish lawgiver, but liberal critics claimed that writing was unknown in Moses' day, that he and his contemporaries were illiterate, and that these books were merely a collection of religious folklore cobbled together by unknown authors hundreds of years after Moses' death. If this were so, we would have to throw the whole Bible out of the window, but the critics' case collapsed in spectacular fashion. In 1904 the British Assyriologist A. H. Sayce showed that 'This supposed late use of writing for literary purposes was merely an assumption, with nothing more solid to rest upon than the critics' own theories and presuppositions,'[29] and that their assumptions crumbled into dust as soon as they could be tested. Sayce went on to show that 'The art of writing in the ancient East, so far from being of modern growth, was of vast antiquity,' and that Egypt and Assyria 'were each emphatically a nation of scribes and readers'.[30] What is more, 'Centuries before Abraham was born, Egypt and Babylonia were alike full of schools and libraries, of teachers and pupils, of poets and prose-writers, and of the literary works which they had composed.'[31] Sayce eventually came to the conclusion that 'The Babylonia of the age of Abraham (much *earlier* than Moses) was a more educated country than the England of George III.'[32] Given the evidence now available, the Bible's assertion that Moses was 'educated in all the wisdom of the Egyptians'[33] is much more believable than the critics' prejudiced notion that he was nothing more than an illiterate nomad.

The Bible has many references to the Hittites, who for centuries occupied the region extending from northern Palestine to the Euphrates, and flourished from the days of Abraham until the time of David, the second King of Israel. When decades of archaeology failed to uncover any signs of the Hittites' existence, sceptics claimed that the Bible's narratives could be dismissed as fiction. Today, we have masses of evidence confirming the Bible's references in great detail, and an entire museum in Ankara, Turkey, is devoted to Hittite relics.[34]

Other critical scholars have even denied that King David of Israel was a historical figure, and have rejected the Bible's claim that a united kingdom preceded the two nations of Judah and Israel, but archaeological finds have long since put the biblical data beyond doubt, and in 1995–1996 the modern state of Israel held a fifteen-month celebration of David's establishment of Jerusalem as the nation's capital.

Archaeologists are not infallible, can rarely account for all the facts, sometimes contradict each other and are often prejudiced, but it is impossible to deny that time and again they confirm the Bible's detailed data. The evidence of archaeology is so powerful that Nelson Glueck, often considered the dean of Palestinian archaeology, wrote of 'the almost incredibly accurate historical memory of the Bible', and even went so far as to say, 'It may be stated categorically that *no archaeological discovery has ever controverted a biblical reference.*'[35] More recently, Alan Millard, Professor of Hebrew and Ancient Semitic Languages at the University of Liverpool, came to an equally emphatic conclusion: 'We affirm that nothing has been found which can be proved to contradict any statement of the Old Testament. Archaeological research is a welcome aid to a richer knowledge of the Bible's message.'[36]

Sir William Ramsay

If Robert Dick Wilson was the nineteenth century's champion in confirming the integrity of Old Testament data, Sir William Ramsay occupied the same position in relation to the New Testament. One of the world's greatest ever archaeologists, Ramsay was Professor of Classical Art and Architecture at Oxford University, Regius Professor of Humanity (the Latin professorship) at Aberdeen University, founder member of the British Academy, holder of nine honorary doctorates from universities in Great Britain, Europe and America, and knighted in 1906 for his distinguished service to the world of scholarship.

Ramsay admitted that in his student years he 'worshipped Wellhausen[37] (a leading German critic), and his early training led him to believe that the New Testament narratives were largely myths, rather than accurate, contemporary historical records. He was convinced, for example, that the Acts of the Apostles was written not by Luke, as the Bible claims, but by an anonymous author who, about 100 years later, put together highly imaginative stories about people he admired.[38] When he began field work in Western Turkey (part of 'Asia' in New Testament language) Ramsay was quite sure that his discoveries would put the final nails in the New Testament's coffin, but he had hardly started when his theories began to come unstuck.

His problems began when he made a major discovery about the exact location of the city of Iconium. The Bible records that when persecuted believers were forced to leave Iconium they 'fled to the Lycaonian cities of Lystra and Derbe and to the surrounding country'.[39] As it was generally believed that Iconium was the chief city of Lycaonia, to speak of people escaping from there to 'the Lycaonian cities of Lystra and Derbe' was rather like saying that people escaped from London to England; it was nonsense, and betrayed basic ignorance of geography. However, and to his great surprise, Ramsay unearthed a mass of evidence to show that in Luke's day Iconium was in the province of Phrygia, *not* Lycaonia. The critics had never gone back further than A.D. 372, when the Roman emperor Valens had made boundary changes which took Iconium into Lycaonia and made it its capital city — Luke 1: Sceptics 0!

The further Ramsay went, the more amazed he became at the way in which the Bible was vindicated; in his own words, 'It was gradually borne in upon me that in various details the narrative showed marvellous truth.'[40] The book in which he wrote those words, *St Paul the Traveller and Roman Citizen*, first published in 1895, hit the world of biblical criticism like a bombshell, but other explosions were to follow. As he pursued his studies, the evidence Ramsay discovered totally convinced him not only that Luke did in fact write Acts of the Apostles, but that he was no ordinary writer: 'Luke is a historian of the first rank; not merely are his statements of fact trustworthy, he is possessed of the true historic sense ... in short, *this author should be placed along with the very greatest of historians*.'[41] Bearing his early prejudices in mind, Ramsay would have been perfectly happy if his discoveries had proved Luke wrong, but a lifetime of investigation led him to a very different conclusion: 'Further study ... showed that the book [Acts] could bear the most minute scrutiny as an authority for the facts of the Aegean world, and that it was written with such judgement, skill, art and perception of truth as to be a model of historical statement.'[42] This assessment was later echoed by E. M. Blaiklock, Professor of Classics at Auckland University, New Zealand, who wrote, 'Luke is a consummate historian, to be ranked in his own right with the great writers of the Greeks.'[43]

Attributes of truth

Another significant piece of corroboration comes from the classical scholar A. N. Sherwin-White, who says that the legal details mentioned in the several trials reported in the New Testament correspond exactly with what we know of Roman practice during the first half of the first century. As the procedures had changed by the time the reports were written, the narratives clearly show that the writers were in direct touch with the facts. Sherwin-White powerfully argues that as a historically reliable source the New Testament compares favourably with the best in the field of classical studies, and goes on to say that sceptics should know better than to downgrade the historicity of the New Testament sources when there is such strong objective evidence in their favour.[44] Brian Edwards agrees: 'The years of patient and careful research and the thousands of pages that William Ramsay devoted to Luke's Gospel and Acts all show that the customs and language, the synagogues, trials, magicians, in fact everything mentioned, reveal a detailed knowledge that could only be written down by an eyewitness of the events.'[45]

To give one specific example of this, it is impressive to notice that references in Acts to the titles of civic officials are uniformly accurate. As has recently been pointed out, 'This was no mean achievement in those days, for they varied from place to place and from time to time in the same place. They were *proconsuls* in Corinth and Cyprus, *asiarchs* at Ephesus, *politarchs* at Thessalonica and *protos* or "first man" in Malta. Back in Palestine, Luke was careful to give Herod Antipas the correct title of *tetrarch* of Galilee. And so on. The details are precise.'[46] Luke seems able to dash off the correct title in every case, in a way that has been compared to the easy and confident way in which an undergraduate at Oxford University would refer to the heads of colleges by their proper titles — the *Provost* of Oriel, the *Master* of Balliol, the *Rector* of Exeter, the *President* of Magdalen, and so on.[47] Nobody unfamiliar with Oxford would find this natural, yet Luke never makes a single mistake with his Roman titles. As facts like these would not have been known by later generations, they provide powerful evidence that they were written by someone familiar with the contemporary culture.

Sherwin-White has no doubt as to what this tells us: 'For Acts, the confirmation of historicity is overwhelming... Any attempt to reject its basic historicity, even in matters of detail, must now appear absurd. Roman historians have long taken this for granted.'[48]

Widening the lens a little, Peter Kreeft points out the unlikelihood of the New Testament being composed in some other way: 'If the Gospels are not eyewitness accounts, then they are a type of fantasy that has absolutely no parallel in all of literature... Some Galilean peasants — fishermen and tax collectors — invented not only the world's most gigantic hoax but a totally unique form of literature.'[49] From the same perspective, Simon Greenleaf, Royal Professor of Law at Harvard University, came to the same conclusion and wrote, 'The essential marks of difference between true narrative and fact and works of fiction are unmistakable ... the attributes of truth are strikingly apparent throughout the Gospel histories.'[50]

An even wider perspective comes from the pen of the German journalist Werner Keller, whose best seller *The Bible As History* was first published in 1956. After years of extensive research in the libraries of many lands, he concluded, 'In view of the overwhelming mass of authentic and well-attested evidence now available, as I thought of the sceptical criticism which from the eighteenth century onward would fain have demolished the Bible altogether, there kept hammering in my brain this one sentence: "The Bible is right after all".'[51]

Secular museums around the world contain vast quantities of inscriptions, documents, coins, utensils, weapons and other artefacts pointing to the Bible's meticulous accuracy. This alone would be sufficient to set the Bible apart from all other literature of its time, and is in striking contrast to much more modern religious literature. Dave Hunt gives a telling example: 'No evidence has ever been found to support the Book of Mormon ... in spite of decades of the most aggressive archaeological exploration throughout North, Central and South America. This Herculean effort, supported by the vast wealth and determination of the Mormon Church, has left no stone unturned in the search for verification of the Book of Mormon, but has come up empty-handed. Not one piece of evidence has ever been found to support the Book of Mormon — not a trace of the large cities it names, no ruins, no coins, no letters or documents or monuments, nothing in writing. Not even one of the rivers or mountains or any of the topography

it mentions has ever been identified!'[52] As Hunt goes on to point out, 'The
Book of Mormon provides one excellent example of the impossibility of
fabricating a make-believe scenario and then trying to convince the world
that it really happened.'[53]

The contrast with the Bible could not possibly be greater. In 1958, reviewing archaeological excavations in the recent past, William F. Albright,
recognized as today's greatest Orientalist, wrote, 'Thanks to modern research we now recognize [the Bible's] substantial historicity. The narratives
of the patriarchs, of Moses and the exodus, of the conquest of Canaan, of
the judges, the monarchy, exile and restoration, have all been confirmed
and illustrated to an extent that I should have thought impossible forty
years ago.'[54] At the end of 1974, *TIME* magazine ran an article entitled
'How True Is the Bible?', which discussed the condition of the Bible after
two hundred years of critical attack. The article came to this conclusion:
'The breadth, sophistication and diversity of all this biblical investigation
are impressive, but it begs a question: Has it made the Bible more credible
or less? ... After more than two centuries of facing the heaviest scientific
guns that could be brought to bear, the Bible has survived — and is perhaps better for the siege. Even on the critics' own terms — historical fact —
the Scriptures seem more acceptable now than they did when the rationalists began the attack.'[55]

The external evidence test asks whether there is contemporary material
to confirm the Bible's statements. The answer could hardly be more positive or emphatic.

Getting it all together

However impressively the Bible may perform when exposed to the bibliographical and external evidence tests, the sceptic will still want to apply the
internal evidence test, which asks whether its essential contents are truth or
error, fact or fiction. This test goes far beyond questions about gaps between manuscripts, the number of copies available, historical dates and
geographical details. Instead, it wants to examine the writers' *message*.
Can we believe that the statements the Bible's writers made about reality,
philosophy, life, morality — and religion — are true and therefore relevant
to everyone who reads them, even 2,000 years after the last of them were
made? This is by far the most difficult and crucial issue, and it cannot be

tested in the same way as we can check matters of history and geography, yet there are at least three important clues which point to the Bible as being uniquely truthful.

To get the first clue in focus, we need to remember that the Bible is not so much a single book as a 'library' of sixty-six separate documents, written by some forty different authors, at intervals stretching over more than 1,500 years. F. F. Bruce outlines something of the variety involved: 'The writers wrote in various lands, from Italy in the west to Mesopotamia and possibly Persia in the east. The writers themselves were a heterogeneous number of people, not only separated from each other by hundreds of years and hundreds of miles, but belonging to the most diverse walks of life. In their ranks we have kings, herdsmen, soldiers, legislators, fishermen, statesmen, courtiers, priests and prophets, a tent-making rabbi and a Gentile physician, not to speak of others of whom we know nothing apart from the writings they have left us. They include history, law (civil, criminal, ethical, ritual, sanitary), religious poetry, didactic treatises, lyric poetry, parable and allegory, biography, personal correspondence, personal memoirs and diaries, in addition to the distinctively biblical types of prophecy and apocalyptic.'[56]

Any honest critic setting out to discredit the Bible should already sense a problem here, but there are more to follow. A credible and comprehensive attack on the Bible requires an expert knowledge of the three biblical languages (Hebrew, Greek and Aramaic), a clear understanding of the context in which each book was written, and an intimate knowledge of the circumstances being addressed in each case. The critic must also be able to identify the author's use of language: was he employing a simile, a localized idiom, metaphor, hyperbole? Is any given story an allegory, a parable or a factual narrative? Even more importantly, is the passage concerned history or prophecy? It would also help if the critic had mastered the civil law of every country and generation represented in the Bible, and the religious and civil customs of all the times and places covered by the Bible's writers.

Now comes the first clue to the Bible's integrity and truthfulness. Many people who have never read it (or have never done so with an open mind) think of it as a disjointed and contradictory heap of bits and pieces, whereas most of those who have studied it carefully come increasingly to the conclusion that it all holds together in a remarkable unity. Its forty or so authors lived at different times and in a variety of cultures and came from many different levels of society. If asked about any controversial subject, they would have had views as diverse as those heard on any of today's media talk shows. Yet without any collaboration or spin-doctoring they combined to produce a volume which is amazingly coherent. The British theologian J. I. Packer underlines the significance of this phenomenon: 'Why do we bind up this collection between the same two covers, call it *The Holy Bible*, and treat it as one book? One justification for doing this — one of many — is that the collection as a whole, once we start to explore it, proves to have an organic coherence that is simply stunning. Books written centuries apart seemed to have been designed for the express purpose of supplementing and illuminating each other... Truly, the inner unity of the Bible is miraculous: a sign and wonder challenging the unbelief of our sceptical age.'[57] This may not be cast-iron proof that the Bible's authors always wrote the truth, but can we imagine a collection of falsehood, or a mixture of truth and falsehood, holding together in this way? By its very nature, error is conflicting, whereas truth is cohesive. The amazing cohesion of the Bible's teaching is a powerful pointer to its integrity.

The critic who fails to see this, and who tries to discredit the Bible by arguing that it contains errors, contradictions and inconsistencies, needs to ask a number of questions before setting his claim in concrete: 'Have I correctly understood the passage concerned? Do I have a clear grasp of the sense in which it uses words or numbers? Have I taken account of any possible nuances in the original language? Do I understand the cultural context? Do I possess all the knowledge currently available on the subject? Am I certain that no further light can be thrown on the passage concerned by textual research, archaeology or any other advance in knowledge?' As the British author Robert Horn reminds us, 'Unsolved problems are not of necessity errors. This is not to minimize the difficulty; it is to see it in perspective. Difficulties are to be grappled with and problems are to drive us to seek clearer light; but until such time as we have total and final light on any issue we are in no position to affirm, "Here is a proven error, an unquestionable objection to an infallible Bible."'[58] In the twentieth century alone, countless so-called 'errors' in the Bible have been completely resolved in the light of modern discoveries, and there is no reason to suppose that the comparatively tiny collection that remains *(no part of which affects the Bible's overall message)* will not become even smaller in the years to come. There is a difference between an unanswered question and proof of a mistake. Time may well prove that, as a modern writer says, 'The difficulty proceeds from our ignorance rather than our knowledge.'[59]

In assessing the integrity of any document, today's literary critics still follow Aristotle's ancient dictum that 'The benefit of the doubt is to be given to the document itself, not arrogated by the critic to himself,' and that one must therefore 'listen to the claims of the document under analysis, and not assume fraud or error unless the author disqualified himself by contradictions or known factual inaccuracies'.[60] Some 2,000 years later, Simon Greenleaf, considered by some to be the world's greatest expert on evidence, laid down the following as his first rule of legal evidence in this kind of case: 'Every document apparently ancient, coming from the proper repository or custody, and bearing on its face no evident marks of forgery, the law presumes to be genuine and *devolves on the opposing party the burden of proving it to be otherwise*'[61] (emphasis added). In the light of the Bible's credentials, which Greenleaf himself accepted, this means that the burden of showing it to be unreliable falls squarely on the sceptic. It is quite a burden. The story is told of an opinionated college student who asked a friend, 'What would you think if I told you that in ten minutes I could produce arguments that would utterly annihilate the Bible?' His friend replied, 'About the same thing I would think if a gnat crawled up the side of Mount Everest and said, "Watch me pulverize this thing with my hind left foot"'!

Telling the future

The second clue to the Bible's integrity can be set in a very modern context. In May 1997 a front-page headline in the *Daily Mail* announced that computers had picked out a hidden code in the Bible 'that predicts every event in history'.[62] On inside pages the claim was modified to read 'every *major* event in history' (the reader had bought the paper by now!) but it was still a startling assertion. Basing his studies on the 304,805 Hebrew letters contained in Masoretic text of the first five books of the Bible (the Hebrew *Torah*), mathematician Eliyahu Rips claimed to have unearthed a remarkable fact. By employing a 'skip-sequence' (missing out a chosen number of letters, running from one to several thousand), key words were thrown up, spelling out events which, when the Torah's words were written, lay hundreds or thousands of years in the future.

Journalist Michael Drosnin jumped on the bandwagon and in *The Bible Code*, first published in 1997, claimed that man's first landing on the moon in 1969, the 1974 Watergate scandal that forced United States President

Richard Nixon out of office, the collision between the Shoemaker-Levi comet and the planet Jupiter in 1994 and the 1995 assassination of Yitzhak Rabin, Prime Minister of Israel, were among many twentieth-century events encoded within words written 3,000 years ago.

Almost inevitably, the book became a best seller, but it was not long before scientists, statisticians and mathematicians were denouncing it. Shlomo Sternberg, holder of the George Putnam Chair in Pure and Applied Mathematics at Harvard University, called Drosnin's book 'complete nonsense',[63] and Sternberg's Harvard colleague Ronald Hendel, editor of *Hebrew Book Review*, dismissed it as a 'journalistic hoax'.[64] Even more devastatingly, the 'skip-sequence' produced equally exciting results when applied to other books. *War and Peace* yielded more than fifty words related to the Jewish festival of Hanukkah, while one researcher found thirteen 'predicted' assassinations of prime ministers, presidents and other public figures when he applied the same 'skip-sequence' to the well-known novel *Moby Dick*![65] Using the so-called 'Bible code' as a means of forecasting the future is on a par with trying to make something of the fact that in the Authorized Version of the Bible the forty-sixth word from the beginning of Psalm 46, and the forty-sixth word from the end spell 'Shakespear'!

In the flood of correspondence which followed Drosnin's *Daily Mail* series, part of one particular letter caught my attention: 'There's a much simpler code in the Bible which doesn't require a computer to decode it. Instead of being confined to the Torah ... this one occurs throughout ... and survives intact when the original languages are translated into modern tongues like English... This earlier code works in a similar way to the new one. Take a letter in the text, skip so many letters, take another letter, skip again, and so on. To try it for themselves, readers need to know only that the number of letters to skip on each occasion is zero.'[66] Very neat! The writer was saying that the Bible's true significance and relevance to *all* the events that have followed its writing are to be based, not on computer-generated collections of random letters taken from its first five books, but on its entire contents. This points not only to the Bible's unity but to another massive clue as to its truthfulness — its use of prophecy.

Dave Hunt has pointed out that while there are no prophecies in the *Qur'an*, in the Hindu *Vedas* or *Bhagavad-Gita*, in the sayings of Buddha, Confucius or in the Book of Mormon, it has been estimated that about 30% of the Bible consists of prophecy of one kind or another, making it unique in religious literature.[67] It is impossible even to summarize such a vast amount of material here, but three examples will give an indication of what we would find if we did.

Around 920 B.C., an unnamed prophet told Jeroboam, who was King of Israel, that his throne would one day be occupied by a king called Josiah, who would sweep away the widespread idolatry which Jeroboam was promoting. This must have seemed nonsensical to the all-powerful Jeroboam at the time, but 300 years later Josiah was enthroned on the death of his father Amon and began to carry out the programme of moral reformation which the prophet had predicted.[68]

Isaiah, who prophesied for forty years from about 740 B.C., predicted a whole series of future events, including the downfall of Jerusalem and the wholesale deportation of the Jews to Babylon. Even more remarkably, he prophesied that their captivity would be ended by someone called Cyrus, who would repatriate the Jews for the specific purpose of rebuilding the temple at Jerusalem. Exactly as forecast, the Babylonians sacked Jerusalem and swept the Jews into captivity. In 539–538 B.C., nearly 200 years after Isaiah's prophecy, the pagan King of Persia conquered Babylon and, as one of his first acts, released all the foreigners the Babylonians had captured, with specific instructions to the Jews that they return to Jerusalem and rebuild their temple. The pagan king's name? Cyrus![69]

Around 600 B.C., Habakkuk prophesied that the Chaldeans would be the future masters of the world.[70] This must have seemed absurd at the time, as the Chaldeans formed an insignificant group of people in Babylon, which had by then become the major world power. Only Egypt seemed likely to pose any future threat to Assyria, and even that was a long shot, yet within a few years the Chaldeans had fulfilled Habakkuk's prophecy to the letter.

Any one of these instances would be impressive, and demand an explanation by the sceptic, but when we put these and other prophecies together the picture becomes truly amazing. In his book *Science Speaks*, Peter Stoner, Professor Emeritus at Westmont College, California, and charter member of the American Scientific Affiliation, has indicated just how amazing it is. From the writings of four of the Old Testament prophets — Isaiah, Jeremiah, Ezekiel and Micah — he identifies eleven specific prophecies about Israel. These concern the land as a whole, the destruction of Jerusalem, the rebuilding of the temple and the later enlargement of the city. Calculating the probability of all eleven prophecies being fulfilled to be one in 8×10^{63}, Stoner gives an illustration of what this means. If we were to scoop together a pile of coins equal in size to 100 billion stars in each of two trillion galaxies in just one second, and then add to the pile at the same rate every second, day and night, for twenty-one years, we would be ready for the test. If we then asked a blindfolded friend to pick out one marked coin from this incomprehensibly massive pile, his chances of doing so would be one in 8×10^{63}, the same as the likelihood that our four prophets could have got things right by guesswork.[71] As even these mind-boggling figures tell nothing like the full story (they apply to just eleven prophecies out of several hundred) the Bible's prophetic element adds an impressive dimension to its integrity and presents an enormous problem to the sceptic.

Other than clinging desperately to this remote possibility, the sceptic's only response is to claim that prophecies were made after the events they predicted. However, this approach is almost always based on the presupposition that such predictions are impossible, and infers that most of the Old Testament authors were either deceived or dishonest. It also ignores the fact that in many cases it is simply impossible to shuffle the dates. The evidence for the dating and fulfilment of the prophecies is such that attempting to use this kind of ploy to discredit the entire prophetic phenomenon is futile. Nor is the problem lessened when we take into account the fact that not a single prophecy made according to the Bible's own criteria (more about this later) has ever been shown to be false. The contrast with claims by today's astrologers, soothsayers, crystal-ball gazers, readers of palms and tea leaves and other assorted con artists could hardly be greater; a January 1995 issue of the *Washington Times* reported, 'In his annual review of would-be tabloid prophets, science writer Gene Emery found that none of the approximately 100 predictions for 1994 that he had studied had come true by late December.'[72]

Persecution; popularity; power

The third clue as to the Bible's integrity has to be seen in the context of its having been more frequently and viciously attacked than any other book in history. A few examples will be sufficient to make the point. Early in the fourth century, the Roman emperors Diocletian and Julian ordered their soldiers to destroy every copy they could find. At one time in those early centuries it was a capital offence to own a Bible. In the thirteenth century, the Roman Catholic Church forbade people to have the Bible in their native tongue. When William Tyndale set about translating it into English early in the sixteenth century, he had to escape to Belgium to do so, and was eventually strangled and burnt to death for his efforts. In modern times, Marxism did everything it could to destroy it. Today, its circulation remains banned in some countries, its teaching is strongly discouraged in others, and it is openly ridiculed by atheists everywhere.

This endless vendetta makes it all the more remarkable that in 1997 the *Daily Telegraph* was able to state, 'The Bible remains the world's best-selling book and its popularity continues to rise.'[73] This claim was based on figures released by the United Bible Societies, which had distributed 19,400,000 complete Bibles in 1996, beating all previous records and a 9% increase on the previous year. In 1996, the world total for all Bible distribution (Bibles, New Testaments, single books and selected portions) was 530,659,106 — and a later UBS report revealed that this rose to some 580 million in 1997, by which time at least one book of the Bible was available in 2,197 languages. A major study published in 1998 revealed that more countries received at least some part of Scripture in their own language in the last forty-five years than in the previous 2,500.[74] The demand in Europe and the Middle East is far greater than the resources to meet it. Even as I write these words, today's mail includes a fund-raising appeal by one organization which had to decline requests for fifteen million Bibles in 1998 and had received from Romania alone over 1,200,000 individual letters asking for a copy. David Hume believed the Bible would soon be looked upon as a discredited relic; shortly after his death his house in Edinburgh became the headquarters of the Edinburgh Bible Society. Voltaire predicted that the Bible would be extinct by 1850; soon after his death his house and printing press in Geneva were taken over by the Swiss Bible Society. Prophecy was clearly not *their* strong suit!

Yet however impressive these figures may be, even they provide no evidence of the Bible's merit. It is theoretically possible that at some time in the future a collection of utter drivel will so capture the imagination of millions that it will easily outsell the Bible. What lifts the Bible above publishers' statistics is the massive moral and spiritual influence it has had, not merely on the lives of individuals, but on communities and nations. Testimonials to this can be found everywhere, and not always in the most expected places. Immanuel Kant confessed, 'The existence of the Bible is the greatest blessing which humanity ever experienced.'[75] The eighteenth-century French philosopher Jean-Jacques Rousseau declared, 'How petty are the books of the philosophers with all their pomp compared with the gospels!'[76] Accusing a fellow philosopher of 'conceited ignorance' when he debunked the Bible, Thomas Huxley went on to say, 'The Bible has been the Magna Carta of the poor and the oppressed down to modern times... Nowhere is the fundamental truth that the welfare of this state in the long run depends on the uprightness of the citizen so strongly laid down. I do not believe that the human race is yet, and possibly ever will be, in a position to dispense with the Bible.'[77]

A whole succession of United States presidents have cited the Bible's powerful and beneficial influence. Abraham Lincoln, the nation's sixteenth president, claimed, 'All things desirable to men are contained in the Bible.'[78] The eighteenth president, Ulysses Grant, urged his people, 'Hold fast to the Bible as the sheet anchor of our liberties; write its precepts on your heart and practise them in your lives. To the influence of this book we are indebted for the progress made in true civilization, and to this we must look for our guide in the future.'[79] Woodrow Wilson, the twenty-eighth holder of the office, declared, 'Give the Bible to the people, unadulterated, pure, unaltered, unexplained, uncheapened, and then see it work through the whole nature.'[80]

Other leading office-holders have expressed similar convictions. When John Jay, the first Chief Justice of the Supreme Court of the United States, lay on his deathbed, and was asked if he had any counsel to give his children, he replied, 'They have the Book.'[81] William Jennings Bryan, secretary of state in the Wilson administration, once said, 'The Bible holds up before us ideals that are within sight of the weakest and the lowliest, and yet so high that the best and the noblest are kept with their faces turned ever upward.'[82] In the opinion of Charles Colson, special counsel to President Richard Nixon in the early 1970s, 'Nothing has affected the rise and fall of civilization, the character of cultures, the structure of government, and the lives of the inhabitants of this planet as profoundly as the words of the Bible.'[83]

'The proof of the pudding ...'

These are fine-sounding sentiments, but is there concrete evidence to back them up? The difficulty here is not in beginning to answer the question, but in knowing when to stop.

Commenting on social and moral progress in the country around the beginning of the seventeenth century, historian John Richard Green wrote, 'No greater moral change ever passed over a nation than passed over England... England became the people of a book, and that book was the Bible.'[84]

When Charles Darwin first visited Tierra del Fuego, he found the inhabitants in a state of misery and moral degradation, but when he returned some years later, after the Bible had been introduced by missionaries, 'The change for the better was so indescribable that he not only testified his astonishment but became a regular contributor to the missionary society.'[85]

Many of the most profound social changes which took place in Great Britain during the nineteenth century were triggered by men and women who found their motivation in Scripture. A handful of examples speak for many others. While he was still a young lawyer, William Wilberforce (1759–1833) began campaigning against the slave trade. By the time he became a Member of Parliament, he was pouring most of his energies into the cause, and slavery was eventually abolished in 1807. Elizabeth Fry (1780–1845) pioneered prison reform in Britain and Europe, sponsored social work among London's homeless, and formed a society for the care and rehabilitation of discharged criminals. The Seventh Earl of Shaftesbury (1801–1885) was at the forefront of revolutionizing the working-class conditions that had been created by the Industrial Revolution, and improving the status and conditions of the mentally ill. He championed the cause of women and children working in mines and collieries, promoted legislation to protect children used as chimney sweeps and devoted a prodigious amount of time to direct social work. Thomas Barnardo (1845–1905) established a home for destitute children in 1870. By the time he died, nearly 60,000 children had been admitted to his homes, 20,000 had been helped to emigrate and a further 250,000 had been given material help of one kind or another.

After the famous mutiny on the *Bounty* in 1789, the nine mutineers were put ashore on Pitcairn Island, along with six native men, ten native women and a fifteen-year old girl. Soon afterwards, someone succeeded in distilling a crude form of alcohol, a 'success' which led to widespread abuse, the deaths of nearly all the mutineers, and several savage murders. Somewhere among the belongings of those who had died, a Bible and *Book of Common Prayer* were found. Reading the Bible led James Adams and Ned Young to a radical change of life and to a determination to build among the natives a society in which the Bible would be the island's rule of life. The change was so dramatic that several years later visitors found what virtually amounted to a model society, with crime unknown and life and property completely safe.

In his well-known book *Miracle on the River Kwai*, Ernest Gordon tells of the amazing transformation which took place in a Japanese prisoner of war camp in Burma between Christmas 1942 and Christmas 1943. In 1942, the prisoners were living in a filthy, muddy mess and subjected to brutal treatment by the Japanese guards. There was hardly any food, and the law of the jungle prevailed — every man for himself. Twelve months later, the camp ground was cleared and cleaned. The bamboo bed-slats had been debugged. Green boughs had been used to rebuild the huts, and on Christmas Day 2,000 men were at worship. What had brought about such an amazing change? During the year, a dying prisoner had shared his last crumb of food with another man who was also in desperate need. Among his belongings someone found a Bible and was convinced that it was this book which contained the secret of its owner's life and of his willingness to deny himself for the benefit of others. By the end of the year, there had been a moral and spiritual revolution in the camp as the prisoners applied the Bible's teaching to their lives.

Some years ago, *Reader's Digest* carried a story entitled 'Shimabuku — the Village that Lives by the Bible'. It told how an advance patrol of American troops liberating the Island of Okinawa were approaching a particular village when they were confronted by two old men carrying a Bible. Suspicious of a trap, they called for the chaplain, who said he felt they could go on. Entering the village, they found it spotless, the fields tilled and fertile, and everything a model of neatness and cleanliness — totally unlike the other run-down villages they had seen. They soon discovered the reason for this amazing contrast. Thirty years earlier, an American missionary on his way to Japan had called at Shimabuku and stayed long enough to leave behind two men who had come to believe in God. He also left a Japanese Bible, which he urged them to study and live by. Without any other outside human help, the community had gradually been transformed. There was no jail, no brothel, no drunkenness, no divorce, a high standard of health and a remarkable spirit of social unity and happiness. Clarence Hall, the war correspondent who wrote the story, quoted the words of his dumbfounded driver: 'So this is what comes out of a Bible... Maybe we are using the wrong weapons to change the world!'

These are some of the headlines, but the small print is even more impressive. On the day these words are being written, and on whichever day they are being read, millions of people all around the world, from every segment of society, are making the reading and study of the Bible part of their chosen lifestyle and would testify to its pervasive influence in their lives. Their testimony is that the Bible presents them with a credible theology, helps them to distinguish between truth and error, offers them a coherent world-view, provides them with stable moral principles, guides them in times of decision, strengthens them in their trials, nourishes their spirits and comforts them in their sorrows. The seventeenth-century minister John Flavel once wrote, 'The Scriptures teach us the best way of living, the noblest way of suffering and the most comfortable way of dying.'[86] Countless millions of people have found Flavel's words endorsed in their own experience, and for Richard Dawkins to suggest that for parents and others to teach children from the Bible is 'mental child abuse'[87] is clearly absurd.

Twisting the truth

Sceptics may try to counter all of this by quoting instances of the Bible being used as justification for many damnable actions over the centuries. The infamous Crusades, holy wars by the Roman Catholic Church in the twelfth and thirteenth centuries to recover the Holy Land from the Muslims, are almost always cited. So is the notorious Inquisition, which the same church set up to punish alleged heretics, and which reached its height in Spain from 1481–1517 when, according to one historian, half a million families were destroyed and nearly 40,000 victims burned alive.[88]

In recent times, many smaller and more localized examples of terror and tragedy have claimed a biblical basis. In 1978 the American minister Jim Jones led over 900 members of his 'People's Temple' cult in Jonestown, Guyana, to commit suicide or allow themselves to be put to death by lethal injection. Ironically, Jones had been voted San Francisco's 'Humanitarian of the year' in 1977. In 1993 over eighty members of the Branch Davidian cult, led by David Koresh, committed suicide in Waco, Texas. In 1997 cult leader Marshall Herff Applewhite persuaded thirty-eight other members of his Heaven's Gate cult to join him in committing suicide near San Diego, California, convinced that the Hale-Bopp comet would whisk their souls to another planet, where they would be reincarnated. In 1998 the *Daily Telegraph* reported that in Uganda, the Lord's Resistance Army, led by Joseph Kony, had displaced at least 200,000 people, abducted almost 8,000 children, and imposed such bizarre and vicious discipline that anyone seen cycling instead of walking had his feet hacked off.[89] The leaders of all four organizations frequently quoted the Bible in support of their teaching — and *Deus Vult!* (God wills it!) was the battle-cry of the Crusades — but there is no justification in the Bible for any of these events. The same applies to the Jehovah's Witnesses' policy of refusing to allow its members to receive blood transfusions. The front cover of a 1994 edition of its magazine *Awake* carried photographs of twenty-six teenagers who had died because they submitted to the cult's directive. The photographs carried the heading, 'Youths who put God first';[90] the truth is that they had been brainwashed into a decision for which the organization had no biblical warrant. The Bible gives a clear warning against those who 'distort ... the ... Scriptures',[91] and it can hardly be blamed for the bizarre, irrational, vicious or cruel behaviour of misguided zealots who have misinterpreted and misapplied its teaching and brought terror and tragedy to so many as a result. The Bible's track record of transforming lives for the better is unparalleled and unscathed.

The spokesmen

We are still pursuing the question as to whether the Bible's message is true or false, fact or fiction. The three clues we have tracked down — its remarkable unity, amazing prophecy and unparalleled moral influence — should catch the attention of any fair-minded person, yet they only prepare the way for the unique and astounding claim the Bible makes for itself: *that it is nothing less than the Word of God.*

We can begin to examine this claim by referring back to the issue of prophecy and noticing the way in which the two are tied together. Old Testament prophets were concerned with more than foretelling future events; they also claimed to be God's spokesmen on all matters of belief and behaviour. At the time of his own commissioning, Moses protested that he had 'never been eloquent' and was 'slow of speech', but God responded, 'Who gave man his mouth? ... Is it not I, the LORD? Now go; I will help you speak and will teach you what to say.'[92] From then onwards, genuine prophets had no hesitation in saying that they were God's mouthpieces and that when they spoke in prophetic mode their message was to be treated as coming directly from God himself. The declarations of Jeremiah, Ezekiel, Hosea, Joel, Jonah, Zephaniah, Haggai and Zechariah are all prefaced with 'The word of the LORD came ...'[93] God is said to have spoken to Isaiah and Daniel in visions.[94] When Amos and Obadiah made prophetic declarations, they said their words were 'what the Sovereign LORD says'.[95] Others, such as Nahum, Habakkuk and Malachi, spoke in the form of an 'oracle',[96] a word specifically used for a declaration by God.

This points to a vitally important factor in the authentication of their message. At a time when the foretelling element in prophecy was a major contemporary issue, believers were naturally concerned to know whether those claiming to be God's spokesmen could be trusted: 'How can we know when a message has not been spoken by the LORD?'[97] The reply Moses gave could not have been clearer: 'If what a prophet claims in the name of the LORD does not take place or come true, that is a message the LORD has not spoken. That prophet has spoken presumptuously. Do not be afraid of him.'[98] It is important to notice that Moses did *not* say, 'If what a prophet claims takes place, the prophet is genuine.' Anybody setting himself up as a prophet might make an accurate forecast from time to time, even if only on a minor matter and by using common sense or some kind of inside knowledge, but this would not be proof of his credentials. Yet nobody claiming to be a prophet could shrug off even *one* failed prophecy on the basis that he was 'only human' and so 'bound to get things wrong from time to time'. A true prophet staked everything on *always* getting it right.

For example, when Micaiah prophesied the death of King Ahab at the battle of Ramoth-gilead, the king was so outraged that he ordered him to be flung into prison on a bread-and-water diet 'until I return safely'.[99] As the penalty for false prophecy was instant execution, and the king already hated Micaiah 'because he never prophesies anything good about me',[100] Micaiah was literally staking his life on his conviction that God had given him the words to speak. What happened? Although the king took the crafty precaution of going into battle disguised as a common soldier, one Syrian arrow, aimed 'at random',[101] found a gap in his armour, and by nightfall he had bled to death.

When a prophet spoke in God's name, nothing could prevent the prophecy coming true. Surely this is powerful evidence that the prophets were more than fortune-tellers who by some fluke sometimes got it right, and their message more than religious rhetoric? Small wonder that John Benton says its 'spectacular use of prediction' is 'probably the most direct evidence for the special involvement of God with the Bible'.[102]

Before leaving the subject of biblical prophecy, we should also note its impressive cohesion, underlined by the way in which many of the prophets referred to each other's ministry and reminded people that it was God's word to them. For example, Jeremiah countered the false claims of a self-styled prophet by a reference to the teaching of 'the prophets who preceded you and me',[103] and Ezekiel claimed that his own words tied in with those of previous 'prophets of Israel'.[104] Even more impressively, Zechariah referred to passages in the writing of Jeremiah and Ezekiel and made it clear that, although these prophets and their own forefathers were long since dead, God's prophetic words had outlived them all and had ongoing integrity and authority.[105] This points to something more than trade union solidarity!

Of the thirty-nine Old Testament books, only seventeen major on prophecy, while seventeen are predominantly history and five poetry, yet the same claim to divine authority runs through them all. Phrases like 'God said', 'God spoke', and 'the word of the LORD came' occur some 700 times in the first five (historical) books alone, some forty times in one chapter, while in one form or another the poetic books point again and again to the same source. When we look at the Old Testament as a whole we find nearly 4,000 direct claims to divine authorship.

Many writers; one Author

New Testament writers were no less emphatic as to the source of their material. The most prolific is Paul, who wrote thirteen (possibly fourteen) of its twenty-seven books, and not only described the Old Testament as 'the very words of God',[106] but was equally certain about his own authority: 'If anybody thinks he is a prophet or spiritually gifted, let him acknowledge that what I am writing to you is the Lord's command.'[107] Later, he commended people who received his message 'not as the word of men, but as it actually is, the word of God'.[108] Laying down instructions on sexual behaviour, he made it clear that 'He who rejects this instruction does not reject man but God.'[109] In all three cases (and there are many others) Paul claimed to be God's mouthpiece and said that his teaching should therefore be accepted without question as having divine authority.

Peter, another major contributor to the New Testament, reminded his readers that Paul had written 'with the wisdom that God gave him',[110] and had no hesitation in including his own writing as part of a body of truth that had come 'from heaven'.[111] John, another New Testament heavyweight, began the last book in the Bible by saying that what he was about to write was 'the word of God',[112] and in almost his final phrase he assured his readers that his words were 'trustworthy and true',[113] having been given to him by 'the Lord, the God of the spirits of the prophets'.

These are merely a few examples of what we find throughout the New Testament. Harold Lindsell notes, 'No one can read any part of the New Testament without being impressed by the fact that the writers convey the sense of divine authority, manifest the badge of truthfulness, and give no impression that what they wrote, or what the other apostles wrote, should or could be doubted by the reader. And no writer gives the impression that what he writes is not to be taken as though it came from the very lips of God himself.'[114] The American scholar B. B. Warfield once said that trying to deny that the Bible claimed to be the Word of God (at least to our satisfaction) was like trying to avoid an avalanche by dodging individual stones.

This is not to say that we are to think of the Bible's human writers as co-authors with God, as they had nothing to do with the *origin* of the message. The Bible's most concise statement on this is to say, 'All Scripture is God-breathed.'[115] Older versions render the last word 'given by inspiration', but this is misleading. 'God-breathed' perfectly translates *theopneustos*, from the noun *theos* (God) and the verb *pneo* (to breathe). As *theopneustos* is in the passive tense, it tells us, not that the writers were *inspired*, but that their writings were *expired*: God breathed out the very words they wrote down. This is exactly why Paul was able to call Old Testament teaching 'the very words of God'.[116] Peter made the same point and said that 'Prophecy never had its origin in the will of man, but men spoke from God.'[117]

It is obvious from the way in which their writings reveal their own character, style and culture that the human writers were not being used in the same way as we use dictating machines, typewriters or word processors. Brian Edwards gives an excellent illustration of this and says that a soldier may deliver an officer's urgent message faithfully and exactly, yet the urgency of his voice and the excitement of his gestures would be his own. As far as the Bible's human writers are concerned, Edwards goes on to say, '[God] allowed them to use their own style, culture, gifts and character, to use the results of their own study and research, to write of their own experiences and to express what was in their mind', yet 'so overruled in the expression of thought and in the choice of words' that 'they recorded accurately all that God wanted them to say and exactly how he wanted them to say it, in their own character, style and language'.[118]

This all tells us that biblical religion is a religion of *revelation*, and there is a sense in which this should not surprise us. It stands to reason that, if an infinitely personal God exists, he is by definition greater than all finite human understanding, and that we could not begin to understand him unless he had revealed himself to us. What is more, if God is our Creator, and has made us in such a way that as human beings we are inherently capable of relationships, and use words to communicate with each other, we might reasonably expect God to communicate with us in a similar way, revealing something of his nature, purposes and will. As the Scottish theologian Bruce Milne puts it, 'Would a wise, intelligent creator leave his creatures to grope in the dark for some clue to his existence without making himself known? The thought is patently absurd. If we suppose further, as many vaguely do, that the creator God is loving, the likelihood of revelation becomes overwhelming; no loving parent would deliberately keep out of a child's sight and range of reference so that it grew up ignorant of its parent's existence.'[119]

We need to emphasize the point that only if God did communicate with us would we know anything about him (or, for that matter, about our own origin and purpose). If God remained silent, we would be incurably agnostic about these things; in C. S. Lewis' words, 'If he can be known at all it will be by self-revelation on his part, not by speculation on ours.'[120] The same thing is true in our own human relationships. The only way in which anyone else can truly know me is as I reveal myself by my words and actions. As we shall see in a later chapter, there are factors which make God's initiative in revealing himself much more significant. The Bible reflects this by asking, 'Can you fathom the mysteries of God?'[121] and by stating that, left to himself, man is incapable of knowing anything about God's nature and will; he simply 'cannot understand them'.[122] Yet God has not left us floundering in ignorance, but in the Bible has used human language to tell us the things we most need to know. We can go one step further and say that, although he has not given us a complete revelation of himself in Scripture, he has given us a perfect one. As the Welsh preacher Derek Swann writes, 'Would a perfect, loving God allow men to write, unsuperintended, about matters of life and death ... and, because of their humanity and stupidity, fudge and muddle the message? The answer must be "No!" If he did, then he would not be a God of love. Because he is a God of love, he has communicated a perfectly clear message which ordinary, humble, seeking human beings can find.'[123]

The sceptic may protest that to say that the Bible is the Word of God because the Bible says it is the Word of God is to argue in circles and, at least on the surface, the criticism is valid; as John Frame admits, 'The God of Scripture tells us in Scripture to go to Scripture.'[124] In normal cases, this would seem to be a self-defeating argument, but the Bible is no ordinary case. In the course of this chapter we have found uniquely impressive evidence of the Bible's integrity in matters of history, geography, prophecy and ethics. This evidence is so powerful and pervasive that it makes it at least reasonable to suppose that its overall message can be trusted. Yet this message is locked into the assertion that it is the Word of God. This argument may not be infallible, but it weakens the charge of circular reasoning by bringing in empirical investigation and logical inference. As R. C. Sproul rightly insists, 'If the Bible is trustworthy then we must take seriously the claim that it is more than trustworthy.'[125] When we do, we face the fact that of all the significant religious literature we have, only the Bible is saturated from cover to cover with the claim that it is God's direct, verbal communication with man. As it proves to be utterly reliable in every other area in which it can be tested, it is both unreasonable and illogical to charge it with making thousands of false and blasphemous statements about its own divine origin.

One other point needs to be borne in mind here. If God is truly the author of Scripture, where else could he tell us to go for an endorsement of his words? As he is by definition the ultimate criterion, what other reference-point could he use to confirm his own existence, character or purposes? One of the New Testament writers makes exactly this point by saying that when God made a covenant with Abraham, 'Since there was no one greater for him to swear by, he swore by himself.'[126]

Pulling all of this together, John Frame is not exaggerating when he goes on to say, 'If God's speech has an obvious location, that location must be the Holy Scriptures. There simply is no other candidate.'[127] We have every warrant for saying that the Bible is exactly what it claims to be, 'the living and enduring word of God'.[128]

The rest of this book is written on that basis.

19.
A God-free zone?

For countless millions of people, drawn from every level of society, the Bible's credentials are beyond question, backed up by their own experience of its reliability, purity and power as its teaching takes hold on their lives. Yet for many others the Bible is an out-of-date irrelevance, of no significance or assistance in getting to grips with the issues which concern twenty-first-century man. One modern phenomenon in particular is a focal point of this diametrical difference: the universal attraction of science. One of the major reasons given for rejecting the Bible's authority and relevance is that modern science has rendered it obsolete. Time and again students and others have told me in no uncertain terms that 'Science disproves the Bible,' that 'Science and religion don't mix,' or that 'Science rules out God.' Opinions vary on whether the 'science versus religion' debate is hotting up or cooling down, but it is difficult to disagree with Edgar Andrews when he says, 'The divorce between science and religion is one of the most significant of our modern philosophical scene.'[1] Nor are articulate atheists shy about pointing out their fundamental opposition to what the Bible teaches. In his book *In the Beginning* Isaac Asimov writes, 'The Bible describes a Universe created by God, maintained by him and instantly and constantly directed by him, while science describes a Universe in which it is not necessary to postulate the existence of God at all.'[2]

Before going any further, we obviously need to establish what we mean by science. This is not as simple as it seems; J. P. Moreland goes so far as to say, 'No generally accepted definition of what science is is agreed on by a majority of philosophers of science.'[3] In ancient times, 'science' was synonymous with 'knowledge', but the word now has a much broader meaning and use, including 'pursuit of [systematic and formulated knowledge] or principles regulating such pursuit'.[4] This immediately tells us (and the relevance of the point will become increasingly obvious as we go along) that science has no essential existence of its own. It is not an entity, but an enterprise, a way of learning by observation and experiment. The French physiologist François Magendie claimed that when he was in his laboratory he had only eyes and ears, and no brain — his way of saying that he did his science as a completely impartial observer, with no agenda except the discovery of truth.[5]

The faith factor

At several stages in this book I have sought to show that nobody is an unbeliever (or, more strictly, a non-believer). In the context of the present chapter, the point needs to be made that while many scientists would claim to have no faith in God, true science is impossible without the principle of faith. Put very simply, the scientist has faith in nature and in himself.

In the first place, scientific work is based on the premise that we live in a rational universe. Scientists assume that all the things they are looking at somehow fit together and work according to a set of fixed laws, such as those of gravity and motion. New discoveries sometimes cause us to revise our understanding of the so-called 'laws of nature', but without the general assumption that there is a sense of order in the universe the scientific process would be futile. The entire scientific enterprise is built on the premise that within this ordered world effects must be related to causes, with no effect greater in quantity or distinct in quality from its cause. Lesslie Newbigin calls this the conviction that 'The universe is rational and that it is contingent,'[6] and says it is no accident that 'modern science was born in a culture which has been shaped for many centuries by this belief'.[7] That shaping was largely carried out by men who were motivated by their conviction that the world they explored came from the hand of an intelligent Creator.

In his superb book, *God, Chance and Necessity*, Keith Ward takes this one step further: 'Science is based on the postulate that one should always seek reasons for why things are as they are. If, every now and again, things just happened for no reason at all, not even for probabilistic reasons, science would come to an end. If I ask, "Why does water boil as it is heated?" I do not expect to be told, "There is no reason at all. It just does." Not

much physics would get started with that attitude, and not many examin-
ations in physics would be passed by candidates who gave that sort of
answer.'[8] Scientists' work will be effective only if nature is the reliable and
comprehensible unity which theism says it is. Entomologist Stanley Beck,
though strongly opposed to theistic creation, concedes that this is the case:
'The first of the unprovable premises on which science has been based is
the belief that the world is real and the human mind is capable of knowing
its real nature... The second and best-known postulate underlying the structure of scientific knowledge is that of cause and effect... The third basic
scientific premise is that nature is unified.'[9]

Beck's words anticipate my second point, which is that the scientist has
faith in himself. Not only does he trust that his eyes and ears are telling him
the truth, but he assumes that he is a rational being, that his rationality is in
tune with the natural world and that he is therefore able to find rational
answers to rational questions. David Broughton Knox makes the point
well: 'Faith is the root of science. For observation itself is based on our faith
that our sensory experience corresponds to reality. Without faith giving us
certitude in our observation, science would not and could not exist. Therefore, science is primarily based on faith, and this is true also if we reflect on
the fact that the forming of axioms, which is fundamental to science, is
grounded in faith. To prove any of the basic rules of logic involves those
rules in the proof. Our certitude with reference to axioms is a product of
the faith structure of our minds... *Faith is the presupposition of all demonstration*'[10] (emphasis added).

None of the assumptions mentioned above — the uniformity and rationality of the universe, the reliability of our senses, and our ability to reach
reliable conclusions based on accurate data — can ever be proved with
philosophical certainty. What is required before any of them can be built
upon is an act of faith, and Albert Einstein recognized where that leads:
'The most incomprehensible fact of nature is the fact that nature is comprehensible.'[11] As we noted in an earlier chapter, he added elsewhere that
faith in the rational validity of the regulations governing the universe belongs 'to the sphere of religion'.[12]

Success, success

Although applied science has led to some enormous problems (imbalance
in the use of natural resources, for example) it has been an exhilarating

success story for the last 300 years. Now at the beginning of the twenty-first century, millions of people are basking in the benefits produced by science and technology. As I write these words, today's *Daily Mail* has a feature highlighting some of the best life-enhancing inventions of the twentieth century which we take for granted. As its 'top ten', the paper chose the vacuum cleaner (invented in 1902), the paper cup (1908), sliced bread (1928), the Mars bar (1932), the shopping trolley (1937), the ring-pull (1962), the hover mower (1963), the baby buggy (1965), the calculator (1972) and the 'Post-it' note (1981).[13] The list is obviously subjective but, as Francis Bridger points out, 'No impartial observer could seriously doubt that without science we would be in a dire state: no electricity, no power of any kind (other than fire perhaps, but even the application of that employs some rudimentary scientific principles), hardly any medicine beyond leeches and magic potions, no life-saving technology and certainly no mechanized transport. For most of us, it is impossible to imagine.'[14]

As an illustration of the progress that has been made, Bridger shows that in seventeenth-century England the average life expectancy of boys born to even the richest families was no more than thirty years, with one-third of them dying before the age of five. (This is in stark contrast to a recent report which gives the male life expectancy in Britain as seventy-four.) In the seventeenth century, one harvest in six failed, leading to widespread starvation, sickness and death. Epidemics were common, with only a dozen plague-free years in London during the 150 years up to 1665, and the few qualified doctors and surgeons were limited to methods of treatment which make us cringe to contemplate.

Science and technology have given us gadgets, devices and equipment to enhance virtually every department of human life, not least our leisure pursuits. Had I been a golfer in the seventeenth century, I would have used a ball consisting of a hatful of boiled feathers stuffed into a (more or less) circular leather pouch; today, I use a perfectly spherical computer-generated ball with advanced, liquid-filled, centre-wound technology and a resilient, high-performance ionomer cover formulation. In listing these features, the makers claim that they combine to produce 'longer, straighter distance and shot-shaping control'. (They often do nothing of the sort, but I suspect the technology is not to blame!) In heavy rain, a seventeenth-century golfer would have got soaking wet (and possibly caught pneumonia). Today, I am protected by a Teflon-coated rainsuit with a hydrophilic laminate outer layer, a capillary-style membrane and a technical mesh dropliner (whatever all that means!) weighing less than 700 grams.

The triumph of technology is more than matched by that of the overall scientific method, which has given us a vastly greater understanding of how nature works, enabling us to bring it under ever closer control and to employ more and more of its resources to meet our material needs. Nor does there seem to be any slackening in the pace of the progress being made. I recently heard an expert in computer technology say that twenty years from now our most advanced systems would seem as dated as the Stone Age artefacts appear to us today. We have come a long way from the time in 1943 when IBM Chairman Thomas Watson suggested there might be a world market for five computers!

No gaps, no God?

In a lecture delivered to working men in 1866, Thomas Huxley outlined the growing triumphs of science at that time, and claimed that science would 'extend itself into all departments of human thought, and become co-extensive with the range of knowledge'.[15] Eventually, he went on, science itself would discover that 'There is but one kind of knowledge and but one method of acquiring it.'[16] Almost exactly 100 years later, Jawaharlal Nehru, the first Prime Minister of India, told his country's National Institute of Science, 'It is science alone that can solve the problems of hunger and poverty, of sanitation and illiteracy, of superstition and deadening custom and tradition, of vast resources running to waste, of a rich country inhabited by starving people... Who indeed could afford to ignore science today? At every turn we have to seek its aid... *The future belongs to science and those who make friends with science*[17] (emphasis added).

These two statements frame a century during which religion often seemed reduced to defending the so-called 'God of the gaps', whose only function was to plug the decreasing number of holes left in the knowledge uncovered by science. At best, he became the deists' God, 'a kind of first cause who, having set the whole process in motion, had retired to watch the consequences from a safe distance'.[18] Today, what Francis Schaeffer called 'modern, modern science'[19] denies God even that role and says that nature operates within a closed system which requires nothing outside of itself. Within this system, science reigns supreme and there is no other source of knowledge about anything. Leaning on his positivism, which we discussed in an earlier chapter, Bertrand Russell spelled out what this means: 'Whatever knowledge is attainable must be attained by scientific means; and what science cannot discover, mankind cannot know.'[20] In the 1998 Oxford debate to which we have referred earlier, Peter Atkins was just as emphatic: 'Use your brains — the most wonderful in the universe — and through your brains you will find you do not need God. There is no necessity for God because *science can explain everything.*'

The idea that science is the only valid test of what we can know and what we should believe is a by-product of what we have called 'nothing-buttery', which reduces everything to atoms and molecules. For those who think in these terms, 'science' has become a virtual deity, invested with omnipotence (giving us increasing control over nature), omniscience (knowing all the answers) and infallibility (telling us that what science claims is beyond dispute). 'God says ...' has been replaced by 'Science says ...', and we must bow in humble submission before any sentence which begins, 'Science proves ...' More than a century ago, the American philosopher J. W. Draper, in his classic book *History of the Conflict Between Religion and Science*, predicted, 'The time approaches when we must make the choice between a quiescent Faith and ever-advancing Science, between Faith with its medieval consolations and Science whose triumphs are sound and enduring.'[21]

For some that time has come, and God must no longer be given houseroom. In 1997 the Harvard geneticist Richard Lewontin declared, 'Our willingness to accept scientific claims that are against common sense is the key to an understanding of the real struggle between science and the supernatural. We take the side of science in spite of the patent absurdity of some of its constructs ... in spite of the tolerance of the scientific community for unsubstantiated just-so stories, *because we have a prior commitment ... to materialism.* It is not that the methods and institutions of science somehow compel us to accept a material explanation of the phenomenal world but, on the contrary, that we are forced by our *a priori* adherence to material causes to create an apparatus of investigation and a set of concepts that produce material explanations, no matter how counter-intuitive, no matter how mystifying to the uninitiated. Moreover that materialism is absolute *for we cannot allow a Divine foot in the door*'[22] (emphasis added).

What Lewontin represents here is not true science but *scientism*, which begins by repudiating all that cannot be reduced to the physical and studied by means of the scientific method. A 'commitment to materialism' comes first, and this shapes the science in such a way that no supernatural explanation can be entertained. This is the line taken by Richard Dickerson, an expert in chemical evolution: 'Science, fundamentally, is a game. It is a game with one overriding and fundamental rule. Rule No. 1: Let us see how far and to what extent we can explain the behaviour of the physical and material universe in terms of purely physical and material causes, without invoking the supernatural.'[23] This approach ignores the basic tenet that in true science the evidence should be followed and tested *wherever* it leads. Instead, scientism rules out a supernatural explanation of anything on the basis of a materialistic theory which predetermines the parameters of the scientific method. This may be 'Rule No. 1' in Dickerson's 'game', but coming to the conclusion before beginning the experiment hardly qualifies as science.

By the same token, demanding scientific proof for the existence of God before believing in him is not acting as a true scientist, and denying the existence of any phenomena which cannot be measured and tested in a laboratory is illogical and naïve. If I stand at the foot of a mountain at midnight and try to illuminate the summit with a pocket-sized lamp I will fail, not because the summit is not there, but because I am using the wrong equipment. To pronounce the universe a God-free zone because science can find no physical trace of him is equally absurd. It is also to be trapped in outdated 'either or' thinking, and takes no account of the recent revolution in thinking about science. As Francis Bridger confirms, 'The self-confident days of rationalism have gone, to be replaced by deep scepticism about the claims of science to have unlocked the secrets of the cosmos or to have discovered reality in all its fulness... Postmodernism has raised far more radically sceptical questions about science than religious protagonists could ever have hoped to get away with.'[24]

All agreed?

Scientism has penetrated people's thinking so deeply that there is now a widespread assumption that science speaks with a united and dogmatic voice, whereas religion is fragmented and uncertain. The story is told of an airline captain who announced to his passengers, 'One of our engines has shut down, but there is no danger, as we can make it safely to our destination on three engines. In case you are still worried, let me tell you that we have four bishops on board today.' One woman summoned a member of the cabin crew and said, 'Could you please tell the captain that I would be far happier if we had three bishops and four engines!' Nobody can brush aside the fact that theologians have their disagreements (usually pounced on with great relish by the secular media, and often blown up out of all proportion), yet the biblical doctrines of God and the nature of man hold together with an impressive consistency. Alister McGrath says that if 'truth' is defined in terms of internal consistency, traditional biblical theology 'scores highly'.[25]

The same can hardly be said of the scientific community. Far from presenting a united front, scientists disagree across a vast spectrum of subjects. As we saw in chapter 13, cosmologists are constantly at loggerheads over issues such as whether the universe had a beginning, and whether it will expand for ever, or reach a certain point and then begin to contract. Experts argue over whether the world as we know it will end in a 'Big Crunch' or whether this will lead to a 'Big Bounce', with the whole process of expansion starting all over again. These are hardly minor matters! The American scholar E. Calvin Beisner highlights other disagreements: 'Some believe in a Big Bang, some in a steady state universe, some in a pulsating universe. Some believe in gradual, Darwinian evolution, some in punctuated equilibrium, some in the creation of specific kinds of life by God. Some of the latter believe in a relatively recent creation, others in creation billions of years ago. Some scientists believe in general relativity, others in spatial particle theory. Some believe in black holes, and some don't.'[26] In other areas, such as the exact nature of electrons and other subatomic particles, uncertainty makes it difficult for scientists to know which side of the argument to take. In a 1999 review of a newly published book on evolution, the *Sunday Telegraph* reported, 'Modern Darwinian evolutionists are among the most bitter of squabblers.'[27] These contradictions and confusions are not a criticism of either science or the scientific method, but they do help to show the danger of equating 'Science says ...' with absolute certainty. The Cambridge biochemist Malcolm Dixon gave a wise warning here: 'It ought not to be overlooked that there are more disagreements and apparent contradictions within science itself than there are between science and religion.'[28]

What's new?

A variation on the idea of scientific certainty is the notion that whatever science says can be set in concrete, but this is equally untrue, and the history of science is paved with examples of scientific 'facts' which have later been discarded.

- Ptolemy's insistence that the earth was at the geographical centre of our universe held sway for 1,300 years until it was disproved by Copernicus and Galileo.
- Nobody disputes Isaac Newton's claim to fame, but twentieth-century scientists have discovered that his laws of physics do not apply to the behaviour of subatomic particles.
- In the eighteenth century, the Scottish chemist Joseph Black introduced a theory of heat which taught that an extra substance (caloric) was added to hot objects and taken away from cold ones, but no scientist believes this today.
- Scientists used to say that a substance called 'ether' filled all space and carried the 'pulling power' between planets, but in 1887 the American physicist Albert Michelson and his colleague Edward Morley conducted a famous experiment which led to the ether idea being abandoned and prepared the way for Albert Einstein to develop the theory of relativity.
- Working at Cold Spring Harbour Laboratory, New York, the British scientist Richard Roberts, who shared the 1993 Nobel Prize for medicine with his American colleague Phillip Sharp, discovered that genes are split up by small inserts of genetic code — called introns — that are thought to control the way genes are read in the body. The discovery, considered fundamental to basic research in biology, as well as for medical research on the development of cancer, flatly contradicted what scientists had previously believed. As Roberts told the *Daily Telegraph* later that year, 'It was one of those discoveries where dogma is overturned.'[29]

A vast number of other examples could be given, but these are sufficient to show that science is in a state of continual change and that in true science dogmatism is out of place. Writing in the *Daily Telegraph* in 1994,

Richard Roberts revealed, 'With science and technology moving so quickly, we face a unique challenge in educating our citizenry about the latest developments. Even in the schools, it can sometimes take so long to change a curriculum that, by the time it is agreed that the latest advances should be taught, they are often out of date.'[30] Even an idea as solidly entrenched as macro-evolution remains tentative at best, and one which must in principle always be capable of being replaced by one which appears at the time to be more credible. Carl Sagan was firmly committed to scientism, and had no place for God, yet even he admitted that true science was always subject to adjustment: 'Scientists, like other human beings, have their hopes and fears, their passions and despondencies, and their strong emotions, which may sometimes interrupt the course of clear thinking and sound practice, but science is also self-correcting... The history of science is full of cases where previously accepted theories and hypotheses have been overthrown to be replaced by new ideas which more adequately explain the data.'[31]

Sagan was not criticizing science, but (quite rightly) commending it, yet his statement helps to make the narrow point which concerns us here, that true science is always provisional, the best we can do at the present time. It is fine to speak of science making progress, but foolish to give the impression that it has arrived. In an educational manual published in 1996, John Burn and Nigel McQuoid, Principal and Vice-Principal of Emmanuel College, Gateshead, put it precisely: 'Science is a humble and persistent search for appropriate models to explain reality. It proceeds by repeated careful observation, measurement and experiment. It deals with hypothesis and theory and is prepared to modify and occasionally abandon established theories and models.'[32] This is perfectly in tune with Karl Popper's conviction that 'Every scientific statement must remain tentative for ever.'[33] In true science, the latest word is never the last word!

Limits

When I was a young boy, we had in our home a book with the enticing title *Enquire Within upon Everything.* Of course the contents never matched the claim, but it snared me into hours of trying to find information about all kinds of subjects. Today, scientism makes claims which match that old book's title. In 1963 the well-known humanist Kay Mouat wrote, 'From biology to botany, sociology to psychology, there is no aspect of life in which science of one kind or another has not something invaluable to contribute.'[34] Be that as it may, scientists have moved on to speak of 'Grand Unification Theories', more popularly known as 'Theories of Everything' (the so-called 'String Theory' is one), and atheists like Peter Atkins claim that we are on the brink of discovering and understanding a complete picture of all reality: 'We are almost there. Complete knowledge is just within our grasp. Comprehension is moving across the earth like a sunrise.'[35] Nor does he think that the final steps to the summit will be very difficult: 'There is nothing that cannot be understood ... nothing that cannot be explained ... everything is extraordinarily simple.'[36]

This all sounds very impressive, but the fanfare is not matched by the facts, and many scientists rightly take a much humbler (and healthier) view, recognizing that even within their own particular discipline 'complete knowledge' is not only beyond their present grasp but will remain so. Geneticist Steve Jones concedes this in his book *The Language of the Genes*: 'It is the essence of all scientific theories that they cannot resolve everything. Science cannot answer the questions that philosophers — or children — ask: why are we here, what is the point of being alive, how ought we to behave? Genetics has almost nothing to say about what makes us more than machines driven by biology, about what makes us human. These questions may be interesting, but scientists are no more qualified to comment on them than is anyone else. In its early days, human genetics suffered from a high opinion of itself. It failed to understand its own limits. Knowledge has brought humility to genetics as to other sciences.'[37]

Jones' down-to-earth humility recognizes the point made at the beginning of this chapter, that science is not an entity but an enterprise, a tool which man is able to use with amazing effectiveness in many areas, yet which remains strictly limited in the purposes it serves. We should no more expect science to produce the answer to every question we ask than we should expect a can opener to be able to launch a spacecraft or a wheelbarrow to distil water. Scientism suggests that the scientific method is the only way to find answers but, as Donald MacKay showed, this is clearly not the case: 'The man who in the name of intellectual integrity tries to win a wife in the way in which he'd tackle a problem in thermodynamics has the wrong idea of what intellectual integrity means, and is very likely to remain a bachelor.'[38]

Scientism has made such inroads into popular thinking that most people fail to recognize that it has many severe limitations. Here are some that come fairly easily to mind:

- Science can produce credible theories as to what happened in the first moments of the universe's existence, some claiming to take us back to within a tiny fraction of a second of the Big Bang. *Science cannot go back beyond the 'zero time point'.* As Edgar Andrews indicates, 'Thus it follows that science, even at its most speculative, must of necessity stop short of offering any explanation or even description of the actual event of origin.'[39]

- Science can speculate as to how the world came into being. *Science cannot explain why it should have done so.* Some fifty years ago Julian Huxley wrote, 'Science has removed the obscuring veil from many phenomena, much to the benefit of the human race; but it confronts us with the basic and fundamental mystery — the mystery of existence in general... Why does the world exist?'[40] More recently, Stephen Hawking has said much the same thing: 'Even if there is only one unique set of possible laws, it is only a set of equations. What is it that breathes fire into the equations and makes a universe for them to govern? ... Although science may solve the problem of how the universe began, it cannot answer the question: why does the universe bother to exist? I don't know the answer to that.'[41]

- Science can demonstrate the consistency of scientific or natural laws in both space and time. *Science cannot tell us how they came to be there, or why they should be exactly as they are.* It can tell us that light travels at 186,282.397 miles per second, but cannot explain why it does not travel faster or slower. Edgar Andrews gives another example: 'If we ask science ... why the law of gravity is an inverse square law with respect to distance, science can do nothing but shrug its mathematical shoulders and reply, "That question lies outside my terms of reference."'[42]

- Science can provide helpful statistics on demographics. *Science cannot explain why human beings exist.* Nor can it tell us why we are self-conscious individuals, or why we should have the slightest interest in asking questions about the meaning and purpose of life. Sir John Eccles, a Nobel Prize-winning pioneer in brain research, confirms that these are questions beyond the competence of science:

'Science cannot explain the existence of each of us as a unique self, nor can it answer such fundamental questions as "Who am I? How did I come to be at a certain place and time? What happens after death?" These are all mysteries beyond science.'[43]

- Science can tell us a great deal about physical and material reality. *Science cannot tell us whether we should expect or hope for more.* Albert Einstein made this clear in *Ideas and Opinions:* 'The scientific method can teach us nothing beyond how facts are related to and conditioned by each other ... knowledge of what is does not open the door directly to what should be. One can have the clearest and most complete knowledge of what *is*, and yet not be able to deduce from that what should be the *goal* of our human aspirations.'[44]

- Science can tell us a great deal about our physical make-up. *Science cannot explain why the mind exists and functions as it does.* In a 1996 *Sunday Telegraph* article Oxford biochemist Arthur Peacocke wrote, 'Science can investigate all the physical aspects of the brain, but there is still something about the mind — and therefore about who you really are — that it cannot get at.'[45]

- Science can enable man to produce nuclear, chemical and biological weapons capable of wiping out the entire human race. *Science cannot remove the causes of war by changing people's attitudes and behaviour.*

- Science can identify Third World needs, provide immediate relief and supply long-term technology to help the countries concerned. *Science cannot eliminate the corruption which often exacerbates the problem.*

- Science can study certain aspects of human behaviour. *Science cannot make any assessment of our deepest convictions.* We know instinctively that peace is better than war, that truth is better than falsehood, and that kindness is better than cruelty. These beliefs are part of the foundation on which viable human society exists, but none of them can be assessed or proved scientifically. Albert Jay Nock puts his finger precisely on the problem: 'When the men of science have said all their say about the human mind and heart, how far they are from accounting for all their phenomena, or from answering the simple, vital questions that one asks them! What *is* the power by which a certain number and order of air vibrations is translated into the processes of great emotional significance? If anyone can answer that question, believe me, he is just the man I want to see.'[46]

- Science can make many aspects of life easier. *Science cannot add to its quality.* In 1991 some 200 scientists, including many social scientists, attended a conference organized by the International Council of Scientific Unions to discuss the likely needs for science and technology in the twenty-first century. John Houghton later assessed the results of their discussion on the theme 'Quality of Life': 'Although we could largely agree on those factors which ideally make up quality of life, as scientists we could say virtually nothing (and there was considerable debate on the issue) about how to achieve it in practice. In particular, how could we overcome the inherent selfishness, greed and other undesirable characteristics shown by human beings? The problems can be described by science, as can the factors which may exacerbate them, *but science cannot solve them*'[47] (emphasis added).
- Science can produce an array of contraceptive devices to reduce the number of unwanted pregnancies (the medical director of London's Margaret Pike Centre proposed in 1999 that ten-year old girls could be given a long-term contraceptive implant). *Science cannot persuade those concerned to behave responsibly and avoid the need for such devices.* If contraception fails, science can enable us to abort foetuses as routinely as we pull teeth, but it cannot identify or address the moral issues involved.
- Science can study the results of human behaviour. *Science cannot explain the principles involved.* It can say nothing about love, justice, freedom, beauty, goodness, joy or peace. It cannot assess ethical values or moral principles, nor can it distinguish between good and bad, right and wrong. To say that science can offer explanations for everything within human experience is to ignore every moral question that has ever been raised.
- Science can specifically study and analyse trends in religious belief and behaviour. *Science cannot supply any reason why either should exist.* The subject is simply outside its terms of reference.

These examples alone severely undermine scientism's claim that only the material world exists and that only scientific explanations are valid or meaningful. In *Nature and the Greeks*, quantum theory expert Erwin Schrödinger writes, 'I am very astonished that the scientific picture of the real world around me is very deficient. It gives a lot of factual information, puts all our experience in a magnificently consistent order, but is ghastly silent about all and sundry that is really near to our heart ... it knows nothing of beautiful and ugly, good or bad, God and eternity. Science sometimes pretends to answer questions in these domains, but the answers are very often so silly that we are not inclined to take them seriously.'[48]

This specific point needs to be driven home by emphasizing the general fact that, although science can be practised only because the universe is controlled by natural law, science cannot account for the law's existence or origin. To say that science can explain everything (or is capable of doing so in principle) is to overlook the fact that *science cannot even explain itself.* It can explain many things in the natural and material world, but can do so only in terms of natural law. Reductionists begin by accepting natural law as 'given', but have no way of explaining why or how it exists.

While this remains outside the scope of science, religion understands that the existence of natural law which we, as rational beings, can comprehend and even admire for its elegance and symmetry, necessarily implies that its cause must be sought in the existence of a transcendent, rational mind, namely God. In Edgar Andrews' judgement, this argument is 'as close to a proof for the existence of God as is possible'.[49]

None of the limitations we have identified represents a flaw in science or in the scientific method; they simply underline the point that science is by definition limited in its valid sphere of reference. Richard Dawkins' statement, 'Truth means scientific truth,'[50] is neither truthful nor scientific.

'Excuse me, gentlemen ...'

During the 1998 Oxford debate Peter Atkins said that religion was 'outmoded and ridiculous', and that it was 'not possible to believe in gods and be a true scientist'.[51] This echoed a statement by Richard Dawkins nine years earlier, when he wrote in the *Daily Telegraph Science Extra*, 'Religion is no longer a serious candidate in the field of explanation. It is completely superseded by science.'[52] On this subject, at least, Atkins and Dawkins never leave one guessing as to what they are saying, but do their dogmatic assertions emerge from any fair reading of the history of science?

The scientific method as we know it began in the sixteenth century, and most of its pioneers were men who believed that the universe was orderly and worth studying precisely because they saw it as the work of an intelligent Creator. When Britain's oldest and most prestigious scientific body of its kind, the Royal Society, came into being in 1662, its founders saw nothing incongruous in dedicating their scientific work 'to the glory of God'. The manifesto of the British Association for the Advancement of Science, drawn up in 1865 and signed by 617 scientists, including many with outstanding reputations, expressed unambiguous belief in the truth and authority of the Bible and its harmony with natural sciences. Over the centuries, trailblazers in many scientific disciplines have been committed believers, motivated by the firm conviction that the natural world obeyed rational laws put in place by the Creator who had revealed himself in Scripture. Counting heads is no criterion of truth but, as we are so often bombarded with the idea that science and belief in God are incompatible, it is worth listening to what some of the truly great scientists have had to say on the subject.

Francis Bacon (1561–1626) was an English philosopher and politician who eventually rose to become Lord Chancellor. In his *Novum organum*, published in 1620, he put forward a new theory of scientific knowledge which became known as the inductive method, stressing the importance of observation and experiment. A devout Bible student, Bacon wrote, 'There are two books laid before us to study, to prevent our falling into error; first, the volume of the Scriptures, which reveal the will of God; then the volume of the Creatures, which expresses his power.'[53]

The German astronomer *Johannes Kepler* (1571–1630), acknowledged to be the father of modern physical astronomy, often said that he was merely 'thinking God's thoughts after him'.[54] The discoverer of the laws of planetary motion, Kepler wrote, 'Since we astronomers are the priests of the highest God in regard to the book of nature, it befits us to be thoughtful, not of the glory of our minds, but rather, above all else, the glory of God.'[55]

The French mathematician, philosopher and scientist *Blaise Pascal* (1623–1662) made massive contributions to hydrostatics, hydrodynamics and differential calculus. As a committed believer, he also wrote prolifically on religious themes, and his *Pensées* (Thoughts) have had worldwide influence ever since. Just before his death he prayed, 'Grant that I may conform to thy will, just as I am, that, sick as I am, I may glorify thee in my suffering.'[56]

The Irish physicist and chemist *Robert Boyle* (1627–1691) has been called the father of modern chemistry, since his precision in defining chemical elements and chemical reactions was a major step in separating the science of chemistry from alchemy. One of the founders of the Royal Society, Boyle was a diligent Bible student, and gave generous financial support to the relief of poverty, the work of Bible translation and evangelism. In his will, he endowed the Boyle Lectures, which were devoted to Christian apologetics, and in his last message to the Royal Society he urged his fellow scientists, 'Remember to give glory to the One who authored nature.'[57]

Boyle's contemporary and fellow believer *John Ray* (1627–1705) was the greatest authority of his day in both botany and zoology. Sometimes known as the father of English natural history, he was another of the Royal Society's founding members. His best-known book, published in 1691, was *The Wisdom of God Manifested in the Works of Creation*, and his personal convictions were clear: 'There is for a free man no occupation more worthy and delightful than to contemplate the beauteous works of nature and honour the infinite wisdom and goodness of God.'[58]

The Danish scientist *Niels Steno* (1638–1686) became the founder of modern geology in pursuing his secondary interest! His initial work lay in the medical field, where he was the first man to trace the human lymphatic system, but his fame now lies mainly in his introduction of the concept of chronology to geological history. In one of his journals he wrote that an unwillingness to look into nature's own works was a sin 'against the majesty of God',[59] and throughout his life he held to a firm belief in a sovereign God who created a universe worth discovering.

The English mathematician and physicist *Sir Isaac Newton* (1642–1727) is universally recognized as one of the greatest scientists who ever lived. He is most popularly known for his discovery of the law of universal gravitation (supposedly inspired by the sight of a falling apple) but he also formulated the three laws of motion and developed calculus into a comprehensive branch of mathematics, now a basic tool in every science. In his greatest work, *Philosophiae Naturalis Principia Mathematica*, written to persuade people 'for the belief of a Deity', he wrote, 'Without all doubt this world ... could arise from nothing but the perfectly free will of God.'[60]

The Swedish biologist *Carolus Linnaeus* (1707–1778) is known as the father of biological taxonomy, having drawn up the system of classification of plants and animals still used today. The Linnean Society of London, founded in his honour, became the focal gathering point for the leading naturalists of the nineteenth century. A firm believer in special creation and the fixity of species, Linnaeus confessed, 'One is completely stunned by the incredible resourcefulness of the Creator,' and stated that he saw everywhere 'an eternal wisdom and power, an inscrutable perfection'.[61]

The outstanding English astronomer *William Herschel* (1738–1822) built some of the greatest reflecting telescopes of his day and catalogued about 800 double stars and some 2,500 nebulae. Best known for his discovery of the planet Uranus in 1781, he was convinced that the skies revealed God's handiwork, and went so far as to say, 'The undevout astronomer must be mad.'[62]

The renowned British chemist and physicist *Michael Faraday* (1791–1867) discovered electromagnetic induction and introduced the concept of magnetic lines of force. He subscribed wholeheartedly to his church's basis of faith, which included the statement: 'The Bible, and it alone, with nothing added to it, nor taken away from it by man, is the sole and sufficient guide for each individual, at all times and in all circumstances.'[63] It is said that in reply to someone who asked him on his deathbed what his speculations were, Faraday underlined his faith in God by saying, 'Speculations? I have none. I am relying on certainties.'

When *Samuel Morse* (1791–1872), the American inventor of the electric telegraph, sent his first message from Washington to Baltimore on 24 May 1844, he testified to his faith by choosing words taken directly from the Bible: 'What hath God wrought!'[64]

The British physicist *James Joule* (1818–1889) was the first to measure the mechanical equivalent of heat, and gave his name to Joule's law, the formula now universally used for calculating the heat produced by electric current moving through a wire. For Joule, nature pointed in one clear direction: 'It is evident that an acquaintance with natural laws means no less than an acquaintanceship with the mind of God therein expressed.'[65]

Joule's contemporary and fellow British physicist, *William Thomson* (1824–1907), who was knighted as the first Baron Kelvin, held the Chair of Natural Philosophy at the University of Glasgow for fifty-three years. His contributions to physics and mathematics rank him with Newton and Faraday, and he received twenty-one honorary doctorates. He established what is now known as the Kelvin Scale of absolute temperatures and gave precise terminology to the First and Second Laws of Thermodynamics. He believed that the coherence of nature and Scripture could be established with 'sober and scientific certainty',[66] and saw God as 'maintaining and sustaining his creation through the exercise of his will'.[67]

The British scientist *James Clerk Maxwell* (1831–1879), who predicted the existence of radio waves, has been called 'the father of modern physics'. Albert Einstein said that Maxwell's achievements were 'the most profound and fruitful that physics has experienced since the time of Newton'.[68]

Maxwell's faith in God ran through all his work, and he is recorded as praying, 'Teach us to study the work of thy hands that we may subdue the earth to our use and strengthen our reason for thy service.'[69]

Born into a family of black slaves, the American scientist *George Washington Carver* (1864–1943) became one of the world's leading agricultural chemists, developing over 400 products from peanuts and sweet potatoes, and was a leading innovator in the new science of chemurgy, the industrial use of agricultural products. Only the third American in history to have a national monument erected in his honour, Carver wrote, 'I love to think of nature as an unlimited broadcasting system through which God speaks to us every hour, if only we will tune him in.'[70]

One of the earliest exponents of the theory of relativity, the British physicist and astronomer, *Arthur Eddington* (1882–1944) dominated the world of stellar astronomy and it was his work on the temperature and stability of stars which led directly to the discovery of the mass-luminance law. It always struck Eddington as absurd that anyone could doubt the existence of God. Drawing an analogy from human relationships, he pointed out that just as we would laugh at philosophical arguments designed to disprove the existence of human friends, so, for a person who has a relationship with God, 'the most convincing disproof is turned harmlessly aside', adding, 'If I may say it with reverence, the soul and God laugh together over so odd a conclusion.'[71]

Even these few examples taken from the huge body of material available prompt some obvious questions. Did these men not meet Peter Atkins' idea of what makes a 'true scientist'? What has Richard Dawkins found that has 'completely superseded' the convictions which governed their lives and gave them such quality and depth? Did their conviction that science is compatible with faith in general, and biblical theism in particular, mean that they were all suffering from a massive delusion?

In this day and age?

In spite of these clear testimonies, which leave Peter Atkins and Richard Dawkins more than somewhat exposed, the impression is often given that in today's world scientists who believe in God are rapidly declining in number, yet this is at odds with the facts. A 1916 survey by the American academic James Leuba revealed that 40% of scientists interviewed said they believed in God,[72] and when *Nature* ran a similar poll in 1997 the result was almost identical.[73] The study of the relationship between science and theology is one of the fastest-growing academic areas in the world. Over 1,000 students in forty-two countries are officially listed as being engaged in this drawing together of disciplines, and there are over seventy institutions and organizations committed to it, among them the Society of Ordained Scientists and the Science and Religion Forum, which alone has about 200 scientists, clergy and lay believers who meet to discuss the insights science and religion can offer each other.[74] In addition, there are flourishing organizations all around the world for scientists who are committed believers. In the United States, the American Scientific Affiliation has about 2,500 members. In Britain, a similar grouping has over 600 members, while other bodies cater for believers in specialized fields such as medicine, pharmacy, ecology, engineering, television and computer technology.

At a personal level, leaders in virtually every scientific discipline give testimonies just as emphatic as those of the giants of previous generations. *God and the Scientists*, a booklet first published in 1997, lists some examples. Sir Robert Boyd, Emeritus Professor of Physics at University College, London, says, 'I worship an unseen God,' and tells how 'getting to know him ... changed my whole world-view'.[75] Professor George Kinoti, one-time Dean of Science at Nairobi University, believes that 'The living world testifies eloquently to the Creator.'[76] Gareth Jones, head of the Anatomy and Structural Biology Department at New Zealand's University of Otago, says that biblical truth is the 'driving force' behind his commitment to treating all human beings with dignity.[77] Owen Gingerich, Professor of Anatomy and the History of Science at Harvard University, states, 'For me, the coherence of my total view of the universe includes a purposeful Creator who continues to act within creation.'[78] Professor Ghillean Prance, until recently Director of London's Royal Botanic Gardens, claims, 'All my studies in science ... have confirmed my faith. I regard the Bible as my principal source of authority.'[79] Sam Berry, Professor of Genetics at University College, London, tells how his extensive research in Antarctica and elsewhere has left him 'more and more convinced that God has revealed himself in both creation and the Bible'.[80]

When all of this is added to the earlier testimonies from so many true giants of science, we have an impressive item of evidence, though in and of itself it does nothing to prove God's existence. If every scientist in the world were to become a believer it would not contribute one whit to God's credibility, yet such an accumulation of facts and statements of faith can hardly be tossed aside as irrelevant. At the very least they call into question atheism's cavalier assertion that true science is incompatible with faith in God.

Enemies or friends?

Until the middle of the eighteenth century, most scientists worked from a religious base, and the first book to argue that science disproved religion was not published until 1875. By then, Thomas Huxley and eight other scientists had formed a secret association known as the X-Club, whose aims included all-out war on religion.[81] In 1874 one of their number, John Tyndall, told the British Association in Belfast, 'We claim, and we shall wrest from theology, the entire domain of cosmological theory. All schemes and systems which thus infringe upon the domain of science must, *in so far as they do this*, submit to its control and relinquish all thought of controlling it.'[82] This militant onslaught on religion developed such a head of steam that a year later Huxley was sure that it had already beaten it to a pulp: 'Extinguished theologians lie about the cradle of every science as the strangled snakes beside that of Hercules; and history records that whenever science and orthodoxy have been fairly opposed, the latter has been forced to retire from the lists, bleeding and crushed if not annihilated; scotched, if not slain.'[83]

This was a gross exaggeration, of course, but Huxley and others succeeded in giving birth to the myth that science and religion are not on speaking terms. Over 125 years later, the myth survives, powerfully promoted by articulate reductionists and quietly nurtured by intellectual and cultural fashion. Writing in his 'Sacred and Profane' column in the *Daily Telegraph* in 1996, Clifford Longley hit the nail on the head: 'Ideas, the origin of which they do not know, trickle down into the thinking of ordinary people, as in the widespread perception that some important scientists or philosophers somewhere — exactly who and when is not clear — have proved that belief in God is unscientific. Intellectual fashion is full of myths of this kind, things "everybody knows" without being able to offer chapter and verse.'[84] The myth that belief in God is unscientific (and therefore untenable) also receives regular injections from the mass media. In the 1990s the *Observer* carried a heavily biased report of a show-piece debate at the Edinburgh Science Festival under the heading, 'God comes a poor second to the majesty of science,'[85] while the *Scotsman* scored it: 'God lost on points.'[86]

Can the myth be dismantled? I believe it can, and that it can be done very simply by correctly defining our terms. When the militant atheist gets into the ring, he is often representing not science but scientism, which presupposes that the whole of reality is composed of *nothing but* atoms and molecules. To make matters worse, he almost inevitably has a grossly distorted view of his opponent. Preparing for a public debate with Richard Dawkins in 1996, William Gosling, Professor of Communications Engineering at Bath University, told *Daily Telegraph* readers, 'Like most atheists, he attacks a God so primitive that few educated believers would recognize the image. If I thought God has the characteristics Dawkins assigns to him, I would share his lack of belief.'[87] When scientism masquerades as science, and then gives its opponent a false identity, it is hardly surprising that the myth flourishes!

A very different picture emerges even when we put true science in the ring with the general idea of religion. Writing in *The Times* in 1994, Fraser Watts, Starbridge lecturer in theology and natural science at Cambridge University, explained: '*I do not know of any research that conflicts with religion.* The problem comes from the ideological position, held by a minority of scientists, that science is the only valid form of knowledge and has got all the answers. Science and religion both have their different stories to tell the world. Science takes a detached, objective view of things, whereas religion focuses on questions about the meaning and purpose of life'[88] (emphasis added). The idea that whereas science deals with facts, religion is a matter of faith at best and superstition at worst misses the point that they speak two different languages because they have two different areas of concern. The fact is that by its own nature science can no more pass judgement on the validity of religion than religion can judge the technical conclusions of science.

The question, 'Does science disprove religion?' is too vague. What we should really be asking is: 'Does true science disprove what the Bible teaches?' (including its teaching about the existence and nature of God, which we will look at in the next chapter). This is a different question altogether, and several things can be said in response.

Firstly, there are many who do see a conflict, but it would be fair to say that this is between the theories of some scientists and the interpretations of some expositors, rather than between the currently accepted facts of science and the text of Scripture. In *The God who is Real* Henry Morris writes, 'Evolutionists, both atheistic and pantheistic, have always vigorously denounced belief in a personal, omnipotent God as unscientific, but the truth is that all the facts of the real world conform perfectly to the existence and creative work of a supernatural Creator.'[89]

Secondly, as the Bible is not a textbook on the natural sciences, it can hardly be criticized for failing to develop these subjects. For example, while it mentions stars, rocks and animals, it is not a research manual on astronomy, geology or biology. Nor, for that matter, does it tell us the height of Mount Hermon, the depth of the Dead Sea, the temperature at which water boils, or the average weight of a fully grown camel. These details are irrelevant to its purpose. Its great concern is with God and man and their relationship to each other. When it deals with man, it majors on his conduct and his destiny, not on his chromosomes and his DNA.

Thirdly, many who would not reject the entire Bible out of hand would say that, while it may be helpful in matters of religion, morals and ethics, the fact that it is not a scientific textbook means that we cannot be expected to trust what it says in scientific matters. This is a plausible argument, but it leaks like a sieve. If the Bible is the Word of God, and not merely a collection of the best religious ideals available at the time, we should expect its science to be as accurate as its theology and, as a matter of historical record, whenever the Bible's statements on natural phenomena have been tested, they have been found to be consistent with contemporary science.

Fourthly, there is a case for saying that the Bible anticipates science. About 750 B.C., the prophet Isaiah wrote that God 'sits enthroned above the circle of the earth',[90] yet it was over 1,000 years later that scientists began to speak of the earth as being spherical. Jeremiah wrote that the stars in the sky were 'countless'.[91] Some 300 years later, Ptolemy reduced this to 1,056, but today's astronomers talk in terms of so many billions that Jeremiah's 'countless' fits very well. Nearly 2,000 years before scientists discovered the distinction between human cells and those of other creatures, Scripture stated, 'All flesh is not the same: Men have one kind of flesh, animals have another, birds another and fish another.'[92] The Bible is not primarily concerned with scientific analysis, yet it has never been proved to be at variance with any known scientific fact. The statement, 'Science disproves the Bible,' is nonsense.

Friends after all

As we saw earlier in this book, Richard Dawkins stoked the fires of the 'science versus religion' debate by stating that faith was 'a cop-out, an excuse to evade the need to think', but this tells us more about Dawkins than it does about science. Even if science, operating within its own limited parameters, uncovered what it claimed to be the clearest evidence for the non-existence of God, this would tell us little or nothing because, as William Gosling puts it, 'We could never be sure that God has not put it there, faking the whole thing.'[93]

Even the most belligerent of atheists occasionally admit this. Having claimed, 'God and immortality, the central dogma of the Christian religion, find no support in science,' Bertrand Russell went on to admit, 'I do not pretend to be able to prove that there is no God.'[94] In the 1998 Oxford debate Peter Atkins took merciless swipes at religion in general and biblical theism in particular, yet his opening words framed a significant escape clause: 'I have to admit from the outset that science cannot disprove the existence of God.'

True science has no reason to disprove the reality of religion, the truth of the Bible or the existence of God, and should have no interest in doing so, because no 'either or' situation exists, as the testimonies earlier in this chapter make clear. Nor do modern advances in any scientific field produce one. Commenting on recent discoveries in cosmology, molecular biology and neurophysiology, James Le Fanu told *Sunday Telegraph* readers in 1996 that these had the effect of reconciling science with religion in a way that was totally unexpected, 'undermining the scientific certainties of the past hundred years'. Noting that these discoveries touched on basic questions such as, 'Where did it all begin?', 'How do we come to be here?' and 'Why should consciousness itself be unique to humans?' Le Fanu went on to say, 'It is only possible to adhere to a strictly materialist view, in which human experience is meaningless — "a farcical accident" — by ignoring the implications of what science has led us to understand. Science can never disprove the existence of God, but one could say *it is making signposts to his existence much more obvious*'[95] (emphasis added). Writing in 1997 about the sense of certainty he found in listening to the eighteenth-century music of Johann Sebastian Bach he concluded, 'Thanks to the onward march of science over the past forty years, it has become ... a lot easier to be certain about the existence of a creator god than it was in Bach's day.'[96]

True science and true religion have always been in perfect harmony with each other, and the biblical theist celebrates science as a method God has given us to investigate the built-in patterns of physical phenomena. Albert Einstein could hardly have put it better when he said, 'Science without religion is lame; religion without science is blind.'[97]

20.
Nothing but the truth – I

Over 2,000 years ago, the wisdom of the ancient world could be summed up in an inscription on the temple to Apollo in the Greek city of Delphi: _Gnothi seauton_ ('Know yourself'). In the middle of the sixteenth century, the great French Reformer John Calvin went one better. In the opening words of his monumental *Institutes of the Christian Religion* he wrote, 'Nearly all the wisdom we possess, that is to say true and sound wisdom, consists of two parts: the knowledge of God and of ourselves.'[1]

The Bible's credentials are such that any serious-minded person concerned about the fundamental issues that have occupied humankind's attention should want to know what it has to say about them. To analyse its teaching on all the major ideas we have discussed thus far would need a book on its own — and a massive one at that[2] — but Calvin points us to the two subjects which obviously frame all the others: the nature of God and the nature of man. In this chapter and the next we will look at these in turn.

In the introduction, we outlined fourteen terms to identify God. As we shall now see, these are all taken from the Bible, and a closer look at them will show how radically they conflict with secular philosophy and with the teachings of the religions and cults we reviewed in chapters 11 and 12.

God is unique

The word 'unique' can be used of something remarkable or unusual, but I am using it here in its primary sense: 'of which there is only one, having no like or equal or parallel'.[3] One of the clearest definitions of God's uniqueness is presented in an unexpected context. Believers at Corinth had apparently asked the apostle Paul's advice about a religious and moral dilemma. Included in cuts of meat on sale in the local market were some which might previously have been connected with idol worship; was it right to buy and eat these? Paul's down-to-earth advice was that, provided they avoided causing problems for any who in their pagan past had been heavily involved in idolatry, they could do as they wished because 'We are no worse if we do not eat, and no better if we do.'[4] However, it is important to notice the doctrine on which his advice was based: 'So then, about eating food sacrificed to idols: We know that an idol is nothing at all in the world and that there is no God but one.'[5]

There are two statements here for the price of one. Positively, we are told that 'There is no God but one.' This endorses the Old Testament *Shema*, the affirmation of monotheism which the Jews repeated morning and evening and to which they clung with fierce tenacity: 'The LORD our God, the LORD is one.'[6] Nothing was more fundamental to their faith; this was the rock on which their whole belief-system was built. God revealed this uniqueness to them again and again, nowhere more clearly than when speaking through the prophet Isaiah:

This is what the LORD says...
'I am the first and I am the last;
    apart from me there is no God...
I am the LORD, and there is no other.'[7]

Negatively, we are told that 'An idol is nothing at all in the world.' In New Testament times, the word 'idol' was commonly used of a natural or man-made object taken to represent some deity or another, though it was sometimes used of the deity itself. Paul says that, whatever the objects, the deities they represented were in fact non-existent. There could hardly be a more positive negative! The Bible is not saying that other gods are inferior, or less attractive, or less influential, but that they are all inventions.

As many contemporary cultures were riddled with idol worship, this was hardly being politically correct! What about the galaxy of gods worshipped by the Greeks and Romans? To give them their Roman names, what of Venus, the goddess of beauty; Diana, the goddess of the hunt; Cupid, the god of love; and Vulcan, the god of fire? Above all, what of Jupiter (Zeus to the Greeks), who was first associated with the heavens, rain, thunder, lightning and harvest, then came to be regarded as the god of hospitality, truth and justice in international relations, and graduated to becoming god of war before ending up as the chief of all the gods? In spite of that impressive c.v., the Bible dismisses all talk of Jupiter and his juniors as claptrap. What is more, it does the same with every one of the countless gods venerated in other cultures: 'For even if there are so-called gods, whether in heaven or on earth (as indeed there are many "gods" and many "lords"), yet for us there is but one God ... from whom all things came and for whom we live.'[8]

None of the myriads of so-called 'gods' which have been promoted throughout human history have existed outside of their inventors' imagination, and all their exciting exploits can safely be filed away as fairy tales. As theologian Leon Morris confirms, 'In all this ordered universe there is no reality corresponding to idols.'[9] God is *the* great reality.

God is personal

God is not a 'thing', or some indefinable power or influence. He is not a principle or concept. He is not cosmic dust or atmospheric energy. Instead, he has all the essential characteristics of personality. Peter Moore goes so far as to say, 'The ultimate fact about the universe is a personal God.'[10]

The Bible reveals God's personality by telling us of his actions:

- He thinks: 'How great are your works, O LORD, how profound your thoughts!'[11]
- He chooses: we are told of 'the people he chose for his inheritance'.[12]
- He cares: believers are urged, 'Cast all your anxiety on him because he cares for you.'[13]
- He gives: Moses tells the people of Israel that they should 'rejoice in all the good things the LORD your God has given to you and your household'.[14]
- He makes (and keeps) promises: at one point in their chequered history, the people of Israel are reminded that 'Not one of all the good promises the LORD your God gave you has failed. Every promise has been fulfilled.'[15]
- He makes known things that could not be known otherwise: he is 'a revealer of mysteries'.[16]
- He shows kindness and mercy: he is 'compassionate and gracious'.[17]

Addressing the 1998 televised debate from Oxford, Peter Atkins said that theists 'believe in absurdities' and are 'committed to intellectual contortion' because they set up 'this absurd idea that there is this *thing* out there, this unknown thing up there that we have to spend our time kowtowing to, and then we have to rationalize what is going on'. Atkins vented his opinions with some relish, but he presented such a caricature of what the Bible teaches that his comments need not be taken seriously. The Bible clearly points to a living, personal Being with a distinct character and nature, in striking contrast to every other 'god' which people have made or imagined. As C. S. Lewis puts it, 'God ... has purposes and performs particular actions ... does one thing and not another, [is] a concrete, choosing, prohibiting God with a determinate character.'[18] The God of Scripture harmonizes not only with the evidence of intelligent design we see in the natural world, but also with human personality, which demands a personal origin, and with our sense of moral obligation to a supreme lawgiver. Unless we presuppose a personal God, we have no way of making sense of our everyday experience of life.

God is plural

Nothing more radically separates biblical theism from other brands than the doctrine of God's plurality — to be more precise, the teaching that God exists as a Trinity of distinguishable persons, most commonly identified in Scripture as the Father, the Son and the Holy Spirit. Although the word 'Trinity' (from the Latin *trinitas*, which means 'threeness') is not in the Bible, Geoffrey Bromiley is right to say that 'The Trinitarian evidence is overwhelming.'[19]

This may seem to contradict the fundamental monotheistic statement, 'The LORD our God, the LORD is one,' but this is not the case. Although there is no natural implication of plurality in the Hebrew *'ehad*, which is translated 'one' here, there are several other biblical statements that clearly point towards this being so. In a remarkable Old Testament incident we are told, 'The angel of the LORD found Hagar.'[20] We might normally assume that the angel concerned was one of the millions of created beings of whom the Bible speaks, but when Hagar refers to him as 'the God who sees me'[21] the angel does not correct her. Again, in an incident involving Abraham it is clear that 'the angel of the LORD'[22] is God himself.

Another strong indication of God's plurality comes in his own words. When the prophet Isaiah was commissioned to his ministry, he heard God saying, 'Whom shall I send? And who will go for us?'[23] However, a strong element of mystery (and an equally strong possibility of misunderstanding) will always be present when considering God's 'threeness' because we have no adequate word in English to express the nature of the different existences within the Godhead. The word 'person' is the nearest we can get, though we must not use it to imply that within the Godhead there are three distinct beings each possessing a different nature.

Over the centuries, many analogies of 'threeness' have been suggested to illustrate the triune Godhead — a man may be a father, a son and a husband; an egg has a shell, a yolk and a 'white'; a human being has memory, understanding and will; an environment comprises light, heat and air — but they all have weaknesses and there is no point in trying to come up with another one which would need to be qualified in one way or another. This is not a cop-out. Instead, it recognizes that trying to reduce God to finite concepts is an exercise in futility. Bruce Milne makes the point well: 'The fact that in this doctrine there are difficulties which burst through the simple formulae constructed out of the raw materials of our human experience is in one sense entirely predictable since God is the transcendent Lord of all being. Indeed, if we did not encounter deep mystery in God's nature there would be every reason for suspicion concerning the Bible's claims.'[24]

Within our understanding of the Trinity's 'threeness' it is important to maintain the individuality of the persons concerned. The Father is not the Son or the Holy Spirit; the Son is not the Father or the Holy Spirit; and the Holy Spirit is not the Father or the Son. Each of these three persons is fully divine, and co-equally so with the other two, so that, in the words of the American theologian Louis Berkhof, 'The whole undivided essence of God belongs equally to each of the three persons.'[25]

Yet the essence of the Trinity goes far beyond a mathematical juggling act. Its heartbeat is that of personal relationships. The biblical picture is that of a loving, mutual indwelling of three persons in each other, something which is the uncreated basis of all created personality and fellowship.

God is spiritual

Strictly speaking, the Bible does not give us a definition of God. The nearest approach to anything like it is its teaching that God is spiritual, that he does not have a body, or any physical or material dimensions: 'God is spirit, and his worshippers must worship in spirit and in truth.'[26] Elsewhere, the Bible uses language that could be taken to mean that God *does* have bodily parts — it speaks of 'the finger of God',[27] 'the mouth of the LORD'[28] and 'the eyes of the LORD',[29] while God tells Isaiah, 'My own hand laid the foundations of the earth,'[30] but these are obviously anthropomorphisms, examples of the way in which God has chosen to reveal himself through human language. As Bob Horn explains, 'God has taken these features of our finite life which he sees can convey by analogy particular aspects of his person or work.'[31] To say, 'God is spirit,' is to say that he has none of the properties belonging to matter. He has no 'parts'; he is simple as opposed to complex, indivisible as well as invisible, and has no limitations of space or distance.

This has important practical implications. As God is spirit, 'His worshippers must worship in spirit and in truth.' This tells us that worshipping God is not merely a matter of externals, such as fine architecture, beautiful music, ornate clothing or elaborate rituals. God is not impressed by what someone used to call 'rites and robes, bells and smells'. A religious performance is not the same as a spiritual experience. God speaks in scathing terms of those who 'honour me with their lips, but their hearts are far from me',[32] leading the American preacher Donald Grey Barnhouse to claim, 'God hates the sanctimonious hallelujah more than he hates the godless curse.'[33] All hypocrisy is corrupt, but religious hypocrisy is contemptible. True worship takes place only when believing men and women approach God honestly, wholeheartedly and submissively.

God is eternally self-existent

God's existence is underived and independent, two related truths which alone would be sufficient to establish his deity. The first says that he is eternal; the Bible speaks of him as 'the eternal God'[34] who is 'from everlasting to everlasting',[35] and God reveals himself as the one 'who is, and who was, and who is to come'.[36] There was never a time when God did not exist, and there will never be a time when he will not exist. He created time, and is not constrained by it in any way. His life does not consist of a succession of days, weeks, months and years — not even an endless succession of them. He is uniquely uncreated; he was not brought into existence by any power or person. In the words of the third-century scholar Novatian of Rome, 'God is beyond origin.'[37]

This concept is totally foreign to us, as on a day-to-day basis we tend to think only in terms of beginnings and ends. Yet Einstein's law of relativity has shown us that time can be altered; when objects travel at extremely high speeds, time can be slowed down or speeded up. We can no longer cling to the old idea that everything originates and operates within what we once thought were the fixed limits of time and space. God's underived existence (the technical term is 'aseity') contradicts no known law of logic or reason, unless we imagine that all living beings must be creatures like ourselves. C. S. Lewis makes the point by saying of God, 'He is not "universal being"; if he were there would be no creatures, for a generality can make nothing. He is "absolute being" — or rather *the* Absolute Being — in the sense that he exists in his own right.'[38]

As we noted in chapter 13, one of the fundamental laws of nature says *Ex nihilo, nihil fit* ('Out of nothing, nothing comes') but the finite laws of nature cannot govern an infinite, eternally self-existent God. To ask, 'Who made God?' posits the answer that there must be someone or something greater than God, yet this would solve nothing, but simply push the question further back. Yet however far back we go, we cannot escape the need for an uncreated Creator. Peter Kreeft and Ronald Tacelli make another important point: 'The question "If God made everything, who made God?" is like asking "Who made circles square?" It assumes a self-contradiction: that the uncreated Creator is a created creature. It extends the law about changing things — that every change needs a cause — beyond its limits, to the unchanging Source of change. God does not need a cause, or a maker, because he is not made or changed. He changes other things, but is not himself changed by anything. There is nothing that comes to be in him, nothing that needs a cause for its coming-into-being.'[39]

God is not only underived, he is completely independent. Every other living being in the universe is dependent on people or things, and ultimately on God, but God is totally independent of his creation: 'He is not served by human hands, as if he needed anything, because he himself gives all men life and breath and everything else.'[40] God has no needs, as we understand them. He can survive on his own. As John Stott insists, 'It is absurd ... to suppose that he who sustains life should himself need to be sustained, that he who supplies our need should himself need our supply. Any attempt to tame or domesticate God, to reduce him to the level of a household pet ... is ... ridiculous.'[41]

God is transcendent

The doctrine of God's transcendence tells us that he is <u>over and above time, space and all finite reality.</u> The Bible says not only that he is 'great, mighty and awesome',[42] but that he is 'exalted as head over all'[43] and that his paths are 'beyond tracing out'.[44]

When the American golfer Tiger Woods spread-eagled the field in the 1997 United States Masters with the greatest winning margin in the history of the tournament, he light-heartedly acknowledged the help of 'the big guy in the sky', while others sometimes speak of God as 'the man upstairs', but the biblical doctrine of God's transcendence means something infinitely more. It tells us that God is distinct and separate from the entire universe and from everything in it. He can no more be confined to space than he can be measured by time: in the Bible's own words, he is the one whom 'the heavens, even the highest heaven, cannot contain'.[45]

This is not to say that God is located somewhere 'away' from the world in remote isolation. Transcendence does not mean remoteness; it means 'otherness'. God is essentially something 'other' than everything else, a higher order of being than any other being in the universe, the absolute in regard to which all else is relative. The Bible records God as telling his people:

> For my thoughts are not your thoughts,
>   neither are your ways my ways...
> As the heavens are higher than the earth,
>   so are my ways higher than your ways
>   and my thoughts than your thoughts.[46]

He cannot be limited by anything else, because he brought everything else into being.

God is immanent

The word 'immanent' comes from the Latin *in* (in) and *manere* (to remain), and theologians use it to convey the fact that, <u>although he is not to be identified with his creation (as in pantheism) God, as an infinite spirit, is present in every part of it.</u> The Bible expresses this in a number of ways. God himself states, 'Do not I fill heaven and earth?'[47] David asks God:

> Where can I go from your Spirit?
>> Where can I flee from your presence?
> If I go up to the heavens, you are there;
>> if I make my bed in the depths, you are there.[48]

Paul reminds his audience at Athens that 'In him we live and move and have our being.'[49]

Contrary to the deists' notion of an absentee landlord, God actively permeates the entire universe, every nook and cranny of it. He is not statically confined to any one place at a time, but is dynamically everywhere at all times. Augustine saw God as 'an infinite circle whose centre is everywhere and whose circumference is nowhere',[50] while C. S. Lewis said, 'If God — such a God as any adult religion believes in — exists, mere movement in space will never bring you any nearer to him or any further from him than you are at this very moment. You can neither reach him nor avoid him by travelling to Alpha Centauri or even to other galaxies. A fish is no more, and no less, in the sea after it has swum a thousand miles than it was when it set out.'[51] A sense of what the seventeenth-century theologian Stephen Charnock called 'God's influential presence'[52] has been of great encouragement and strength to millions of believers throughout human history; on the other hand, anyone thinking that God is safely out of range is making a fundamental and ultimately fatal mistake.

God is omniscient

The Bible establishes God's omniscience in a number of ways. It says not only that he is 'a God who knows',[53] but that he is 'perfect in knowledge'.[54] Using one of the analogies we came across earlier, it says that 'The eyes of

the LORD are everywhere.'[55] Pulling these and other biblical statements together, we see that God's knowledge is timeless, immediate and total.
Whereas we learn one thing after another, and need to retrieve or recall
information in order to have it at our immediate disposal, this is not the
case with God. He never has to learn or remember anything. What is
more, nothing takes him by surprise; as far as God is concerned, there is
never an unexpected event around the corner. His knowledge embraces
eternity as well as time. There is nothing for him to discover.

The Bible repeatedly emphasizes one practical facet of God's omniscience — his total knowledge of human experience and behaviour,
thoughts as well as words, intentions as well as actions. The Old Testament
says that God's eyes are open to 'all the ways of men',[56] while the New
Testament is even more emphatic: 'Nothing in all creation is hidden from
God's sight. Everything is uncovered and laid bare before the eyes of him
to whom we must give account.'[57] The phrase 'laid bare' is based on the
Greek *trachelos* ('neck'), which has an interesting history, including its use
in criminal trials, when a dagger was fixed, point upwards, just below the
neck of the accused, forcing the person concerned to face the court and
look straight into the judge's eyes. The Bible's use of this particular word
tells us that there is never a moment of privacy from God, and that no set
of circumstances can provide cover from his gaze.

During the first week in Lent each year, many people in Basle, Switzer-
land, abandon their moral inhibitions in the carnival of *Fastnacht* and, as
the revellers all wear masks, it is difficult to know who is kicking over the
traces with whom. In an attempt to counter this loose behaviour, the local
Salvation Army places posters around the city announcing *Gott sieht hinter
deine Maske* ('God sees behind your mask'), words reflecting the Bible's
statement that 'A man's ways are in full view of the LORD, and he examines
all his paths.'[58] Our past, present and future, our thoughts, words and deeds,
our attitudes, ambitions, hopes and fears are all an open book to the one
who says, 'I the LORD search the heart and examine the mind.'[59] Nor does
God's knowledge of us begin at birth: God told Jeremiah, 'Before I formed
you in the womb I knew you.'[60]

God is immutable

The biblical doctrine of God's immutability tells us that his character and
purposes are not subject to change of any kind. Whereas we live in an

ever-changing universe, surrounded by nature which is always in a state of flux, and find ourselves being continuously moulded and matured by experience, God says, 'I the LORD do not change.'[61] His character is absolutely constant, for the simple reason that no greater power can be brought to bear upon him so as to effect change of any kind, nor can his purposes ever be frustrated or deflected.

To say that God is immutable is not to say that he is inactive. God is not the metaphysical equivalent of a concrete block. On the contrary, Scripture reveals a vigorous, energetic and dynamic God who performs 'great and awesome deeds'[62] (of which holding the universe in place is just one). His immutability speaks not of inaction, but of his constancy, consistency and dependability; in the Bible's words, he 'does not change like shifting shadows'.[63] Among other things, this means that every one of God's promises, warnings and commands are geared to what the Bible calls 'the unchanging nature of his purpose'.[64]

God is holy

At a critical moment in his nation's history, and in his own life, the prophet Isaiah had a vision of heaven in which he saw God 'seated on a throne, high and exalted' and surrounded by angels crying:

> Holy, holy, holy is the LORD Almighty;
> the whole earth is full of his glory.[65]

In the last book in the Bible the apostle John also records a vision of heaven in which God's throne is surrounded by celestial beings calling out:

> Holy, holy, holy
> is the LORD God Almighty,
> who was, and is, and is to come.[66]

The repetition of the word 'holy' was a common Jewish form of emphasis, but these are the only places in Scripture in which we find the same word repeated twice. The significance of this is underlined by the fact that of all the words used to speak of God's attributes, 'holy' is used more than any other.

The Bible uses the word 'holy' in two senses. The primary meaning relates to ideas such as 'separateness' or 'otherness'. When used of God, it indicates one who is in a class of his own, uniquely majestic, glorious and awe-inspiring. To speak of God's holiness in this way is virtually the same as to speak of his transcendence. J. I. Packer says, 'The basic thought that the word carries is of God's separateness from us and of the contrast between what he is and what we are,'[67] while John Piper elaborates: 'The holiness of God is the absolutely unique, infinite value of his majestic glory. To say that our God is holy means that he is beautiful beyond degree in the magnificence of his glory, and that his value is infinitely greater than the sum of the value of all created things.'[68] In this use of the word, the holiness of God is synonymous with his infinite glory, something which is beyond human understanding and influence. C. S. Lewis maintained, 'A man can no more diminish God's glory by refusing to worship him than a lunatic can put out the sun by scribbling the word *darkness* on the walls of his cell.'[69]

The Bible also speaks of God as being holy in the ethical sense of the word. Time and again he is called 'the Holy One';[70] his eyes are said to be 'too pure to look on evil';[71] he 'cannot tolerate wrong';[72] his 'right hand is filled with righteousness';[73] 'God is light: in him is no darkness at all.'[74] These and related statements in Scripture tell us that God is morally impeccable; in Bruce Milne's words, 'His very being is the outshining and outpouring of purity, truth, righteousness, justice, goodness and every moral perfection.'[75]

Unlike all other beings, God has no moral flaws, weaknesses, blemishes, shortcomings or disabilities. Simply put, 'There is no one holy like the LORD.'[76] He is 'majestic in holiness'.[77] The nineteenth-century American theologian James Boyce called God's holiness 'the sum of all excellence and the combination of all the attributes which constitute perfection of character'.[78]

The moral perfection of God's character forms the basis of all moral distinctions. As John Benton says, 'God's own character is the fundamental basis for what is right and just. He is the holy God who is the foundation of all creation. His character is what is right and good, and all that offends against the holy character of God is therefore wrong, and wrong in the most absolute sense.'[79] God's character is what enables us to say that we live in a moral world. In morality (as in everything else) Protagoras' 'Man, the measure' must give way to 'God the measure'.

God is loving

It has been suggested that 'God is love'[80] is 'probably the greatest single statement about God in the Bible',[81] and it is not difficult to see why this has been said, as the theme of God's love permeates Scripture from cover to cover. Even if we ignored sixty-five of the Bible's sixty-six books, and confined ourselves to the Psalms, we would read about God's 'great love'[82] and his 'unfailing love'.[83] We would be told that he is 'abounding in love'[84] and reminded over thirty times that his love 'endures for ever'.[85] We would read that God was 'gracious and compassionate',[86] and that his love is expressed in his 'many kindnesses'[87] and his 'unfailing kindness',[88] and we would hear one of the psalmists ask, 'How can I repay the LORD for all his goodness to me?'[89]

Yet we need to recognize that 'God is love' says much more than 'God loves', as if loving was just one of his many activities. 'God is love' tells us that his essential nature is love, that love is of his very essence. 'God is love' was true before there was anyone or anything in creation for him to love. God's love is an eternal attribute which inheres in his Trinitarian being. The Father loves the Son and the Holy Spirit, the Son loves the Father and the Holy Spirit, and the Holy Spirit loves the Father and the Son. The 'threeness' of God is at the very heart of the statement, 'God is love,' and tells us that God is not a forlorn or lonely being who needs anything he creates as an object of his love.

This leads to the truth that *all* of God's actions are loving, even those which seem to our finite minds to be the reverse. The depth and breadth of God's love are utterly beyond our limited human understanding. J. I. Packer calls God's love his 'cosmic generosity',[90] yet it is specifically linked to his free, spontaneous, sovereign purpose to bring people into a living and eternal relationship with himself as members of his family. Those who experience God's love in this way can join one of the New Testament writers in exclaiming, 'How great is the love the Father has lavished on us, that we should be called children of God!'[91]

God's loving nature explains the very existence of love in human relationships. In *The Selfish Gene*, Richard Dawkins admits, 'Much as we may wish to believe otherwise, universal love and the welfare of the species as a whole are concepts which simply do not make evolutionary sense,'[92] but the Bible pinpoints their divine origin by stating, 'We love because he first loved us.'[93] The only logical basis for human love is one which has an inherently loving Godhead as the driving force behind the universe. John Benton is not overstating the case when he says that 'Without God there is no rationale for love.'[94]

If 'God is love' has a claim to being the Bible's greatest single statement about God, it is also one of the most misunderstood. Many misinterpret it to mean that God is a 'soft touch', a benevolent father-figure with a re-laxed attitude about beliefs and behaviour, a kindly carer who is long on pardon and short on punishment. This supposes that God's love in some way overrides his other attributes, and especially his holiness, but this is wishful thinking and is fundamentally flawed, as God's holiness is the sum total of all his moral perfections. In his superb book *Knowing God*, J. I. Packer writes, 'The God who is love is first and foremost light, and senti-mental ideas of his love as an indulgent, benevolent softness, divorced from moral standards and concerns, must therefore be ruled out from the start. God's love is a holy love.'[95] We shall see some of the implications of this shortly.

God is Creator

The Bible's opening words could not be simpler, nor could they be more inclusive: 'In the beginning God created the heavens and the earth.'[96] As the Hebrews had no single word to describe the universe, the phrase *hassamayim we'et ha'ares* ('the heavens and the earth') was the one they used to speak of all reality. As the American scholar Douglas Kelly explains, '"The heavens and the earth" is a way of saying "everything that exists", whether galaxies, nebulae or solar systems, all things from the farthest reaches of outer space to the smallest grain of sand or bacterial microbe on planet earth.'[97] Quoting the Nicene Creed's affirmation that God is 'the Creator of all things', Kelly goes on to say, '"All things" include the various ranks of angels, and every form of life, from whales to elephants to viruses. "All things" include every form of energy and matter; the speed of light, nuclear structure, electromagnetism and gravity, and all the laws by which nature operates.'[98]

Words recorded by the Old Testament writer Nehemiah typify the way in which the Bible frequently expresses the totality of God's creation: 'You alone are the LORD. You made the heavens, even the highest heavens, and all their starry host, the earth and all that is in it, the seas and all that is in them.'[99] The stupendous scope of God's creation may be reflected in what comes across (at least in its English translation) as an understatement: at one point in the Genesis creation narrative we read, 'He also made the stars,'[100] rather as we might slip in, 'By the way ...' A writer of fiction, anxious to impress his readers, might not be expected to gloss over billions of stars and millions of galaxies in just five words!

In the clearest possible way, the Bible tells us that God is the uncreated Creator of everything else, and its opening words, 'In the beginning...', tell us that not even time is excluded. Time as we understand it was brought into being by God just as certainly as he created space and matter. Once upon a time there was no time. 'In the beginning' marks the emergence of time out of eternity. Over fifteen centuries ago Augustine wrote, 'It is idle to look for a time before creation, as if time can be found before time. If there were no motion of either a spiritual or corporal creature, by which the future moving through the present would succeed the past, there would be no time at all. A creature could not move if it did not exist. We should, therefore, say that time began with creation rather than that creation began with time. Both are from God. For from him and through him and in him are all things.'[101] God is the sovereign Creator and Controller of time. He brought time as we know it into being and will eventually bring it to an end, when the temporal present will give way to the infinite future of 'the age to come'.[102]

Before going any further, we must avoid any distortion of the majestically simple words of the first sentence in Genesis. God did not create the universe out of any kind of pre-existing substance. Whereas we make things by shaping existing materials, theologians rightly speak of God creating everything *ex nihilo*. While the phrase 'out of nothing' is not actually found in the Bible, the idea of creation *ex nihilo* certainly is: 'The universe was formed at God's command, so that what is seen was not made out of what was visible.'[103] Nor was 'nothing' some kind of negative entity which God overcame to bring into being what we know as concrete reality: 'nothing' means exactly what it says. Nor did God make the world out of himself, as a cosmic extension of his own being. God is original and uncreated, and does not exist in the same way as the world. Instead, as H. R. Rookmaaker puts it, '[God] is the Creator of that world, of all that exists, the Maker of existence itself.'[104] In the Bible's own words, 'God is the builder of everything.'[105]

As we might expect, the Bible is more concerned with questions of meaning than mechanism. For example, it does not give us a detailed explanation of *how* creation took place. Instead, it merely says of the universe and everything in it, 'The LORD ... commanded and they were created.'[106] Some theists see this as contradicting the Big Bang theory as presently understood, but others see no conflict here between science and Scripture. In *Thinking Clearly about God and Science*, David Wilkinson, a Fellow of the Royal Astronomical Society, sees the Big Bang theory as '*currently* the best model we have which describes how God did it', and goes on to say, 'Genesis 1 complements that description with the fundamental truth that the purpose, the source of order and faithfulness of the Universe can only be found in this Creator God.'[107] The word I have emphasized is important!

Nor does the Bible tell us *when* creation took place. In *As You Like It*, William Shakespeare wrote, 'This poor world is almost 6,000 years old,'[108] but the most famous estimate of the earth's age was made by the Irish scholar James Ussher, who became Bishop of Armagh in 1625. Working on the basis of somewhat complicated genealogies and other Old Testament data, Ussher came to the conclusion that creation took place in 4004 B.C. His 'guesstimation' became so widely accepted that by the end of the nineteenth century most English Bibles put Ussher's date in the margin opposite the opening verse of Genesis. In 1825, the Cambridge scholar John Lightfoot fine-tuned things by saying that the first human being was created at 9 a.m. on 23 October 4004 B.C., a speculation which led someone to comment drily that, as a careful scholar, Lightfoot was unable to commit himself further than that!

The massive gap between the positions of those who say that the earth is millions of years old and those who claim that a straightforward reading of Scripture teaches an earth only about ten thousand years old at most is impossible to dissolve, and Ian Taylor notes that each of the popular attempts to reconcile Genesis with science on this issue 'mixes more or less science with more or less Scripture and produces a result more or less absurd'.[109] The issue is well discussed elsewhere;[110] here, we need only recognize that the Bible's specific focus is not on a precise chronology but on the comprehensive fact that 'God ... made heaven and earth and sea and everything in them.'[111] God is the Author of everything (which means, incidentally, that he is the *true* origin of species).

While the age of the earth is not our prime concern at this point, the Bible *is* clear on an even more radical issue, the reason why there should be a universe at all. Stephen Hawking raises the subject towards the end of *A Brief History of Time*: 'Up to now, most scientists have been too occupied with the development of new theories that describe *what* the universe is to ask the question *why*. On the other hand, the people whose business it is to ask *why*, the philosophers, have not been able to keep up with the advance of scientific theories.'[112] He then goes on to say that if we should ever discover why we and the universe exist, 'it would be the ultimate triumph of reason — for then we would know the mind of God'.[113] The Bible provides this precise answer to the ultimate question Hawking raises:

You are worthy, our LORD and God,
    to receive glory and honour and power,
for you created all things,
    and *by your will* they were created...[114] (emphasis added).

This tells us that God did not create because he had to, but because he chose to. It also implies that nothing in creation needs any justification beyond the fact that in his infinite wisdom God willed it to be, and in his infinite power brought it into being. The universe exists to reflect the majesty of its Creator, whose free, independent and sovereign will is the originating cause of all things: 'By the word of the LORD were the heavens made, their starry host by the breath of his mouth.'[115] There is confirmation of this at the end of the creation narrative, where we are told, 'God saw all that he had made, and it was very good.'[116] God called creation 'good', not because he made it, but because it conformed to his wishes and reflected his perfect nature.

Atheists protest that a creationist world-view is a matter of faith, *but so is any approach to reality which dispenses with God.* Limited as it is to what is observable, measurable and repeatable, science alone can never get at the ultimate facts, while philosophy has come up with so many unsatisfying (and often contradictory) notions that C. S. Lewis came to the conclusion: 'No philosophical theory which I have yet come across is a radical improvement on the words of Genesis, that "In the beginning God made heaven and earth".'[117] Although there are some theists who believe that creation by a self-existent and eternal Being is philosophically demonstrable, the Bible settles for this: '*By faith* we understand that the universe was formed at God's command.'[118]

As a card-carrying atheist, Richard Dawkins dismisses this out of hand and ranks the Bible's teaching with the Hindu myth about the world being created in a cosmic butter-churn and the West African notion that the world was created from the excrement of ants. In a 1996 television programme he claimed, 'It has no more status than hundreds, thousands of creation myths around the world,'[119] but he is clearly unqualified to make such a statement and his myopic view is widely rejected. According to science historian Frederic Burnham, many scientists are coming to consider God's creation of the universe 'a more respectable hypothesis today than at any time in the last 100 years'.[120]

not read yet ↕ ## God is Ruler

The most succinct biblical statement of this is the declaration, 'The LORD reigns,'[121] words which tell us that God rules as King in the most absolute sense of the word. As R. C. Sproul indicates, God's sovereignty is essential to his essence: 'The moment we negotiate on this point, or dilute the concept of sovereignty, we are playing around with God's character... If God is not sovereign, God is not God.'[122]

The Bible makes it clear that God's reign takes in all reality. He rules over the lives of individual human beings: 'Many are the plans in a man's heart, but it is the LORD's purpose that prevails.'[123] He rules over all earthly authorities: 'The king's heart is in the hand of the LORD; he directs it like a watercourse wherever he pleases.'[124] He rules over international affairs: 'Dominion belongs to the LORD and he rules over the nations.'[125] He rules over the natural world: 'The LORD is exalted over all the nations, his glory above the heavens.'[126] He rules over the spiritual world: he is 'far above all rule and authority, power and dominion, and every title that can be given, not only in the present age but also in the one to come'.[127] God's reign could not be more comprehensive: 'His kingdom rules over all.'[128] The nineteenth-century American theologian John Dagg got it absolutely right when he wrote, 'He has everything in the universe under his immediate and perfect control.'[129]

This revelation of God's sovereignty is vastly different from the deists' idea of God, which has been well illustrated by Russell Stannard, Professor of Physics at the Open University: 'They regard God as the divine groundsman who prepares the cricket pitch, marks it out, cuts the grass and erects the stumps. But then, having done his bit, he retires to the pavilion for the duration of the match.'[130] This does not remotely resemble the God of the Bible, who is active, not passive, a 'hands-on' ruler, not an unconcerned spectator. What is more, his kingdom is not a democracy. He does not rule by referendum, set up sub-committees, or consult focus groups before making decisions or taking action. He needs no advice or consent for anything he chooses to do, nor can anyone prevent him from doing exactly as he pleases: 'No one can hold back his hand or say to him: "What have you done?"'[131] Instead, he 'works out everything in conformity with the purpose of his will'.[132] God is a law unto himself, he rules over everything and everyone, and is under no obligation to account for anything he does. Peter Moore is right to say, 'History is "his story" and, in an unfathomable combination of divine sovereignty and human will, God is the master chess-player, moving his chessmen forward and back in anticipation of the final moment when all that opposes him will be checkmated and his reign will be universally recognized.'[133]

Such sovereignty presupposes unimaginable power, which the Bible attributes to God, either directly or indirectly, on virtually every page. The clearest evidence of this is the fact that titles such as 'the LORD God Almighty' are used by him or given to him nearly 350 times.[134] The Septuagint, the first Greek translation of the Old Testament, rendered the Hebrew word for 'Almighty' as *pantokrator*, from *pas* (all) and *kratos* (power, strength, dominion). It was the perfect word to reflect God's omnipotence, which is underlined by his own rhetorical question: 'I am the LORD, the God of all mankind. Is anything too hard for me?'[135]

God does have one radical limitation, which is that he cannot do anything inconsistent with his own nature. The Bible gives two clear examples of this, saying that 'It is impossible for God to lie,'[136] and that 'He cannot disown himself,'[137] but there must obviously be other qualifications to our understanding of God's omnipotence. As his power must necessarily be consistent with his perfection, it clearly excludes things which are self-contradictory. For example, God is unable to draw anything shorter than a straight line between two points, to determine that something is both right and wrong at the same time, or to make an object that is both circular and square. The hoary chestnut, 'Can God make a rock so heavy that he would be incapable of lifting it?' can be ignored for the same kind of reason. Nor can God change the past. Not even God can make Napoleon win the Battle of Waterloo in 1815, John F. Kennedy lose his 1960 bid for the presidency of the United States, or England win football's World Cup in 1998, or cricket's equivalent in 1999. Yet these limitations in no way affect the Bible's insistence that God 'rules for ever by his power'.[138]

God is Judge

God's role as the Judge of all mankind is in harmony with the fact that the Bible reveals his wrath as well as his love. In the Old Testament alone, more than twenty different Hebrew words, spread over nearly 600 important passages, are used to express God's wrath, and A. W. Pink is not exaggerating when he points out, 'There are more references in Scripture to the anger, fury and wrath of God than there are to his love and tenderness.'[139] Many people find this difficult or impossible to accept, as it seems to offer a God who blows hot and cold as the mood takes him, but this kind of thinking fails to understand that God's anger is not to be confused with temper, pique or irritation and that it is never arbitrary or unjustified. When the Bible speaks of God's anger it uses words which show it to be the necessary, consistent and personal reaction of his holiness, what the Welsh theologian Eryl Davies calls 'the controlled and permanent opposition of God's holy nature to all sin'.[140] R. C. Sproul rightly says that if people would think soberly for five seconds they would realize their error in imagining that God is not a God of holy anger: 'If God is holy at all, if God has an ounce of justice in his character, indeed if God exists as God, how could he possibly be anything else but angry with us? We violate his holiness, we insult his justice, we make light of his grace. These things can hardly be pleasing to him... But a God of love who has no wrath is no God. He is an idol of our own making, as much as if we carved him out of stone.'[141] Simply put, without God's anger against evil, he would cease to be holy, and his love would degenerate into sentimentality.

As far as sin of any kind is concerned, God has zero tolerance. He makes no exceptions, cuts no deals and sweeps nothing under the carpet. Nor is he turning a blind eye while humanity as a whole ignores or sidelines him: 'God is a righteous judge, a God who expresses his wrath every day.'[142] This tells us that although he is 'a forgiving God, gracious and compassionate, slow to anger and abounding in love',[143] his anger is operating in the world here and now. There have been devastating examples of this in natural disasters (how interesting that they are sometimes called 'acts of God'!) while, at a personal and individual level, minds are darkened, perspectives distorted, perceptions dulled, spiritual awareness reduced and characters debased as people (mostly without knowing it) suffer the consequences of their godless lifestyles.

Yet nothing the Bible says about the way God expresses his righteous anger against sin in the present world lessens the reality of what it calls 'the coming wrath',[144] a day of universal and final reckoning, when the God who brought mankind into being calls every member of the human race before the bar of his awesome justice. Nothing in Scripture is clearer than this. One New Testament writer says that 'Man is destined to die once, and after that to face judgement.'[145] Another says that 'Each of us will give an account of himself to God,'[146] and warns, 'Do not be deceived: God is not mocked. A man reaps what he sows.'[147]

At this point, many people find themselves wrestling with two conflicting ideas. In the first place, they realize that the concept of accountability is built into the very fabric of human life. The British preacher David Watson rightly noted, 'The whole fabric of society would collapse without it,' and went on to ask, 'Why should there be anything odd about the fact that a created being must give account of his life to his Creator? It is plain common sense.'[148] Without a perfect and final judgement, moral values are rendered meaningless, and there are simply too many loose ends, something which leads J. I. Packer to claim, 'No man is entirely without inklings of judgement to come.'[149]

However, many people find it impossible to square the idea of eternal punishment with the concept of a God whose love is said to pervade everything he does. They find themselves going along with liberal theologians like John Hick, who said that such an action would be 'totally incompatible with the idea of a God as infinite love',[150] and C. H. Dodd, who claimed, 'In the end, no member of the human race is left outside the scope of salvation.'[151]

Not surprisingly, such universalism is hugely popular. It fits perfectly with today's easygoing attitude to personal morality, and its reluctance to get to grips with ultimate spiritual issues. As John Robinson wrote in 1969,

'We live, in this twentieth century, in a world without judgement, a world where at the last frontier post you simply go out — and nothing happens. It is like coming to the Customs and finding there are none after all. And the suspicion that this is in fact the case spreads fast; for it is what we should all like to believe.'[152] For many people, our future meeting with God is seen as some kind of celestial prize-giving, from which nobody leaves empty-handed. When the notorious British criminal Ronnie Kray, a violent psychopath and pervert, died in prison in 1995, the *Daily Mail's* Rosemary Anne Sisson assured her readers, 'His sins — and there were many — were forgiven in the moment he met God.' A few weeks later, when the British entertainer Kenny Everett, a practising homosexual famous for his smutty humour, died of an AIDS-related disease, the minister at his funeral said, 'He will be a very welcome guest in heaven.' This may have gone down well at the time, but the idea that God automatically wipes the slate clean at death and welcomes everyone into his holy and eternal presence, regardless of their earthly beliefs and behaviour, conflicts radically with Scripture, where we read that 'The LORD is a God of justice,'[153] that 'Right-eousness and justice are the foundation of his throne,'[154] and that 'He has set a day when he will judge the world with justice.'[155] For some, that day will lead to an eternity of unimaginable and uninterrupted joy, where there will be 'no more death or mourning or crying or pain'.[156] For all others, it will lead to an eternity of uninterrupted 'torment'[157] and 'agony',[158] where God's wrath will be 'poured out like fire'.[159] There is no alternative destiny, and nobody will be able to avoid the moment of truth, when every one of us must appear before 'the Judge of all the earth'.[160] Trying to avoid God is an exercise in catastrophic futility, and J. I. Packer is right to say, 'As our Maker, he owns us and, as our Owner, he has a right to dispose of us.'[161]

Before turning to what the Bible says about man, we need to summar-ize the specific ways in which its doctrine of God conflicts with the secular philosophies, religions and cults we reviewed in earlier chapters. As God's uniqueness implies his existence, this alone rules out nihilism, naturalism, materialism, the atheistic brands of rationalism, existentialism and deter-minism, and atheistic religions such as Confucianism and Taoism. His uniqueness also precludes animism, polytheism (including Hinduism and Shinto) as well as dualistic religions such as Zoroastrianism; it is also in direct conflict with the bizarre mishmash of ideas promoted by the New Age Movement. The personhood of God (to say nothing of his 'threeness') rules out the ancient philosophy of monism, which says that all reality consists of one basic, impersonal stuff or essence. It is also incompatible with Buddhism and Sikhism and with what is taught by the Church of Scientology. The single statement, 'God is spirit,' demolishes pantheism, which says that God is everything and everything is God, and in so doing it sweeps aside a raft of pantheistic cults including Christian Science, Divine Light, EST, Hare Krishna, the Rajneesh Foundation, the Theosophical Society, TM, the Unification Church, Unity and Yoga. It also outlaws Mormonism, which teaches that God has a material body. The Bible's Trinitarian teaching flatly contradicts Islam, while 'God is love' goes far beyond the Islamic concept of Allah and anything taught in Baha'ism. Finally, the Bible's teaching on God's personhood and his judgement of humanity is a far cry from the ideas promoted by the Jehovah's Witnesses.

The Bible's doctrine of God is as distinctive as its own credentials.

21.
Nothing but the truth – II

In the early part of his *Institutes of the Christian Religion*, John Calvin underlined the merit of the motto, 'Know yourself,' which we mentioned at the beginning of the previous chapter. He wrote, 'With good reason the ancient proverb strongly recommended knowledge of self to man. For if it is considered disgraceful for us not to know all that pertains to the business of human life, even more detestable is our ignorance of ourselves, by which, when making decisions in necessary matters, we miserably deceive and even blind ourselves!'[1]

The jewel in the crown

As we have seen, centuries of atheistic and agnostic thinkers have taken up the Greeks' challenge and suggested wagonloads of perspectives on the human race. Many of these were based on materialism, naturalism and determinism, in which man is seen as an animated machine which mysteriously came into existence for no intelligent reason and with no meaningful future. Jacques Monod spoke for many of them when he wrote, 'Man at last knows that he is alone in the unfeeling immensity of the universe, out of which he emerged only by chance. Neither his destiny nor his duty have been laid down.'[2]

The Bible paints a very different picture, saying that humankind is the jewel in the crown of God's creation. There are clear pointers to this in the first chapter of Genesis. In referring to the origin of things, the writer uses two Hebrew verbs, *bara'* (usually translated 'create') and *'asah* (usually translated 'make'). As far as our present subject is concerned, the significant thing is that *bara'* is used of just three distinct events — the first existence of matter ('God *created* the heavens and the earth'),[3] the first existence of conscious life ('God *created* ... creatures')[4] and the first existence of human life ('God *created* man').[5]

The British scholar E. F. Kevan showed that *bara'* stands 'exclusively for the act of divine production which brings into existence something entirely new'.[6] This obviously makes it the right word to use of the creation of 'the heavens and the earth' *ex nihilo*, and bringing conscious life into existence is clearly another distinct stage in the overall creation narrative, while the third use of *bara'* separates the creation of man from the previous two stages. As Kevan goes on to say, *bara'* does not necessarily exclude existing materials — we are told in Genesis 2 that 'The Lord God formed man from the dust of the ground'[7] — but it does point to 'the achievement of something completely new, *and without any causal relationship to preceding agencies*'.[8] This makes *bara'* exactly the right word to use of the separate, 'instantaneous' creation of humankind as an entirely new order of being, whereas it sits awkwardly with the idea that over the course of millions of years man gradually evolved from other, more primitive species.

We find in Genesis 1 three other powerful indications that human beings are radically superior to the rest of creation. The first is the dominion God gave them over the natural world: 'Be fruitful and increase in number; fill the earth and subdue it. Rule over the fish of the sea and the birds of the air and over every living creature that moves on the ground.'[9] Those who equate human beings with animals in terms of status and rights collide head-on with Scripture, which tells us that God has placed man on a higher level altogether and 'put everything under his feet'.[10]

Woven into this derived authority over the earth is the responsibility to 'work it and take care of it'.[11] This so-called 'dominion mandate' makes it clear that the natural world is not to be treated as if it were some kind of divinity, nor raised to such a status that man loses his distinctive significance, nor ruthlessly ravaged for short-term material gain. Instead, as Douglas Kelly confirms, 'The dominion mandate of Genesis teaches man both to respect and to subdue nature so as to shape it in a direction that will reflect the beauty, order and glory of its Creator.'[12] Simply put, this means that man is a steward, given the responsibility of carrying out his Maker's wishes and taking care of his Master's property.

The second indication of humankind's superiority is the way in which the creation of the first human beings is given such an emphasis by the repetition of the word *bara'* at one particular point:

So God *created* man
   in his own image,
in the image of God
   he *created* him;
  male and female
   he *created* them [13] (emphasis added).

This kind of emphasis occurs nowhere else in the entire creation narrative, and it is difficult to escape the impression that the writer is describing an event of greater significance than anything else in his story. Francis Schaeffer suggests that by repeating the word 'created', 'it is as though God put exclamation points here to indicate that there is something special about the creation of man'.[14]

The third indication is even stronger: 'God created man *in his own image.*' The Bible nowhere spells out in so many words what this means, but Schaeffer is right to say that man is 'created to relate to God in a way that none of the other created beings are'.[15] As God is spirit, and has no physical or material properties, being made in his image has nothing to do with size, weight, shape, or any other kind of concrete calculation. Nevertheless, the Bible insists that being made in the image of God means to be like him in certain respects, something not said of anything else in the entire created order. Likeness to God gives mankind what Douglas Kelly calls 'the highest possible spiritual, transcendent reference'.[16]

The American theologian Samuel Waldron reminds us that 'Everything that makes man man is involved in his being the image of God.'[17] What this means was spelled out in earlier chapters, but we should underline some of the main features here. Primarily, to be made in God's image or 'likeness' means to have personality, to have powers of thought, feeling and will which go far beyond the brute instincts of purely animal life. In James Montgomery Boice's words, 'To say that an animal possesses something akin to human personality is meaningful only to a point. Personality, in the sense that we are speaking of it here, is something that links humanity to God but does not link either humanity or God to the rest of creation.'[18] Creation in the image of God distinguishes man from all other life-forms. He has a unique level of intelligence, an ability to reason and an acutely self-conscious capacity to evaluate himself. He has a conscience, an ability to recognize ethical values, to distinguish between right and wrong, and to make moral choices, rather than act by blind or irrational instinct.

He has a capacity to love and to be loved in personal, social relationships; as John Calvin put it, 'Man was formed to be a social animal'[19] (and in this way to mirror the Trinity). He can express himself in language, something which can never be accounted for by evolution and which implies that God created us to communicate with each other and with him. Above all, man is a unity of body and soul. He has a spiritual dimension, a unique capacity to relate to God, to worship him and to live in fellowship with him. The Bible is hardly exaggerating when it says that we are 'fearfully and wonderfully made'.[20]

The Bible's definition of man as being made 'in the image of God' is the clinching reason for his sense of dignity. Without this, one is hard put to see how we can claim that a human being has any more dignity than a donkey. Francis Schaeffer elaborates: 'No matter who I look at, no matter where he is, every man is created in the image of God as much as I am. So the Bible tells me who I am. It tells me how I am differentiated from all other things. I do not need to be confused, therefore, between myself and animal life or between myself and the complicated machines of the second half of the twentieth century. Suddenly I have value, and I understand how it is that I am different. I understand how it is that God can have fellowship with me and give me revelation of a propositional nature... Any man, no matter who he is ... is made after the likeness of God. A man is of great value not for some less basic reason but *because of his origin*'[21] (emphasis added).

Disaster

Man came into being with a perfect moral and spiritual nature. He was what Samuel Waldron calls 'the animate or living visible replica of God'.[22] He was not merely innocent, or in a morally 'neutral' state, but positively good; we are specifically told that 'God made mankind upright.'[23] However, man's 'true righteousness and holiness'[24] were not set in concrete. He was not created as a robot, but as a morally responsible agent able to exercise free will, and with his inclinations open to development or deterioration. For some time (the Bible gives no clue as to how long a period) man gladly chose to render God unqualified obedience, as a result of which faultless people lived in a flawless environment in a perfect relationship with each other and in complete harmony with their Maker. God's assessment of the situation was concise and comprehensive: he 'saw all that he had made, and it was very good'.[25] Francis Schaeffer explains why it is impossible to overstate what this means: 'This is not a relative judgement, but a judgement of the holy God who has a character and whose character is the law of the universe. His conclusion: "Every step and every sphere of creation, and the whole thing put together — man himself and his total environment, the heavens and the earth — conforms to myself." '[26]

Things have changed! At a specific moment in history, man chose for the first time to disbelieve God's words and disobey his directions, and at that moment 'sin entered the world'.[27] This is not the place to discuss whether all the specific details in the Genesis account of what theologians call 'the Fall' are to be taken literally or figuratively, but the message is clear. God's warning had been that the moment man sinned, 'You will surely die.'[28] As Adam lived for many years after his disastrous disobedience, does this mean that God lied, or changed his mind and decided to let him off with a 'slap on the wrist'? The answer to the question becomes clear when we understand that in biblical language death never means cessation but *separation*, as Alec Motyer correctly says, 'There are no biblical grounds for saying that "death means the end".'[29] When our first parents sinned, their souls were not annihilated, leaving them to exist as one-dimensional vegetables; in many ways they carried on living much as they had done before the Fall. Yet their spiritual relationship with God was shattered. Instead of delighting in the consciousness of his presence, they 'hid from the LORD God among the trees of the garden'.[30] They had not forfeited their spiritual existence, but they had lost their spiritual life. Alienated, ashamed and afraid, they were now living in a state of spiritual death, their communion with God a thing of the past and the purpose of their existence in ruins.

A Scottish friend of mine tells of visiting a farm in the Hebrides and seeing a derelict old car being used as a chicken coop. It was still recognizable as a car, but no longer able to fulfil the function for which it was originally made. In the same way, fallen man did not become less than man, but he did become less than man was intended to be. He had not lost the natural likeness of God (he continued to be a personal and morally responsible being) but he did lose God's moral likeness. E. F. Kevan is right on the mark: 'The sin of the first man has far more in it than an external failure to do what he was told. It meant that an attitude of distrust of God's goodness had entered the heart of man which, having brought him to rebellion against God, had injected a poison into his moral being that left him suspicious of God and hostile to him.'[31]

There was more to follow. The penalty incurred by human sin involved not only spiritual death (the separation of the soul from God) but physical death (the separation of the soul from the body), and God pronounced this second part of the death sentence by telling Adam, 'Dust you are and to dust you will return.'[32] For the first time, Adam's body became prone to decay, disease and deterioration, with his physical death a foregone conclusion. Death was not built into man's original make-up, nor is it part of what it is to be human. God created man to live, not die. In his original state, man was not subject to death, even though being given free will exposed him to the possibility of it. If Adam had not sinned, he would never have died (spiritually or physically) but would have been sustained for ever in a perfect, unfallen state. Death entered the world as an unnatural intrusion, a foreign invader — and a killer.

How we became what we are

This may all sound like nothing more than very ancient history, and so far removed from life in the twenty-first century as to be totally irrelevant, but two biblical statements lock us into these events as firmly as if they were breaking news. The first tells us that human reproduction first took place *after* the Fall. It was when Adam's nature had been polluted by sin that he began to father children, and he did so 'in his *own* likeness, in his *own* image'.[33] It is impossible to miss the significance of this. At creation, Adam reflected God's perfection; when he began to have children, they reflected his own pollution. From then on, like poison dumped at the source of a river, Adam's corrupt nature flowed down to every succeeding generation. Centuries after Adam's fall, David acknowledged, 'Surely I was sinful at birth, sinful from the time my mother conceived me.'[34] 'In the New Testament, Paul lumped believers and unbelievers together and said, 'Like the rest, we were by nature objects of wrath.'[35] Now the poison has reached our generation. We do not become sinners because we sin; we sin because we are sinners, caught up in the flow of Adam's fall.

This is vehemently contested by those who have a distorted view of the love of God, but Paul makes it clear that we are not born in a state of innocence or moral neutrality, but that, because of our inherited sinful nature, we begin life already under God's righteous wrath. Assuming it has been carried to term, a baby has already been a sinner for nine months the day it is born. Before its umbilical cord is cut and it begins to live independently of its mother, its nature is already inclined to live independently of its Maker. Sinful tendencies and desires are all in place, waiting to express themselves in the sinful words, thoughts and actions which will follow as surely as night follows day. If this sounds like fundamentalist 'Bible-punching', it is worth noting what Thomas Huxley had to say on the subject: 'The doctrines of original sin, of the innate depravity of man ... appear to me to be vastly nearer the truth than the liberal, popular illusions that babies are all born good, and that the example of a corrupt society is responsible for their failure to remain so.'[36]

The second biblical statement locking us into Genesis says that 'Sin entered the world through one man, and death through sin, and in this way death came to all men, because all sinned.'[37] The point being made here is that when Adam sinned he did so as the head and representative of the entire human race and that, because humanity is an integrated whole, he took the whole species with him. When Adam sinned, we sinned; when Adam was pronounced guilty, we were pronounced guilty; when Adam was sentenced to spiritual and physical death, so were we, and we ourselves provide living — and dying — evidence of the fact.

Theologians speak of man's fallen condition as 'total depravity', but the term is so widely misunderstood that it might be better to think of it as 'radical depravity'. The Bible does not teach that people are unable to tell right from wrong, nor that they are incapable of appreciating goodness or doing things which are helpful, nor that every person is as sinful as it is possible to be, nor that each individual human being commits every kind of sin to the same extent. Radical depravity does not mean utter depravity. What it does mean is that the effects of the Fall have permeated every component of every member of the human race, with the result that all human experience and activity is tainted to some degree. It was a recognition of human depravity which led Mark Twain to write, 'If man could be crossed with the cat, it would improve man, but it would deteriorate the cat'![38]

As we have already seen, the body is affected: the Bible bluntly says that 'Your body is dead [that is, subject to death] because of sin'.[39] The mind is affected: the Bible speaks of people 'darkened in their understanding',[40] with the result that they 'cannot understand' biblical truths, which are 'spiritually discerned'.[41] In this state, man's entire perspective on life is fatally distorted; he is unable to acquire what Francis Schaeffer calls 'true knowledge'.[42] The will is affected: men have lost their desire and ability to conform to God's purposes and have instead become 'slaves to sin',[43] unable by themselves to escape its relentless grip. The conscience is affected: it can become 'seared as with a hot iron',[44] deadened to such an extent that it virtually ceases to function. The emotions, desires and imagination are affected: the Bible openly charges us with 'gratifying the cravings of our sinful nature and following its desires and thoughts'.[45]

This is certainly a far-reaching condemnation, but endorsement of it can often be found outside of Scripture, such as in this 1989 statement in *The Times* by the then British prime minister Margaret Thatcher: 'For years when I was young and in politics with all my hopes and dreams and ambitions, it seemed to me and to many of my contemporaries that if we got to an age where we had good housing, good education and a reasonable standard of living, then everything would be set and we should have a fair and much easier future. We now know that this is not so. *We are up against the real problems of human nature*'[46] (emphasis added).

The Bible tells us that these problems are part and parcel of the terrible alienation produced by sin, something which runs right through our modern culture. Man is separated from God, unable to fulfil the purpose for which he was created and restlessly searching to find the answers to his spiritual needs. He is also separated from himself, and has become a tangled network of psychological pressures and problems, plagued by guilt, fear, shame, insecurity and anxiety. He is separated from other men, a rift reflected throughout human society. Children's tantrums, family tensions, teenage rebellion, lovers' tiffs, political in-fighting, racial prejudice, religious sectarianism, civil wars and international confrontations all stem from the fact that fallen human nature is a catalyst for conflict; as the Bible puts it, man is 'born to trouble as surely as sparks fly upward'.[47] Finally, he is separated from nature. Having lost full dominion over it, he now wrestles with enormous ecological problems, none of which were present at creation, while nature itself, dislocated by the entrance of sin into the world, is in what the Bible calls 'bondage to decay',[48] and has been 'groaning as in the pains of childbirth right up to the present time'.[49]

All of this ties in with a brilliant analogy by the prophet Isaiah: 'We all, like sheep, have gone astray, each of us has turned to his own way.'[50] Stuart Briscoe makes this comment: 'There is a strange anomaly called humanity, a contradictory entity called people. We have on the one hand the ability to be incredibly creative and unbelievably destructive; wonderfully kind and abysmally cruel; the ability to build up and tear down; the ability to be very generous and to be thoroughly mean. We can be one thing to one person and the opposite to another, we can be one person at work and another at home. How in the world do we describe the conflicting nature of humanity? You can't describe it by saying humans are innately good or innately evil, or how do you explain the combination? There is only one way I know, and that is to say that we were made by God in his image and there are still the vestiges of his goodness in us that allow us to be creatively kind and good, but we are fallen — we're sheep with that innate tendency to wander, to go astray, to turn every one to our own way.'[51]

The most clinical analysis in Scripture of man's fallen state is to be found in Paul's letter to the Romans, and in one particular passage he pinpoints the defining factors. The passage is so important that we need to set it out in full and then take the remainder of this chapter to draw out its meaning:

> The wrath of God is being revealed from heaven against all the godlessness and wickedness of men who suppress the truth by their wickedness, since what may be known about God is plain to them, because God has made it plain to them. For since the creation of the world God's invisible qualities — his eternal power and divine nature — have been clearly seen, being understood from what has been made, so that men are without excuse.
>
> For although they knew God, they neither glorified him as God nor gave thanks to him, but their thinking became futile and their foolish hearts were darkened. Although they claimed to be wise, they became fools and exchanged the glory of the immortal God for images made to look like mortal man and birds and animals and reptiles.
>
> Therefore God gave them over in the sinful desires of their hearts to sexual impurity for the degrading of their bodies with one another. They exchanged the truth of God for a lie, and worshipped and served created things rather than the Creator — who is for ever praised. Amen. [52]

Without specifically identifying them as such, Paul clearly includes professing atheists and agnostics in those he has in mind, and he can hardly be accused of beating about the bush. His language is direct and dramatic and goes to the very heart of humanity's fallen state. For our present purposes we will divide the passage into seven sections and (without changing their meaning in any way) look at them in a different order from the one in which they originally appear.

Revelation

Although he goes far beyond this elsewhere, Paul states that the very existence of the natural world is a powerful pointer to the reality and nature of God:

> ... what may be known about God is plain to them, because God has made it plain to them. For since the creation of the world God's invisible qualities — his eternal power and divine nature — have been clearly seen...

This is the background against which the rest of the passage should be read. Just as the rift between God and man is not of God's making, so God cannot be held responsible for anybody's atheism or agnosticism. The fact of his existence is as clear as daylight: 'God has made it plain to them.'

Theologians call this 'general revelation', as distinct from the fuller 'special revelation' which God gives in Scripture, and Paul's statement agrees with other biblical declarations. He does not say that God reveals himself to man's physical sight; elsewhere in the New Testament we are told, 'No one has ever seen God.'[53] Nor does he say that God's general revelation tells us everything that can be known about him. Indeed, for all that we are told in the fuller revelation of Scripture, the reality of God's transcendence means that he will always be beyond our complete understanding. When the Bible asks, 'Can you fathom the mysteries of God? Can you probe the limits of the Almighty?'[54] it is obvious what our reply should be. Nevertheless, God has revealed certain things about himself, and has done so 'since the creation of the world'. God is not hiding away in some remote, unreachable part of the universe, nor is he playing hard to get. Instead, he has provided us with a massive and spectacular visual aid to assure us of his existence and presence — the entire created order. In a brilliant statement of this, David writes:

The heavens declare the glory of God;
    the skies proclaim the work of his hands.
Day after day they pour forth speech;
    night after night they display knowledge.
There is no speech or language
    where their voice is not heard.
Their voice goes out into all the earth,
    their words to the ends of the world. [55]

Immanuel Kant said that it was impossible to reason from visible nature to an invisible God; Paul says exactly the opposite, and states that certain things about God, 'his eternal power and divine nature', are 'clearly seen'.

Nor has God left us with a mere handful of enigmatic clues which can make sense only to the most brilliant of philosophers and theologians. He has made his presence 'plain'. We are completely surrounded by God's faithful and obvious self-revelation. John Calvin says that God's revelation of himself in nature is 'so apparent that it ought not to escape the gaze of even the most stupid tribe'.[56] As clearly as we can look at a painting and know that there was an artist, or hear a beautiful symphony and know that there was a composer, so, when we look at the bewildering variety, intricacy and beauty of the natural world, we can tell that there is a Creator.

In 1979 the British astronomer Bernard Lovell, then Professor of Radio Astronomy at the University of Manchester and director of the experimental station at the Nuffield Radio Astronomy Laboratories at Jodrell Bank, wrote a book entitled *In the Centre of Immensities*, described by the publishers as 'a brilliant summation of current cosmology and an illumination of life itself'. In a newspaper interview he gave at the time, Lovell said that his own emotions at the discoveries he had made were like those of Albert Einstein, 'a rapturous amazement at the harmony of natural law, which reveals an intelligence of such superiority that, compared with it, all the systematic thinking and acting of human beings is an utterly insignificant reflection'.[57] Paul uses an apparent oxymoron to say the same thing: 'God's invisible qualities ... have been clearly seen.'

Before we move on to the second section of Paul's passage, it is important to realize that God's general self-revelation is not limited to external objects which man sees with his physical eyes. There is a strong case for saying that the phrase *phaneros en autois* — 'plain to them' — should be translated 'plain *in* them'. This does not invalidate anything we have said, but it adds the important dimension that man's own being is included. The distinguished Dutch theologian Cornelius Van Til says, 'By the idea of revelation, then, we are to mean not merely what comes to man through the facts surrounding him in his environment, but also that which comes to him by means of his own constitution... The revelation that comes to man by way of his own rational and moral nature is no less objective to him than that which comes to him through the voice of trees or animals.'[58]

This ties in with what we said earlier about man being made in the image of God. In particular, it reminds us that human beings have not only an ethical awareness, a natural instinct by which they can distinguish between right and wrong, but an innate sense that this moral faculty is God-given and God-related. Paul underlines this later in Romans, when he says that even those without the special revelation of Scripture have God's standards 'written on their hearts, their consciences also bearing witness, and their thoughts now accusing, now even defending them'.[59] This moral consciousness was damaged when man fell into sin, but it was not destroyed. When even the most entrenched atheist passes judgement on his own behaviour, or on the behaviour of others, he is confirming that he is under the authority of a divine moral code and that God has 'made it plain'. Van Til goes on to say that men's efforts 'to destroy or bury the voice of God that comes to him through nature, which includes his own consciousness' can never succeed because even 'the most depraved of men cannot wholly escape the voice of God'.[60]

Proposition number 3

In the introduction to this book, we put forward three propositions. The first of these stated that only a minority of people are atheists. We established this by reviewing the results of opinion polls from around the world which showed that in response to a vaguely worded question such as 'Do you believe in God?', only about 20% responded in the negative. Our second proposition stated that most people in the world are atheists. It took us twelve chapters to establish this, and we did so by setting people's philosophical and religious ideas alongside what we later saw to be a biblical definition of God. We are now about to see that when the issue is looked at from another perspective the third proposition holds good: *nobody is an atheist.*

Paul establishes this when he says of fallen man in general, and atheists and agnostics in particular, that *'They knew God,'* and that their denial of him was therefore *'without excuse'*. As we can be sure that Paul has a correct conception of God, the key word here is obviously 'knew'. The verb *ginosko* ('to know') has a great variety of uses in the New Testament, from a general understanding to the most intimate of personal relationships. As the context makes clear, Paul is using it here to speak of intellectual and instinctive awareness. There is no conflict between this and his statement to the Corinthians that 'The world through its wisdom did not know [God].'[61] The message to the Corinthians is that philosophical speculation, claiming its own autonomy, is based on a defective world-view, and can never lead people to a true and intimate knowledge of God. The message to the Romans is that all human beings (including speculative philosophers) have an awareness of deity, a knowledge of God which exists at some level of their thinking and which is programmed into their constitutions. As the eighteenth-century German physicist G. C. Lichtenberg wrote, 'Belief in God is an instinct as natural to man as walking on two legs.'[62]

In 1998, I heard the British doctor and broadcaster Jonathan Miller tell a radio audience, 'I was a cradle atheist,'[63] but the Bible assures us that he was no such thing. The knowledge of God which Paul means here is bred into a person's being and runs through his psyche as surely as blood runs through his veins; in John Calvin's words, 'Men of sound judgement will always be sure that a sense of divinity which can never be effaced is engraved upon men's minds.'[64] What is more, this knowledge is indelible and can never be lost. Even those who sink to the very dregs of human society carry with them some sense of God's reality and requirements. To quote Calvin again, 'Yet that seed remains which can in no wise be uprooted: that there is some sort of divinity; but this seed is so corrupted that by itself it produces only the worst fruits.'[65]

This single statement — 'They knew God' — is sufficient to establish the biblical proposition that nobody is an atheist. We can be as emphatic about this as Cornelius Van Til: 'There are no atheists... Metaphysically speaking then, both parties, believers and unbelievers, have all things in common. They have God in common, they have every fact in the universe in common. And they know they have them in common. All men know God, the true God, the only God. They have not merely a capacity for knowing him but actually do know him.'[66] While those who deny the existence of God are commonly called atheists, it would be more in line with biblical teaching to call them antitheists, as they deliberately set themselves against the knowledge of God which they have.

Paul specifically addresses this later, when he says that 'They did not think it worthwhile to retain the knowledge of God.'[67] As we should expect, Paul's choice of words is perfect, though the meaning is slightly blurred in this particular translation. The phrase 'did not think it worthwhile to retain' means 'did not approve, or like', while the word translated 'knowledge' has a prefix which intensifies its meaning and refers to 'clear and exact knowledge ... a knowledge which has a powerful influence on the knower'.[68] What Paul is saying is that atheists (for the sake of simplicity we shall continue to use the word) put God on trial and, when they find he is not to their liking, they refuse to give him their endorsement. In other words, they have knowledge of God, but refuse to acknowledge him. J. B. Phillips' paraphrase may be very near the mark: 'They considered themselves too high and mighty to acknowledge God.'[69] What is certain is that those who want to live godless, self-centred lives have a vested interest in keeping God out of their thoughts.

This leads us to Paul's second phrase, an indictment that such men are 'without excuse'. The word he uses is *anapologotes*, which literally means 'without defence'. This is the language of the law court, and Paul deliberately uses it to pronounce the atheist guilty in the sight of the God he refuses to acknowledge. Nobody can claim with Bertrand Russell that there is not enough evidence for a person to believe in God. God speaks to man externally, in a dazzling demonstration of 'his eternal power and divine nature', and this alone leads Stuart Olyott to say, 'Nobody can plead that he is ignorant of the existence of God. It can clearly be seen that there is an Unseen.'[70] Yet God also speaks to man internally, giving him an indelible sense of the divine and prompting his conscience to respond to a powerful moral instinct.

The American Bible expositor William Hendriksen pulls all of this together and gives a good illustration of what this meant in Paul's day: 'Even without the benefit of such products of human invention as microscope and telescope, they were able to reflect on the vastness of the universe, the fixed order of the heavenly bodies in their courses, the arrangement of the leaves around a stem, the cycle of the divinely created water-works (evaporation, cloud formation, distillation, pool formation), the mystery of growth from seed to plant — not just any plant but the particular kind of plant from which the seed originated, the thrill of the sunrise from faint rosy flush to majestic orb, the skill of birds in building their "homes" without ever having taken lessons in home building, the generous manner in which food is supplied for all creatures, the adaptation of living creatures to their environment (for example, the flexible soles of the camel's feet to the soft desert sands), etc., etc. In addition to this voice of God in the works of the creation, there was also the voice of that same God in conscience. The evidence was overwhelming. And still no response of adoration and gratitude. Then surely their conduct is inexcusable!'[71]

By definition, agnostics are in the same boat, because when they say that they are not persuaded by the evidence, the fault lies not with God but with them. God has ensured that those who question his existence, along with those who reject him out of hand, have not a shred of moral integrity in doing so. When they try to argue rationally, they are admitting that there is such a thing as transcendent reason. When they make moral assessments, they are forced to lean on a transcendent basis of morality. Denying the true source of these transcendent norms is deliberate wrong-headedness, as nobody can plead a lack of either information or instinct to point them in the right direction. God's revelation is universal, and so is man's knowledge of it. The Bible makes it clear that those who reject God outright, and those who claim to be sitting on the fence, are refusing to acknowledge what they know to be true. On that basis alone proposition number 3 holds good: there are no atheists.

The coiled spring

not read yet

Paul now presses home his indictment with the specific charge that, although God's eternal power and divine nature are *'understood from what has been made'*, those who reject him *'suppress the truth by their wickedness'*. The word 'understood' translates *kathoraō*, which literally means 'clearly seen'. Nature does not tell us the whole story, but its message is loud and clear: it points to the truth that it has a divine Creator of stupendous power. The word 'suppress' is from the verb *katechō*, which means 'to hinder, hold down or restrain'. It is the word we would use about hostages being held against their will. R. C. Sproul says that the picture is that of pressing down with force against something that is exercising a counter-force: 'The image that comes into my mind would be a giant steel spring, which would take the full weight of a human being to press down.

Because of the tension, if the person lets go for a second, the spring will shoot right up.'[72]

This is exactly the point Paul is making. Those of whom he is speaking know something of the truth about God (enough to render them guilty if they reject him or question his existence) but they do everything they can to imprison it and to prevent it challenging their world-view and lifestyle. There is more than enough evidence to convince them that there is a God, but they have a natural hostility to the God it reveals. Ludwig Feuerbach's claims that 'Knowledge of God is self-knowledge,'[73] and that religion is 'the dream of the human mind'[74] could hardly be further from the truth. Genuinely biblical religion is not a dream to the atheist; *it is a nightmare*, letting loose a God of truth, holiness and justice who makes non-negotiable moral demands on him and calls him to surrender his autonomy. James Montgomery Boice is right: 'Nearly everything that can be known about God is repugnant to the natural man in one way or another. So he represses the evidence that would lead him in the direction of a true knowledge of God.'[75] The great eighteenth-century American theologian and philosopher Jonathan Edwards went even further and said that such people 'would kill God if they could get at him'.[76]

As they are unable to get rid of God, atheists concentrate on squeezing him out of their thinking but, as the Scottish theologian Sinclair Ferguson explains, this, too, is a futile exercise: 'According to the New Testament, there is no escape from the knowledge of God, even if I am an unbeliever. I may seek to repress it, but I cannot escape it. There are no ultimate atheists, only theists who argue against what, in the deepest recesses of their being, they know to be true: God is. We cannot succeed in our struggle permanently to suppress that knowledge. We certainly cannot do so consistently. This is God's world, and all who live in it must borrow from God's capital in order to do so.'[77] Cornelius Van Til used to give an illustration of this last point by picturing a little girl slapping her father's cheeks while being held in his lap: she could not do even this unless her father made it possible.

The unpaid bill

Having insisted that those who rejected God did so in spite of the fact that they 'knew him', Paul adds the double-barrelled accusation that *'They neither glorified him as God nor gave thanks to him.'* Of all the defects the

Bible finds in atheists, these are two of the most obvious. God's glory is a very familiar biblical theme and, as Bruce Milne says, it 'carries us to the heart of all that is essential to his being as God'.[78] In other words, it gathers together everything that makes God God, the one who by definition transcends all finite reality, of which he is the eternally self-existent and self-sufficient Creator. Time and again there is a link in the Bible between the glory of God and the revelation of his being. We are told not only that 'The heavens declare the glory of God,'[79] but that 'The whole earth is full of his glory.'[80] This not only speaks of the reality of his presence, it endorses Paul's earlier statement that God has 'made it plain'.

Among the many commandments in Scripture is one which in a sense includes all the others: 'Ascribe to the LORD the glory due to his name.'[81] 'Ascribe' translates the Hebrew word *yahab*, which basically means 'to bring, present, bear'.[82] It goes without saying that human beings can never add to God's essential glory, nor can they contribute to it in any way, but they are commanded to bring before God, in an attitude of worship and submission, an acknowledgement of all his glorious attributes. It is obvious from other passages in the Bible that this involves much more than the observance of religious rituals and ceremonies. God says in no uncertain terms that when these are devoid of true worship they are not merely unacceptable but 'detestable'.[83] On holiday in the Republic of Ireland in 1998, my wife and I passed a group of men milling around outside a church during a Sunday morning service. A local friend told us that this happened every Sunday, and that this was their way of 'going to church' without getting involved! This was hardly giving to God the glory due to his name — but neither was any ceremony that may have been going on inside the church that did not genuinely come from the believing hearts of those taking part.

The glory due to God's name is the greatest unpaid bill in the world. Commenting on Psalm 104, which speaks of the sun, moon, the earth, and living plants and creatures, Martyn Lloyd-Jones wrote, 'Everything in creation manifests the glory of God by obeying the law of its nature; man alone does not do so.'[84] According to Scripture, those who reject God, refuse to acknowledge his glory and have no interest in honouring him by the quality of their lives are in practical terms sub-human; they are failing to meet God's specification for human beings.

Almost as an illustration of what he has just written, Paul goes on to accuse those he has in mind of ingratitude: they neither glorified God as

they should, 'nor gave thanks to him'. A number of years ago, I was invited to speak at a school in Plymouth. Before I spoke, a Moody Institute
of Science film was shown. I found it compelling, but the students obviously thought otherwise, and the film had to be stopped twice while members of staff restored some sort of order. As soon as the film ended, the
headmaster introduced me. As I walked on to the stage, quite sure that the
students would very quickly 'give me the bird', I decided on shock tactics.
'Let me ask you a very unusual question,' I began. 'Have you ever seen a
pig giving thanks to God before eating its food?' This produced a puzzled
murmur, so I repeated the question and asked them to shout out the answer.
There was a loud and unanimous 'No!' 'Then let me ask you another
question,' I went on. 'Do *you* give thanks to God before eating your food?'
This produced another bewildered buzz, but as soon as I interrupted by
asking, 'What is your answer?', a massive 'No!' echoed around the hall.
'Thank you very much,' I responded. 'That is a great help to me. You see,
I have never been to this school before, and I knew nothing about you.
Now I know at least one thing: as far as giving thanks for your food is
concerned, you are on the same level as the pigs!' To my great relief, the
shock tactics worked a treat and (to mix my metaphors) from then on they
were as quiet as mice. I admit this was a pretty crude approach, but why
would any atheist want to object?

Ingratitude is a miserable trait, but a common one; Fyodor Dostoevsky
went so far as to say, 'I believe that the best definition of man is the ungrateful biped.'[85] Two factors spark Paul's allegation of man's ingratitude
to God.

The first is that God is not only our Creator but the source of everything
for which we have cause to give thanks. Addressing the members of Athens
city council, Paul told them that God 'gives all men life and breath and
everything else',[86] and reminded them of the statement by the sixth-century
B.C. Greek poet Epimenedes that 'In him we live and move and have our
being.'[87] Writing to people in Corinth who were boasting that they were
better or more gifted than others, Paul asked, 'What do you have that you
did not receive?'[88] Elsewhere in the New Testament we are told that God
'gives generously to all',[89] and that every 'good and perfect gift is from
above, coming down from the Father of the heavenly lights'.[90] Persistent
ingratitude to such a generous Giver, who 'causes his sun to rise on the
evil and the good, and sends rain on the righteous and the unrighteous',[91]
is inexcusable.

The second factor behind Paul's accusation is the Bible's repeated assertion that we *should* give thanks to God. To give just three examples, we are told, 'Give thanks to the LORD, for he is good';[92] 'Sing to the LORD with thanksgiving';[93] 'Enter his gates with thanksgiving and his courts with praise; give thanks to him and praise his name.'[94] Nor is our thanksgiving to be limited to the best of times, when everything in life seems to be going our way. Instead, we are told to 'give thanks in all circumstances'[95] and reminded that we should be 'always giving thanks to God the Father for everything'.[96]

By and large, these factors are ignored in today's society. Countless millions go through the average day with no conscious appreciation of God's goodness and kindness to them, and without ever giving thanks to him for his gracious provision of their needs. Even 'Thank God!' is often meaningless, or no more than a superstitious nod in the general direction of Deity, while vast numbers of people are more likely to read their horoscopes and thank their 'lucky stars'. It may seem strange to some that Paul should list ingratitude in his denunciation of atheistic behaviour, but this misses the point that giving thanks to God is not a suggestion but an instruction. Failing to thank God is not weakness but wickedness on the part of those who refuse to give God the place in their hearts, minds and lives which he deserves and demands.

Fools!

The fifth section in our analysis of Paul's defining statement in Romans takes in two extended but related phrases. He says of the people he has in mind that:

> Their thinking became futile and their foolish hearts were darkened. Although they claimed to be wise, they became fools and exchanged the glory of the immortal God for images made to look like mortal man and birds and animals and reptiles... They exchanged the truth of God for a lie, and worshipped and served created things rather than the Creator — who is for ever praised — Amen.

Having refused to give God his rightful place in their hearts, minds and lives, 'their thinking became futile' — and the word 'became' establishes the connection between this section and the previous one. It confirms that the so-called 'primal religions' are a degeneration from the original worship of the one true God. Geoffrey Wilson calls this 'the *coup de grace* to the modern myth of man's unaided ascent from primitive animism to the lofty summit of monotheism'.[97] William Ramsay's extensive research led him to the same conclusion: 'For my own part, I confess that my experience and reading show nothing to confirm the modern assumptions in religious history, and a great deal to confirm Paul. Wherever evidence exists, with the rarest exceptions, *the history of religion among men is a history of degeneration*'[98] (emphasis added). Man has not risen from many gods to one, but fallen from one God to many, or to none.

Paul highlights two stages in this decline. In the first place, 'Their thinking became futile.' The word 'thinking' translates *dialogismos* (from which we get 'dialogue'), while 'futile' means 'empty, vain or worthless'.[99] When people refuse to accept divine revelation, they are inevitably reduced to human speculation, to tossing around religious and philosophical ideas in the hope of finding something that will be intellectually and morally satisfying. It is a hopeless quest, because when God is not in his rightful place man's entire world-view is out of focus. R. C. Sproul comments, 'It should not surprise us that brilliant thinkers compose very intricate, complex systems of philosophical thought that rise up in opposition against the character of God. In fact, if a person is logically consistent, there is a certain sense in which the more brilliant he is, the further he will remove himself from the conclusion of the existence of God.'[100]

Paul then goes an important step further and says that 'Their foolish hearts were darkened.' In biblical terminology, the heart usually means the central core of a person's being, the mainspring of his thoughts, words and actions, and the key word here is 'foolish', which Paul later endorses by saying that these people 'became fools'. In Western society today, foolishness usually refers to ignorance or stupidity, but in biblical language it has a much deeper dimension. In the Old Testament, David twice says, 'The fool says in his heart, "There is no God."'[101] The word 'fool' translates the Hebrew *nabal*, which carries a sense of moral perversity. The Old Testament scholar Derek Kidner illustrates this by saying that the assertion is treated in Scripture, 'not as a sincere but misguided conviction, but as an irresponsible gesture of defiance'.[102] Paul's word 'foolish' translates the Greek *asunetos*, which means 'without insight or understanding',[103] while his later word 'fools' comes from *mōros*, which basically means 'dull, sluggish, stupid',[104] but which also includes the idea of something losing the purpose for which it exists.

Pulling all of these meanings together gives us an important biblical perspective on atheism. When men reject God, their thinking is distorted, their wills are perverted and their emotions cannot function properly. *Their own independent ideas about reality are automatically flawed by their fundamental presupposition that no self-existent supernatural Being exists.* As a result, they have to explain existence without creation, design without planning, a universal moral code without a transcendent lawgiver and life without a supernatural origin. As an example of this last point, they are reduced to agreeing with evolutionist Sidney Fox's absurd suggestion that 'In the beginning, life assembled itself.'[105]

This kind of thinking obviously opens the door to extremely liberal views on matters such as eugenics, genetic engineering and euthanasia. Francis Crick has been reported as saying that if a new-born infant does not pass certain tests regarding its genetic endowment it forfeits its right to live;[106] he has also proposed compulsory death for everyone at eighty years of age.[107] The same distorted thinking has revolutionized the abortion scene. During the past thirty years, abortion has become one of Britain's major growth industries, with nearly five million pregnancies terminated. Few people would now pretend that abortion is not available on demand, and in 1997 Marie Stopes International Clinics offered women ten-minute abortions which 'would be carried out quite easily in a working woman's lunch hour'.[108] It has been estimated that whereas the chances of being killed by a terrorist in this country are one in 420,000, the chances of being killed in the womb are one in five. We now live in a world in which seals and whales have more legal rights than unborn infants.

The Bible makes it clear that the atheist's problem is not merely intellectual deficiency but moral obtuseness. So-called human 'ignorance' is not excusable, it is culpable. Men's hearts are 'darkened', not because the light is not shining, but because they have deliberately drawn the blinds. In the Bible's own words, 'Light has come into the world, but men loved darkness instead of light, because their deeds were evil.'[109] Atheism is not a neutral position, and nor, for that matter, is agnosticism. Nobody is an atheist by accident, but by deliberately setting himself against God's clear revelation of himself (and therefore of issues which flow from his existence). Commenting that atheism 'may be learned, taught and adapted, but it cannot be neutral',[110] the British preacher Robert Sheehan gives a simple illustration. A child visiting an art gallery would ask of an exhibit, 'Who painted that?' On a visit to a science museum, the question would be: 'Who invented that?' As Sheehan writes, 'He is by nature a creationist. Paintings have painters; inventions have inventors. Which child (or adult) would *naturally* ask, "By what process did that painting (or invention) evolve by chance?" ... Cross the road to a natural history museum and a child (and adult) would *naturally* respond in the same way. He would see in God's handiwork God's imprint. He would look for a creator... Atheism may be taught, but it is contrary to nature.'[111]

Knowledge of God is so deeply embedded in the human constitution that atheists and agnostics can be classified as eccentrics, and as guilty eccentrics at that. R. C. Sproul nails the main point down: 'Atheism and agnosticism are not merely defective theories that need to be corrected by further study and more information. They are sin for which men are called to repent because God has made himself known to them.'[112]

Idolatry; immorality

In our next section, Paul moves from the general to the particular, and points up two specific areas in which atheism expresses itself. The first is idolatry:

> They ... exchanged the glory of the immortal God for images made to look like mortal man and birds and animals and reptiles... They exchanged the truth of God for a lie, and worshipped and served created things rather than the Creator — who is for ever praised. Amen.

His repetition of the word 'exchanged' is significant for two reasons. In the first place, it confirms that religion has not evolved upwards, but has devolved downwards, beginning with belief in the one true God and degenerating to idolatry. Secondly, it underlines the fact that man is constitutionally religious, and that the human spirit abhors a vacuum. Sin has not destroyed man's religious capacities or desires, it has simply diverted them to the worship of man-made idols and ideas. James Montgomery Boice notes, 'The universality of religion on this planet is not due to men and women being seekers after God, as some have argued. Rather, it is because they will not have God, yet need something to take God's place.'[113] In G. K. Chesterton's famous phrase, 'People think that when they do not believe in God they believe in nothing, but the fact is that they will believe in anything.'[114]

The worship of idols made in the likeness of human beings, birds, animals and reptiles is widely recorded in biblical and secular history, and is still practised today. There is a tragic insanity about these forms of idolatry, in that people worship the very things over which God originally gave humankind dominion. Yet idolatry comprises much more than these gross and senseless practices. Worshipping false ideas of God is an obvious example of the same thing. People want a God who is powerful and loving enough to meet their needs and get them out of trouble, but not one who is holy and just, demands obedience and punishes sin. As the God revealed in Scripture does not meet their specification, they invent others to take his place. As they push God out of the back door, they welcome self-made idols in at the front door, and nothing more cruelly demonstrates humankind's fallen state than the way in which people 'exchange the truth of God for a lie' and seek to worship deities who are nothing more than figments of their own imagination.

One of the Old Testament writers ridicules the pagan idols of his day by saying:

> They have mouths, but cannot speak,
>   eyes, but they cannot see;
> they have ears, but cannot hear,
>   noses, but they cannot smell;
> they have hands, but cannot feel,
>   feet, but they cannot walk;
>   nor can they utter a sound with their throats.[115]

Far from being limited to an ancient and localized culture, these words are powerfully up to date. In a 1998 report in the *Daily Telegraph*, a spokesman for the Pagan Federation told of many people turning away from traditional beliefs, and said that up to 200,000 pagans in Britain saw themselves as the modern representatives of an ancient religion based on worshipping the sanctity of nature.[116] A 1999 report spoke of there being some 400 religious cults in Britain and claimed that their number was 'growing by the month'.[117]

Idolatry is not limited to overtly religious practices; it invades every area of human culture. Anything which occupies the place in a person's life which rightly belongs to God, and therefore betrays a grossly distorted sense of values, comes under the same condemnation. In today's 'must-have' society, material possessions are an obvious example, and Scripture specifically speaks of 'greed, which is idolatry'.[118] The Swiss author Guy Appéré says that this particular form of idolatry is 'sometimes difficult to unmask, being hidden behind deceptive appearances such as caution, economy and prudence',[119] but the Bible clearly shows that it can become a substitute for God by warning, 'You cannot serve both God and Money.'[120] Writing elsewhere, Paul pinpoints another danger area when he says of some people that 'Their god is their stomach.'[121] Food and drink have undoubtedly become gods to many people, but the principle extends far beyond the dining room. It includes all who worship at the altar of their own appetites. Paul's core complaint against these people is this: 'Their mind is on earthly things.'[122] Their only concern is to accumulate and en-joy what this life has to offer. If God is anywhere on their agenda, he is included in 'Any Other Business'. One's own career, the arts, science, a cultural movement, physical fitness, a non-biblical religion, and even per-sonal reputation are other danger areas. So is sport, either as a player or a fan. To give one simple example of the latter, a few months after the Ameri-can baseball player Mark McGwire hit a season's record seventy home runs in 1998, the ball he hit to set the new mark was sold at auction in New York for £1,800,000.[123]

Atheistic ideas, such as the theory of macro-evolution, or rationalism, can also become 'gods' but, like all the others, they are escape routes from our responsibility to the one true God. Idolatry is Scripture's fundamental prohibition: the first of the Ten Commandments reads, 'You shall have no other gods before me,'[124] while the second specifically forbids the making and worship of idols.[125] Far from being a mere technicality, idolatry, in any way, shape or form, is a capital offence against the majesty of God.

Paul next goes on to pinpoint immorality as another area in which athe-ism often expresses itself, and writes of those engaged in 'sexual impurity' and in 'the degrading of their bodies with one another'. It is no coinci-dence that Paul was writing from Corinth, a city notorious not only for its idolatry but for its sexual debauchery, with 1,000 prostitutes attached to the temple of Aphrodite. Although nobody would suggest that all (or even most) atheists are sexual deviants, the connection between idolatry and immorality has a long history. When I first visited Greece in the late 1960s, my interpreter told me that two major trends were sweeping through the country's universities. The first was atheism; the second was immorality.

In the text we are studying, Paul refers to sexual depravity in general, but he later specifies women who 'exchanged natural relations for unnatural ones',[126] and men who 'abandoned natural relations with women', were 'inflamed with lust for one another' and 'committed indecent acts with other men'.[127] To put it bluntly, he is condemning all homosexual and lesbian practices. This will be firmly resisted in today's society by those with a so-called 'gay rights' agenda, but Scripture shows that their resistance indicates their slavery, not their liberty. Paul clearly says that such practices stem from the 'sinful desires' of those involved and result in the 'degrading of their bodies'. The word 'degradation' translates the Greek *atimia*, which literally means 'dishonour, disgrace, ignominy'.[128] Those who behave in this way not only refuse to honour God, they also dishonour themselves, however passionately they may argue otherwise. As R. C. Sproul explains, 'Part of the sinfulness of sin is seen when people begin to call the truth a lie, or call a lie the truth. They begin to call good, evil, and evil, good. There is virtually no sin known to the human race for which somebody hasn't put forth a learned and sophisticated ethical defence that it is in fact really good.'[129] There is no clearer example of this than in the way 'gay rights' activists try to commend what God condemns.

Fools' wisdom

Paul's final indictment against those he had in mind is that they *'claimed to be wise'*. It is easy to see why he should include this, as by definition atheism and hard-core agnosticism virtually exclude genuine humility. Atheists claim the ability to rule out God's existence, and hard-core agnostics claim to know that the knowledge that God exists is beyond us. Atheism and pride have always been a perfect fit for each other. Some 3,000 years ago, one Old Testament author wrote:

> In his pride the wicked does not seek him;
>   in all his thoughts there is no room for God...
> He says to himself, 'Nothing will shake me'...
>   'He won't call me to account.'[130]

Another referred to arrogant sinners who reduce God to the level of an empty, powerless idea and dare to ask, 'How can God know? Does the Most High have knowledge?'[131] Today's atheists use the same kind of language. As we saw in chapter 16, Peter Atkins has no hesitation in dismissing theology as 'fantasy', and Richard Dawkins scoffs at theism and calls it 'ignominious, contemptible and retarded'.[132] On the other hand, Dawkins is certain that atheism occupies the intellectual high ground; in a 1996 article in the *Independent* he asked, 'Have you ever met an uneducated atheist?'[133]

There is a tragic irony here. Far from being able to make dogmatic assertions about the most important issues in life, *fallen man is fundamentally incapable of valid, independent insight about anything.* Although they claim to be wise, atheists and hard-core agnostics have turned their backs on the one who alone 'gives wisdom to the wise and knowledge to the discerning'.[134] As God is the source of all true wisdom, it is hardly surprising to read elsewhere in Scripture, 'The fear of the LORD is the beginning of wisdom,'[135] and 'The fear of the LORD is the beginning of knowledge.'[136] The 'fear' the writers have in mind is not the terror that drives people away from God, but a sense of awe and reverence which leads to humble submission and joyful obedience. To fear God is to take him seriously, and to respond properly. Corrupt religions tend to generate panic or presumption, while true biblical religion calls men to acknowledge their Maker as being both great and gracious and as the ultimate reference-point for every question they will ever have to face.

God's response to man's rejection

As we have now seen, Paul's picture of those who reject God is devastating. In the light of God's clear revelation of himself, their attitude is without excuse. They wickedly suppress the truth and neither glorify God nor thank him as they should. Morally obtuse, they turn their backs on him and choose to worship idols and ideas of their own, some sinking to vile immorality. As if this were not bad enough, they add insult to injury by arrogantly claiming that their conclusions and conduct stem from their superior wisdom, which assures them that God is non-existent or irrelevant and that they can confidently 'do their own thing'. As we shall see in a moment, Paul summarizes all of this in two words — 'godlessness' and 'wickedness'. The word 'godlessness' translates the Greek *asebeia*, which refers to 'impiety toward God ... lack of reverence'.[137] It indicates rebellion against God's majesty and authority, a determination to rule God out of one's thinking and conduct. The word 'wickedness' translates the Greek *adikia*, which is 'the comprehensive term for wrong, or wrong-doing, as between persons'.[138] When used separately, 'godlessness' refers to religious perversity and 'wickedness' to moral perversity, but here they are closely linked and, as the rejection of God's authority leads inevitably to moral evil of one kind or another, the New English Bible makes the connection well by referring to 'godless wickedness'.

God's response is inevitable:

> The wrath of God is being revealed ... against all the godlessness and wickedness of men... God gave them over...

As we saw in chapter 20, the Bible documents God's anger in hundreds of places. To take just one example, the Israelite leader Joshua warned a mass rally of his people, 'He is a holy God; he is a jealous God. He will not forgive your rebellion and your sins. If you forsake the LORD and serve foreign gods, he will turn and bring disaster on you.'[139] This will hardly make popular reading in today's permissive society, where sin is trivialized to the point at which almost any kind of behaviour is swept under the carpet but, as Robert Mounce notes, 'All caricatures of God which ignore his intense hatred of sin reveal more about man than about God.'[140] In his perfect holiness, God is utterly intolerant of sin, and cannot overlook anything which falls short of his own perfection.

God's anger is shown in Scripture to be his settled, personal reaction to sin of every kind, yet it is never portrayed as being irrational or capricious. It is never blind fury. God never goes 'over the top', never loses his temper. His anger is always justified and righteous, yet the Bible warns us that it is serious, consistent and passionate, and Paul's use of the present tense — 'is being revealed' — confirms the Old Testament statement that God 'expresses his wrath every day'.[141] Far from sitting idly on the sideline while men ridicule or reject him, God is actively expressing his righteous anger in human history. The Bible records spectacular examples of this in its records of a catastrophic and universal flood,[142] the destruction of the cities of Sodom and Gomorrah[143] and a series of devastating plagues upon Egypt,[144] and we have every reason to believe that many so-called 'natural disasters' since have the same significance.

God's judgement is not always 'wholesale', but often falls on individuals. In the Old Testament, we are told that Judah's arrogant king Uzziah was struck down with leprosy.[145] In the New Testament, we read that Ananias and Sapphira, who deliberately lied to God and to the early church leaders about a financial fiddle, were suddenly struck dead,[146] and that the self-indulgent ruler Herod Agrippa I, who viciously persecuted the church, was suddenly felled by a gruesome and fatal disease.[147] The ultimate cost of dishonesty, greed, drug addiction, alcoholism, immorality and violence to modern society, families and the individuals concerned can also be included, along with the incalculable psychological damage done to those with godless lifestyles.

Yet the most severe punishment for sin is reserved for those of whom Paul says, 'God gave them over,' in other words, those he abandoned. The Bible tells us that God is 'compassionate and gracious' and 'slow to anger',[148] and records many examples of his 'kindness, tolerance and patience',[149] but makes it equally clear that his patience is not endless. In the lives of some, there comes a time when God cries, 'Enough!' and turns his back on those who have determinedly turned their backs on him. He can hardly be criticized for this. Those who have arrogantly rejected his love and grace receive perfect justice as 'a positive punishment for culpable ignorance and wilful sinfulness'.[150]

It is pointless to speculate when that moment comes in any given person's life, but these are some of the clear danger signals: when a person deliberately rejects God because he feels no need for him, or because he feels God will interfere with his lifestyle; when he arrogantly dismisses the Bible as an irrelevance; when he has no conviction of personal sin; when he feels that this life is the beginning and end of his existence, and that he is free to indulge himself in any way he chooses, without any fear of eternal consequences. A person thinking and acting like this is risking the greatest catastrophe of all, God executing perfect justice and repaying him in kind by abandoning him for ever.

P.S.

Does God believe in atheists? The answer depends on precisely what the question means. If it means, 'Does God recognize that there are people to whom he has not revealed himself in any way, who are therefore not in any proper sense answerable to him for their ignorance, and for whose eternal destiny he has made no wise and just provision?', the answer is 'No'. If the question means, 'Does God recognize that there are people who have deliberately rejected his self-revelation to them and who are therefore the proper objects of his holy and eternal anger?', the answer is 'Yes'.

22.

The case against God

In the late 1990s Serbia carried out a ruthless campaign of so-called 'ethnic cleansing' in the province of Kosovo, killing thousands of Albanians and sweeping hundreds of thousands more into neighbouring countries. Among the reported atrocities was the systematic raping of young women by Serb soldiers. One Kosovar woman told the news media of an incident in which, after she and seven others had been separated from their families and gang-raped, four of them were killed, including one woman who was seven months pregnant. Another woman from the same village told how soldiers separated ten women from their families and raped them by the roadside saying, 'We are not going to shoot you, but we want your families to see what we are doing.' 'It was then,' she told reporters, 'that I came to know that God did not exist.'[1]

It is unlikely that anyone reading this book will ever have suffered from such depravity, yet it is not difficult to understand why this traumatized woman should make such a statement. It was not a formal declaration of philosophical atheism, but a passionate cry from the heart. How could she believe in a God who would allow such barbarity to take place and not lift a finger to stop it?

In his book *All in the Mind*, first published in 1999,[2] Ludovic Kennedy rehashes a number of traditional atheistic ideas, but majors on a catalogue of crimes committed in the name of religion. He then suggests that these alone prove the non-existence of God but, as Paul Vallely pointed out in his *Independent* book review, 'There is a leap of logic here ... for though the awful inventory may discredit the use to which religion has been put, it does not necessarily undermine faith itself.'[3] As Vallely rightly says, Kennedy is guilty of sloppy thinking here, and we saw in chapter 18 that evil done in

God's name is a prostitution of biblical teaching. However, we do need to examine the much wider question of how the existence of the God revealed in Scripture can be squared with the reality of evil and suffering in any way, shape or form. This will be the focus of the next two chapters.

Until the seventeenth century, evil and suffering were not generally thought to pose any threat to traditional theism. In the view of the philosopher Alasdair McIntyre (atheist turned theist), the issue was 'an incentive to enquiry, but not a ground for disbelief'.⁴ Reporting on his own research, Alister McGrath says, 'I spent many years working through the major works on ... theology written between the twelfth and sixteenth centuries, and cannot recall any of them treating the reality of suffering as obstacles to ... faith.'⁵ His findings are endorsed by McIntyre, who argues in *The Religious Significance of Atheism* that 'The God in whom the nineteenth and twentieth centuries came to disbelieve had been invented in the seventeenth century.'⁶

The 'invention' came during the Enlightenment, when it was claimed that questions about God's existence and nature could be settled by reason alone. In that setting, the existence of evil and suffering clashed with the Enlightenment's philosophical model of God as an abstract being, chiselled out of human ideas of omnipotence and goodness. The two could not possibly co-exist and, as evil and suffering were unquestionable realities, God had to go. Enlightenment thinking has been in decline for some time now, yet in these early days of the twenty-first century the global reality of evil and suffering is a sustained and powerful argument in the atheist's case against God. In a *Daily Telegraph* article written in 1995, Clifford Longley wrote, 'The existence of evil, of suffering especially, is one of the most common causes of religious doubt in the modern age,'⁷ while Paul Johnson is even more emphatic: 'The problem of evil drives more thoughtful people away from religion than any other difficulty.'⁸

The strongest way of formally presenting the case against God pulls together ideas put forward by a variety of thinkers, including the Greek philosopher Epicurus in the third century B.C., the seventeenth-century French sceptic Pierre Bayle and Bertrand Russell in the twentieth century. In a series of premises and conclusions, the argument usually runs along these lines:

1. Evil and suffering exist in the world.
2. If God were omnipotent, he would be able to prevent these things.

3. If God were wholly good (specifically, if he were a God of love), he would want to prevent them.
4. If there were an omnipotent and wholly good God, then evil and suffering would have no place in the world.
5. Therefore, there is no such being as an omnipotent and wholly good God.

At first glance, the logic seems simple and watertight. As nobody can deny the pervasive presence of evil and suffering, surely it can be taken for granted that a God who could and would banish all of them must be a figment of human imagination? In his classic work *The Problem of Pain*, C. S. Lewis makes the point by focusing on how one particular aspect of the issue is presented: '"If God were good, he would wish to make his creatures perfectly happy, and if God were almighty he would be able to do what he wished. But the creatures are not happy. Therefore God either lacks the goodness, or power, or both." This is the problem of pain, in its simplest form.'[9] On the face of it, there seems little room for manoeuvre here, and for many people the point is not worth discussing; as Stephen Evans says, 'When posed by the atheist or the hostile agnostic, the question about suffering is not really a question, but an assertion.'[10] This is why it deserves our close attention.

In the course of this book we have looked at many of the objections raised against the arguments for theism, but the problem of evil goes much further. For millions who have suffered its effects in one way or another, it brings into question the whole idea of God's existence, while hard-core atheists claim that it proves their case. The existence of evil and suffering is said to make belief in God logically incoherent; it is inconsistent to believe that an omnipotent and wholly good God can co-exist with the malign realities which human beings have to face in every part of a world he created and controls.

Wherever we stand on the issue, we can all agree that the problem is not a hypothetical one, something conjured up by philosophers and theologians shut away in their ivory towers. Evil of every kind, pain, suffering and injustice are universal facts of life, and nobody is totally exempt from them. Writing of one aspect of the issue, the American minister D. James Kennedy says, 'This world is a source of endless suffering that comes in a variety of forms — physical, emotional, relational and spiritual. It erupts as rage, settles in grief, hides in sorrow, or burrows in depression. Few things in life are certain, but pain is one of them.'[11] The simple fact of the matter is that all we have to do is to live long enough and we will suffer in one way or another.

The contemporary philosopher Alvin Plantinga claims that 'Of all the antitheistic arguments, only the argument from evil deserves to be taken seriously.'[12] Be that as it may, one can ignore the problem only by committing intellectual suicide, and theists cannot duck the issue. For the remainder of this chapter we will try to state this aspect of atheism's case as fairly as possible, then look at some unsuccessful attempts to justify God's co-existence with evil. In the next chapter, we will examine theism's response.

Unnatural nature

Two kinds of evil are put forward as denying the existence of God. The first is *natural evil*, things which happen when nature gets out of joint, while the second is *moral evil*, usually thought of in terms of 'man's inhumanity to man',[13] but including his abuse of other sentient creatures and even of nature itself.

The problem of evil arises largely in connection with the teleological argument, the so-called argument from design, which we examined in chapter 13. David Hume and others stressed that the world reveals not only order but disorder, and not even the most fervent theist can deny this. Nature produces both benefits and losses; the human body functions beautifully, but decays horribly; human beings behave well at times, yet at other times act in such a way as to show that, in Hume's own words, 'Man is the greatest enemy of man.'[14] Theists point to order and design as support for believing in God, but atheists point to their opposites as proof that God is non-existent. As David Hare asked in the *Daily Telegraph in* 1996, 'If everything that is good in the world is to be proffered and celebrated as evidence of God's existence, then what are we to make of the bad?'[15]

It is not difficult to find atheistic ammunition. In 1920 some 200,000 people were killed when a series of earthquakes devastated 300 square miles of China's Kansu province, and just three years later another 160,000 perished in Japan when quakes struck Tokyo and Yokohama. Up to 10,000 earthquakes occur every year, and though many are so small that they do no significant damage, others combine to take a terrible toll on life and property.

Volcanoes, named after Vulcan, the Roman god of fire, can be equally terrifying and destructive. In A.D. 79, Mount Vesuvius, near Naples, in modern Italy, erupted and buried the nearby towns of Pompeii and Herculaneum, killing over 10% of their population. In 1631, an even more explosive eruption killed 18,000 people. There are up to 600 active volcanoes in the world today, including Mount Etna, in Sicily, which may have been active for 3,000 years. Its most notable eruptions included one in 1169, which killed 15,000 people in the neighbouring town of Catania, another exactly 150 years later when 20,000 were engulfed, and one in 1928 which wiped out the town of Muscati. Other volcanoes have produced less dire results, but still draw attention to the danger they represent. On 18 May 1980 Mount St Helens, in the north-western United States, blew its top and 1,300 feet of its peak collapsed or blew outwards, filling twenty-four square miles of an adjacent valley. Fifty-seven people were killed and over four billion board feet of usable timber, enough to build 150,000 homes, was damaged or destroyed.

Floods, hurricanes and tidal waves have also had devastating results. In 1887 no fewer than one million people were drowned when China's Hwang-ho River overflowed its banks. When Hurricane Andrew hit the United States in 1992, it drained one-tenth of the global insurance industry's reserves in a single night. When Hurricane Mitch, dubbed 'The Storm of the Century', hit Central America in 1998, 12,000 people were drowned or crushed to death and millions left homeless following torrential rain and winds of up to 150 miles per hour. In 1953 a record spring tide wreaked havoc on both sides of the North Sea, with nearly 2,000 people in Holland and over 300 in England swept to their deaths. In the last major natural disaster of the twentieth century some 30,000 people were swept to their deaths when freak rains hit Venezuela in December 1999.

Fire has often been a great friend to the human race, but it can also be a frightening enemy. History books still give headlines to the Great Fire of London, which destroyed four-fifths of the city in 1666, and the disastrous fire which wiped out the entire business district of Chicago in 1871, but countless others, large and small, have combined to cause incalculable death and destruction.

The *1999 World Disasters Report* of the International Federation of Red Cross and Red Crescent Societies said that the previous year had produced a record number of natural disasters, and forecast an even greater number of 'superdisasters' because of human-driven climate change, environmental degradation and population growth. The report said that events including Hurricane Mitch and the El Nino weather system, together with declining soil fertility and deforestation, drove twenty-five million 'environmental refugees' from their land and into shanty towns around the fast-growing cities of the Third World, a figure representing 58% of the total refugee population worldwide. Fires, droughts and floods from El Nino alone claimed 21,000 lives, and the natural disaster bill for 1999 was more than £55 billion.[16]

These are the headline-makers, but they are by no means the only natural phenomena atheists cite in their attacks on God's existence. Avalanches, blizzards, drought, famine, landslides, lightning, monsoons, plagues, pestilence, subsidence and typhoons, as well as devastating extremes of heat and cold, also draw attention to the fact that, as the scientist and theologian John Polkinghorne admits, we live in 'a world with ragged edges, where order and disorder interlace with each other'.[17] How can theists claim that an omnipotent, wise and loving God presides over this catastrophic chaos?

Titanic, Aberfan, Chernobyl

Some of these 'ragged edges' involve a human element, and three very different incidents in the twentieth century will serve to illustrate countless others.

When the British liner *Titanic*— 883 feet long, 92 feet wide and weighing 46,328 tonnes — was launched in 1911, she was the largest movable object made by man. Setting new standards of safety, she was said, before her maiden voyage began on 11 April 1912, to be so well constructed that 'God himself couldn't sink this ship'. Yet on 14 April she struck an iceberg in the North Atlantic and, in the greatest maritime disaster in history, sank with the loss of over 1,500 lives.

The second incident took place on 21 October 1966, when a slag-heap loosened by persistent rain slid into the coal-mining village of Aberfan in South Wales. The black slime slithered down the hillside and burst into the classrooms of the local junior school. Five teachers and 109 children were suffocated by the foul-smelling mud, and the village's final death count was 116 children and twenty-eight adults.

The third example had ramifications on a vast scale. On 26 April 1986 two explosions destroyed the core of Unit 4 in the RBMK nuclear reactor in Chernobyl, a town just over eighty miles north of Kiev, in the Ukraine. The explosions sent a shower of hot, highly radioactive debris and graphite high into the air and exposed the destroyed core to the atmosphere, releasing radiation roughly equivalent to a thousand times that of the atomic bombs which destroyed Hiroshima during the Second World War.

The fire took two weeks to extinguish, and by then a catastrophic chain of events had been set in motion. Only some thirty people were killed at the time, but in 1991 the *Economist* reported that the accident 'may yet cause up to 300,000 deaths'.[18] Some 800,000 children in the Ukraine were put at risk of contracting leukaemia. 20% of the population of Belarus' more than ten million people, living in twenty-seven cities and over 2,600 villages, had to be moved from areas contaminated by radiation. Radioactive fallout from the incident was detected from Finland to South Africa, and a report in a 1990 edition of the *Los Angeles Times* estimated that it might take $400 billion and up to 200 years to remove the effects of the Chernobyl catastrophe.[19]

Aberfan numbed a nation, while the names *Titanic* and Chernobyl remain synonymous with disaster, suffering and the loss of human life, yet these three tragedies represent millions of other accidents and incidents, large and small, which take place every day, producing untold human misery and helping to convince the atheist that talk of a caring and controlling God is nothing more than cruel rhetoric.

Nasty neighbours

A related item on the atheist's list of charges against God is the existence of so many plants and creatures hostile to others, and especially to man. The simplest way of pinpointing this is to quote two men committed to convincing others that God is fantasy and not fact. The well-known nineteenth-century American sceptic Robert Green Ingersoll wrote:

> Can the intelligence of man discover the least wisdom in covering the earth with crawling, creeping horrors that live only upon the agonies and pangs of others? Can we see the propriety of so

constructing the earth that only an insignificant portion of its surface is capable of producing an intelligent man? ...

What would we think of a father who should give a farm to his children, and before giving them possession should plant upon it thousands of deadly shrubs and vines; should stock it with ferocious beasts and poisonous reptiles; should take pains to put a few swamps in the neighbourhood to breed malaria; should so arrange matters that the ground would occasionally open and swallow a few of his darlings; and, besides all this, should establish a few volcanoes in the immediate vicinity, that might at any moment overwhelm his children with rivers of fire? ... Should we pronounce him angel or fiend?[20]

In a debate held in the 1990s at the University of California at Irvine, Gordon Stein asked his opponent, 'If all living things on the earth were created by a God, and he was a loving God who made man in his own image, how do you explain the fact that he must have created the tapeworm, the malaria parasite, the tetanus germ, polio, ticks, mosquitoes, cockroaches and fleas?' Like Ingersoll, Stein added a rider which brought in the evidence we considered in the previous section, and pointed out that 'Earthquakes and fires kill adults, babies and animals without distinction, as well as destroying churches and hospitals.'

Moral madness

When we turn to the question of moral evil, modern atheism almost always begins with Nazism's ruthless anti-Semitism. Francis Bridger goes so far as to say, 'The case against the existence of God can be summed up in two words: "the Holocaust".'[21] Where was God when six million Jews were being systematically exterminated, when men, women and children were being gassed twenty-four hours a day for three years? In *The Journey Back From Hell* Anton Gill gives a gruesome glimpse into the horrors of Auschwitz, where four million Jews met their end: 'The furnaces in the crematoria became so hot that the firebricks cracked, and additional burning pits had to be dug. Once started, the flames were fuelled with the fat that had run off the burning bodies. As at this period it was not considered worth gassing babies and small children, [the SS] would throw them live into the gutters of boiling human fat.'[22] It is almost literally sickening to write and read these words, yet these things happened within my lifetime and within a few hours' travel of where I live. Much more to the point, they happened in a world which theists claim to be under the complete control of a just and loving God. It is not difficult to see why the atheistic philosopher Walter Kaufmann, who lost family members in the Holocaust, called such evil 'a complete refutation of modern theism'.[23]

Yet, for all its horror, the Holocaust is just one incident in centuries of human slaughter, much of it in the formal context of war. It has been estimated that in the past 4,000 years there have been fewer than 300 without a major war, a fact leading someone to make the wry suggestion that peace was merely the time when everybody stopped to reload.

The twentieth century was hailed by many as the beginning of a millennium of peace, but this empty idealism turned sour in 1914, and the First World War, believed by some to be 'the war to end all wars', left thirty million dead on its battlefields. To help avoid a repetition of this madness, the League of Nations was founded in 1920, with the maintenance of peace as its primary aim, yet less than twenty years later almost all of its members were caught up in the Second World War, which eventually cost over ninety million lives. In 1946, the League of Nations was disbanded in favour of the United Nations Organization, established with the aim of freeing succeeding generations from what it called 'the scourge of war'. Yet for nearly half a century the world was subject to the so-called Cold War and lived under the threat of nuclear extinction. At one point the nuclear powers had stockpiled the equivalent of 100 tons of high explosive for each human being on the planet, leading United States president John F. Kennedy to warn the United Nations General Assembly in 1961, 'Every man, woman and child lives under a nuclear sword of Damocles, hanging by the slenderest of threads, capable of being cut at any moment by accident, miscalculation or madness.' In 1967, Britain's Secretary of State for Defence admitted, 'This has been the most violent century in history. There has not been a day since the end of the Second World War when hundreds have not been killed by military action.'

Even this dismal diagnosis did not include the untold millions of Chinese who lost their lives during the Cultural Revolution which had begun a year earlier, and since then we have had the Cambodian killing fields, the catastrophic war in Vietnam, genocide in several African countries and elsewhere, endless conflict in the Middle East and civil war on virtually every continent.

All of this is grist to the atheists' mill, and they openly deride the idea that an omnipotent and benevolent God presides over this moral mayhem. During the Second World War, the British novelist H. G. Wells wrote, 'If I felt there was an omnipotent God who looked down on battles and deaths and all the waste and horror of this war — able to prevent these things — doing them to amuse himself, I would spit in his empty face.'[24] In a similar vein, the British art critic Brian Sewell told in a 1996 *Sunday Telegraph* article how the evils of war had eventually driven him to atheism. Referring to armed conflict in places like Bosnia, Tibet, Ethiopia, Vietnam and East Timor, he concluded, 'Bring these and a thousand other such matters to the bar of judgement and one is left only with a profound scepticism both about the human instruments and God himself.'[25] In the same article he told how his decision had come after years of battling through adolescent uncertainty: 'After watching a world gone mad with greed and aggression ... I ceased to believe in God and abandoned faith and its observance.'[26]

If corporate aggression is sometimes cited by atheists to support their case, so too are acts of violence carried out by individuals, especially those against apparently innocent victims. The Dunblane massacre is an obvious example (see page 145), but countless others could be given. As I write, the news headlines belong to Mark Barton, a forty-four-year-old American chemist who bludgeoned his wife and their two children to death before killing nine people working in stockbrokers' offices in Atlanta, apparently because he had sustained heavy losses in trading stocks and shares on the Internet. For all the civilizing advances said to have been made in modern society, shooting, knifing, strangling, mugging, rape, sodomy, torture, child abuse and other acts of aggression are all common currency in today's world. Sometimes the sheer depravity almost defies belief. In April 1992 Andrei Chikatilo, described by friends as 'kindly, retiring and respected',[27] confessed to a Russian court that he had murdered fifty-three boys, girls and young women, disembowelled them and eaten parts of their remains. Mercifully, Chikatilo's case is exceptional, but every day violent behaviour brings suffering and misery to millions. Can we really believe that an omnipotent God who, according to the Bible, 'loves righteousness',[28] deliberately allows this horrific state of affairs to continue?

Unfair shakes of the dice?

The eighteenth-century American statesman Daniel Webster once said, 'Justice is the great interest of man on earth,'[29] while theologian Rousas John Rushdoony has written, 'The whole of recorded history is one great longing for justice.'[30] This may be stretching things a bit, but there is no denying that an instinct for justice is deeply embedded in the human psyche. We instinctively feel that people should get what they deserve, that right should be rewarded and wrong punished. What is more, we want these principles carried out to the letter.

In his *Autobiography*, the nineteenth-century British philosopher John Stuart Mill (ironically Bertrand Russell's godfather, though he insisted that this was 'in the purely secular sense')[31] described himself as 'one of the very few examples in this country who has not thrown off religious belief, but never had it.'[32] Of all his arguments for atheism, none was more passionately expressed than what he had to say about the absence of divine justice in the world. In a section headed 'Three Essays on Religion' he wrote:

> If the law of all creation were justice, and the creator omnipotent, then in whatever amount suffering and happiness might be dispensed to the world, each person's share of them would be exactly proportioned to that person's good or evil deeds... No one is able to blind himself to the fact that the world that we live in is totally different from this, insomuch that the necessity for redressing the balance has been deemed one of the strongest arguments for another life after death, which amounts to an admission that the order of things in this life is often an example of injustice, not justice.
>
> If it be said that God does take sufficient account of pleasure and pain to make them the reward or punishment of the good and the wicked, but that virtue itself is the greatest good and vice the greatest evil, then these at least ought to be dispensed to all according to what they have done to deserve them; instead of which every kind of moral depravity is entailed upon the multitude by the fatality of their birth, through the fault of their parents, or society, or of uncontrollable circumstances, certainly through no fault of their own. *Not even on the most distorted and contracted theory of good which was ever framed by religion or philosophical fanaticism can the*

government of nature be made to resemble the work of a being at once good and omnipotent[33] (emphasis added).

In a nutshell, Mill was saying that an omnipotent God of absolute justice would see that everyone got his or her perfectly just deserts. Good would always, obviously, and in exactly the right measure, be rewarded, while evil would always, obviously, and in exactly the right measure, be punished, and nobody would suffer because of agencies over which he had no control. This is clearly not happening, and time and again we see our cosy clichés overturned. Not infrequently, people get away with murder (literally and metaphorically), the good die young, the innocent suffer, cheats frequently prosper and crime often pays — and handsomely at that. How could a God who 'loves justice'[34] allow such blatant and universal injustice to have its way?

To give just one example of inequality, there seems to be little justice in the distribution of the world's wealth. A survey published in 1999 reported that the income gap between the richest fifth of the world's people and the poorest had increased from thirty to one in 1960 to seventy-four to one in 1997.[35] The 200 richest people in the world were said to be worth as much as the poorest 2.25 billion (41%) of the world's population,[36] while three people alone (Bill Gates and Paul Allen of Microsoft and investor Warren Buffet) were said to be richer than the world's poorest forty-three *countries.*[37] What price a God who 'does not show favouritism'?[38]

The Kennedys

Sometimes groups and individuals seem to have been dealt a bizarre mixture of cards, some extravagantly good, others almost unbelievably bad. In the second half of the twentieth century, one family of Kennedys were said to be the nearest thing the United States had to royalty. Their wealth, talent, flair and influence were the stuff of romantic fiction, and their achievements were truly remarkable. The patriarch, Joseph Kennedy Sr, was a self-made millionaire who became his country's ambassador to Britain from 1937 to 1940. In 1960 John F. Kennedy became the thirty-fifth president of the United States. Two of his brothers, Robert (Bobby) and Edward (Ted), were elected senators, and both ran for president, while the next generation included a congressman and a lieutenant governor. The

Washingtonian magazine once predicted that 256 Kennedys would be holding political office by 2050 and 4,096 by the end of the twenty-first century.[39]

Yet the Kennedys' triumphs were matched by their tragedies. In 1944 Joseph Kennedy Jr was killed in a plane crash. In 1948 his sister Kathleen met a similar fate in Saint-Bauzille, her husband having been killed a few months after their wedding. In 1963, and following an earlier stillbirth, the president's son, Patrick Bouvier Kennedy, died when he was just two days old. Three months later, on 22 November 1963, the president was assassinated in Dallas at the age of forty-six. In 1968 his brother Robert was gunned down by a Palestinian immigrant. In 1969 Ted Kennedy drove his car off a bridge on Chappaquiddick Island, killing his passenger Mary Jo Kopechne. Four years later, Robert's second son Joseph was involved in a car accident which left a female passenger paralysed from the waist down. In the same year, Edward Kennedy Jr had his right leg amputated after contracting cancer. In 1984 Robert's son David, aged twenty-nine, died of a cocaine overdose. In 1994 John F. Kennedy's widow, Jacqueline Kennedy Onassis, died of cancer. In 1999 John F. Kennedy Jr, his wife and her sister were killed when he crashed his private plane into the sea off Martha's Vineyard on America's east coast. Commenting on the last of these tragedies, *Newsweek* said, 'A curse seems to haunt the family'[40] — but where was the Bible's loving, caring God when the bullets were flying and the planes falling?

The global hospital

If the sudden deaths of those cut down in their prime are sometimes quoted to help make the atheists' case, so too are all forms of human disease, especially those which are terminal. Linking this with a facet of entropy, or disorder, that we noted earlier, William Miller wrote, 'To what divine purpose and in what loving brain was a scorpion forged? What holy chastening is intended when babies are deformed in mind or body? Is it God's will that two-thirds of the world's population are undernourished? ... Any hospital will show a gallery of pain which is almost unbearable to the viewers... If there is a God, he is responsible.'[41]

By that token, God has a lot to answer for, as there are grounds for saying with Francis Bridger that 'The history of the human race is nothing less than the history of suffering.'[42] Earlier today, in a local hospital ward, a day-old baby cried as I held her in my arms, a telling symbol of the fact that from birth to death we are prone to pain. Even 'simple' complaints can be very painful: cramp, muscle spasms, toothache, migraine, fibrositis, ingrowing toenails, shingles, sciatica, rheumatism, neuralgia, frozen shoulder, a slipped disc. Other problems are more serious and can cause terrible distress: Autism, Down's syndrome, meningitis, tuberculosis, epilepsy, muscular dystrophy, ankylosing spondylitis, Parkinson's disease, rheumatoid arthritis, multiple sclerosis (MS), myalgic encephalomyelitis (ME), motor neurone disease and poliomyelitis, to say nothing of the terrible scourge of cancer. In addition to these physical problems, we are exposed to a whole raft of complex and at times baffling disorders, such as Alzheimer's disease, clinical, psychotic and manic depression, paranoia and schizophrenia. How does this frightening catalogue of disease and disintegration tie in with the Bible's assurance that God is 'faithful to all his promises and loving towards all he has made'?[43]

To make matters worse, the human race is dying at the rate of over 250,000 a day, and nobody can escape the cull. In the words of Fred Carl Kuehner, 'Death is the most democratic institution on earth... It allows no discrimination, tolerates no exceptions. The mortality rate of mankind is the same the world over: one death per person.'[44] Death comes to young and old, good and bad, rich and poor, weak and strong — and, for that matter, to theist and atheist alike. It may come slowly or suddenly, accidentally, deliberately or by natural causes — but it comes. Our cradle stands in the grave. What we call living is the process of dying, and the writer and reader of these words are both involved in it.

Where does God fit into this morbid scenario? Can we believe that an all-powerful and all-loving God who 'does whatever pleases him'[45] is the builder and manager of a global hospital, has brought all its patients into being, and ensures that none of them leaves alive? How can such a being be one of 'abundant goodness'?[46] John Stuart Mill wrote that a divine being who could not measure up to the goodness he found in his fellow men did not even deserve to be called good, and if such a being could sentence him to hell for refusing to do so, then 'to hell I will go'.[47] Those who, with Mill, find it morally repugnant that such a world as ours could be the loving creation of a perfectly good and all-powerful Deity are just as defiant.

God off the hook?

One response to the atheist's charge has been the attempt to answer the question, 'Why does God allow evil?' by proposing what is known as a theodicy. The word 'theodicy', from the Greek *theos* (God) and *dike* (justice) was coined in 1790, when the German mathematician and philosopher Gottfried Leibniz, who shares with Isaac Newton the distinction of having discovered the universal calculus, published his book *Essais de Theodicée sur la bonté de Dieu.*

Theodicy asks the question: 'How can the justice of an almighty God be defended in the face of evil, especially human suffering and, even more particularly, the suffering of the innocent?' Put more simply, theodicy is a rational attempt to justify God.

Leibniz's theodicy is extremely complicated, but we can sketch out some of its main features here. It rests on his idea that God created the best of all possible worlds but, as it was not in itself divine, it was less than perfect, and what Leibniz called 'physical evil' and 'moral evil' flowed from this fact. Simply put, this model says that human beings sin because they were created as part of a finite (and therefore imperfect) universe. As R. C. Sproul points out, in this theodicy, 'not only is God exonerated ... but so is man'.[48] God has done the best he could (he could not have created a perfect universe without its including another independent, infinite God — which would be a nonsense) and man's evil tendencies flow automatically from the fact that he is not divine.

This may sound feasible, but it can hold together only if we accept that to be a finite creature is to be what Leibniz calls 'metaphysically evil', something which cuts across the divine verdict on his creation: 'God saw all that he had made, and it was very good.'[49] What is more, Leibniz's idea that man's moral and spiritual fall was unavoidable contradicts the Bible's insistence that he is not the victim of circumstances, but truly and actually guilty in the sight of a holy God. At a critical point in his nation's history, the Old Testament priest Ezra expressed what this means in personal experience: 'O my God, I am too ashamed and disgraced to lift up my face to you, my God, because our sins are higher than our heads and our guilt has reached to the heavens.'[50] Nowhere does Scripture allow us to plead deficiencies in heredity, environment or personal psychology as reasons for determining our behaviour. We stand individually responsible to obey God.

Leibniz's theodicy also says that since evil is the inevitable consequence of things as they are, it is in effect *necessary* in order to throw into relief the virtues of goodness, in the same way that an artist uses light and shade in a painting. In other words, if there were no evil we would be unable to define good, as we should have no standards of comparison. This argument has become very popular in recent years, but it can be rejected on two counts. Firstly, if the experience of evil is necessary to an ultimate appreciation of good, then God himself would need to experience it, something ruled out by the Bible's teaching that 'God is light,' and that 'In him there is no darkness at all.'[51] Secondly, as theodicies based on Leibniz's model say nothing clear about the existence of natural evil, they fail to make their case. There is no logical reason why a perfect world should require the existence of evil.

More of the same

Leibniz tries to justify God, but ends up by replacing him with a feeble substitute. Other theodicies do the same thing by robbing God of one or other of his attributes.[52] In *Why Do Bad Things Happen to Good People?*, the Jewish rabbi Harold Kushner popularized the idea that although evil does exist and God is all-loving, he is not all-powerful. Much as he would like to abolish evil (and he was doing the best he could), God had not yet worked out how this could be done. In Kushner's own words, 'Bad things do happen to good people in this world, but it is not God who wills it. God would like people to get what they deserve in life, but he cannot always arrange it. Even God has a hard time keeping chaos in check and limiting the damage evil can do.'[53] In putting forward this concept of what some theologians call 'theistic finitism', Kushner actually proposed that we should lend God a hand by praying for him (although he was unable to suggest a suitable being to whom our petitions could be presented). The basic and fatal flaw in Kushner's theodicy is that it robs God of his sovereignty, clashing headlong with the Bible's assertion that he 'works out everything in conformity with the purpose of his will'.[54]

John Stuart Mill had a theodicy which was tied in to one version of dualism and traced the problem back to creation. In this model, evil and suffering flow from the fact that 'the substance and forces of which the universe is composed'[55] were in some way sub-standard. God did the best he could with what he had, but it was not good enough to produce perfection: 'The Creator did not know how to do it; creative skill, wonderful as it is, was not sufficiently perfect to accomplish his purposes more thoroughly.'[56] There are other theodicies along the same lines, but they all ignore the Bible's insistence that at creation God was not working with material (substandard or otherwise) which happened to be lying around, but that by his sovereign decree all reality outside of himself was brought into being *ex nihilo*, and then pronounced 'very good'.[57] Mills' theodicy replaces the Creator with a mere builder.

Another version of theistic finitism compromises God's wisdom. When at the time of the Aberfan disaster a clergyman was asked by a BBC reporter how he could reconcile this with his faith in God, he replied, 'Well, I suppose we have to admit that this is one of those occasions when the Almighty made a mistake.'[58] Yet his reply was worse than the tragedy itself. It replaces a God to whom 'belong wisdom and power'[59] and whose 'way is perfect'[60] with one who cannot always be trusted to get things right and is liable at times to let them get out of hand.

Another attempt to get God off the hook says that his transcendence puts him above and beyond the moral law which he lays down for his rational creatures. This would mean that God could violate his own moral standards without compromising his justice or goodness. Put even more specifically, this theodicy says that God's status outside the moral law means that it would not be evil of him to allow evil. At first glance, this seems to be a more promising approach, but it fails to take account of the bedrock biblical principle that *God's law is a reflection of his own character*. This is clearly stated in the early part of the Old Testament, where details of the moral law are given in the context of the overriding command, 'Be holy, because I am holy',[61] a principle repeated throughout Scripture.[62] None of God's characteristics is more clearly expressed in the Bible than his holiness, which he in turn requires of his people and, as John Frame explains, 'We can be assured that God will behave according to the same standards that he prescribes for us, except insofar as Scripture declares a difference between his responsibilities and ours.'[63] God could no more violate his own moral code than he could cease to exist. The so-called *ex lex* ('outside the law') argument is a non-starter.

We will take space to mention just two other theodicies. In *The Quest For God*, first published in 1996, Paul Johnson takes a very unusual line: 'God is infinitely curious, just as he is infinitely everything else which is desirable, and curiosity is clearly one reason why he brought the universe into existence in the first place. God's curiosity in observing humanity is more likely to be stimulated and satisfied if humankind has to struggle both against the consequences of choosing evil instead of good, and against the objective facts of evil in nature — often overcoming or mitigating those evils by his or her own ingenuity.'[64] Johnson admits, 'I do not pretend this is a complete answer,'[65] but in truth it is no answer at all. We have not a shred of biblical evidence to support the idea that God brought the universe into being out of curiosity, and the chilling picture of God allowing evil's universal presence and devastating effects purely for the purpose of stimulating and satisfying his inquisitive nature directly contradicts his omniscience and has not a shred of biblical warrant.[66]

Finally, there are those who put forward a theodicy which denies that evil and suffering exist and writes them off as an illusion caused by our inability to see things as they really are. When Guru Mahoraj Ji was asked, 'How does suffering exist; do you know?', he replied, 'Evil is nothing. Evil is ignorance of our mind.'[67] Mary Baker Eddy, the seminal theologian of the self-styled Christian Science movement, wrote, 'Sin, sickness and death are states of mortal mind — illusions,'[68] but this absurdity even contradicts Christian Science's own blatant pantheism. As Jay Adams points out, 'They implode their own belief by this internally-inconsistent self-contradictory explanation. If there is no such thing as evil, if God is all (as they also teach), then this all-knowing god of which every human being is a part cannot err, and there is no such thing as mortal mind.'[69]

Another version of the same kind of theodicy comes to the conclusion that there can be no intrinsic evil in the universe because God is perfectly good, but the glaring weakness here is that there is no reason to think that the negative and painful things we see and experience are an illusion. What is more, if they are an illusion, then the illusion itself is evil. There is little to choose between evil and suffering that are objectively real and a psychological disorder which imagines they are, nor is a God who allows such miserable illusions, and the pain and suffering they bring, an improvement on the one this particular model seeks to replace.

The theodicies we have considered do nothing to lessen the problem of evil, which arguably remains atheism's strongest card. Does theism have a credible response?

23.

The case against the case against God

Thirteen years spent in and around the Guernsey law courts have left me with an endless fascination for the judicial process. Soap operas leave me cold, but real-life courtroom drama always gets my attention. In many trials, a critical point comes when the prosecuting counsel sits down and the case for the defence begins. Although I know that at that point I have heard only a one-sided presentation, there are times when the prosecution case seems so strong that one is hard-pressed to know what can be said to counter it.

In the previous chapter, we have been listening to the case for atheism, challenging the claim that the universe is governed by an omnipotent and all-good God. It has been a multi-pronged attack: the natural world is out of joint, resulting in death and destruction on a massive scale; other disasters take a heavy toll of life and property; nature is red in tooth and claw; armed conflict continues to slaughter people in their thousands; individual acts of aggression and violence are widespread; social disorder is part of the fabric of society; in spite of brilliant advances in science and medicine, we are still subject to a frightening array of diseases and disorders; and we are all heading for the grave, where everything we value comes to nothing.

It is such an impressive case that, after many years of careful analysis, Richard Swinburne admitted, 'Anyone with any moral sensitivity must consider the fact of pain and suffering to constitute a *prima facie* objection to the existence of an all-powerful and all-good God.'[1] God's lawyers would seem to have their work cut out, but before we hear them it will help to be reminded of the main structure of the atheists' argument:

1. Evil and suffering exist in the world.
2. If God were omnipotent, he would be able to prevent these things.
3. If God were wholly good (specifically, if he were a God of love), he would want to prevent them.
4. If there were an omnipotent and wholly good God, evil and suffering would have no place in the world.
5. Therefore, there is no such being as an omnipotent and wholly good God.

What is more ...

The charge is serious enough as it stands, but many sceptics have embellished it by claiming that the responsibility for most of the world's suffering can be laid at the door of religion itself. In the eighteenth century Voltaire went so far as to say, 'Theological religion is the enemy of mankind.'[2] In more recent years Madalyn Murray O'Hair's entrenched atheism included the claim, 'Religion has caused more misery to all of mankind in every stage of human history than any other single idea,'[3] while in 1997, Larry Flynt, America's best-known pornographer, told viewers of the programme *Larry King Live*, 'Religion has caused more harm than anything since the beginning of time.'[4] Nobody can deny that religious fervour has sometimes had disastrous consequences, and we gave examples of this in chapter 18. Yet these tragedies pose no threat to biblical theism, as they occurred when people were promoting or defending non-biblical religions, or when they wrenched the Bible's teaching out of shape to suit their own fanatical agendas. Suggesting that these disprove God's existence is an unwarranted leap of logic.

On the other hand, atheism's record is truly terrible. In 1991 the British journalist William Rees-Mogg told readers of *The Times*, 'The emotional power of religious belief can reinforce evil as well as oppose it, yet no religious tyranny in history has matched that spawned by atheism.'[5] Even if we confined ourselves to just one example from the last completed century of human history, the evidence for this is overwhelming; during these ten decades more people were killed by atheistic states than in all other wars throughout history. It was atheism, not religion (of any kind) which triggered Nazism and led to such wholesale slaughter. In *The Rise and Fall of the Third Reich*, journalist William Shirer indicated that the Nazi regime's ultimate goal was to destroy biblical religion and substitute 'the old paganism of the early German gods and the new paganism of the Nazi extremists'.[6] It was atheism, not religion, which fuelled the Marxist-Leninist agenda and resulted, directly or indirectly, in the deaths of over sixty million men, women and children in Eastern Europe in the space of fifty years. It was atheism, not religion, which crushed the life out of seventy million people in Mao Tse-tung's China and left 1.3 million dead in Pol Pot's Cambodia.

Religion had no part to play in China's Tiananmen Square massacre in 1989, when the People's Liberation Army killed 2,600 peaceful demonstrators and injured another 10,000. Religion was not the cause of the genocide perpetrated in recent years on Rwanda, Congo and Sierra Leone, nor of so-called 'ethnic cleansing' in Bosnia and Kosovo. Time and again I have heard sceptics cite thirty years of violence in Northern Ireland as a recent example of the misery caused by religion, yet 100 visits to the Province have shown me that the sectarianism which has cost over 3,000 lives is basically political, whatever religious affiliation the culprits may claim. None of the bombing, shooting and burning in the Balkans and Northern Ireland was aimed at getting people to change their religious ideas.

Few things cause more misery in modern society than the epidemic breakdown of marriage relationships, and Britain is now known as the 'divorce capital of Europe', with a 1999 report showing that the average British marriage now lasts just 510 weeks. Is it seriously suggested that religion is the major cause of marriage breakdown and divorce, and of the ensuing emotional and psychological trauma caused to tens of thousands of children in Britain alone? Does religion lie behind this country's crime figures — or those of any other country? Is religion usually the catalyst for wife-battering, robbery, rape or child abuse? As the vehement charge against religion is so inclusive, we are entitled to broaden the counter-attack. Is religion the main culprit when industrial and domestic accidents take place? Is religion responsible for most of the carnage on our roads? Does religion cause natural disasters, or trigger most of the injuries or diseases which land people in doctors' surgeries or hospital beds? O'Hair and Flynt may be enthusiastic and eloquent atheists, but they are hopeless historians and, as far as the present issue is concerned, are not even on speaking terms with the truth. Whatever else may be said, their accusations leave biblical theism untouched.

Cows over the moon

In the last chapter, we looked at a number of theodicies, attempts to justify God in allowing evil to exist. These were framed in response to atheism's claims that the existence of evil is logically inconsistent with the belief in an omnipotent and all-good God. As the issue of logic underpins atheism's position, it needs to be tackled head-on, but the theist has no need to explain *why* God should allow evil to exist or continue, nor to show *how* God does this. All he has to do on this point is to show that there is no logical contradiction in the co-existence of God and evil, and he can do so simply and effectively.

In *Return to Reason*, first published in 1990, the American philosopher Kelly James Clark gives an amusing explanation of the difference between logical and physical impossibility: 'Given certain physical laws, it is physically impossible — given laws of gravity, the weight of cows, and the propulsive power of cow legs — that cows jump over the moon, or that human beings fly. However, both of these states of affairs are logically possible — their obtaining violates no laws of logic.'[7] Atheism says that there is no *possible* way for God and evil to co-exist, but this is not the case, as any state of affairs that does not violate the laws of logic is logically possible. What is more, atheism is wide open to a clinching counter-attack because, in answering the case, the theist is not restricted to the *plausible*, but can bring in any scenario that is *possible*.

If we construct a state of affairs in which, to quote Clark, 'cows have a strong penchant for moon-hopping' and 'legs as strong as an interstellar rocket',[8] there would be no reason why they should not do so as easily as we walk down the road. This is very different from talking about square circles, or things existing and not existing at one and the same time. These are logical impossibilities; lunar-hopping cows are not. Nor — whatever problems it might raise — is the co-existence of God and evil. Atheism's claim that there is no possible way for this to be the case goes too far.

Why good and evil?

We drew attention to another fundamental flaw in the atheist's case back in chapter 17, but this is the point at which to pursue it. If the believer has a problem in explaining the existence of evil in a world created and ruled by God, the unbeliever has the much greater problem of explaining how, in a world without God, he can speak of anything as being either good or evil. In order to use the 'problem of evil' argument against a theistic world-view, the atheist must show that his own definition of evil is meaningful, which is precisely what he is unable to do. Over 2,000 years ago, Socrates showed that in order to make a distinction between particulars, in which one is good and the other is evil, you must begin with a universal or abso-lute. Without an infinite reference-point, the atheist can never speak of 'good' or 'evil' in an absolute sense, nor, for that matter, can he explain why there is a difference between them.

In a debate about the existence of God held at the University of Califor-nia at Davis in 1993, Edward Tabash, a vehement atheist, challenged his opponent by declaring, 'If the God of the Bible actually exists, I want to sue him for negligence for being asleep at the wheel of the universe when my grandfather and uncle were gassed to death in Auschwitz.'[9] It might be thought that nobody would want to question an emotional reaction to the Holocaust, but what is the basis for any moral complaint about what Hitler did to the Jews if God does not exist? In a godless universe, what one 'animal' does to another 'animal' is ethically irrelevant, and there is no moral basis for anger or outrage against anything. Whatever happens hap-pens, and that is all there is to it.

An atheistic world-view advocates freedom of belief, expression and choice, and says that evil is related to these at an individual or corporate level, but it is easy to see how this concept implodes, because those said to commit evil are not really doing so *according to the values that they have chosen for themselves*. On this basis, Hitler's slaughter of the Jews can be defended just as easily as it can be condemned, since in the absence of an absolute, transcendent moral standard, there can be no such thing as an observance or breach of it. In an atheist's universe, an action can be said to produce unhappiness or pain, but it cannot be said to be absolutely, radically wrong. As we saw in an earlier chapter, the most that a leading atheist spokesman like Gordon Stein can say is, 'Evil is by definition in an atheist's universe that which decreases the happiness of people... The thing is evil which causes more people to be unhappy.' Yet when he faces the question, 'How do we know this?' he is forced to reply, 'Well, we don't know it. It's a consensus, just like morality in general is a consensus.' This is seriously defective as an answer. In some societies, people usually re-spect their neighbours, while in others they occasionally eat them; are the rights and wrongs of these cases a matter of consensus, or preference? It is difficult to see how we can rationally discuss the problem of evil if definitions are decided by a show of hands. The fact is that a sense of right and wrong is 'there', regardless of cultural considerations and, as Peter Kreeft and Ronald Tacelli insist, 'The very fact of our outrage at evil is a clue that we are in touch with a standard of goodness by which we judge this world as defective, as falling short of the mark.'[10] However strong the atheist's argument from evil may seem at first glance, an even more compelling case can be made for saying that the existence of evil points *towards* God rather than away from him.

Interviewed in 1995 by the *Sunday Telegraph's* John Morrish, the passionate homosexual campaigner Peter Tatchell said that his 'very strong sense of knowing the difference between right and wrong'[11] stemmed from his strict religious background. Tatchell is now a staunch atheist, but he admits that it was his belief in God, not his atheism, which enabled him to distinguish good from evil. This should hardly surprise us. If there is no transcendent moral lawgiver, there can be no universal moral law. If there is no such law, there is no such thing as essential good. If there is no such thing as essential good, there can be no such thing as essential evil. As Robert Morey rightly says, 'The problem of evil does not negate the existence of God. It actually requires it.'[12]

In other words, paradoxical as it may seem, Alvin Plantinga is entitled to claim, 'There is a *theistic* argument *from* evil, and it is at least as strong as the antitheistic argument from evil.'[13] We have already seen that there is no such thing as a logical problem of evil, and we could actually rework atheism's classic attack in the following way to show that the existence of evil is indirect proof that God *does* exist:

1. If God does not exist, transcendent, objective values of good and evil do not exist.
2. Evil does exist.
3. Therefore objective values exist, and some things are really, basically, fundamentally bad.
4. Therefore God exists.

As we saw in chapter 21, God is much more than a transcendent moral being (he is eternal, self-existent and omnipotent, for instance), yet as soon as the atheist draws a distinction between right and wrong, his whole case begins to fall apart.

By the same token, the atheist is also faced with what Lord Hailsham, the former Lord Chancellor, calls 'the problem of good'. In his autobiography, he makes the point like this:

> You do not get out of your philosophical troubles arising out of the fact of evil by rejecting God. For, as I have tried to point out before, the real problem is not the problem of evil, but the problem of good, not the problem of cruelty and selfishness, but the problem of kindness and generosity, not the problem of ugliness, but the problem of beauty.
>
> If the world is really the hopeless and meaningless jumble which one has to believe it to be if once we reject our value judgements as nothing more than emotional noises, with nothing more in the way of objective truth than a certain biological survival value for the species rather than the individual, evil then presents no difficulty because it does not exist. We must expect to be knocked about a bit in a world which consists only of atoms, molecules and strange particles. But how, then, does it come about that we go through life on assumptions which are perfectly contrary to the facts, that we love our wives and families, thrill with pleasure at the sight of a little bird discreetly dressed in green and black and white, that we rage at injustice inflicted on innocent victims, honour our martyrs, reward our heroes, and even occasionally, with difficulty, forgive our enemies and do good to those who persecute us and despitefully use us? No, it is light which is the problem, not darkness. It is seeing, not blindness... It is love, not callousness. The thing we have to explain in the world is the positive, not the negative. *It is this which led me to God in the first place*[14] (emphasis added).

By saying that our need is to explain 'the positive, not the negative', Lord Hailsham is not saying that evil needs no explanation, but that, without God, good poses an even greater problem.

The understandable mystery

When the English television personality Jill Dando was shot dead outside her London home in 1999, a card attached to one of the floral tributes laid at the spot soon afterwards simply asked, 'Why?', the one-word question which dominates the whole 'problem of evil' debate. Consistent atheists brush it aside, and their bleak materialism dismisses Dando's death as yet another meaningless event, but the overwhelming human instinct is to recognize her killing as evil and not as something that can be shrugged off as 'one of those things'. Where can we look for answers?

In *Pages from God's Casebook*, first published in 1962, the Australian doctor John Hercus wrote about the way he and his colleagues answered patients' questions about illness or disease and explained what had gone wrong with the 'machinery'. He then went on to say, 'But sometimes we hear the other question, the big question. "Why? What have I done to deserve this? Why should I have to get polio right in the middle of my university course? Why should my little boy be killed? Why should my wife get cancer? Why did my coronary artery occlude?" And I must bow my head, humbled, as I answer, "I'm trained only in a Medical School. I can tell you only *how* it happened. If you want to know *why* this happened, you shouldn't ask your doctor. You should ask your Maker."'[15]

The theist agrees, and in response to the wider question of evil and suffering in general he turns to the Bible, 'the living and enduring word of God'.[16] As no other religion or philosophy can produce a credible explanation, and some never even address the problem, this certainly puts him on the right track, yet even the Bible does not give off-the-shelf, clear-cut or comprehensive answers to every query which the subject raises. To the critical atheist, this must sound like the ultimate cop-out: 'The theist is happy to lean on logic when it suits him to do so, but when we come to the strongest argument against belief in God, he labels it "mystery" and slams the door against rational discussion and logical conclusions.' This is heavy hitting, but the theist can make at least three immediate responses to the charge that he is running scared.

Firstly, although the believer does not have a full and final explanation for the existence of evil, the fact is that no one has a complete answer. What is more, and as we have just seen, the atheist has the additional problem of finding an explanation for the origin of good. To insist that every question about evil and suffering must have a clinical and comprehensive answer is to engage in metaphysical 'nothing-buttery' and reduce God to nothing more than a logical proposition or a mathematical formula. The fact that God is consistently wise,[17] just,[18] true[19] and faithful[20] shows that he is perfectly consistent and cannot contradict himself, but this is not to say that we can strip him down and understand how he works, as if he were an internal combustion engine or a computer.

Secondly, to insist on answers to all the questions involved is to assume that God owes us an explanation for everything he has done, or is doing, but there can be no logical basis for such an assumption, and there is no warrant for it in Scripture. The Bible clearly establishes that God is beyond our complete understanding:

> Oh, the depth of the riches of the wisdom and knowledge of God!
>   How unsearchable his judgements,
>   and his paths beyond tracing out! [21]

Should this surprise us? Elsewhere in Scripture we are told that 'The foolishness of God is wiser than man's wisdom,'[22] that is to say, not even the highest exercise of human wisdom can approach an understanding of why God acts as he does. God's infinite transcendence means that there are issues on which as finite human beings we are simply unqualified to pronounce a definite verdict. In his careful study *How Long, O Lord?*, Don Carson writes, 'The mystery of providence defies our attempt to tame it by reason. I do not mean it is illogical; I mean that we do not know enough to be able to unpack it and domesticate it.'[23] Why should believing this be thought illogical?

Questions raised by some of the Bible's most firmly grounded believers confirm the conflicts raised by the issue of evil and suffering. The prophet Jeremiah asked God, 'Why does the way of the wicked prosper? Why do all the faithless live at ease?'[24] Job, a man who was 'blameless and upright' and who 'feared God and shunned evil',[25] faced the same problem: 'Why do the wicked live on, growing old and increasing in power?'[26] The prophet Habakkuk, a man of outstanding faith, nevertheless found himself asking God, 'Why do you make me look at injustice? Why do you tolerate wrong?'[27] One obvious reason why questions like these can be asked is that we often understand things by analogy, yet there are no complete analogies within a finite creation from which we can understand the ways of an infinite Creator. As Don Carson confirms in *Divine Sovereignty and Human Responsibility*, 'There is an unbridgeable ontological gap between the personal transcendent God and finite man, and this gap brings about the breakdown of all analogical arguments designed to picture the mode of divine causation.'[28]

Nothing we have said in this section means that there is no rhyme or reason for the way God works, nor that he is other than 'righteous in all his ways'.[29] Writing in *The Quest for God* that throughout his life he has been 'amazingly fortunate', and that this disqualifies him from advancing justification for God's tolerance of evil, Paul Johnson goes on, 'But, having thus disqualified myself, I am still convinced that God sees infinitely further than the rest of us, that he has reasons for all things, and that in his good time there will be explanations forthcoming for all he has done, or does not do, or permits to happen.'[30] This may cut no ice with the atheist, but Johnson's confidence has a firm biblical foundation.

Thirdly, to be left with doubts is not the same as being left in the dark. In one of the most famous passages in the New Testament, the apostle Paul writes, 'For now we see in a mirror dimly, but then face to face.'[31] The word 'dimly' translates the Greek *en ainigmati*, the noun being one from which we get our English word 'enigma'. In Paul's day, a mirror would have been made from burnished metal and the image somewhat blurred, but it would still have given the user *some* indication of whatever it was reflecting. On the issue of evil and suffering there are enigmas, grey areas, apparent anomalies and what seem at times to be downright contradictions, yet even in our finite, fallen state we are not left entirely in the dark about God and his ways. To say that something is mysterious is not to say that we can know nothing about it. John Frame goes so far as to say that 'The whole Bible addresses the problem of evil, for the whole story turns on the entrance of sin and evil into the world and on God's plan for dealing with it.'[32] In the remainder of this chapter, we will sketch in the contours of what it says.

God is God

During the debate at Davis referred to earlier, Edward Tabash referred to God as a 'cosmic egomaniac' and a 'moral monster', and then issued the following challenge: 'If you are listening, and you are really there, show yourself right now. Manifest on the stage. Do a colossal miracle. Levitate this building. Show me something more than ancient hearsay from the depths of antiquity to prove your existence. And if you do not meet my challenge, I say to you, if you are awake and listening, that you are violating your moral duty to manifest yourself, considering that you yourself have erected such harsh penalties to befall all those of us who do not believe. If there is such a penalty to be paid for disbelief, then you must, to be fair, give us greater evidence to induce that belief.'

As none of Tabash's demands were met, he claimed to have proved his case, but this only added ignorance to arrogance. A God who allowed himself to be pulled around in this way would be surrendering the very qualities which make him God. Did Tabash, a self-styled expert on atheism (and a lawyer to boot) not grasp this? What if other atheists insisted on more radical action? Should we expect God to answer their demands for instant wealth, promotion, business achievement, sporting success, or a cast-iron guarantee against injury or ill-health? A deity who granted these (and was forced to do so to prove his own existence) bears as much resemblance to the God of Scripture as a genie popping out of a bottle and asking, 'What can I do for you?' By definition, God acts on his terms, not ours. This is the basic reality which must govern our thinking as we continue to respond to atheism's charge that God cannot co-exist with evil and suffering.

It is not difficult to imagine what would happen if God always stepped in to correct our mistakes, or to prevent suffering of any kind, regardless of how man behaved. As Brian Edwards says, 'Man would be even more convinced that he is infallible and can live perfectly well without God.'[33] We might imagine God acting in such a way if man's uninterrupted happiness was the ultimate end of all reality, but the Bible never allows us to harbour such a self-centred illusion.

Atheism nevertheless maintains that an omnipotent God would be able to prevent evil and its effects. The theist's response is not merely to state that God *is* omnipotent, but to assert that he is *actively* omnipotent, exercising 'hands-on' sovereignty over all other reality. In the Bible's words:

> The LORD does whatever pleases him,
> in the heavens and on the earth,
> in the seas and all their depths. [34]

God has no 'no-go' areas. Times and seasons, upheavals in the natural world (as well as its normal processes), weather patterns, political decisions, civil and international wars, human choices and relationships, incidents and 'accidents' of every kind — the Bible teaches that all are under the control of the one who is 'enthroned as King for ever'.[35] The Bible insists that nothing in the entire universe happens by chance, and that no detail of created reality is beyond God's government. We are told that not even a sparrow falls to the ground apart from God's will[36] and that 'Even the very hairs of your head are numbered.'[37]

God's sovereignty is pervasive throughout Scripture, but it is far from popular outside of it. The nineteenth-century British preacher C. H.

Spurgeon claimed, 'No doctrine in the whole Word of God has more excited the hatred of mankind than the truth of the absolute sovereignty of God,'[38] yet those who flatly refuse to accept God's rights are often passionate in asserting their own. In *Deliver Us From Evil*, Ravi Zacharias tells of taking part in an open-line talk programme from an American university when one of the callers raised the subject of abortion and asked for his comment on her assertion that the freedom to abort was her moral right. In response, Zacharias pointed out that on virtually every university campus on which he had debated the issue of God's existence, someone challenged God's goodness by pointing out all the evil in the world, especially the gratuitous evil that seems purely the result of a whim. When a plane crashes, why does God arbitrarily allow some people to die and some to survive? Surely this kind of decision shows that God must be evil and not good? Zacharias then went on: 'My question to you, madam, is this. When you arrogate the right to yourself to choose who may live in your womb and who may die, you call it your moral right. But when God exercises the same right, you call him evil. Can you explain this contradiction to me?'[39] The caller responded with what Zacharias calls 'anger and verbal frustration', but she could not wriggle out of her dilemma.

The Bible emphasizes the comprehensiveness of God's sovereignty by making it clear that in the exercise of his divine right God is as completely in control of evil as he is of good. He specifically tells the prophet Isaiah:

I am the LORD, and there is no other...
I form the light and create darkness,
    I bring prosperity and create disaster;
    I, the LORD, do all these things. [40]

Another Old Testament writer underlines this: 'Is it not from the mouth of the Most High that both calamities and good things come?'[41] When the prophet Amos warns Israel of an imminent military invasion he asks, 'When disaster comes to a city, has not the LORD caused it?'[42] It is important to notice that there is not a drop of dualism here. Even the most dreadful disaster is caused, not by some unidentified, malignant co-deity, but by the sole and sovereign God of the universe.

This inevitably raises the question of the relationship between divine sovereignty and human responsibility, which many people believe to be incompatible. If God is absolutely sovereign, directing and controlling everything, how can human beings be free to make moral choices and then be held accountable for their actions? If, on the other hand, human beings are free moral agents, how can God be said to be totally in control? Atheism would argue that in either case God becomes less than theists make him out to be; he loses either his right to judge or his claim to rule.

Early in the Old Testament there is a clear illustration of the way in which the Bible counters this. The Hebrew patriarch Jacob had twelve sons, of whom his favourite was Joseph, the second youngest. When Joseph brashly told his brothers of having dreams which featured them in an inferior position to him, they decided to kill him, but eventually settled for selling him to a caravan of Ishmaelites on their way to Egypt. In a remarkable series of promotions, Joseph eventually became prime minister, and under his leadership Egypt built up surplus stocks of grain at a time when neighbouring countries were hit by famine. When Joseph's brothers went to Egypt to buy food, they unknowingly found themselves dealing with the very man they had brutally abused as a teenager. Recognizing who they were, Joseph graciously forgave them, and claimed, 'It was not you who sent me here, but God,'[43] adding some time later, 'You intended to harm me, but God intended it for good to accomplish what is now being done, the saving of many lives.'[44]

It is important to notice exactly what is being said here. We are not told that Joseph's brothers took the initiative, and that God interrupted to change the course of events. Nor are we told that the brothers' ill-treatment of Joseph replaced God's planned method of getting him to Egypt. Instead the words, 'You intended ... but God intended...', make it clear that while the brothers were fully responsible for their evil actions, God was actively and intentionally at work at every point. This illustration alone (there are many others) is sufficient to show that as God is both 'good and upright',[45] it must be the case that he stands behind good and evil in somewhat different ways. Don Carson elaborates: 'To put it bluntly, God stands behind evil in such a way that not even evil takes place outside the bounds of his sovereignty, yet the evil is not morally chargeable to him: it is always chargeable to secondary agents, to secondary causes. On the other hand, God stands behind good in such a way that it not only takes place within the bounds of his sovereignty, but it is always chargeable to him, and only derivatively to secondary agents.'[46] In other words, human beings alone can properly be blamed for evil, and God alone can properly be praised for good.

Nobody can fully grasp how this can be the case, but submission to Scripture is an infinitely wiser course than what Don Carson calls 'our frankly idolatrous devotion to our own capacity to understand'.[47] Discussing the relationship between God's sovereignty and man's responsibility, Paul makes a critically important statement: 'One of you will say to me: "Then why does God still blame us? For who resists his will?" But who are you, O man, to talk back to God?'[48] Commenting on this, the Welsh preacher Geoff Thomas asserts, 'In these words is the total biblical philosophy as to the relationship between God's willing of everything that happens to us and our own responsibility for the things we do. Both truths stand on the basis of their own independent testimony in the Scriptures. Our duty is to believe them both... We will always freely choose the very thing that God has planned for us. The Lord's purposes will be fulfilled and man will be held accountable for his every sin.'[49]

As an epilogue to Joseph's story, I recall a minister friend in South Africa asking me to visit an elderly believer in a Johannesburg hospital. About a week earlier, he had been thrown out on to the street by a young shopkeeper angry at him for trying to return a defective tool he had recently bought there. The man was rushed to hospital with a broken arm and severe bruising, but tests carried out when he was admitted revealed an unsuspected heart condition which would have killed him within days had it not been attended to. When I visited him he was recovering successfully from a multiple cardiac bypass — and rejoicing in the fact that, while his attacker had intended to harm him, 'God intended it for good'.

One further thing can be said in rounding off this section. The Bible asserts or implies the omnipotence of God on every page but, as we saw in chapter 20, this does not mean that he can do absolutely anything. Instead, it means that he can do *anything consistent with his revealed nature and eternal purposes*. By choosing to do certain things, God has ruled out other possibilities. Having created man with free will, he would not then step in and prevent its misuse, which inevitably led to suffering. Not even an omnipotent God would have created human beings with genuine moral freedom and at the same time have ruled out the possibility of their doing wrong. As Stephen Evans points out, 'A person who is free and yet cannot choose wrongly is a person who is both free and not free. *Not even God could create such a "round square"* '[50] (emphasis added).

As we shall see shortly, all the world's suffering would have been prevented if God had created human beings as robots, permanently

programmed to behave impeccably towards their Creator, their fellow creatures and nature as a whole, and with no potential or opportunity to choose
or develop personal relationships. Would atheists settle for such an arrangement? Would they be happy to live under a cosmic tyrant who prevented them ever causing hurt or harm by exercising rigid control over all
their thought-patterns and actions? Would atheists seriously go along with
Andy Warhol and claim, 'The world would be easier to live in if we were
all machines'?[51] Would they honestly prefer to be puppets? Freedom of
choice without choice's effects is a non-starter; as C. S. Lewis wrote, 'It is
no more possible for God than for the weakest of his creatures to carry out
both of two mutually exclusive alternatives *not because his power meets
an obstacle, but because nonsense remains nonsense, even when we talk
it about God*[52] (emphasis added). Far from there being a logical conflict
between the existence of evil and an omnipotent God who created humankind with genuine moral freedom, exactly the opposite is the case.

By the same token, would atheists settle for a God who prevented all
natural disasters by interrupting the laws of physics without notice, even if
this meant leaving us unable to rely on them at any point? If we added this
to what we have already seen, it would paradoxically bring about even
more suffering because, as Francis Bridger rightly says, 'We should be
reduced to such a state of physical, social and psychological instability that
life would fall apart.'[53]

Suffering and love

We can respond much more briefly to atheism's charge that the existence
of evil is incompatible with a God of love who would by definition eliminate the possibility of suffering in a universe he created and controls.

Theists are certainly happy to endorse the definition. In chapter 20, we
concentrated on what some of the psalmists said about God's love, but
the same truths are expressed from Genesis to Revelation, filling out the
fundamental fact that 'God is love.'[54] J. I. Packer calls God's love 'the
supreme and most glorious manifestation'[55] of his goodness. The Bible
speaks of God's 'abundant goodness',[56] and time and again we are told,
'Give thanks to the LORD, for he is good; his love endures for ever.'[57] At
one point, David declares:

The LORD is gracious and compassionate,
    slow to anger and rich in love.
The LORD is good to all;
    he has compassion on all he has made. [58]

Believers rejoice in statements like this, yet atheists latch on to them just as avidly and claim that if a God of such grace, love and goodness really existed, and truly did have 'compassion on all he has made', he would never even expose them to the risk of suffering, let alone fail to put an end to it if it should somehow occur.

Three things can be said in response to the charge.

Firstly, how can we know that there cannot be good reasons for God to allow suffering? If we accept that God's thoughts and ways are 'higher' than ours, how can we know that he did not act wisely in exposing humankind to the risk of suffering? Can we say with certainty that he would want to prevent *any* possibility of pain? Do love and risk-prevention necessarily go together? In Britain alone, hundreds of children are killed or injured in traffic accidents every year. One sure way to prevent this kind of thing would be for parents to keep their children confined to the house, but would that be an acceptable alternative to exposing them to the risk of an accident? Wise parents may give a teenager sensible guidelines on the choice of friends and the conduct of personal relationships, but they will not be ruthlessly dictatorial. They will realize that the young person concerned will need a measure of freedom if he or she is to become a mature adult. As Stephen Evans says, 'Good persons do not necessarily eliminate all the suffering they can... Rather, they prevent suffering where it is possible to do so *without harming some more important goal*' [59] (emphasis added). Without a perfect understanding of God's 'goal', are we in a position to pass judgement on his actions?

Secondly, as C. S. Lewis noted, 'The problem of reconciling human suffering with the existence of a God who loves is insoluble only so long as we attach a trivial meaning to the word "love", and look on things as if man was the centre of them.' [60] The biblical picture of God's love is not one of sloppy sentimentalism, or what Lewis calls 'a senile benevolence that drowsily wishes you to be happy in your own way'. [61] It is not a wishy-washy attitude which cheerfully leaves man free to 'do his own thing' regardless of the consequences. Instead, as Alec Motyer puts it, it is 'part and parcel of the very nature of God himself', [62] and as such it is pure, righteous, wise and perfect. God's great concern is not to satisfy man's appetite for what he considers to be success, happiness or well-being, but 'to impart *himself*, and so all good, to other persons, and to possess them for his own spiritual fellowship'[63] (emphasis added).

Thirdly, God demonstrates the reality and depth of his love by his willingness to enter into and share the trauma of human suffering. He is not a remote, unfeeling deity, unable to understand our pain, unwilling to do anything about it, and content to watch us twisting in the wind. On the contrary, the Bible reveals a God who is prepared to accept more suffering than we can ever imagine in order to fulfil his perfect purposes and to bring into a transforming and eternal relationship with himself 'a great multitude that no one could count, from every nation, tribe, people and language'.[64] No discussion of the problem of evil and suffering makes sense without taking this into account, but the structure of this book means that we must delay doing so until the final chapter.

Blame and cause

When tragedies hit the front pages, God often gets the blame, yet there are often much clearer ways of explaining what went wrong. For example, people shake their fists at God when they hear of the world's starving millions, yet he has provided the means of producing more than sufficient food for everyone on the planet. In many cases, it is man's greed, corruption or mismanagement which lead to people dying of hunger. Nor are these the only man-made causes of starvation. Millions are dying of hunger in India while Hinduism treats cows as sacred and forbids their use as food. Can God be blamed for unbiblical religious dogma which allows people to die while surrounded by the means of keeping them alive?

Can God be directly and obviously blamed for deaths caused by such things as floods, famine, volcanoes and earthquakes? James Sire points the finger elsewhere: 'It is at least possible that if human beings had continued in the will of God, they would have discerned the limits set by their environment. The ravaging effect of floods could be prevented if we avoided living on floodplains. Famine is often a consequence of bad farming, not just erratic weather. Had we not fallen, perhaps we would have been better farmers and better predictors of future weather. Volcanoes and earthquakes seem harder to predict, but who knows what we might know about our environment had we developed science and technology as unfallen creatures?'[65]

There are sometimes other factors which directly implicate man. These words are being written as Turkey reels from the impact of an earthquake registering 7.4 on the Richter scale and said to be the country's worst disaster in modern times. In just forty-five seconds, over 15,000 people were killed and more than 200,000 rendered homeless. Yet even as the rescue teams try desperately to find signs of any remaining survivors, blame is already being laid at the door of 'corrupt or incompetent contractors who ignored elementary earthquake precautions'.[66] Turkish newspapers are claiming that of 600 buildings erected by one well-known contractor, 550 collapsed; the builder is said to have fled the country.

Can God be blamed for catastrophic events triggered by human decision-making? What about the three we identified in the last chapter? On the night *Titanic* went down, the weather was pleasant and clear, and in any case she was equipped with Marconi's new wireless telegraph system, which was monitored around the clock. The ship's captain had been unconcerned about five different warnings of drifting ice in the course of 14 April, and the ship sailed safely on. That evening, when the wireless operator on duty received a sixth warning, he failed to realize its significance, and tucked it under a paperweight on his desk. It never reached the captain, and when a lookout in the crow's nest spotted the fatal iceberg at 11.40 that night, *Titanic* was just thirty-seven seconds away from disaster. Is there a straight line from a wireless operator's lack of concentration to the non-existence of God, or to defects in his character? Again, the original design of *Titanic* called for thirty-two lifeboats, but the owners felt that so many would make the boat deck look cluttered, and reduced the number to twenty, giving a total lifeboat capacity of 1,178 for a liner capable of carrying over 3,500 passengers and crew. Does this help to make the case for atheism?

When Aberfan was hit, one man sent a contribution to the disaster fund with a footnote, 'Don't mention God to me, there isn't one' — but is this a logical or fair conclusion to draw? The subsequent enquiry into the tragedy laid the blame fairly and squarely at the door of those responsible for building a slag-heap over a stream and so close to a school. Previous, smaller slips should have warned those involved not to continue adding to the man-made mountain of waste. The enquiry spoke of 'bungling ineptitude' and concluded, 'Our strong and unanimous view is that the Aberfan disaster could and should have been prevented.'[67] In other words, it was the result of human error, and a local minister was perfectly justified in saying, 'I defy any coroner to call this an act of God.'[68]

The same can be said about Chernobyl. The day before the accident, the Unit 4 reactor was shut down for routine maintenance, but an important test was run without a proper exchange of information and co-ordination between the team in charge of the test and the personnel in charge of the operation and safety of the reactor. The official report of the International Atomic Energy Agency came to a clear conclusion as to where the blame for the disaster lay: 'The accident can be said to have flowed from deficient safety culture, not only at the Chernobyl plant, but throughout the Soviet design, operating and regulatory organizations for nuclear power that existed at that time.'[69] Chernobyl was a catastrophe of truly terrifying proportions, but can God be held responsible for those in charge not operating a suitable 'safety culture'?

Is God at fault when an aeroplane crashes as the result of pilot error or faulty equipment? In 1999 the *Sunday Telegraph* said that the tragedies which hit the third generation of the Kennedys had been mostly self-inflicted.[70] This was certainly true in the case of John F. Kennedy, Jr, who insisted on taking off in conditions which deterred more experienced pilots, and while he was still using a crutch after breaking his ankle two months earlier. Can God be put in the dock for these risks being taken? Is he to blame for injuries and deaths caused by drivers under the influence of drink or drugs? Can he be held to account for deficient urban planning, misguided agricultural policies, or the pollution of the atmosphere in pursuit of technological goals? Is God at fault when drinking habits lead to cirrhosis of the liver, cigarette smoking to cancer or sexual promiscuity to AIDS? Is he responsible for the suppressed hatred, anger, bitterness and envy which are often the direct cause of serious illness or worse?

Yet misery and suffering are not free-standing; they have their roots in the sinfulness of humanity's fallen nature. In a telling New Testament passage, 'evil thoughts, sexual immorality, theft, murder, adultery, greed, malice, deceit, lewdness, envy, slander, arrogance and folly' are said to come 'from within'.[71] Simply put, man is morally and spiritually defiled. Nor is this evil itself a separate substance or entity. We know this because God is the Creator of all reality outside of himself, and could not bring into existence anything in conflict with his own perfect nature. No created reality is evil in itself, not even the constituent parts of nature, such as volcanic lava which buries towns, or the water which sweeps thousands to their deaths. Nor is any man-made device, from a knuckle-duster to a nuclear warhead. The problem lies elsewhere.

The Bible's definition of evil could not be more concise: 'Sin is lawlessness.'[72] 'Lawlessness' is the negative form of the Greek *nomos* (law) and could literally be translated 'no law'. Evil is not a substance, but a spirit, an attitude. Evil is neither original nor eternal, nor does it provide a basis for dualism, as God alone is the supreme and only eternal Being. It is the deliberate rejection of God's sovereign right to rule over his creation.

The first rebellion against God's rule was by Satan, a created angel or spirit, who persuaded many others to join him[73] and who was directly instrumental in persuading Adam and Eve that if they were to throw off God's authority and disobey his command not to eat of 'the tree of the knowledge of good and evil'[74] they would 'be like God'.[75] Their intimate personal relationship with God and their enjoyment of his lavish provision meant that God's instruction was perfectly reasonable, and an ideal way of testing their willingness to obey what God said simply because he said it; but they failed the test, and at that moment 'sin entered the world'.[76]

The consequences were awesomely disastrous. As we saw in chapter 21, their relationship with God was shattered, leaving them alienated, ashamed and afraid, the world's first dysfunctional family. Not only were man's circumstances ruined, so was his very nature. As a psychosomatic being, sin affected every part of him, leaving his mind, heart, will, conscience and emotions unable to function as they once did. Made 'in the image of God',[77] he became a shadow of his former self, and for the first time was prone to decay, disease and death. What is more, his decisions and actions became governed by a nature that was now 'hostile to God';[78] put another way, man lost his freedom not to sin.

This ruined, corrupt nature was then transmitted to every generation of human beings from that day onwards. As the head and representative of the human race, Adam dragged the whole species down with him. When he sinned, 'all sinned',[79] and Paul spoke for all of us when he said that we are 'by nature objects of [God's] wrath'.[80] When our first parents sinned, they brought down sorrow, pain and suffering not only upon themselves but upon every succeeding generation, to whom their sinful nature has been transmitted. Whatever reasons God may have had for allowing it, evil is our fault, not his. Lawlessness, the urge to reject God's rule and run our own lives, is embedded in our fallen human nature, and all the suffering we face hinges on that fact. The word 'suffering' would not exist if man had not shaken his fist in his Creator's face.

Not *every* separate experience of pain is the direct result of a specific sin, but every one of them can be traced back to man's initial disobedience. As Don Carson points out, 'If ... we see such suffering as the effluent of the fall, the result of a fallen world, the consequence of evil that is really evil and in which we ourselves all too frequently indulge, then however much we may grieve when we suffer, we will not be taken by surprise.'[81]

Yet sin had even wider consequences; it affected not only the whole human race but the entire cosmos. After Adam had sinned, God told him, 'Cursed is the ground because of you.'[82] One of the Bible's clearest ways of stating this is to say that the whole of creation is 'in bondage to decay', and that ever since sin entered the world it has been 'groaning as in the pains of childbirth right up to the present time'.[83] A previously perfect system, reflecting the holy character of its Creator, has been turned into one which is prone to earthquakes, floods, tornadoes and other natural disorders. In ways which we can never fully grasp, but which includes *every* part of creation which is adverse to man, sin has knocked the cosmos out of kilter. For all its beauty, colour, variety and vibrancy, the world we see all around us bears little resemblance to the original creation which God pronounced 'very good'.[84] We live in a fallen world, and the whole creation is groaning in pain under the curse of God's judgement upon it.

To what purpose?

Martin Luther used to say that God sometimes acts in ways which are obviously consistent with his revealed nature, and that when he does so this is *opus proprium Dei* (the proper work of God). At other times, however, God acts in ways which might seem to contradict his nature. Luther called this *opus alienum Dei* (the strange work of God), and it is not difficult to see why people should put evil and suffering in this category. What purpose can God have in these? Can good come out of evil? What possible benefits can suffering bring?

We must begin our answer with a question which, in one form or another, we have asked several times already: can finite creatures really expect to fathom the infinity of God's thinking? Those who state that suffering is too high a price to pay for achieving whatever higher purpose

God may have in mind are claiming to have a better idea than God of how all created reality should have been programmed. Can we treat such a claim seriously?

Even before turning to the Bible, it is not difficult to think of a number of ways in which evil and suffering can lead to positive results. For all its cost in life and property, the Great Fire of London led to vastly improved building techniques and a much healthier environment for future generations. Other tragedies have led to better construction codes, improvements in the design of cars, ships, trains and aircraft, better working conditions and improved safety regulations. Injury and disease have triggered amazing advances in medical research, leading to more effective drugs, medication and surgical procedures. They have also drawn out a whole range of virtues such as love, pity, sympathy, compassion, patience, gentleness and selfless service, sometimes with very far-reaching results. When Jean Henri Dunant heard of 40,000 men killed or wounded at the Battle of Solferino in 1859, he not only took a lead in organizing humanitarian help on the spot, but three years later wrote a book which inspired the founding of the International Red Cross. Seeing his own nine-year-old boy die of diphtheria intensified Thomas Barnardo's desire to rescue orphans and other needy children, and resulted in Barnardo's Homes, which have helped to rehabilitate many thousands of young people over the years.

Even without human intervention, pain helps to save countless lives. A world without pain would be one in which injury and disease would wreak even greater havoc than they do. Dr Paul Brand, famous for his pioneering work in the fight against leprosy, once spent three years trying to invent an artificial pain system for limbs that had lost their feeling. When he realized that he could never match man's built-in warning system, he abandoned the project, saying, 'Thank God for inventing pain. I cannot think of a greater gift I could give my leprosy patients.'[85]

When we do turn to the Bible, we do not find evil and suffering brushed aside as illusory or irrelevant. Instead, we are told of many ways in which they serve God's transcendent purposes. We can only mention some of these here, and then only briefly, but even this will be enough to show that we can go far beyond atheism's bleak acceptance that evil and suffering 'just happen'.

In the first place, as we noted in chapter 21, the Bible cites many instances of God using natural disasters, including earthquakes, floods, famine, drought and pestilence to express his righteous anger against those who blatantly reject his right to rule and to execute summary judgement on them,[86] and the same means are at his disposal today. There are also cases of God striking individual people dead as a direct and immediate punishment for sin,[87] and these too are to be seen as ways in which God 'works out everything for his own ends — even the wicked for a day of disaster'.[88]

By the same token, adversity points towards the reality of universal and final judgement. At one point, the Bible records two tragic news items, one reporting that Jews worshipping at the temple in Jerusalem had been mown down by Roman soldiers, and the other that a tower inside the city had collapsed, killing eighteen people. On hearing the news, many people assumed that God had struck the victims down for gross wickedness, but this was not the case.[89] Although there are obviously examples of a particular sin leading directly to specific suffering, the Bible shows that, generally speaking, we are not entitled to trace suffering back to a given sin. It records an incident when some people wanted to know whether a man had been born blind as a direct result of his own sin (which they apparently thought could have been committed in the womb!) or that of his parents.[90] They were roundly told that neither was the case, but that his apparently helpless condition was 'so that the work of God might be displayed in his life',[91] a verdict confirmed in the most remarkable way soon afterwards, when he was completely cured.

In the two tragedies we are considering, those who died were not 'worse sinners'[92] or 'more guilty than all the others living in Jerusalem'.[93] The lesson to be learned from the news reports was very different: 'Unless you repent, you too will all perish.'[94] Those discussing these tragic events were not to waste time speculating on what wickedness might have triggered them. Instead, they were to consider their own spiritual condition, and ask whether their relationship with God was such that they need not fear what the Bible calls 'the coming wrath'.[95] Modern global news media bring us similar reports every day, and these generate strong emotions, yet the Bible shows that they should also cause us to reflect on our own mortality and on our need to be ready to meet 'him to whom we must give account'.[96] In fact, such disasters are early intimations of far worse to come at the final judgement.

Nor does God confine his warnings to events which make the headlines. C. S. Lewis famously pointed out that all personal suffering may serve the same purpose: 'God whispers to us in our pleasures, speaks in our conscience, but shouts in our pains; it is his megaphone to rouse a deaf world.'[97] For many people, life is utterly self-centred. If God features in their thinking at all, it is merely as an emergency service to be called in when the going gets tough, or when they have a particular need. Such people need to be reminded that, for all his achievements, man is not at the centre of the universe, nor is he in ultimate control of any part of it. God often uses suffering of one kind or another to help people get their thinking straight, find a proper sense of perspective and rearrange their priorities.

Lessons learned in the crucible of suffering have often fitted the sufferers to help others. Paul tells his friends at Corinth that believers' experience of God's help in times of suffering is not merely for their own benefit, but 'so that we can comfort those in any trouble with the comfort we ourselves have received from God'.[98] In his perceptive book *Facing Suffering*, the Irish preacher Herbert Carson writes, 'To comfort others we need to learn to be sensitive to their deepest needs. A superficial word of passing sympathy only mocks by its sheer formality. What is required is the sympathy which comes right alongside and feels and grieves with the sufferer. But much sensitivity may itself be learnt through much pain, for it is true that some of the great sympathizers have been — and perhaps still are — great sufferers.'[99]

When believers read the Bible, they may see at least six other ways in which suffering can have positive results.

In the first place, there are times when *it develops confidence in God's transcendent wisdom*. When Job asked for an explanation of his traumatic experiences, especially in the light of his own spiritual integrity, God had the perfect opportunity to give him a neatly packaged theodicy, but he did no such thing! Instead, he told Job that he could charge God with being uncaring or unjust *only if he showed that he could at least match the divine wisdom and power.*

> Where were you when I laid the earth's foundation?
>   Tell me, if you understand...
> Will the one who contends with the Almighty correct him?
>   Let him who accuses God answer him! [100]

This alone should convince us that God is less interested in answering our questions than in strengthening our faith. Job eventually got the message and his response to God's challenge was not to say, 'Now I can see the whole picture,' but, 'I am unworthy — how can I reply to you? I put my hand over my mouth.'[101] Job recognized that he had no right to be given an explanation of God's ways. Have we? Do we have any right to know what God is thinking, or exactly why he acts as he does? Some years ago, nothing was a greater help to my wife in emerging from a frightening cloud of depression than the realization that God is under no obligation to explain anything he causes or allows to come into our lives, but that he calls us to trust him in the dark. Doing so has sometimes led to remarkable expressions of submission to God's gracious sovereignty. When Job's wife told him to blame God for what was happening, he replied, 'Shall we accept good from God, and not trouble?'[102] Robert Fyall has pointed out that the Hebrew word for 'trouble' indicates that Job was not saying that when adversity comes we must grin and bear it, but that 'Whatever happens we must continue to love God, trust him and keep on walking with him.'[103] In Greece, I once met a blind believer who had had both legs amputated, yet he told me, 'I have no complaint against God. These legs belonged to him anyway, so he is entitled to do whatever he likes with them.'

A <u>second</u> way in which God sometimes uses evil and suffering is to *provide a focal point for the believer's faith*. Living in Judah around 600 B.C., the prophet Habakkuk was genuinely puzzled by God's apparent indifference in the face of the country's moral degradation. When God told him that, in response to his prayerful concern, Judah would be invaded by the vicious Babylonians, Habakkuk had even more cause to be baffled, but his conviction of God's overruling wisdom and love was such that even the threat of a 'scorched-earth' invasion could not destroy it:

Though the fig tree does not bud
    and there are no grapes on the vines,
though the olive crop fails
    and the fields produce no food,
though there are no sheep in the pen
    and no cattle in the stalls,
yet I will rejoice in the LORD,
    I will be joyful in God my Saviour. [104]

<u>Thirdly</u>, suffering is meant to be *spiritually productive*. In fact, there is a certain kind of maturity that comes only through the discipline of suffering. Paul was a living example of this and well qualified to write, 'We ... rejoice in our sufferings, because we know that suffering produces perseverance;

perseverance, character; and character, hope.'[105] Later in the New Testament, James encouraged his fellow believers to cultivate a positive perspective in 'trials of many kinds',[106] knowing that 'the testing of your faith develops perseverance'[107] and would lead them to become 'mature and complete, not lacking anything'.[108] Just as winter contributes to producing healthy crops, so painful experiences often play an important role in developing strength of character.

Fourthly, the Bible specifically speaks of *the value in God's disciplining of believers* and speaks of 'the corrections of discipline' as 'the way to life'.[109] One New Testament writer says, 'God disciplines us for our good, that we may share in his holiness,' and adds that although 'no discipline seems pleasant at the time', it eventually produces 'a harvest of righteousness and peace for those who have been trained by it'.[110] When parents discipline their children for their own good, only an unthinking critic would accuse them of being loveless tyrants. Wisely exercised discipline builds character; sentimental indifference destroys it. One of the psalmists confessed to God:

> Before I was afflicted I went astray,
>   but now I obey your word...
> It was good for me to be afflicted
>   so that I might learn your decrees. [111]

This kind of thinking goes against the grain of a culture which puts personal happiness and self-indulgence at the top of the human agenda, but generations of believers have endorsed its truth.

Fifthly, *suffering reminds us of our physical frailty, and of our dependence upon God.* It teaches us that life is more than health and strength. When he was at the peak of his powers, Paul was plagued by an unspecified 'thorn in the flesh'. When God did not grant his prayer for healing, Paul realized that his infirmity was not a punishment but a form of protection; in his own words, it was 'to keep me from being conceited'.[112] Reflecting on this, and on all the other pressures and problems he faced, he went so far as to say, 'I delight in weaknesses, in insults, in hardships, in persecutions, in difficulties. For when I am weak, then I am strong.'[113] Suffering helped him to see that any physical, moral or spiritual power he possessed had been granted to him by God, making arrogance irrational and out of place.

In the <u>sixth</u> place, trials *divert our attention from the brevity of time to the vastness of eternity*. In the context of his own traumas Paul wrote, 'So we fix our eyes not on what is seen, but on what is unseen. For what is seen is temporary, but what is unseen is eternal.'[114] Herbert Carson is helpful here: 'The things which are seen have incredibly potent influence upon us, until they are shown up, in the context of suffering, to be so much passing show.'[115] He goes on to give the example of a woman who, at a time when the family had been vigorously debating the choice of new wallpaper for the lounge, was diagnosed as having cancer. How trivial and irrelevant their discussion seemed in the light of the sombre reality she now had to face! It has been said that some people never look up until they are laid on their backs, and there are countless examples of sudden traumas causing people to give serious thought to the fact that, as a friend of mine has put it, 'We are not here to stay; we are here to go.' Put more bluntly, suffering should encourage us to reflect that we are 'destined to die'[116] and help us to set our minds 'on things above, not on earthly things'.[117]

The centre of gravity of God's discipline is not time but eternity, and God uses suffering, not only to detach his people's minds from preoccupation with the temporal, but to remind them of the greater goal he has in mind for them. Commenting on this, Herbert Carson writes, 'Slum clearance is not an end in itself, simply to satisfy the town planners; its ultimate aim is to move people to better homes. So in all God's dealings, which at times may appear harsh, he is gently and graciously preparing us for removal. To change the analogy, like a gardener loosening the soil around the roots before transplanting, so the Lord breaks up the soil of our comfortable living and our persistent materialism. The fork which the heavenly gardener uses is a painful one, but the ultimate aim is a new flowering in paradise.'[118] The Bible nowhere offers believers an insurance policy against suffering, but it does point to a way of coping with it through living faith in God, who is 'near to all who call on him, to all who call on him in truth'.[119]

Apocalypse later

Another serious flaw in atheism's case is to assume that because we do not see an obvious 'here-and-now' solution to the problem of good and evil, one which is clearly being carried out on a continuous basis, the theist's God is incapable of supplying one. If such a God existed, surely he would be handing out prizes and punishments non-stop, all of them commensurate with the good or evil which prompted them? According to the atheist, the fact that this is not happening points to his being a myth and not a reality.

The Bible has two specific things to say in response. In the first place, it teaches that if God were to change his policy to one of instantaneous reward and punishment, the whole world would immediately become a vast cemetery, with not a single person left to comment on the change. One of the psalmists makes the point in the form of a rhetorical question: 'If you, O LORD, kept a record of sins, O Lord, who could stand?'[120] He is not suggesting that God is unaware of any of the world's evil, but that if he put every sin 'on the record' and then exacted on the spot whatever punishment was due, nobody would escape, and the issue of rewards would not come into play. In an earlier psalm, David draws attention to God's gracious dealings with humankind by saying, 'He does not treat us as our sins deserve or repay us according to our iniquities.'[121] Here, God's generosity and patience are said to be in direct contrast to what someone has called 'the heavy-handed wrath of man, who loves to keep his quarrels going and to nurse his grievances'.[122] Finally, the prophet Jeremiah, who was persecuted, ostracized, humiliated, beaten, put in the stocks and thrown into a cistern of mud, all because he refused to compromise his religious principles, says that only one thing prevented even worse happening to him: 'Because of the LORD's great love we are not consumed, for his compassions never fail.'[123] To pull these three statements together, the Bible is telling us that if we understood the holiness of God, and were fully aware of the true nature of sin, we would gasp in astonishment that God did not punish us more frequently and more severely.

The atheist's case at this point is often framed in the context of justice: 'How can a God of justice allow so much injustice to take place under his very nose?' In the light of what the Bible teaches, the theist is entitled to respond by asking some questions of his own. How much justice does the atheist really want? Where should God draw the line? Should he punish bank robbers, but turn a blind eye to people who fiddle their expenses? Should he clamp down on massive tax fraud, but sweep small items of dishonesty under the carpet? Should he punish perjury, but gloss over white lies? Should he be ruthless with rapists, but lenient with muggers and bullies? How should he react to those who consistently ravage their consciences? Even more to the point, *what should he do about those who wilfully deny*

his existence? One has only to ask questions like these to show that demands for a God of justice may have more cant than conviction.

The second thing the Bible has to say is that the picture of evil and
suffering must be seen in a broader context than the here and now. Atheists assume that, because evil and its effects are still rampant, nothing has
been done to counter it, but the Bible says that something radical *has*
been done. As we shall see in our final chapter, God has intervened so
decisively in the evil-suffering syndrome that the entire universe will eventually bear witness to his full and final triumph over it. Speaking on BBC
Radio's *Start the Week* in 1999, author Salman Rushdie said, 'The world
is a very provisional place.'[124] He was not making a religious comment, but
he could not have expressed biblical truth more clearly. Sin and suffering
were never part of God's original intention and he has provided a means
whereby they can be fully and finally removed from a person's experience.
In language which is in dazzling contrast to the specific experience of sin
and its effects in this world, the Bible speaks of 'a new heaven and a new
earth',[125] where there will be 'no more death or mourning or crying or pain'
because 'the old order of things' will have 'passed away'.[126]

In *The Big Questions*, Rod Garner writes, 'Without a belief in the here-
after, the moral case against God is overwhelming.'[127] Even if we limited
our thinking to the issue of justice and proportionality, we would seem to
be living in a madhouse. Babies are starving to death in Third World countries off whose shores tycoons luxuriate on board their yachts. Hundreds
live on the streets in London's 'cardboard city', within walking distance of
stadia where footballers demand upwards of £30,000 a week for their
services. Defenceless pre-teenagers are gang-raped, while pimps make a
fortune out of prostitution. There seems little room for the doctrine of a
just God here, but the Bible tells us to 'judge nothing before the appointed
time',[128] when God will 'judge the world with justice'.[129] Any assessment of
fairness based entirely on what takes place here and now is premature at
best and hopelessly distorted at worst. God has not yet done all the totting
up.

If the atheist asks how such gross irregularities can ever be corrected,
and how there can ever be a perfect righting of these and all other wrongs,
he is unwittingly selling the pass. On atheism's own claim that an all-powerful
God could defeat all evil and an all-good God would do so, the theist can
argue that as this has not yet happened, we can be certain that it *will*
happen in the future. God's own character demands and guarantees that

evil will finally be defeated. The Bible tells us that history is not cyclical but linear, that it is going somewhere, that God is going to take the raw materials of the cosmos and transform them into a state of perfection, 'a new heaven and a new earth, the home of righteousness'.[130] There *will* be an apocalypse (a revelation of God's perfect moral adjustment), when justice will not only be done, but be seen to be done; when the wicked will no longer prosper and the righteous no longer suffer, when the problem of evil will be fully, finally and obviously settled beyond all doubt and dispute — but the Bible tells us that this state of affairs lies in the future, not in the present.

It was his unshakeable confidence in this that enabled Paul to brush twenty years of trauma aside as 'light and momentary troubles'[131] and to assure his fellow believers that 'Our present sufferings are not worth comparing with the glory that will be revealed in us.'[132] Atheists dismiss this as talk of 'pie in the sky when we die', but mockery contributes nothing to their case.

The real world

Evil and suffering are not subjects which can be filed away, pulled out for discussion when the fancy takes us, then tucked away again until we decide to take another look at them. They are an inescapable part of human experience, and need to be wrestled with at that level. They touch every one of us, sometimes gently, and at other times with crushing and frightening force, either personally, within our own family circles, or indirectly as they arise among friends and acquaintances, or in the wider world.

The atheist's response is to see them as evidence for the non-existence of God, but any honest reading of history provides literally countless examples of those who have suffered greatly (and at times, by human reasoning, unjustly) yet whose faith in God has not disintegrated but deepened as a result. It has been said that a person with an experience is never at the mercy of one with an argument. This dictum needs to be handled with care, as it can be used to justify all kinds of eccentric ideas and outrageous behaviour. Yet when the interpretation of events consistently ties in with biblical teaching, it is a powerful endorsement of revealed truth. The atheist has an argument, a hypothesis which says that evil and suffering 'just happen' in a mindless, godless universe; those whose faith has been tested and deepened in the furnace of affliction have an experience, one which cannot be brushed aside. Choosing examples is like taking a spoonful of water from an ocean, and I will limit myself to two from the Bible, one from the seventeenth century and a few from very recent history.

In the Old Testament, nobody gives a clearer testimony than Job, whose name has become a byword for personal trauma. He was enormously wealthy (at a time when prosperity was measured by livestock, he owned 7,000 sheep, 3,000 camels, 500 yoke of oxen and 500 donkeys), had a large number of servants and was the father of seven sons and three daughters. He had so much going for him that he was rated 'the greatest man among all the people of the East'.[133] As if that were not enough, his moral and spiritual foundations were rock solid: he was 'blameless and upright; he feared God and shunned evil'.[134] Yet none of these things could shield him from suffering. In one day, all his livestock was stolen or slaughtered and all ten of his children died when a violent storm struck the house in which they were holding a party.[135]

It is difficult to imagine anyone suffering more in a single day, but Job's troubles were far from over. His own health began to deteriorate. He was covered with boils, his skin began to peel off, he suffered from anorexia and halitosis, his eyes grew weak, his teeth began to rot, he was hit by a 'triple whammy' of fever, insomnia and depression, and to cap it all he had to cope with friends whose advice only made matters worse and a nagging wife who at one point told him to 'Curse God and die!'[136] The way in which Job worked his way through all of this makes for gripping narrative, and the high point comes when Job expresses his faith in God in one of the best-known statements in the Old Testament: 'Though he slay me, yet will I trust in him.'[137]

The New Testament example is the apostle Paul, a dynamic spiritual leader whose religious convictions and actions led to his suffering years of bitter persecution and hardship. In a letter to friends at Corinth he compared his experience with that of people who were boasting of their record of service: 'I have worked much harder, been in prison more frequently, been flogged more severely, and been exposed to death again and again. Five times I received from the Jews the forty lashes minus one.[138] Three times I was beaten with rods, once I was stoned, three times I was shipwrecked, I spent a night and a day in the open sea, I have been constantly on the move. I have been in danger from rivers, in danger from bandits, in danger from my own countrymen, in danger from Gentiles; in danger in the city, in danger in the country, in danger at sea; and in danger from false brothers. I have laboured and toiled and have often gone without sleep; I have known hunger and thirst and have often gone without food; I have been cold and naked.'[139]

To a detached onlooker, this might seem like a poor return for over twenty years of selfless service, but Paul saw it not as punishment, but as a privilege. At one point we find him, along with Silas, a fellow believer, 'praying and singing hymns to God' in the middle of the night. They were not having a sentimental 'sing-along' in the relaxed comfort of someone's home, but were being held in a prison in Philippi with their feet 'fastened ... in the stocks', after having been 'stripped and beaten' and 'severely flogged'.[140] Yet some time later, Paul told friends at Rome, 'We ... rejoice in our sufferings'![141] Later still (and by fascinating coincidence) he wrote to believers at Philippi from imprisonment in Rome, 'If I am being poured out like a drink offering on the sacrifice and service coming from your faith, I am glad and rejoice with all of you. So you too should be glad and rejoice with me.'[142]

In the latter part of the seventeenth century, a body of Scottish believers strongly resisted the efforts of successive kings to foist an episcopal system of church government on their country and opposed the idea of the Divine Right of Kings. These so-called Covenanters (they had signed solemn dec- larations setting out their convictions) were viciously persecuted, and when Charles II's dragoons captured Richard Cameron and his friends as they met for prayer and Bible study at Airdsmoss, they cut off his head and hands. Later, they put them in a sack and took them to Cameron's father, Alan, who was being held in an Edinburgh gaol. When they asked the prisoner, 'Do you know them?', he kissed the blood-stained remains and said, 'I know them, I know them. They are my son's, my own dear son's. It is the Lord. Good is the will of the Lord, who cannot wrong me nor mine, but has made goodness and mercy to follow us all our days.'[143]

The first modern example is a survivor of the Holocaust. Quoted in *The Times* by Dan Cohn-Sherbok, he said that he had never questioned God's action (or inaction) while he was an inmate of Auschwitz: 'It never oc- curred to me to associate the calamity we were experiencing with God — to blame him or believe in him less, or cease believing in him at all because he didn't come to our aid.' He then went on, 'God doesn't owe us that, or anything. We owe our lives to him. If someone believes that God is re- sponsible for the death of six million because he didn't somehow do some- thing to save them, he's got his thinking reversed.'[144]

The Romanian preacher Richard Wurmbrand spent fourteen years in a Communist prison, three of them in solitary confinement, yet he looked back on this vicious cocktail of evil, injustice and suffering with no regrets, having discovered that throughout it all his faith had flourished: 'The Communists believe that happiness comes from material satisfaction; but alone in my cell, cold, hungry and in rags, I danced for joy every night... Sometimes I was so filled with joy that I felt I would burst if I did not give it expression.'[145]

On 30 July 1967, Joni Eareckson, a vivacious, athletic American teenager, went swimming with friends in Chesapeake Bay. It was meant to be a delightful end to a beautiful summer day, but a terrible diving accident left Joni paralysed for life from the shoulders down. In seconds, her entire life was changed from one of vigorous activity and independence to one of apparent helplessness, yet the story of her spiritual growth through thirty years of trauma has been an inspiration to countless people all around the world. Now a mature, confident, happily married woman (and a brilliant mouth-painting artist), Joni looks back on her accident not as a stumbling-block but as a stepping-stone: 'My accident was not a punishment for my wrongdoing — whether or not I deserved it. Only God knows *why* I was paralysed... Relaxed and in God's will, I know he is in control. It is not a blind, stubborn, stoic acceptance, but getting to know God and realize he is worthy of my trust. Although I am fickle and play games, God does not; although I have been up and down, bitter and doubting, he is constant, ever-loving.'[146]

On 8 November 1987, Gordon Wilson and his twenty-year-old daughter Marie went to the war memorial in the small Northern Ireland market town of Enniskillen to take part in the Remembrance Day service, but as they stood alongside a hall used as a community shelter they were hit by the explosion of a bomb planted by IRA terrorists, and found themselves buried by tons of rubble from the demolished building. When the dust finally settled, eleven people lay dead or dying and over sixty were injured; Marie was one of the dying. Interviewed later on television, Gordon Wilson expressed a faith that was in brilliant contrast to the acrimony and recrimination that filled the airwaves: 'I do not feel any bitterness. I prayed for the terrorists who planted the bomb.' He did have one question, but even that came within the framework of his faith: 'Why did it have to be Marie and not me? I have had a good innings. She was young and had her life before her. Still, I know that it is all part of a greater plan. We cannot see it all, but God is in control.'[147]

In April 1994 my friend Stuart Latimer, pastor of a thriving church in South Carolina, went to Trinidad to preach at an Easter conference. Late on a Saturday night, he was robbed by armed gunmen who then shot him in the right knee at close range with a 16-gauge shotgun, destroying the knee-joint and doing severe damage to adjacent bones. Four operations followed, the last of them a thirteen-hour procedure to reconstruct and graft broken bones and to replace muscle and connective tissue. Writing to tell friends what had happened, Stuart's assistant asked, 'How are we to view an incident such as this? Our settled conviction that God is absolutely sovereign teaches us to trust him in all things. Although we may not understand all of his purposes, we know that *God is too righteous ever to do wrong, too loving ever to be unkind, too wise ever to make a mistake, and too powerful ever to be frustrated.* It is to our gracious and sovereign God we look for strength and help'[148] (emphasis added).

In the course of the last twenty years, five of my friends have been murdered, all of them strong believers actively involved in sharing their faith with others. The last of these was Mike Pollard, a sixty-two-year-old schoolteacher who over a period of twenty-five years risked fines, imprisonment or worse, ferrying Bibles, medical supplies and other help to believers living behind Eastern Europe's infamous Iron Curtain. Ironically, it was when the Cold War was over that Mike was killed. On a mercy mission to Hungary in 1997, he and his wife Jo had parked their camper van for the night in a lay-by on the outskirts of Nyiregyhaza when they were woken by three young men masquerading as police and demanding a 'fine' for illegal parking. An hour later, the Pollards were disturbed again, and when Mike tried to drive off he was smashed to death with an iron bar. Jo was also left for dead, and emergency medical services eventually found her with a broken nose and jaw, a badly damaged breastbone and severe strangulation marks around her throat. The killers were found within twenty-four hours and eventually sent to prison. At their trial, Jo told the court that she bore them no ill-will. Visiting two of them in prison some time later (the third declined to meet her), Jo assured them of her forgiveness. Two years later, she told the *Telegraph Magazine,* 'Terrible as it all was, there was so much of God in what happened subsequently that I never felt alone. It strengthened my faith a tremendous amount. I miss Michael dreadfully. But I don't think God makes mistakes. Though it would be much nicer to have [Mike] around, I accept what has happened. I have complete and utter peace.'[149]

These nine cases represent millions of believers who would testify that their experience of suffering, and often injustice, has left them with even stronger faith in the sovereignty, goodness and faithfulness of God. To put it another way, they would claim that their faith in God has transformed their whole attitude to evil and its consequences. Are all of these people freaks or fakes? Are they all lying? Are they all bamboozled or brainwashed? Are they all suffering from what Richard Dawkins calls 'a virus of the brain'? Does their united testimony have no more weight than the atheist's illogical and untested hypothesis?

The atheistic alternative

Brian Edwards begins his helpful little book *Not By Chance*, subtitled 'Making Sense out of Suffering', by telling of a routine visit to his doctor's surgery. As he was turning to leave, the doctor suddenly asked him, 'How can you believe in a God who allows all the suffering in the world today?' He had apparently been asking the question for years, but had never been given a satisfactory answer. Edwards responded as best he could in the few minutes available to him, then ended by issuing a perfectly reasonable challenge: 'You may find my explanation unsatisfactory, but at least with a belief in God I do have an answer to give; with no belief in God you face the same problem without any answer.'[150]

The doctor conceded that at least they were agreed on that point, and it is difficult to see how he could have done otherwise. Logically speaking, and were he right in his core belief, the atheist would have no problem with the existence of evil (other than in handling the suffering it causes). Believing that human beings are chemical and biological accidents, with no transcendent reason for existence, the atheist living in a godless world would have no questions to ask. But people *do* ask questions, at times passionately and urgently, and when they do the atheist has no answers to give. Fatalism (the only creed available to the atheist on this issue) is fine in theory, but in a suffering world the most it can offer to those who are being hurt is Bertrand Russell's 'unyielding despair'.[151]

Interviewed in the *Daily Telegraph* in 1992, Richard Dawkins had the honesty to bite the bullet: 'Suppose that some child is dying of cancer, we say, "Why is this child dying; what has it done to deserve it?" The answer is, there's no reason why ... there's no reason other than a series of historical accidents which had led to this child dying of cancer. No reason to ask why.' When reminded that this is precisely the question that people *do* ask, Dawkins' only response was: 'That's their problem.'[152]

Just over a year later, twelve children and their teacher, returning home after attending a concert in London's Royal Albert Hall, were killed in an accident on the M40. Writing about it afterwards, Dawkins said that such events were meaningless, and precisely what one should expect in a world with no intelligent Creator: 'Such a universe would be neither good nor bad in intention. It would manifest no intentions of any kind. In a universe of blind physical forces and genetic replication, some people are going to get hurt, other people are going to get lucky, and you won't find any rhyme or reason in it, or any justice. The universe that we observe has precisely the properties that we should expect if there is, at bottom, no design, no purpose, *no evil and no good*, nothing but blind, pitiless indifference'[153] (emphasis added).

Dawkins must be given full marks for consistency here, but how does his bleak doctrine play out in *real* life? Here are parents with a child deformed at birth, children born with a congenital disease as the result of their parents' promiscuous lifestyles, an old-age pensioner lying in a pool of blood after being savaged by a passing hooligan, a promising sportswoman sidelined for life by damage to a cruciate ligament, a happy young mother who suddenly discovers that she has breast cancer, a successful businessman who notices the first signs of Parkinson's disease, an innocent pedestrian mown down by a drunken driver and paralysed for life, a haemophiliac who has contracted AIDS by being infected with HIV during a blood transfusion. Talk of a sovereign, loving God may not provide instant or totally satisfying answers to their instinctive questions, but all that atheism has to offer these people is: 'That's your problem.'

Can thinking, feeling, hurting, questioning people live with this? Is it sufficient to tell them that the material world we see around us is the only reality there is, and that looking for truth, values, meaning or hope is pointless? Can we brush even the horror of the Holocaust aside as a meaningless event in a meaningless world in which there is 'no evil and no good'? Heinrich Himmler, the violent anti-Semite who ran Hitler's notorious *Schutzstaffel* (SS), and later became head of the infamous secret police force, the Gestapo, rejoiced in the extermination of the Jews as a 'glorious page in our history, never before, never again to be written'.[154] In a meaningless, valueless world, who can contradict him? The Jewish theologian Eliezer Berkavits asks the obvious question here: 'If there is no possibility for a transcendental value-reference, if existence as such is fundamentally meaningless and man alone is the creator of values, who is to determine what the values are going to be, or what the man-made meaning is to be? Man of course. *But which man?*'[155] (emphasis added).

If the Holocaust raises massive problems for the theist, it raises even greater ones for the atheist, who has no appeal to transcendent values but is left with what Albert Camus called 'that hopeless encounter between human questioning and the silence of the universe'.[156] Francis Bridger makes the point well: 'What has atheism to say to the burning children? That the Holocaust "was just one of those things"? That it was merely an unfortunate fact of history? That it was a meaningless event in a meaningless cosmos? None of these is acceptable. Atheism is the most cruel hypothesis of all. For it says that in the end injustice cannot be righted, suffering cannot be redeemed, evil triumphs after all. *There is nothing more the atheist can say to the victims of Auschwitz*'[157] (emphasis added). Nor can he say more to anyone who wrestles with the problem of evil and suffering.

In conclusion ...

For all its length, this chapter has done little more than sketch in the outline of some of the issues involved. There are grey areas we have not addressed, loose ends left dangling and questions unanswered. Though it could hardly be otherwise, some theologians have suggested that Scripture *does* supply an overall answer to the problem of evil. When the Pharaoh of Egypt obstinately refused to release a captured nation of Hebrew slaves, Egypt was punished with a succession of plagues. As Pharaoh still dug his heels in, God warned him that he and all the Egyptians could have been wiped out in one fell swoop, then added, 'But I have raised you up for this very purpose, that I might show you my power and that my name might be proclaimed in all the earth.'[158] This is a remarkable statement of God's sovereignty, yet this apparently straightforward explanation of why God tolerates evil people (and, by implication, all forms of evil) raises a host of other questions. Why would God risk being misunderstood by many people and rejected by others? Why would he choose something utterly foreign to his nature in order to reveal what that nature is? Was there no other way for God to demonstrate his character than by allowing evil to wreak such havoc?

The fact that God has not told us the answers to those questions means that, however hard we lean on God's statement to Pharaoh, evil and suffering still retain an element of mystery, yet the force of that mystery is not nearly enough to establish the atheist's case. As R. C. Sproul explains, 'While we cannot explain the existence of evil, that is no reason for us to disregard the positive evidence for God. To deny what we know on the basis of what we do not know is not only bad theology, but bad science as well.'[159]

Earlier in this chapter we touched on the fact that God has entered intimately into the reality of human suffering. It is impossible to discuss this any further without showing that he did so in the course of taking radical action to punish evil and eventually to destroy it. We will do this now, as we consider the most powerful evidence for his existence.

24.
The last word

Throughout this book, and especially from chapter 13 onwards, I have sought to identify and address the problems of being an atheist. These have ranged from the scientific to the philosophical, from the existence of matter to the origin of life, and from evolution to ethics. As far as I know, I have at least touched on all but one of atheism's major stumbling-blocks. The remaining problem (and avoiding any mention of it has not been easy, especially in some chapters) is not a scientific theory, a philosophical proposition or a social construct, but one particular human being. Atheists cannot avoid tackling him head-on; this chapter will show what happens when they do so.

The population of the world is increasing by over 70,000 a day, and the current total of people who have ever lived has been put at about sixty billion. The overwhelming majority of these have lived and died virtually unknown. Some have left behind temporary ripples, and others have influenced thousands or millions of people through their work, teaching or example. Comparatively few can be said to have left a major and permanent mark on the history of our planet, with rulers, politicians, philosophers, scientists and religious leaders strongly represented in this select group. Yet one person dominates all the others in such a way as to make him truly unique — a man in sixty billion. Even some of the world's most articulate sceptics have endorsed this: H. G. Wells called him 'easily the dominant figure in history', and concluded that no historian could portray the progress of humanity honestly without giving him the 'foremost place'.[1] This assessment is all the more remarkable when seen in the apparently modest context of his life.

- We have no record of his date of birth, yet all the world's chronology is linked to it.
- He never wrote a book, yet more books have been written about him than about anyone else in history, and the output is still accelerating. The nearest thing we have to his biography has now been translated in whole or in part into over 2,000 languages.
- He never painted a picture, or composed any poetry or music, yet nobody's life and teaching have inspired a greater output of songs, plays, poetry, films, videos and other art forms. One film, based on his recorded words, has been produced in over 100 languages and has already been seen by more people than any other film in history.
- He never raised an army, yet millions of people have laid down their lives in his cause, and every year thousands more do so.[2]
- Except for one brief period during his childhood, his travels were limited to an area about the size of Wales,[3] but his influence today is worldwide, and his followers constitute the largest religious grouping the world has ever known.[4]
- He had no formal education, but thousands of universities, seminaries, colleges and schools have been founded in his name.
- His public teaching lasted just three years, and was restricted to one small country, yet purpose-built satellites and some of the world's largest radio and television networks now beam his message around the globe.
- He set foot in just two countries, yet an organization committed to his cause[5] claims to make regular flights to more countries than any commercial airline.
- He was virtually unknown outside of his native country, yet in the current issue of *Encyclopaedia Britannica* the entry under his name runs to 30,000 words.
- He is by far the most controversial person in history. Nobody has attracted such adoration or opposition, devotion or criticism, and nobody else's teaching has ever been more fervently received or more fiercely rejected. For centuries, every recorded word he spoke has been relentlessly analysed by theologians, philosophers and others. On the day this sentence is being written (and read), millions of people are studying what he said and did, and trying to apply the significance of his words and actions to their lives.

- Even the most dyed-in-the-wool sceptics must acknowledge that this man was something special, and any open-minded student of human history should agree that he deserves meticulous attention.
- His name is Jesus, who lived and died about 2,000 years ago.

He presents an enormous problem for the atheist.

Anybody there?

That last sentence needs a rider, as some atheists have tried to dissolve the problem by contesting the fact that Jesus ever existed. To give just one example, Bertrand Russell rehashed ideas put forward by cynical nineteenth-century German scholars and concluded, 'Historically, it is quite doubtful whether Jesus ever existed at all, and if he did we do not know anything about him.'[6] One hardly knows whether to laugh or cry. Quite apart from the mass of data in the Bible, the credentials of which were confirmed in chapter 18, at least nineteen celebrated authors in the first and second centuries (who shared Russell's atheism but were somewhat better placed to comment) record more than 100 facts about Jesus. These give details of his birth, life, teaching and death, all without the slightest hint that he was not a real historical person. These writers include the distinguished Jewish historian Flavius Josephus, Suetonius, official historian of the Roman Imperial House, Cornelius Tacitus, another eminent historian who was also Governor of Asia, and Pliny the Younger, a Roman proconsul in Bithynia in Asia Minor and 'one of the world's great letter-writers, whose letters have attained the status of literary classics'.[7]

Very little literature from their time has survived, making it all the more remarkable that these historians, seeking to record the major events of their day, should devote reams of writing to a penniless peasant who lived in a scruffy little town (Nazareth) in a remote part (Galilee) of one of the world's smallest countries (Palestine), especially as they all rejected the main thrust of his teaching, Tacitus calling it a 'mischievous superstition'.[8] The second-century Greek philosopher Celsus went even further, and in *The True Doctrine* mounted a ruthless, sarcastic attack on virtually every aspect of Jesus' teaching, yet even he made some eighty allusions to New Testament quotations and never once claimed that he was merely deriding a myth, as Jesus never really existed. No wonder the British anthropologist and historian James Frazer concludes that doubts cast on the historical reality of Jesus are 'unworthy of serious attention'.[9] As Paul Johnson wrote in the *Daily Mail* on Good Friday 1997, the argument that Jesus never existed has been 'demolished' ... by 'the march of historical research'.[10]

One of us

Although Jesus stands out from all the rest of humankind, he is not detached from them. He is a genuine human being, not some kind of biological freak or extra-terrestrial alien. The Bible traces his family tree back through over forty generations,[11] and the ongoing evidence for his normal humanity is overwhelming, as we can easily confirm.

There is the evidence of *his physical life*. Like any other Jewish boy, he was circumcised when he was eight days old, in accordance with Old Testament law.[12] His physical development was perfectly normal; in one chapter alone he is successively described as a 'baby',[13] a 'child'[14] and a 'boy'.[15] He had to be taught to crawl, stand, walk, feed himself, wash, dress, write and go to the toilet. He knew what it was to be hungry,[16] thirsty,[17] tired,[18] and physically weakened by suffering and stress.[19] Soon after he died, his body was pierced with a spear, and an eyewitness's report of a 'sudden flow of blood and water'[20] is exactly how a layman might describe blood and serum flowing from a post-mortem rupture of the pericardial sac.

There is the evidence of *his intellectual life.* Just as he had all the usual physical limitations (he could not stand on the day he was born, jump 100 feet in the air, or be in two places at once), so he had intellectual limitations. Although there is no record of his being in error, there were apparently things he did not know. When he wanted to feed a crowd of people, he asked his followers, 'How many loaves do you have?'[21] When a distraught father brought his demon-possessed son to him, he asked, 'How long has he been like this?'[22] When he visited Bethany four days after a friend had died, he enquired, 'Where have you laid him?'[23]

There is the evidence of *his emotional life*. Jesus not only had a genuinely human body and mind, he also experienced a great range of human emotions. He told his followers, 'I have called you friends.'[24] We are told of his close relationship with one particular family that 'Jesus loved Martha and her sister and Lazarus.'[25] There were times when he showed flashes of anger. When his followers tried to stop parents bringing their children to him, he was 'indignant'.[26] When members of a strict religious sect were plotting to have him killed, 'He looked around at them in anger ... deeply distressed at their stubborn hearts.'[27] Nor was he a great fan of political correctness: he called the crafty King Herod 'that fox',[28] false prophets 'ferocious wolves',[29] the Pharisees a 'brood of vipers',[30] 'blind fools',[31] 'white-washed tombs'[32] and 'hypocrites'.[33] When he saw black-marketeering and swindling going on in the temple in Jerusalem, he drove the racketeers out in an explosion of anger.[34] Perhaps no emotion more clearly illustrated his genuine humanity than his anger, yet it was always *righteous* anger, with never a tinge of personal pique or resentment. Far from outlawing anger, the Bible commends it and says, 'Be angry, and yet do not sin.'[35] As Martyn Lloyd-Jones commented, 'The capacity for anger against that which is evil and wrong is essentially right and good.'[36]

He expressed great sorrow. Looking over Jerusalem at a time when he knew it was heading for disaster, 'He wept over it.'[37] He showed great sympathy and compassion. When he came across a deaf-and-dumb man, he expressed his feelings with 'a deep sigh';[38] when he saw crowds of people in religious and spiritual confusion, 'He had compassion on them.'[39] There is no record of him laughing, but parts of his teaching had humorous undertones and we are told that when his followers reported on a particularly successful mission, 'He was full of joy.'[40]

There is the evidence of *his spiritual life*. He knew what it was to be tempted. He underwent at least one extended assault which lasted for nearly six weeks,[41] and in the course of his life he was 'tempted in every way, just as we are'.[42] He prayed — we are specifically told of twenty-five instances, including at least one occasion when 'he offered up prayers and petitions with loud cries and tears',[43] but these obviously represent a lifetime of intercession. He regularly attended public worship: we are told that 'On the Sabbath day he went into the synagogue, as was his custom.'[44] He studied the Bible: he constantly quoted the Old Testament, and with one exception always did so from memory.[45] He also fasted,[46] not because he was on a diet, but as a spiritual discipline laid down in the Old Testament and which he commended to others.[47]

The evidence of his physical life, his intellectual life, his emotional life and his spiritual life establish beyond question that Jesus was one of us, a genuine human being. Yet in several significant ways he was unique. Evidence for this can be found all over the Bible, but for our present purposes we will keep to six specific ways in which Jesus stands alone.

Great expectations

In the first place, *the announcement of his birth was unique*. From the time when it was first reduced to writing, the Old Testament was never treated by the Jews as a man-made anthology of unrelated material. Instead, they recognized it as the Word of God, focused on his dealings with their own nation — his 'chosen people'[48] — in particular and with all mankind in general. Woven into this was God's promise that at some point in time he would break into human history by sending someone who would fulfil to perfection the roles of prophet, priest and king, establish God's righteous reign on the earth and meet men's deepest spiritual needs. This great ruler and deliverer came to be known as 'the Anointed One'.[49] The English translation of this Hebrew title is 'the Messiah', while we translate the New Testament Greek equivalent, *ho christos*, as 'the Christ'. Prophecies about the coming Messiah can be found throughout the Old Testament, culminating in this assurance by Malachi: 'The messenger of the covenant, whom you desire, will come.'[50] The voice of prophecy then fell silent for 400 years; what is more, all the Messianic predictions remained unfulfilled.

Everything changed when Jesus came on the scene. Invited to read from the Old Testament during a service in his local synagogue in Nazareth, he deliberately chose a Messianic passage written by Isaiah, read it aloud, then added, 'Today this scripture is fulfilled in your hearing.'[51] The inference was inescapable: Jesus was claiming that when the prophet wrote about the Messiah he was writing about him. In the weeks and months which followed, Jesus stepped up his insistence that this was the case, and he was soon in conflict with the religious establishment, especially the Pharisees and Sadducees, who had a vested interest in preserving the status quo.

If they felt they could pressurize Jesus into softening or abandoning his claim, they were mistaken, and he was soon drawing on all three sections of the Old Testament — the Law, the Poetical Books and the Prophets — to press his message home. When his enemies were plotting to kill him, he referred to their great lawgiver Moses and told them point-blank, 'If you believed Moses, you would believe me, for he wrote about me.'[52] Later, he said that their opposition was in fulfilment of a psalm in which the Messiah says, 'They hated me without reason.'[53] Knowing that the prophet Daniel had spoken of the Messiah as 'one like a son of man',[54] Jesus deliberately referred to himself as the 'Son of Man' no fewer than seventy-eight times.[55] Elsewhere, he pulled the whole of the Old Testament together and claimed,

'These are the Scriptures that testify about me.'[56] His claim was clear and confident, and the New Testament provides convincing data to show that it was valid.

About 2,000 years earlier, God had told Abraham that through his offspring 'all nations on earth will be blessed'.[57] This means that twenty centuries before Jesus was born every other family on earth except Abraham's was out of the running as far as producing the Messiah was concerned. Other Old Testament prophecies indicated that the Messiah would come from a line taken directly through Abraham, Jacob, the tribe of Judah (bypassing eleven others), Jesse and David. This alone precludes most of the human race, but there are two other significant pointers.

One of the Messianic prophecies said that the tribe of Judah would provide Israel with all its kings *until the Messiah came.* 'The sceptre will not depart from Judah ... until he comes...'[58] As Judah's government collapsed with the destruction of Jerusalem in A.D. 70, *Jesus was born just before the deadline.*

The second pointer is the prophecy which told where the Messiah would be born:

But you, Bethlehem Ephrathah,
    though you are small among the clans of Judah,
out of you will come for me
    one who will be ruler over Israel.[59]

There were two Bethlehems, one in the region of Ephrathah in Judea and the other seventy miles to the north, in Zebulun. Jesus was born 'in Bethlehem in Judea',[60] a tiny village where no one else of major importance has been born since Micah's remarkable prophecy, which was made some 700 years before Jesus arrived.

A student once suggested to me that when Jesus realized he had been born in Bethlehem and into a family descended from David, he decided to stake a claim to fame by fulfilling all the other Messianic prophecies. This is hardly original, and less than convincing. The nineteenth-century Oxford scholar Henry Liddon drew attention to the fact that Jesus fulfilled to the letter no fewer than 332 Old Testament prophecies.[61] These covered his family's social status, his lifestyle, his general demeanour, his teaching and his amazing powers. Even more remarkably, they included minute details of the events surrounding his death. It has been calculated that twenty-nine Messianic prophecies were fulfilled in the final twenty-four hours

of his life alone. The prophets said that he would be forsaken by his followers,[62] betrayed for thirty pieces of silver (which would then be used to buy
a potter's field),[63] wrongly accused,[64] tortured and humiliated[65] (in response
to which he would not retaliate),[66] executed along with common criminals,[67] and put to death by crucifixion[68] (a form of execution never carried
out by the Jews). Prophets also foretold that at the time of his death he
would pray for his executioners,[69] none of his bones would be broken,[70] his
body would be pierced[71] and people would cast lots to see who would get
his clothing.[72]

Is it seriously suggested that a hoaxer could (or would) have arranged
for all of these things to happen in order to lodge a false claim to be the
Messiah? In *Science Speaks*, Westmont College's Peter Stoner evaluates
the biblical data using scientific principles of probability, and at one point
calculates the chance of just forty-eight of the Messianic prophecies being
fulfilled in one person as one in 10^{157}. To illustrate what this means, he uses
an electron, something so small that, at the rate of 250 a minute, it would
take 190 million years to count a line of them one inch long. At the same
rate, a cubic inch of electrons would take 190,000,000 x 190,000,000 x
190,000,000 years to count. Stoner then says that if we took this number
of electrons, marked one of them, stirred them all together, then asked a
blindfolded friend to find the one we had marked, his chance of selecting
the right one would be the same as that of one man fulfilling even forty-
eight of the more than 300 Messianic prophecies. He concludes that to
reject the Bible's claims that Jesus is the Messiah is to reject a fact 'proved
perhaps more absolutely than any other fact in the world'.[73] As he refers to
the quantity of electrons used in his illustration as 'a large number',[74] we
can hardly accuse him of being given to exaggeration! Writing in the *Sunday Times* in 1998, Ludovic Kennedy airily dismissed all the Messianic
prophecies as 'bogus'.[75] This may shorten the discussion, but only by shelv-
ing the data.

The 'no-man' man

The second factor which marks Jesus out from the rest of humankind is
that *his conception was unique*. When speaking about the beginning of his
earthly life, people usually refer to the 'virgin birth', but this phrase can be
misleading, in that there is no evidence of anything unusual about his birth
as such. As far as we know, Jesus' actual birth took place in the normal

way; what is unique is not how he *left* his mother's womb, but how he *entered* it, and the Bible could not be more emphatic. When his mother, Mary, found herself pregnant she declared, 'I am a virgin';[76] Mary's husband, Joseph, 'had no union with her until she gave birth to a son';[77] Jesus was born 'before they came together'.[78] These three statements make it crystal clear that she was *virgo intacta* when she became pregnant, and that she remained so until after Jesus was born.

As there is no other record of human parthenogenesis (the female egg dividing itself without male fertilization), sceptics have produced a wagon-load of theories seeking to undermine the Bible's record. It is suggested that as the Jews were rather puritanical about sexual matters, and considered intercourse to be in some way 'unclean', the story was invented to avoid the Messiah being tainted in any way. Yet as there is no hint of Jewish squeamishness about sexuality elsewhere in the New Testament, this idea relies on supposition, not substance. Others have suggested that the story is an attempt to match or outdo tales of how pagan gods and other religious leaders came into being. Buddha's mother claimed that a white elephant with six tusks 'entered my belly'.[79] The mother of the Greek god Perseus was said to have been impregnated with a shower of rain containing Zeus. Alexander the Great was alleged to have been the result of an illicit union between his mother Olympus and Zeus, who had cunningly turned himself into a snake for the occasion. The suggestion that Jesus' virgin conception is another such yarn suffers from two fatal flaws. The first is that there is not a shred of evidence that the New Testament writers had even heard of these exotic fantasies; the second is that their crude sensuality is in stark contrast with the simplicity and purity of the Bible's narrative which, as the scholar Robert Gromacki notes, was 'bathed in holiness'.[80]

A more direct attack comes from those who say that virgin conception would be a miracle, a contradiction of known scientific law and that, as miracles can be ruled out, what we have recorded in the Bible is not a fact but a fairy-tale. Liberal theologians have sometimes joined sceptical scientists in pushing this line. Early in the twentieth century the American minister Harry Emerson Fosdick wrote that the birth of Jesus was recorded 'in terms of a biological miracle that *our modern minds cannot use*'[81] (emphasis added), but this is hardly a sensible approach. In 1969 Norman Anderson's book *Christianity: the Witness of History* included a lengthy section on miracles, yet by 1985, when the book was reissued under the revised title of *Jesus Christ: the Witness of History*, this particular section was reduced to a few lines. Anderson explained that the main reason for doing so was 'because the one-time insistence of scientists on the uniformity of nature and her "laws" is today much less obtrusive; for physicists, doctors and others have come increasingly to realize that the exceptional and unexpected does happen from time to time and that cause and effect do not invariably follow the normal pattern'.[82]

This tells us that rejecting the possibility of miracles is decidedly unscientific. This was made clear in a 1984 letter to *The Times*, written by the President of the Linnean Society and fourteen leading scientists, most of them university professors: 'It is not logically valid to use science as an argument against miracles. To believe that miracles cannot happen is as much an act of faith as to believe that they can happen... Miracles are unprecedented events. Whatever the current fashions in philosophy or the revelations of opinion polls may suggest, it is important to affirm that science (based as it is on the observation of precedents) *can have nothing to say on the subject*'[83] (emphasis added).

We ought also to mention one compromise solution on offer. This suggests that the virgin conception *was* a case of parthenogenesis (which has been observed in some lower mammal forms, though without any viable young developing). However, this theory collapses because of the genetic make-up of human beings. The male has x and y chromosomes, while the female has x and x, which means that, even if Mary's pregnancy had been triggered off by some unique biological freak, the child born as a result would have been female, as no y chromosome would have been present to produce a male.

Pre-natal reports

Some of the clearest evidence for Jesus' virgin conception comes from Luke, who was a medical practitioner, but the first pre-natal indications of the miracle to come were announced by Old Testament prophets. One of the most remarkable of these came about 700 years before Jesus was born when, through the prophet Isaiah, God promised Ahaz, the eleventh King of Judah, 'Therefore the Lord himself will give you a sign: The virgin will be with child and will give birth to a son.'[84]

Critics have objected that Isaiah's word for 'virgin' (the Hebrew *almah*) could simply mean 'young woman' and that, if he had wanted to make her virginity clear, he would have used the word *bethulah*. However, this argument has three major weaknesses. In the first place, another prophet uses *bethulah* to describe someone 'grieving for the husband of her youth' (and presumably therefore not a virgin).[85] Secondly, the Septuagint translators always rendered *almah* as *parthenos*, a Greek word which can only mean 'virgin'. As the Septuagint dates from around 300 B.C., we can hardly accuse them of manipulating their translation to accommodate the birth of Jesus. Thirdly, of the nine occasions in which the word *almah* is used in the Old Testament, it is not once clearly used of a woman who is not in fact a virgin. Martin Luther once offered 100 *gulden* to anyone who could show that *almah* ever referred to a married woman (adding that the Lord alone knew where he would get the money!). There were no takers. The American theologian and linguist Edward J. Young is on record as stating that *almah* 'is never, as far as the present writer knows, either in the Old Testament or outside, used of a married woman'.[86]

Another pre-natal report was filed about 600 years before Jesus was born: 'The LORD will create a new thing on earth — a woman will surround a man.'[87] There are no fewer than six important facts contained in these few words. Firstly, God himself — 'the LORD' — would bring the event about. Secondly, it would be unique — 'a new thing'. Thirdly, the location was specified; the literal meaning of 'on earth' is 'in the land' (i.e. of Judah). Fourthly, although 'a woman' would be involved, there is no mention of a husband or father. Fifthly, the word 'surround' is used elsewhere in the Old Testament of a river winding its way through or around a country,[88] and of God bringing comfort to one of his people,[89] and conveys a beautiful picture of a mother conceiving and enclosing a child within her womb. Sixthly, in speaking of a 'man', the prophet did not use one of three most common Hebrew words available (*adam, ish* or *enosh*) but specifically chose *geber*, the root meaning of which is to be strong or heroic. This very word was the one used of the Messiah 100 years after this particular prophecy, when God called him 'the man *(geber)* who is close to me'.[90]

Problems

Because God is said to be involved in the event, atheists will obviously have a fundamental, presuppositional problem with the Bible's clear insistence that Jesus was born of a virgin, but I suggest that the record poses other difficulties for them.

Difficulties virgin birth makes for atheists

- Why did the early church invent a story which would immediately invite a storm of ridicule and contempt? As David Kingdon writes, 'You do not invent a story about an engaged woman conceiving a child and claiming that no man was involved if you want [the story] to gain easy acceptance among Jews, for they held pre-marital chastity in such high regard that a woman could be stoned to death if proved to have been unchaste before marriage.'[91] Nor would much headway be made among the Gentiles, who were much more relaxed about sexual matters, and would have been likely to dismiss the story as a dirty joke.
- Would New Testament writers try to counter grotesque pagan birth stories by inventing something just as likely to deter prospective recruits?
- Why did a medical practitioner like Luke never retract his evidence, despite all the pressure that he must have faced?
- Why was the story not refuted by anyone within the church during the first two centuries, when the first Christian creeds were being formulated? Surely someone would have suggested dropping such an embarrassing item from its manifesto?
- Why have no contemporary records produced a credible alternative story of the birth of Jesus?
- Why has the church always treated Mary with such reverence (some even going to the unbiblical lengths of worshipping her) if she was no more than a common-or-garden fornicator?
- How could the church reconcile the illegitimate conception of Jesus with its insistence that God calls for chastity before marriage?

Both by Old Testament prophecy and New Testament narrative, the Bible makes it clear that Jesus entered the world in a uniquely miraculous way. When Mary questioned her part in this astonishing event, an angel told her that 'Nothing is impossible with God.'[92] Those words remain the ultimate response to contemporary sceptics of every description. A virgin conception led to a virgin birth.

Words, deeds, character

In the third place, Jesus stands apart from the rest of humanity in that *his life was unique*, a fact which comes into focus in at least three areas.

From an early age, Jesus was marked out by his words. When he was just twelve years old, his dialogue with religious leaders in the temple courts in Jerusalem left people 'amazed at his understanding and his answers'.[93] Eighteen years later, when he claimed to be the fulfilment of Isaiah's Messianic prophecy, those who heard him 'were amazed at the gracious words that came from his lips'.[94] When his religious enemies were closing in, temple guards sent to arrest him were awestruck by his teaching and skulked back to the chief priests and Pharisees complaining, 'No one ever spoke the way this man does.'[95] At the end of what is now known as the Sermon on the Mount, the crowds 'were amazed at his teaching, because he taught as one who had authority, and not as their teachers of the law'.[96] Their reaction was hardly surprising. Can finer moral doctrine be found anywhere else? Are there any more fundamental spiritual principles than those contained in his opening words, now known as the Beatitudes?[97] Is there a finer prayer than what we now call 'the Lord's Prayer'?[98] Is there any higher ethical standard than 'Love your enemies'?[99] Can moral instruction rise beyond 'Be perfect'?[100] Has anyone bettered the so-called Golden Rule: 'In everything, do to others what you would have them do to you'?[101]

Broadening his assessment to take in all of Jesus' teaching, Geoffrey Thomas writes, 'He speaks on marriage; he speaks on divorce; he speaks on creation; he speaks on the human heart and its predicament. He speaks on death and on eternity. He pronounces inerrantly on every single item that you and I will ever meet in life.'[102] The American historian Bernard Ramm says of the words Jesus spoke, 'They are read more, quoted more, loved more, believed more and translated more because they are the greatest words ever spoken. And where is their greatness? Their greatness lies in the pure, lucid spirituality in dealing clearly, definitively, and *authoritatively* with the greatest problems that throb in the human breast.'[103]

People were not only astonished by Jesus' words, but by his *actions*, and specifically by the miracles he performed. At one point we are told that in addition to his extensive preaching and teaching ministry he healed people 'who were ill with various diseases, those suffering severe pain, the demon-possessed, those having seizures and the paralysed'.[104] Elsewhere, he is on record as curing blindness,[105] deafness,[106] dumbness[107] leprosy,[108] lameness,[109] fever[110] and paralysis.[111] Virtually all the healings were instantaneous and, in brilliant contrast to the records of 'faith healers' past and present, *there is no recorded case of a relapse*. On at least three occasions, he brought a dead person back to life: a twelve-year old girl within an hour or two of her death,[112] a man whose body was being carried to the cemetery[113] and another who had lain in the grave for four days.[114]

He also showed authority over the natural elements. During a crossing of the Sea of Galilee, one word from him brought an end to a storm so violent that experienced sailors had been terrified of being drowned.[115] He was able to tell local fishermen exactly where fish could be caught, even when they seemed to think there were none to be had.[116] As a wedding guest, he rescued an embarrassing situation by turning water into the day's finest wine.[117] He once fed over 5,000 hungry people with a handful of bread and fish,[118] and on another occasion did the same thing for a crowd of over 4,000.[119] It has even been suggested that Jesus may have performed more miracles in a given day than are recorded in the whole of the Old Testament.

If Jesus' teaching and actions left his contemporaries baffled, his _character_ has drawn endless admiration, sometimes from the most unlikely sources. The famous nineteenth-century British historian (and sceptical rationalist) William Lecky referred to Jesus as 'the highest pattern of virtue' and 'the strongest incentive to its practice', and admitted that his life 'has done more to regenerate and soften mankind than all the disquisitions of philosophers and all the exhortations of moralists'.[120] Lecky's contemporary, the German theologian David Strauss, who set out to debunk most of the Bible, was forced to concede that the life of Jesus 'remains the highest model of religion within the reach of our thought'.[121]

These are stunning character references, but the Bible goes even further and declares that although 'tempted in every way, just as we are' he was '_without sin_'.[122] The evidence for this comes from his enemies,[123] his followers (including Saul of Tarsus, who once led a personal crusade to destroy Jesus' early followers but was eventually persuaded that he 'had no sin')[124] and his inner circle of friends who, after scrutinizing him at close quarters for three years, came to the conclusion that he was 'righteous'[125] and 'without blemish or defect'[126] and that he 'committed no sin'.[127]

Yet perhaps the most remarkable testimony is Jesus' own claim to be sinless. The Bible and subsequent history are full of great men's confessions of personal sin. Israel's King David acknowledged, 'I have sinned greatly.'[128] The great prophet Isaiah admitted, 'I am a man of unclean lips.'[129] Job, the most upright man of his day, cried out, 'I despise myself and repent in dust and ashes.'[130] The apostle Paul called himself 'the worst of sinners'.[131] Augustine wrote of his 'foulness' and of the 'carnal corruptions of my soul'.[132] In the eighteenth century, Jonathan Edwards, who was possibly the finest theologian and philosopher America had ever produced, and was once described as 'one of the most holy, humble and heavenly-minded men the world has seen since the apostolic age',[133] said that as far as he was concerned the wickedness of his heart looked 'like an abyss infinitely deeper than hell'.[134]

Jesus presents a totally different picture, in that he showed no consciousness whatsoever of personal sin. Speaking of his relationship with God, he said quite openly, 'I always do what pleases him.'[135] Has anyone else in history ever credibly made such a claim? Faced with a highly critical audience steeped in biblical teaching on morality, and looking for any excuse to humiliate him, he threw down the gauntlet by asking, 'Can any of you prove me guilty of sin?'[136] Not even his severest critic dared to pick it up. Elsewhere, he claimed complete mastery over temptation by stating that the devil 'has no hold on me'.[137] Jesus never blushed with shame, never had a guilty conscience, never regretted anything he said, thought or did, never had any reason to apologize and never asked or prayed for forgiveness. Small wonder that the famous nineteenth-century French humanist Ernest Renan once wrote of him, 'His beauty is eternal, and his reign shall never end. Jesus is in every respect unique, and nothing can be compared with him.'[138]

'I am'

The fourth way in which Jesus stands out from all other human beings is that *his claims were unique*. When he was at the peak of his career, the great American boxer Muhammad Ali used to promote himself by claiming, 'I am the greatest!' and other people over the centuries have made similar boasts about their talent, power or influence. Yet Jesus is beyond comparison. He fulfilled all the Old Testament prophecies about the Messiah, he was born of a virgin, he lived a sinless life, his teaching has never been equalled and his miracles were astonishing in their range and number. This tends to put even the finest boxing champion in perspective! Although the Bible's verdict on his life means that he could never be accused of conceit, he often spoke about himself, and in the most extraordinary terms. He claimed, 'I am the bread of life,' and promised, 'He who comes to me will never go hungry, and he who believes in me will never be thirsty.'[139] He claimed, 'I am the light of the world,' and pledged, 'Whoever follows me will never walk in darkness, but will have the light of life.'[140] He claimed, 'I am the way and the truth and the life,' and added, 'No one comes to the Father except through me.'[141] Nobody else in history has ever made credible claims to meet other people's spiritual hunger, give infallible wisdom and be the exclusive means of entering a right relationship with God, yet Jesus made another set of claims which transcended even these. Taken together, they amounted to this: *he claimed to be God.* Although he is never on record as using the phrase 'I am God', there are at least six instances in which he made the same stupendous claim using other words.

When nit-picking religious leaders complained about him healing a paralysed man on the Sabbath day, Jesus answered them by saying, 'My Father is always at his work to this very day, and I, too, am working.'[142] That may seem innocuous to us, but there is more to it than meets the modern eye. Jesus was telling them that God was not bound by their legalistic interpretation of the Sabbath law. What is more, Jesus claimed to be working in the same way that God was working. Whatever one was thinking and doing, so was the other. The Jews had no doubt what he meant; he was 'making himself equal with God'[143] — *and Jesus did nothing to correct their interpretation of his words.*

In a later discussion about the Old Testament patriarch Abraham, Jesus responded to a question by stating, 'Before Abraham was born, I am![144] This was certainly an unusual answer, especially as they were not asking him about his age, but about his identity: 'Are you *greater* than our father Abraham?'[145] What makes the reply so startling is that 'I AM' was one of the names by which God revealed himself in the Old Testament. When giving Moses certain instructions for his people, God said, 'This is what you are to say to the Israelites: "I AM has sent me to you."' [146] 'I AM' is a title which speaks of absolute, timeless self-existence, qualities which can be true only of God, yet Jesus quietly used it about himself. Those listening to him had no doubts about what he meant; they immediately 'picked up stones to stone him',[147] a clear sign that they were accusing him of the blasphemy of claiming to be divine. As J. C. Ryle, the first Bishop of Liverpool, commented, 'All claims to evade this explanation appear to me to be so preposterous that it is a waste of time to notice them.'[148]

Later still, Jesus brought a teaching session to an end by stating, 'I and the Father are one.'[149] The crucial point here is that 'one' is not masculine, but neuter; Jesus was not claiming to be one in person with God, but one in essence or nature. Once more, his enemies 'picked up stones to stone him',[150] and again they made it clear why they did so. When Jesus asked them, 'I have shown you many great miracles from the Father. For which of these do you stone me?',[151] they replied, 'We are not stoning you for any of these ... but for blasphemy, because you, a mere man, claim to be God.'[152] If this was a catastrophic misunderstanding on their part, *why did Jesus not correct them?*

When one of his disciples asked him, 'Lord, show us the Father and that will be enough for us,' Jesus replied, 'Don't you know me, Philip, even after I have been among you such a long time? Anyone who has seen me has seen the Father. How can you say, "Show us the Father"? Don't you believe that I am in the Father, and that the Father is in me?'[153] Jesus was not claiming to *be* the Father, but was indicating that in his own distinct life and personality he was revealing all of God's nature and character that it was possible and necessary for any human being to know on this earth; it was a clear claim to deity.

The fifth incident took place a few hours before his death, when Jesus prayed, 'And now, Father, glorify me in your presence with the glory I had with you before the world began.'[154] The phrase 'in your presence' is a rather weak translation of words which mean much more than 'alongside' or 'in the same place'. Literally, they mean 'along with yourself'. They speak of Jesus taking up again a heavenly status which he had possessed by divine right before time began. This either makes the prayer blasphemous balderdash or tells us that Jesus is addressing God on equal terms. In the light of what we have already discovered, is it difficult to decide between those two alternatives?

The sixth of these claims was made at the end of his last day of freedom, when Jesus was being taken into custody by a detachment of soldiers. Fully aware of what was about to happen, Jesus asked the approaching troops, 'Who is it you want?' When they replied, 'Jesus of Nazareth,' he told them, 'I am he.'[155] This all seems perfectly straightforward, yet the soldiers' reaction was amazing: 'When Jesus said, "I am he," they drew back and fell to the ground.'[156] At that point, Jesus was offering no resistance and appeared helpless, yet an entire detachment of hand-picked troops collapsed in a heap — hardly commando material! The only credible explanation seems to lie in the phrase Jesus used to identify himself. Translators have added the word 'he' in order to round out the sentence, yet what Jesus actually said was *'ego eimi'* ('I am'). But why should four syllables flatten a squad of soldiers? The only answer that fits is that there was something about the majesty and glory of the words (the divine title we noted earlier) and the way in which they were spoken that swept the troops to the ground in a spectacular demonstration of the presence and power of God.

When we put these six claims together, and add the other available biblical data, we can easily agree with the American educator William Biederwolf when he wrote, 'A man who can read the New Testament and not see that Christ claims to be more than a man can look all over the sky at high noon on a cloudless day and not see the sun.'[157] Sceptics sometimes try to evade the central issue here by conceding on the one hand that Jesus was an outstanding moral example while denying on the other hand his deity, but C. S. Lewis has long since torpedoed this ploy: 'I am trying here to prevent anyone saying the really foolish thing that people often say about him: "I'm ready to accept Jesus as a great moral teacher, but I don't accept his claim to be God." That is the one thing we must not say. A man who was merely a man and said the sort of things Jesus said would not be a great moral teacher. He would either be a lunatic — on a level with the man who says he is a poached egg — or else he would be the devil of hell. You must make your choice... You can shut him up for a fool, you can spit at him and kill him as a demon; or you can fall at his feet and call him Lord and God. But let us not come up with any patronizing nonsense about his being a great human teacher. *He has not left that open to us. He did not intend to.*'[158]

Endorsement of Jesus' claims to deity are to be found all over Scripture. I have examined many of these elsewhere,[159] but we can note two here. Their particular significance is that they speak of Jesus doing things which only God *could* do — create and sustain the universe. Paul says of Jesus, 'By him all things were created: things in heaven and on earth, visible and invisible, whether thrones or powers or rulers or authorities; all things were created by him and for him.'[160] It would be difficult to make a statement of that importance clearer or more comprehensive. Paul then goes on to say of Jesus that 'In him all things hold together'[161] — in other words that it is his power and wisdom which prevent our cosmos from becoming chaos. It is perfectly clear that only of God could these two statements be made, and that no other human being in history has been credibly able to match Jesus' claim.

The substitute

The fifth way in which Jesus stands out from the rest of humanity is that *his death was unique*. Biographers seldom spend much time on the deaths of their subjects — it is their lives that matter — but Jesus is a striking exception to the rule. It has been calculated that about 40% of the Gospel of Matthew, 60% of the Gospel of Mark, over 30% of the Gospel of Luke and nearly 50% of the Gospel of John are given over to the events leading up to and surrounding the moment when Jesus was put to death by crucifixion when he was in his early thirties. Later, the apostle Paul, who wrote most of the New Testament, summed up his message by saying, 'We preach Christ crucified,'[162] and reminded friends at Corinth, 'I resolved to know nothing while I was with you except Jesus Christ and him crucified.'[163] If we include the contributions of the other writers, it is impossible to disagree with Leon Morris when he says, 'The cross dominates the New Testament.'[164]

It is equally obvious that Jesus saw his death as being the consummation of his life, not merely its conclusion. As the time drew near he said, 'It was for this very reason I came to this hour.'[165] Two earlier life-threatening situations had been defused 'because his time had not yet come',[166] but on the night of his arrest he began a prayer with the words: 'Father, the time has come.'[167] For Jesus, death was to be a triumphal climax to his life's work. As John Stott puts it, 'The hour for which he had come into the world was the hour in which he left it.'[168] This explains why 2,000 years later the universally recognized symbol of the movement Jesus started is not one which relates to his conception, character or creed, but a cross, a replica of the cruellest instrument of execution in the ancient world, and one which was banned nearly 1,500 years ago.

What is so special about the death of Jesus? After all, death itself is universal and inescapable; the whole world is a hospital, and every person in it a terminal patient. Nobody has to ask, 'Is there death after life?', but everybody should surely ask another question: *'Why?'* Why should every one of us have to face what J. I. Packer calls this 'malevolent monstrosity'?[169] In the course of my work in the Registrar-General's office in Guernsey, I wrote out hundreds of death certificates, and I can still remember the strange emotion I often felt when completing the column headed 'Cause of Death'. Sometimes, the words were frighteningly long — 'arteriosclerotic degeneration of the myocardium' — while at other times 'cancer' said it all, yet these and countless others tell us only part of the story. To discover the rest, we must turn to the Bible.

As we saw in the previous chapter, our first parents were created in God's perfect moral and spiritual image, but that perfect relationship was shattered by their catastrophic rebellion. They died spiritually and began to die physically, and it was in this fallen and dysfunctional state that they became the original ancestors of the entire human race. This means that whereas they *became* sinners, we were *born* that way; David acknowledged, 'Surely I was sinful at birth, sinful from the time my mother conceived me.'[170] What is more, we share Adam's guilt as well as his corruption, the penalty as well as the pollution: 'Sin entered the world through one man, and death through sin, and *in this way death came to all men*, because all sinned.'[171] Here is the answer to the 'Why?' By his sin, Adam ruined all those he represented, and the evidence for man's inherent spiritual death is his inevitable physical death.

The Bible links sin and death so fundamentally that it speaks of 'the law of sin and death'.[172] Elsewhere it warns, 'The wages of sin is death'[173] and that 'Sin, when it is full-grown, gives birth to death.'[174] The law of sin and death is part of the moral fabric of the universe. Before man sinned, death was impossible; since he sinned, death has been inevitable, and the ultimate and eternal outcome for those who die physically while still dead spiritually is to be 'punished with everlasting destruction and shut out from the presence of the Lord and from the majesty of his power'.[175] This is the background to the Bible's insistence that the death of Jesus was unique in two ways.

Firstly, it was the only truly *voluntary* death in human history. Death is not an option for any one of us; in the Bible's words, we are all 'destined to die'.[176] Not even suicides decide to die — they merely choose the day, the time, the place and the method. Death is the final item on our earthly agenda and we cannot avoid reaching it. We are all sinners and we all die. As Jesus was without sin he was not subject to 'the law of sin and death'; he was outside of death's jurisdiction. Yet he died, and made it crystal clear that he did so of his own volition. On one occasion he told his hearers, 'No one takes [my life] from me, but I lay it down of my own accord.'[177] At the time of his arrest, he rejected violent resistance and told one of his companions, 'Do you think I cannot call on my Father, and he will at once put at my disposal more than twelve legions of angels?'[178] Jesus could have been delivered at any time he wished, but he chose otherwise. Even clearer evidence comes from the moment of his death, when he 'cried out again in a loud voice' and 'gave up his spirit'.[179] Both phrases are important. The first tells us that Jesus did not die of physical exhaustion, unable to continue any longer. The second literally means, 'He sent his spirit away,' like a master dismissing a servant. The Bible specifically states, 'No man has power to retain the spirit, or authority over the day of death,'[180] yet here again Jesus proved the exception to the rule and showed that he had complete authority over the entire process of dying. As Augustine wrote some 400 years later, 'He gave up his life *because* he willed it, *when* he willed it and *as* he willed it.'[181]

Secondly, it was the only truly *vicarious* death in human history. We are all moved by stories of those who sacrifice their own lives to rescue others, or even take the place of the condemned, yet what Jesus did was infinitely more significant. When he died on behalf of others and in their place, he took upon himself the penalty for sin which they had incurred. The uniqueness of Jesus' substitutionary death lay in the fact that, although he was innocent of all sin, his death was a sin-bearing and atoning sacrifice. This tremendous truth is to be found in Old Testament prophecy and in New Testament narrative and teaching. Isaiah had written about a suffering servant who would bear the sins of others and die in their place[182] and, at a last meal with his disciples, Jesus quoted from the passage concerned and told them that 'What is written about me is reaching its fulfilment.'[183] Elsewhere in the New Testament, Paul writes, 'While we were still sinners, Christ died for us';[184] Peter says, 'Christ died for sins once for all, the righteous for the unrighteous, to bring you to God';[185] and John adds, 'Jesus Christ laid down his life for us.'[186] God's perfect holiness demands that all sin — every sin — must be punished, and when Jesus took the place of others, he became as accountable for their sins as if he had been responsible for committing them.

Those who see the death of Jesus as nothing more than an example of how to endure suffering with meekness, courage and dignity are missing the central thrust of the Bible's message, as one illustration will be sufficient to demonstrate. Jesus spoke of his death as being 'for the forgiveness of sins',[187] but how could an example, however brilliant, achieve this? As John Stott explains, 'A pattern cannot secure our pardon... An example can stir our imagination, kindle our idealism and strengthen our resolve, but it cannot cleanse the defilement of our past sins, bring peace to our troubled conscience or fetch us home to God.'[188] The death of Jesus *was* an example, but it was much more than that. It was the only occasion in human history when one human being volunteered to take upon himself the appalling yet just penalty which God imposes on sinners. It was unique.

The suffering God

There is one further way in which Jesus stands out from the rest of the human race, but before we examine it we need to take on board a vitally important truth we touched on in the last chapter, one which ties together our last two sections and without which the significance of Jesus' death will be lost.

In chapter 23, we saw that God is not a distant, uncaring despot, unable to understand human suffering and unwilling to do anything about it. In our last two sections, we have noted the Bible's teaching that Jesus is divine and that he willingly took upon himself the physical and spiritual death which God rightly imposes on those who reject him. Pulling all of this together, we are faced with the amazing fact that when Jesus died on the cross, *God himself was suffering in the place of others, and paying the penalty for their sin.*

Far from insulating himself against suffering, God is the supreme sufferer in the universe. In the person of Jesus Christ, he has come to us in our desperate and self-imposed plight. He has entered into the deepest suffering of the human race, and in the death of 'his own Son'[189] has provided the means by which the punishment for human rebellion can be turned aside and he can graciously forgive evil and bring the evildoers concerned into a living and eternal relationship with himself.

Two things stand out when we give serious thought to this. The first is that *God's justice was not compromised.* The Bible tells us that 'All have sinned and fall short of the glory of God,'[190] and that 'The wages of sin is death,'[191] yet also makes it clear that when Jesus died in the place of others, and on their behalf, he became as accountable for their wickedness as if he had been responsible for it. As a result, he received in his own body and spirit the full fury of God's holy anger against evil. The Bible specifically says that God acted in this way 'to demonstrate his justice'.[192] The death of Jesus involved no 'back-room deal' or sleight of hand. Nor was it a spectacular but empty gesture. Isaiah anticipated the true meaning of it when he wrote:

He was pierced for our transgressions,
  he was crushed for our iniquities;
the punishment that brought us peace was upon him,
  and by his wounds we are healed. [193]

Secondly, *the death of Jesus reveals God's amazing love*. Just as emphatically as the Bible tells us that the death of Jesus demonstrates God's unflinching justice, his unwillingness to gloss over sin and 'let bygones be bygones', so it tells us that in that death 'God demonstrates his own love for us in this: While we were still sinners, Christ died for us.'[194] In what some believers would call the greatest statement in Scripture, Jesus himself said, 'God so loved the world that he gave his one and only Son, that whoever believes in him shall not perish but have eternal life.'[195]

Those who claim that there cannot be a God of either justice or love have failed to grasp that in the death of Jesus he is seen to be both. As Alister McGrath puts it, 'God suffered in Christ. He *knows* what it is like to experience pain. He has travelled down the road of pain, abandonment, suffering and death... God is not like some alleged hero with feet of clay, who demands that others suffer, while remaining aloof from the world of pain himself. He has passed through the shadow of suffering himself ... and, by doing so, transfigures the sufferings of his people.'[196]

The long silence

Outside of Scripture, I have never come across anything that makes the point about God identifying himself with human suffering more powerfully than these words:

> At the end of time, billions of people were scattered on a great plain before God's throne. Most shrank back from the brilliant light before them. But some groups near the front talked heatedly — not with cringing shame but with belligerence. 'Can God judge us?'
>
> 'How can he know about suffering?' snapped a pert young brunette. She ripped open a sleeve to reveal a tattooed number from a Nazi concentration camp. 'We endured terror ... beating ... torture ... death!'

In another group a black man lowered his collar. 'What about this?' he demanded, showing an ugly rope burn. 'Lynched for no crime but being black!'

In another crowd, a pregnant schoolgirl with sullen eyes. 'Why should I suffer?' she murmured. 'It wasn't my fault.'

Far out across the plain were hundreds of such groups. Each had a complaint against God for the evil and suffering he had permitted in his world. How lucky God was to live in heaven where all was sweetness and light, where there was no weeping or fear, no hunger or hatred! What did God know of all that men had been enforced to endure in this world? For God leads a pretty sheltered life, they said.

So each of these groups sent forth their leader, chosen because he had suffered the most. A Jew, a black, a person from Hiroshima, a horribly disabled arthritic, a thalidomide child. In the centre of the plain they consulted with each other.

At last they were ready to present their case. It was rather clever. Before God could be qualified to be their judge, he must endure what they had endured. Their verdict was that God should be sentenced to live on earth — as a man! Let him be born a Jew. Let the legitimacy of his birth be doubted. Give him a work so difficult that even his family will think him out of his mind when he tried to do it. Let him be betrayed by his closest friends. Let him face false charges, be tried by a prejudiced jury and convicted by a cowardly judge. Let him be tortured. At last, let him see what it means to be terribly alone. Then let him die in agony. Let him die so that there can be no doubt that he died. Let there be a whole host of witnesses to verify it.

As each leader announced the portion of his sentence, loud murmurs of approval went up from the throng of people assembled. When the last had finished pronouncing sentence there was a long silence. No one uttered another word. No one moved. For suddenly all knew that God had already served his sentence. [197]

Man alive!

We can now return to the sequence of factors which mark Jesus out from the rest of the human race. The sixth way in which this is true is that *his resurrection was unique.* Jesus died at about three o'clock on a Friday afternoon, and was buried less than three hours later in a cave carved out of a rock face in a nearby garden, after which the entrance to the tomb was covered by 'a big stone'.[198] To prevent Jesus' disciples from removing the body, the Roman governor Pontius Pilate posted a detachment of soldiers at the tomb and had his own official seal attached to the stone.[199]

By Sunday morning, *the body had gone.* At least five people who visited the site said so,[200] and not a single contemporary is known to have doubted it. What is more, Jesus' followers were soon risking their lives on the streets of Jerusalem by branding his murderers as 'wicked men'[201] and announcing that he had been 'raised ... from the dead'.[202] Their message has been the linchpin of the Christian church ever since, and has successfully withstood every attempt to dislodge it. I have written elsewhere about these attacks,[203] but a thumbnail sketch of some of them will be useful here.

'The tomb was not empty.' This is woefully weak: why did the authorities not encourage people to visit it and see for themselves?

'The first visitors all went to the wrong tomb.' Yet we are specifically told that at least two of them had been present at the burial just thirty-six hours earlier and 'saw the tomb and how his body was laid in it'.[204] What is more, the tomb had been donated by Joseph of Arimathea, a prominent local citizen;[205] would he have forgotten the location of his own carefully chosen burial plot?

'The body was stolen by a person or persons unknown.' There is not a shred of evidence for this, let alone any opportunity or motive. As Norman Anderson wryly comments, 'A Jew of that period could scarcely be suspected of stealing bodies on behalf of anatomical research!'[206]

'The Roman authorities removed the body.' They obviously had the opportunity, but why would they have done so? Why post a guard in the first place? If they had moved the body elsewhere, why did they not produce it when Jesus' followers began to announce his resurrection?

'The Jewish authorities removed the body.' As they were hand in glove with the Romans, and knew of prophecies that Jesus would rise from the dead after three days, they had both opportunity and motive for hiding it

elsewhere for *four* days, when they could then squash the 'Jesus move-ment' at birth. Then why did they resort to arresting, imprisoning, flogging and executing the first Christian preachers when they could have killed off their movement by producing the body? The Jewish authorities' silence speaks volumes.

'Jesus' disciples removed the body.' This was the story cobbled together by the frantic religious authorities, who circulated the rumour that the dis-ciples had snatched the body while the guards were asleep,[207] but it runs into an avalanche of problems. Would every one of the guards have fallen asleep on duty, knowing as they must have done that such an offence attracted the death penalty? How did the disciples manage to break open the seal, roll away the massive rock and take the body away without a single soldier noticing what was going on? If the guards *were* asleep, how did they know who had stolen the body? Did the body-snatchers leave a visiting card? If the guards were awake, how (and why) did a handful of men who had run into hiding 'with the doors locked for fear of the Jews'[208] suddenly pluck up enough courage to tackle an armed squad of soldiers and risk the death penalty for breaking the governor's official seal — all for the purpose of taking possession of a body already in the safe keeping of one of their friends? Why is there no record of their ever being charged with a capital offence? The brilliant second-century theologian Tertullian scornfully dismissed all the body-snatching theories by adding another — that perhaps a gardener had removed the body to prevent crowds of visi-tors from damaging his vegetables!

'Jesus never actually died.' This is the so-called 'swoon theory', which was popularized in the eighteenth century, but has long since been comprehen-sively discredited, not least by pointing out that Pontius Pilate called for an official report from the officer in charge of the execution squad, and only released the body to Joseph of Arimathea when he had this first-hand confirmation of the prisoner's death.[209] The swoon theory asks us to be-lieve that after a succession of savage beatings by Roman soldiers, and being left for hours nailed by the hands and feet to a wooden beam and a vertical pole, Jesus lost consciousness, but remained alive, even when his body was ripped open by a soldier's spear in order to ensure that he had died. We must believe that nobody noticed any sign of life throughout the removal and burial of the body, and that later, revived by the cool air or

the strong-smelling spices with which he had been embalmed, Jesus came out of coma, wriggled free from the tightly-wound grave-clothes, pushed aside the rock sealing the tomb, overcame the soldiers, ran off naked (the grave-clothes were left behind) and, by the time he met with his disciples a few hours later, had made such a complete recovery that he persuaded them he had conquered death and begun a radiant new life. Surely only the grossly gullible could swallow such nonsense? Even if we did, we also have to believe that after more than thirty sinless years Jesus was suddenly transformed into a monstrous liar. It is hardly surprising that even an arch-sceptic like David Strauss had no hesitation in dismissing this whole scenario as 'impossible'.[210]

On the other hand ...

Evidence for the truth of Jesus' resurrection is plentiful and persuasive, and is backed up by some surprising credentials. In the first place, there is no description of the resurrection. If the disciples had made up the whole story, surely they would have included a dramatic eyewitness account? Secondly, at a time when a woman's testimony was thought so worthless that it was not considered binding in Jewish law, the first post-resurrection appearance of Jesus is said to have been to a woman.[211] Would the disciples have scuppered their own scheme by building on such a flimsy foundation? Thirdly, while the different narratives agree on the essentials, they are not identical, and it is virtually impossible to fit them into a precise chronological order. This may seem like a weakness in the case, but it is exactly the opposite: if the disciples had invented the story, would they not have made sure that all the loose ends were tied up?

The positive evidence begins with the fact that *the Bible records six independent, written testimonies* (three of them by eyewitnesses) telling of eleven separate appearances over a period of forty days. Sceptics have suggested that these 'appearances' were hallucinations, but this line of attack founders on the fact that they fail to meet the necessary criteria. Those to whom Jesus appeared included a number of women,[212] a sceptical brother,[213] several fishermen,[214] a brilliant intellectual engaged in a vicious crusade to wipe out his followers,[215] and a close friend who had remained deeply sceptical even when others assured him that they had met the risen Jesus face to face.[216] He appeared in a garden, in a home, on a roadside, out in the country, on the seashore and on a hillside. He appeared at many different times of day, and hardly ever in places where he and his disciples had spent time together. What is more, he appeared not merely to individuals but to two, three, seven, eleven and on one occasion several hundred people at once.[217]

It is difficult to discount the force of this accumulation of evidence. Writing as a distinguished medical expert, Arthur Rendle Short says that 'The resurrection appearances break every known law of visions.'[218] A friend of mine once shocked 200 students at a school assembly by cutting the headmaster's tie in two with a pair of scissors. She then went on to say something like this: 'Imagine that on your way home this afternoon you met a friend and told him that you had seen the assembly speaker chop the headmaster's tie in two. Your friend would probably think you were pulling his leg, but supposing three other students who were there at the time told him the same story, and then that tomorrow thirty others did so. Now imagine that by the end of the week all 200 students present at the assembly told your friend the same thing. Would it be reasonable for him to doubt them?' My friend made a good point. When Paul told friends at Corinth that Jesus appeared 'to five hundred of the brothers at the same time' he added, '*most of whom are still living*'.[219] Those who doubted Jesus' resurrection were at liberty to interrogate hundreds of witnesses, all of whom would have confirmed the fact. As one scholar has explained, 'Hallucination involving five hundred people at once and repeated several times is unthinkable.'[220]

One other thing: why should hallucinations convince the disciples that Jesus had risen from the dead? They had been utterly demoralized by his death, and resurrection was the last thing they expected. The first women at the tomb went to anoint his remains, not to arrange a press conference announcing his return to life! In their contemporary culture, it would have been much more natural to presume that they had seen a ghost. Francis Bridger points out that 'This would have been much more plausible to their contemporaries, since belief in resurrection was uncommon and outlandish. If they truly had wanted to convince as many people as possible, they would have been much better off avoiding the notion of the resurrection altogether.'[221]

A second striking piece of evidence for Jesus' resurrection is *the sudden transformation of the disciples* from a dejected, faithless and depressed rabble, cowering behind locked doors, to a fearless and dynamic band of believers, prepared to face persecution, imprisonment and execution rather than deny their convictions.[222] Something objective must have happened to kindle such a radical change, and this tremendous transformation from cowardice to courage leads Norman Anderson to claim that it is 'far and away the strongest circumstantial evidence for the resurrection'.[223] The disciples' transformation was what convinced Charles Colson that the biblical account of Jesus' resurrection was true. The Nixon administration had tried to cover up its burglary of the Democrats' Watergate offices but, in less than a month, three of those involved had gone to the Department of Justice to turn state evidence, and Richard Nixon's presidency was doomed. Some time later Colson wrote, 'In my Watergate experience I saw the inability of men — powerful, highly motivated professionals — to hold together a conspiracy based on a lie... Yet Christ's followers maintained to their grim deaths by execution that they had in fact seen Jesus Christ raised from the dead. There was no conspiracy... Men and women do not give up their comfort — and certainly not their lives — for what they know to be a lie.'[224] As John Stott comments, 'Hypocrites and martyrs are not made of the same stuff.'[225]

The next piece of evidence brings the previous one up to date. Within a few years, enemies of the new movement accused its leaders of having 'caused trouble all over the world'.[226] By the early part of the fourth century, the movement was recognized as the official religion of the Roman Empire, which had tried to kill it off at birth. Some 2,000 years later, it has become the largest religious movement the world has ever known, and its origin is to be found, not in some new moral teaching, nor in an original slant on social issues, nor in a trendy new style of worship, but in one simple, stupendous fact: *the resurrection of Jesus*.

How convincing is the evidence for the resurrection? In a document found among his private papers, Lord Lyndhurst, one of the greatest minds in British legal history, wrote, 'I know pretty well what evidence is; and I tell you, such evidence as that for the resurrection has never broken down yet.'[227] The distinguished legal counsel Sir Edward Clarke was just as certain: 'As a lawyer I have made a prolonged study for the events of the first Easter Day. To me the evidence is conclusive, and over and again in the High Court I have secured the verdict on evidence not nearly so compelling.'[228] Lord Darling, a former Chief Justice of England, concluded: 'There exists such overwhelming evidence, positive and negative, factual and circumstantial, that no intelligent jury in the world could fail to bring in a verdict that the resurrection story is true.'[229] Small wonder that American author D. James Kennedy writes, 'The Grand Canyon wasn't caused by an Indian dragging a stick, and the Christian Church wasn't created by a myth.'[230]

The resurrection of Jesus is unique in the most radical sense: he is the only person raised from the dead and never to die again. There are several instances, in both Old and New Testaments, of people being miraculously raised from the dead, but in each case the person concerned had to suffer the trauma of death all over again. However, 'Since Christ was raised from the dead, he cannot die again; death no longer has mastery over him.'[231] Having submitted to death once, on behalf of others, he has triumphed over it for ever, and countless millions of people, in every section of society, testify to the moral and spiritual dynamic he brings to their lives.

The fly and the elephant

In *God in the Dock*, C. S. Lewis wrote, 'What are we to make of Jesus Christ? This is a question which has, in a sense, a frantically comic side. For the real question is not what we are to make of Christ, but what is he to make of us? The picture of a fly sitting deciding what it is going to make of an elephant has comic elements about it.'[232] Lewis' analogy is brilliant, yet the two questions are linked by the Bible's teaching that a person's assessment of Christ is fundamental in determining his or her destiny. The birth, life, claims, death and resurrection of Jesus clearly constitute a serious problem for the atheist, and brushing them aside is an escape hatch not open to the honest, serious thinker. *Jesus demands a verdict*, and there are just four options available.

The first is that he was _evil_ — specifically, that he was a blasphemous liar, a blatant hypocrite and a callous deceiver. On this view, he knew perfectly well that he was not divine, yet he deliberately toyed with people's tangled emotions. When he saw them groaning under the burden of religious rules and regulations which brought them no relief, 'harassed and helpless, like sheep without a shepherd,'[233] he cruelly promised the forgiveness of sins and eternal life to all who trusted him,[234] knowing full well that he was lying through his teeth. Does that chime with the record of a loving, gracious, gentle, sympathetic teacher, who so clearly had his finger on the pulse of spiritual reality, who 'went around doing good,'[235] and who caused people to be 'amazed at the gracious words that came from his lips'?[236] Even an entrenched sceptic like John Stuart Mill called Jesus 'the ideal representative and guide of humanity',[237] while the nineteenth-century arch-liberal Ralph Waldo Emerson, whose thinking was permeated with pantheism, was forced to admit that Jesus was 'the most perfect of all men that have yet appeared'.[238] If Jesus was a charlatan, how has he become the inspiration for so much goodness in society, especially in the giving of help to those in need? If the character of Jesus and his influence on others point to something essentially evil, rational discussion is pointless.

The second option is that he was *deluded*, especially about his own identity. This sounds a more promising approach, enabling us to dismiss his claims while commending his character, but it misses the point that his teaching and his claims were welded together. To give just one example, he spoke not only about 'the kingdom of God',[239] and 'the kingdom of heaven',[240] but also about '*my* kingdom',[241] and clearly inferred that these were identical. The distinguished historian Kenneth Scott Latourette points out the significance of this: 'It is not his teachings which make Jesus so remarkable, although these would be enough to give him distinction. It is a combination of the teachings with the man himself. *The two cannot be separated*'[242] (emphasis added). Jesus was either much more than a great teacher, or he was much less, and to say that he was right in the whole flow of his teaching but wrong on its greatest theme is to be neither sensible nor honest.

The third is that he was *mentally deranged*. This is certainly radical, but far from original. In his own day there were those who said, 'He is demon-possessed and raving mad. Why listen to him?'[243] Insanity is frightening and mysterious, and sometimes leads people to make the most absurd claims about themselves. Norman Anderson tells of playing football for his school against a team from what was then known as a lunatic asylum, one of whose patients firmly believed that he was a poached egg.[244] Yet such absurd claims are matched by unstable character traits in those concerned. Is this what we find in the life of Jesus? Far from being emotionally unbalanced, irrational, eccentric and self-absorbed, we find him balanced, utterly composed and constantly taken up with the needs of others; healing the sick, feeding the hungry, encouraging the sad and comforting the bereaved. Bernard Palmer's medical expertise leads him to this diagnosis: 'There are no mood swings, depressive episodes or the schizophrenic's tendency to be out of touch with reality. On the contrary, [his biographers] paint a picture of somebody who is eminently sane, balanced and reliable — a tough, compassionate, practical man who drew love and respect from all who met him.'[245] His teaching clearly reflects this. If the Sermon on the Mount is an expression of insanity, we urgently need a global epidemic of it! Those who honestly examine the character of Jesus, listen to his words and conclude that he was a madman are telling us nothing about Jesus, but a great deal about themselves

This leaves just one alternative. Writing to people who lived in a culture in which heretical ideas about God and man and their relationship to each other were rife, Paul told them that Jesus was 'the image of the invisible God',[246] that 'God was pleased to have all his fulness dwell in him,'[247] and that 'In Christ all the fulness of the Deity lives in bodily form.'[248] Elsewhere, he referred to 'our great God and Saviour, Jesus Christ',[249] and stated that, in the person of Jesus, God 'appeared in a body'.[250] The writer of Hebrews was equally clear, and described Jesus as 'the radiance of God's glory and the exact representation of his being'.[251] These statements all confirm that when Jesus claimed, 'I and the Father are one',[252] he was telling the truth.

No other option is available. If Jesus is not evil, deluded or deranged, he is *exactly who Scripture declares him to be* — 'the true God and eternal life'.[253]

Where does that leave the atheist?

Where does it leave *you*?

Notes

Preface
1. Mortimer J. Adler, *The Great Ideas: A Syntopicon of Great Books of the Western World,* vol. I, Encyclopaedia Britannica, p.543.
2. Cited in *Daily Telegraph,* 7 November 1997.
3. C. Stephen Evans, *The Quest for Faith,* Inter-Varsity Press, p.28.
4. As the English language does not have a pronoun for referring to persons without carrying an implication of gender, I am following custom by referring to God as 'he', but without any implication of maleness.

Introduction
1. C. S. Lewis, *God in the Dock,* ed. Walter Hooper, William B. Eerdmans Publishing Co., p.100.
2. Os Guinness, *The Dust of Death,* Inter-Varsity Press, p.349.
3. Alister McGrath, *Explaining Your Faith,* Inter-Varsity Press, p.89.
4. George Mavrodes, *Belief in God,* Random House, p.46.
5. *International Bulletin of Missionary Research,* January 1991, cited in *Act on the Facts*, MARC Europe, pp.75-6.
6. Patrick Johnstone, *Operation World,* (Fourth Edition), STL Books/WEC Publications, p.33.
7. *What Americans Believe,* Regal Books, p.201.
8. European Value Systems Study Group 1986, cited in *LandMarc,* High Summer 1989.
9. Cited by Andrew Knowles, *Finding Faith,* Lion Publishing, p.16.
10. Cited in *Act on the Facts,* p.158.
11. *Ibid.*
12. *Believing in Britain,* BBC Radio 4, 2 January 1995.
13. *British Social Attitudes Survey,* undertaken by Social and Community Planning Research, published by Gower Publishing Co. Ltd.
14. *Daily Telegraph,* 16 December 1999.
15. European Value Systems Study Group 1986, cited in *LandMarc,* High Summer 1989.
16. *The Concise Oxford Dictionary of Current English,* Seventh Edition, Clarendon Press, p.1109.
17. *Ibid.,* p.425.
18. George Harrison, *Beatles* magazine, February 1968.
19. David Elton Trueblood, *Philosophy of Religion,* Harper & Brothers, p.54.
20. John Robinson, *Exploration into God,* SCM Press, p.46.
21. Lewis Carroll, *Alice Through the Looking Glass,* Penguin Popular Classics, p.100.
22. *Concise Oxford Dictionary,* p.54.
23. Cited by Jostein Gaarder, *Sophie's World,* Phoenix House, p.116.

Chapter 1 — The Greeks had words for it
1. See especially James George Frazer, *The Golden Bough* (1890), which examined the development of human thought with reference to magic, religion and science.

2. Robert Brow, *Religion: Origins and Ideas,* Tyndale Press, p.11.
3. *Ibid.*
4. Johann Warneck, *The Living Forces of the Gospel,* Oliphant, Anderson and Ferrier, p.99.
5. Edward G. Newing, 'Religions of Pre-literary Societies', in *The World's Religions,* ed. Norman Anderson, Inter-Varsity Press, pp.11-12.
6. Andrew Lang, *The Making of Religion,* Longmans & Green, p.18.
7. Max Muller, *History of Sanskrit Literature,* p.559.
8. Flinders Petrie, *The Religion of Ancient Egypt,* Constable, p.4.
9. Stephen Langdon, *Semitic Theology,* vol. 5 in *Mythology of All Races,* Archaeological Institute of America, p.xviii.
10. Edward G. Newing, 'Religions of Pre-literary Societies', in *The World's Religions,* p.14.
11. *Daily Telegraph,* 4 December 1998.
12. Charles S. MacKenzie, 'Classical Greek Humanism', in *Building a Christian World View,* vol. 1, ed. W. Andrew Hoffecker, Presbyterian & Reformed Publishing Co., p.32.
13. Ross A. Foster, 'Cosmologies of Philosophical Speculation', in *Building a Christian World View,* vol. 2, ed. W. Andrew Hoffecker, Presbyterian & Reformed Publishing Co., p.22.
14. James Thrower, *A Short History of Western Atheism,* Pemberton Books, p.17.
15. Guinness, *The Dust of Death,* p.220.
16. Charles S. MacKenzie and W. Andrew Hoffecker, 'Greek Epistemology: Plato and Aristotle', in *Building a Christian World View,* vol. 1, p.219.
17. Cited by William Raeper and Linda Smith, *A Beginner's Guide to Ideas,* Lion Publishing, p.10.
18. Plato, *Laws,* 886.
19. *See* Plato, *Laws,* XI, 907a-910d; pp.1462-5.
20. Plato, *Laws,* vol. 7, trans. Jowett, pp.769-70.
21. *Sunday Telegraph,* 19 January 1997.
22. Jostein Gaarder, *Sophie's World,* Phoenix House, p.89.
23. MacKenzie, *Building a Christian World View,* vol. I, p.43.
24. Cited in *Sunday Telegraph,* 19 January 1997.
25. Epicurus, letter to Menoeceus.
26. John D. Currid, 'From the Renaissance to the Age of Naturalism', in *Building a Christian World View,* vol. 1, p.139.
27. William H. Halverson, *A Concise Introduction to Philosophy,* Random House, p.394.
28. Lewis, *God in the Dock,* p.137.
29. George Roche, *A World Without Heroes,* George Roche and the Hillsdale College Press, p.118.
30. MacKenzie, *Building a Christian World View,* vol. I, p.47.
31. Thrower, *A Short History of Western Atheism,* p.38.
32. R. C. Sproul, *Reason to Believe,* Zondervan Publishing House, p.104.
33. Ravi Zacharias, *A Shattered Visage,* Wolgemuth & Hyatt, p.2.
34. Paul Johnson, *The Quest for God,* Weidenfield and Nicolson, p.18.
35. B. A. G. Fuller, *A History of Philosophy,* vol. II, Rinehart and Winston, p.581.
36. Peter Kreeft and Ronald Tacelli, *Handbook of Christian Apologetics,* Monarch Publications, p.371. Although I am happy to quote with approval from this title, I should add that since it was first published in 1995, Peter Kreeft has expressed certain theological views with which I would take issue.
37. Henry M. Morris, *The Long War Against God,* Baker Book House, p.208.
38. John Toland, *Pantheism.*
39. C. S. Lewis, *Miracles,* Collins, p.86.
40. *Ibid.*
41. Rodney D. Holder, *Nothing but Atoms and Molecules,* Monarch Publications, p.153.
42. *See* for example Grace M. Jantzen, *God's World, God's Body,* Darton, Longman and Todd; Sallie McFague, *Models of God,* SCM Press.
43. Cited in *Ground Zero,* October-November, 1996, C T Communications, p.18.
44. *Christian News,* 21 March 1994, p.8.
45. Gene Edward Veith, *Loving God With All Your Mind,* Crossway Books, pp.121-2.
46. Kreeft and Tacelli, *Handbook of Christian Apologetics,* p.374.
47. Johnson, *The Quest for God,* p.44.

Chapter 2 — Movers and shakers

1. Colin Brown, *Philosophy and the Christian Faith*, Tyndale Press, pp.17-18.
2. C. G. Thorne, 'Middle Ages', in *The New International Dictionary of the Christian Church*, ed. J. D. Douglas, the Paternoster Press, p.658.
3. John M. Frame, *Apologetics to the Glory of God*, Presbyterian & Reformed Publishing Co., p.114.
4. Paul Helm, 'Thomas Aquinas', in *New International Dictionary of the Christian Church*, p.61.
5. Robert G. Clouse, 'Thomas Aquinas', in *The History of Christianity*, Lion Publishing, p.288.
6. Brown, *Philosophy and the Christian Faith*, p.34.
7. Cited by Thrower, *A Short History of Western Atheism*, p.63.
8. *Ibid.*, p.68.
9. Cited by Robert G. Clouse, 'Francis Bacon', in *New International Dictionary of the Christian Church*, p.95.
10. Cited by Gaarder, *Sophie's World*, p.169.
11. Guinness, *The Dust of Death*, p.5.
12. Cited by Kenneth Clark, *Civilisation*, John Murray Ltd, p.104.
13. Robert G. Clouse, 'Erasmus', in *The New International Dictionary of the Christian Church*, p.350.
14. See Brown, *Philosophy and the Christian Faith*, p.33.
15. Norman Geisler, *Christian Apologetics*, Baker Book House, p.171.
16. Stephen Hawking, *A Brief History of Time*, Bantam Books, p.122.
17. *Ibid.*, pp.140-41.
18. *Ibid.*, p.13.
19. Geisler, *Christian Apologetics*, p.171.
20. Cited by V. James Mannoia, 'Rationalism and Empiricism', in *Building a Christian World View*, vol. 1, p.267.
21. René Descartes, *Meditations on First Philosophy* (IV).
22. Ravi Zacharias, *Can Man Live Without God?*, Word Publishing, p.197.
23. Cited by Ronda Chervin and Eugene Kevane, *Love of Wisdom*, Ignatius, p.212.
24. Geisler, *Christian Apologetics*, p.45.
25. Ayn Rand, cited in *Washington Times*, 21 September 1997.
26. *Washington Times*, 21 September 1997.
27. *Ibid.*
28. See *History of Christianity*, p.484.
29. Benedict De Spinoza, *Ethica Ordine Geometrico*, Part I, Proposition xiv.
30. *Ibid.*, Part I, Proposition xviii.
31. Cited by Paul Hazard, *The European Mind 1680-1715*, p.9.
32. John Locke, *An Essay Concerning Human Understanding*, II.i.2.
33. Mannoia, *Building a Christian World View*, vol. 1, p.273.
34. *Ibid.*, p.270.
35. Brown, *Philosophy and the Christian Faith*, p.73.
36. David Hume, *Treatise*, I.1.6.
37. Paul Helm, 'David Hume', in *New International Dictionary of the Christian Church*, p.490.
38. David Hume, *Enquiry Concerning Christian Understanding*, C. W. Hendel.
39. Brown, *Philosophy and the Christian Faith*, p.72.
40. *Ibid.*, p.69.
41. See H. J. Blackman, *et. al.*, *Objections to Humanism*, Greenwood Press.
42. Hume, *Enquiry Concerning Human Understanding*.
43. Clark H. Pinnock, *Reason Enough*, the Paternoster Press, p.16. Although I am happy to quote with approval from this title, I should add that since it was first published in 1980, Clark Pinnock has expressed certain theological views with which I would take issue.
44. See *Life of the Haldanes*, p.600.
45. Thrower, *A Short History of Western Atheism*, p.106.
46. See R. C. Sproul, *If there's a God, why are there atheists?*, Tyndale Press, p.22.
47. See Paul Hazard, *European Thought in the Eighteenth Century*, pp.407-8.
48. Cited by Gaarder, *Sophie's World*, p.261.
49. Ernst Cassirer, *The Philosophy of the Enlightenment*, trans. Fritz C. A. Koelln and James P. Pettegrove, Beacon, p.134.

50. Cited by Zacharias, *Can Man Live Without God?*, p.201.
51. See the introduction to Immanuel Kant, *Prologomena to Any Future Metaphysics.*
52. Immanuel Kant, letter dated 4 May 1793, *Gesammelte Schriften*, XI, p.429 (No. 574).
53. Immanuel Kant, *Critique of Pure Reason*, Introduction, p.41.
54. Brown, *Philosophy and the Christian Faith*, p.96.
55. R. C. Sproul, *Lifeviews*, Fleming H. Revell, p.161.
56. Kant, *Critique of Pure Reason*, p.528.
57. Immanuel Kant, *Religion with the Limits of Reason Alone*, p.40.
58. Sproul, *If there's a God, why are there atheists?*, p.23.
59. Zacharias, *Can Man Live Without God?*, p.202.
60. *Ibid.*, p.203.
61. Brown, *Philosophy and the Christian Faith*, p.105.
62. *Ibid.*, p.106.

Chapter 3 — Conflict and confusion
1. Cited by Currid, in *Building a Christian World View*, vol. 1, p.143.
2. Colin Brown, 'Friedrich Schleiermacher', in *History of Christianity*, p.541.
3. Nicola Hoggars Creegan, 'Schleiermacher as Apologist', in *Christian Apologetics in the Post-modern World*, ed. Timothy R. Phillips and Dennis L. Okholm, Inter-Varsity Press, p.62.
4. Friedrich Schleiermacher, *On Religion: Speeches to Its Cultured Despisers*, trans. Richard Crouter, Cambridge University Press, pp.77-8.
5. *Ibid.*, p.39.
6. Friedrich Schleiermacher, *The Christian Faith*, p.12.
7. Creegan, 'Schleiermacher as Apologist', p.67.
8. *Ibid.*
9. Schleiermacher, *The Christian Faith*, p.194.
10. See Geisler, *Christian Apologetics*, p.71.
11. *Ibid.*
12. Paul Tillich, *Biblical Religion and the Search for Ultimate Reality*, pp.82-3.
13. Rudolf Otto, Introduction to the Harper Torch Books edition of Schleiermacher's *On Religion: Speeches to Its Cultured Despisers*, pp.vii-viii.
14. Bertrand Russell, cited by Alain de Botton, *Daily Telegraph*, 24 May 1997.
15. Oonagh McDonald, 'Georg Wilhelm Friedrich Hegel', in *New International Dictionary of the Christian Church*, p.457.
16. Georg Hegel, *The Phenomenology of the Mind*, p.86.
17. McDonald, 'Georg Wilhelm Friedrich Hegel', in *New International Dictionary of the Christian Church*, p.457.
18. Georg Hegel, *The Philosophy of Religion, II*, p.104.
19. Cited in Karl Popper, *The Open Society and Its Enemies*, 4th ed., Princeton University Press, 2:31.
20. Søren Kierkegaard, *Journals*, p.187.
21. Johnson, *The Quest for God*, p.8.
22. Kreeft and Tacelli, *Handbook of Christian Apologetics*, p.373.
23. Ludwig Feuerbach, 'The Essence of Religion', in *Sämliche Werke*, VII, p.434.
24. Cited by Currid, *Building a Christian World View*, vol. 1, p.151.
25. Cited by Alister McGrath, *Bridge-Building*, Inter-Varsity Press, p.133.
26. Eduard von Hartmann, *Geslichte der Logik*, vol. 2, p.444.
27. Cited by Saul K. Padover, *Karl Marx: An Intimate Biography* (abridged edition), New American Library, p.280.
28. Karl Marx, 'Thesen über Feuerbach' in *Werke*, vol. 2, p.4.
29. Cited by Currid, in *Building a Christian World View*, vol. 1, p.157.
30. Karl Marx, *Economic and Philosophical Manuscripts*, p.85.
31. *Ibid.*, p.41.
32. Karl Marx, 'Zur Kritik der hegelschen Rechtphilosophie', in *Werke*, vol. 1, p.379.
33. Cited by Charles S. MacKenzie, 'Marxism: A Communist Society', in *Building a Christian World View*, vol. 2, p.319.
34. V. I. Lenin, *Religion*, Lawrence and Wishart Ltd, pp.11-12.

35. Letter to Maxim Gorky, 13 January 1913.
36. Nikolai Lenin, *Selected Works,* vol. XL, Lawrence and Wishart Ltd, pp.675-6.
37. See Paul Johnson, *Modern Times,* Orion Books Ltd, p.277.
38. See Roy Medvedev, *Let History Judge: the Origins and Consequences of Stalinism,* (trans. New York 1971), pp.70-71.
39. See Johnson, *Modern Times,* p.548.
40. Cited by Johnson, *Modern Times,* p.563.
41. *Political Change in Wartime: the Khmer Krahom Revolution in Southern Cambodia 1970–1974,* paper given at American Political Science Convention, San Francisco, 4 September 1975.
42. See Johnson, *Modern Times,* pp.654-7.
43. MacKenzie, *Building a Christian World View,* vol. 2, p.315.
44. Johnson, *The Quest for God,* p.10.
45. *Ibid.,* p.25.
46. MacKenzie, *Building a Christian World View,* vol. 2, pp.303-4.
47. Cited by Benton, *One World, One Way,* Evangelical Press, pp.53-4.
48. *Daily Telegraph,* 10 November 1997.
49. Johnson, *Modern Times,* p.788.
50. Johnson, *The Quest for God,* p.27.
51. Zacharias, *A Shattered Visage,* p.18.
52. Friedrich Nietzsche, 'The Madman', a section of 'Gay Science' in *The Portable Nietzsche,* ed. Walter Kaufman, Viking, p.125.
53. Friedrich Nietzsche, *The Joyful Wisdom,* No.343, p.275.
54. Friedrich Nietzsche, *Thus Spake Zarathustra,* trans. R. J. Hollingdale, Penguin, p.42.
55. Cited by Zacharias, *A Shattered Visage,* p.59.
56. Zacharias, *ibid.,* pp.60-61.
57. Viktor Frankl, *The Doctor and the Soul: Introduction to Logotherapy,* Knopf, p.xxi.
58. Zacharias, *A Shattered Visage,* p.19.
59. Brown, *Philosophy and the Christian Faith,* p.140.

Chapter 4 — Impossible things before breakfast

1. Cited by Michael Poole, *A Guide to Science and Belief,* Lion Publishing, p.95.
2. Brown, *Philosophy and the Christian Faith,* p.147.
3. Charles Darwin, *The Autobiography of Charles Darwin,* ed. Nora Barlow, Collins, p.87.
4. Cited in John Brooke, *A Guide to Science and Belief,* p.99.
5. Charles Darwin, *More Letters of Charles Darwin,* ed. Francis Darwin and A. C. Seward, John Murray, 2:170.
6. Charles Darwin, *The Life and Letters of Charles Darwin,* vol. 3, John Murray, pp.312-13.
7. The story of Lady Hope's discussion with Darwin has been flatly denied by evolutionists, and even some creationists have doubted its authority. For an interesting review of the evidence, see M. Bowden, *The Rise of the Evolution Fraud,* Sovereign Publications, pp.188-9, and Ian Taylor, *In the Minds of Men,* TFE Publishers, pp.134-7.
8. S. S. Chawla, 'A philosophical journey to the West', in *The Humanist,* September/October 1964, p.151.
9. R. J. Rushdoony, *The Mythology of Science,* Craig Press, p.41.
10. Cited by Poole, *A Guide to Science and Belief,* p.95.
11. Søren Lovtrup, *Darwinism: the Refutation of a Myth,* Croom Helm, p.60.
12. Desmond King-Hele, *Doctor of Revolution: The Life and Times of Erasmus Darwin,* Faber & Faber.
13. Morris, *The Long War Against God,* p.178.
14. Cited by Loren C. Eisley, 'Alfred Russel Wallace' in *Scientific American,* February 1959, p.80.
15. Morris, *The Long War Against God,* p.173.
16. G. G. Simpson, see Foreword to *Origin of the Species,* 6th edition, Collier Books, p.5.
17. J. Huxley, T. Dobzhansky, R. Neibuhr, O. L. Reiser, S. Nikhilananda, *The Book that Shook the World,* University of Pittsburgh Press.
18. Cited by M. Bowden, *The Rise of the Evolution Fraud,* Sovereign Publications, p.56.
19. Cited in 'John Lofton's Journal', *Washington Times,* 8 February 1984.
20. Charles Darwin, *Life and Letters of Charles Darwin,* vol. 1, p.232.

21. *Ibid.,* vol. 2, p.157.
22. Cited by H. Enoch, *Evolution or Creation,* Evangelical Press, p.145.
23. Michael Denton, *Evolution: A Theory in Crisis,* Adler & Adler, p.69.
24. Cited by Denton, *ibid.*
25. *Ibid.,* p.70.
26. G. G. Simpson, cited by M. Bowden and J. V. Collyer, 'Quotable Quotes for Creationists,' in *Creation Science Movement,* Pamphlet No. 228, January 1982, p.1.
27. Carl Sagan, *Cosmos,* Random House, p.27.
28. H. J. Muller, 'Is Biological Evolution a Principle of Nature that has been well established by Science?' (Privately duplicated and distributed by author, 2 May 1966).
29. Theodosius Dobzhansky, 'Changing Man', in *Science No. 155,* p.409.
30. René Dubos, 'Humanistic Biology', in *American Sciencist No. 53,* p.6.
31. Cited by John Wright, *Designer Universe,* Monarch Publications, p.61.
32. Julian Huxley, 'Evolution after Darwin', in *Issues in Evolution,* vol. 3, Sol Tax, Chicago University Press, p.41.
33. Cited by Ian T. Taylor, *In the Minds of Men,* TFE Publishing, p.396.
34. Cited by Kristin Murphy, 'United Nations', Robert Muller — A Vision of Global Spirituality', in *The Movement Newspaper,* September 1983, p.10.
35. Cited by Phillip E. Johnson, *Darwin on Trial,* Monarch Publications, p.9.
36. Cited by Bowden, *The Rise of the Evolution Fraud,* p.56.
37. Thomas Huxley, *Life and Letters of Thomas Henry Huxley,* vol. 2, ed. L Huxley, Macmillan, p.193.
38. See *Concise Oxford Dictionary,* p.334.
39. E. Mayr, *Population, Species and Evolution,* Harvard University Press, p.10.
40. Cited by Currid, in *Building a Christian World View,* vol. 1, p.154.
41. Cited in *Christianity on Trial,* Book 2, Lion Publishing, p.36.
42. Frame, *Apologetics to the Glory of God,* p.197.
43. Richard Dawkins, *The Blind Watchmaker,* W. W. Norton, pp.6-7.
44. Taylor, *In the Minds of Men,* p.177.
45. Richard Dawkins, 'The Necessity of Darwinism', in *New Scientist,* No. 94, p.130.
46. Denton, *Evolution: A Theory in Crisis,* p.55.
47. Cited by Johnson, *Darwin on Trial,* p.20.
48. C. H. Waddington, *Mathematical Challenges to the Neo-Darwinian Interpretation of Evolution* (The Wistar Institute Symposium Monograph No. 5), ed. P. S. Moorhead and M. M. Kaplan, Wistar Institute Press, pp.13-14.
49. Denton, *Evolution: A Theory in Crisis,* p.62.
50. Sylvia Baker, *Bone of Contention,* Evangelical Press, p.19.
51. Pierre Grassé, *Traité de zoologie, Tome VIII,* Masson.
52. Pierre Grassé, *Evolution of Living Organisms,* Academic Press, p.103.
53. Julian Huxley, *Evolution in Action,* Harper & Brothers, p.41.
54. Magnus Vergbrugge, *Alive: An Enquiry into The Origin and Meaning of Life,* Ross House Books, p.12.
55. *Ibid.,* p.11.
56. Baker, *Bone of Contention,* p.19.
57. Verbrugge, *Alive: An Enquiry into the Origin and Meaning of Life,* p.13.
58. René Chauvin, *La biologie de l'esprit,* Editions du Rocher, pp.23-4.
59. Malcolm Bowden, *Science vs Evolution,* Sovereign Publications, pp.52-3.
60. Cited by Edward F. Block, *Special Creation vs Evolution,* Southwest Bible Church, p.5.
61. See Johnson, *Darwin on Trial,* p.175.
62. G. A. Kerkut, *Implications of Evolution,* cited in Baker, *Bone of Contention,* p.8.
63. Charles Darwin, *The Origin of Species,* J. M. Dent & Sons, Ltd, pp.292-3.
64. David M. Raup, 'Conflicts between Darwin and Palaeontology', in *Field Museum of Natural History Bulletin,* vol. 50, p.25.
65. Mark Ridley, *Darwin Up to Date,* IPC, p.5.
66. Scott M. Huse, *The Collapse of Evolution,* Baker Books, p.30.
67. R. H. Rastall, 'Geology', in *Encyclopaedia Britannica,* 1954 edition, vol. 10, p.168.
68. Cited by Norman Macbeth in *Darwin Retried,* Delta, pp.37-8.

69. Johnson, *Darwin on Trial*, p.54.

70. Henry M. Morris, *Evolution and the Modern Christian*, Presbyterian & Reformed Publishing Co., p.33.

71. See Norman Myers, 'Extinction Rates Past and Present', in *Bioscience* 39, January 1989.

72. Steven M. Stanley, *Macroevolution: Pattern and Process*, W. M. Freeman, p.39.

73. Cited by Luther D. Sutherland, *Darwin's Enigma*, Master Book Publishers, p.63.

74. Barbara J. Stahl, *Vertebrate History*, cited by Johnson, *Darwin on Trial*, p.74.

75. *Daily Telegraph*, 24 September 1998.

76. Johnson, *Darwin on Trial*, p.77.

77. Tom Kemp, 'The Reptiles that became Mammals', in *New Scientist*, vol. 92, p.583.

78. Mayr, *Population, Species and Evolution*, p.253.

79. See Bowden, *Science vs Evolution*, pp.21-4 and Appendix 1.

80. Francis Hitching, *The Neck of the Giraffe: Where Darwin Went Wrong*, Ticknor and Fields, p.34.

81. Charles Darwin, *The Descent of Man*, vol. 1, p.204.

82. *The Guardian*, 21 November 1978.

83. Taylor, *In the Minds of Men*, p.212.

84. See Taylor, *In the Minds of Men*, p.215.

85. Marvin Lubenow, *Bones of Contention*, Baker Books, p.65.

86. *Daily Telegraph*, 29 April 1998.

87. Cited by W. A. Criswell, *Did Man Just Happen?*, Zondervan Publishing Co., p.86.

88. Taylor, *In the Minds of Men*, p.227.

89. *Ibid.*, p.228.

90. *Encyclopaedia Britannica*, 1929 edition, vol. 14, p.767.

91. Taylor, *In the Minds of Men*, p.237.

92. *Ibid.*, p.244.

93. Louis Leakey, 'Finding the World's Earliest Man', in *National Geographic*, September 1960, p.421.

94. Taylor, *In the Minds of Men*, p.245.

95. See Arthur Keith, 'The Taungs skull', in *Nature*, 116 (4 July 1925), p.11.

96. See John Reader, *Missing Links*, Collins, p.173.

97. See also *Creation ex Nihilo*, vol. 11, No. 2, p.8.

98. Jeremy Beadle was a lightweight British television personality at the time.

99. *Daily Telegraph*, 25 February 1994.

100. Phillip Johnson, privately circulated article cited by Bowden, *Science vs Evolution*, p.227.

101. David Pilbeam, 'Rearranging our family tree' in *Human Nature*, June 1978, p.45.

102. Charles Darwin, in a letter to Asa Gray, 5 September 1857, *Zoologist*, 16:6297-99, see p.6299.

103. Stephen Jay Gould, 'The return of hopeful monsters,' in *Natural History*, vol. LXXXVI(6), June-July 1977, p.24.

104. Stephen Jay Gould, *The Panda's Thumb*, W.W. Norton & Co., p.184.

105. Cited by Johnson, *Darwin on Trial*, p.59.

106. Jeremy Rifkin, *Algeny*, Viking Press, p.188.

107. N. Eldridge and S. J. Gould, 'Punctuated Equilibria: An Alternative to Phyletic Gradualism', in *Models in Palaeobiology*, ed. T. L. M. Schopf, Freem, Cooper & Co.

108. Luther D. Sunderland, *Darwin's Enigma*, p.104.

109. Cited *ibid.*, p.144.

110. Lubenow, *Bones of Contention*, p.182.

111. Marcel P. Schutzenberger, 'Algorithms and the Neo-Darwinian Theory of Evolution', in *Mathematical Challenges to the Neo-Darwinian Interpretation of Evolution*, p.75.

112. D. M. S. Watson, *Nature*, vol. 124, p.233.

113. Cited by A. J. Monty White, *Wonderfully Made*, Evangelical Press, p.33.

114. B. G. Ranganathan, *Origins*, Banner of Truth Trust, p.22.

115. Cited by Sol Tax and Charles Callender, *Evolution After Darwin*, vol. 3, University of Chicago Press, p.43.

116. *Ibid.*, p.45.

117. Cited in *The Advocate*, 8 March 1984, p.17.

118. Carroll, *Alice Through the Looking Glass*, p.84.

Chapter 5 — The legacy

1. Charles Darwin, *The Illustrated Origin of Species,* abridged by Richard E. Leakey, Faber & Faber, p.216.
2. Letter from Charles Darwin to Joseph Hooker, July 1880, cited in *Charles Darwin, Life and Letters,* vol. 2, ed. F. Darwin, John Murray, p.324.
3. Cited by Adrian Desmond and James Moore, *Darwin,* Penguin, p.497.
4. See Holder, *Nothing But Atoms and Molecules?,* p.69.
5. G. M. Trevelyan, *Social History of England,* Longman, Green and Co., pp.565-6.
6. Denton, *Evolution: a Theory in Crisis,* p.67.
7. Morris, *The Long War Against God,* p.156.
8. Denton, *Evolution: a Theory in Crisis,* p.358.
9. *New Catholic Encyclopaedia,* vol. 5, Mc Graw-Hill, p.689.
10. Dawkins, *The Blind Watchmaker,* p.ix.
11. Wolfgang Smith, *Teilhardism and the New Religion,* Tan Books, p.2.
12. *Ibid.,* p.5.
13. Phillip E. Johnson, *Evolution as Dogma: the Establishment of Naturalism,* Houghton Publishing Co., pp.1-2.
14. See Criswell, *Did Man Just Happen?,* p.89.
15. Edgar Andrews, *Christ and the Cosmos,* Evangelical Press, p.23.
16. Cited by Roche, *A World Without Heroes,* p.238.
17. Colin Patterson, keynote address at American Museum of Natural History, New York City, 5 November 1981.
18. Andrews, *Christ and the Cosmos,* p.42.
19. E. Mayr, 'Evolution', in *Scientific American No. 239,* September 1978, p.47.
20. George M. Marsden, 'Creation versus Evolution: No Middle Ground', in *Nature* No. 25, 13 October 1983, p.574.
21. Cited by R. L. Wysong, *The Creation-Evolution Controversy,* Inquiry Press, p.31.
22. Andrews, *Christ and the Cosmos,* p.25.
23. See Charles Darwin, *Origin of Species,* 6th edition (1971), p.x.
24. Roche, *A World Without Heroes,* p.234.
25. Cited by C. Mann, 'Lynn Margulis: Science's Unruly Earth Mother', in *Science,* No. 252, pp.378-81.
26. D. M. Lloyd-Jones, *Romans, An Exposition of Chapter 8:17-39,* Banner of Truth Trust, p.56.
27. Leonard Zuzne, *Names in the History of Psychology,* John Wiley, p.112.
28. Charles Darwin, *The Descent of Man,* 2nd edition, A. L. Burt Co., p.178.
29. Thomas Huxley, *Lay Sermons, Addresses and Reviews,* Appleton, p.20.
30. Morris, *The Long War Against God,* p.60.
31. Gertrude Himmelfarb, *Darwin and the Darwinian Revolution,* Chatto & Windus, pp.343-4.
32. Cited by Otto Scott, 'Playing God', in *Chalcedon Report No. 287,* February 1986, p.1.
33. See Allan Chase, *The Legacy of Malthus,* University of Illinois Press, p.134.
34. Ernst Haeckel, *Anthropogenie oder Entwicklungsgeschichte des Menschen,* translated in 1879 under the title *The Evolution of Man: A popular exposition of the principal points of human ontogeny and phylogeny,* Appleton, p.93.
35. Ernst Haeckel, *The Wonders of Life,* Harper, p.21.
36. *Ibid.,* p.118.
37. *Ibid.,* p.119.
38. Arthur Keith, *Evolution and Ethics,* G. P. Putnam's Sons, p.28.
39. *Ibid.,* p.230.
40. Cited by Robert E. C. Clark, *Darwin: Before and After,* Paternoster Press, p.730.
41. Cited by Francis Schaeffer, *How Shall We Then Live?,* Revell, p.151.
42. Edward Simon, 'Another Side to the Evolution Problem', in *Jewish Press,* 7 January 1983, p.24B.
43. Cited by Currid, *Building a Christian World View,* vol. 1, p.158.
44. Karl Marx, in a letter to Friedrich Engels, 19 December 1860, after reading Darwin's *Natural Selection.*
45. Friedrich Engels, in a letter to Karl Marx, 12 December 1859.
46. Cited by Himmelfarb, *Darwin and the Darwinian Revolution,* p.348.
47. Charles Darwin, *The Origin of Species,* Everyman's Library edition, reprinted 1967, p.463.
48. Dawkins, *The Blind Watchmaker,* p.5.

49. William Provine, 'Influence of Darwin's Ideas on the Study of Evolution', in *Bioscience*, 32, June 1982, p.506.

50. *Everyman*, BBC Television, 9 September 1996.

51. C. S. Lewis, *Poems*, Harcourt Brace Jovanovich, pp.55-6.

52. Rifkin, *Algeny*, p.244.

53. *Ibid.*, see p.255.

54. Cited by Taylor, *In the Minds of Men*, p.422.

55. William Provine, 'Scientists, Face it! Science and Religion are Incompatible', *The Scientist*, 5 September 1988, p.10.

56. Keith, *Evolution and Ethics*, p.15.

57. Edgar Andrews, *God, Science and Evolution*, Evangelical Press, p.20.

58. Cited by Enoch, *Evolution or Creation*, p.146.

59. J. Holmes, *Science*, 1939, p.121.

60. Michael Ruse and Edward Wilson, 'Evolution and Ethics' in *New Scientist* 208, 17 October 1985, pp.51-2.

61. *Everyman*, BBC Television, 8 September 1996.

62. Julian Huxley, *The Human Frame*, George Allen & Unwin, p.47.

63. John R. W. Stott, *Issues Facing Christians Today*, Marshall Morgan & Scott, p.18.

64. Dave Hunt, *A Cup of Trembling*, Harvest House Publishers, p.379.

65. *Charles Darwin, Life and Letters*, vol. 1, ed. F. Darwin, John Murray, p.249.

66. Morris, *The Long War Against God*, p.148.

67. Theodosius Dobzhansky, 'Ethics and Values in Biological and Cultural Evolution', *Zygo in, the Journal of Religion and Science*, as reported in *Los Angeles Times*, 16 June 1974, part 4, p.6.

68. *Daily Telegraph*, 14 July 1981.

69. René Dubos, 'Humanistic Biology', in *American Scientist*, No. 53, March 1965, pp.10-11.

70. Keith Ward, *God, Chance and Necessity*, Oneworld Publications, pp.176-7.

71. W. H. Murdy, 'Anthropocentrism, a Modern Version', in *Science Digest* No. 82, 28 March 1975, p.1169.

72. Richard Dawkins, *The New Humanist*, vol. 107, No. 2.

73. Edgar Andrews, *From Nothing to Nature*, Evangelical Press, p.2.

Chapter 6 — Every man for himself

1. *The Chambers Dictionary*, Chambers Harrap Publishers, p.590.

2. Søren Kirkegaard, *The Journals of Søren Kirkegaard*, ed. and trans. Alexander Dru, Oxford University Press, p.44.

3. Cited by Bruce Milne, *Know the Truth*, Inter-Varsity Press, p.112.

4. *Pears Cyclopaedia*, p.J18.

5. Brown, *Philosophy and the Christian Faith*, p.130.

6. Roy Clements, *God and the Gurus*, Inter-Varsity Press, p.6.

7. Martin Heidegger, *The Way Back Into the Ground of Metaphysics*.

8. *Ibid.*

9. J. McQuarrie, *An Existential Theology*.

10. B. A. G. Fuller, *Philosophy*, p.608.

11. Brow, *Religion: Origins and Ideas*, p.101.

12. See Jean-Paul-Sartre, *Existentialism and Human Emotions*, the Citadel Press, p.15.

13. Jean-Paul Sartre, *Existentialism and Humanism*, trans. Philip Mairet, Methuen, pp.32-3.

14. *Ibid.*, p.56.

15. *Ibid.*, p.33.

16. Jean-Paul Sartre, *The Rebel*, p.75.

17. Jean-Paul Sartre, *Existentialism and Humanism*, pp.33-4.

18. *Ibid.*

19. Jean-Paul Sartre, *Being and Nothingness*, trans. Hazel E. Barnes, Methuen, p.566.

20. Jean-Paul Sartre, *Nausea*, Penguin Books, p.162.

21. *Ibid.*, p.191.

22. See Zacharias, *Can Man Live Without God?*, p.211.

23. Sproul, *Lifeviews*, p.46.

24. Johnson, *Modern Times*, p.655.
25. See Zacharias, *Can Man Live Without God?*, p.211.
26. Jean-Paul Sartre, *Words*, Penguin Books, pp.62-5.
27. *Ibid.*
28. *Ibid.*
29. Johnson, *The Quest for God*, p.22.
30. *Ibid.*
31. *National Review*, 11 June 1982, p.677.
32. See *National Review*, 11 June 1982, p.677.
33. Brown, *Philosophy and the Christian Faith*, p.185.

Chapter 7 — Five steps to nowhere
1. Cited by Karl Lowith, *Meaning in History*, University of Chicago Press, p.63.
2. *Ibid.*, p.66.
3. Sproul, *Lifeviews*, p.49.
4. *Daily Telegraph*, 29 March 1994.
5. *Ibid.*
6. *Ibid.*
7. Cited by Peter Moore, *Disarming the Secular Gods*, Inter-Varsity Press, p.38.
8. Alex MacDonald, *Love Minus Zero*, Christian Focus Publications, p.135.
9. Bruce Springsteen, *Born in the USA*, CBS.
10. Arthur Koestler, *The Ghost in the Machine*, Hutchinson & Co. Ltd, p.267.
11. *Daily Mail*, 1 December 1995.
12. David Cook, *Blind Alley Beliefs*, Pickering & Inglis, pp.120-21.
13. *Concise Oxford Dictionary*, p.685.
14. William Shakespeare, *Macbeth*, Act V, Scene V.
15. Cited by Edyth Draper, *Draper's Book of Quotations for the Christian World*, Tyndale House Publishers, p.237.
16. See David Watson, *In Search of God*, Falcon Books, p.33.
17. Dale Rhoton, *How Much For the Man?*, Send the Light Trust, p.5.
18. Cited in *This I Believe*, ed. J. Marsden, Random House, p.48.
19. *Observer*, 19 February 1995.
20. *Daily Mail*, 6 June 1997.
21. *Observer*, 19 February 1995.
22. Francis Schaeffer, *Death in the City*, Inter-Varsity Press, p.17.
23. Roche, *A World Without Heroes*, p.192.
24. Johnson, *The Quest for God*, p.6.
25. *TIME* Magazine, 7 April 1980.
26. J. P. Moreland, *Scaling the Secular City*, Baker Book House, p.197.
27. Frame, *Apologetics to the Glory of God*, p.102.
28. Lewis, *God in the Dock*, p.22.
29. Sproul, *Reason to Believe*, p.119.
30. Lewis, *God in the Dock*, p.24.
31. Cited by Currid, *Building a Christian World View*, vol. 1, p.151.
32. Cited by Johnson, *The Quest for God*, p.20.
33. *Ibid.*
34. *Ibid.*
35. *Ibid.*
36. Cited by Currid, *Building a Christian World View*, vol. 1, p.153.
37. P. W. Atkins, *The Creation*, W. H. Freeman & Co., pp.vii-viii.
38. Michael Cosgrove, *The Essence of Man*, Zondervan, p.34.
39. See Robert A. Morey, *The New Atheism and the Erosion of Freedom*, Presbyterian & Reformed Publishing Co., p.104.
40. Cook, *Blind Alley Beliefs*, p.35.
41. John Benton, *Looking for the Answer*, Evangelical Press, pp.38-9.
42. Kreeft and Tacelli, *Handbook of Christian Apologetics*, p.227.

43. Morey, *The New Atheism and the Erosion of Freedom*, p.106.
44. *Concise Oxford Dictionary*, p.261.
45. John Gerstner, *Reasons for Faith*, Soli Deo Gloria Publications, pp.198-9.
46. Schaeffer, *Death in the City*, pp.92-3.
47. Cited by Joseph Wood Krutch, *The Meaning of Man*, Grosset and Dunlap, p.122.
48. Cook, *Blind Alley Beliefs*, p.37.

Chapter 8 — Protagoras rides again
1. Guinness, *The Dust of Death*, p.20.
2. *Ibid.*, p.5.
3. Sproul, *Lifeviews*, p.160.
4. Peter Gay, *The Enlightenment: An Interpretation*, Alfred A. Knopf, Inc., p.417.
5. John A. T. Robinson, *Honest To God*, SCM Press, p.47.
6. *Ibid.*, pp.48-9.
7. J. I. Packer, *Keep Yourselves from Idols*, Church Book Room Press, p.5.
8. *Sunday Times*, 30 November 1997.
9. *Ibid.*
10. Anthony Freeman, *God In Us*, SCM Press, p.3.
11. *Ibid.*, p.9.
12. *Ibid.*, p.10.
13. *Ibid.*, p.25.
14. *Ibid.*, pp.69-70.
15. *Daily Telegraph*, 29 July 1994.
16. *The Times*, 5 August 1994.
17. *Sunday Telegraph*, 9 April 1995.
18. *Daily Telegraph*, 25 November 1997.
19. Gerstner, *Reasons For Faith*, p.12.
20. Dan Beeby, *Treasure in the Field*.
21. *Human Manifesto I and II*, ed. Paul Kurtz, p.10.
22. *Ibid.*, p.13.
23. *Ibid.*
24. *Daily Telegraph*, 20 June 1997. Kennedy's book, *All in the Mind*, was published in 1999 by Hodder & Stoughton.
25. Cited by Smith, *Building a Christian World View*, vol. 1, p.168.
26. *Ibid.*
27. Kreeft and Tacelli, *Handbook of Christian Apologetics*, p.19.
28. *Daily Telegraph*, 31 August 1992.
29. Andrew Miller, *Real Science, Real Faith*, ed. R. J. Berry, Monarch Publications, pp.94-5.
30. Blaise Pascal, *Pensées*, trans. H. F. Stewart, Random House.
31. Francis Crick, *The Astonishing Hypothesis, the Scientific Search for the Soul*, Simon and Schuster, p.3.
32. Atkins, *The Creation*, p.35.
33. Richard Dawkins, *The Selfish Gene*, Oxford University Press, p.v.
34. Dawkins, *The Blind Watchmaker*, p.10.
35. Fred Hoyle, *The Nature of the Universe*, Penguin Books, pp.120-21.
36. B. F. Skinner, *Beyond Freedom and Dignity*, Alfred A. Knopf, Inc., p.202.
37. J. S. Jones, *The Language of the Genes*, HarperCollins, p.xi.
38. Cited by Cook, *Blind Alley Beliefs*, p.40.
39. Morey, *The New Atheism and the Erosion of Freedom*, p.102.
40. *Daily Mail*, 29 October 1998.
41. J. B. S. Haldane, *Possible Worlds*, p.209.
42. See H. J. Blackman, *Objections to Humanism*, Constable, pp.105-6.
43. *Encyclopaedia Americana*, vol. 1, p.604.
44. John H. Hick, *The Existence of God*, Macmillan, p.186.
45. Joseph Lewis, *The Bible Unmasked*, Freethought Publishing Co., p.15.
46. Freeman, *God In Us*, pp.69-70.

47. D. H. Lawrence, *Fantasia of Unconsciousness*.
48. John Benton, *One World One Way*, Evangelical Press, pp.73-4.
49. C. S. Lewis, *Mere Christianity*, Collins, pp.45-6.
50. Zacharias, *A Shattered Visage*, p.138.
51. Jean-Paul Sartre, *Existentialism and Humanism*, p.34.
52. Francis Schaeffer, *The Church at the End of the Twentieth Century*, The Norfolk Press, p.25.
53. Johnson, *Modern Times*, p.5.
54. Allan Bloom, *The Closing of the American Mind: Education and the Crisis of Reason*, Simon and Schuster, p.25.
55. Fyodor Dostoevsky, *The Brothers Karamazov*, Penguin Books, p.733.
56. Cited by Albert Camus, *The Rebel*, p.58.
57. *The Times*, 20 June 1997.
58. Josh McDowell and Don Stewart, *Concise Guide to Today's Religions*, Here's Life Publishers, p.447.
59. *Daily Telegraph*, 30 June 1997.
60. Cited by J. Andrew Kirk, *Loosing the Chains*, Hodder & Stoughton, p.53.
61. *Newsweek*, 8 September 1997.
62. Roger Scruton, *Modern Philosophy*, Sinclair and Stevenson, p.6.
63. Lee Carter, *Lucifer's Handbook*, Academic Associates, p.112.
64. Robert L. Johnson, cited in Smith, *Building a Christian World View*, vol. 1., p.173.
65. Cited by Sproul, *Lifeviews*, p.70.
66. Cited by Michael Green, *Man Alive!*, Inter-Varsity Press, p.12.
67. Bertrand Russell, *Why I am not a Christian*, Simon and Schuster, p.107.
68. *Ibid.*, p.111.
69. *Moody Monthly*, September 1980.
70. Stott, *Issues Facing Christians Today*, p.19.
71. Cited by Kreeft and Tacelli, *A Handbook of Christian Apologetics*, p.135.
72. Gerstner, *Reasons for Faith*, pp.73-4.
73. Cited by Kreeft and Tacelli, *A Handbook of Christian Apologetics*, p.135.
74. M. J. Savage, *Life After Death*, cited in Augustus H. Strong, *Systematic Theology*, Pickering & Inglis, p.989.
75. Arthur C. Custance, *The Sovereignty of God*, Baker Book House, p.328.
76. Dave Hunt, *Whatever Happened to Heaven?*, Harvest House Publishers, p.13.
77. Schaeffer, *Death in the City*, pp.86-7.
78. Sheldon Vanauken, *A Severe Mercy*, Hodder & Stoughton, p.203.
79. Woody Allen, *Woody Allen on Woody Allen*, Faber & Faber, p.105.
80. R. C. Sproul, *Table Talk*, October 1993, Ligonier.

Chapter 9—The dogmatists
1. See Camille B. Wortman and Elizabeth F. Loftus, *Psychology*, Knopf, p.408.
2. Cited by William Raeper and Linda Smith, *A Beginner's Guide to Ideas*, Lion Publishing, p.74.
3. McGrath, *Bridge-Building*, p.136.
4. Leslie Paul, *Attitudes to Christian Belief*, p.133.
5. B. R. Hergenbahn, *An Introduction to Theories of Personality*, Prentice-Hall, p.19.
6. *Ibid.*
7. Ernest Jones, *Sigmund Freud*, vol.1, p.22.
8. Anthony C. Thiselton, 'An Age of Anxiety', in *History of Christianity*, p.601.
9. Sigmund Freud, *The Future of an Illusion*, trans. W. D. Robson-Scott, Doubleday, p.20.
10. Cited by Thiselton, *History of Christianity*, p.602.
11. Zacharias, *A Shattered Visage*, p.17.
12. Thiselton, *History of Christianity*, p.601.
13. Johnson, *Modern Times*, p.6.
14. *Newsweek*, 18 December 1995.
15. Peter C. Moore, *Disarming the Secular Gods*, Inter-Varsity Press, p.109.
16. C. G. Jung, *Modern Man in Search of a Soul*, Harcourt, Brace & World, Inc., p.120.
17. Moore, *Disarming the Secular Gods*, p.70.
18. Clark H. Pinnock, *Reason Enough*, Paternoster Press, p.112.

19. Jones, *Sigmund Freud,* vol. 2, p.394.
20. Johnson, *Modern Times,* p.171.
21. Brown, *Philosophy and the Christian Faith,* p.226.
22. Bertrand Russell, *Religion and Science,* Oxford University Press, p.243.
23. See Zacharias, *Can Man Live Without God?,* pp.208-9.
24. Charlie Broad, Professor of Moral Philosophy at Cambridge, cited by Zacharias, *ibid,* p.209.
25. *The Listener,* 2 March 1978.
26. Ronald H. Nash, *Faith and Reason,* Zondervan Publishing House, p.53.
27. Cited by Gary Scott Smith, 'Naturalistic Humanism', in *Building a Christian Worldview,* vol. 1, p.174.
28. Bertrand Russell, 'The Scientific Outlook', in *In Search of Truth,* Nelson, p.150.
29. Russell, *Why I am not a Christian,* p.107.
30. Cited by Smith, *Building a Christian Worldview,* vol.1, p.169.
31. Russell, *Why I am not a Christian,* p.20.
32. Moreland, *Scaling the Secular City,* p.230.
33. Russell, *Why I am not a Christian,* pp.115-16.
34. *Ibid.,* p.107.
35. Kreeft and Tacelli, *Handbook of Christian Apologetics,* p.249.
36. A. J. Ayer, *Language, Truth and Logic,* pp.115-16.
37. William and Mabel Sahakian, *Ideas of the Great Philosophers,* Harper & Row, p.100.
38. Isaac Asimov, 'An Interview with Isaac Asimov on Science and the Bible', in *Free Enquiry 2,* Spring 1982, p.9.
39. Etienne Borne, *Atheism,* Hawthorn Books, p.8.
40. *Encyclopaedia of Philosophy,* ed. Paul Edwards, Macmillan, p.175.
41. Martin Robinson, *The Faith of the Unbeliever,* Monarch Publications, p.81
42. Madalyn Murray O'Hair, *What on Earth is an Atheist?,* Arno Press, p.38.
43. *Ibid.,* p.43.
44. Paul Edwards, *Encyclopaedia of Unbelief,* vol.1., Prometheus Books, p.xiii.
45. *Daily Telegraph Science Extra,* 11 September 1989.
46. *Independent,* 22 March 1993.
47. *Daily Telegraph,* 9 January 1994.
48. Gordon Stein, *An Anthology of Atheism and Rationalism,* Prometheus Books, p.3.
49. George Smith, *Atheism: The Case Against God,* Prometheus Books, p.7.
50. Morey, *The New Atheism and the Erosion of Freedom,* p.46.
51. See James W. Sire, *Why Should Anyone Believe Anything at All?,* Inter-Varsity Press, p.14.
52. Robinson, *The Faith of the Unbeliever,* p.78.
53. Cited by Os Guinness, *The American Hour,* Free Press, p.172.
54. *Evangelicals Now,* October 1998.
55. Private letter to the author, 3 November 1998.
56. Antony Flew, *The Presumption of Atheism,* Pemberton, p.14.
57. Michael Scriven, *Primary Philosophy,* McGraw-Hill, p.103.
58. *Ibid.*
59. Nash, *Faith and Reason,* p.18.
60. Lewis, *God in the Dock,* pp.52-3.
61. B. C. Johnson, *The Atheist Debater's Handbook,* Prometheus Books, p.23.
62. Karl Popper, *The Logic of Scientific Discovery,* Unwin Hyman Ltd, p.278.
63. McGrath, *Bridge-Building,* pp.115-16.
64. Dawkins, *The Selfish Gene,* p.198.
65. Rem B. Edwards, *Reason and Religion,* Harcourt Brace Jovanovich, p.222.

Chapter 10 — The impossible option

1. *Daily Telegraph,* 13 August 1996.
2. Thomas Henry Huxley, 'Agnosticism' in *An Anthology of Atheism and Rationalism,* ed. Gordon Stein, Prometheus Books, pp.43-4.
3. *Ibid.*
4. Frag. 4.

5. See Thrower, *A Short History of Western Atheism*, p.29.

6. Hume, *Enquiry Concerning Human Understanding*.

7. Huxley, *An Anthology of Atheism and Rationalism*, p.44.

8. Leslie Houlden, *The Myth of God Incarnate*, ed. J. Hick, SCM Press, p.125.

9. Robinson, *The Faith of the Unbeliever*, p.57.

10. D. A. Carson, *The Gagging of God*, Apollos, p.74.

11. *Evangelicals Now*, April 1998.

12. *Ibid.*

13. *Observer*, 26 December 1993.

14. *Ibid.*

15. *Daily Telegraph*, 1 September 1995.

16. Carson, *The Gagging of God*, p.23.

17. *Ibid.*

18. Richard Rorty, *Consequences of Pragmatism*, University of Minneapolis Press, p.xiii.

19. *Evangelicals Now*, April 1998.

20. Carson, *The Gagging of God*, p.544.

21. *The Times*, 9 March 1996.

22. Ayer, *Language, Truth and Logic*, p.115.

23. Cited in the *Daily Telegraph*, 14 September 1996.

24. Bernard Palmer, *Cure for Life*, Summit Publishing Ltd, p.72.

25. Cited by Hunt, *Whatever Happened to Heaven?*, p.14.

26. John Dryden, *Aurengzebe*, 4.1.

27. See William James, *The Will to Believe*, Dover, pp.1-30.

28. William James, *The Will to Believe*, pp.29-30.

29. Evans, *The Quest for Faith*, p.32.

30. Gerstner, *Reasons for Faith*, p.14.

31. Geisler, *Christian Apologetics*, p.20.

32. Cited by Moore, *Disarming the Secular Gods*, p.111.

33. Somerset Maugham, *The Summing Up*, Penguin Books, p.179.

34. Aldous Huxley, *Ends and Means*, pp.270ff.

35. David Hume, *Dialogues Concerning Natural Religion*, Bobbs-Merrill, p.214.

36. G. K. Chesterton, *Orthodoxy*, Doubleday & Co., p.150.

37. Geisler, *Christian Apologetics*, p.20.

38. Cited by Earle Albert Rowell, *Prophecy Speaks: Dissolving Doubts*, Review and Herald Publishing Association.

39. See Leith Samuel, *The Impossibility of Agnosticism*, Victory Booklets, p.32.

Chapter 11 — Masks

1. See Eryl Davies, *Truth Under Attack*, Evangelical Press, p.224.

2. See *Pears Cyclopaedia*, Book Club Associates, p.J7.

3. Buddhagosa, 'Path of Purity', *Man in Buddhism and Christianity*, YMCA Publishing House, p.119.

4. John B. Noss, *Man's Religions*, Macmillan Co., p.146.

5. Huston Smith, *The Religions of Man*, Harper & Row, p.140.

6. Josh McDowell and Don Stewart, *Concise Guide to Today's Religions*, Scripture Press, p.309.

7. Leslie Lyall, 'Confucianism', *The World's Religions*, ed. Norman Anderson, Inter-Varsity Press, p.222.

8. *Ibid.*, p.219.

9. Noss, *Man's Religions*, p.88.

10. See Patrick Johnstone, *Operation World*, STL Books/WEC Publications, p.216.

11. Guinness, *The Dust of Death*, p.211.

12. Noss, *Man's Religions*, p.88.

13. *Sunday Telegraph*, 11 January 1988.

14. Norman Anderson, *The World's Religions*, Inter-Varsity Press, p.91.

15. Muhammad Abul Quasem, *Salvation of the Soul and Islamic Devotions*, Kegan Paul International, p.32.

16. Cited by Annemarie Schimmel, 'The Prophet Muhammad as a Centre of Muslim Life and Thought', *We Believe in One God*, ed. Annemarie Schimmel and Abdoljavad Falaturi, the Seabury Press, p.35.

17. Cited by Norman Geisler and Abdul Saleeb, *Answering Islam,* Baker Books, p.140.
18. See Abdiyah Akbar Abdul-Haqq, *Sharing Your Faith with a Muslim,* Bethany Fellowship, pp.128-9.
19. Michael Nazir-Ali, *Frontiers in Muslim-Christian Encounter,* Regnum Books, p.133.
20. Cf. Sura 3:138; 39:31, etc.
21. Cf. Sura 18:110; 40:57; 41:5; 47:21; 48:2; 80:1-10, etc.
22. Anderson, *The World's Religions,* p.98.
23. Cited by Joseph Gudel, *To Every Muslim an Answer,* Simon Greenleaf School of Law, p.72.
24. See Anis S. Shorrosh, *Islam Revealed,* Thomas Nelson Publishers, p.35.
25. Hunt, *A Cup of Trembling,* pp.240-41.
26. Kenneth Cragg, *The Call of the Minaret,* Oxford University Press, p.37.
27. *Ibid.,* pp.37-8.
28. Maurice Bucaille, *The Bible, the Qur'an and Science,* trans. Pannell and Bucaille, pp.120-21.
29. See Nazir-Ali, *Frontiers in Muslim-Christian Encounter,* p.133.
30. Anderson, *The World's Religions,* p.115.
31. Cited by S. M. Zwemer, *The Moslem Doctrine of God,* American Tract Society, pp.58-9.
32. *Ibid.,* p.60.
33. William A. Miller, *A Christian's Response to Islam,* Presbyterian & Reformed Publishing Co., p.72.
34. Cited by Zwemer, *The Moslem Doctrine of God,* p.21.
35. Schimmel and Falaturi, *We Believe in One God,* p.85.
36. McDowell and Stewart, *Concise Guide to Today's Religions,* p.375.
37. C. G. Pfander, *The Mizabnu'l Haqq,* Light of Life, p.187.
38. Sura 76:4-22.
39. Colin Chapman, *Christianity on Trial, Book 2,* Lion Publishing, pp.70-71.
40. Sura 51:56.
41. Shorrosh, *Islam Revealed,* p.31.
42. Isma'il R Al Faruqi, *Islam,* Argus Communications, p.5.
43. Sura 9:5.
44. See Hunt, *A Cup of Trembling,* p.161.
45. *The Times,* 30 March 1996.
46. *Daily Telegraph,* 13 February 1997.
47. Cited by Nigel McCullough, *Barriers to Belief,* Darton, Longman and Todd, p.53.
48. *Daily Telegraph,* 20 February 1996.
49. Anderson, *The World's Religions,* p.115.
50. Clark B. Offner, 'Shinto', *The World's Religions,* p.191.
51. Nafusa Hurai, 'Shukyositeki no Mati no Tokushitsu', ('The Character of Shinto viewed from a History of Religious Perspective') in *Deai ('Encounter'),* May 1969, p.40.
52. Sokyo Ono, *The Kami Way,* International Institute for the Study of Religions, pp.3-4.
53. K. Singh, *Abingdon Dictionary of Living Religions,* Abingdon Press, p.691.
54. Robert E. Hume, *The World's Living Religions,* Charles Scribner's Sons, p.103.
55. *Daily Telegraph,* 22 April 1999.
56. *Pears Cyclopaedia,* p.J51.
57. Lyall, *The World's Religions,* p.226.
58. Noss, *Man's Religions,* p.274.
59. *Daily Telegraph,* 3 June 1996.
60. *Daily Telegraph,* 28 May 1996.
61. Malcolm Muggeridge, *Jesus Rediscovered,* Collins, p.148.
62. Sproul, *Reason to Believe,* p.39.

Chapter 12 — Deviations

1. John Coleman, *Concilium,* New Religious Movements, T. & T. Clark, p.161.
2. Mary Baker Eddy, *Christian Science Journal,* January 1901.
3. Mary Baker Eddy, *Miscellaneous Writings,* p.16.
4. *Ibid.,* p.13.
5. Cited by Davies, *Truth Under Attack,* p.248.
6. *Ibid.,* p.250.
7. *Ibid.,* p.179.

8. *Questions people ask about the training,* p.2.
9. Adelaid Bry, *EST: 60 hours that transform your life,* Avon, p.200.
10. William Greene, *EST: Four days to make your life work,* Pocket Books, p.131.
11. Werner Erhard, *East-West,* p.5.
12. Cited by J. Oswald Sanders, *Heresies Ancient and Modern,* Marshall, Morgan & Scott Ltd, p.74.
13. J. Stafford Wright, 'Jehovah's Witnesses', in *The New International Dictionary of the Christian Church,* p.528.
14. *The Watchtower,* 15 July 1960.
15. J. J. Ross, cited by Davies, *Truth Under Attack,* p.113.
16. Joseph Smith, *History of the Church,* 4:461.
17. Joseph Smith, *Doctrines and Covenants,* 6:5.
18. Joseph Smith, *King Follett Discourse,* p.9.
19. Editors of *Body, Mind and Spirit, The New Age Catalogue,* Doubleday.
20. Marilyn Ferguson, *The Aquarian Conspiracy: Social Transformation in the 1980s,* J. P. Tarcher, Inc., p.23.
21. Joseph Adolph, 'What is the New Age?', *New Age Journal,* Winter 1988, p.9.
22. From promotional material from 'The Center for New Age Light'.
23. Randall N. Baer, *Inside the New Age Nightmare,* Huntington House, p.115.
24. Cited in *Young Life* (undated), p.6.
25. Baer, *Inside the New Age Nightmare,* p.102.
26. Cited in *Christian World News Review,* October 1989.
27. Baer, *Inside the New Age Nightmare,* p.84.
28. Cited in *Young Life,* p.6.
29. Rifkin, *Algeny,* p.244.
30. Benton, *One World, One Way,* p.63.
31. Julia Duin, *Christianity Today,* 23 April 1982, p.39.
32. Cited by Davies, *Truth Under Attack,* p.254.
33. *The Times,* 29 January 1986.
34. *The Theosophical Movement,* p.112.
35. H. P. Blavatsky, *Key to Theosophy,* Aryan Theosophical Press, p.63.
36. *Ibid.*
37. Cited by Sanders, *Heresies Ancient and Modern,* p.90.
38. United States District Court, District of New Jersey, Civil Action No. 76-341.
39. Maharishi Mahesh Yogi, *Transcendental Meditation,* p.266.
40. Maharishi Mahesh Yogi, *Science of Being and Art of Living,* revised edition, p.276.
41. Cited by Davies, *Truth Under Attack,* p.139.
42. Sun Myung Moon, *Christianity in Crisis,* p.98.
43. *TIME* magazine, 30 September 1974.
44. Cited by Davies, *Truth Under Attack,* p.144.
45. Cited by McDowell and Stewart, *Concise Guide to Today's Religions,* p.153.
46. *Unity,* August 1974, p.140.
47. Charles Fillimore, *Jesus Christ Heals,* Unity School of Christianity, p.31.
48. Dave Hunt, *The Seduction of Christianity,* Harvest House Publishers, p.110.
49. See Davies, *Truth Under Attack,* p.238.

Chapter 13 — Matter matters

1. Cited by Brown, *Philosophy and the Christian Faith,* p.224.
2. Stephen Hawking, *A Brief History of Time,* 1995 Edition, Bantam Books, pp.139-40.
3. Donald B. De Young, *Astronomy and the Bible,* Baker Book House, p.57.
4. Wright, *Designer Universe,* p.51.
5. *Daily Mail,* 16 April 1996.
6. *Daily Telegraph,* 28 June 1996.
7. *Daily Telegraph,* 15 February 1997.
8. *Daily Telegraph,* 9 September 1997.
9. *Sunday Times,* 23 November 1997.
10. *Ibid.*

11. D. Adams, *The Hitchhiker's Guide to the Galaxy:* The Original Radio Scripts, Pan Books, p.39.
12. *Observer,* 9 April 1995.
13. Peter Atkins, *Creation Revisited,* Penguin, p.3.
14. Keith Ward, *God, Chance and Necessity,* Oneworld Publications, p.24.
15. *Ibid.,* p.33.
16. Cited by L. Barnett, *The Universe and Dr. Einstein,* Morrow, p.95.
17. Cited by Ray Comfort, *God Doesn't Believe in Atheists,* Bridge Publishing, p.28.
18. Donald MacKay, *Real Science, Real Faith,* ed. R. J. Berry, Monarch Publications, p.200.
19. *Sunday Telegraph,* 31 August 1997.
20. Simon Mitton, *Exploring The Galaxies,* Faber & Faber, p.177.
21. Stanley L. Jaki, *Science and Creation,* University Press of America, p.2.
22. Hawking, *A Brief History of Time,* p.6.
23. See *Sunday Times,* 22 February 1998.
24. Isaac Asimov, 'In the Game of Energy and Thermodynamics You Can't Even Break Even', *Journal of the Smithsonian Institute* (June 1990), p.6.
25. William Lane Craig, *Reasonable Faith,* Crossway Books, p.103.
26. Michael Behe, *Darwin's Black Box,* The Free Press, p.245.
27. John Gribbin, 'Oscillating Universe Bounces Back', *Nature,* 59 (1976), p.15.
28. Cited by Craig, *Reasonable Faith,* p.103.
29. Duane Dicus, *et al.,* 'The Future of the Universe', *Scientific American* (March 1983): p.101; Duane Dicus, 'Effects of Proton Decay on the Cosmological Future', *Astrophysical Journal* 252 (1982), pp.1-9.
30. Hawking, *A Brief History of Time,* p.103.
31. *Ibid.,* p.151.
32. *Sunday Telegraph,* 31 August 1997.
33. Behe, *Darwin's Black Box,* p.247.
34. George Smoot and Keay Davidson, *Wrinkles in Time,* Avon Books, p.283.
35. Cited by Timothy Ferris, *The Whole Shebang: A State-of-the-Universe(s) Report,* Simon & Schuster, p.167.
36. *Ibid.*
37. Hawking, *A Brief History of Time,* p.11.
38. David Wilkinson, *God, the Big Bang and Stephen Hawking,* Monarch Publications, p.148.
39. Smoot and Davidson, *Wrinkles in Time,* p.145.
40. Ferris, *The Whole Shebang,* p.147.
41. Hawking, *A Brief History of Time,* p.13.
42. *Stephen Hawking's Universe,* BBC 2, 30 August 1997.
43. *Sunday Telegraph,* 31 August 1997.
44. Plato, *Timaeus,* Loeb Classical Library, vol. 7, *Plato's Dialogues,* trans. R. G. Bury, William Heinemann Publishers, pp.52-3.
45. *Daily Mail,* 30 April 1999.
46. Andrews, *God, Science and Evolution,* p.35.
47. *Daily Telegraph,* 6 April 1998.
48. Atkins, *Creation Revisited,* p.143.
49. Richard Feynman, *The Character of Physical Law,* MIT Press, p.27.
50. David Darling, *New Scientist* (2047), p.49.
51. Ward, *God, Chance and Necessity,* p.40.
52. Atkins, *Creation Revisited,* p.143.
53. Ward, *God, Chance and Necessity,* p.49.
54. Lewis, *God in the Dock,* pp.77-8.
55. Ward, *God, Chance and Necessity,* p.19.
56. *Ibid.,* p.23.
57. Peter Atkins, *The Creation,* W. H. Freeman & Co., p.115.
58. See Hawking, *A Brief History of Time,* pp.189-93.
59. See Ferris, *The Whole Shebang,* pp.248-9; 259-63 and Hawking, *A Brief History of Time,* pp.145-6; 154.
60. Hawking, *A Brief History of Time,* pp.156-7.
61. Ward, *God, Chance and Necessity,* pp.23-4.

62. Paul Davies, *The Mind of God,* Touchstone Books, p.226.

63. Cited by David Wilkinson and Rob Frost, *Thinking Clearly about God and Science,* Monarch Publications, p.31.

64. Plato, *Laws* 12.996e.

65. Aristotle, *On Philosophy.*

66. Cicero, *The Nature of the Gods,* 2, 97, 132-3.

67. Minucius Felix, *Dialogue.*

68. Cited by Raeper and Smith, *A Beginner's Guide to Ideas,* p.38.

69. Cited by Wilkinson and Frost, *Thinking Clearly about God and Science,* p.199.

70. Cited *ibid.,* p.148.

71. Cited *ibid.,* p.201.

72. Isaac Newton, *Principia,* cited in DeYoung, *Astronomy and the Bible,* p.115.

73. William Paley, *Natural Theology,* pp.3-4.

74. *Ibid.,* p.13.

75. Cited by H. N. Brailsford, *Voltaire,* Oxford University Press, p.122.

76. Immanuel Kant, *Critique of Pure Reason,* trans. Norman Kemp Smith, St. Martin's Press, p.528.

77. *Ibid.,* p.520.

78. *Ibid.*

79. David Hume, *Dialogues Concerning Natural Religion,* ed. Nelson Pike, Bobbs-Merrill, p.222.

80. *Ibid.,* p.214.

81. *Theological Dictionary of the New Testament,* ed. Gerhard Kittel and Gerhard Friedrich; trans. Geoffrey W. Bromiley, William B. Eerdmans Publishing Co., p.460.

82. Richard Swinburne, in *Philosophers Who Believe,* ed. Kelly James Clark, Inter-Varsity Press, p.193.

83. Hawking, *A Brief History of Time,* pp.135-6.

84. Dawkins, *The Blind Watchmaker,* p.147.

85. Cited by Wilkinson and Frost, *Thinking Clearly about God and Science,* p.22.

86. Rod Garner, *The Big Questions,* SPCK, pp.9-10.

87. Cited by Wilkinson and Frost, *Thinking Clearly about God and Science,* p.33.

88. John Houghton, in *Real Science, Real Faith,* ed. R.J.Berry p.46.

89. See Roger Penrose, *The Emperor's New Mind: Concerning Computers, Minds and the Laws of Physics,* Oxford University Press, pp.339-45.

90. See Smoot and Davidson, *Wrinkles in Time,* p.296.

91. *Ibid.*

92. Davies, *The Mind of God,* p.16.

93. *Ibid.,* p.232.

94. Paul Davies, *God and New Physics,* Touchstone Books, p.188.

95. *Ibid.*

96. 'Science of the Sacred', *Newsweek,* 28 November 1994.

97. Hawking, *A Brief History of Time,* p.139.

98. Fred Hereen, *Show Me God,* Day Star Publications, pp.207-8.

99. Hawking, *A Brief History of Time,* p.138.

100. Smoot and Davidson, *Wrinkles in Time,* p.110.

101. *Ibid.,* see pp.110-12; 293.

102. Hawking, *A Brief History of Time,* p.134.

103. Cited by John Polkinghorne, *One World,* SPCK, p.58.

104. John Barrow and Joseph Silk, *The Left Hand of Creation: The Origin and Evolution of the Expanding Universe,* Basic Books, p.206.

105. Ferris, *The Whole Shebang,* p.16.

106. *Ibid.,* pp.304-5.

107. John Gribbin and Martin Rees, *Cosmic Coincidences,* Bantam Books, p.247.

108. Cited by Wilkinson, *God, The Big Bang and Stephen Hawking,* p.108.

109. See Ferris, *The Whole Shebang,* pp.180-81 for support.

110. J. L. Mackie, *The Miracle of Theism,* Clarendon Press, p.141.

111. G. F. W. von Leibniz, 'Nature and Grace', *Selections,* p.527.

112. Richard Swinburne, *Philosophers Who Believe,* p.191.

113. Hawking, *A Brief History of Time,* 2nd edition, pp.232-3.

114. Cited by Ferris, *The Whole Shebang*, p.275.
115. Davies, *The Mind of God*, pp.15, 226.
116. Ward, *God, Chance and Necessity,* p.16.
117. Cited by Russell Stannard, *Doing Away with God?*, Marshall Pickering, p.80.
118. Cited by Wilkinson and Frost, *Thinking Clearly about God and Science*, p.23.
119. *The Guardian*, 4 May 1995.
120. Taylor was writing before the British railway system was privatized.
121. Richard Taylor, *Metaphysics*, 2nd edition, Prentice-Hall, p.115.
122. *Ibid.*, pp.118-19.
123. Ronald H. Nash, *Faith and Reason*, Zondervan Publishing House, p.142.
124. Wilkinson and Frost, *Thinking Clearly about God and Science*, p.41.
125. Wright, *Designer Universe*, p.120.
126. Dawkins, *The Selfish Gene*, p.xi.
127. Ward, *God, Chance and Necessity*, p.59.
128. Davies, *God and the New Physics*, p.189.
129. Hawking, *A Brief History of Time*, p.140.
130. William Lane Craig, *The Kalam Cosmological Argument*, Barnes and Noble, p.149.
131. *New York Times*, 25 June 1978.
132. *Ibid.*

Chapter 14 — Such is life

1. *The Concise Oxford Dictionary of Current English*, p.580.
2. *Ibid.*, p.34.
3. *New Encyclopaedia Britannica*, 15th edition (1974), vol. 22, p.964.
4. Cited by Ian Ridpath in *Signs of Life*, Penguin Books, p.179.
5. Cited by G. Claus and P. P. Madri, Annals of New York Academy of Sciences, p.394.
6. H. N. Nininger, cited *ibid.*, p.395.
7. F. Hoyle and C. Wickramasinghe, *Space Travellers*, University College of Cardiff Press, p.32.
8. F. Hoyle, *Of Men and Galaxies*, University of Washington Press, p.43.
9. *Daily Telegraph*, 8 August 1996.
10. *Sunday Times*, 11 August 1996.
11. *Ibid.*
12. *Daily Telegraph*, 8 August 1996.
13. *Ibid.*
14. *Daily Telegraph*, 16 January 1998.
15. *Ibid.*
16. *Daily Telegraph*, 18 July 1998.
17. *Dictionary of National Biography* (1961-1970), p.474.
18. F. Crick, *Life Itself: Its Origin and Nature*, MacDonald, pp.15-16.
19. Henry M. Morris, *The Biblical Basis for Modern Science*, Baker Book House, p.235.
20. Denton, *Evolution: A Theory in Crisis*, p.271.
21. Manfred Eigen, *Steps Towards Life*, Oxford University Press, p.11.
22. V. A. Firsoff, *Life Beyond Earth — A Study in Exiobiology,* Hutchinson, cited by L. R. Croft, *How Life Began,* Evangelical Press, p.149.
23. See *TIME*, 11 October 1993, p.71.
24. William Shakespeare, *Antony and Cleopatra*, Act III, Scene 7.
25. Cited by René J. Dubos, *Louis Pasteur: Freelance of Science*, Charles Scribner's Sons, p.395.
26. Moreland, *Scaling the Secular City*, p.53.
27. Cited by Johnson, *Darwin on Trial*, p.101.
28. L. R. Croft, *How Life Began*, Evangelical Press, p.42.
29. Johnson, *Darwin on Trial*, p.102.
30. *Sunday Telegraph*, 10 December 1995.
31. Johnson, *Darwin on Trial*, p.103.
32. Edgar Andrews, *God, Science and Evolution*, Evangelical Press, p.13.
33. *Sunday Telegraph*, 10 December 1995.

34. T. S. Kuhn, *The Structure of Scientific Revolutions,* 2nd edition, University of Chicago Press, p.69.
35. See John Gribbin, *Genesis,* Oxford University Press, pp.191-2.
36. *Cracking the Code,* BBC 2, 1 September 1993.
37. Carl P. Haskins, 'Advances and Challenges in Science in 1970', in *American Scientist,* vol. 59, May-June 1971, p.298.
38. See *Mathematical Challenges to the Neo-Darwinian Interpretation of Evolution,* ed. P. Moorhead and M. Kaplan, Wistar Institute, Philadelphia.
39. Leslie Orgel, 'Darwinianism at the Very Beginning of Life', in *New Scientist,* 15 April 1982, p.150.
40. R. E. Dickerson, 'Chemical Evolution and the Origin of Life', in *Scientific American,* vol. 239, No. 3, September 1978, p.62.
41. Gerald Joyce and Leslie Orgel, 'Prospects for Understanding the Origin of the RNA World', in *The RNA World,* ed. R. F. Gesteland and J. F. Atkins, cited by Michael Behe, *Darwin's Black Box,* the Free Press, p.172.
42. Behe, *Darwin's Black Box,* p.171.
43. G. A. Kerkut, *Implications of Evolution,* Pergamon Press, p.150.
44. Henry M. Morris, *The God who is Real,* Baker Book House, p.18.
45. Crick, *Life Itself,* p.88.
46. F. Hoyle, 'The big bang in astronomy', *New Scientist,* 92, p.521.
47. F. Hoyle and C. Wickramasinghe, *Evolution From Space,* J. M. Dent & Co., p.28.
48. *Daily Express,* 14 August 1981.
49. *Ibid.*
50. *Ibid.*
51. Cited by *The Intellectuals Speak about God,* ed. Roy Abraham Varghese, Regnery Gateway, p.33.
52. *Science Today,* BBC Radio 4, 30 November 1981.
53. *Reader's Digest,* January 1963.
54. Denton, *Evolution: A Theory in Crisis,* p.324.
55. *Concise Oxford Dictionary,* p.153.
56. Cited by Ravi Zacharias, *Can Man Live Without God?,* Word Publishing, p.85.
57. Sproul, *Reason to Believe,* p.108.
58. Michael Poole, *A Guide to Science and Belief,* Lion Publishing, p.116.
59. Cited by J. Bronowski and B. Mazlish, *The Western Intellectual Tradition,* Penguin Books, p.311.
60. Frame, *Apologetics to the Glory of God,* p.103.
61. John Benton, *Is Christianity True?,* Evangelical Press, p.48.
62. Jacques Monod, *Chance and Necessity,* Collins, p.134.
63. Denton, *Evolution: A Theory in Crisis,* p.250.
64. *Ibid.,* pp.328-9.
65. Dawkins, *The Blind Watchmaker,* p.18.
66. Behe, *Darwin's Black Box,* p.39.
67. *Ibid.,* p.42.
68. Darwin, *Origin of Species,* 6th edition, New York University Press, p.154.
69. Behe, *Darwin's Black Box,* p.69.
70. *Ibid.,* p.97.
71. Dawkins, *The Selfish Gene,* p.16.
72. Dawkins, *The Blind Watchmaker,* p.139.
73. Ward, *God, Chance and Necessity,* p.117.
74. *Ibid.,* pp.108-9.
75. George Wald, 'The Origin of Life' in *The Physics and Chemistry of Life,* Simon and Schuster, p.12.
76. F. B. Salisbury, 'Natural Selection and the Complexity of the Gene', in *Nature,* vol. 224 (217) 1969, 25 October, pp.342-3.
77. Richard Dawkins, *Climbing Mount Improbable,* Viking, p.66.
78. Cited by Scott M. Huse, *The Collapse of Evolution,* Baker Book House, p.3.
79. *Scientific American,* August 1954.
80. Richard Dawkins, 'The Necessity of Darwinism' in *New Scientist,* No. 94, 15 April 1982, p.130.
81. Ward, *God, Chance and Necessity,* p.112.
82. Hubert P. Yockey, 'A Calculation of the Probability of Spontaneous Biogenesis by Information Theory' in *Journal of Theoretical Biology,* p.67.

83. 'The Rocket' was the name given to a steam railway engine built by the British inventor George Stephenson in 1829. It won a prize of £500 for maintaining an average speed of twenty-nine miles per hour.

84. Lewis, *God in the Dock*, pp.210-11.

85. Cited by Wilkinson, *Thinking Clearly About God and Science*, Monarch Publications, p.124.

86. Behe, *Darwin's Black Box*, p.252.

Chapter 15 — Glory and rubbish

1. Blaise Pascal, *Selections From 'The Thoughts'*, trans. Arthur H. Beattie, Appleton-Century-Crofts, p.68.

2. Cited by Andrew Knowles, *Finding Faith*, Lion Publishing, p.13.

3. Christopher Darlington Morley, cited in Draper, *Quotations for the Christian World*, Tyndale House Publishers, p.109.

4. Cited by Dave Hunt, *In Defense of the Faith*, Harvest House Publishers, p.22.

5. *The Book of Knowledge*, vol. 4, The Waverley Book Co., p.140.

6. Anthony Smith, *The Human Body*, BBC Books, p.132.

7. *Ibid.*

8. Isaac Asimov, 'In the Game of Energy and Thermodynamics, You Can't Even Break Even', in *Smithsonian*, June 1970, p.10.

9. *Daily Telegraph*, 28 December 1994.

10. *Evangelical Times*, September 1996.

11. *Daily Telegraph*, 28 December 1994.

12. *Ibid.*

13. Letter from Charles Darwin to Asa Gray, cited by John Greene, *Darwin and the Modern World View*, p.44.

14. Russell, *Why I am not a Christian*, p.107.

15. *Daily Telegraph*, 28 December 1997.

16. *60 Minutes*, 22 April 1994.

17. Isaac Newton, *Optiks*, pp.369-70.

18. *Sunday Telegraph*, 30 March 1997.

19. C. Everett Koop, in *Scientists Who Believe*, ed. Eric C. Barrett and David Fisher, Moody Press, pp.158-9.

20. Cited by Ray Comfort, *God Doesn't Believe in Atheists*, Bridge Publishing, p.34.

21. *Sunday Telegraph*, 31 March 1996.

22. Cook, *Blind Alley Beliefs*, p.37.

23. *Sunday Telegraph*, 17 April 1994.

24. *Oxford Illustrated Encyclopaedia*, Oxford University Press, Foreword.

25. *Daily Mail*, 11 April 1998

26. See *Daily Mail*, 17 March 1996.

27. See *Daily Telegraph*, 21 January 1995.

28. *Sunday Telegraph*, 29 May 1994.

29. *Ibid.*

30. *Ibid.*

31. *Daily Telegraph*, 22 July 1998.

32. *Daily Mail*, 16 April 1998.

33. *Daily Telegraph*, 30 August 1997.

34. *Daily Mail*, 19 May 1998.

35. *Daily Telegraph*, 18 May 1998.

36. See *Daily Telegraph*, 11 February 1999.

37. *The Times*, 3 August 1994.

38. David Berlinski, *Black Mischief: The Mechanics of Modern Science*, William Morrow and Co., p.270.

39. Roche, *A World Without Heroes*, p.103.

40. Karl Popper, in Karl Popper and John Eccles, *The Self and its Brain*, Springer International, p.144.

41. Herbert Schlossberg, *Idols for Destruction*, Thomas Nelson, p.171.

42. Cited by Draper, *Quotations for the Christian World*, p.406.

43. Arthur Koestler, *The Ghost in the Machine*, Picador, p.19.

44. See Douglas F. Kelly, *Creation and Change,* Christian Focus Publications, p.222.
45. Noam Chomsky, *Rules and Representations,* Columbia University Press, p.139.
46. *Ibid.,* pp.38-9.
47. See Kelly, *Creation and Change,* p.223.
48. Benton, *Is Christianity True?* p.90.
49. J. H. John Peet, *In the beginning, God created ...,* Grace Publications, p.61.
50. M. Ruse, *Darwinism Defended,* Addison Wesley, p.108.
51. *Daily Telegraph,* 13 March 1994.
52. John Rendle-Short, *Reasonable Christianity,* Evangelical Press, p.72.
53. Richard Dawkins, *River Out Of Eden,* Weidenfeld & Nicholson, p.120.
54. Ward, *God, Chance and Necessity,* p.142.
55. H. R. Rookmaaker, *Art and the Public Today,* L'Abri Fellowship, p.20.
56. *Daily Telegraph,* 18 August 1998.
57. Fyodor Dostoevsky, *The Brothers Karamazov,* trans. Constance Garnett, The Modern Library, p.297.
58. Benton, *Is Christianity True?,* p.92.
59. Cited by Draper, *Quotations for the Christian World,* p.406.
60. Peet, *In the beginning, God created ...,* p.63.
61. *Ibid.*
62. C. S. Lewis, *Mere Christianity,* Macmillan, p.21.
63. Garner, *The Big Questions,* pp.75-6.
64. R. B. Kuiper, *God-centred Evangelism,* Banner of Truth Trust, p.129.
65. John Houghton, *The Search for God,* Lion Publishing, p.143.
66. Roche, *A World Without Heroes,* p.101.
67. Ronald Nash, *Faith and Reason,* Zondervan Publishing House, p.138.

Chapter 16 — Pointers

1. Cited by Bernard Palmer, *Cure for Life,* Summit Publishing Ltd, p.10.
2. Andrew Knowles, *Finding Faith,* Lion Publishing, p.9.
3. Rheinalt Nantlais Williams, *Faith Facing Facts,* Coverdale House Publishers, p.35.
4. Leo Tolstoy, *Memoirs of a Madman,* cited in Colin Wilson, *The Outsider,* Pan, p.164.
5. Cited by Peter A. Angeles, *Critiques of God,* Prometheus Books, p.296.
6. Rebecca West, in *What I Believe,* Allen and Unwin, p.176.
7. Cited by Ravi Zacharias, *Can Man Live Without God?,* Word Publishing, p.31.
8. Cited by Johnson, *Darwin on Trial,* p.114.
9. William Provine, 'Scientists, Face it! Science and Religion are Incompatible', in *The Scientist,* 5 September 1988, p.10.
10. *In The Psychiatrist's Chair,* BBC Radio 4, 28 July 1993.
11. *Observer,* 9 April 1995.
12. Dawkins, *The Selfish Gene,* p.xi.
13. *Ibid.,* p.x.
14. *Ibid.,* p.21.
15. *Sunday Telegraph,* 22 March 1998.
16. *Ibid.*
17. *Ibid.*
18. *Ibid.*
19. Ward, *God, Chance and Necessity,* pp.140-41.
20. Dawkins, *River out of Eden,* p.96.
21. Ward, *God, Chance and Necessity,* pp.138-9.
22. Ludwig Wittgenstein, *Note-books, 1914-1916,* trans. G. E. M. Anscombe, eds. Anscombe and Wright, Oxford, p.16.
23. Aldous Huxley, *Ends and Means,* Chatto & Windus, p.273.
24. Cited by Martin Esslin, *The Theatre of the Absurd,* Penguin, p.23.
25. *Idea,* July — September 1994, p.11.
26. David Eccles, 'The Christian View of Time', in *Frontier,* August 1970, pp.153-4.
27. *Ibid.*

28. José Luis Martin Descalzo, cited by Michael Scott Horton, *Mission Accomplished,* Evangelical Press, p.25.
29. Cited by Raeper and Smith, *A Beginner's Guide to Ideas,* p.144.
30. Roche, *A World Without Heroes,* pp.107-8.
31. Joseph Gaer, *What the Great Religions Believe,* Dodd, Mead & Co., p.16.
32. Richard Cavendish, *The Great Religions,* Arco Publishing, p.2.
33. Samuel Zwemer, *The Origin of Religion,* Loiseaux Brothers, p.26.
34. See *Daily Mail,* 30 July 1998.
35. See Peter Anderson, *Talk of the Devil,* Word (UK) Ltd., p.9.
36. *Ibid.,* p.17.
37. Martin Bell, *In Harm's Way,* Penguin, p.72.
38. *Ibid.,* p.74.
39. Morris, *The Long War Against God,* p.293.
40. Wilhelm Schmidt, *Origin of the Idea of God,* cited by Zwemer, *The Origin of Religion,* pp.14-15.
41. Johnson, *Modern Times,* p.700.
42. Don Feder, *The Jewish Conservative Looks at Pagan America,* Huntington Press, p.54.
43. *Observer,* 16 April 1995.
44. *Sunday Telegraph,* 30 June 1996.
45. Johnson, *The Quest For God,* pp.9-10.
46. UKCH: *Religious Trends,* No. 1, 1998/1999, 6.3.
47. *Daily Telegraph,* 27 September 1996.
48. *Evangelism Today,* February 1997.
49. *Daily Telegraph,* 9 September 1996.
50. Jonathan Sacks, *The Persistence of Faith,* Weidenfeld Paperbacks, p.71.
51. *TIME,* 26 December 1969.
52. *TIME,* 7 April 1980.
53. *USA Today,* 15 October 1996.
54. Ralph Reed, *Politically Incorrect: The Emerging Faith Factor in American Politics,* Word, p.5.
55. *Daily Telegraph,* 12 April 1996.
56. *Observer,* 16 April 1995.
57. *The Times,* 15 May 1995.
58. *Observer,* 16 April 1995.
59. Pinnock, *Reason Enough,* p.40.
60. *Sunday Telegraph,* 31 January 1993.
61. *Devout Sceptics,* BBC Radio 4, 6 September 1997.
62. *Sunday Telegraph,* 25 February 1996.
63. *Sunday Times,* 22 March 1998.
64. Edward Young, *Night Thoughts,* 5.177.
65. *Sunday Telegraph,* 5 January 1997.
66. *Daily Telegraph,* 22 January 1996.
67. Chay Blyth, *The Impossible Voyage,* Hodder & Stoughton, p.214.
68. *Ibid.,* p.85.
69. Cited by Charles T. Glicksberg, *Literature and Religion,* Southern Methodist University Press, pp.221-2.
70. Cited by Draper, *Quotations for the Christian World,* p.412.
71. Cited by Guinness, *The Dust of Death,* p.332.
72. Carl Gustav Jung, *Psychotherapists or the Clergy?,* cited *ibid.,* p.330.
73. *Daily Telegraph,* 13 July 1996.
74. Cited by Draper, *Quotations for the Christian World,* p.658.
75. Charles Edward Locke, cited *ibid.,* p.24.
76. Edmund Burke, *Reflections on the Revolution in France,* cited in *The Portable Conservative Readers,* Penguin Books, p.27.
77. Lewis, *Mere Christianity,* p.118.
78. Muggeridge, *Jesus Rediscovered,* p.154.
79. Cited by Draper, *Quotations for the Christian World,* p.230.
80. *Daily Telegraph,* 22 April 1992.

81. Fred Carl Kuehner, 'Heaven and Hell', in *Fundamentals of the Faith,* ed. Carl F. H. Henry, *Christianity Today,* p.24c.

82. Sigmund Freud, *The Complete Psychological Works,* vol. 14, cited by Eryl Davies, *Condemned for Ever!,* Evangelical Press, p.13.

83. Alex MacDonald, *Love Minus Zero,* Christian Focus Publications, p.136.

84. McGrath, *Bridge-Building,* p.71.

85. *Ibid.,* pp.70-71.

86. *Daily Telegraph,* 25 May 1994.

87. Muggeridge, *Jesus Rediscovered,* p.57.

88. *Daily Express,* 18 August 1996.

89. *Ibid.*

90. Kenneth Williams, *Just Williams,* Fontana/Collins, p.130.

91. John Bunyan, *Pilgrim's Progress,* Thomas Nelson, p.166.

92. David Potter, *Evangelical Times,* August 1979.

93. *Daily Telegraph,* 25 May 1994.

94. Woody Allen, 'Death [a play]', in *Without Feathers.*

95. See John Blanchard, *Whatever Happened to Hell?,* Evangelical Press.

96. *Daily Telegraph,* 25 May 1994.

97. Muggeridge, *Jesus Rediscovered,* p.99.

98. Ernest Becker, *The Denial of Death,* Free Press, p.26.

99. Bunyan, *Pilgrim's Progress,* p.166.

100. Cited by Guinness, *The Dust of Death,* p.257.

101. Muggeridge, *Jesus Rediscovered,* p.118.

102. Zacharias, *A Shattered Visage,* p.94.

103. *Ibid.,* p.102.

104. Stephen Travis, *The Jesus Hope,* Word Books, p.72.

105. Zacharias, *A Shattered Visage,* p.95.

106. John Donne, *Sermons,* No. 57, 1628.

107. Lewis, *God in the Dock,* p.108.

108. Anthony O'Hear, *Beyond Evolution,* Clarendon Press, p.204.

109. *Sunday Telegraph,* 18 October 1998.

110. Dawkins, *The Blind Watchmaker,* p.188.

111. *Ibid.,* p.93.

112. *Sunday Times Magazine,* 11 February 1996.

113. P. W. Atkins, *The Creation,* W. H. Freeman & Co., pp.36-7.

114. *Sunday Times Magazine,* 11 February 1996.

115. Lewis, *God in the Dock,* p.138.

116. *Life and Letters of Charles Darwin,* ed. Frances Darwin, Johnson reprint, p.285.

117. Francis Schaeffer, *The God Who is There,* Hodder & Stoughton, p.88.

118. David Lack, cited by Guinness, *The Dust of Death,* p.351.

119. C. S. Lewis, *Broadcast Talks,* cited in Frederick P. Wood, *Facing Facts and Finding Faith,* Marshall, Morgan & Scott, p.24.

120. C. S. Lewis, 'Is Theology Poetry?', in *The Weight of Glory and Other Addresses,* Macmillan, pp.91-2.

121. Cited by Zacharias, *A Shattered Visage,* p.81.

122. Wolfhart Pannenberg, *Basic Questions in Theology,* SCM, p.201.

Chapter 17 — Status and standards

1. R. C. Sproul, *In Search of Dignity,* Regal Books, pp.18-19.

2. Knowles, *Finding Faith,* p.8.

3. *Daily Telegraph,* 16 January 1996.

4. *Daily Telegraph,* 11 August 1996.

5. *Daily Mail,* 29 October 1997.

6. *Daily Telegraph,* 24 March 1998.

7. See Sproul, *In Search of Dignity,* p.92.

8. Robert Burns, 'Man was made to mourn'.

9. *Daily Telegraph,* 19 May 1994.

10. *The Times,* 27 July 1994.
11. *Daily Telegraph,* 30 July 1994.
12. Bell, *In Harm's Way,* p.297.
13. *Daily Telegraph,* 7 April 1996.
14. BBC television news, 29 January 1996.
15. *Sunday Times,* 14 June 1998.
16. Morey, *The New Atheism and the Erosion of Freedom,* p.158.
17. William Lane Craig, *Reasonable Faith,* Crossway Books, p.59.
18. Paul Oestreicher, *Thirty Years of Human Right* (The British Churches' Advisory Forum on Human Rights, 1980).
19. Jean Rostan, *Humanly Possible,* cited by John Stott, *Issues Facing Christians Today,* Marshall, Morgan & Scott, p.296.
20. C. S. Lewis, 'The Weight of Glory', in *Screwtape Proposes a Toast,* Collins, p.109.
21. See Gary Scott Smith, 'Naturalistic Humanism', in *Building a Christian World View,* vol. 1, p.170.
22. Jacques Monod, *Chance and Necessity,* p.145.
23. CNN News, reported in 'Focus on Faith', Premier Radio, 11 March 1998.
24. *Daily Mail,* 22 June 1998.
25. Julian Huxley, *The Humanist Frame,* ed. Huxley, George Allen & Unwin, p.47.
26. Stott, *Issues Facing Christians Today,* p.118.
27. Cited by Martin Mawyer, *Fundamentalist Journal 7,* June 1988.
28. *Ibid.*
29. Marvin Harris, 'Our Pound of Flesh', *Natural History* 88 (August–September 1979), p.36.
30. James Rachels, *Created from Animals: The Moral Implications of Darwinism,* Oxford University Press, p.198.
31. *Ibid.,* p.194.
32. Lubenow, *Bones of Contention,* p.197.
33. *Daily Telegraph,* 6 April 1998.
34. William Shakespeare, *Macbeth,* Act V, Scene V.
35. *Sunday Telegraph,* 12 March 1997.
36. *Ibid.*
37. BBC Radio 4 News, 10 May 1998.
38. *Daily Telegraph,* 8 June 1998.
39. *Daily Telegraph,* 27 March 1998.
40. *Sunday Times,* 29 March 1992.
41. Peter Singer, 'Sanctity of Life or Quality of Life', in *Pediatrics,* July 1983, p.129.
42. Peter Singer, *Practical Ethics,* Cambridge University Press, p.48.
43. Ward, *God, Chance and Necessity,* p.143.
44. Dawkins, *The Blind Watchmaker,* p.200.
45. Jacob Bronowski, *The Identity of Man,* Penguin, p.8.
46. Sproul, *In Search of Dignity,* pp.93-4.
47. Thomas Paine, *The Rights of Man,* pp.47-8.
48. *Daily Telegraph,* 17 August 1998.
49. Stott, *Issues Facing Christians Today,* pp.143-4.
50. Cited by Raeper and Smith, *A Beginner's Guide to Ideas,* p.38.
51. Evans, *The Quest For Faith,* p.46.
52. Cicero, *de Legibus,* cited in Joseph Fletcher, *Situation Ethics,* Westminster Press, p.77.
53. Cited by Draper, *Quotations for the Christian World,* p.97.
54. *Sunday Telegraph,* 25 February 1996.
55. Lesslie Newbigin, *The Gospel in a Pluralistic Society,* SPCK, p.163.
56. *Evangelicals Now,* July 1998.
57. See Nigel MCullough, *Barriers to Belief,* Darton, Longman and Todd, p.74.
58. *Sunday Times,* 4 January 1998.
59. *The Times,* 12 February 1994.
60. *The Times,* 14 February 1994.
61. *Daily Telegraph,* 23 April 1996.
62. *Ibid.*

63. *Daily Telegraph,* 17 January 1995.
64. *Ibid.*
65. Paul Kurtz, *Forbidden Fruit,* Prometheus Books, p.73.
66. *Observer,* 6 October 1957.
67. Benton, *Is Christianity True?,* p.96.
68. C. S. Lewis, 'The Poison of Subjectivism', in *Christian Reflections,* ed. Walter Hooper, Eerdmans, pp.74-5.
69. Lewis, *God in the Dock,* p.21.
70. John A. T. Robinson, *Honest to God,* SCM, p.116.
71. *Ibid.,* p.118.
72. Brown, *Philosophy and the Christian Faith,* p.214.
73. James Montgomery Boice, *Foundations of the Christian Faith,* vol. II (God the Redeemer), Inter-Varsity Press, p.85.
74. Gertrude Himmelfarb, *The De-moralisation of Society: From Victorian Virtues to Modern Values,* Knopf, p.9.
75. Kreeft and Tacelli, *Handbook of Christian Apologetics,* p.77.
76. Knox, *Not By Bread Alone,* p.2.
77. *Observer,* 27 February 1994.
78. *Daily Telegraph,* 30 August 1995.
79. *Observer,* 28 January 1996.
80. *Daily Telegraph,* 7 July 1994.
81. Benton, *Is Christianity True?,* p.95.
82. S. E. Stumpf, in discussion in J. R. Elkington, 'The Changing Mores of Biological Research': A Colloquium on Ethical Dilemmas from Medical Advances at the American College of Physicians', *Annals of Internal Medicine,* 1967, Supplement 7.
83. Peter Atkins, *Creation Revisited,* Penguin, p.23.
84. Dawkins, *The Selfish Gene,* p.3.
85. *Ibid.,* p.215.
86. O'Hear, *Beyond Evolution,* p.214.
87. Kreft and Tacelli, *Handbook of Christian Apologetics,* p.379.
88. Guinness, *The Dust of Death,* p.160.
89. Cited by Owen Chadwick, *The Secularisation of the European Mind in the Nineteenth Century,* Cambridge University Press.
90. Michael Ruse and Edward Wilson, 'Evolution and Ethics', *New Scientist* 208, 17 October 1985, p.50.
91. Michael Ruse and Edward Wilson, 'Moral Philosophy as Applied Science', *Philosophy,* 61 (1986), p.186.
92. Francis Crick, *The Astonishing Hypothesis, the Scientific Search for the Soul,* Simon and Schuster, p.3.
93. *The Darwin Debate,* BBC 2, 28 March 1998.
94. *Daily Telegraph,* 31 August 1992.
95. *God — For or Against?* Channel 4.
96. Zacharias, *A Shattered Visage,* p.138.
97. Thomas Huxley, *Evolution and Ethics and Other Essays,* Romanes Lecture 1893, D. Appleton, p.80.
98. Rodney D. Holder, *Nothing But Atoms and Molecules?,* Monarch Publications, p.21.
99. *Sunday Telegraph,* 1 July 1997.
100. Cited *ibid.*
101. Michael Ruse, *Evolutionary Naturalism,* Routledge, p.241.
102. *Ibid.,* p.290.
103. See Karl Popper, *Objective Knowledge: An Evolutionary Approach,* Oxford University Press, pp.223-4.
104. *Daily Telegraph,* 1 May 1996.
105. *Ibid.*
106. *Daily Telegraph,* 4 February 1997.
107. O'Hear, *Beyond Evolution,* p.212.
108. *Daily Mail,* 17 August 1998.
109. Hunt, *In Defense of the Faith,* p.41.

110. Jean-Paul Sartre, *Existentialism and Human Emotions,* the Citadel Press, p.22.

111. Cited by Palmer, *Cure for Life,* p.96.

112. Michael Ruse, *Evolution and Religion,* cited in O'Hear, *Beyond Evolution,* p.140.

113. Moreland, *Scaling the Secular City,* p.115.

114. Peter C. Moore, *Disarming the Secular Gods,* Inter-Varsity Press, p.137.

115. See Craig, *Reasonable Faith,* p.56.

116. Publilius Syrus, *Moral Sayings,* trans. Darius Lyman, cited in *The International Thesaurus of Quotations,* George Allen & Unwin, p.105.

117. William Shakespeare, *Hamlet,* Act III, Scene I.

118. Peter Ustinov, *Dear Me,* Mandarin, p.281.

119. Johnson, *The Quest for God,* pp.2-3.

120. Cited by Wood, *Facing Facts and Finding Faith,* p.28.

121. Holder, *Nothing But Atoms and Molecules?,* p.130.

122. Lewis, *Miracles,* p.42.

123. *Concise Oxford Dictionary,* p.724.

124. Frame, *Apologetics to the Glory of God,* p.99.

125. Evans, *The Quest for Faith,* p.48.

126. Cited by Draper, *Quotations for the Christian World,* p.95.

127. Private letter to the author, 3 November 1998.

128. Kreeft and Tacelli, *Handbook of Christian Apologetics,* p.75.

129. Richard Taylor, *Ethics, Faith and Reason.*

Chapter 18 — The book that speaks for itself

1. C. Sanders, *Introduction to Research in English Literary History,* MacMillan Co., pp.143ff.

2. Norman L. Geisler and William E. Nix, *A General Introduction to the Bible,* Moody Press, p.361.

3. F. J. A. Hort and B. F. Westcott, *The New Testament in the Original Greek,* Macmillan Co., p.2.

4. Geisler and Nix, *A General Introduction to the Bible,* p.365.

5. Hort and Westcott, *The New Testament in the Original Greek,* p.2.

6. Philip Schaff, *Companion to the Greek Testament and the English Versions,* Harper & Brothers, p.177.

7. *Ibid.*

8 See Geisler and Nix, *A General Introduction to the Bible,* p.367.

9. Frederic G. Kenyon, *Our Bible and the Ancient Manuscripts,* Harper & Brothers, p.23.

10. F. F. Bruce, *The Books and the Parchments,* Fleming H. Revell Co., p.178.

11. 'Codex' is the name for an early form of book, made by sewing together leaves of writing material. Codices were often made from papyrus or longer-lasting vellum.

12. Frederic G. Kenyon, *The Bible and Archaeology,* Harper & Row, p.288.

13. Cited by Holder, *Nothing But Atoms and Molecules?,* p.203.

14. Geisler and Nix, *A General Introduction to the Bible,* p.263.

15. Cited by René Pache, *The Inspiration and Authority of Scripture,* Moody Press, p.164.

16. For these and other details, see Samuel Davidson in *Hebrew Text of the Old Testament,* 2nd edition, p.89 as cited in *A Dictionary of the Bible,* vol. IV, ed. James Hastings, p.949.

17. Kenyon, *Our Bible and the Ancient Manuscripts,* Harper & Brothers, p.43.

18. Wheeler Robinson, cited in Josh McDowell, *Evidence That Demands a Verdict,* Campus Crusade for Christ, p.58.

19. Kenyon, *Our Bible and the Ancient Manuscripts,* p.38.

20. Brian H. Edwards, *Nothing But the Truth,* Evangelical Press, p.175.

21. Cited by Edwards, *ibid.,* p.135.

22. *Ibid.,* p.140.

23. Robert Dick Wilson, *A Scientific Investigation of the Old Testament,* Moody Press, pp.70-71.

24. Cited by Edwards, *Nothing But the Truth,* p.135.

25. See Genesis 14.

26. Wilson, *A Scientific Investigation of the Old Testament,* p.22.

27. Robert Dick Wilson, *Is The Higher Criticism Scholarly?,* cited by Edwards, *Nothing But the Truth,* p.134.

28. Edwards, *Nothing But the Truth,* p.289.

29. A. H. Sayce, *The 'Higher Criticism' and the Verdict of the Monuments*, SPCK, p.28.
30. *Ibid.*, p.29.
31. *Ibid.*
32. *Ibid.*, p.35.
33. Acts 7:22.
34. See Hunt, *In Defense of the Faith*, p.69.
35. Nelson Glueck, *Rivers in the Desert: History of Neteg*, Jewish Publications Society of America, p.31.
36. Cited by Edwards, *Nothing But the Truth*, p.294.
37. *Ibid.*, p.142.
38. *Ibid.*
39. Acts 14:6.
40. William Ramsay, *St Paul the Traveller and Roman Citizen*, Baker Book House, p.7.
41. William Ramsay, *The Bearing of Recent Discovery on the Trustworthiness of the New Testament*, Hodder and Stoughton, p.222.
42. *Ibid.*, p.85.
43. E. M. Blaiklock, *The Acts of the Apostles*, Wm. B. Eerdmans Publishing Co., p.89.
44. See A. N. Sherwin-White, *Roman Society and Roman Law in the New Testament*, Clarendon Press, cited by Clark H. Pinnock, *Reason Enough*, Paternoster Press, p.77.
45. Edwards, *Nothing But the Truth*, p.148.
46. C. Everett Koop and Francis A. Schaeffer, *Whatever Happened to the Human Race?*, Crossway Books, p.176.
47. See F. F. Bruce, *The New Testament Documents: Are They Reliable?*, Inter-Varsity Press, p.82.
48. Sherwin-White, *Roman Society and Roman Law in the New Testament*, cited by Koop and Schaeffer, *Whatever Happened to the Human Race?*, p.175.
49. Peter Kreeft, *Between Heaven and Hell*, Inter-Varsity Press, p.80.
50. Cited by Hunt, *In Defense of the Faith*, p.144.
51. Werner Keller, *The Bible as History*, Hodder & Stoughton, p.x.
52. Hunt, *In Defense of the Faith*, p.156.
53. *Ibid.*
54. William F. Albright, *The Christian Century*, 19 November 1958, p.1329.
55. *TIME*, 30 December 1974.
56. Bruce, *The Books and the Parchments*.
57. J. I. Packer, in foreword to Edmund P. Clowney, *The Unfolding Mystery*, Inter-Varsity Press, pp.8-9.
58. Robert Horn, *The Book that Speaks for Itself*, Inter-Varsity Press, p.86.
59. B. M. Palmer, *Theology of Prayer*, Sprinkle Publications, p.71.
60. See John Warwick Montgomery, *History and Christianity*, Inter-Varsity Press, p.29.
61. Simon Greenleaf, *The Testimony of the Evangelists: Examined by the Rules of Evidence Administered in Courts of Justice*, Baker Book House, p.2.
62. *Daily Mail*, 28 May 1997.
63. *TIME*, 9 June 1997.
64. Cited in *The Berean Call*, February 1998.
65. *Christian News*, 13 October 1997.
66. *Daily Mail*, 4 June 1997.
67. Hunt, *In Defense of the Faith*, p.74.
68. Compare 1 Kings 13:1-2 with 2 Kings 21:25 - 22:2 and 2 Kings 23:15-18.
69. Compare Isaiah 44:28 with Ezra 1:1-3.
70. See Habakkuk 1:6-11.
71. See Peter W. Stoner, *Science Speaks*, Moody Press, pp.67-96 for this and other illustrations.
72. *Washington Times*, 7 January 1995.
73. *Daily Telegraph*, 13 May 1997.
74. Patrick Johnstone, *The Church is Bigger than you Think*, Christian Focus Publications.
75. Cited by John Blanchard, *Gathered Gold*, Evangelical Press, p.15.
76. Cited in Draper, *Quotations for the Christian World*, p.36.
77. Thomas Huxley, *Contemporary Review*, cited in Earle Albert Rowell, *Prophecy Speaks: Dissolving Doubts*, Review and Herald Publishing Association, p.91.

78. Cited by Draper, *Quotations for the Christian World,* p.35.
79. Cited by John Blanchard, *More Gathered Gold,* Evangelical Press, p.26.
80. Cited by Draper, *Quotations for the Christian World,* p.36.
81. *Decision,* October 1971, p.7.
82. Cited by Draper, *Quotations for the Christian World,* p.39.
83. Cited by John Blanchard, *Sifted Silver,* Evangelical Press, p.17.
84. John Richard Green, *A Short History of the English Bible,* cited in *The Book of Knowledge,* vol.1, Waverley Book Co., p.452.
85. A. Rendle Short, *Why Believe?,* Inter-Varsity Fellowship, p.62.
86. Cited by Blanchard, *Gathered Gold,* p.17.
87. *Everyman — Science Friction,* BBC television, 8 September 1996.
88. Walter M. Montano, *Christian Heritage,* cited in Loraine Boettner, *Roman Catholicism,* Banner of Truth Trust, p.510.
89. *Daily Telegraph,* 8 October 1998.
90. *Awake,* 22 May 1994.
91. 2 Peter 3:16.
92. Exodus 4:10-12.
93. Jeremiah 1:2; Ezekiel 1:3; Hosea 1:1; Joel 1:1; Jonah 1:1; Zephaniah 1:1; Haggai 1:1; Zechariah 1:1.
94. Isaiah 1:1; Daniel 7:1.
95. Amos 3:11; Obadiah 1.
96. Nahum 1:1; Habakkuk 1:1; Malachi 1:1.
97. Deuteronomy 18:21.
98. Deuteronomy 18:22.
99. 1 Kings 22:27.
100. 1 Kings 22:8.
101. 1 Kings 22:34.
102. John Benton, *Looking for the Answer,* Evangelical Press, p.14.
103. Jeremiah 28.8.
104. Ezekiel 38:17.
105. See Zechariah 1:1-6.
106. Romans 3:2.
107. 1 Corinthians 14:37.
108. 1 Thessalonians 2:13.
109. 1 Thessalonians 4:8.
110. 2 Peter 3:15.
111. 1 Peter 1:12.
112. Revelation 1:2.
113. Revelation 22:6.
114. Harold Lindsell, *God's Incomparable Word.*
115. 2 Timothy 3:16.
116. Romans 3:2.
117. 2 Peter 1:21.
118. Edwards, *Nothing But the Truth,* p.53.
119. Milne, *Know the Truth,* p.20.
120. C. S. Lewis, *God in the Dock,* p.144.
121. Job 11:7.
122. 1 Corinthians 2:14.
123. Private letter to the author, 23 November 1998.
124. John Frame, 'Scripture Speaks for Itself' in *God's Inerrant Word,* ed. John Warwick Montgomery, Bethany Fellowship, p.185.
125. Sproul, *Reason to Believe,* pp.31-2.
126. Hebrews 6:13.
127. Frame, *Apologetics to the Glory of God,* p.121.
128. 1 Peter 1:23.

Chapter 19 — A God-free zone?
1. Andrews, *God, Science and Evolution,* introduction.
2. Isaac Asimov, *In the Beginning,* Crown, p.13.
3. Moreland, *Scaling the Secular City,* p.199.
4. *Concise Oxford Dictionary,* p.939.
5. See *Crusade,* July 1956, p.9.
6. Lesslie Newbigin, *The Gospel in a Pluralist Society,* S.P.C.K., p.20.
7. *Ibid.*
8. Ward, *God, Chance and Necessity,* p.22.
9. Stanley D. Beck, 'Natural Science and Creationist Theology', *Bioscience* 32, October 1982, p.739.
10. David Broughton Knox, *Not by Bread Alone,* Banner of Truth Trust, p.14.
11. Cited by Victor F. Weiskopf, 'The Frontiers and Limits of Science', *American Scientist* 67, July-August 1977, p.405.
12. Cited by Frost, *Thinking Clearly about God and Science,* Monarch Publications, p.33.
13. *Daily Mail,* 26 January 1999.
14. Francis Bridger, *Why Can't I Believe?,* Triangle Books, p.5.
15. Thomas Huxley, *Collected Essays,* vol. 1, p.41.
16. *Ibid.*
17. *Proceedings of the National Institute of Science of India* 27A (196): 564.
18. Robinson, *The Faith of the Unbeliever,* p.43.
19. Francis Schaeffer, *The Church at the end of the Twentieth Century,* The Norfolk Press, p.16.
20. Bertrand Russell, *Religion and Science,* Oxford University Press, p.243.
21. See *Sunday Telegraph,* 7 April 1996.
22. R. Lewontin, *New York Review of Books,* 9 January 1997.
23. Cited by Behe, *Darwin's Black Box,* p.238. Dickerson's essay is in *Journal of Molecular Evolution,* 34, 277 (1992).
24. Bridger, *Why Can't I Believe?,* p.31.
25. McGrath, *Bridge-Building,* 208.
26. E. Calvin Beisner, *Answers for Atheists, Agnostics and Other Thoughtful Skeptics,* Crossway Books, pp.115-16.
27. *Sunday Telegraph,* 28 February 1999.
28. Cited by Michael Poole, *A Guide to Science and Belief,* Lion Publishing, p.32.
29. *Daily Telegraph,* 12 October 1993.
30. *Daily Telegraph,* 23 April 1994.
31. Carl Sagan, 'Velikovsky's Challenge to Science', cassette tape 186-74, produced by the American Association for the Advancement of Science.
32. John Burn and Nigel J. McQuoid, *Christianity and the School Curriculum,* the Christian Institute, p.20.
33. Karl Popper, *The Logic of Scientific Discovery,* Unwin Hyman Ltd, p.280.
34. Cited by Bridger, *Why Can't I Believe?,* p.11.
35. *Ibid.,* p.10.
36. *Ibid.,* p.11.
37. J. S. Jones, *The Language of the Genes,* HarperCollins, p.xi.
38. Donald MacKay, *Where Science and Faith Meet,* Inter-Varsity Fellowship, pp.15-16.
39. Andrews, *God, Science and Evolution,* p.35.
40. Julian Huxley, *Essays of a Humanist,* p.112.
41. Stephen Hawking, *Black Holes and Baby Universes,* Bantam Books, p.90.
42. Andrews, *God, Science and Evolution,* p.36.
43. John Eccles, 'Science Can't Provide Ultimate Answers', *US News and World Report,* February 1985.
44. Albert Einstein, *Ideas and Opinions,* p.41.
45. *Sunday Telegraph,* 17 April 1996.
46. Cited by Roche, *A World Without Heroes,* pp.132-3.
47. Houghton, *The Search For God,* pp.213-14.
48. Erwin Schrödinger, *Nature and the Greeks,* cited in Wilkinson, *Thinking Clearly About God and Science,* p.67.
49. Private letter to the author, 25 February 1999.

50. *Independent,* 23 December 1991.

51. *Daily Telegraph,* 6 April 1998.

52. *Daily Telegraph Science Extra,* 11 September 1989, p.xi.

53. Cited by Henry M. Morris, *Men of Science — Men of God,* Master Books, p.15.

54. *Ibid.,* p.13.

55. *Ibid.*

56. Cited Dan Graves, *Scientists of Faith,* Kregel Publications, p.58.

57. *Ibid.,* p.63.

58. *Ibid.,* p.66.

59. *Ibid.,* p.72.

60. Isaac Newton, *Philosophiae Principia Mathematica,* cited by Holder, *Nothing But Atoms and Molecules?,* pp.60-61.

61. Cited by Graves, *Scientists of Faith,* p.82.

62. Cited by Morris, *Men of Science — Men of God,* p.30.

63. *Ibid.,* p.37.

64. Numbers 23:23, Authorized Version.

65. Cited by Graves, *Scientists of Faith,* p.153.

66. *Ibid.,* p.146.

67. Cited by Colin A. Russell, 'The Conflict Metaphor and its Social Origin', *Science and Christian Belief,* vol. no. 1, April 1989, p.26.

68. See Morris, *Men of Science — Men of God,* p.67.

69. Cited by Graves, *Scientists of Faith,* p.153.

70. *Ibid.,* p.164.

71. *Ibid.,* p.169.

72. See *Daily Telegraph,* 3 April 1997.

73. *Nature,* vol. 386, pp.435-6.

74. See McCullough, *Barriers to Belief,* p.84.

75. *God and the Scientists,* C.P.O. — Design & Print, p.2.

76. *Ibid.,* p.4.

77. *Ibid.,* p.6.

78. *Ibid.,* p.8.

79. *Ibid.,* p.10.

80. *Ibid.,* p.11.

81. See Holder, *Nothing But Atoms and Molecules?,* p.71.

82. Cited by Colin A. Russell, 'The Conflict Metaphor and its Social Origins', *Science and Christian Belief,* vol. 1, No. 1 (April 1989), pp.5-8, 22.

83. Thomas Huxley, *Darwiniana: essays,* Macmillan, p.52.

84. *Daily Telegraph,* 14 June 1996.

85. Cited by Russell Stannard, *Doing Away With God?,* HarperCollins, p.4.

86. *Ibid.*

87. *Daily Telegraph,* 3 September 1996.

88. *The Times,* 10 December 1994.

89. Henry Morris, *The God who is Real,* Baker Book House, p.35.

90. Isaiah 40:22.

91. Jeremiah 33:22.

92. 1 Corinthians 15:39.

93. *Daily Telegraph,* 3 September 1996.

94. Russell, 'What I believe', in *Why I am not a Christian,* p.50.

95. *Sunday Telegraph,* 7 April 1996.

96. *Sunday Telegraph,* 30 March 1997.

97. Albert Einstein, 'Science and Religion', *Out of My Later Years,* cited by Rhoda Thomas Tripp, *The International Thesaurus of Quotations,* George Allan & Unwin, p.564

Chapter 20 — Nothing but the truth – I

1. J. Calvin, *Institutes of the Christian Religion,* vol. 1, ed. John T. O'Neille, trans. Ford Lewis Battles, p.35.

2. For a superb popular treatment, see J. I. Packer, *Knowing God,* Hodder & Stoughton.
3. *Concise Oxford Dictionary,* p.1173.
4. 1 Corinthians 8:8.
5. 1 Corinthians 8:4.
6. Deuteronomy 6:4.
7. Isaiah 44:6; 45:5.
8. 1 Corinthians 8:5-6.
9. Leon Morris, *The First Epistle of Paul to the Corinthians,* Tyndale Press, pp.125-6.
10. Moore, *Disarming the Secular Gods,* p.158.
11. Psalm 92:5.
12. Psalm 33:12.
13. 1 Peter 5:7.
14. Deuteronomy 26:11.
15. Joshua 23:14.
16. Daniel 2:47.
17. Psalm 103:8.
18. Lewis, *Miracles,* p.81.
19. Geoffrey W. Bromiley, 'The Trinity', *Baker's Dictionary of Theology,* ed. Everett F. Harrison, Pickering & Inglis, p.531.
20. Genesis 16:7.
21. Genesis 16:13.
22. See Genesis 22:1-18.
23. Isaiah 6:8.
24. Milne, *Know the Truth,* p.63.
25. Louis Berkhof, *Systematic Theology,* Banner of Truth Trust, p.88.
26. John 4:24.
27. Exodus 8:19.
28. Deuteronomy 8:3.
29. Deuteronomy 12:25.
30. Isaiah 48:13.
31. Horn, *The Book that Speaks for Itself,* p.39.
32. Isaiah 29:13.
33. Cited by Blanchard, *More Gathered Gold,* p.105.
34. Deuteronomy 33:27.
35. Psalm 90:2.
36. Revelation 1:8.
37. Novatian, *De Trinitate,* xxxi, 190.
38. Lewis, *Miracles,* p.87.
39. Kreeft and Tacelli, *Handbook of Christian Apologetics,* p.105.
40. Acts 17:25.
41. John R. W. Stott, *The Message of Acts,* Inter-Varsity Press, p.285.
42. Nehemiah 9:32.
43. 1 Chronicles 29:11.
44. Romans 11:33.
45. 1 Kings 8:27.
46. Isaiah 55:8-9.
47. Jeremiah 23:24.
48. Psalm 139:7-8.
49. Acts 17:28.
50. Cited by Blanchard, *Gathered Gold,* p.121.
51. C. S. Lewis, 'The Seeing Eye', in *Christian Reflections,* ed. Walter Hooper, Harcourt Brace Jovanovich, pp.167-8.
52. Stephen Charnock, *The Existence and Attributes of God,* vol. 1, Baker Book House, p.369.
53. 1 Samuel 2:3.
54. Job 37:16.
55. Proverbs 15:3.

56. Jeremiah 32:19.
57. Hebrews 4:13.
58. Proverbs 5:21.
59. Jeremiah 17:10.
60. Jeremiah 1:5.
61. Malachi 3:6.
62. Deuteronomy 4:34.
63. James 1:17.
64. Hebrews 6:17.
65. Isaiah 6:1, 3.
66. Revelation 4:8.
67. J. I. Packer, *Hot Tub Religion,* Tyndale House Publishers, p.52.
68. *Evangelicals Now,* April 1998.
69. Cited by Draper, *Quotations for the Christian World,* p.238.
70. e.g. Psalm 22:3.
71. Habakkuk 1:13.
72. Habakkuk 1:13.
73. Psalm 48:10.
74. 1 John 1:5.
75. Milne, *Know the Truth,* p.68.
76. 1 Samuel 2:2.
77. Exodus 15:11.
78. James P. Boyce, *Abstract of Systematic Theology,* reprinted by Christian Gospel Foundation, p.93.
79. Benton, *Is Christianity True?,* p.97.
80. 1 John 4:8.
81. William Barclay, *The Letters of John and Jude,* Saint Andrew Press, p.117.
82. Psalm 69:13.
83. Psalm 33:5.
84. Psalm 103:8.
85. e.g. Psalm 118:1-4,29.
86. Psalm 111:4.
87. Psalm 106:7.
88. Psalm 18:50.
89. Psalm 116:12.
90. Packer, *Knowing God,* p.136.
91. 1 John 3:1.
92. Dawkins, *The Selfish Gene,* p.2
93. 1 John 4:19.
94. Benton, *Is Christianity True?,* p.42.
95. Packer, *Knowing God,* p.134.
96. Genesis 1:1.
97. Douglas Kelly, *Creation and Change,* Christian Focus Publications, p.45.
98. *Ibid.*
99. Nehemiah 9:6
100. Genesis 1:16.
101. Augustine, *The Literal Meaning of Genesis,* vol. 1: *Ancient Christian Writers,* No. 41, ed. Quasten *et. al,* trans. John H Taylor, Newman Press, pp.153-4.
102. Matthew 12:32.
103. Hebrews 11:3.
104. Rookmaaker, *The Creative Gift,* p.140.
105. Hebrews 3:4.
106. Psalm 148:5.
107. David Wilkinson, *Thinking Clearly about God and Science,* p.41.
108. William Shakespeare, *As You Like It,* Act 4, Scene 1.
109. Taylor, *In the Minds of Men,* p.364.
110. e.g. in Kelly, *Creation and Change.*

111. Acts 14:15.
112. Hawking, *A Brief History of Time,* p.193.
113. *Ibid.*
114. Revelation 4:11.
115. Psalm 33:6.
116. Genesis 1:31.
117. Lewis, *Miracles,* p.37.
118. Hebrews 11:3.
119. *Everyman* — '*Science Friction*', BBC 2, 8 September 1996.
120. Cited in *Christianity Today,* 12 December 1994.
121. Psalm 97:1.
122. R. C. Sproul, *Table Talk,* February 1998, Ligonier.
123. Proverbs 19:21.
124. Proverbs 21:1.
125. Psalm 22:28.
126. Psalm 113:4
127. Ephesians 1:21.
128. Psalm 103:19.
129. J. L. Dagg, *Manual of Theology and Church Order,* Gano Books, p.75.
130. Stannard, *Doing away with God?,* p.111.
131. Daniel 4:35.
132. Ephesians 1:11.
133. Moore, *Disarming the Secular Gods,* p.17.
134. e.g. Jeremiah 44:7.
135. Jeremiah 32:27.
136. Hebrews 6:18.
137. 2 Timothy 2:13.
138. Psalm 66:7.
139. A. W. Pink, *The Attributes of God,* Reiner Publications, p.75.
140. Eryl Davies, *The Wrath of God,* Evangelical Movement of Wales, p.11.
141. R. C. Sproul, *The Holiness of God,* Tyndale House Publishers, pp.224, 228.
142. Psalm 7:11.
143. Nehemiah 9:17.
144. 1 Thessalonians 1:10.
145. Hebrews 9:27.
146. Romans 14:12.
147. Galatians 6:7.
148. David Watson, *My God is Real,* Falcon Books, p.36.
149. Packer, *Knowing God,* p.172.
150. John Hick, *Death and Eternal Life,* Collins, p.200.
151. C. H. Dodd, *New Testament Studies,* University Press, p.119.
152. J. A. T. Robinson, *On being the Church in the World.*
153. Isaiah 30:18.
154. Psalm 97:2.
155. Acts 17:31.
156. Revelation 21:4.
157. Revelation 14:11.
158. Revelation 9:5.
159. Nahum 1:6.
160. Genesis 18:25.
161. Packer, *Knowing God,* p.156.

Chapter 21 Nothing but the truth – II

1. Calvin, *Institutes of the Christian Religion,* vol. 1, p.241.
2. Jacques Monod, *Chance and Necessity,* Alfred A. Knopf, p.180.
3. Genesis 1:1.

4. Genesis 1:21.
5. Genesis 1:27.
6. E. F. Kevan, *The New Bible Commentary,* ed. A. M. Stibbs, F. Davidson, E. F. Kevan, Inter-Varsity Press, p.77.
7. Genesis 2:7.
8. Kevan, *New Bible Commentary,* p.77.
9. Genesis 1:28.
10. Psalm 8:6.
11. Genesis 2:15.
12. Kelly, *Creation and Change,* p.224.
13. Genesis 1:27.
14. Francis A. Schaeffer, *Genesis in Space and Time,* Hodder & Stoughton, p.33.
15. *Ibid.,* p.47.
16. Kelly, *Creation and Change,* p.219.
17. Samuel E. Waldron, *A Modern Exposition of the 1689 Baptist Confession of Faith,* Evangelical Press, p.84.
18. James Montgomery Boice, *The Sovereign God* (Foundations of the Christian Faith, vol. 2), Inter-Varsity Press, p.195.
19. Cited by Milne, *Know the Truth,* p.99.
20. Psalm 139:14.
21. Schaeffer, *Genesis in Space and Time,* p.51.
22. Waldron, *Modern Exposition of the 1689 Baptist Confession,* p.84.
23. Ecclesiastes 7:29.
24. Ephesians 4:24.
25. Genesis 1:31.
26. Schaeffer, *Genesis in Time and Space,* p.55.
27. Romans 5:12.
28. Genesis 2:17.
29. J. A. Motyer, *After Death,* Hodder & Stoughton, p.40.
30. Genesis 3:8.
31. *Crusade,* November 1958.
32. Genesis 3:19.
33. Genesis 5:3.
34. Psalm 51:5.
35. Ephesians 2:3.
36. Cited by Custance, *The Sovereignty of Grace,* p.91.
37. Romans 5:12.
38. Cited by Draper, *Quotations for the Christian World,* p.405.
39. Romans 8:10.
40. Ephesians 4:18.
41. 1 Corinthians 2:14.
42. Schaeffer, *Genesis in Space and Time,* p.99.
43. Romans 6:16.
44. 1 Timothy 4:2.
45. Ephesians 2:3.
46. *The Times,* 27 September 1989.
47. Job 5:7.
48. Romans 8:21.
49. Romans 8:22.
50. Isaiah 53:6.
51. *Evangelism Today,* June 1997.
52. Romans 1:18-25.
53. John 1:18.
54. Job 11:7.
55. Psalm 19:1-4.
56. Calvin, *Institutes of the Christian Religion,* vol. 1, p.51.

57. *Daily Mail*, 13 February 1979.
58. Cornelius Van Til, *Christian Apologetics*, Presbyterian & Reformed Publishing Co., pp.32-3.
59. Romans 2:15.
60. Van Til, *Christian Apologetics*, p.33.
61. 1 Corinthians 1:21.
62. Cited by Blanchard, *Sifted Silver*, p.110.
63. *Saturday Night Fry*, BBC Radio 4, 1 August 1998.
64. Calvin, *Institutes of the Christian Religion*, vol. 1, p.45.
65. *Ibid.*, p.51.
66. Cornelius Van Til, *The Defense of the Faith*, Presbyterian & Reformed Publishing Co., p.153.
67. Romans 1:28.
68. Bullinger, *A Critical Lexicon and Concordance to the English and Greek New Testament*, p.436.
69. J. B. Phillips, *Letters to Young Churches*, Geoffrey Bles, p.4.
70. Stuart Olyott, *The Gospel as it Really is*, Evangelical Press, p.9.
71. William Hendriksen, *Romans: 1-8*, Banner of Truth Trust, p.71.
72. R. C. Sproul, *Romans*, Christian Focus Publications, p.35.
73. Ludwig Feuerbach, *The Essence of Christianity*, trans. George Eliot, Harper & Row, p.12.
74. *Ibid.*, p.xxxix.
75. Boice, *The Sovereign God*, p.33.
76. Cited by Blanchard, *More Gathered Gold*, p.74.
77. Sinclair Ferguson, *The Pundit's Folly*, Banner of Truth Trust, p.45.
78. Milne, *Know the Truth*, p.64.
79. Psalm 19:1.
80. Isaiah 6:3.
81. Psalm 96:8.
82. *Theological Wordbook of the Old Testament*, vol. 1, ed. R. Laird Harris, Moody Press, p.368.
83. Isaiah 1:13.
84. D Martyn Lloyd-Jones, *Romans: An Exposition of Chapter 1: The Gospel of God*, Banner of Truth Trust, p.382.
85. Cited by Blanchard, *More Gathered Gold*, p.169.
86. Acts 17:25.
87. Acts 17:28.
88. 1 Corinthians 4:7.
89. James 1:5.
90. James 1:17.
91. Matthew 5:45.
92. 1 Chronicles 16:34.
93. Psalm 147:7.
94. Psalm 100:4.
95. 1 Thessalonians 5:18.
96. Ephesians 5:20.
97. Geoffrey B. Wilson, *Romans*, Banner of Truth Trust, p.27.
98. William Ramsay, *The Cities of St Paul*, p.17.
99. Spiros Zodhiates, *The Complete Word Study Dictionary: New Testament*, AMG Publishers, p.948.
100. Sproul, *Romans*, p.38.
101. Psalms 14:1; 53:1.
102. Derek Kidner, *Tyndale Old Testament Commentaries: Psalms 1-72*, Inter-Varsity Press, p.79.
103. Zodhiates, *The Complete Word Study Dictionary: New Testament*, p.282.
104. Kenneth S Wuest, *Romans in the Greek New Testament*, Wm B. Eerdmans Publishing Co., p.32.
105. S. Fox, *New Scientist*, 1969, p.450.
106. *Pacific News Service*, January 1978.
107. *Sunday Telegraph*, 23 February 1997.
108. *Daily Mail*, 28 June 1997.
109. John 3:19.
110. Robert J. Sheehan, *The Word of Truth*, Evangelical Press, p.35.
111. *Ibid.*, pp.35-6.

112. Sproul, *Romans,* pp.39-40.
113. Boice, *The Sovereign God,* p.34.
114. Cited by Blanchard, *More Gathered Gold,* p.14.
115. Psalm 115:5-8.
116. *Daily Telegraph,* 20 November 1998.
117. *Sunday,* BBC Radio 4, 17 January 1999.
118. Colossians 3:5.
119. Guy Appéré, *The Mystery of Christ,* Evangelical Press, p.96.
120. Luke 16:13.
121. Philippians 3:19.
122. *Ibid.*
123. *Daily Telegraph,* 14 January 1999.
124. Exodus 20:3.
125. Exodus 20:4.
126. Romans 1:26.
127. Romans 1:27.
128. Zodhiates, *The Complete Word Study Dictionary: New Testament,* p.286.
129. Sproul, *Romans,* p.46.
130. Psalm 10:4, 6, 13.
131. Psalm 73:11.
132. *Daily Telegraph,* 12 April 1996.
133. *Independent,* 19 December 1996.
134. Daniel 2:21.
135. Psalm 111:10.
136. Proverbs 1:7.
137. Zodhiates, *The Complete Word Study Dictionary: New Testament,* p.269.
138. W. E. Vine, *Expository Dictionary of New Testament Words,* vol. IV, Oliphants, p.174.
139. Joshua 24:19-20.
140. Robert Mounce, *The Book of Revelation,* Wm B. Eerdmans Publishing Co., p.295.
141. Psalm 7:11.
142. See Genesis 6-9.
143. See Genesis 19.
144. See Exodus 7-12.
145. See 2 Chronicles 26.
146. See Acts 5:1-11.
147. See Acts 12:19-23.
148. Exodus 34:6.
149. Romans 2:4.
150. G. T. Thomson and F. Davidson, *New Bible Commentary,* p.943.

Chapter 22 — The case against God

1. Sky News, 12 April 1999.
2. Ludovic Kennedy, *All in the Mind,* Hodder & Stoughton.
3. *Independent,* 3 February 1999.
4. Alasdair McIntyre, 'Is Understanding Religions Compatible with Believing?', in *Rationality,* ed. B. R. Wilson, Blackwell, p.73.
5. McGrath, *Bridge-Building,* p.140.
6. Alasdair McIntyre and Paul Ricoeur, *The Religious Significance of Atheism,* Columbia University Press, p.14.
7. *Daily Telegraph,* 24 March 1995.
8. Johnson, *The Quest for God,* p.61.
9. C. S. Lewis, *The Problem of Pain,* Geoffrey Bles, p.14.
10. Evans, *The Quest for Faith,* p.92.
11. D. James Kennedy, *Skeptics Answered,* Multnomah Books, p.124.
12. Alvin Plantinga, 'A Christian Life Partly Lived', in *Philosophers Who Believe,* p.72.
13. Robert Burns, 'Man was made to mourn' (1786).

14. Hume, *Dialogues Concerning Natural Religion,* p.60.
15. *Daily Telegraph,* 13 July 1996.
16. *Daily Telegraph,* 24 June 1999.
17. John Polkinghorne, *Science and Providence,* SPCK, p.67.
18. *Economist,* 27 April 1991.
19. *Los Angeles Times,* 20 June 1990.
20. Cited by John Allan, *I Know Where I'm Going,* Lutterworth Press, pp.102-3.
21. Bridger, *Why Can't I Believe?,* p.47.
22. Anton Gill, *The Journey back from Hell,* Grafton Books, pp.26-7.
23. Cited by Frame, *Apologetics to the Glory of God,* p.150.
24. H. G. Wells, *Mr Britling Sees it Through,* Merrimack Pub. Corp.
25. *Sunday Telegraph,* 17 April 1996.
26. *Ibid.*
27. *Daily Mail,* 15 April 1992.
28. Psalm 33:5.
29. Daniel Webster, on Mr Justice Story, 12 September 1845.
30. Rousas John Rushdoony, *Salvation and Godly Rule,* ed. Carl F. Henry, p.380.
31. Cited by Thrower, *A Short History of Western Atheism,* p.130.
32. John Stuart Mill, *Autobiography, The Essential Works of John Stuart Mill,* Bantam Classics, p.34.
33. John Stuart Mill, *Three Essays, The Essential Works of John Stuart Mill,* Bantam Classics, p.386.
34. Psalm 11:7.
35. *Daily Telegraph,* 13 July 1999.
36. *Daily Mail,* 13 July 1999.
37. *Ibid.*
38. Romans 2:11.
39. Cited in *Daily Telegraph,* 18 July 1999.
40. *Newsweek,* 26 July 1999.
41. William Miller, *The God I Want,* Constable, p.52.
42. Bridger, *Why Can't I Believe?,* p.48.
43. Psalm 145:13.
44. Fred Carl Kuehner, 'Heaven and Hell', in *Fundamentals of the Faith,* ed. Carl F. H. Henry, *Christianity Today,* p.24c.
45. Psalm 115:3.
46. Psalm 145:7.
47. Cited by Thrower, *A Short History of Western Atheism,* p.132.
48. Sproul, *Reason to Believe,* p.123.
49. Genesis 1:31.
50. Ezra 9:6.
51. 1 John 1:5.
52. For a detailed review of theodicies, see Henri Blocher, 'Christian Thought on the Problem of Evil: Part II,' *Churchman* 99 (1985): pp.101-30.
53. Harold Kushner, *Why do Bad Things Happen to Good People?,* Avon Books, pp.42-3.
54. Ephesians 1:11.
55. Cited by Bridger, *Why Can't I Have Faith?,* p.61.
56. *Ibid.*
57. Genesis 1:31.
58. Cited by Brian Edwards, *Not By Chance,* Evangelical Press, p.14.
59. Job 12:13.
60. 2 Samuel 22:31.
61. Leviticus 11:44-45.
62. e.g. at 1 Peter 1:15-16.
63. Frame, *Apologetics to the Glory of God,* p.168
64. Johnson, *The Quest for God,* p.64.
65. *Ibid.*
66. The clearest biblical statement as to God's reason for bringing the universe into being is at Revelation 4:11.

67. *Divine Light*, January 1972.
68. Mary Baker Eddy, *Science and Health* (1906 edition), p.283.
69. Jay Adams, *The Grand Demonstration*, EastGate, p.16.

Chapter 23 — The case against the case against God
1. Swinburne, 'The Vocation of a Natural Theologian,' in *Philosophers Who Believe*, ed. Kelly James Clark, Inter-Varsity Press, p.200.
2. Cited by Johnson, *The Quest for God*, p.19.
3. Cited by Wade Burleson in *Atheistic Quotations*, published privately, p.147.
4. *Larry King Live*, CNN, 13 January 1997.
5. *Times*, 9 September 1991.
6. William Shirer, *The Rise and Fall of the Third Reich*, Simon and Schuster, p.240.
7. Kelly James Clark, *Return to Reason*, William B. Eerdmans Publishing Co., p.66.
8. *Ibid.*, p.67.
9. *Penpoint*, vol. 15, No. 1, January 1994.
10. Kreeft and Tacelli, *Handbook of Christian Apologetics*, pp.122-3.
11. *Sunday Telegraph*, 23 April 1995.
12. Morey, *The New Atheism and the Erosion of Freedom*, p.153.
13. Alvin Plantinga, 'A Christian Life Partly Lived', in *Philosophers Who Believe*, p.72.
14. Lord Hailsham, *The Door wherein I Went*, Collins, pp. 41-2.
15. John Hercus, *Pages From God's Casebook*, Inter-Varsity Fellowship, p.20.
16. 1 Peter 1:23.
17. See Proverbs 3:19.
18. See Zephaniah 3:5.
19. See Psalm 33:4.
20. See Deuteronomy 7:9.
21. Romans 11:33; see also Isaiah 55:8-9
22. 1 Corinthians 1:25
23. D. A. Carson, *How Long, O Lord?*, Inter-Varsity Press, p.226.
24. Jeremiah 12:1.
25. Job 1:1.
26. Job 21:7.
27. Habakkuk 1:3.
28. D. A. Carson, *Divine Sovereignty and Human Responsibility*, Marshalls.
29. Psalm 145:17.
30. Johnson, *The Quest for God*, p.65.
31. 1 Corinthians 13:12, New American Standard Bible.
32. Frame, *Apologetics to the Glory of God*, p.153.
33. Edwards, *Not By Chance*, p.19.
34. Psalm 135:6.
35. Psalm 29:10.
36. Matthew 10:29.
37. Matthew 10:30.
38. C. H. Spurgeon, *Spurgeon at his Best*, ed. Tom Carter, Baker Book House, p.199.
39. Ravi Zacharias, *Deliver us from Evil*, Word Publishing, pp.111-12.
40. Isaiah 45:5,7.
41. Lamentations 3:38.
42. Amos 3:6.
43. Genesis 45:8.
44. Genesis 50:20.
45. Psalm 25:8.
46. Carson, *How Long, O Lord?*, p.213.
47. *Ibid.*, p.226.
48. Romans 9:19-20.
49. *Evangelical Times*, December 1989.

50. Evans, *The Quest for Faith,* p.94.
51. Cited by Dale Rhoton, *How Much for the Man?,* Send the Light Trust, p.3.
52. Lewis, *The Problem of Pain,* p.16.
53. Bridger, *Why Can't I Believe?,* p.75.
54. 1 John 4:16.
55. J. I. Packer, *Knowing God,* Hodder & Stoughton, p.136.
56. Psalm 145:7.
57. *See* e.g. Psalm 118:1.
58. Psalm 145:8-9
59. Evans, *The Quest for Faith,* p.93.
60. Lewis, *The Problem of Pain,* p.36.
61. *Ibid.,* p.35.
62. Motyer, *After Death,* p.15.
63. W. N. Clarke, cited by Augustus H. Strong, *Systematic Theology,* Pickering & Inglis, p.264.
64. Revelation 7:9.
65. James W. Sire, *Why Should Anyone Believe Anything at all?,* Inter-Varsity Press, p.184.
66. *Sunday Times,* 22 August 1999.
67. Cited by Edwards, *Not By Chance,* p.16.
68. *Ibid.*
69. IAEA's International Nuclear Safety Advisory Group (INSAG), *The Chernobyl Accident: Updating of INSAG-1* (*INSAG-7,* 1992, p.24).
70. *See Sunday Telegraph,* 18 July 1999.
71. Mark 7:21-22.
72. 1 John 3:4.
73. *See* e.g. Ezekiel 28:12-19; Jude 6; Revelation 12:3-4a, 7-9.
74. Genesis 2:17.
75. Genesis 3:5.
76. Romans 5:12.
77. Genesis 1:27.
78. Romans 8:7.
79. Romans 5:12.
80. Ephesians 2:3.
81. Carson, *How Long O Lord?* p.48.
82. Genesis 3:17.
83. Romans 8:21-22.
84. Genesis 1:31.
85. Cited in *Heroes,* ed. A. Spangler and C. Turner, Inter-Varsity Press, p.14.
86. *See* e.g. Genesis 7:1-24; Exodus 7:14 - 11:10; 1 Samuel 14:15.
87. *See* e.g. 1 Samuel 25:38; 2 Samuel 6:7; Acts 12:23.
88. Proverbs 16:4.
89. *See* Luke 13:1-5.
90. *See* John 9:1-2.
91. John 9:3.
92. Luke 13:2.
93. Luke 13:3.
94. Luke 13:5.
95. 1 Thessalonians 1:10.
96. Hebrews 4:13.
97. Lewis, *The Problem of Pain,* p.81.
98. 2 Corinthians 1:4.
99. Herbert Carson, *Facing Suffering,* Evangelical Press, p.58.
100. Job 38:4; 40:2.
101. Job 40:4.
102. Job 2:10.
103. Robert Fyall, *How does God treat his Friends?,* Christian Focus Publications, p.23.

104. Habakkuk 3:17-18.
105. Romans 5:3-4.
106. James 1:2.
107. James 1:3.
108. James 1:4.
109. Proverbs 6:23.
110. Hebrews 12:10-12.
111. Psalm 119:67,71.
112. 2 Corinthians 12:7.
113. 2 Corinthians 12:10.
114. 2 Corinthians 4:18.
115. Carson, *Facing Suffering,* p.61.
116. Hebrews 9:27.
117. Colossians 3:2.
118. Carson, *Facing Suffering,* pp.61-2.
119. Psalm 145:18.
120. Psalm 130:3.
121. Psalm 103:10.
122. Derek Kidner, *Psalms 73-150,* The Tyndale Old Testament Commentaries, Inter-Varsity Press, p.366.
123. Lamentations 3:22.
124. *Start the Week,* BBC Radio 4, 5 April 1999.
125. Revelation 21:1.
126. Revelation 21:4.
127. Garner, *The Big Questions,* p.53.
128. 1 Corinthians 4:5.
129. Acts 17:31.
130. 2 Peter 3:13.
131. 2 Corinthians 4:17.
132. Romans 8:18.
133. Job 1:3.
134. Job 1:1.
135. See Job 1:13-19.
136. Job 2:9.
137. Job 13:15, Authorized Version.
138. The maximum penalty the Jewish law allowed was forty lashes (see Deuteronomy 25:3). To be sure of observing the law punctiliously, this was in practice reduced to thirty-nine. To all intents and purposes, Paul was given the heaviest punishment possible.
139. 2 Corinthians 11:23-27.
140. See Acts 16:22-25.
141. Romans 5:3.
142. Philippians 2:17-18.
143. See Jock Purves, *Fair Sunshine,* Banner of Truth Trust, p.51.
144. Cited by Nigel McCullough, *Barriers to Belief,* Darton, Longman and Todd, p.66.
145. Richard Wurmbrand, *In Search of God,* W. H. Allen, p.54.
146. Joni Eareckson, *Joni,* Pickering & Inglis, pp.206-7.
147. *Evangelical Times,* December 1987.
148. Letter dated April 1994, written on behalf of People's Bible Church, Greenville, S. Carolina.
149. *Telegraph Magazine,* 31 July 1999.
150. Edwards, *Not By Chance,* p.11.
151. Russell, *Why I am not a Christian,* p.116.
152. *Daily Telegraph,* 31 August 1992.
153. *Daily Telegraph,* 10 May 1995. These views are adapted from Dawkins' book *River Out of Eden.*
154. Cited by Bridger, *Why Can't I Believe?,* p.70.
155. Eliezer Berkovits, *Faith after the Holocaust,* KTAV Publishing House, p.71.
156. Cited by Bridger, *Why Can't I Believe?,* p.72.

157. Bridger, *ibid.*
158. Exodus 9:16.
159. Sproul, *Reason to Believe,* p.129.

Chapter 24 — The last word
1. *American Magazine,* July 1922.
2. David Barrett, editor of *World Christian Encyclopaedia,* cited in *Evangelical Times,* December 1987, puts the figure at 330,000.
3. Wales is just under 7,500 square miles, about the same size as New Jersey, the fifth smallest state in the U.S.A.
4. See the 1998 *Guinness Book of Records.*
5. Mission Aviation Fellowship.
6. Russell, *Why I am Not a Christian.*
7. F. F. Bruce, *Jesus and Christian Origins Outside the New Testament.*
8. Cited by Benton, *Is Christianity True?,* p.58.
9. Cited by Frost, *Thinking Clearly About God and Science,* p.188.
10. *Daily Mail,* 28 March 1997.
11. See Matthew 1:1-17; Luke 3:23-38.
12. See Luke 2:21.
13. Luke 2:16.
14. Luke 2:40.
15. Luke 2:43.
16. Matthew 21:18.
17. See John 4:7.
18. John 4:6.
19. See Luke 23:26.
20. John 19:34.
21. Mark 6:38.
22. Mark 9:21.
23. John 11:34.
24. John 15:15.
25. John 11:5.
26. Mark 10:14.
27. Mark 3:5.
28. Luke 13:32.
29. Matthew 7:15.
30. Matthew 12:34.
31. Matthew 23:17.
32. Matthew 23:27.
33. Matthew 15:7.
34. See Matthew 21:12-13.
35. Ephesians 4:26, New American Standard Bible.
36. D. M. Lloyd-Jones, *Darkness and Light,* Banner of Truth Trust, p.226.
37. Luke 19:41.
38. Mark 7:34.
39. Matthew 9:36.
40. Luke 10:21.
41. See Matthew 4:1-11.
42. Hebrews 4:15.
43. Hebrews 5:7.
44. Luke 4:16.
45. The exception is at Luke 4:18-19.
46. See Matthew 4:2.
47. See Matthew 6:16.
48. Isaiah 65:9.
49. Daniel 9:25.

50. Malachi 3:1.
51. Luke 4:16-21.
52. John 5:46.
53. John 15:25; see Psalms 35:19; 69:4.
54. Daniel 7:13.
55. e.g. Matthew 16:13.
56. John 5:39.
57. Genesis 22:18.
58. Genesis 49:10.
59. Micah 5:2.
60. Matthew 2:1.
61. Cited in William Hendriksen, *A Commentary on the Gospel of John,* Banner of Truth Trust, p.430.
62. See Zechariah 13:7; Mark 14:50.
63. See Zechariah 11:12-13; Matthew 26:15; 27-1-10.
64. See Psalm 35:11; Matthew 26:60.
65. See Isaiah 50:6; Matthew 26:67-68.
66. See Isaiah 53:7; Matthew 27:14.
67. See Isaiah 53:12; Matthew 27:38.
68. See Psalm 22:16; Luke 23:33.
69. See Isaiah 53:12; Luke 23:34.
70. See Psalm 34:20; John 19:33, 36.
71. See Zechariah 12:10; John 19:34,37.
72. See Psalm 22:18; John 19:23-24.
73. Stoner, *Science Speaks,* p.110.
74. *Ibid.,* p.108.
75. *Sunday Times,* 27 December 1998.
76. Luke 1:34.
77. Matthew 1:25.
78. Matthew 1:18.
79. Cited by Thomas Boslooper, *The Virgin Birth,* Westminster Press, p.139.
80. Robert G. Gromacki, *The Virgin Birth,* Baker Book House, p.180.
81. Cited by G. W. McPherson, *The Virgin Birth,* Yonkers Book Co., p.7.
82. J. N. D. Anderson, *Jesus Christ: The Witness of History,* Inter-Varsity Press, p.80.
83. *The Times,* 13 July 1984.
84. Isaiah 7:14.
85. Joel 1:8.
86. Edward J. Young, *Thy Word is Truth,* Banner of Truth Trust, p.144.
87. Jeremiah 31:22.
88. Genesis 2:11,13.
89. Psalm 71:21.
90. Zechariah 13:7.
91. David Kingdon, *Banner of Truth* magazine, cited by Benton, *Is Christianity True?,* p.56.
92. Luke 1:37.
93. Luke 2:47.
94. Luke 4:22.
95. John 7:46.
96. Matthew 7:28.
97. Matthew 5:3-12.
98. Matthew 6:9-13.
99. Matthew 5:44.
100. Matthew 5:48.
101. Matthew 7:12.
102. *Evangelical Magazine of Wales,* October-November 1996, p.12.
103. Bernard Ramm, *Protestant Christian Evidences,* Moody Press, p.170.
104. Matthew 4:24.
105. See Matthew 9:27-30.

106. See Mark 7:31-37.
107. *Ibid.*
108. See Luke 17:11-19.
109. See John 5:1-9.
110. See Mark 1:29-31.
111. See Matthew 9:1-8.
112. See Mark 5:21-43.
113. See Luke 7:11-17.
114. See John 11:1-44.
115. See Mark 4:35-41.
116. See Luke 5:1-11.
117. See John 2:1-11.
118. See Matthew 14:13-21.
119. See Matthew 15:32-39.
120. William E. Lecky, *History of European Morals from Augustus to Charlemagne,* D. Appleton & Co., p.8.
121. Cited by Wilbur Smith, *Have you Considered Him?,* Inter-Varsity Press, p.11.
122. Hebrews 4:15.
123. See Matthew 27:1-4.
124. 2 Corinthians 5:21.
125. 1 John 3:7.
126. 1 Peter 1:19.
127. 1 Peter 2:22.
128. 2 Samuel 24:10.
129. Isaiah 6:5.
130. Job 42:6.
131. 1 Timothy 1:16.
132. Augustine, *The Confessions of St Augustine,* trans. E. B. Pusey, J. M. Dent & Sons, p.21.
133. Ashbel Green, *Discourses Delivered in the College of New Jersey,* p.317.
134. Cited by Iain Murray, *Jonathan Edwards,* Banner of Truth Trust, p.102.
135. John 8:29.
136. John 8:46.
137. John 14:30.
138. Cited by Frank Mead, *The Encyclopaedia of Religious Quotations,* Fleming H. Revell, p.57.
139. John 6:35.
140. John 8:12.
141. John 14:6.
142. John 5:17.
143. John 5:18.
144. John 8:58.
145. John 8:53.
146. Exodus 3:14.
147. John 8:59.
148. J. C. Ryle, *Expository Thoughts on the Gospels,* vol. 3, Baker Book House, p.132.
149. John 10:30.
150. John 10:31.
151. John 10:32.
152. John 10:33.
153. John 14:8-10.
154. John 17:5.
155. John 18:4-5.
156. John 18:6.
157. Cited by Mead, *The Encyclopaedia of Religious Quotations,* p.50.
158. C. S. Lewis, *Mere Christianity,* Macmillan Co., pp.40-41.
159. See John Blanchard, *Will the Real Jesus Please Stand Up?,* Evangelical Press, pp.133-60.
160. Colossians 1:16.

161. Colossians 1:17.
162. 1 Corinthians 1:23.
163. 1 Corinthians 2:2.
164. Leon Morris, *The Cross in the New Testament,* Paternoster Press, p.365.
165. John 12:27.
166. John 7:30, 8:20.
167. John 17:1.
168. John R. W. Stott, *Basic Christianity,* Inter-Varsity Press, p.29.
169. J. I. Packer, *God's Words,* Inter-Varsity Press, p. 203.
170. Psalm 51:5.
171. Romans 5:12.
172. Romans 8:2.
173. Romans 6:23.
174. James 1:15.
175. 2 Thessalonians 1:9.
176. Hebrews 9:27.
177. John 10:18.
178. Matthew 26:53.
179. Matthew 27:50.
180. Ecclesiastes 8:8, Revised Standard Version.
181. Cited by M. R. Vincent, *Word Studies in the New Testament,* Associated Publishers and Authors, p.82.
182. See Isaiah 53.
183. Luke 22:37.
184. Romans 5:8.
185. 1 Peter 3:18.
186. 1 John 3:16.
187. Matthew 26:28.
188. Stott, *Basic Christianity,* p.92.
189. Romans 8:3.
190. Romans 3:23.
191. Romans 6:23.
192. Romans 3:25.
193. Isaiah 53:5.
194. Romans 5:8.
195. John 3:16.
196. McGrath, *Bridge-Building,* p.144.
197. *The Long Silence* originally appeared in the 1960s in the British student magazine *Voice.* The author is unknown.
198. Matthew 27:60.
199. See Matthew 27:62-66.
200. See Mark 16:1-8; John 20:1-9.
201. Acts 2:23.
202. Acts 2:24.
203. See Blanchard, *Will the Real Jesus Please Stand Up?,* pp.103-31.
204. Luke 23:55.
205. See Luke 23:50-53.
206. Anderson, *Jesus Christ: The Witness of History,* p.129.
207. See Matthew 28:11-15.
208. John 20:19.
209. See Mark 15:42-45.
210. D. F. Strauss, *The Life of Jesus for the People,* vol. 1, Williams and Norgate, p.412.
211. See John 20:14-18.
212. See Matthew 28:8-9; John 20:14-18.
213. See John 7:5; 1 Corinthians 15:7; Galatians 1:19.
214. John 21:1-14.

215. 1 Corinthians 15:8.
216. John 20:24-28.
217. 1 Corinthians 15:6.
218. Short, *Why Believe?*, p.51.
219. 1 Corinthians 15:6.
220. W. H. Griffith Thomas, *The Principles of Theology,*
221. Bridger, *Why Can't I Have Faith?*, p.116.
222. See e.g. Acts 4:1-18.
223. Anderson, *Jesus Christ: The Witness of History*, p.146.
224. Charles A. Colson, *Kingdoms in Conflict*, p.70.
225. Stott, *Basic Christianity*, p.49.
226. Acts 17:6.
227. Cited by Wilbur M. Smith, *Christian Apologetics.*
228. Cited by Stott, *Basic Christianity*, p.46.
229. Cited by Michael Green, *Man Alive!*, Inter-Varsity Fellowship, p.54.
230. D. James Kennedy, *The Gates of Hell Shall Not Prevail*, Thomas Nelson Publishers, p.21.
231. Romans 6:9.
232. Lewis, *God in the Dock*, p.156.
233. Matthew 9:36.
234. See e.g. Luke 5:20; John 3:36.
235. Acts 10:38.
236. Luke 4:22.
237. Cited by Josh McDowell, *Evidence that Demands a Verdict*, Campus Crusade for Christ, p.109.
238. Cited by Mead, *The Encyclopaedia of Religious Quotations*, p.52.
239. e.g. Mark 1:15.
240. e.g. Matthew 13:24.
241. e.g. John 18:36.
242. Kenneth Scott Latourette, *A History of Christianity,* Harper & Row, p.44.
243. John 10:20.
244. Anderson, *Jesus Christ: The Witness of History*, p.9.
245. Palmer, *Cure For Life,* p.19.
246. Colossians 1:15.
247. Colossians 1:19.
248. Colossians 2:9.
249. Titus 2:13.
250. 1 Timothy 3:16.
251. Hebrews 1:3.
252. John 10:30.
253. 1 John 5:20.

Index of names

Note: Some entries refer to the sources of quotations who are not named in the text.

Index of subjects

Scripture index

A wide range of excellent books on spiritual subjects is available from Evangelical Press. Please write to us for your free catalogue or contact us by e-mail.

Evangelical Press
Faverdale North Industrial Estate, Darlington, Co. Durham, DL3 0PH, England

Evangelical Press USA
P. O. Box 84, Auburn, MA 01501, USA

e-mail: sales@evangelical-press.org

web: www.evangelical-press.org